Letters from St. Petersburg
A Siamese Prince
at the Court of the Last Tsar

To Paul Suan

Best wishes for a

HAPPY NEW YEAR ,2018

From John Inga

Monmouth , 27th. December ,2017

R I V E R
BOOKS

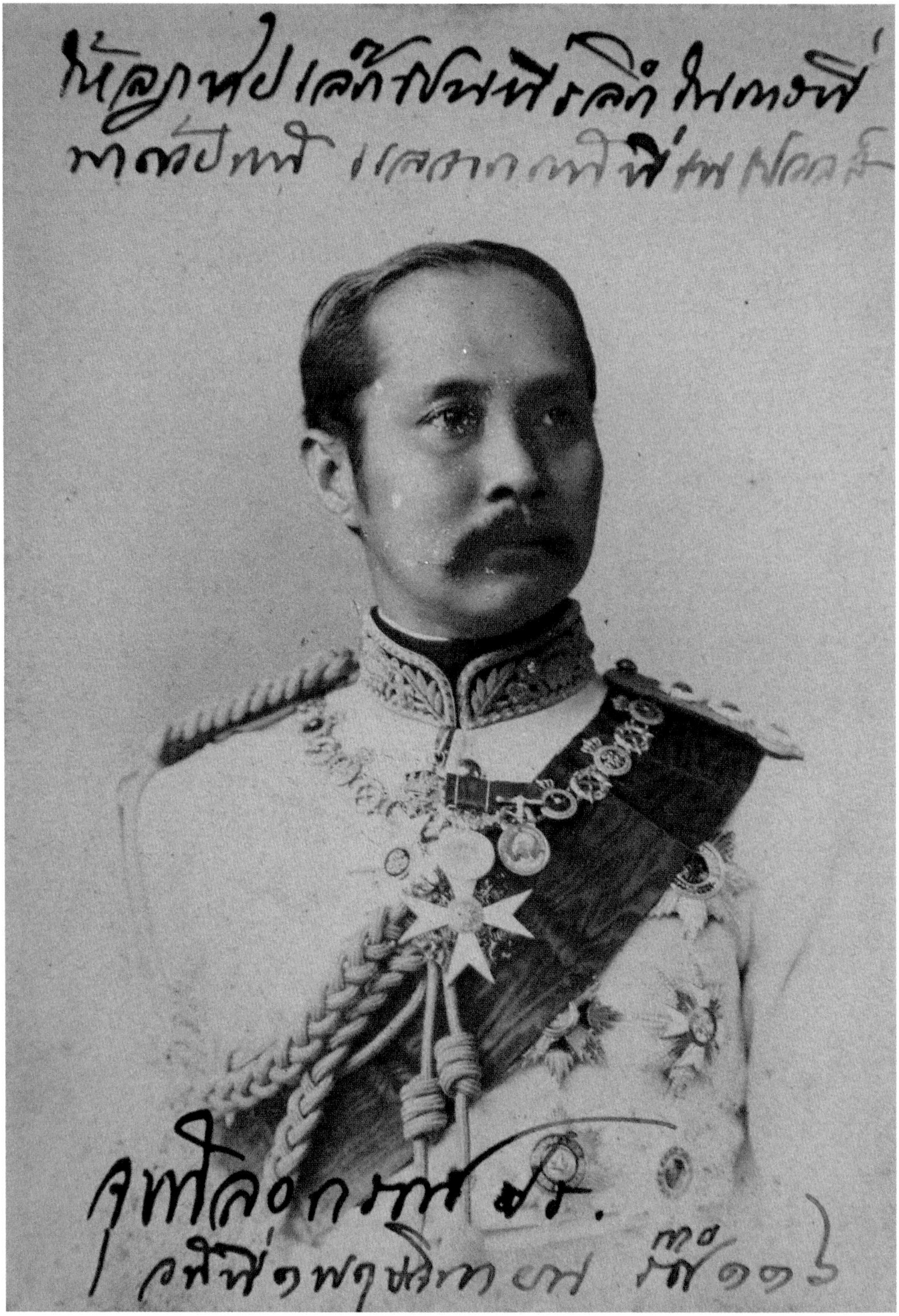

Letters from St. Petersburg
A Siamese Prince
at the
Court of the Last Tsar

Translation and Commentary by Narisa Chakrabongse
Edited by Narisa Chakrabongse and Paisarn Piemmettawat

This book is dedicated to my beloved sons, Hugo Chulachak
and Dominic Puwasawat, that they may enjoy researching
their heritage and learn how their great grandfather was
dedicated and brave, sensible and a risk taker, beloved both
by his father and the last Tsar of Russia.

First edition published in 2017 by
River Books Co. Ltd.
396 Maharaj Road, Tatien, Bangkok 10200 Thailand
T: (66 2) 622-1900, 224-6686
F: (66 2) 225-3861
E: order@riverbooksbk.com
www.riverbooksbk.com

Editor Narisa Chakrabongse
Production supervision Paisarn Piemmettawat
Design Narisa Chakrabongse

ISBN 978 616 7339 58 0

Printed in Thailand by Sirivatana Interprint Public Co., Ltd.

*Cover: King Chulalongkorn and Prince Chakrabongse,
photographed during the prince's trip home in 1899.*

*Back cover: The Tsar and Prince Chakrabongse, c. 1903.
Prince Chakrabongse, Katya and Chula, 1908.*

*Frontispiece: Photograph given to his son by King
Chulalongkorn and inscribed: To my son Lek as a souvenir of
our trip to Naples and our parting there, Chulalongkorn, 1st
November 1897.*

Contents

INTRODUCTION

The letters written between King Chulalongkorn (r. from 1868) and his son Prince Chakrabongse (1883-1920) cover a period of 15 years, beginning in 1896 and ending with the King's death in 1910. In all, there are some 281 letters. 70 from the King and over 200 from Prince Chakrabongse. The prince was sent to study in Tsarist Russia and thus the letters written from that country provide a fascinating insight into the Corps des Pages[1] (where he was enrolled), Tsar Nicholas II[2] and the Imperial family, the role that Siam occupied in Russia's attempts to gain a foothold in the East, and the way Siam hoped Russia could help apply pressure to keep the French[3] from encroaching on her borders.

While still Tsarevich, Nicholas had visited Bangkok in 1891 as part of his Eastern Tour, which culminated in the opening of the eastern end of the Trans-Siberian railway in Vladivostok in 1893. Although he only stayed in Bangkok for five days, he was lavishly entertained by King Chulalongkorn, establishing a friendship which continued throughout their lives.

Prince Chakrabongse

Prince Chakrabongse was born on 3rd March 1883. He was the 40th child of the King and the 13th son, although one had only lived a few days. His mother, Queen Saovabha (1861-1919), was half-sister to the King and one of four princesses elevated to queens. When he was born, his mother was only 21 years old and had already had three children: Princess Bahurad, born December 1878, Prince Vajiravudh (1880-1925), aged three when Chakrabongse was born, and Prince Tribej (1881-1887). In 1887, the year in which Chakrabongse turned four, two of his full brothers died, first his younger brother, Prince Siriraj (1885-1887), aged only one and a half, and, later in the year, Prince Tribej (1881-1887), who was only six. In the previous years, his mother had had several miscarriages. Therefore Queen Saovabha must have been very preoccupied and it is hard to imagine the childhood of these boys brought up in the Grand Palace[4]. Nevertheless, Chakrabongse seems to have been her favourite child, as the letters will later show.

Tsarevich Nicholas (later Tsar Nicholas II) in Thailand in March, 1891. On his left is King Chulalongkorn, on his right, Crown Prince Maha Vajirunhis.

In addition to his full brothers, Prince Chakrabongse had six older half brothers: Prince Kitiyakara Voralaksana, Prince of Chantaburi (1874-1931), Prince Rabi Badhanasakdi, Prince of Rajaburi (1874-1920), Prince Pravitra Vadhanodom (1875-1919), Prince Chirapravati Voradej (1876-1913), Prince Maha Vajirunhis, Crown Prince (1878-1894) and Prince Abhakara Kiartivongse, Prince of Chumphon (1880-1923), as well as numerous sisters. Just nine months older than him, were Prince Paribatra Sukhumbhand, Prince of Nakhon Sawan (1881-1944) and Prince Purachatra Jayakara, Prince of Kamphaeng Phet (1881-1936). Prince Chakrabongse was particularly close to several of his brothers, especially the Crown Prince, but in England often saw several more. Later, younger brothers, such as Prince Rangsit Prayurasakdi (1885-1951), followed to Europe and Prince Chakrabongse, when passing through Berlin to St. Petersburg, often met with those studying in Germany, as well as inviting some to Russia, even at dangerous times.

King Mongkut (r. 1851-1868), Rama IV, had realised the importance of a wide education, including learning English, but he did not send his children abroad, instead employing the somewhat infamous

The book commemorating the Tsar's trip to the East in 1890-91 was published by Prince Esper Ukhtomsky, who later met Prince Chakrabongse in St. Petersburg.

Anna Leonowens as governess. It was only in the reign of his successor, King Chulalongkorn, with increasing threats from colonial expansion by Britain[5] and France, that the King decided to send his sons abroad. Accordingly, they were sent to learn foreign languages and then to military colleges in England, Germany and Denmark.

In 1881, a group of nine Siamese princes were sent to Europe, including the King's younger brother Prince Svasti Sobhon (1865-1935), then only 16. In 1885, four of the King's eldest sons were sent to England for a year (Prince Rabi, Prince Kitiyakara, Prince Chira and Prince Pravitra), before returning once again to continue their higher education. In a letter written to his sons in 1885, the King emphasized that the purpose of overseas study was not to become westernized but to become modernized, as he recognised the need for technical expertise. Prince Chakrabongse was the ninth son to be sent to England, following in the footsteps of his full brother Prince Maha Vajiravudh, the Crown Prince. From the account of King Chulalongkorn's trip to Europe in 1897, it seems that only when the King visited Tsar Nicholas II in August was it decided that Prince Chakrabongse should study in Russia.

Why was Russia chosen?

Clearly the successful trip made by Nicholas to Siam when Tsarevich was one factor, but furthermore King Chulalongkorn could see that after the Paknam Incident[6] in 1893, when the country risked becoming a French protectorate, Siam needed a counterweight to the French and British. Accordingly, Prince Damrong[7] was sent to represent Siam at the coronation of Nicholas II in 1896. Another factor may well have been that Tsar Nicholas offered to pay for Prince Chakrabongse's education in its entirety. This was different from in other European countries where the money had to come from the Siamese treasury.

King Chulalongkorn's trip to Europe

As part of his efforts to show that Siam was a civilised country and to create alliances through personal friendships among monarchs, in 1897 King Chulalongkorn made an extensive trip to Europe.

During the trip, two of his sons, Crown Prince Vajiravudh and Prince Chakrabongse, already studying in England, accompanied their father for certain visits and thereby became acquainted with foreign royalty.

Before the trip, the Tsar had spoken highly of the Siamese King to the Austrian Emperor Franz Joseph I (1848–1916), who in turn spoke to the German Kaiser Wilhelm II. As a result these two monarchs treated King Chulalongkorn as a royal equal. The tour began in Italy on 14th May and, after meeting with the Italian King, Umberto I and His Holiness the Pope (Leo XIII 1878-1903), King Chulalongkorn travelled to Switzerland, Austria and Hungary, before resuming his friendship with Tsar Nicholas II at Peterhof. The King then visited King Oscar II in Sweden, King Christian IX in Denmark, Kaiser Wilhelm II in Germany, Queen Wilhelmina in the Netherlands, King Leopold II in Belgium, King Alfonso XIII, under the regency of his mother Queen Maria Christina, in Spain and King Carlos I in Portugal. The Prince of Wales officially welcomed King Chulalongkorn for his five week visit to Great Britain, during which time he called on Her Majesty Queen Victoria at her Isle of Wight residence. The stay in England was particularly long, as many of his sons were being educated there.

Because of the strains between Siam and the

French Republic, France had originally not been included. However, having heard of the reception given to King Chulalongkorn by other European Heads of State, President Faure of France sent his special train to Brussels (where King Chulalongkorn had been visiting King Leopold II) to invite the Siamese King. The reception in France, on 11th September 1897, was suitably regal and wherever he went, King Chulalongkorn was cheered by the French people.

The letters

All the letters from the King are in Thai, as are most of those from the prince, but a few are in English as the head of the Siamese Legation in St. Petersburg, Phraya Mahibal, wanted to ensure that Prince Chakrabongse maintained his good English.

From 1902 onwards, some telegrams are included in their chronological position. These were written using a code and were deciphered into English at the Siamese legation in St. Petersburg.

Included from late 1897 to mid-1898 are 18 letters to his family from one Pavel Nicholaivich Ardachev, a young PhD student engaged to teach Russian to the prince while he was still in England.

In early 1906, a few letters are included from Prince Chakrabongse to his future wife Ekaterina Desnitskaya (known as Katya)[8], before they eloped to Constantinople. Read in conjunction with the formal letters to his father, they provide a fascinating insight into his state of mind at that time.

When Prince Chakrabongse left for Europe in 1896 he was only 13, but his letters already show a maturity that belies his years. The first group recount details of his voyage and the people and places encountered, then comes a long a gap in 1897, partly because his father arrived in Europe for his foreign tour but also, in all likelihood, because some letters were lost. On the other hand, 1896 and 1897 are rich in letters from the King, who was clearly missing one of his favourite sons.The prince's letters in early 1898 recount his progress in learning Russian and his anxiety to leave England and find a young Siamese man to accompany him. The second half of the year is full of his impressions of Russia, his first meeting with the Tsar and his studies at the Corps des Pages.

As the prince was writing to the King, albeit his father, his letters are of necessity somewhat formal and, no doubt, he concentrated on subjects he felt

were appropriate. Thus there are many details of whom he saw and how he was received.

From Prince Chakrabongse's reports, it is clear that the Tsar treated Prince Chakrabongse like an adopted son and thus the doors of the entire Imperial family were open to him, as were those among the royal houses of Europe, given that many Grand Dukes and Grand Duchesses had married various members of the German royal families. In addition, by attending the elite Corps des Pages school, he met many senior generals and army officers. Later letters discuss events of the day, such as assasinations and the Russo-Japanese war of 1904-05.

The letters from King Chulalongkorn to Prince Chakrabongse vary greatly in tone and length. Some of the early ones, such as from his Javanese tour, are long, detailed and difficult to translate. Others are short and to the point. Some show the extent to which the King missed his son, in particular those written in 1896 when they had parted from each other relatively recently. Thus a letter of 24th June 1896 ends with the words: "…how can I stop thinking about you? I really don't know what to do".

Later several letters reflect his annoyance with the French or exhaustion after several visits by foreign dignitaries, while others show his anxiety at a child's illness, or sorrow at another child's death.

Gaps in the letters typically occur when father and son were together, such as in 1897, or in 1899 between June and August, when the prince returned home to Thailand for a holiday, and again in mid-1903-early 1904 when he made his second, longer trip home.

By May 1906, Prince Chakrabongse was back for good in the recently built Paruskavan Palace, having secretly married Katya in Constantinople. The anger felt by the king was given expression in two letters, as well as, one imagines, in person. If Prince Chakrabongse replied, those letters have been lost. In 1907, King Chulalongkorn made a second trip to Europe and there are only two letters from that year. 1908 saw the birth of Katya and Prince Chakrabongse's only child, Chula, and a harsh letter from the King refusing to allow the boy to be a member of the royal family. However, by 1909, the King's anger had dissipated and he began writing to Prince Chakrabongse more and asking his help in arranging things, or complaining to him about the behaviour of

May 7th 1901.

My dear father,

Since I wrote to you last time we have had three more examinations at the Corps. On the 28th of last month there was the exam on the Russian language, on the 30th - on mechanic and on the 4th - on artillery.

I am glad to be able to say that I received full marks on all subjects.

To-day we ought to have had a parade of all the troops of the military district of Petersburg, in which we also take part. The review has been

He asked me to give him my photograph in order that he might be able to show it to his coreligionists. I of course acceded to his request. When taking leave of me the officer took my hand up to his forehead and on the whole expressed such respect that I was moved. I wished him every happiness and prayed him to express to his people my joy at knowing that there are so many coreligionists of mine in this country.

Hoping you are quite well and with best love

I remain

Your very affectionate son

Lek

Top: *Part of a letter dated 22nd July 1901 from King Chulalongkorn to Prince Chakrabongse.*

Above: *One of the relatively few letters in English from Prince Chakrabongse.*

other princely ministers. By 1910, a mood of greater irritation and despondency is apparent in the King's letters. For his part, Prince Chakrabongse's letters focus on work, apart from one of the penultimate ones cleverly persuading the King to let him represent Siam at the Coronation of King George V and thereby take Katya on a trip home.

In their totality the letters reflect an intense and close relationship between a father, who was also the King, and one of his favoured sons. They also shed light on a fascinating and volatile period in Thai and Russian history.

Note from and Translator and Editor

As most of the letters have been translated from Thai, inevitably some of the flavour has been lost. However, I have tried to echo the language of both King Chulalongkorn and Prince Chakrabongse as far as possible. Only about eight letters have been excluded, mainly because they were just two-line answers from King Chulalongkorn. On two occasions some lines have been cut to avoid offence. Any excisions are indicated by a dotted line. However, the entire collection can be consulted online at the British Library.

My co-editor, Paisarn Piemmettawat, and I have endeavoured to provide footnotes to people and events mentioned in the letters as far as possible. Some names transliterated into Thai from English and Russian have proved impossible to find and we would be grateful for comments on incorrect transliterations or identifications. Nicknames used for some of the brothers, aunts, uncles and great aunts are also problematic. Thus the Crown Prince is referred to by Prince Chakrabongse as Toonmom or Toonkramom Toh, while his younger brother is simply called Eeyd Lek. In the index, the nicknames are included in a bracket and are cross referenced. Siamese civil service titles, Phaya, Chao Phraya, etc, and their names, which can change when rising up the ranks, are also somewhat complicated. We have tried to only use the name or title which fits with the chronological context within which the person is mentioned.

For the English edition, we have changed the *Rattanakosin Sok* dates[9] to Common Era ones and in both editions we begin each year in January in the western manner, rather than in April as in old Siam. However, in Thai, the *Rattanakosin Sok* date is included after the Buddhist Era date. For Russian dates, we give the Gregorian date, as this is what Prince Chakrabongse used, although in some letters he mentions that the Russian dates are behind.

Photographs come mainly from private collections or the National Archives, Bangkok. However, we have also researched photographs from other archives and the Internet and established the sources to the best of our ability.

This is a book Paisarn and I have been working on for many years. Only the prospect of celebrating 120 years of Thai-Russian relations in 2017, of which my grandfather is an important part, has given us the impetus to complete our work.

The Letters and the British Library

When I was 15, my mother, Elisabeth Chakrabongse (Lisba, 1915-1971) was dying in Cornwall and I remember her going through boxes of letters and trying to sort them out. About 14 years later, when I was in Bangkok researching the book on my grandmother, *Katya and the Prince of Siam*, I realised that some of the letters were missing.

Then, some 22 years ago, Paisarn rang me up one Sunday morning to say that a collection of letters was coming up for auction at Christies, that he thought they were connected with my father and I must go along to view them at once. I went to Christies that afternoon and a pleasant woman produced the box files full of letters. As I went through the first box, I saw labels pinned on the various sections in my mother's distinctive handwriting. The moment I told the woman that I thought the letters were mine, her manner changed and the files were taken away from me. I immediately began research to prove successfully that the letters were mine, but I was unable to say when they might have been taken or whether I had lost them between clearing out my house in Cornwall or selling a house in the Cotswolds. An injunction was obtained to stop the auction and I was able to acquire the letters for a relatively small sum. An added complication was that the then Thai ambassador to London was intent on buying them to present to His Late Majesty King Bhumibhol Adulyadej.

The whole matter was very traumatic, with various parties in Thailand being divided as to whether I should fight to get the letters back, or allow the ambassador to purchase them. I talked about this with my close friend the late Henry Ginsburg, who worked at the British Library, and he suggested that the library might be a safe home for them and would also enable scholarly research. As my father, the historian Prince Chula (1908-1964), had ended up spending more of his life in Great Britain than Thailand, I felt he would have been pleased with this decision. Accordingly in 2001, the letters were duly presented to the library where they remain to this day.

Getting ready to leave

King Chulalongkorn did not generally travel to Singapore to bid farewell to sons bound for the long sea voyage to Europe. On this occasion, however, he decided to combine the send-off with a trip of his own – to Java, an island he had first visited some 26 years ago. The king had been unwell and had still not recovered from the exhaustion and anxiety of the Paknam affair three years previously.

Accompanying him were Queen Saovabha, for whom the trip was a welcome antidote to missing her son, another of the king's sons, Prince Pravitra, and Princess Valaya Alongkorn, the daughter of Queen Savang Vadhana, who had been adopted by Queen Saovabha, on account of her having no daughters.

While in Singapore, last photographs were taken of the royal couple and their son, together with group photographs of the entourage and local officials.

From left to right: Prince Rabi Badhanasakdi, Phraya Abhaya Ronariddhi, Prince Chakrabongse, King Chulalongkorn, Mr. John Anderson (the Siamese Consul), and Prince Damrong.

1. The Corps des Pages was an elite military school in St. Petersburg, see page 111 for more details.

2. Tsar Nicholas II (1868-1918, r. 1894-1918). Between 1890-91 when Tsarevich he made an Eastern Journey. He was in Bangkok in March 1891. In Japan he was almost assassinated. The tour encouraged Nicholas, when Tsar, to look eastward expanion and also made him dislike Japan.

3. The French were a constant worry to Siam with their expansionist policy on Siam's eastern border. They are mentioned frequently in the king's letters.

4. A walled compound enclosing the Emerald Buddha temple and many throne halls, the Grand Palace was both the royal residence of the King and his family and the seat of government.

5. Relations with the British were better than with the French, although there were tensions over the three states of Kelantan, Trengganu and Kedah on the Malay Peninsula. Many British advisors were employed by the Siamese government.

6. The Paknam Incident of July 1893 occurred when three French ships were fired on by the Siamese fort at the mouth of the Chao Phraya, as part of the Franco-Siamese war. The French then blockaded Bangkok which ended the war.

7. Prince Damrong Rajanubhab (June 1862-1943) was King Chulalongkorn's half brother. He was C-in-C of the Army in 1887 and Minister of Education, as well as being responsible for provincial reform. He was the most influential person after the King.

8. See *Katya and the Prince of Siam*.

9. In 1888, King Chulalongkorn changed the dating system to be based on the founding date of the Chakri dynasty, namely 6 April 1782, with that year up to 6 Apri 1783 being year I.

Prince Chakrabongse and his mother, Queen Saovabha, taken just before he left for Europe. Neither look particularly happy.

ไวย หลวงศักดิ์   มหามาตยอภิบาลกุก มุนีรัง มหา   ฯ   ฤ

From left front row: Phraya Sirisatsathid, Prince Sommot Amarabandh, Prince Sanpasartsubhahitch, Prince of Nakhon Rajasima, Prince Rajburi Direkriddhi, King Chulalongkorn, Prince Chakrabongse, Phraya Thamjanya Nukulmontri.
Back row: Luang Sakdi, Rajamat, Phraya Apaironrith, Prince Mahisara Rajaharudaya, Phraya Montrisuriyawongsa, Mr. John Anderson, Phraya Anuchitcharnchai.

A photograph of the farewell published in Le Petit Journal, *May 1896*

Colombo
23 May 1896

Your Majesty

Ever since I respectfully bade Your Majesty farewell and left the port of Singapore, I have been sitting and gazing out to sea from the stern of the boat. They raised the royal elephant flag[1] on the central mast, while the French flag flew from another mast. Even the 'in port mast' had the elephant flag above the French one but only for a short while. As soon as we were out at sea they took all the flags down. At 5 pm they came and took the three *mom chao* princes[2] to have supper with the children. I went down to see them and saw that our children were eating much better than the older ones. Once they'd finished our children grumbled that the food wasn't tasty. So it was decided that tomorrow they'll eat with the grown ups. At 6 o'clock they rang the bell for dinner. The captain arrranged a separate table for the Thai contingent but in the same room.

I must report on what the eating and drinking is like. At 10 in the morning I have coffee in my room. We have another meal at 1 pm and then at 3 pm tea. At 6 pm we have dinner and at 9 pm some supper.

One of the good things about this boat is that the passengers don't see any messy things at all unless they are mischievous and poke about where they shouldn't. So you don't see the food, or the animals. In other words the fancy people are kept towards the bow of the boat, unlike on the *Maha Chakri*[3] where you see people lying around.

One thing I forgot to tell Your Majesty is that the captain complained a lot to Toonmom Aa[4] about how sad he was that he forgot his French decoration abroad and couldn't wear it to welcome him.

LE "SAGHALIEN"

SS Saghalien was a French passenger steamer built in 1880 and owned by the Messegeries Maritimes. It was used for the Far East routes.

An engraving of Prince Chakrabongse published in
Le Petit Journal, *1896.*

Toonmom Aa has said he will send a report to Your Majesty. Only the captain has come to sit on our table in order to explain various things to us over dinner. He is very amusing but constantly intersperses his conversation with French which Teacher Carter[5] translates. He is very strange when he translates Thai into French as he mixes in a lot of Thai words. Then when he speaks Thai he mixes in a lot French. Up on deck is very comfortable but at night it is too dark being rather poorly lit. Today there has been no waves because we are near Sumatra.

On the 20th, I became acquainted with two passengers – a millionaire American and his wife. He speaks English very well and the wife talks a great deal. She wants to visit Thailand. Today there were no waves again. I looked at the map at midday. They raised the flags to indicate we were at the mouth of the port of Din Ding (where *Wasadree* sank). Also at this time, although I haven't finished the letter, I wanted to tell Your Majesty that in the past two days I have been thinking about Your Majesty a great deal.

21st. As soon as I woke up I felt that the sea was

very rough. I felt rather sick but had to force myself to have a shower and get dressed. Then I had to lie in my room until it was time for breakfast. Then I went up on deck but I couldn't walk around as normal and had to lie down all day. Lunch had to be taken on deck and I didn't go down to the room all day as it was very hot. The porthole had to be kept closed otherwise sea water would come in. So I had to lie up on deck all day.

22nd. When I woke up it didn't feel as if the waves had abated in any way, but I didn't feel as sick as the day before. I went down to have a shower and got dressed with great ease. Then, however, I had to go up on deck but at mealtime was able to go downstairs. As time passed I didn't feel too sick and was able to write this letter to your majesty.

Since leaving you I have been fine and have thought of Your Majesty a great deal.

According to the schedule the ship should arrive tomorrow and we will have to go and pay respects to the tooth relic in Kandy so I won't have time to write to you, which is why I am writing now although I will be able to report on tomorrow's events later.

Also I would be grateful if Your Majesty could tell all the members of the royal family and court officials that I am thinking of them very much.

I beg to remain Your Majesty's obedient servant,
Chakrabongse

1. Elephant Flag. The image of a white elephant on a red ground facing the hoist was created by King Mongkut in 1855. In 1916 the flag was changed to a white elephant in royal regalia and in 1917 the tricolour Thai flag was introduced two months after Siam entered the First World War.

2. *Mom Chao* is the lowest level of princely rank equivalent to His/Her Serene Highness. The three *mom chao* princes accompanying Chakrabongse to study in the UK were HSH Prince Nibandh Phanuwongse (1885-1934); HSH Wibul Sawwaddiwongse Sawadikul; HSH Tavorn Mongkolwong Chaiyan.

3. Maha Chakri. This royal steam yacht of 2,290 tons was built in the Leith shipyards in 1892. After 24 years in royal service, she was sold on and sank near Faro in 1921.

4. His Royal Highness Prince Bhanurangsri Savangwongse (1859-1928), was the 45th child of His Majesty King Rama IV and 4th child of Her Majesty Queen Dhepsirindra, and the younger and favourite brother of His Majesty King Chulalongkorn. He was father to Prince Paribatra Sukhumbhand (1881-1944) and Prince Nibandh who were also on the boat. The latter was only 11 at this time. Chakrabongse referred to him as Toonmom Aa (*Aa* meaning an uncle who is a younger brother to one's father and Toonmom being a shortened form of Toonkramom and used for a prince/princess of *chaofa* rank, or the highest level).

5. Cecil A. Carter, had been tutor to Crown Prince Maha Vajirunhis (June 1878-January 1895) and was later author of *The Kingdom of Siam 1904* and a report on Thai students in 1916.

Saghalien
31st May 1896

Your Majesty

I informed Your Majesty in my last letter that I would give you details of the arrival in Colombo in my next letter and so I will now do this in detail.

On the 24th at 9 am we had sight of the island of Sri Lanka in the distance which gradually got nearer and nearer. At 11 in the morning we saw the light-house of Contra head which is the southernmost point of Sri Lanka. From there the boat turned and sailed north. At just after 2 pm we saw a small town which also has a lighthouse called Poynter Kell. Looking through binoculars I could see only one large building, the rest being small structures. The ship sailed on and at 4 pm we saw a hotel in an area of Colombo with the city visible on a point way in the distance. The ship gradually approached and I felt uneasy, wishing to reach Colombo as soon as possible. Originally the captain had said the ship would reach Colombo around midday, but because there were Thai princes on board he would try and get there faster at around 10 am. Then he said we would arrive around 4 pm, but when 4 pm came, we still weren't there. This made me very angry with the captain.

In fact, on that day in the morning there were very few waves, but by the afternoon as we approached Colombo, the waves increased and a par-

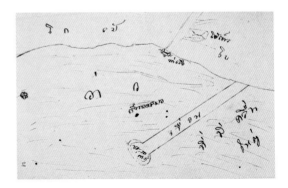

Sketch map drawn by Prince Chakrabongse showing the breakwater and the bay.

ticularly large wave broke over the roof of the boat. I was so keen to get to the shore which I had been star-ing at all the time. I was not sick but I felt sorry for Phra Nai Siri[1]. He hasn't been well at all. I shouldn't report this to you, but he has vomited many times. Meanwhile the boat was getting ever nearer to Colombo, until at almost 6 pm the boat passed in front of the city, the guns fired a 21-gun salute and the ship moored in the port at 6 pm.

When we got close to the town we could see the water pounding on the breakwater. It looked like a very impressive fountain or something reminiscent of Niagara falls. I examined this structure and was impressed that they managed to build something going straight out into the sea and able to withstand constant buffeting by strong waves. I should explain that the place where the the breakwater stands, is a small bay from where they constructed the breakwa-ter out to the point with a lighthouse at the end. The area inside the breakwater is large and completely calm, as shown in the plan which I have enclosed.

Once the ship had docked, the aide-de-camp of the governor came aboard. He was a Singhalese man born here. He was dark skinned and wearing a frock coat and top hat with a distinguished air. He spoke very good English. In addition a monk of the Maha Nikaya[2] Buddhist sect also came aboard. Toonmom Aa received them in the appropriate manner and then

The lighthouse in Colombo.

Colombo docks, looking out to sea.

we disembarked into the boat that they had provided. Tan Supadi and other Buddhist monks were waiting, as well as many onlookers. There was nowhere to walk and someone read an address welcoming Toonmom Aa, after which we pushed through the crowd to get into a car to the Grand Oriental Hotel which was close by. We went up to our room and received Tan Supadi who came to present monk paraphenalia which he asked us to present to Tan Sumankala. We learnt from him that there are some 10,000 Buddhist monks of which 6,000 were the Maha Nikaya sect and 4,000 were the Dhammayuttika Sect. In addition, 400 are of peculiar affiliation, including one Thai monk who was robed in white and wore a bun like a Brahmin and was asking for money for his passage back to Siam. As we saw that he came with a priest, Toonmom Aa gave him money to go home. He had had no idea how to get back. At 7.30 we had dinner together with the governor's ADC.

The governor himself had gone up to Kandy because there is going to be a ball on the birthday of Queen Victoria on the 26th so we didn't meet him here. Once we had had dinner a Singhalese man, who spoke good English, came with a picture showing the Buddha imprinting his footprint. There was also a Burmese man who said he was the nephew of Phraya Sirimon who lives in Bangkok. He brought a

Burmese bible to give to us. We rested for a while and then got in the car to tour the town. It is rather a mediocre place and cannot compete with Singapore in any way. On the other hand, it is pleasant and peaceful. We drove to the sea which is called Golfed. There were large waves and a delightful cool breeze. We also drove to a large pond which was quite impressive as well as passing a temple called Victoria. Then we drove straight to the railway station. We got on the train at just after 9 pm, which was a special train for ministers[3]. There were lots of seats so we didn't have to sleep sitting up. At 10 o' clock the train departed. I had heard that the route was very beautiful but as it was night time nothing could be seen. At 11 pm it started to rain. I went to sleep and at around midnight the train reached Kandy station.

25th. We had to wake at 4 am to have some tea and come down to await the horse carriage until almost 6 am. The ADC of the governor (another *farang*[4]) in uniform went in front with two more behind. We were able to look around the town which

1. Later known as Chao Meun Sri Soraruk (Peng Bunnag).
2. The Maha Nikaya Buddhist sect is the predominant sect of modern Thai Buddhism; the Dhammayuttika Nikaya is the other one. Both are Theravada Buddhist sects as is the Buddhism of Sri Lanka.
3. The 74-mile single-track Colombo-Kandy railway line was opened in 1867.
4. *Farang* is how Thais frequently refer to westerners.

Temple of the Holy Tooth, Kandy (Side View).

The Temple of the Tooth, c. 1890s.

The stupa holding the tooth, c. 1890s.

seemed even quieter than Colombo. However, the weather here is very pleasant. The town also has a large pond with an island in the middle. We reached the place where the Buddha's tooth is kept. I had thought the building would be large but in fact it was very small and I didn't realise the carriage would be able to draw up alongside the chapel. The chapel itself wasn't how we understand the word. Strictly speaking it shouldn't be called a chapel as it has several storeys. As we walked up the steps they beat the drums very loudly, explaining that it was because the Buddha's tooth was about to appear. We had to go up two more storeys before reaching the room where the tooth is housed. It is a tiny, little room about the same size as that of the Banya Hall in Wat Bavornives[5]. It is divided into two, one section slightly larger than the other. The smaller room is where the tooth is kept and is covered in elaborate gold. Up there we met a senior caretaker who was impressively dressed but kept his hat on inside the small room. The room had a large stupa on a base with horses and elephants (on either side). In front were standing eight monks but there were no other offerings. The stupa itself is decorated with many beautiful gems donated by previous kings. At first I had planned to go down on the floor in full salutation, but once inside, it was not possible as there was not enough room. They hadn't made any arrangements for us to pay our respects and

the Buddhist monks remained standing there. If I had gone down on the floor somebody would probably have stood on my back, because the area was thronged with local Singhalese people who had come up to have a look because the tooth relic is only open on special occasions. Suddenly two of the monks went up and took off the various decorations, before opening the stupa. Inside was another stupa and then yet more stupa, over four in all, before reaching the final box decorated with rubies. When this was opened, the tooth was finally revealed. I had a look and saw that it was two inches long. It didn't look like a human tooth, but rather a tiny elephant tusk. I lit candles and joss sticks and withdrew to allow others have a look. I also went in to see the golden Buddhist scriptures sent out by King Borommakot of Ayutthaya[6]. Then I came out and got back into the car, which drove down the same way before ascending the hill to Government House. The Governor[7] came down to meet us on the ground floor and invited us up to the reception room where we exchanged the conventional pleasantries.

This governor has only been in Sri Lanka for three months. He seems a good man. His name is Sir A. E. Havelock. Then he invited us down for breakfast, which consisted of tea and some toast. After this, we went back to the station, accompanied by both the Sri Lankan and *farang* aide-de-camps who saw us off and talked to Toonmom Aa until it was almost time to say goodbye. At 8.10 am the train left Kandy station. This time I made a great point of looking at the scenery along the way, which is alleged to be so beautiful. I had my notebook ready to note down a report for Your Majesty. Once the train had gone a certain distance, I saw beautiful scenery on either side with streams, valleys and mountains, as well as tea trees on the ridges of the hills. Everything is very green, nowhere is arid and there are lots of rice fields along the track. However, the bunds between the field are small and the fields lack order or a uniform size.

At 2.30 pm the train waited at a station in order to allow the other trains to pass through. Near the station is a monument to a certain Mr Dawson, the man who built the road from Colombo to Kandy, a distance of 74 miles. After that, one could see a valley between the mountains and the road below, with tiny figures walking, seeming as small as children, all amidst hills and trees. It was all very beautiful. After this came the first tunnel (blasted through the mountain), followed by lots of rice fields. It was like being in a balloon and looking down. Then we entered a second tunnel and a third. The latter was very long and, in the middle, it was so dark we could not see each other's faces. Then came another cutting and a high mountain known as Bible Rock, followed by the fourth tunnel, which was also long, before reaching Sensation Rock, a cliff to the left of the track. While we were coming along this delightful route, I said to Toonmom Aa that I was thinking about Your Majesty a lot, as you would have loved this part of the trip. However well I described the scene, could not in any way compare with seeing it yourself. I said I would have to rebuke Toonmom Chai[8] and tell him that not coming this way was like not coming to Lanka at all. I added that if you were to come in the *Maha Chakri* royal yacht, you would have to come when it was very calm, otherwise the boat would roll too much.

After this we reached the fifth tunnel. On leaving this one, there were a lot of twists and turns, which enabled us to see the train steaming ahead. Then came the sixth tunnel. Along the way on the left were inlets. We could see rice fields, as I mentioned before.

Then came a large stream, pulsating down the mountain. Some of these mountains are layered like steps, which are very dramatic. On the right of the track, are mountains with waterfalls from time to

The railway line near Kandy.

time. The seventh tunnel was also so long that you couldn't see anyone's face when we were inside, but it was a bit shorter than the one before. On exiting, there were many valleys, then at 3.20 the train stopped again. From then on, the rain began falling off and on until today, starting and stopping all the time. The eigth tunnel was also long and the ninth came immediately after, although it was shorter. By now there was some forest on the left. At around 3.30, we started to descend from the mountains onto a plain and it was not so interesting, so I hardly need to describe it. At 3.35, we came to a station where four to five trains were waiting to go to Colombo.

5. The Banya Hall was a small European style built by King Rama III for Prince Mongkut (later king) when he was a monk at Wat Bavornives (1824-1851)

6. King Barommakot of Ayutthaya (r. 1733-1758). During his reign he revived links with Sri Lankan Buddhism.

7. Governor A. E. Havelock. Sir Arthur Elibank (1844-1908) was governor of Ceylon from 1890, and of Madras in 1895, so in fact he was not the governor at this time, but perhaps he had come back specially?

8. Prince Paribatra Sukhumbhand (June 1881-January 1944). was the 33 son of King Chulalongkorn. As his mother was a queen, Queen Sukumala Marasi, Prince Chakrabongse used the appellation Toonmom Chai to refer to his half brother. Prince Paribatra went to study in Germany.

They were waiting for the train coming from Colombo. At that time I had my breakfast. Then at 5 minutes to 4, the train left the station and shortly thereafter crossed a wide river. At 4.10, it halted at another station for just a minute. Now there were rice fields on either side for about a *sen*[9], before the mountains. There were also often forests alongside the track, alternating with the rice fields. Then we crossed a river again, which might have been the same one as before. Then came more forests and hills, followed by the river running alongside the track. At 4.21, we passed another train in the station and briefly saw the river again. I asked a railway official what it was called and he said it is the Kalu Ganga and is the same one throughout. At 4.30 we crossed the river again and at 4.33 the train stopped to allow those who were in the front carriage to come and eat in this carriage before moving off. Then we came to the 11th tunnel, which was the last. On emerging from it we passed a pond with water lilies. At 5 pm, the train stopped in a station to let those who had been eating return to their carriage. This stretch had many flooded fields along the track but nothing else of interest. At 5.50 the train pulled into Colombo and we transferred from the train to a horse carriage.

Phra Sumangkla came to see Toonmom Aa and got into the carriage too. It was raining and we looked around the town which was pretty awful – dirty and not beautiful. All the streets were rain drenched. It was almost worse than Bangkok. We came to the port and got back on the *Saghalien*. The boat was full of people selling things, but the produce was terrible. At 1.03 pm, the ship weighed anchor and left Colombo. As soon as we were outside the breakwater, the waves were large, but not as bad as before. Once the boat left and I had eaten, I had to go to bed because I was so sleepy having slept only five hours the night before.

Today I am really very tired, but it was certainly great fun and I was very sad at having to come back to the ship.

On the 26th, the ship continued her course without incident and there was not much wind. Nor is there anything to report from the 27th or 28th. There were no waves. However, on the 30th it was rough all day and through the night until dawn. It was quite scary and Phra Nai Siri thought about waking me. As for Phra Borirak[10], he thought the boat was going to sink and prepared a piece of cork to help him swim. In fact, I woke often during the night as the waves were very loud and were crashing on the deck. I was rather frightened too, as tomorrow is the 31st which

Two of the many tunnels on the Kandy-Colombo line.

Aden and recount more details later.

Since leaving Colombo I have been well and am thinking about Your Majesty very much. Incidentally, since entering the area before the Red Sea, it has been incredibly hot – the same as in Thailand, or even worse – and I imagine that the Red Sea itself will be even hotter. Please tell the royal family that I have been thinking of everyone whilst enjoying myself sightseeing, as in the past we used to go travelling together. If they were here with me now, I am sure I would have had an even better time.

I beg to remain Your Majesty's obedient servant
Chakrabongse

can lead to thing all sorts of things[11].

On the morning of the 31st, the sea became calmer and, at 9am, we saw the Cape of Guardafui on the African coast[12]. By 10, we could see it clearly, and by 11, we sailed past the point where many ships have been wrecked. However, I was not afraid, as the sea was calm and the ship sailed on to take on coal in Aden. It had earlier planned to stop at Djibouti, but the coal there had run out. It should reach Djibouti tomorrow around 4 pm or thereabouts. However, the mail box for this ship will be taken off at 1 pm, so I will have to report to Your Majesty before reaching

In addition, I would like to dedicate to Your Majesty the merit that I received in paying my respects to the

9. A *sen* is a Thai unit of measurement equal to 40 m.

10. Phra Boribak was later Phraya Maitri Wirachakrid (Pum Bunnag).

11. 31st May was the anniversary of the date when Queen Sunanta Kumari (November 1860-May 1880) drowned and so was considered very inauspicious.

12. Cape of Guardafui is a headland in Somalia, which forms the geographical apex of the Horn of Africa.

Map produced by Messageries Maritimes, one of the main shipping lines between Europe and the East, c.1890s.

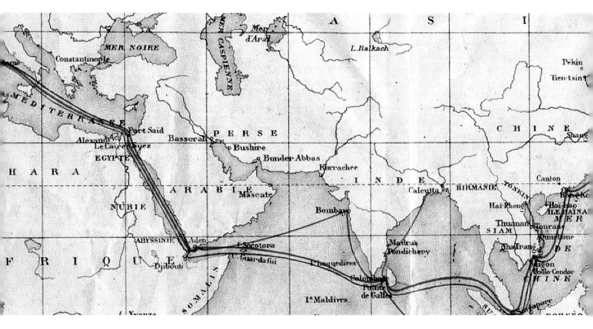

Front row from left to right: Prince Rabi, Chao Chom Manda Chum, Queen Saovabha, King Chulalongkorn, Prince Damrong, Chaiyan and Krom Luang Sampasart.

Back row: Dr. Reytter (royal physician), Head of the botanical gardens, Jamin Raja Madhya, Jamin Wayaworanat, the deputy of the gardens, and at far right, the Assistant Resident.

Hotel van Horek, Garoet
24 June 1896

Dear Lek

I have had no time to forget you! In particular, every time I go riding I always talk about you. I received your letter from Colombo here. I like the way you write and have shown it to many people who all said that you write well. The places we have visited are Batavia [see opposite]; Buitenzorg[1], which has a beautiful Botanical garden; Cipanas[2], an area of Jakarta with hot springs and the place where the Governor General[3] resides and Sindang. These latter two places require going up a 7,000-foot mountain, but the roses are really beautiful. Prince Rabi[4] said that in Europe they are hardly as beautiful as this, as the temperature here is perfect. Then we came to Garoet[5]. It

is a quiet, provincial town, but the weather is good. We stayed a week. We also went to Bandung[6], Cianjur and Sukabumi. The first was the town where the officials lived just like with us. The second city is for ministers, *Raden Adipati*, and the third city is for more junior officials. We are also going to go to Solo[7], which is the Dutch equivalent of our Khmer territories[8], as they rule themselves. There are many strange customs. Our trip here is a lot of fun, as we understand each other easily. The words for places or desires here are not like Malay at all, as the language is mainly Sanskrit, and thus the theatrical performances are of the *Mahabharata*, *Ramakien* or else *Inao*[9]. So we enjoy them all. The people are sort of Hindu, and sing and dance. They are allowed to drink and the women are not required to hide themselves.

The countryside is mountainous and full of water

but not like in Singapore. The mountains go as high as 7,000-8,000 feet. They are so clever in their water management from the top of the mountain to the foot. Wherever the path goes, so does the water, so they can grow crops all the year round. One can in fact say that for these people water is power. Machinery hardly needs to use electricity at all. But it made me depressed about our country, when I see how well developed it is, despite being a colony. Nothing is just done for show, but simply for its benefit. It doesn't matter if it's not beautiful. They are so good at producing something beneficial. In other areas we could perhaps follow suit, but with regard to irrigation and people, we can't compete. They have up to 20 million and, since we've been here, finding somewhere with no people, somewhere that is virgin forest such as at Chom Bung, is not possible.

However, there is a lot of oppression. So everyone is dragooned into making roads, for example. But on the other hand this is instead of taxes. In terms of a feeling of fear, our country is much freer. If someone is important they have to kneel down. If someone just visited Batavia they would think that it is not very different from Singapore, but, once in the interior, it is a different story. Their governance is simple and there is little bureaucracy. They are allowed largely to govern themselves. So there is an official who controls the locals and around 2-3 overseers for 100,000 people, namely an assistant official, a chief inspector and his assistant. For one district, there is a senior official, a chief clerk, a chief inspector, a deputy inspector and an assistant. If it is a district with seven cities, there will be a committee of around 25 people for around 1,000,000 citizens. The populace seem to be very happy. They use very little money and receive it

Batavia

This city, now present-day Jakarta, was the capital of the Dutch colonial empire. The King's journey to Java aimed both to restore his health and act as a trial run for his trip to Europe in 1897. At the time, Java was part of the Dutch East Indies, which, after the collapse of the Dutch East India Company in 1800, was brought under Dutch government control. As the King was to observe in his two letters, the colonial social order was based on rigid racial and social structures, with the two legal classes being the colonialists (soldiers, administrators, managers, teachers and pioneers) and the "natives", the indigenous population. The term Indonesia did not come into use for the geographical location until the late 19th century. The prime aim of the Dutch was to secure access to cash crops and natural resources, as well as the profitable trade in spices.

Comparisons with Siam

In both these letters, in particular the second, longer one, King Chulalongkorn tries to find similarities with Siam, such as similar dance drama performances or certain peoples, customs and traditions.

---

1. Buitenzorg is present-day Bogor. Originally the capital of the Sunda kingdom, it was the summer residence of the Governor Generals. At that time it was one of the most westernized cities.

2. Cipanas is the site of the wooden 'palace' of the former Dutch Governor Generals of the Dutch East Indies.

3. The Governor General of the Dutch East Indies was Carel Herman Aart van de Wijck (governed 1893-99).

4. Prince Rabi Badhanasakdi, Prince of Rajaburi (1874-1920).

5. Garut (in Dutch: Garoet) was a hill station for the Dutch elite.

6. About 180 km southeast of Batavia and connected by railroad since 1880. Tea-growing area.

7. Present-day Surakarta.

8. In the Java letters, the king makes comparisons with Siam throughout, with greater or lesser success.

9. All three dance dramas were also performed in Siam.

regularly, so that for 20 years now they have had no debt. They have money to send home, it's just not that much. The Dutch are rather gloomy. They hardly have dinner parties and rarely meet up. One aspect of what we refer to as the 'Dutch yoke' can be seen in the fact that every evening between 7 and 8.30 they go and see each other and sit around a table in rocking chairs chatting. They all have dinner in their homes just with their wives and children.

One of the things that I really wanted to see, I have achieved, namely volcanoes[10]. I even went and walked in a crater, which is like a broken dish. One enters through the crack and can walk around the bottom, but it's very steep. Imagine riding a horse up the Golden Mount. If the horse does not die en route it will bring you back. But it didn't even get as far as half way. Your mother and I are very well, but Eeyd Lek[11] has been unwell twice with a fever because he went swimming and had an upset stomach as usual. I plan to reach Bangkok in August. Please tell Toh[12] that I will write to him on another occasion, as it's so hard to find time. I received his letter, but it arrived after yours, so I'll have to reply later. If you see Sadet Na Toh[13] or Toonmom Aa, tell them that I am thinking of them and want to write, but it's just more than I can manage as we're rushing here and rushing there with no time at all. And while I'm here, I want to see as much as possible as is my habit. As you know, I'll go and see anything not to have spare time on my hands. But nothing is certain. I am so tired.

Pravitr[14] has arrived and we met up in Bandung. Now that he is with me he, seems very Thai and not as severe and serious as I had imagined. I think I'll be able to use him for work. Nevertheless, how can I stop thinking about you? I really don't know what to do.

Chulalongkorn

King Chulalongkorn on horseback en route to Papandayan volcano.

10. The king visited several volcanoes. The first was Papandayan, southeast of Bandung and near Garut. In 1772, an eruption and ensuing avalanche had destroyed 40 villages and killed nearly 3,000 people.

11. Eeyd Lek was the nickname of Prince Asdang Dejavudh, Prince of Nakhon Ratchasima (1889-1924). He was a younger brother of Prince Chakrabongse.

12. Toh, meaning large in Thai, was the nickname of Crown Prince Vajiravudh, born 1 January 1881 and Prince Chakrabongse's elder brother by two years. Later King Vajiravudh (r. 1910-1925).

13. Sadet Na Toh, meaning Prince Uncle Toh, was a younger full brother of Queen Saovabha, Prince Svasti Sobhon. *Na* is an aunt or uncle who is younger than one's mother.

14. HRH Prince Pravitra Vadhanodom (1875-1919) was the 15th child of King Chulalongkorn and only child of Chao Chom Manda Cham.

King Chulalongkorn posing on top of the Bromo volcano.

King Chulalongkorn wrote in his letters that he had longed to visit and examine volcanoes.

Arrival in Batavia, May 25th, 1896. His Majesty King Chulalongkorn (centre, white suit) walking with Mr Carel van de Wijck, the Governor-General of the Dutch East Indies.

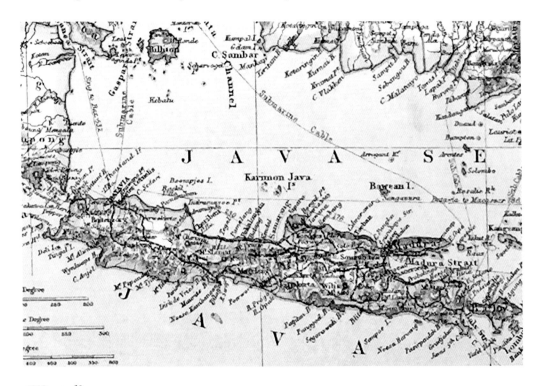

1902 map of Java.

The royal yacht Maha Chakri.

Royal yacht Maha Chakri

30 July 1896

To my son Lek

I feel that this may be the only day on which I can keep my promise and briefly write to you about the journey, as tomorrow we will reach Singapore and it is unlikely that I will have any free time and would have to wait to write from Bangkok, which would be too long. After leaving Garut, we have been having a rest in Maos which is a district beween Surabaya and Batavia in the county of Banjur Mas. From Maos onwards, it is the east of Java. The west and east halves of Java are very different from each other in many ways, both in terms of the geography and the people, as I will tell you. On the west, the countryside is completely mountainous. There are some large fields, it is true, but they are several hundred, or even one thousand, feet above sea level and are surrounded by mountains. There are very few low-lying rice fields and most are stepped such as you described on the way to Kandy. I asked those who had been to Kandy, such as Prince Damrong, who once came and praised them to me when he first got back, and he had to admit they were not a patch on those here. The eastern half, in contrast, is a flat plain like at home. The fields are mainly large and are planted with indigo or sugar cane, but there are still a lot of mountains, which are further away. There is no doubt that the land on the east site is more fertile than that on the west, and the people on the east and the centre of the country are the true Javanese, with a distinct lan-

guage. On the east, bordering the sea, are some people from the island of Madura[1], many of whom live in Surabaya and also have a distinct language. Those from Sunda don't mix with them, and vice versa. But Javanese are found everywhere and, in the centre, one finds a mix of all three ethnicities. If one arrived first on the west and learnt the language of that region, by the time you reach the east, or the centre, no one would understand you. Thus the word for committee member on the east is *Waedan* and on the west *Waedono*. The title of the same person such as *Senapati* on the west, on the east will be *Senopati*. In other words, *aa* is changed into *o*. However, if one tries to invent things and change some *o*'s in line with the Madot language, it doesn't work because the *o* has various complications and when in the middle of the word there are 2-3 *o* sounds. Things that should be *o* are not, and one has to start again. The Dutch themselves have made it more confusing, as they pronounce the words strangely, such as Baengkok, even though they know they haven't got it right. Their pronounciation is weird anyway. They speak English as if they are actors. So the word Pappanda they pronounce Papandaa. Other times they use the pronunciation of the Javanese, just as the way people in the capital say things so it is also slightly off. It's as if Nakhon was suddenly the capital and Bangkok a provincial town. Thus, the town known as Surakarta, they pronounce Surakatta, or someone called Prapuwiyaya, they call Prapuwee-yaayo. Malay is used as a common language by all, although the ordinary people don't understand it on the whole. Trying to find an interpreter among these three groups of people is rather hard and they have different characteristics.

The Javanese are intelligent, but they are slight of build and, especially among the royals, there is no one

The Javanese rice fields and irrigation were admired by the King.

---

1. Madura is an island off the northeastern coast of Java and is separated from the main island by a narrow strait.

who is taller than we are. They are polite, but do everything annoyingly slowly[2]. They seem ignorant of speed and even drive very slowly. Erecting a bamboo hut takes a whole month, while for the Sultan to sign his name requires a clerk to come in and check the document letter by letter, taking an hour.

The Sundanese[3] are rather uncouth. They are well built, but not very bright. They also do things very slowly and use old-fashioned methods, which have been in use for 2,000 years or so. An example is the short wooden tubular musical instrument known as an *angklung*[4]. They are a moral people, however, and nobody smokes opium or drinks. So for that reason in the Priyungka region, the Dutch prohibit the sale of opium and there are no liquor shops. On the Madura side, the people are well built and muscular. They do not wear their hair in a topknot like the Javanese and Sundanese, but rather in the Malay style. They like taking employment and are not afraid of work. When carrying things along the road, they use their heads, unlike the Javanese and Sundanese. However, they are fierce and always carry a knife. It is forbidden to touch anyone and they get annoyed by small things. If someone just glances at their wife, they will stab him. In towns where there are many Madurese, such as Surabaya or Pasurawon, there is a stabbing every day. The day I arrived in Pasurawon, I saw a knife fight and the wounded man being carried off almost dead. I went to Kamel, which is the port town of Madura and has only a few houses. On that day they had been two stabbings. In constrast, on the Sunda side, stabbings or court cases are rare. The Javanese fall between the two, being neither very good, nor very quarrelsome. Among these three ethnic groups, the Chinese can be anywhere[5]. On the west side, the Chinese are looked down on, whereas on the east, the Chinese are looked up to, because they are more pros-

perous than the Dutch, wealthy largely as a result of sugar-cane plantations. Overall, they understand things better than the *farang*.

Now I will return to the account of my journey. I went to stay in Maos for one night. The next day we took the train to Cilacap which is a port on the Indian Ocean side. It is the only town there and the Dutch planned to make it into a big city like Batavia. They made roads and built a barracks, as well as warehouses as big as those in Batavia. Moving troops from there to Yogja (or Yogjakarta), which is another capital city is easy. It was established at the time when the Diponegoro[6] revolt was suppressed 40 years ago. Then there was such a serious outbreak of malaria that no one could live there. Nowadays, it is a deserted town, which looks like Nakhon Sri Thammarat. It is the first time I have seen an abandoned town in Java. Only the roads have been kept in good condition. There are no roads which compare with those in Java. It's not that they have invested a lot of money in creating new roads. In fact, they are the old military tracks, like those Chao Phraya Bodindecha[7] used to go to Cambodia. They are well maintained and there are tracks linking all the important towns. In total, there must be 1,000s of tracks crossing the whole island. One can use a two-horse carriage to go gently along for two or three hours. They pack the roads with hard gravel and there are good walking tracks too. The rivers are mainly shallow or have been channelled using stone or coal, so they are not used for transport but irrigation, with a system of dams and channels. Before the water reaches the sea, it has been truly well used and this is the great resource of Java.

From Maos, we went to Yogjakarta, the old capital from the beginning of the Mataram dynasty[8], a dynasty that still rules today but whose capital was moved to various places, finishing up in Surakarta.

---

2. Throughout this letter, the King frequently complained about how slow the Javanese were.

3. The Sundanese on the western side of Java were very different from the Javanese. They practiced dry- not wet-rice farming and had a simpler way of life, with a less rigid social hierarchy.

4. The *angklung* is a percussion instrument, in which carved bamboo tubes are attached to a bamboo frame. The base of the instrument is held in one hand and it is struck with the other, to produce a resonant pitch.

5. The Chinese were regarded as 'foreign Orientals' by the Dutch and had difficulty acquiring land. They were also educated in separate schools. Some picked spices, others were middlemen for tax collection, making them unpopular with the locals.

Batavia was, and remains, the main centre, of the Chinese population and it was the most important trading port.

6. Prince Diponegoro (1785-1855) opposed Dutch colonial rule and played an important role in the Java War of 1825-30.

7. Chao Phraya Bodindecha (Sing Singhaseni), 1777-1849, was a top general and Minister of Civilian Affairs during the reign of King Rama III. He led the campaign to Cambodia in the 1840s.

8. The Mataram dynasty was the last major independent Javanese kingdom before the island was colonised by the Dutch. It was the dominant political force, radiating from the interior of Central Java from the late 16th century until the early 18th century. In 1755, after much internecine strife, it was divided into the Yogyakarta Sultanate and Surakarta.

Above and below right: King Chulalongkorn and his party.
In the top photograph, the king wears boots for riding.

One of the things the king commented on were traditional
Javanese houses, here in Sundanese style.

Performers at the court of Surakarta.

At this point, the kings split the kingdom into two. Today, the former kingdom of Mataram is in two parts, but the new arrangement has endured over seven generations. The head of the Surakarta dynasty is the Susuhunan[9], which means saint in Mohamadism. Both kingdoms are rather similar and both have a Front Palace[10]. This arose because the Dutch were unable to quash the rebels. When they saw that the royals were fighting each other, they stepped in to broker a deal and divide up the territory. They could then take some for themselves and let the remainder be independent. There is thus a second king in the capital, but he has no power to inherit the throne[11] and has to accept that the main king has a son who is the crown prince, referred to as *Pangeran Adipati* and equal in status to the Front Palace. So both Front and Main Palaces have a crown prince. There is another person who is similar to the *kaew fa* of Cambodia. These two positions are not hereditary, but depend on the will of the Sultan and the Resident, who can appoint a younger brother or a son to the Front palace or the Main palace.

Apart from going to the residency, I did not go into any homes at all.

The palace is known as the *kraton*. It is in an old quarter, like the home of Prince Noruebal[12]. There are narrow streets with higgledy piggledy walls everywhere. However, the palace itself is very spacious with an entrance like our Front Palace. Javanese city planing traditions require that a wide lawn, known as an *alun-alun*, is installed first and this is used to spread sand and plant a ficus tree. If it is in the capital, two trees are planted in the middle with others surrounding it. If it is an ordinary town, just one tree suffices. The capital has two such spaces – a large one to the north and a smaller one to the south. The palace habitually faces north. Around the *alun-alun* on the north, are many buildings known as *prasaebun* for the royals who are *pangeran*, those who are from a different family or *raden adipati* and important officials, *pupatti* [should be *priyayi*] The rulers of tribute states come to pay their respects twice a year.

In front of the palace is a spacious pavilion with brick columns, an earthen floor and a woven bamboo roof in order to hold audiences once a year. In the interior, there is a square hall rather like the *kuti* of Zen priests. It is known as a *pendopo*[13] and is used for receiving female relatives. It is beautifully carved and

9. Susuhunan was the title used by the monarchs of Mataram and then by the hereditary rulers of Surakarta.

10. Front palace. The explanation that follows shows King Chulalongkorn attempting to compare the palace set up in Java with that in Siam. In the latter, the Front Palace was occupied by the Second or Deputy King and was more or less powerful according to the personalities involved, sometimes causing a lot of trouble, as was the case in late 1874-early 1875 in Siam, when the Second King attempted to block some of King Chulalongkorn's reforms. The office of Deputy King was abolished during the reign of King Rama V. This led King Rama V to view the institution of the Front Palace in a negative way.

11. The succession was determined by the Sultan and the resident. In his account, the king uses the various titles as used at the Yogyakarta court. *Adipati* can be loosely translated as Duke and *Pangeran* as prince.

12. Prince Noruebal Mukkhamataya was the elder brother of Queen Debsirindra and, thus, uncle to King Chulalongkorn. He received a special title, as did other relatives on the King's mother's side.

13. This open-sided pavilion on four columns is a basic element of Javanese architecture.

14. *sok* = 50 cm, *wa* = 2 metres

adorned with gold leaf. Going further inside is the throne hall which must have a massive bed which can be as large as 10 *sok* by 3 *wa*[14] depending on one's rank. These huge beds have a mattress over the whole thing with large cushions. Half the bed consists of triangular cushions and pillows lining the headboard. In front of the bed are carvings of a woman and a man dressed in wedding regalia. Two small shelves are for food offerings and this is where the house spirits reside. When newly-weds first lie on the bed, the spirits are invited to go and lie there with them, but otherwise it is just a shrine. Such spirit shrines are found throughout Java no matter whether in the home of a king or an ordinary person.

If it is the residence of a Sultan or a prince who has hereditary arms or regalia known as *pusaka*[14] such as a kris, these are kept on the altar whenever they are away. In fact, they would rather die than give up their kris. I'm telling you about the Javanese home all at once so I don't have to repeat it.

We arrived in the evening.

The next day, the Sultan[15] came to see us. He was dressed half formally in a fashion difficult to describe, but I'll try. He was wearing trousers of patterned material, wrapped around with a piece of cloth four times as wide as a sarong. It was slightly pleated on the left with the edge trailing on the floor. He wore a white Indian-style shirt, the thick collar coming up to his chin. It was buttoned from the collar down the front with 12 buttons. His jacket was velvet and was slightly like our Thai style ones. He was wearing one of his own decorations namely commander and the lion of the Dutch as another. A diamond watch chain hung across his chest and he wore another around his neck. His hair was worn in a bun in the form of a dragonfly, in which there was a diamond butterfly brooch and a diamond comb. His hair was enclosed in a black sheath with gold mesh like a wrist band for sewing. He wore shoes studded with diamonds but no stockings. He had a kris tucked at the back of his outfit. When he arrived, he got down from the Resident's car and took his arm, holding it in the fash-

ion of a lady. One of his sons served as aide-de-camp and held the edge of his cloth. At first I thought that he was feeling weak, but then when the Crown Prince got down, the Assistant Resident jumped up to lead him also. It was quite comical and I felt awkward that the Dutch were humouring them in this way and treating them like a European lady going into church for her wedding. We were all hiding our smiles, but talking to him, it was clear he was a very polite man. However, he did not ask me anything at all as that would have been seen as a sign of disrespect, so I had to hold forth alone. Once he had gone, we went on visiting the *kraton*. I have to complain somewhat about the way they receive guests in Java. When you reach the palace gates, the guard receives you and you don't have to take their hand. The soldier guarding the door wore a coat of that patterned material, had a

Sultan Hamengkubowono VII.

14. *Pusaka* within the Javanese and the Malay world refers to family heirlooms passed down from ancestors. The *pusaka* can have specific names and titles as well as supernatural attributes.

15. The Sultan at that time was Hamengkubowono VII (r. 1879-1921).

kris in his belt and carried a spear. When he salutes, he touches the end of the kris with his right hand. Once you've gone through the door, the *raden adipati* called Premier and eight *Patinayakos* come to greet you. These are soldiers as in Europe, but look a bit scruffy. Penetrating further inside were the *Pangeran adapati* and Pangeeran. We had to shake hands with about 20 people. The royal steed and old fashioned soldiers were also standing to receive us in the court-yard. In the next room was the Pangeran Adipati Hanum, the Crown Prince with a gold umbrella. Six senior people (*tao kae*) bearing the things came out to meet me. When they reached me, they crouched down and raised their hands with their fingers level with their nose in salutation. Then they opened their arms as if to lead me in. I froze and would not let them lead me in. They were very surprised as to why I would not let them lead me. So I had to explain why, and then he walked in ahead of me.

The Sultan came out to meet me outside the *pen-dopo*. He did not *wai*, but shook my hand and then held out his arm. I hesitated again. He looked suspicious, as if I was offended about something. After-wards, I cross-examined the Assistant Resident and understood that it was an Indonesian tradition for the lesser person to lead the senior person into their home. When the Governor General visits, he is also led in in that way. They were afraid that I was being haughty. When the Governor General receives the Sultan, he leads him in too, but because he is the sen-ior figure he uses his left arm. Once I knew this, I allowed myself to be led in this way and it was fine all the way to Solo. At first I could barely contain my laughter, and was amused again when there were three people to be led. Thus, when we went to the ball, I led in your mother and he was leading me in turn. The *farang* just smiled, but all this leading is too much. Any time one just moves from one's chair, the resident's arm is next to the Sultan at all times.

And the wife is rushing around trying to keep up. The tradition is the same in both cities.

In the inner courtyard, the officials and pages stood in their hundreds, wearing coats and *koluk*, a fez-like hat. Upon reaching the *pendopo*, your mother and I sat in the middle with the Sultan on my left. The *ratu*, his wife sat on your mother's right and so on, according to rank. First there was *pinphat* music[16] and we drank tea. Then the host must ask: "Would you like some tea?", to which we were expected to say "yes". The person holding the tea tray, then came over and knelt down. The Sultan, or whoever is the host, must then pour the tea. Then we had to ask, "Do you want some sugar?" The host will nod and we then had to put the sugar into both cups, while saying just a lit-tle. Then the host adds the milk and we had to say just a little. Finally, both parties drink their tea and sit still until the *pinphat* music finishes. Then the ciga-rettes are brought round and he asks whether you want a cigarette. Once you've taken one, the servant brings a set of betel leaves or coconut leaves depend-ing on availability. The orchestra continues. After the third cigarette, came a tray of drinks. On the one tray were two sets, each with eight glasses. A servant with a cabinet of alcoholic drinks followed behind. This time we were asked what we wanted to drink. It was rather awkward, as one could not say "No". However, when one gave an answer, they did not understand as the names of the drinks were strange. So we had to point to this or that and take whatever came. Whatever we chose, the Sultan had to follow suit and take it from the same tray, while bowing back and forth. They don't get on with things, and there was music to accompany the alcoholic drinks. This cus-tom is so tiring. If you meet someone three or four times on the same day, each encounter requires the same ceremony. The Dutch homes have adopted it too. After that, whatever you want to do is allowed. The time wasted by this formality is at least 15 min-utes and sometimes as much as half an hour.

The performances put on for guests are: *Srimpi*, or *serimpi*, with four dancers and the *bedhaya* with nine dancers. They wear sarongs with no front fold, known as *gone,* and the hem is kept long and trails on the ground, so that during the dance it can be kicked this way and that. They wear a short-sleeved velvet top with upturned shoulders and a scarf hanging down to the knees on both sides and a girdle with

16. *Pinphat* music refers to Thai classical music performances. In this case, the indigenous Javanese music must have been similar enough for the King to use the same term.

17. The *Srimpi/Serimpi* and *bedhaya* are the classical dances asso-ciated with the royal palaces of Yogyakarta and Surakarta. The *Srimpi* dance is soft and slow, with highly stylized hand positions and poses. The *bedhaya* is more sacred and there are many taboos connected with its performance. The dances epitomized the elegant nature of the court and were an important symbol of the ruler's power.

Wayang kulit *(shadow puppet) performance in the royal court.*

another belt on top. A belt is tied around, either in three layers or one, with a sword in front. They wear rings on six fingers and a headdress with spikes stuck into their hair, which is gathered in a bun with a tail piece hanging down. The bun is held in place by a net of jasmine flowers, while the hanging hair is also enclosed with a net. There are diamond hairpins like the back of a Thai-style tiara. The front of their arms and their feet are dusted with yellow cumin powder, while their eyebrows are shaved and then redrawn to resemble a *khon* mask[18]. Round the eyes, the cumin powder is wiped off to leave bare skin and this makes their eyes seem really large. The *unalom* symbol is drawn in the centre of their forehead, using charcoal. The orchestra walked out in front, but to get to the throne hall along a passageway of about 10 *wa* they took half an hour. There was an old woman walking out in front like Mayurachatra[19], wearing a knife a little like the one I sent you, and then sitting in the meditation posture, but with knees high in order to read a long eulogy, before the dancing began. The procession of dances is similar to the *lakhon luang rum banleng*[20]. There is a story and a plot, but to explain it would take too long. The costumes and traditions are rather convoluted in both cities, but are not too different from each other. Apart from this, there was a *wayang orang*[21] and other things which we had seen before. They were all *lakhon nok*[22], while in Jogja they perform genuine court dramas with no deviation from traditon.

Above: Two photographs showing a group of dancers performing the bedhaya.

18. *Khon* masks were worn for the Thai masked dance drama based on the *Ramakien*, the Siamese version of the *Ramayana*.

19. In the tonsurate ceremony for young princes and princesses held in the Grand Palace in Bangkok, an older lady from the Inside part of the palace would led the procession holding an item of regalia called Mayurachatra, which was a bunch of peacock feathers.

20. & 22 *Lakhon luang rum banleng* and *Lakhon luang* were dance dramas performed only in the court. *Rum banleng* means danced to music. *Lakhon nok*, footnote 22, were performances for the general public.

21. *Wayang orang* is a classical dance performance with themes from the *Ramayana* or *Mahabharata*. The performances are highly stylised.

The exterior (above) and interior (below) of the pendopo *of the palace in Surakarta.*

Court musicians in the palace in Surakarta.

The royal Siamese party, Dutch officials and local Javanese outside a traditional house.

Javanese officials in Surakarta.

In Solo, the performance was like those by Chao Phraya Mahindra[23] at Manunyaya (the real Mongkol Chaiya), or a play like those of Phraya Deves[24]. The banquet consisted of eating while watching, but once again we had to do everything in concert. If we didn't eat, he couldn't either. We knew that he had not eaten, so had to eat everything for his sake. But in Solo, all the royal relatives were ordered to come out, including one as old as our Princess Man Kien[25]. Pravitra was led by this lady and got very anxious. The receptions begin about 9 pm and do not finish until around 2 am, which can become very tedious.

The Susuhunan[26] is worth talking about more than anyone else. We had all said that he was rather crazy, but in fact he is not mad at all. He is a young man who was born into a life of knowing nothing about the world except enjoying *serempi* and *bedhaya*. The Dutch have done their utmost to keep him sequestered and to prevent him from knowing anything. When I tell you the following anecdote, you will see it's true. He related it himself and I have asked other people. An American woman went to see him and he asked her if America was large or small. She said it was large. He asked her how many assistant residents there were. She said there were none. He replied that his country had five assistant residents. How can you blame him for this? He has faults, and the mind of a child. If he thinks of something, he has to say or do it. There is nothing he thinks he can't say or do. Decorations are the things he loves most in the world. Everything else – women, ships or treasure – he can without, but not decorations. The first time we met, before talking of anything else, he asked me what decorations I was wearing and kept stroking them, so that in the end we talked of nothing else. In our party, he liked those who were wearing decorations and called them over to touch the various

The Susuhunan, Pakubuwono X, wearing many decorations on his velvet jacket.

medals and offer that person a drink or cigarettes. Luang Sunthorn[27], the interpreter, happens to have a lot of decorations and so the Susuhunan gave him a watch with a gold strap. If someone has only a few decorations, whether a royal or a commoner, he ignores them completely. Unfortunately those without decorations go in first and, seeing those with decorations behind, he takes their hand or claps them on the shoulder. Indeed, he rushes to those who have decorations to such an extent that it's become habitual.

If anyone is going to visit, he asks first if they have decorations. If they don't, he receives them poorly, but if they do, he receives them well and wears five stars he has designed himself. The only problem is that they look like those belonging to Toonmom[28],

23. Chao Phraya Mahindrasakdi Dhamrong (Peng Benyakul) 1821-1894 was influential in developing Thai theatre in the reigns of Kings Rama IV and Rama V. He was also a choreographer and theatre designer, as well as having a commercial theatre. Later his troupe, led by his sons, went to St. Petersburg, while Prince Chakrabongse was there.

24. Chao Phraya Deves Wongwiwat was in charge of the Telegraph office, but also encouraged the *khon* troupes to include dance performances. The King is linking what he sees in Java to comparable performances in Siam.

25. Princess Man Kien was a daughter of King Rama II, who lived to a great age. The King was comparing an old Javanese lady to her.

King Chulalongkorn, Pakubuwono X and their entourages.

which we used to wear for fun at New Year. This whole obsession with decorations is not entirely his fault. The Dutch are also fairly keen. When he received the Crown of Siam Second Class[29], he practically leapt in the air and whomsoever he met, be it a page or a teaboy, he showed it off.

Another rather unattractive thing is their dress. From Susuhunan downwards, all his relatives wear powder on their faces like princes about to undergo their tonsurate. Their eyebrows are shaven and then redrawn so they slant up like in Chinese opera. Their moustaches are also shaved off and drawn to resemble a hook or bow. One of the *pangerans* has drawn a beard on his chin with charcoal and has a few measly hairs like an elephant. It really looks ridiculous rather than impressive. Susuhunan is better turned out than the rest. If one thinks of him as a character in a dance drama, he is good looking and could definitely be the lead. However, he is very thin and looks rather unhealthy. As for his conversational skills, they are first class and he acts as if we have been friends for a century. He felt comfortable asking me how many wives and how many children I have, and told me how many he has. With such and such a dancer, he has a child, with that one not yet, and that one is not yet his wife. He took me inside as far as his living quarters and got his wives to come and sit with us. There were over 50 betel nut sets[30]. In the end, he went to see us off at the station. Wherever he goes, a hunchbacked woman and an old woman accompany him. There was one old lady, like our Tao

Worachan[31], called *Raden Adipati* who was one of his father's wives. She was well turned out and looked like our lady. She has found maybe 13 to 14 dwarves to act as servants and they crawled here and there under the tables and beside the chairs. Your mother said she liked them when she was seated, as they were quick and efficient, but did not like it when she was walking as she was scared to trip over them.

There was a review of soldiers in both cities, but it was odd that the soldiers performed the Kachentara Sanam[32] just like ours. There were children and

26. The rulers of Surakarta, Susuhunan, traditionally adopted the reign name of Pakubuwono, in this case Pakubuwono X (r.1893-1939). It was well known that he was obsessed with orders and decorations, as will be seen in the King's account.

27. Luang Sunthorn Kosa. Born in Penang, his original name was Koyulay Na Ranong (1868-1965). He became a royal page to King Rama V, before leaving to study law in England. He then returned to royal service with the title Luang Sunthorn Kosa in the legal department of the Foreign Office. In 1891 he accompanied Prince Damrong on his tour of European capitals. He was to accompany the King on his first trip to Europe in 1897.

28. Toonmom here refers to King Rama IV and was a shortened version of his title, used only by immediate family members.

29. The Most Noble Order of the Crown of Thailand was established in 1869 by King Rama V for Thais, the royal family, government employees and foreign dignitories. The second class had the title Knight Commander.

30. Betel nut chewing was very common in Southeast Asia and each wife would be given a special set as an item of regalia.

31. Tao Worachan was a position held by one of the senior ladies of the Inside (the area of the Grand Palace where men were not allowed).

32. The Kachentara Sanam was a special ceremony instituted by King Rama IV, in which elephants were paraded in front of the King and sprinkled with holy water.

adults, all swaying about. They marched in time to the *pinphat* orchestra and danced as well. Those who wanted to give them some refreshment could not just go up to them, but had to dance as well. And all the servers carrying food were members of the royal family. Their rank[33] is that of *ratu* meaning consort. The other wives are known as *raden*. The children of *ratuweba* when still young are called *dusadee raden mas*. When they are older and can wear coats they are made *dusadee pangeran*. The children of *raden* of any age are *raden mas* and later *pangeran*. The children of *pangeran* are *raden mas*. The children of *raden mas* are *raden mas punyi* , the same level as *mom rajawongse*, the ranks declining in some eight stages before they become commoners. However, the *raden mas* level, who are not children of the king, can be elevated to *pangeran,* like our *krom meun*, and *mas punyi* can be elevated to *raden mas* in the manner of *phra ong chao*.

Hearing about their lives, makes me feel sorry for them. The wretched Dutch are true oppressors in every way, but it's too long to write about. If you can, get hold of the book *History of Java* by Thomas Stamford Raffles[34] printed in 1817 and you will learn about everything. You will learn how the Front Palace went to the *farang* asking to be appointed king. How once appointed, he was very stupid and never revived his fortunes. Today he is still alive and has been able to pass on the crown, because the Dutch are not very brave. Whatever they do, they are in a quandary but despite that they have included him. The Front Palaces of both cities habitually dress in Western clothes, because they are afraid that otherwise they will have to sit on the floor or make salutation according to existing traditions. However, if they dress in

the Dutch way, they don't have to sit on the floor and don't need to make the traditional *wai* greeting. Nevertheless, they do all still *wai* even when dressed in Western clothes, so the only benefit is they can sit in chairs. When in Javanese dress, they must sit on the floor, or, if they are royal, they can sit on the *pendopo*, although each time they take a step they must *wai*. So by the time they reach the top, they have *wai*'d many times. Officials sit on the ground; no rush mats are provided and the dust is about two inches thick.

I must stop talking about the palace and the royal family now and talk about the ordinary people in the regions of these two cities. They look extremely poor, because the officials and royals have to take advantage of them in order to get by. They, in turn, are in debt to the Dutch up to their ears, as they had to borrow money from them to quash the Toroh revolt[35]. Even if they didn't ask the Dutch to crush it for them, they were charged a very high price. They added sums for this and that and, once they had helped them, the Dutch were masters of the country. They also take bribes or sometimes extort money brazenly, such as happened with Susuhunan. Someone appointed by the *farang* waited till he was on his own, whereupon he was forced to agree that once they had taken the city, Susuhunan would give the Dutch 5,000 oxcarts of rice every year. Before he could even answer, the Dutchman called his fellow countryman and Pupaditama together to thank Susuhunan and sent him a letter to sign. Susuhunan could see no way out. If he made a fuss and refused the Dutch would abandon him in favour of the old ruler, so he signed. The Dutch became even more greedy and pushy. Then, once he became king, there was no rice to give them. So the Dutch costed the rice and added interest. Susuhunan just let it go on and allowed them to take what they could. There are many such agreements and people are still living on the benefits of them today. The Dutch give the two kings an allowance of 6,600 guilders each, but from that they have to support their relatives and their court. Just the women alone in the palace come to 6,000 or 7,000. Those living in the *kraton* are over 50,000. The owner of the land allows villagers to come and scrape a living as long as they give half to him. On the Dutch side, they simply levy taxes and get them to do road building, join the police, or collect taxes. The citizens of both these polities are treated the same, and then they have

33. King Chulalongkorn compares how royal ranks within the Surakarta dynasty decline in a similar way to that in Siam. *Mom rajawongse* is the second lowest rank and is not at prince or princess level, but indicates the child of a prince. *Krom meun* is a rank given to a prince or princess in addition to their birth title.

34. Thomas Stamford Raffles (1781-1826), better known as the founder of Singapore, was lieutenant-governor of Java between 1811-14, after the British invasion of 1811 during the Napoleonic Wars. Returning to Britain, he wrote the book read by the king.

35. Toroh is situated in what was formerly the Mataram kingdom.

36. *Kum* = 31. ml.

37. Prambanan is an 9th century Hindu temple compound in Central Java dedicated to the Trimurti. The King is incorrect in stating that Prambanan is earlier than Borobudur. Borobodur was also built in the 9th century but during the Sailendra dynasty.

Engraving of the ruins of Prambanan.

Borobudur, c. 1900.

to deal with the Dutch as well, so hence are very poor. For their clothes, they have to wear a greenish indigo for both the sarong and the top, as they are not allowed to dress above their station. Those who work for the *farang* can wear whatever patterned cloth they like, forbidden or not, and look much better dressed.

Despite all this, one cannot find a single rich Javanese. The wealthy are either Dutch or Chinese. All other nations are inferior to them and can't even pretend to be rich. All ethnicities are dragooned into being soldiers. The English also took advantage. On the other hand, there are many good things about the Dutch. They run things well. They are not a people who seek position or rank, but rather seek money and happiness. The government is run like a business and they economize like a plantation millionaire. The country is as prosperous as it could be, but has developed slowly. It is almost impossible to find any empty space even at the tops of the mountains. All the large trees on Java legally belong to the government. They have been harvested over the past one hundred years. Now it is impossible to find a teak tree of 5 or 6 *kum* [36]. I think they have been replanting, but they are not usable yet. That's enough on this subject.

Now I'm going to talk about various sites. When I was in Jogja, I went to see two Brahmin temples. The third was Prambanan[37]. This temple, dedicated to Shiva and Vishnu, was built in 1018 according to the Javanese calendar, the same period when Atisha came from India. The Javanese calendar is 75 years behind the Christian one. At that time, the Hindu King established his capital at Prambanan. He was part of the Inao[38] family, about which we have a dance drama. The complex was begun by the great

The pierced chedis *on the upper level of Borobudur, c.1900*

One of the reliefs from Borobudur.

38. *Inao* is a popular Thai epic poem written by King Rama II and based on the Javanese tale of Prince Panji.

The royal party at Borobudur, 1896.

One of the giant figures mentioned by King Chulalongkorn.

grandfather of Inao. At that time, Buddhism had also arrived in the country and so Borobudur was built. At Prambanan, the workmanship is exceptional with individual *prangs* for the different gods. Some are still buried under the ground and await excavation, but many are still standing. There are also large sandstone figures and lintels carved with the *Ramakien*. They say it is better than Angkor Wat, but I don't think so.

Borobudur is in Kedu province. It is built on the top of a hill some 300 feet high and built over nine levels. The five lower tiers are redented with 12 corners and indented to 20 like at Prambanan. The upright walls and the lotus base are carved with *Jataka* tales and the Life of the Buddha. Behind the uprights, there are porches with Buddha images. Measuring two *keub*[39] across their lap, there are 100s of images. On the top level, there are another three tiers which are circular and have *chedis*. The pierced bell shapes also house Buddha images. In the middle of the last one, is a large *chedi*. On all these levels, apart from a large band around the *chedi*, there are no other carvings and their craftsmanship seems crude. The five lower levels and the four upper ones do not seem to go together at all. It looks as if they were constructed at different times, just like the Golden Mount[40], which started to subside and then was left for a while until the small *chedi* was built on top. What is really beautiful is the Buddha image at Candi Mendut[41], near Borobudur. One cannot find its equal. Another ancient site was that in the town of Singhasari[42]. There is a huge giant there, which must weigh more than 30 tons. The calves of the seated figure are buried beneath the earth, but the portion above ground must be at least 12 feet high. As I imagine you won't want to know any more about this topic, I'll stop here.

I will tell you more about our journey. We left Jogja and went to stay at Borobudur for three nights. While there, we visited Magelang which is a large town in Kedu province. We inspected the barracks and the hospital. It is all very well arranged. Your mother was thrilled by the *Foi Fa* tree at the Resident's house. It was 10 *sok* tall and covered in flowers from the tip to the lower boughs. Its smell permeated everywhere. On our return to Jogja, we went to Solo and then left Solo for Surabaya. The government railway only goes as far as Jogja, and so we had to take a company train from there on. Surabaya is a prosperous trading town, but it is hot and the water is not very clean. Nowadays, it is even more flourishing than before, because the commercial train which use to run to Pasuruan now comes to Surabaya, as the former town is difficult to access. That town is rather run down now. I wanted to cross the water to see the capital of Madura, as the island is famous in Javanese chronicles. The road to go to Bangalan is only 12 Dutch miles, but there were no horses so we could only visit Kamel. That was truly delapidated because there is not enough water and they can only grow corn. There are no high mountains so all the rain falls on Java. We went to see the Lloyd and Government marine yard. They boasted that there was nowhere to equal it anywhere in the world. It is very large and impressive, but the word 'world' refers only to the Javanese world. We stayed in Pasuruan for one night. The town is large but very quiet. The club can hold 200 people and at first had 170 members. But now there are only 70 left. It's not that there is less business. There are plentiful fish stocks and many sugar cane plantations on the plain and coffee on the hills. The sugar cane fields come right up to the houses. The reason it has declined is because of the train going to Surabaya instead.

After that, we went to stay in Tosari[43] for six nights. It's 6,000 feet up and of all the mountain routes in Java none of them can beat that to Tosari. The carriage can go right to the summit. In terms of a dramatic view, here is not as beautiful as Priyanka, but in terms of somewhere to relax and wander about, this is better. From 2,000 metres downwards, the vegetation is tropical with bamboo and bananas growing abundantly. Then, up to 3,000 feet, there are no more bananas or bamboo but rather large trees and coffee. After 5,000 feet, there are only pine trees and tree ferns. I asked people who had been to Europe and they said it was not like Europe at all, but rather like Japan. It was very cold. During the day the thermometer never went above 70 degrees and no lower than 54, but at night it was never above 64 and the lowest was 48. The houses are not built for the cold as the walls are either woven bamboo or pine. The windows have glass panes and there were no stoves. Some people wore two pairs of trousers and two tops. Even with five blankets, it still felt cold. I only used two blankets, and some days even threw one of them off. Your mother used only one or none at all, just a

Candi Mendut

thin sheet. Life in Tosari begins with breakfast and then riding. The routes are like going up and then down a roof. So we would descend 4-500 feet and then ascend 5-600 feet continuously until we reached our destination. The roads are extremely well made, but they need to be, as it is quite different from the Jipanus Sindanglaya side where the hills are larger and easier to climb. On this side there are just peak after peak. The *farang* have made a garden at one point growing vegetables and keeping cattle. They sell fresh milk and butter. I had not eaten any for 25 years and it tasted really delicious. I know some people think it smells, but I can eat it all. There was a rose garden which gave your mother great pleasure and we went there twice. There were many other temperate flowers such as tulips and fuschias. In addition, there were many fruits such as strawberries, raspberries and wild flowers growing along the track. Then, we would come back for lunch and have a rest or do various things before going out again around 5 pm. We had dinner around 8.30, before bed at around 10.30 or 11. The people here are known as Buddhists, but, having observed their rituals and behaviour, I could see no trace of Buddhism at all. They are people who

39. *Keub* = 25 cm.

40. Golden Mount. Wat Saket, the name of the temple within which the mount stands, already existed in the late Ayutthaya period. King Rama III decided to build a large stupa in the middle but it collapsed and the rubble formed the hill on which a much smaller *chedi* was built early in the reign of King Rama V.

41. Candi Mendut is a 9th century Buddhist temple 3 km east of Borobudur and slightly earlier. Having been discovered in bushes in 1834, restoration began in 1897, the year after the King's visit.

42. Singhasari was the site of a 13th century Buddhist kingdom with a temple still remaining.

43. Tosari is a village in the Tengger Mountains of East Java, Indonesia. It is near Pasuruan and is on the way to nearby Mount Bromo.

The royal group on horseback in front of Mount Bromo.

were Hindu when Islam was ascendant in 1475 CE and they escaped into the hills. They still keep to their old religion, but hide their three gods and in fact have reduced them to one, namely Pratorokuru, who is the main god on the summit of Mount Semeru – the highest mountain on Java and also a volcano. They accept circumcision, but do not worship Mohammed. They observe the five precepts, but otherwise are rather dissolute and it's all rather puzzling.

Cultivation on steep mountains some 800-900 feet high requires the aid of a walking stick when planting corn or vegetables. Some of the peaks are higher than the streams and depend on rainwater alone. They eat a mixture of corn and potato for seven months, and corn alone for five. Their houses are surprisingly beautiful and very clean. They are stepped and well organised in rows, and there are quite a lot of people. However, they are very superstitious. Whoever proclaims something, they believe it. I almost missed out on participating in a ceremony as they thought it might be seen as a misdeamenour. The Controller and Raden Tumahong took three days

44. Bromo is an active volcano, set within a plain called the Sand Sea. King Chulalongkorn was particularly keen on visiting volcanoes as the letter reveals.

45. The *paal* is a Dutch unit of measure equal to 1506.94 metres.

46. Look Ying refers to Princess Valaya Alongkorn, Princess of Bejraburi (1884-1938). She was the daughter of King Chulalongkorn and Queen Savang Vadhana, but was brought up by Queen Saovabha, Prince Chakrabongse's mother.

to persuade them. They were going to delay it, and said that people should go and see it in Surabaya first. Then, after three days passed, he came back and reported that the people who had seen it believed that they shared the same religion. Only then did they agree to perform the ceremony. I will talk about it when I tell you about Bromo[44].

Going to Bromo was a big event. The route was up hill and down for nine *paal*[45]. One *paal* is equivalent to almost one and a half English miles. When we reached the hill that was the mouth of the crater it was 9,000 feet above sea level. We went down some 800 feet to the so-called Sand Sea. People looked small and only just over a *sok* high and horses the size of sheep. There were smaller mountains inside: one was Bromo and the other Badok. They are smooth and covered with ash and sand set within a plain of sand. From the rim to Badok is three *paal*, while the whole circuit is 10 *paal*. Coming down from the edge of the crater is like climbing down a wall. You cannot ride down. Inside the crater is sandy and a light wind blew up from time to time, smoothing down the surface. We rode across the crater floor for three and a half *paal* and reached the group, where a pavilion for resting had been set up with paraphernalia for a ceremony. The offerings of food in baskets were lined up in front. The Brahmin priests each had a brass vase decorated with the 12 Chinese year animals and filled with water and a bunch of flowers. Stones from the volcano were lined up and a fire was lit to burn incense. All 30 recited prayers. Then they dipped the flowers in water and sprinkled water all about. The chanting started with Om and then mumbled on. It was rather like Vietnamese monks softly chanting Namo. The praying completed, the offerings were borne to the foot of the mountain, where they stopped to pay homage to the gods looking after it before beginning the ascent. We rode horses up the winding path which was sandy and thick with mud and large stones – some as heavy as 3-4 tonnes.

When we were nearly at the top, the sand became mixed with ash and we sank in up to our ankles and slipped about. We still had to go up another 230 steps before reaching the crater mouth which was also 800 feet from the interior. Once there, we could see the smoke rising which was not very exciting, but the sound was incredibly loud. Coming from Tosari some 4 miles away, you could already hear it. Although peering down it didn't look very deep, if you throw a stone in, it does not reach the bottom. They say it is 800 feet deep. The locals go down into the middle where fire comes up in gas jets. At night you can see it flaring up from the mouth of the chimney, but we just saw the smoke and some boiling in certain places. It looked more frightening than Papandayan, as if it was coming up in a strange way. Those who went up did not make a fuss like those at Papandayan. They just seemed a bit dazed. Look Ying[46] fainted when she got to the top and had to be carried down. The mouth of the crater is 3 ½ miles wide and 5 *paal* in circumference. The funny thing is that if the smoke from Mount Bromo increases, that from Mount Semeru, which is three days journey away but seems very close, diminishes and vice versa. The smoke from Semeru when it erupts is like a newly extinguished fire, a coal fire, or the smoke from a petroleum fire. These two volcanoes arose together and are very ancient, being mentioned in early Javanese chronicles. Often they are dangerous. A year ago, Mount Semeru was very much so. The younger brother of the owner of the hotel in Tosari was tending to his coffee plantation, when the volcano suddenly erupted. He and his wife and children, together with 70 workers died without trace and were buried in the ash. Bromo erupted the last time three years ago, but it was not a big one. Ash and lumps of lave fell within the crater. However, when the Controller before this one went

Mount Bromo, c.1900s.

to look at the mouth of the mountain, two or three rocks fell down only around three yards away. He panicked and ran away with all speed. At the moment, around 22 volcanoes are active, of which I have seen eight. We joked that if all of them erupted at once, the Dutch would certainly all go to heaven, leaving only Susuhunan and *srimpi* and *bedhaya*. These two words have lodged in my mind. Coming back down, the Brahmins had eaten and said their prayers. They kissed the feet of your mother and my knee, blessed us and left. There were more things related to the ceremony, but it went on so long I won't relate it.

On the way back, we stopped to see the Colony, the community which the administration has set up as an experiment so that mixed race people who are wrong doers can live here and earn a living, such as poor Dutch people who have been caught thieving. It is after a German model, and perhaps you can enquire about it. They then use them as witnesses in their Report. Apparently it works. We came back down and stayed in Pasuruan another two nights. I saw Susuhunan hold the Sra Sanan mentioned in the *Inao* story. There were around 500 *waedono* and *desa* riding horses, all dressed and covered in ash in the old- fashioned way, but the dance was not good. We went to Singhasari and Melang[47] one day and then to Kediri[48]. It was near the Willisamara volcano and would only have taken three hours, but we did not go as we had no time. The next day we stopped off to see the place called Mdium, a large town in the province of the same name. In truth it means middle ie Matayom. We reached Samarang on the same day. There is nothing much to see there, but the city has changed from the past and I couldn't recognise anything. It was incredibly hot and almost unbearable. I could not sleep for two nights and had to come down and sleep on the boat. Whenever I had to stay in a two-storeyed hotel, I was not happy if it was full above and we were below. The next day, I received the Resident and the Krom Karn saw us off and we left in the ship. The next day we stoped at Cirebon[49], a reasonably-sized port town, but again very hot. The only thing to see was the mountain of the Sultan Pi Eiy, because there are three sultans there. It is very large but the workmanship is poor. It looks a bit like the Susorn sea where Phra Narai relaxed in Lopburi[50].

So my trip to Java ends here. In the boat I have not been able to eat for two days, but it began two days ago on our arrival in Semarang and so has been four days now. I have been weak and I was worried I would lose weight. However, today I am a bit better. I've put on weight and felt much stronger and was better on my horse than when I was in Ratchaburi. I could ride all day without feeling that tired. My stomach was also normal. However, if I eat too much rice or chilli, I risk an upset stomach. Fancy food seems to be better, but if it is not tasty I can't eat it at all.

This letter is already extremely long, so I'll stop now. I think about you and talked about you all the time. I forgot to tell you one thing. I went close to a Mount Chakraphuwano in Banyumas region, which is known as Khao Look Chai Lek[51].

Chulalongkorn

Opposite: King Chulalongkorn in Javanese dress, 1896. See his comments about this in the following letter on page 46.

47. Melang was the seat of government of the ancient Singhasari kingdom.

48. Kediri was a Hindu Javanese kingdom from 1042-1222. Wilis volcano, referred to by the king as Wilismahara, is nearby.

49. A treaty of 1705 saw Cirebon become a Dutch protectorate, which, as the king mentioned, was administered by three sultans.

50. Phra Narai refers to King Narai (r.1656-1688) who moved his palace to Lopburi. In the middle of a large reservoir, the so-called Susorn Sea, he built a pavilion for relaxation.

51. Meaning "My Son Lek Mountain".

Hurricane House, Singapore
3rd August 1896

To my son Lek

I have arrived in Singapore and am staying in Hurricane House[1] again, because the boat has to take on coal. The Governor[2] came to visit me again. The reception on the boat went of well. This time round, Look Mai Chum had both rambutans and mangosteens. I didn't have any. We went into Raffles Hotel and called over the chef who is from Surabaya. All the food we had in Java was very Indian in taste. Bandong was better than the *farang* food in Surabaya. I am going back to Bangkok and I am sure I will think about you again for a good while. While I was travelling this last time, I thought about you always, but it was not as painful as before. I have gradually got used to it. Nong Eeyd Noi[2] was very ill, while I was away. Your mother was in a terrible state, but now we have news that he is better. I'm afraid he seems to be rather prone to illness. The various photographs I will send again once I am in Bangkok. I took a picture of me in Indonesian dress, which was given to me by the Sultan. If I send it to you you will be amused. I look more like a bantam cockerel than anything else (see page 45). Tomorrow morning we will go back on the boat. Tell Pen[4] that I have followed his instructions to the letter.

You have written nice long letters and I am sorry that I haven't answered, but it is busy from dawn to

Hurricane House in the 1880s.

dusk, as you have seen. The news I have for you is that Sanpetch[5] dances the *tantak* very well, but in the ceremony for the company will likely have *srimpi bedhaya* and *tantak*. Apart from that I've told you everything and Pen also probably knows.

Chulalongkorn Por Ror

Group photograph taken at Istana Tyersall, the Sultan of Johor's palace in Singapore. Seated from left to right: Chaochom Manda Chum Krairiksh, (on the ground) ADC to the Sultan Daud bin Sulaiman, Sultan Ibrahim, Queen Saovabha, King Chulalongkorn, Ungku Maimunah, Prince Damrong, a Johor lady and sister of the Sultan. It was taken on 2nd August, 1896.

Amorn Phiman Manee Throne Hall
25th September 1896

To my son Lek

Chameun Sri[1] came back at the end of my birthday party. He told me all the news of you and also brought the four cushions, which you sent back for Sadet Yai[2]. I was very pleased that you took the trouble to find something she could use. If she was still alive, she would have used them for sure. Also they weren't expensive. It shows that you are not forgetful and the words are funny. Now they can be distributed to her heirs, divided into four: one for presenting to the monks, one for me, one for Tan Klang[3] and one for Tan Lek[4].

These days, I am trying to clear my outstanding work and so have not answered your letters, but it's a bit better now and I'll answer you when I'm free.

The raffle prizes from the mail boat, which you said you had sent to me, your mother and your younger brothers, have not arrived. Your mother goes on and on about these things and was getting ready to really love them. But now we have to wait and have no idea where they have gone. Anyway, your mother does love the cushions, even though she says that the workmanship in Bangkok is better.

Chulalongkorn Por Ror

Princess Sudaratana Ratchaprayoon, Sadet Yai.

Letter opposite
1. The house on Orchard Road was purchased by the King in the 1890s, through Tan Kim Ching, the Thai Consul. Today it remains the Royal Thai embassy. King Chulalongkorn made his first foreign trip to Singapore in 1871.

2. Sir Charles Mitchell, governor from February 1894 to December 1899.

3. Nong Eeyd Noi was the nickname of Prince (later King) Prajadhipok (1893-1941), the youngest son of King Chulalongkorn and Queen Saovabha. Being 10 years younger than Prince Chakrabongse, their time in England did not overlap

4. Prince Benbadhanabongse (September 1882-November 1909) was the son of King Chulalongkorn with Chao Chom Manda Morakot. He was very musical and later had a band. It is possible that the King had consulted him about a dance performance.

5 Sanpetch refers to Chameun Sampapetch Pakdi (But Penkul) (1858-) He was in royal service for many years with various titles. When his father, Chao Phraya Mahindrasakdi, died he took over the dance troupe, taking them to Europe.

Letter above
1. Chameun Sri was Chameun Sri Soraraskha (Peng Bunnag). Chameun Sri was one the ranks given to royal pages.

2. Sadet Yai refers to HRH Princess Lamom, later Princess Sudaratana Ratchaprayoon (1818-1896), the aunt of Queen Debsirindra, mother of King Chulalongkorn. When the king's mother died when he was 8 years old, Princess Lamom looked after him and his brothers. As a result the King loved and respected her very much.

3. Tan Klang, meaning middle prince, was the nickname the King used for his brother, HRH Prince Chaturonrasmi, Krom Phra Chakrapadibongse (1856-1899).

4. Tan Lek, meaning small prince, was the nickname the King used for his youngest brother, HRH Prince Bhanurangsi Savangwongse (1859-1928).

From left: Prince Abhakara, Prince Purachatra, Prince Paribatra, Prince Chirapravati, Prince Sommatiwongse, King Chulalongkorn, Prince Yugala, Crown Prince Maha Vajiravudh, Prince Chakrabongse, Prince Vudhijaya, Prince Dilok, Prince Benbadhanabongse.

1897 The king's visit
Studies in England

SUPPLÉMENT ILLUSTRÉ

LES HOTES DE LA FRANCE

After several letters detailing his voyage to England in 1896, there are only six letters from Prince Chakrabongse to his father in this year and three from the King. It is likely many letters have been lost. In addition, during his European tour, King Chulalongkorn and Prince Chakrabongse did spend a certain amount of time together and so had no need to write. Prince Chakrabongse was certainly with the King in Darmstadt, which is where he met Tsar Nicholas II, and he also accompanied his father to Spain and Portugal.

The first country King Chulalongkorn visited was Italy, where he arrived on 13th May. He then went to Switzerland before returning to Rome and going on to Russia where he arrived on 3rd July, having travelled via Poland. He stayed at Peterhof Palace outside St. Petersburg for one week, before voyaging to Stockholm, where he arrived on 13th July. and left on 20th July. The King arrived in Belgium on 9th September and left for Paris on the 11th.

While the King was away, Queen Saovabha, presided over the Regency Council.

Amorn Phiman Manee Throne Hall
16th February 1897

Dear Lek

I'm sure you must think that I am not thinking of you, just as I do when you end your letters in a formulaic way by saying that you are thinking of me. Then, it seems almost like the end of an official letter, along the lines of, "and to conclude", "may I take the opportunity to express". In truth I have been muttering that you may think me rather dull these days, as you must be becoming rather smart. You are the only one, apart from Prince Paribatra, who wrote to his mother, who has said you are looking forward to seeing me soon. It's true that on this trip I feel like a bit like a country bumpkin coming up to town, so by all means make suggestions. Perhaps I can find some finery to make me look good. But I doubt that I can manage to drink a magic potion to try and match those fancy fellows. My only worry, is that we won't have that many days together as the time is short and there are many places to go. I really want to sit down and discuss things with you to the full. I am only sorry that your mother is ill and so I cannot leave until November, a fact that has become news. Whenever I say I am going, she starts to cry. Nevertheless, I have to harden my heart and go, as if I don't make it this time, I doubt there will be another chance, as I get older every day. However, if I did not think there would be some benefit, I wouldn't go. Having fun and sightseeing are not important and I worry about my duties, but I am steeling myself to endure hardship and go. The whole affair with Tan Lek is awful and I am very worried about it. In fact, I didn't hear it from anywhere else first, but only from the letter he wrote. It's very messy and when I read it, it's almost laughable. The situation is that six months have been refunded now. You can compare it to Prince Vora Sakdaphisan. He said the various princes agreed to like that. I teased him, saying if I come I would not have to be Prince Wongsa Dhirajasanit, or first old then young. Finally I said that Tan Lek was drunk before he knew anything about it. It was some three months and now he still has not arrived. So I am still worried although the fact he has left makes it easier. I am so happy we are going to see each other. That's it for now.

Chulalongkorn Por Ror

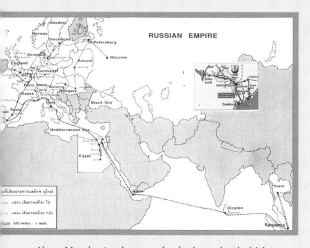

Above: Map showing the route taken by the royal yacht, Maha Chakri.

Right: This image of King Chulalongkorn and Tsar Nicholas II set the tone for the rest of the visit.

Trip to the Court of Spain. Seated in the front: King Chulalongkorn and the Regent of Spain, Queen Maria Christina. King Alfonso XIII stands behind King Chulalongkorn and Prince Chakrabongse next to him. Crown Prince Vajiravudh stands behind Queen Christina.

Reunited in England: King Chulalongkorn and Prince Chakrabongse.

Hotel Royal de la Paix, Florence
14th June 1897

Dear Lek

I have planned to write to you for many days now, but have been unable to find the time until I received your letter dated the 9th of this month. I had already been complaining that once the children had gone back, the house would be quiet. I went to Rome and was received very well, but felt so tired. You can say I almost died if you like. Coming here I've had a little more time to myself, but still am at the mercy of the six professors, namely the sculptor and the various portrait painters. They are much fussier than I've ever experienced. First, I must sit here, then there, for an hour or so, or sometimes half an hour. I always have to look as if I am almost smiling, as looking too severe is not allowed. I also have to do other things, such as dress up and make as if I am about to write something. Anything he cannot see, he can't paint. It's not just my face or my figure, but my entire outfit. And he also tried to get me to tell him what your mother was like. As for the dress, the lace was too poor and he said he could not paint it. So we had to buy 25 *chang* more. I also had to telegram to get my ceremonial gown sent over. In addition, I had to promise that this winter I would send Toh and you over for him to see. I had to do every gesture and posture, sitting till I was really tired. On the other hand, watching him work was really quite fun. It's just when it was two days, it seemed too long. The pictures he is working on are two half-length portraits of me and your mother, and two full-length ones. Professor Gordigiani is the artist. One of his pictures is in the Art Gallery already.

Then there is a picture of me, your mother and our children, all seven of us, by Professor Gelli[1]. Finally, there are two portrait busts by Charles Summers[2] in Rome, two profile portraits in relief and another full length portrait of me, by Professor Fantacchiotti[3]. I still have to take photographs as well. They fuss around from morning to night. It's not very pleasant here, as its hot and stuffy. Lots of people have upset stomachs as it is not healthy. However, I have been fine. Please tell Pen and Vudh[4] that I have received their letters and think of them all.

Chulalongkorn

Full-length portraits of the King and Queen by Michele Gordigiani (1835-1909), a well-known Italian portraitist. Previously, among others, he had painted Queen Victoria in 1867 and King Victor Emmanuel II and the Count Cavour.

Above and below: Marble busts of King Chulalongkorn and Queen Saovabha by by Charles F. Summers.

Group portrait of King Chulalongkorn, Queen Saovabha and their five sons by Eduardo Gelli. From left standing is Prince Asdang (Eeyd Lek), standing at the back is Crown Prince Vajiravudh (Toh), standing behind the Queen on the left is Prince Chakrabongse (Lek), seated on the stool is Prince Chudadhuj (Tiw) and, on the lion skin, Prince Prajadhipok (Eeyd Noy).

. Eduardo Gelli (1852-1933) was a painter of genre and ortraits born in Savone. In 1886, he had painted a portrait of he Emperor of Austria.

. Charles F. Summers (1858-1945) was an Australian sculptor vorking in Rome. He was the son of a more famous father vith the same name.

. Cesare Fantacchiotti (1844-1922) a Florentine sculptor.

.Vudhijaya Chalermlabh, Prince of Singburi (1883-1947), enbadhanabongse, Prince of Phichai (1882-1909)

Two profile medallions of Queen Saovabha and King Chulalongkorn by Cesare Fantacchiotti.

Prince Bhanurangsi (Tan Lek) is seated in the centre.
Standing from left to right: Prince Benbadhanabongse (Pen),
Prince Paribatra (Toonmom Chai), Prince Chakrabongse

(Lek), Prince Svasti (Sadet Na Toh) and Crown Prince Maha
Vajiravudh. Seated at the front are Prince Purachatra and
Prince Abhakorn (Abha).

18th November 1897

Your Majesty

During this week only a few things are worth recounting. On Sunday we walked down to see the soldiers training in the Military Academy at Camberley (Sandhurst) before going to church. It is known as the Church Parade. On such occasions, the general in charge usually comes to inspect and it is something that people like to see. In truth, it's nothing special. All that happens is the cadets come out and line up to wait for the general. When he comes, he just walks by and isn't really inspecting. Whether he notices anything or not, I don't know because he is so old he's almost in his dotage. After that he waits while they march past and takes the salute before everyone goes on their way.

For us, one funny thing was that Siddhi[1] is now at this officer school, so we were kept amused trying to spot him.

Then this Wednesday, in the evening, they had a show at the school including fencing, sword fighting, stick fighting and performing gymnastics. There were lots of cadets in the audience and they clapped no matter what. It was rather noisy. The hall where the performance took place was a sea of red, with the cadets all wearing their mess jackets. It looked really impressive.

My studies at the moment consist of English, as we have not been able to find a Russian teacher yet. But my homework is almost as if it has been decided already. I am impatient to start studying, so that I can learn the basics. Whenever I go and meet someone, they all exclaim how difficult Russian is, but I think the British make a big fuss about such things and are not good at languages. That's why they protest that its so difficult, but I think I'll be fine with it. The students take turns to come down and stay for two days, so I can chose which one to take with me. Four people have come down so far. I rather like the one called Nai Poum[2], who came with Your Majesty during Your Majesty's visit, but I need to check over the others as well.

I think of Your Majesty at all times without fail.

I beg to remain Your Majesty's obedient servant,

Chakrabongse

1. Mom Rajawongse Siddhi Sudhasana (later General Phraya Wisidhiwongse Wudhikrai).

2. At this time, the prince was trying to choose companion to accompany him to Russia. Poum Sakara was born on 23 January 1883, so was two months older than Prince Chakrabongse. He studied at Debhsirin school, winning a government scholarship.

Elsenwood Camberley
2nd December, 1897

Your Majesty

I have received you letter from Egypt and I was really pleased.

Since the 30th November, I have now moved to this new house. In the evening Dr Yarr[1] comes to look after things. Such as Mr Hume[2] does for Toonmom Toh. The house is the same size as Graitney, but is better in terms of the rooms and facilities.

Mr. Ardachev[3] and Nai Nok Yoong[4] arrived here in the evening yesterday. The teacher is very good. He is fun to talk to, but does not speak English very well and is always speaking French. I can understand a lot, although I can't really speak it. We have started learning Russian. There are 35 letters, so many more than English and its also written differently so its quite confusing. It's very difficult to make the sounds as a lot of the sounds are in one's throat. Such as H for example is really difficult. The language itself is like Latin in that it has different declensions and conjugations.

One thing that is similar to Thai is that in speaking to the king etc one uses different language according to their rank. Here is an example of a Russian word. *Zdravstvouytye* means "Good Day" and is written like this in English. Another word *Throupyaume* means good bye but written in English is *Proshaite*. I've written these words so you can see how they are. The *shtsh* sound using five letters is combined in one like this ULY.

I and Nai Nok Yoong can hardly think of anything except studying Russian and we speak making lots of mistakes all the time.

I really hope that in these five months I will learn enough to be able to know a little and that I will be able to talk to the Emperor. I am sure he will be surprised that coming from England I can speak Russian.

I think about Your Majesty very much. When I have some spare time, I always think about Your Majesty and feel very lonely.

I beg to remain Your Majesty's obedient servant,
Chakrabongse

A very damaged photograph of Charles Vernon Hume, military governor of the Crown Prince.

1. Dr. Michael Thomas Yarr (1862-1937) was a surgeon and later major-general, who between 1895-1900 was personal physician to Crown Prince Maha Vajiravudh.

2. Colonel Charles Vernon Hume (1860-) taught military history to Prince Vajiravudh and Prince Chakrabongse while they were studying in England. For three years, he was military governor to the Crown Prince of Siam. In 1911, he entered the service of the Siamese government.

3. Pavel (Paul) Nicholaivich Ardachev was Prince Chakrabongse's Russian tutor.

4. Nai Nok Yoong refers to Nok Yoong Wisetkul (later Luang Abhirak and then Phraya Surintaracha). He accompanied Prince Chakrabongse to St. Petersburg and taught him Thai.

During this period, it was essential that a Russian teacher was engaged to prepare the Prince for his life in Russia. The Siamese legation found a young Russian historian Pavel (Paul) Nicholaivich Ardachev, who was researching his Ph.D. thesis in Paris on the political administration of France in the 18th century.

Ardachev wrote many letters to his relatives about teaching Russian to the young Siamese prince. His 18 letters from London are so captivating and witty, if sometimes melodramatic, that significant abstracts are included in this chapter. His remarks about his young pupil and about London one hundred years ago are incisive and of historical value. In the light of recently discovered archive documents, it is clear that the relationship between the teacher and his pupils was very close, as the Prince and his comrade Nai Poum (who joined the Prince later) remained in touch with Ardachev throughout their years in Russia and maybe even afterwards.

In conjunction with the weekly letters written to his father by Prince Chakrabongse, these letters are an invaluable source of information concerning the life of Prince Chakrabongse and Crown Prince Maha Vajiravudh in England, their studies, daily routine, entertainments and travelling. It was in October 1897 that Paul Ardachev was offered the post of tutor. It is not known who contacted him, but possibly Mr. Girse (the Russian envoy in Brussels, mentioned below) recommended him. The choice is surprising as Ardachev was unknown, did not know English well, and had not gained his Ph.D. On the other hand, Russian tutors may have been hard to find.

Paris. 10th October 1897.

Recently I've been to London, invited by the Siamese legation, where I've got the offer to teach Russian and French to the second son of the King of Siam, who lives now not far from London (40 *versts*, 1 versta – 3,500 ft.) With the letter of reference from Girse I went to the Siamese legation and introduced myself to the secretary, a young Italian, and the envoy himself. The envoy is a Siamese, speaking good English, but not French. It turned out, that I would have to stay in England (how terrble!) in the suburbs of

London till spring. My salary will be 20 pounds a month (around 190 roubles), of course, board and lodging all provided....

The main problem, which is bothering me, is my poor knowledge of English (I can read, but not speak), and the Prince, whom I am going to teach Russian and French, speaks good English, but not French. So, the answer will be probably negative. . .

London
November 22nd 1897

Dear Father and Kolya,

Having dined at the expense of the King of Siam, I am sitting in the reading-room, impatient to share my news with you.

After the first visit to the Siamese legation, I went to see the site of the fire[1]. It occupies a vast territory, around twenty streets, separated by police lines. The fire took place in the centre of London; I suppose you know the details from the Russian newspapers. At 3.30 p.m. I paid a second visit to the Siamese legation and was lucky to meet with the minister. . . . I entered the spacious and luxurious office and saw a small, rather young and intelligent looking Siamese – a very lively, quick, nimble and cheerful man. He immediately sprang to his feet, greeted me merrily and without ceremony. There is no arrogance or the so-called English stiffness in him. Our conversation was cordial, but not excessively familiar, a manner I got used to in Paris. The Siamese turned out to be more of a Parisian, than an Englishmen, in spite of his English education. He couldn't say a thing in French, but spoke English, like a native speaker. It was rather hard to talk to him, so I had to enlist the help of the secretary, who translated some difficult phrases and my answers when I was not able to make a sentence. From this visit I got a good impression of the Siamese, and, I hope, produced the same on them. They saw me to the door with great courtesy, even helping me on with my coat. Nevertheless, the final decision was not taken. Probably, the minister didn't want to take responsibility, so he offered the following solution: I will spend 2-3 days in Camberley as a trial, an offer I accepted. The idea seems an excellent

1. There appears little or no information about this fire, which according to the letter caused a lot of damage.

one, as it will help to prevent misunderstandings on either side. During three days I'll manage to find out who I am dealing with, and find some "insuperable obstacle" in case I don't like them or they don't like me. But I think we will get on well. I like the Siamese, and, who knows, maybe they will reconcile me with the English as well. The minister promised that Dr. Yarr, the personal physician of the Prince, would visit me tonight or tomorrow in the morning and introduce me to His Highness.

Yours, *Panya*

London

23rd November 1897

I've just returned to my hotel with Dr. Yarr. We went along the streets, noisy as hell, and dark as Tartarus, covered by an impenetrable screen of smoke and mist. Street lamps and the lights in the houses twinkle through it like live coals all day long, though it is not really daytime, but rather a parody of night. It is even darker than the June nights in St. Petersburg[1]. Frankly speaking, I've never been in such atmosphere. I am so sorry for the poor people, who are doomed to live in this hell on Earth. I hope that it will be different in the suburbs of London, at least Dr. Yarr assures me it will be so. He is a very nice young man of 35. It is amazing that individual English people are better than the people as a whole. Fortunately (for me) his French is rather good and between my fruitless attempts to speak English, we turn to this neutral language. Yarr has lived in France and has travelled widely, though has never been to Russia. He came to me yesterday in the evening, and today I've been in his company from 11 a.m. till 3.30 p.m. We had lunch together, than took an underground; a railway, which spreads in all directions under London for a distance of more, than 200 *versts*. The trains go every three minutes from early morning till late at night. You can go through London from end to end in several minutes (for a few pence). The railway partly runs under Thames. There are stations on each *versta* and one can come back to light through big spacious wells.

1. In fact, in June it barely gets dark in St. Petersburg, so he must be emphasizing how dark it was.
2. The expression "the exotic Prince" exemplifies the attitude of many Russian people to Siam and other Asian countries at the time.

The plan, developed yesterday, went wrong as the Siamese minister decided that my preliminary visit to Camberley was unnecessary. So after lunch, Yarr and I went to the embassy and the minister announced that he accepted my conditions and asked me to assume office from December 1. Thus, with God's help, my new pupil will be the first Siamese Prince who will know the Russian language and maybe in time will come to love Russia. He will probably be placed in some educational institution in Russia, most likely the Corps des Pages. As a matter of fact, the secretary of the Siamese embassy in Paris told me that the idea to give the Prince an education in Russia had been suggested to King Chulalongkorn by His Majesty the Tsar, during the visit of the former to Russia. The eldest son of the King (the heir) was brought up in England in the English manner, the third – in Germany, in the German manner, and the second obviously is destined to be brought up in Russia and in the Russian manner. I have to confess, that the prospect of laying the foundation for the Russian education of an Asian Prince, who may become a King in his time, pleases my national pride.

Besides, I like the idea of becoming closer acquainted with this country (of which, frankly speaking, I am not over fond) and those features of life in England that I had missed during my previous short visits. I hope I'll get a lot of new impressions. As for my new pupil, Dr. Yarr says, that he is a gifted boy, but a little bit sluggish. Though I would be very surprised if he had said that the exotic[2] prince was extremely diligent. From my point of view, it is better to have a bright, but lazy pupil, than a complete dunce.

At first, it will be difficult for both of us, for me to speak English and for my pupil to understand me. So now I have to apply myself to the language. I think in a month or so, I will be able to speak fluently and understand everything easily. After that everything will run smoothly. Another question is, how much can the Siamese Highness learn in five months? Taking into consideration, that the conditions are totally new and unfamiliar to him. He has never heard Russian or French speech and the monologues of the teacher during the lessons will not be of much help. But if the Prince desires to learn these languages as ardently as I desire to teach him, than the result is guaranteed. We will see.

Best wishes. *Your Panya*

On November 24, Ardachev returned to Paris from Folkstone by the ship "*Luisa Dagmara*". After several days putting his affairs in order before the final departure and copying documents in the archives and National library, he returned to London on 29th November and from there left for Camberley, the residence of his new pupil, where he was to live in the company of Dr. Yarr – the oldest of them all – and the two Siamese companions of the Prince, making five people altogether. Crown Prince Maha Vajiravudh lived with his own court not far from Camberley. Ardachev was fascinated with the surroundings, which seemed to him, like an episode from the Arabian Nights.

Elsenwood. Camberley. Surrey.

5th December 1897

Dear Father

I congratulate you on your name day and wish you all the best. As for me, I will celebrate my name day in such unbelievable surroundings, that I could never have dreamed of – to find oneself in the heart of England, under the same roof as the son of the king, to be the teacher of the Asian prince! Anyway, since last Tuesday I am living in an English mansion and teaching Russian and French to Prince Chakrabongse and his companion, the young courtier Nai Nok Yoong. I am quite satisfied with the beginning . . . and only hope it will continue along the same lines.

After various problems on arrival, when his luggage got left on the train from Folkstone, Ardachev arrived at the Siamese embassy.

Phaya Visudh, the envoy, welcomed me kindly, as usual. They gave me a spacious, luxurious and comfortable apartment in English style. I unpacked hastily and changed for dinner, putting on a tailcoat. At 7 o'clock we had dinner. There were ten persons, mostly men, as the host is a bachelor. I occupied an honoured place, on the left of the host, who was unbelievably nice. Some of the fellow diners were Siamese, working for the embassy, some were Englishmen. Only two could speak French. With the envoy I just managed to talk in English a little.

In the morning, I went to do some shopping and returned by 1 p.m. By that time Nai Nok Yoong had arrived from Elsenwood to show me the way. We left at 4 p.m. for Victoria station in two coaches, as I had a lot of luggage. Unfortunately, we arrived just in time to see the rear lights of the train and to hear its final whistle. So we had to take a roundabout route and arrived in Camberley at 6.30 p.m. Again we took two coaches and after 15 minutes ride – along a smooth road, through parks, widespread here – we approached the big three-storey building with pointed roof in English cottage style.

The account of Ardachev's first meeting with his pupil is one of the most important and moving passages of his correspondence. First impressions can often be the most perceptive and he gives a detailed description of the Prince's appearance and character:

In the doorway I saw Dr. Yarr. Next to him stood a miniature, black-eyed, black-haired boy with expressive and deep oriental eyes and a clever face, rather more southern European, than Asian in type. It was Prince Chakrabongse in person. In spite of his tiny figure, he conducts himself with great dignity, and there was nothing artificial in his manner. He showed great confidence in every movement, every word. The first minutes were extremely important for both of us, as it was difficult to understand each other. I was the first to speak with him in French. He answered monosyllabically with a heavy accent and then began to talk with me in English. I did the same thing – answered monosyllabically in English and addressed him in French. Diamond cuts diamond. I realized it was a kind of a small battle between pupil and teacher, and this first encounter would determine the outcome of this war. The first contact between a teacher and pupil is always a battle in a way, and if the teacher gives in, it is as good as lost. I knew that, if I had shown any awkwardness in my behavior with this Prince-pupil, I would have lost the battle and any hope of having an influence on him. In fact nobody won – it was a draw where we both managed to hold our positions.

The Prince probably felt that I was a worthy opponent and we soon got on very well. Instead of fighting, we started working together on the basis of mutual cooperation, both striving for one aim. My pupil obviously feels my sincere desire to teach him and our work has been in full swing from the very beginning. I only hope it will continue. My second pupil, Nai Nok Yoong, is much older and not so talented as his younger classmate, but is very attentive and industrious.

I arrived in Elsenwood in the evening, just before dinner. After dinner at 8 o'clock, we all left for the neighbouring estate (five minutes walk) to visit the elder brother of the Prince (the heir), who lives separately with his own court. I was introduced to the Crown Prince and got acquainted with his English and Siamese courtiers. Among them I met the London envoy, whom I knew well. The Crown Prince is two years older than my pupil, his upbringing seems to be in strong English hands and he speaks fairly good English, as far as I can judge after a short conversation. On the whole he has been made very British, which I suppose is all for the good, as there is no barrier to the British influence in these surroundings. "My Prince" has also been made rather British, but will I try to force it out with my Russian influence. It pleases me that at least one member of the Siamese Royal family will be considerably Russified for the first time.

Yours, *Pasha*

These first letters are full of enthusiasm and exude the atmosphere of a countryside idyll. Ardachev, who, as he confessed, hated England, was delighted with Camberley, his surroundings and house in Elsenwood and, of course, his pupil.

Elsenwood
15th December 1897

Dear Father and Kolya

Camberley is a small town 45 *versts* from London by rail. Elsenwood, where we live, is a country estate two *versts* from Camberley, surrounded by the adjoining similar estates and verdant parks of pine trees. The whole area is one big park, divided into estates with comfortable manor houses. Each house has a name. Thus the neighbouring house, occupied by the Crown Prince is called Graitney. Near the gate of our house, just across the road, there is a small red post with the mail-box, which is emptied by a postmen four times a day on weekdays, and once on Sunday. In the same manner, he empties all the boxes,

attached to numerous red posts along the road, and delivers the mail to the post office in Camberley, from where the letters are sent to all corners of the world. The same postman brings the mail three times a day on weekdays and once on Sundays. For registered letters, it is not so convenient, as I have to pick them up in Camberley. However, it is very easy, the roads here are cleaner than the streets in Moscow. Yesterday I walked without galoshes and my feet remained clean. I didn't wear my coat, as this seems to be a local habit and everyone walks about lightly dressed as in summer. The weather is really warm and the lawns are emerald green. I am pleasantly surprised by the British climate. I suppose its ill repute is due to London, famous for its fogs. It is amazing, but the climate, the weather and even the sky, 40 *versts* away from London are absolutely different. Today, for example, the weather is really delightful, with a bright caressing sun. Even in France such winter weather is uncommon. On a day like this our small community likes to cycle. I also have a bicycle, which is now out of order due to my numerous trips, so I have had to give it in for repair.

The life of our mixed colony, consisting of representatives from three nations, speaking four languages (English, French, Russian and Siamese) has developed a well-established, stable life. We get up at 8 o'clock in the morning and have English breakfast at half past 8 (tea and a light hot meat or fish dish with cold meat snacks: Yorkshire ham, roast beef etc.). I am not used to such an abundance of foodstuffs in the morning and content myself with a cup of coffee with milk and butter. At half past 9, the Prince and Nai Nok Yoong go to Graitney to learn English, maths, geography and horse riding with the Crown Prince, sometimes till 11 o' clock, sometimes till 1 p.m. At half past one we have lunch, consisting of one rich, hot, meat dish, some cold snacks, vegetables and dessert. Between lunch and tea there is free time and everyone does what he wants, sometimes we go for a walk together. At five o'clock – tea, with the inevitable cake. From half past 6 till half past 8, I teach my Siamese baby birds. Sometimes we study between 11 a.m. and 1 o'clock, if they come back early from Graitney. From time to time they work alone on the lessons I give them, but usually I supervise them, thus things get going much better, especially at the beginning.

So far I have only compliments for my pupils,

particularly for the prince, who has exceeded all my expectations. His progress is really amazing. I have never dealt with such an attentive, gifted and industrious pupil. Moreover, he always works with pleasure and in good spirits. If you just heard the bursts of merry laughter from our classroom, you would never imagine that we are working and working hard, almost furiously. The harder we work, the louder and merrier we laugh. The louder we laugh, the better are our results. If the teacher or the pupil has a sour look, nothing will come of it. We are far from this, thank God. Maybe we are getting along so well, because we remain in a cheerful mood and laugh all the way. Anyway, the prince does amazingly well and for the two weeks we have been studying, he has already left behind his elder companion.

Unfortunately, the Christmas vacation, lasting from December 19th till January 3rd will cause an unfavorable break in our study and progress. The prince and his elder brother are going to visit another brother, who lives 200 *versts* away from here, and after that to London to celebrate New Year. Dr. Yarr and me are also planning to join the celebration at the Siamese embassy. As for Christmas, I'll probably spend it here, as Dr. Yarr leaves for Ireland and Nai Nok Yoong for London. I am not longing to go to London, it would be nicer to visit Paris, but I can't afford the trip now. Tomorrow in the morning our small community will celebrate a great event: King Chulalongkorn will return to Bangkok, the capital of Siam after his nine-month travel to Asia and Europe! Prince Chakrabongse writes to his father weekly in Siamese, Dr. Yarr also writes to the King in English every week. It takes a month for the letter to reach Bangkok. At half past seven the bell rings, announcing that it is time to change into tailcoats for dinner according to the English tradition. At 8 o'clock – dinnertime. The dinner is rather more French than English, with French wines and fruits from all parts of the world, for example bananas from India. It is a five-course meal: soup, fish, meat and vegetables, dessert and, according to a strange English custom, some hot dish, very spicy and peppery. I tasted it once and got so sick, that I have had to refuse it for good. Finally, fruit and coffee, which I usually avoid, as it causes insomnia. After dinner we all relax, reading newspapers and magazines by the fireplace. After a while come the visitors from Graitney, the

Crown Prince and his devoted suite. They immediately start playing billiards in the big room. They play without cues and jump and jerk a lot, moving their arms and legs wildly. At half past 10 or 11 o'clock they leave, having drunk a glass of mineral water with several drops of old, very strong and flavored Scotch (as is customary in England). By half past 11 we are all usually in bed, and dead silence falls over the house.

The house is always in perfect order, in spite of the presence of many servants. Actually, there are half a dozen of them, more than one for each of us. However, they are so perfectly trained, that there is no need to give them orders, not to mention reprimands.

Elsenwood, Camberley
December 5, 1897

Dear Mother, Lyuda and others,
I am writing from my new place, where I have been living since December in quite unusual and unexpected surroundings. From December 1, I have been the teacher of Prince Chakrabongse. the 14-year old son of the Siamese King, who is assigned to get his education in Russia and has been already registered as Russian officer. I got this offer through the Russian embassy in Paris and accepted it, because it doesn't stand in the way of my research activities, not to mention my patriotic feelings, as I will probably Russify the future King of this Asian country, which has never come under Russian influence. I consider my present job, not like ordinary teaching, but as a service for my homeland, which is now so far away from me.

Unfortunately, I am pressed for time (till May 1). Nevertheless, I hope to teach Russian to my Siamese Prince within these five months. So, when he comes to Russia, he will feel at home. The first steps are encouraging. I have never met such a clever and gifted pupil. Let's hope that he will continue in the same way and will not lose his enthusiasm for learning the language of my great homeland. I look forward to the moment when he speaks more or less decent Russian. So far we communicate in French (which he understands badly), or English (I am not very good at). Nevertheless, we are on very good terms and I am fascinated by my wonderful pupil, who was, by the way, described to me, as being "slightly lazy". Maybe, this weakness is present in his nature, but I try to replace it by other feelings, mostly of pride, honor and duty. Thus I told him: "We have to learn Russian. This language is very difficult and we have no time. But we will manage, if we work hard. I rely on your good will, your feeling of honor and duty. You belong to the Russian Army. The knowledge of Russian is a matter of honour and duty for you. Imagine how pleased the Tsar will be when he hears your Russian speech. Besides, one who knows Russian will be welcomed in Russia with much more enthusiasm, than a person, who doesn't. So, let us not waste our time and proceed to work."

Such were my opening words, spoken in French, and these simple but sincere words must have impressed my pupil a lot. It seems I've touched the right chord, as he is very proud, noble and ambitious (in a good sense). At once, he started working. By the end of the first day, my pupil was already able to write in Russian, and knew a dozen Russian words. The first words, written and spoken by him were "Russia", "Russian language". Then we turned to names of household items and everyday objects. So, after several lessons, we can exchange short questions and answers. If we continue in this manner, success is guaranteed. One of these days I will write a report about our results to the Siamese envoy in London. My host, Dr. Yarr has probably already written the same to the King of Siam. Dr. Yarr enjoys the confidence of the King, and Prince Chakrabongse is in his charge in England. We two are the only Europeans in the house, as the others are the prince and his Siamese companion, a young man of 20, who also studies Russian but is not so talented as his younger classmate. …

Dr. Yarr is very nice, and we have become friends. In addition, he speaks good French and is the only person in the house with whom I can talk freely. He is the real master of the house and reports about all the events in Elsenwood directly to the King. Yesterday we caused a sensation by our Russian expressions, such as: very well, thank you, hello (ochen horocho, blagodaryu, zdravstvuyte). We also gave Dr. Yarr a Russian name and patronymic – Phoma Phomich, as his English name is Thomas, as well as his father's. We all had a lot of fun, especially Dr. Yarr himself.

Best wishes.

Your loving Panya

Elsenwood
18th December 1897

Dear Father

I congratulate you heartily on your name day. It is 7 o'clock p.m. now (10 in Russia). I've just returned from the station in Camberley. Dr. Yarr, Nai Nok Yoong and me were in London to see off my Siamese baby bird, his brother and companions. They all left to visit another brother, who lives 150 *versts* away from London. Our Christmas vacation has begun. This two-week break will of course adversely affect our studies, which, as I have already mentioned, have exceeded all my expectations. I suppose, it is because my pupil expresses the same ardent longing to learn, as I have to teach him.

Moreover, he is brilliantly gifted. I say "he" in singular, because, unfortunately, the same cannot be said of my other pupil. Every day, he is falling behind more and more, hampering our results, which makes me nervous. But I find consolation in my small Prince Chakrabongse Chulalongkornovich (as I call him in Russian), on whom I concentrate all my pedagogic efforts, and our studies are going swimmingly. He is unbelievably attentive and never complains. I am extremely surprised by his tenacity, as he is able to stand two or two and a half hours of hard intellectual work with only one short 10-15 minute break (that is how long our lesson usually lasts). Sometimes Nai Nok Yoong looks completely worn out, but my little Prince remains fresh and strong.

"Are you tired", I would ask him in Russian, and he answers also in Russian, "Not yet". And goes on working with all his might, in cheerful mood with laughter. However, I try not to go too far and stop this "torture", when I consider it is time. It is really a pleasure to have such a pupil. . . He is amazingly even tempered and very serious, a characteristic of children surrounded and brought up mostly by adults. During my lessons, he becomes animated and perks up, as healthy children usually do. The little prince is really radiant with health. As for good manners, I would wish that any prince, Asian or otherwise, could be as well mannered as this little Asian prince, brought up amongst all the servility of the Asian court (I had an opportunity to see this incredible servility, looking through photos). Here is a small detail: when we met for the first time, the

Prince sat down, only after I had taken my seat. At our lessons, he always takes his seat after me. Generally speaking, the young Prince arouses my esteem and sympathy in every respect.

19th December 1897

Today is my name day. What a strange place to celebrate it. By the way, nobody knows about it except me. What for? It is a family occasion. My soul is with you, and it is enough for me. Dr. Yarr handed me the invitation from the Siamese envoy to spend Christmas with him. I accepted it with gratitude. Of course, I am not eager to go to London, but it is much better than to stay all alone in Elsenwood for 10 days. So far we have agreed to leave Elsenwood on December 23. . . . Our entire colony from Elsenwood and Graitney (where I am the only Russian element) is going to join us for the New Year celebrations. I will take advantage of this visit to get better acquainted with London, one of the greatest capitals in the world. . .

God bless you.

Your Panya

The Siamese legation,
23 Ashburn Place
25th December 1897

Dear Mother and Lyuda

I've been living for three days in the Siamese legation in London. The place is crowded, mostly with Siamese, including Prince Purachatra, one of the King's sons (aged 15). We have had a good time; the Siamese treat me with respect, mostly due to my nationality, I guess. This makes me really proud. At the table I sit next to the prince. The Siamese Envoy is very kind and gentle. Christmas day was very gloomy. Not a ray of light, only smoky fog and darkness. I have been suffering from a severe headache since I arrived here. On the first day I got so sick from charcoal poisoning (charcoal fumes), that I even threw up. You can't imagine what London is like at the moment, a real Tartarus. Elsenwood is completely different. But I would have felt even worse if I had spent Christmas there all alone.

Good luck and a Happy New Year.

Your loving Panya

25th December 1897
London

My dear Father and Kolya

I wish you a Merry Christmas and a Happy New Year. I have just received your letters from Camberley. On December 23rd, on the day of my arrival, the fog was so thick, that all the local trains were late. It took us an hour to get from the station to the Siamese legation, though the distance is only 5 *versts*. The coachmen had to get out and take the horse by the bridle. Otherwise it would have been dangerous, as we couldn't see other coaches at a distance of ten metres but only their lamps, flickering through fog and smoke. In some places it was so dark, that only the rump of our horse could be seen, but not its head. The coachman even lost his way and barely found the legation. When we arrived at last, I felt so sick, that I could hardly walk. After an hour I felt even worse (nausea and headache) and felt so sleepy that I was almost unconscious. I slept till midday, but got up, feeling much better. Probably I was starting to acclimatize to the atmosphere of London. What bothers me is that I can't work, and even read with difficulty, the fog having penetrated my head. It is hardly possible to see anything outdoors and I am afraid of not finding the way back. However, today it has cleared a little. By the way, the locals are surprised by my indisposition. They are used to such an atmosphere. . .

Best wishes.

Yours Panya

London
29th December 1897

I had just started sorting your letters when suddenly I heard: "Zdravstvuyte" [hello].

In front of me – my dear Lek, radiant and blooming, a picture of health. He has just returned from his trip, accompanied by his band of younger brothers. I was overjoyed to see that, contrary to my apprehensions, he hadn't forgotten his two-week Russian, or maybe just a little. At dinner I waited for a temporary pause in the flow of English and Siamese words and exchanged some Russian phrases with my pupil. He responded willingly, as usual, and amazed this Anglo-Siamese community with his knowledge of the Russian language.

By the way, there were seven Chulalongkorn-ovichs [sons of King Chulalongkorn, Russian patronymic] at the table. Yesterday the brother of the King, who is staying in England, arrived. The King himself is in Siam now. We talked a little (his French is tolerable). He also knows Paris very well and Russia to some extent. Last year he visited Russia with the King – a very nice, gentle, talkative and cheerful man, with not a shadow of arrogance[1]. Unfortunately, he disappeared soon, and I haven't seen him since. Yesterday I was at the circus with Prince Purachatra and other Siamese. It was the biggest and most magnificent circus I've ever seen. The circuses in Paris and Berlin cannot be compared to it. Three days ago we were at the theatre, this is all my entertainment in London. Fortunately, I feel much better now, as possibly I have got used to the atmosphere, or maybe the wind has cleared away the heavy fog. . . . . I remain a convinced London-phobe, though my Anglophobia has considerably subsided. I understand that London and England are two different things. London is wonderful, one of the miracles of the world, but I can't help hating it!

London
31st December 1897

During the first days in London, I suffered from smoke and fog, now I have started suffering from the English spleen, which envelops the local atmosphere. It resembles seasickness, in that you can stand firm, oppose it, struggle and boast, but sooner or later, you will succumb. Now I know from experience, what this famous English spleen is like. Neither in Russia nor in France have I ever been in such a dismal depressed mood, which gets even worse from the impossibility of exchanging a lively, hearty word with anybody. I am a stranger among strangers here. Not a single friend among this gloomy human ocean. How I wish to go to the country! There, in the company of the people, who have become, maybe not close, but familiar to me, I feel less strange. Moreover, to my despair, the only man I could talk with, Dr. Yarr, seldom appears at the legation. He is already back from Ireland, but has a lot of friends and relatives here, and, of course, prefers to spend his time with them. As for my Lek, I meet him only at the table, as he is

always away with his younger brothers. Other Siamese can't keep me company, as we can't even talk to each other and, frankly speaking, don't have much in common.

The sense of loneliness has even dulled my interest to London, which deserves interest. But I hated it at first sight, and this feeling of irritation is getting stronger and stronger, poisoning my sightseeing efforts. Nevertheless, I will get acquainted with this Leviathan and let you know by a separate letter. At this very minute a butler has come, carrying your letters on a silver tray. It is strange, that you haven't got the photos of my pupil, his brother the Crown Prince and their royal father. Maybe I've confused the address, as I have become rather absent-minded. My Prince has given me an excellent official photo, and I will keep it as a token.

Tomorrow I am going for an all night-vigil to the Russian church; it was very difficult to find it here. . . I am really impatient to return to Elsenwood and start work.

The correspondence resumed on January 18. In the first letter Ardachev writes about another very successful pedagogical trick of his – a debating society where he could discuss various topics with his pupils, both in Russian and English. Of course, it was done mainly for the prince, as his companion Nai Nok Yoong was obviously at the bottom. Nai Poum had now joined the class and, after some problems with Nai Nok Yoong, Ardachev continues full of praise for his Chulalongkornavich, as he called him.

I've got one more pupil: two weeks ago a new companion joined us, a 16-year-old Siamese, who has been studying for several months at one of the English colleges. This boy is very industrious, but rather slow witted. Of course we creep along at a snail's pace. So, I try to concentrate all my attention on the Prince, wishing him to speak Russian by April. By that time we will have to part: I will leave for Paris, and he for Russia. During my first lessons with this new pupil (Poum), another Chulalongkornovich, namely Prince Purachatra[1], who studies at one of the English colleges, came here on a visit. (If you remember I had got acquainted with him in London at

---

1. This must be Prince Damrong.

1. Prince Purachatra Jayakara, Prince of Kamphaeng Phet (1881-1936) was two years older than Prince Chakrabongse. Later involved with the development of the Siamese railways.

Christmas). As a joke, I suggested he join as my new pupil; he accepted with great pleasure, and spent almost all his vacation time with us, learning Russian, fulfilling tasks given by me, and proving himself a willing and gifted pupil.

I have to confess, I was deeply impressed by this 17-year-old Prince, who preferred to work, instead of taking rest. As a result he learnt to write and read Russian, decline and conjugate a little, and even learn by heart a small poem: "Mountain peaks"[1].

Both my official pupils had learnt this poem by that time and liked it very much. Prince Purachatra became so enthusiastic about the Russian language, that he even decided to take lessons at his college, as there is an Englishman there who teaches Russian. I can only imagine what this son of Albion can teach. At the same time, Dr. Yarr expressed a desire to take part in our lessons, so I had to deal with five pupils simultaneously. Dr. Yarr also managed to learn the alphabet and several colloquial phrases in Russian. These different pupils explain why I wrote how busy and tired I was. Fortunately, this hard time is over. Prince Purachatra has left for his college. Dr. Yarr took several lessons and quit. . .

Nevertheless, I have to take trouble over my three pupils 4-5 hours a day. The rest of the time I devote to studying the English language and my Ph.D. I've already written about the debut of the Graitney Debating Society. It was even better than I expected. The statement of my opposer, Prince Chakrabongse, was defeated by the majority: 6 votes against to 4 votes for. So far the same fate has overtaken all the proposers, including the first one, proposed by the Crown Prince at the first meeting of the Society. Lek has proved himself the best orator. I suppose it is due to the absolute lack of shyness, which is characteristic of him and distinguishes him from his other brothers.

Best wishes

Yours Panya

Elsenwood
10th February 1898

The Prince and I are doing very well; we have begun to speak Russian a little. As usual he is working willingly and cheerfully. As for his elder companion, I have completely given up on him, as all my efforts to teach him something have proved useless. Poum, on the contrary, is an industrious and well-bred student. But his results cannot be compared to the Prince's. It takes him two days to learn a lesson, which the Prince learns in two hours. But I am sure he will make progress, as he expresses a sincere desire to learn.

Yours Panya

Elsenwood
4th March 1898

Dear Father and Kolya

Yesterday we celebrated the birthday of Prince Chakrabongse. The Crown Prince, with his Siamese suite, was present. Several toasts were proposed in English, Siamese and, in conclusion, in Russian (by me). The Prince was the only person at the table, who understood fully my several impromptu phrases. As a birthday present, I gave him a book by Leo Tolstoy *Childhood, Boyhood and Youth*, especially ordered and sent from Russia. It will be the first book he will read in Russian. The envoy gave him an illustrated *Russian History* in English. By the way, the Prince is an ardent reader, and spends almost all his free time with a book, although so far he reads only in English.

Yesterday, it was finally decided to postpone the Prince's departure till the end of May (instead of the end of April). They also asked me to stay till that time. I agreed with great pleasure: the deadline of my trip is July 1, so one month will be quite enough to finish my work in Paris. Thus my stay in England will last for 6 months, from the beginning of December till the end of May. At least I hope so, provided that the Siamese 'idol', whom I am unlucky to have among my pupils, will not make my further stay here absolutely impossible[1]. You can see him in the photo (page 74), and if the eyes are indeed the mirrors of the soul, you can judge about his soul by these mirrors. Tomorrow, I am again proposing in English at the Graitney Debating Society. By the way, I've organized a similar debating society in Elsenwood, consisting of

---

1. A Russian variant of a well-known Goethe poem, translated by Lermontov.

1. Ardachev is writing about Nai Nok Yoong, which shows he was still causing trouble.

2. Orenburg is Russian city. Most likely, Ardachef's brother Kolya was the editor of this newspaper, as Ardachef often sent him articles, later the paper went bankrupt.

five members. The first meeting took place on Wednesday, when I was elected the chairman and the Prince the honorary secretary. He wrote the society rules from dictation after each clause had been put for discussion and voting. Russian is the official language of the society, but as the majority knows it badly, Lek was appointed official interpreter. These meetings will be good language practice for my students, or at least for the best one, the Prince, as I don't expect much from the other two. I also enclose my snapshot of the Prince, though not very good one. He is holding an Orenburg newspaper.

Wish you good luck.

Yours Panya

April 5th 1898

Dear Father and Kolya

Christ has arisen! I wish you happy Easter. Today is the first day of the local Easter, Palm Sunday in Russia. There is hardly anything to write about Easter here, as it doesn't differ from the usual Sunday. Easter vacation began four days ago and the house is full of Lek's younger brothers. Some of them stay with us, some in Graitney. I sit at my desk for hours on end, making only short cycling breaks from time to time. The roads here are rather good, though the French ones are even better. The weather is fine, sometimes even hot. On Wednesday we all are going to take a bicycle ride and visit an English family, living 25 *versts* away from Elsenwood. . .

Elsenwood.
15th May 1898

Dear Kolya

Best wishes for your name day.

. . .

At last we've received news from Paris: The Siamese minister in Paris got a letter from Count Muraviev, with the notification that his Majesty the Tsar invites the Prince to come to St. Petersburg by the beginning of July and takes the responsibility for his upbringing and education. Besides, the Prince will live in the Winter Palace. So he will be welcomed in Russia with such honours as his brother, the Crown Prince, could never dream of in England.

The departure is scheduled for May 25th. Chakrabongse will spend a few days with his brothers

(he calls them cousins, as they were born by other wives, not the Queen, there is only one Queen, and the Crown Prince is her eldest son). On June 3rd, he will come to Paris and then in a few days, accompanied by the Siamese envoy, he will go to St. Petersburg via Berlin.

Yours Panya

The Siamese legation, London.
May 27, 1898

Yesterday, all our party, loaded with luggage, left for London. Only Dr. Yarr will stay in Elsenwood for a while to look over the accounts. The envoy again kindly invited me to stay at the legation. We went to exhibitions, the theatre, and yesterday the Royal Military Tournament. What a splendid show!

Paris
3rd June 1898

It was so sad to leave London, especially because Mr. Visudh (the envoy) was so kind and gentle. Dr. Yarr and one of my pupils saw me to the station (Lek and his companion went out for the day). We exchanged friendly good-byes, including with the pupil, who used to annoy me [Nai Nok Yoong]. I hope to see them again in Paris tomorrow. . .

I have got a very nice letter today from Nikolai Nikolaevich Girse, who recommended me to the Siamese. Here is his letter:

Dear Pavel Nikolaevich

Thank you for the letter. I am sure that the talented Prince should be very grateful to you, as you put your heart and soul into your work. In my opinion and according to your reference, this nice young man will not forget his teacher, who has begun his Russian education.

I remain sincerely yours
N.N. Girse

Ardachev was to accompany the prince to Russia, write some articles about him and remain on friendly terms. This first encounter with a Russian teacher clearly set Prince Chakrabongse on a very favourable course for his future life in Russia.

Raenong House, Penang
7th December 1897

Dear Lek

I received your letter dated 6th November with great pleasure. I had been saying every day that I wanted news of Toro[1], but I never thought that he would play a role with such results as quickly as that. I thought he would go to sleep. He escaped and only Phraya Non[2] was caught, because "he was not quick enough for Fijaka'. He had the nerve to play a lot but it's a good think that there has been some straight talking. Doing the right thing won't have much effect, because it won't last as long as he stays abroad. So long as I don't have confidence in him. . . I don't know what is wrong but I have to talk about him every day. I really want to know what will happen next. On the way here the waves were very rough. It was difficult to get to sleep. Staying here is unbelievably boring. I want to arrive so I can know what's happening. I am affected by the heat and have not eaten any game yet, as my stomach doesn't feel so good. In truth it was probably because of the rough sea. I felt sick and couldn't really eat, so I had an upset stomach. There was not one who did not take some stomack pills.

In Bangkok they are preparing to receive me. Apparently they are genuine in wanting to do this. In fact since I have been king there has never been such a big affair as this time. I am worried that everyone who is taking part is hoping for some benefit in showing themselves en masse and I am not sure how I will really be able to help them, which will be a bad thing later. So I've been a bit embarrassed and haven't been able to be really happy about it. I've just asked that it not be too extravagant. On the other hand, if I cut it back too much, they will be sad and think that I have become too arrogant or am suspicious. They will blame me in some way, so I can't do the right thing. All I keep thinking is that the fact they are receiving me in this way, means that they are tricking me and if I'm unprepared they will be laughing behind their hands.

I received a letter from your mother complaining that she is jealous that I am always writing to her and not telling her anything apart from I've arrived at so and so and that my letters are boring. And she says that the children of others write nicely.

I think about you so much that I feel weak and I have to do so much to do and am always worrying. It's not fun at all. I will leave here tomorrow. They say it will be rough. When I left Singapore, it was terrible. So now I've turned into a seasick person.

From your loving father,
Chulalongkorn

---

1. Toro was a private nickname the king used when referring to his half brother Prince Svasti.

2. Phraya Non later was known as Phraya Kraikosa (Tut Singhaseni). He was Siamese ambassador in Berlin at this time.

Letter Opposite
1. Phraya Visudh Suriyasak (1867-1916) was born Pia Malakul and served in the Ministry of Education and the Home Office. Between 1897-1899, he was special ambassador to London and the governor of Crown Prince Maha Vajiravudh. Later he was responsible for various educational reforms.

2. Frederick William Verney (1846-1913) was a clergyman, a barrister, a Siamese diplomat and a Liberal party politician. In 1883, he was appointed English Secretary and Counsellor to the legation of Siam in London. In 1870 he had married Maude Sarah Williams (died 1937). Chakrabongse remained close to them both and visited when he came back to England from Russia.

Frederick William Verney.

Elsenwood, Camberley
10th December 1897

Your Majesty

During the week, there was a play in Camberley performed at Sandhurst. We all went down to see it yesterday. It is called "Our Flat" and concerns a writer who has eloped with the daughter of a wealthy man and rented a house together. The man has written sevеrl books but they are not good at all. This bit was really funny. Afterwards, when he wrote a book no one would print it, and if he wrote a play no one would act in it, so they got poorer and poorer. Meanwhile the woman's father was angry and would not give them any money. So now the couple were at their wits' end and the creditors were pressing. The woman decided to write a play and send it out under an assumed name. People took it on and she got some money. Her father, seeing his daughter getting poor, could not resist and asked her to go and live with him and forgave her. The story was simply that, but it had a twist and many more funny moments. Mr Olivier was one of the actors and he was very good indeed and terribly funny. He played the owner of the theatre that accepted the musical written by the woman.

Regarding the student who is to be chosen to accompany me to Russia, we have come to a decision, but I need to hear from Your Majesty which one Your Majesty would like. I trust that Phraya Visudh[1] has informed you about this in detail already.

I have started having riding lessons in the officer training school. They teach very well. I only started yesterday and will go twice a week.

I beg to remain Your Majesty's obedient servant,
Chakrabongse

Elsenwood, Camberley
16th December 1897

Your Majesty

Nowadays, I am having riding lessons in the Military Academy. The training is just as it is for the cadets and I am taught to practice standing to attention, on guard, and so forth, before mounting the horse. The horses are very tall and I can hardly get on, even though it is the smallest one they have. It is very intelligent and understands all the commands given by the instructor. When told to do something, it does it

Phraya Visudh Sorasak.

immediately and I don't need to do anything. The important thing is to keep one's legs pressed in tightly and sit upright, one's chest sticking out. These large horses certainly have a very irregular gait. If you don't squeeze your legs in tight, you will fall off and sustain a blow to your chest. Cantering is quite comfortable but you have to be careful when it turns and I almost fall off every time. Today they made me try not wearing stirrups and it was really hard. My legs ached so much because I had to grip really tightly and there was nothing to help me except my own knees. Most people usually fall off when turning, or when they are really exhausted and can't grip any more. Today I managed to escape and haven't fallen off, because I didn't ride without stirrups for very long. Today Mr and Mrs Verney[2] are going to come here and will stay in Graitney. I hope I will hear some news regarding Your Majesty's trip to Egypt.

Today is the day Your Majesty will arrive back in Bangkok. I am thinking of how happy everyone will be there and how they must be having a good time. When I think about it, I want to come home.

I beg to remain Your Majesty's obedient servant,
Chakrabongse

Chalcot Westbury, Wilts
23rd December, 1897

Your Majesty

Mr Phipps[1] has invited Toonkramom Toh and myself to stay during the winter holidays. They have arranged that there will be a play and want us to help out.

On the 18th, Phraya Rajawallapa[2] brought Toonkramom Toh and myself up to London. On that day, it was extremely foggy and all the trains were delayed. We had to wait at Camberley station for an hour and so arrived in London two hours later than we had planned.

On the 19th, we stayed in London another day and went to visit various people such as Mr. Thomson[3].

On the 20th, we came down to Chalcot. Mr Crake[4] brought us down. He had gone up to London to buy various props for the play, which we are going to perform next week. It will take place in the church and is for charity. Lots of people have bought tickets, so I don't think there will be enough seats.

Today Mr Phipps took Toonkramom Toh, Pi Pen and me to have lunch with Lord Bath, whose house is at Longleat. It is about one hour away from here. I am sure Your Majesty must have heard about this renowned house, which is enormous. We just walked around, but if we were to see the whole thing, I think we would have been exhausted. Mr Phipps knows Lord Bath well and so we were well received and shown a lot. The old books are very interesting and the house is huge with many rooms. In truth it is too large for a single couple and so half of it is closed up. Lady Bath has been unwell but now she is much better and able to walk again.

I am thinking of Your Majesty very much.

I beg to remain Your Majesty's obedient servant,

Chakrabongse

Prince Chakrabongse, Prince Benbadhana and Mr Crake, their English teacher.

30th December 1897

Your Majesty

On the 27th and 28th of this month, we took part in the play in the school in Tilton Mars near Chalcot. Mr Phipps, his wife and children are supporters of the school, so all the profit from the play is given to the church and the school.

On the 27th, the play was performed in the evening for the lower classes such as the farmers, maids, etc, as a trial run. It was packed and those who wanted a good seat came at least an hour early. We performed two plays. The first was called "Freezing A Mother-in-Law". Toonmom Toh, Pi Pen, Mr. Crake, Mr Phipps' children and two other women were the actors. It is a good story, but not very amusing. Toonmom Toh as his Mother-in-Law were very good, while everyone found Mr Crake, as an old man was very funny, although I did not think he acted very well. The second play was called "Who is Who". It is a comedy and lots of fun. Toonmom Toh, Mr Crake and the Phipps children, the two other women and myself took part. Toonmom Toh played an old person and he shuffled around very well. One Phipps girl played a maid and was really good, just like a real maid. She was probably the best out of all the female actors. I also played a servant,

---

1. Mr Phipps was guardian to Prince Chakrabongse. They stayed in touch over the years.
2. Lieutenant Colonel Phraya Rajawallapanusith was the son of Sut Bunnag. He was born in 1855. After starting life in the royal pages, he was ADC to Crown Prince Vajiravudh when he was in England and continued in his service thereafter.
3. Mr Thomson was possibly John Thomson the photographer.
4. Mr Crake was English teacher to the Thai princes.

who had just arrived and gone into service. I was a maid who was always showing off and talking rubbish. The old man who was boss thought that she must be a gentlewoman and that the gentlewoman was a maid so everything got muddled.

The evening of the 27th passed off well and the audience were very appreciative, laughing like mad. That evening we were all exhausted as inside the theatre it was so hot and we all had to speak loudly and dance around. So at the end, we were spent. On the 28th, we performed in the afternoon for all the rich people and gentlefolk of the area. Lots of people came from far and wide and squeezed in just as on the previous day. At first, we were rather anxious because the weather was bad with rain and we thought no one would come, but the performance went well just as before. But I don't think it was quite as good and there were some slight hitches. The money raised was several tens of pounds, but there were a lot of expenses. Nevertheless, there was a profit to support the church and the school. On the 29th morning, Mr Crake brought all six of us up to London as Phraya Visudh had ordered that we should all come back a bit earlier and it was a bit of a rush to get our things together.

In the evening of that day, we went to see Barnums Circus show, which had just come over from America. They have set up in Olympia. The show was really massive. First of all we went to see the various animals and the freaks, such as a man and a woman as tall as giants, a dwarf and a fat lady, a woman with a long beard and a person with two bodies. I really don't like these sorts of things, as I find them disturbing and rather repellent. For example, I can't help thinking that the woman with a beard is very fake. Nevertheless upon staring at her face, I could see she was a real woman. Her hair and beard were very long. It was black like an Indian and it seems it was encouraged to grow deliberately.

I also went to see the cinematograph. It was the Jubilee Queen and was very good. It was all a bit too fast, however, and I did not spot Toonmom Toh[1], as when it got to the foreign royalty, they cut the end and I couldn't see him. The circus itself started after 8 pm. They played this and that as usual such as various insects who had been trained to do certain things in the same hall. There were three groups doing different things at the same time. As a result one doesn't know where to look first and it made me quite dizzy, but

Prince Chakrabongse, Crown Prince Maha Vajiravudh and Mr Crake.

it was very well done. They say that these people were brought over from the Sudan. They probably were, and the performing and dancing were just like the real thing. I liked the way the man twirled his revolver around with one hand. The gun whizzed round very fast and it was most impressive.

On the evening of the 30th, we went to see a pantomime at the Drury Lane theatre, but it was not a patch on last year. Nevertheless the set and all the costumes were very beautiful. The first act was about a world of orchids and everyone was dressed as orchids. The backcloth was also of orchids. The lighting was really magnificent and when the designer came out and bowed he received very loud applause.

I plan to stay in London until Sunday, Toonmom Toh's birthday. As for the play that we performed in Westbury, I am sure Toonmom Toh has already written to you about it in detail and sent you the programme.

I think about Your Majesty without cease.

I beg to remain Your Majesty's obedient servant,

Chakrabongse

1. The Crown Prince had been invited to the celebrations for Queen Victoria's Diamond Jubilee.

Six brothers, from left to right: Prince Purachatra, Prince Benbadhanabongse, Crown Prince Maha Vajiravudh, Prince Abhakara, Prince Paribatra and Prince Chakrabongse. Photographed shortly before Prince Chakrabongse left for Russia.

In the first half of 1898, Prince Chakrabongse was still in England preparing to leave for Russia. Three long letters from the King discuss the details of the trip – who would accompany him and when would he leave. In mid-June the Prince and his entourage left by boat and train via Berlin, together with Ardachev, his tutor. After arriving in Russia, in late June, there are around 20 letters from Prince Chakrabongse detailing his arrival, his meeting with the Emperor and Empress, and summer in Peterhof where he fell from his horse. Then comes an account of moving into his quarters in the Winter Palace and beginning his studies in the Corps des Pages. There are no letters from the King for the second half of the year.

Prince Yugala Dighambara, known as Somdet Chai.

Opposite above: Prince Vudhijaya Chalermlabh.

Elsenwood, Camberley, Surrey
6th January 1898

Your Majesty

I was delighted to receive Your Majesty's letter dated 7th December from Penang.

Since Prince Toro made a big scene that time in Paris, he has been silent and there has been nothing further. While I was in London this time, he crossed over from Paris to stay with me. He said he had come to say goodbye to us and his various friends in England before going back to Bangkok. At first when Phraya Visudh went to meet him at the station, he made as if he was going to stay at the embassy, but then was not sure. After Phraya Visudh had been with him, he asked whether there was a hotel room available and so he stayed in Bailey's Hotel as usual, but came to eat at the embassy all the time and everything was fine. There was no fuss. In fact, he seemed a different person. On the 1st in the evening, he went back to Paris and said goodbye very politely. I hear that he is going to go stop off to visit Egypt before going home. It's as if he thinks that if he can't go to Egypt, he'll be missing out. You can't look at everything as if you are missing out. The wives and children of Krom Naret[1] all went to see him off in Genoa. They really are a group who are very loyal to each other.

On the 1st of this month which was the birthday of Toonmom Toh, we all had a dinner, albeit not a large one. A few of us also went to see a play.

Then on the next day, the 2nd, we came back down to Camberly, as the holiday was over. Somdet Chai[2], Prince Vudh and Prince Dilok[3] came to stay at Camberley too as they are still on holiday, and Chao Khun Visudh arranged for them to come down here as he thinks that is is better than staying in London.

My studies have begun again now. I am doing more Russian and have completed all the declensions and I seem to be groping towards getting things right.

Pi Purachatra has also come down to stay and will remain for the duration of his holidays.

I beg to remain Your Majesty's obedient servant,

Chakrabongse

---

1. Prince Naret Worarit (1855-1925) was Minister of Municipal Government.

2. Somdet Chai refers to Prince Yugala Dighambara, Prince of Lopburi (1882–1932). He was a year older than Prince Chakrabongse, but he does not call him Pi because he was the son of King Chulalongkorn and a princess.

3. Dilok Nabarath, Prince. 1884-1912. In 1907 he completed a degree in agriculture in Germany.

Bannakom Soranee Throne Hall
January 1898

A corner of the Bannakom Soranee Throne Hall in the Grand Palace, used by the king as his private study.

Dear Lek

I have received a letter dated 18th November and one dated 6th December, but haven't replied. And now another has arrived. I could say I am very busy and haven't had time, but that isn't really it. I am busy, but it's more about putting on blazers to receive people than real work. Nowadays, they give me little to do. The aim is to stop me wheezing, but I think even if they took 100 percent away, I wouldn't feel better. I have a tightness in my chest. It is as if when I had just come back I felt 50 % well, which has diminished to 25%. When I first arrived I felt lazy and didn't want to work in the Thai way. It was around 5% out of 100. Now it has increased to around 20% but I feel lazy, unlike when I was in Europe around 25 %.

No one seems worried because I have been like this for a long time when preparing to receive people. In truth we are very ready. I have never met either the *farang* or the Thai. I am saying in a teasing way that I don't want to flatter or be flatterd. I am pleased in a way not to have met them, but am worried that it won't follow through and I will get blamed. Will it be worth the effort? I feel like I have a heavy weight on my shoulders and can't move in any direction.

In the two letters you sent, I can see that you are truly trying to learn a new language. It seems really difficult and I'm worried it will take a long time. Your mother is grumbling about this as well.

As for the student who is going to accompany you, you speak of Nai Poum, but there is still time to choose. I have heard from Phraya Visudh that the choices are between Nai Poum, Nai Tiem[1] and Nai Manit[2]. Nai Manit doesn't seem to be up to much and would probably go as a pair with Nai Poum. Nai Tiem has the advantage of coming from a good family. I can talk to him, but the most important thing is that we choose someone who is intelligent, reliable and can be loyal in the future. If Poum can be that person, it would be excellent. If he is someone who is intelligent and has good knowledge, not being from a good family doesn't matter and may even be a benefit, so that he can continue to perform his duties in the future. I will therefore tell Phraya Visudh to take your preference as the determining factor.

I am thinking of you such a lot. Nowadays there are few young princes. It's no fun and I don't have anything special to relate. When there is more time, I will find some more stories to tell you.

Chulalongkorn

1. Nai Tiem Bunnag (1879-) was adopted by Prince Bhanurangsi aged three. At 13 was sent to England to be a soldier. He entered military service in 1898 and in 1901 became ADC to Prince Paribatra.
2. Nai Manit Manitayakul was the son of Chao Phraya Norraratratchamanit.

Elsenwood, Camberley, Surrey
13th January 1898

Your Majesty

Mr Verney has sent down various things, which Your Majesty bought for me in Egypt. I am really thrilled and thank Your Majesty so much. The things are beautifully made and I think if they were large things such as a cupboard or such like, they would be very impressive.

In addition, Phraya Visudh has sent Your Majesty's telegram regarding the student who should go to Russia to Colonel Hume and he has shown it to me here. I am very pleased that Your Majesty agrees that Nai Poum should go, as he is a really good person. The colonel and Dr Yarr also agree that he is the most suitable.

I also would have liked to take Nai Tiem as he is someone I know very well and Chao Khun Decho[1] begged me to take him along. I had intended to check him out and if there had been no objection to take him. However, once he was here and we talked about the idea of going, it was clear he was not totally convinced. He wants to be a British soldier as he had already prepared for that, and is about to enter Sandhurst very shortly. He did not say directly that he did not really want to go, but I could see from what he said that he felt he had done various things already and that this would be like starting all over again and other negative things. In fact, Nai Tiem is very English and so to try and convince him that there could be other things in this world better than England would be hard. Nai Poum, on the other hand, is someone who had just arrived and is not yet obsessed with England and can think to the future. He is fully committed to coming with me. I think that Phraya Visudh will arrage for him to come down here very shortly.

Nai Nok Yoong is still rather lonely and I'm not entirely sure why. He is partly a government funded student and partly paying his own way. He is still like a student, but has to come and work like a government official so I would like to request that he receives a salary in the same way as Luang Sorasit[2].

What he should be called has still not been decided. Should he be referred to as a Gentleman-in-

Nai Nok Yoong.

Waiting, what should his Thai name be, and what uniform he should wear? But these decisions are not that important. As he is going to Russia, the name he will use can be decided later, although the sooner the better otherwise he'll be somewhat indeterminate in status.

Tomorrow there will be a Russian exam based on what we have studied and next week an English exam.

I beg to remain Your Majesty's obedient servant,
Chakrabongse

1 Chao Khun Decho refers to Chao Phraya Surawongse Vadhanasak (Toh Bunnag) Nai Tiem's natural father. He graduated from Sandhurst and was in government service. He accompanied King Chulalongkorn to Europe as his personal ADC.

2. Luang Sorasit Yanukarn. Former name Um Intharayothin (1871-). At that time he was ADC to HRH Crown Prince Maha Vajiravudh.

Elsenwood, Camberley
20th January 1898

Your Majesty

On Monday 17th of this month, Colonel Hume took all of us up to London to hear Mr Smyth[1] talk about his experiences in Thailand when in the service of the Royal Siamese government.

At 8 pm we left the embassy to go to London University which is where the meetings of the Royal Graphical Society [sic] are held. Sir Clements Markham[2], the President, came to receive Toonmom Toh at the door and invite him inside to the musem room, where there were various ink sketches by Mr Smyth and some Thai artefacts. The sketches were really good and were of subjects such as the Chakri Throne Hall, which he captured extrememly well. There were also some oils by Mr Nurberry, but they were really bad. Today, all those who had something to do with Thailand and lived in London were there, together with some others.

Once it was time, we were invited into the lecture room. The President opened the meeting and announced that today the Crown Prince of Siam had come to visit. After that, Mr Smyth got up and read his lecture about Thailand.

Today he was talking about the Malay Peninsula from Chumporn down to Songkhla and Pattalung. The places he described were all ones I had visited when I accompanied Your Majesty. He also mentioned Lang Suan, Chaiya, Lakhon[3]. He seemed to really like Sam Roi Yod and he described the tale of Ta Mong Lai[4]. I was very amused. He gave a very good account and the audience seemed to enjoy it very much. While he was speaking, there were slides like a foreign film and pictures of the various towns. The first picture was of Phraya Petchaburi[5] whom he praised as being very intelligent. As for Phraya Chaiya, it seemed as if they got on very well and he praised him profusely. Once Mr Smyth had finished, the president asked whether there were any questions or comments to make about Thailand. He mentioned the names of several people but none of them got up. These included some of those who had criticised us such as Aman, but no one got up. Eventually Mr Werr got up and praised Mr Smyth and Thailand in various ways. One other person got up called Byers and asked about the various races inhabiting the Malay peninsula. Mr Smyth explained and he was satisfied.

In addition, Mr Smyth played a small bamboo flute (*kaen*) for people to listen to. They loved it and clapped loudly and he had to play it twice more. In the end the leader of the committee voted to than Mr Smyth and the evening was over. However, the meeting went on in the museum room for a long time and people asked lots of questions as is normal.

On the 18th, we came back down here. By the way, my Russian and English exams are finished and I imagine that Phraya Visudh will have sent you a report.

I beg to remain Your Majesty's obedient servant,

Chakrabongse

An sketch of Lakhon from Five Years in Siam by Herbert Warrington Smyth

1. Herbert Warington Smyth (1867-1943 was a British traveller, writer, naval officer and mining engineer who served the government of Siam as Secretary of the Dept of Mines from 1891-95, DG from 1895-97. Between 1898-1901 he was secretary of the Siamese Legation. He was the author of *Five years in Siam: from 1891-1896*.

2. Prince Chakrabongse has made a mistake with the name. It was in fact the Royal Geographical society as evidenced by the fact that Sir Clements Markham (1830-1916) was President of the society from 1888-1900.

3. Lakhon is today called Nakhon Sri Thammarat.

4. Ta Mong Lai is a Thai folk tale from Western Thailand.

5. This refers to the governor of Petchaburi province who at that time was Phraya Amarintharachai (Tien Bunnag).

6. The governor of Chaiya at that time was Kum Sriyapai who was a Southerner.

Elsenwood, Camberley
27th January 1898

Your Majesty

On the 24th, Pi Purachatra left here. He is going to stay with Mr and Mrs Verney before going back to Harrow. I am sad he has gone away as the more time we spend together, the more fun we have.

This is first day that Toonmom Toh went to Sandhurst. Yesterday he went there in advance to report in and they read his name out in the hall.

Today is the first day of actual classes. He had to go at 8 in the morning and came back in the evening.

One thing is that we have set up a new club here called the Graitney Debating Society so that we are forced to use English and speak it more fluently. It has been decided that there will be a debate once a week during which we will argue with each other. One person will express an opinion about something such as 'Bicycles are a bad thing' and then another has to say that they are good and give reasons. The others all then join in saying why they are good or bad. There is a rule that any member of the group who sits silent without saying anything for two sessions, will be fined a shilling.

The chairman and the secretary changes every week, and he who is secretary this week is likely to be chairman the next. If anyone wants to agree to something in the meeting, and someone else disagrees, it has to be put to the vote, with the chairman having the deciding vote. We have only had two debates, but it seems fun.

Colonel Hume gives a lecture every week also concerning various aspects of warfare in history and how the British were victorious. An example is how General Woolf attacked Quebec.

I am well and think of Your Majesty always.

I beg to remain Your Majesty's obedient servant,
Chakrabongse

Crown Prince Maha Vajiravudh in his Sandhurst uniform.

Elsenwood, Camberley
3rd February 1898

Your Majesty

On Saturday there was another meeting of the debating society. The topic for that day was "It would be a good thing if disagreements between nations were to be solved by arbitration rather than by warfare". One side said it was good and the other that it was bad. However, the topic was a bit too difficult and so no one felt comfortable talking about it.

Nowadays, the weather here is terrible. First cold and then hot. They had said that this year would be very cold, but that was wrong because until now it hasn't been cold at all.

Today I went riding in the manège, fell off and lay on the ground. However, I was not hurt, just dirty and my hair was full of sawdust.

I am very well and happy and all my studies are going well.

I beg to remain Your Majesty's obedient servant,
Chakrabongse

Elsenwood, Camberley
10th February 1898

Your Majesty

As yesterday was a half day at the Military Academy, Camberley, Toonkramom Toh invited Pi Pen, Phraya Raja, Luang Sorasit and myself to go and have tea at his college.

His room is nice but rather small, as it is used both as a bedroom and a sitting room for receiving guests all in one. However, in his room he has put a sofa instead of a bed so it looks more like a sitting room than those of others.

The cadets need to buy their own tea and cakes and they can buy whatever they like. Those we had yesterday were delicious, because Toonmom Toh bought the best and we ate a great deal as we couldn't bear to waste them.

Wednesday is traditionally a day of relaxation for the cadets and lots of them have guests to tea. This one and that one invite their friends and an added bonus in the afternoon is that there is a brass band.

Nai Poum has now arrived here and is studying Russian. However, he cannot join the same class as me. Accordingly, my teacher has decided to take Nai Nok Yoong into the same class as Nai Poum, leaving me in the top class on my own, as Nok Yoong can't really keep up. At this point, Nai Poum is at the lowest level and can't keep with Nai Nok Yoong and so he has to stop studying for a while.

One question is whether Your Majesty wants Nai Poum to be part of the court or not. If he is to be a part, he will need a uniform of some sort. My feeling is that if Your Majesty were so gracious as to allow him to be a cadet as well and if he could wear the uniform, it would be a good thing and later he could be a soldier as well.

It is almost time for us to go. I really hope that I will be able to speak Russian to a certain extent. My teacher says that to get really good results would take two years.

I beg to remain Your Majesty's obedient servant,
Chakrabongse

Crown Prince Maha Vajiravudh in the uniform of a Sandhurst cadet.

Elsenwood, Camberley
17th February 1898

Your Majesty

I have received Your Majesty's letter and am really pleased.

I looked in the court circular and saw how Your Majesty was received this time in magnificent fashion. It was clear how much the officials and populace love Your Majesty – something that was very gratifying.

I couldn't help noticing and being amused when comparing Your Majesty's reception this time with when *farang* arrive. It was so extravagant, like the vehicle procession from Reun Pae to the palace.

Regarding Nai Poum, I am very pleased that Your Majesty has said I can make whatever decision I like. Since we have been together, I can observe that he is a good person in every way and very aware of things around him. The thing I did not like about Nai Tiem was that he was too English in his thinking, with no Thai character left. Phraya Decho came and asked me to take his son but I did not definitely say yes, as I said I had to choose the one who was most appropriate.

I am still anxious about my Russian studies and that they will take too long. The teacher says it will take two years for me to be able to speak well. This language is very strange in that it is so difficult to speak, that the reading is easy by comparison and the opposite of Chinese. People on the whole say that it is the most difficult language to learn in the world. Nevertheless, I am not one for giving up and am determined to study it and succeed, as it will be of great benefit if Russia feels closer to us and does not treat us as foreigners. The teacher says all the time that when I go to Russia, people will like me very much because I can speak the language, so even if I make mistakes, he says I must speak.

I have told you about Nai Nok Yoong and Nai Poum in my previous letter and I hope it will all be decided when Prince Damrong leaves.

I am well and happy and think of Your Majesty constantly. I hope that I will be able to see Your Majesty in Europe again at least once.

I beg to remain Your Majesty's obedient servant,

Chakrabongse

One of the celebratory arches erected for the King's return.

Queen Maria Christina of Spain with her children. King Alfonso XIII is in the middle.

Letter Opposite
1. Queen Maria Christina of Spain (1885–1902), who was Regent for her son Alfonso XIII (1886–1931).

2. HRH Prince Chaiyantamongkol (1855-1907), one of the sons of King Mongkut.

3. HRH Prince Chirapravati Voradej, the Prince of Nakhon Chaisri (1876-1913). He attended the coronation of Nicholas II and was in the first group of King Rama V's children sent abroad, being away from 1885-1896. In 1891 he went to study at the Royal Danish Military Academy, graduating in 1894 and serving in the Royal Danish Army. In 1901, he was appointed Commander of the Department of Military Operations, equivalent to Commander in Chief of the Army.

4. King Alfonso XIII was the son of Alfonso XII. His mother Maria Christina acted as Regent. See above.

5. Jules Albert Defrance (1860-1936) was minister at the French legation in Bangkok between 1895 to 1907. Interestingly, the king refers to him as François de Franz.

Bannakom Throne Hall
18th February 1898

To my son Lek

I have received a letter from the Queen Regent of Spain[1] in answer to the letter sent from Seville. She sent some pictures – an envelope for Chaiyan[2], one for Chira[3], one for you. There are various pictures (the envelopes were not sealed so I could see them). However, in your envelope there was a letter from King Alfonso[4]. Again it was not sealed. He understood that you would come back to Bangkok with me. There was a picture in the envelope with no name on. It was a picture of three women and another of mother and child. The large photograph is mounted on card and one is inscribed on the back to me. There seemed to be nothing for Toh, or maybe it was sent to England, I don't know. However, the pictures which were sent on their own are rather strange, as in the Queen's letter to me she simply says she is sending pictures to my children and younger brothers, but not to me. In the letter from King Alfonso, it says that all the pictures are for you. So I am sending the photograph with another on the back to you as well. As for the picture of a mother and child, I would like that one, as I think you don't like large pictures as they are difficult to transport. So I am exercising my rights and keeping it. The Order of Maria Luisa encrusted with diamonds was sent at the same time. In the letter it says it is for your mother. I will get her to write a thank you letter and will explain about the pictures which I have sent to you. Please write to King Alfonso and, if you can, try and keep in touch with him. This letter is referred to by the Bangkokians as Lek's letter.

I have received your letters dated 10th, 16th, 23rd and 30th December, as well as the 6th of January. I was happy to hear your news, to see the report by your teacher and to hear in your own words that you are really trying with Russian. As for Nai Poum, I am happy that he is intelligent, although I am a bit sorry

about Nai Tiem as he is the son of a gentleman. Once I had given my permission by telegram many days ago, Phraya Decho had his wife come in and beg your mother for you to take him as well, saying that her son was very keen now. The fact that Phraya Decho wants this is from the best motives, but unfortunately it's too late now and so that's that. As for taking you to Russia, I think it is unlikely that Prince Damrong will go because at the moment he is in talks with the French. We are meant to exchange views, but the French have not said anything and so we haven't said anything either. We suggested arbitration but the French would not agree and I understand that at the moment they don't want to agree to anything, as it is near their elections. Francois de Franz[5] has not yet arrived and the French in Bangkok are quiet, with no trouble but I expect they are in consultation with each other.

My reception in Bangkok was good in every way. The open air *khon* performance[6], which was a large event was far better than I could have imagined. It was rather like the ancient towns in the Great Exhibitions, such as Old Brussels which you saw. The only thing was that here it was a *khon* performance or a procession. I have told you about the various exhibitions and they tried to make it like that. However, the shops nowadays don't have very much, only boats carved in the prison. I bought some boats and I asked Krom Sambassatra[7] to send them to Phraya Visudh to distribute to my children. I think you could even give them to *farang*. In Bangkok this year it is not very cold, but it's been chilly for a long time. In January, when it was the time of the fair, it was cool all month which was very good. In contrast, this February has been so hot, it's no fun at all.

Toro has arrived. His mouth looks like a gecko from trying to be a real Thai by chewing betel, but he wipes his mouth with a handkerchief. His face was red in stripes. He said that the reason he made a scene was so that I would allow him to come back. It's still not certain which way he will go. He is not someone who is constant. Coming to see your mother, he did not mention you at all, praising only Toh. I think it must be some plan to stop her being too keen on you.

I think about you so much. I feel that time passes slowly before we will see each other again.

Chulalongkorn

6. The *khon* performed in honour of the King on 2nd February 1898 featured the episode from the *Ramakien*, when Phra Ram returns victorious to Ayutthaya.

7. HRH Prince Thongthaem Sambassatra, seen as the father of Thai cinema. In June, 1897, "the wonderful Parisian cinematograph" was shown in Bangkok, the first known film screening in Thailand. The same year, the film of King Chulalongkorn's visit to Europe was brought to Thailand, along with camera equipment bought by the prince.

Elsenwood, Camberley, Surrey
24th February 1898

Your Majesty

Now another person, called Hale, has joined us in our riding lessons. I also know his elder sister. At the moment he rides really badly. His back is bent and he almost fell off many times, but that's what it's like at the beginning.

I have looked in the newspapers and seen how Your Majesty was received on Your Majesty's return from Europe. It was a huge affair and looks great fun. The blessing that the Sankaraj made on behalf of the entire Sangha was very impressive.

The feast in Lao style also seemed most entertaining and the Calling the Spirits ceremony must have been loud and strange. If I had been there, I might not have been able to contain my laughter.

By the way, everyone here has now become amateur photographers and we all go off together. I have sent you a picture of me. Mr Ardachev, my teacher, took it for me.

Last evening, Dr Yarr gave a practical lecture on biology and explained how to tie a bandage if you have hit your head or broken a bone, etc.

I hope that everyone in Thailand is well and happy.

I think of Your Majesty always.

I beg to remain Your Majesty's obedient servant,
Chakrabongse

Bannakom Soranee Throne Hall
3rd March 1898

To my son Lek

Today is your birthday and I have already sent a telegram to wish you well and given some money to you mother. Now I want to send you all good wishes for your health and happiness, together with success in your studies which you have begun.

Your letter of 13th January discussing the position of Nai Nok Yoong, I did not answer straight away as I was consulting and giving instructions. In fact, it has been sorted out, but being swamped with work I have not had time to write. I will answer the various points in order. At present, any discussion with the French does not look as if it will be successful. Monsieur Defrance has still not arrived, but the clashes with the French are much less. There is a date for releasing the prisoners with a promise that they will agree to release Phra Yot[1] as well. My intention is for the Emperor to decide whether the agreement is fair, but saying that is one thing, it is quite another to achieve it through government channels. Accordingly, there is as yet no schedule for Prince Damrong to depart. So if you decide that May is the month, then Phraya Suriya[2] will have to be the one to take you.

Concerning who is to go with you, it was originally thought in Bangkok that if you were to go to Russia on your own, an ambassador should be appointed. Then Phraya Suriya suggested that a secretary should be appointed as Chargé d'Affaires. But I thought about this further and decided that

One of the arches erected to celebrate the King's return.

establishing a secretary would look suspicious in the eyes of other countries as we have no trade with Russia. Another issue is that a secretary cannot request an audience with the Tsar and so it has been decided that someone should be appointed as your Guardian or Governor, but with the opportunity to discuss official business. How this would work in practice, Chao Phraya Abahya Raja[3] still wants to think more about. For this position we have chosen Phra Prom Surin who was Phraya Cholburi and is skilled in diplomacy. Nai Nok Yoong will be there as your Thai teacher, Nai Poum is there as your class-mate. All these three have official positions and will take a salary from the Royal Household and I will increase their salary in the New Year.

I will write a letter to the Emperor outlining my thoughts on this and also ask him about any arrange-ments for your education, which is the right thing to do and we will pay as much as we can. Then I will get Phraya Suriya to arrange everything. I am afraid that in Paris at the moment there won't be anything, but it seems the only way to find out what the Emperor has arranged is to ask the French ambassador via Count Muraviev[4] and arrange things with Phraya Suriya. When you are ready, then there will be a let-ter to the Emperor and Empress Marie and anyone else that I know. Phraya Chol[5] will bring this letter to Phraya Suriya. This has just been decided and if it changes in anyway I will tell you again.

By the way, your letters of 20th and 27th January and 3rd February have been received, as well as a letter from Phraya Visudh with your exam report. I am very pleased by your firm intentions to succeed.

Affairs in Bangkok are going along as usual. I can't say things are going backward or standing still but they are progressing slower than I would wish. All the events surrounding my return are over. The party for all the women who received decorations, included various tables and a raffle, stalls and competitions among the women. They all had a great time. The only problem was it was terribly hot and I did not feel well. The heat definitely makes people very lazy. There's no doubt about it – I just have to observe

myself. I don't feel as energetic as when I'm in Europe and my behaviour becomes more Thai every day, which makes me feel a bit fed up. I think about trying to be chic, but it seems impossible to be smart here.

There is one thing I wanted to tell you. Chira has become engaged to Ying Pravas[6], but she is still young so he has to wait. He was in a rush because he and Pravitra were fighting over her. However, her mother and father were not that keen on Pravitr. . . I feel a bit sorry for him.

Toro has arrived in Bangkok. He is now very calm and he doesn't seem to be going for any one. But as ever, one can't be sure as far as he is concerned.

At the moment I am feeling very lazy. I would love to get on the tram in Lisbon. It was such fun, even if it made me feel a bit sick as it was so bumpy. What it really means is I am thinking of you.

Chulalongkorn

---

1. Phra Yot was Phra Yot Muang Kwang, a Thai provincial gover-nor, accused of murdering a French military officer.

2. Phraya Suriya Nuvat (Kert Bunnag), the Siamese Minister who was representing King Chulalongkorn in Europe, residing in Paris, received an additional appointment to the Russian Imperial Court.

3. Chao Phraya Abahy Raja refers to Gustave Rolin Jacquemyn (January 1835-January 1902), the General Advisor. Expert in international law, he met Prince Damrong in Cairo in December 1891. Prince Damrong offered him the job and he wished "to ensure that respect for international law enabled a small, threat-ened country to resist the major powers." He played a key role in negotiating the aftermath of the Franco-Siamese war of 1893, which endured for 15 years. In 1906, Siam ceded Nakhon Province in Cambodian territory to French Indochina; and in the Anglo-Siamese Treaty of 1909, gave up claims to Kedah, Kelantan, Perlis and Terengganu in Upper Malaya.

4. Count Mikhail Nikolayevich Muraviev (1845-1900), Russian statesman and Minister of Foreign Affairs from 1897 to his death. He initiated the Hague Peace Conference, but died suddenly after a meeting with Sergei Witte and Alexei Kuropatkin where Witte blamed Muraviev for the situation in China.

5. Real name Sawat Phumirat (1867-1927), entered royal service when young and rose through the ranks to provincial positions in the 1890s, as well as governor of Cholburi, hence his title. In April 1898, he was elevated to Phraya Mahibal Boriraksha as governor to Prince Chakrabongse. In 1899, he was appointed Siamese ambassador to St. Petersburg.

6. HSH Princess Pravas Svasti Sonakul (1883-1902). They had two daughters and a son.

Elsenwood, Camberley, Surrey
3rd March 1898

Your Majesty

On the 1st of this month, Colonel Hume took me and Pi Pen to see a concert in Aldershot which is about 6 miles from here. At the concert we met various members of the English aristocracy, namely the Duke and Duchess of Connaught[1] and Prince and Princess Christian[2]. I had met the latter once before when I saw the Russian Emperor in Darmstadt[3], but he couldn't remember me. However, I know the Duke of Connaught and he came and shook hands with me and chatted nicely.

The concert had some singing and violin playing. It was so good that everyone exclaimed that they had never thought that Aldershot could have such an excellent concert. The woman sang like the one we heard in Paris when she sang Lakshmi. She produced a vibrato sound in her throat and did not need music. She was good but the pieces were rather short.

Today it rained a lot, so everyone who went in an open carriage was freezing cold. Doctor Yarr came too and when he got back he had a cold.

Today is my birthday, so there will be a party for all the Thais who are in Camberley.

I am thinking of Your Majesty all the time. I did not receive Your Majesty's good wishes for my birthday and am a bit upset, but it may not yet have arrived.

I beg to remain Your Majesty's obedient servant,
Chakrabongse

Right: The Duke of Connaught in 1890 from Vanity Fair.

Elsenwood, Camberley
11th March 1898

Your Majesty

Your Majesty's telegram wishing me a happy birthday arrived late because it got held up in London at the post office here. Nevertheless, it still made me very happy and I am deeply grateful to Your Majesty.

On the 3rd, Toonkramom Toh, Pi Pen, Phraya Raja and Luang Sorasit came to dinner here and there were speeches and so forth as is customary, but they were in three languages, namely Thai, English and Russia, which was rather unusual.

On the 4th, Colonel Hume gave a lecture on the army at Waterloo in the time of Napoleon. It was very good but is not yet completed and there will be more.

Doctor Yarr gave a lecture on various medical issues regarding first aid before the doctor arrives. This last session related to people falling into the water. It was very weird. Another debating society has been established like that at Graitney, but this time only using Russian. It is really hard to talk to each other, although Doctor Yarr knows quite a few words.

I am well and happy and think of Your Majesty all the time.

I beg to remain Your Majesty's obedient servant,
Chakrabongse

---

1. The Duke of Connaught, Arthur William Patrick Albert; (1850 -1942), was the third son of Queen Victoria. Between 1893-98 he had command of the Aldershot District Command.

2. Prince Christian of Schleswig Holstein (1831-1917) was a minor German prince who became part of the British Royal family when he married Princess Helena (1846-1923), third daughter of Queen Victoria.

3. Prince Chakrabongse did not accompany King Chulalongkorn to Russia in 1897, but instead joined the royal party in Darmstadt when the Emperor was also there.

Bannakom Throne Hall
11th March 1898

To my son Lek

I received another letter dated 10th February, just at the moment when I was about to write to you.

I have now written to the Emperor that you are preparing to go. I have sent a copy for you to see as well. I want you to be ready by May even though that does not mean it will definitely be then, as the letter to the Emperor, despite being a personal letter, due to the Emperor's high standing, has had to be sent via various ambassadors and will probably take longer than a normal letter. Another thing is that being the Emperor, he has a lot of duties and may take a long time to give the order. So all I could do was to explain to Phraya Suriya that our firm intention is that if the Emperor sets a date via Count Muraviev or via the ambassador, he is not to wait to inform me. If he sees that he has not yet proposed a date, but just answers the letter, then Phraya Suriya can say that it can be as late as the end of May, or even better, the beginning of June, as it won't be so cold.

As Nai Poum is going to study alongside you, he must be a cadet, but whether he should be received by the Emperor or not is difficult to judge. In Russia they take questions of rank very seriously, but if it isn't the moment for rank, they are just like ordinary people. He should prepare a suit for the possibility, but whether he gets an audience, all depends on how things are organised in Russia and I will tell the Ministry of War. However, for Nai Nok Yoong I think it would be harder as he is not a soldier. To transfer him into the military when he is a grown up and not a student is difficult. To make him an officer, he would then have to participate in military chat. I think he will have to be a civilian, wearing evening dress or maybe Siamese court dress of the fifth level. If he has a chance to have an audience, I would like to think more on this. Phraya Chol will probably leave Bangkok quite soon now.

Phraya Mahibal at the time of his appointment as ambassador in St. Petersburg.

Russia and England are being very provocative with each other at the moment, but I hope it won't lead to fighting. I don't think that it will flare up so easily. It's like dogs snapping at each others heels, or like threatening those of us in the East.

Chulalongkorn

Prince Chakrabongse before leaving for Russia.

Elsenwood, Camberley, Surrey
24th March 1898

Your Majesty

This is the day on which all the schoolchildren of the public schools in England, who have joined the military corps in their schools, namely the Public School Corps, come together for an inspection in Aldershot. There are some light exercises and then a parade.

We all got on our bicycles to go and watch. However, we were a little bit late as we had to pick up Toonmom Toh from the Military Academy and he had to get changed which took a long time. When we arrived we had missed the fighting, but saw them marching past the general. These boys do not have the appearance of soldiers at all. They have not been well trained at the schools. They complain every time and this is because the teachers are not military men, but put on uniforms and pretend to be captains in charge. It looks really bad. Some of them have beards and wear glasses. However, there was one group – I don't know from which school – who looked good and more soldierly. In the whole gathering, there were three Thai boys, namely Nai Tiem, Phraya Decho's son, Nai Chot, the son of Phraya Montri and Nai Krasien, the son of Phraya Intornthep. Nai Tiem is in the Malvern College group and looked worthy of being a soldier. Nai Krasien just played the trumpet. All of the boys must be very tired, judging by their manner when they were walking back. The weather was terrible, with snow almost all the time, which spoiled things a great deal.

I am well and happy and thinking about Your Majesty.

I beg to remain Your Majesty's obedient servant,
Chakrabongse

P. S. A newspaper here called the *Court Circular* had a strange piece of news, namely that they had heard that the King of Siam was not going to send his second son to stay in Russia as previously planned, because someone had suggested that it would be better not to send him as it would cause a rift with England. The editor commented that the King of Siam was intelligent to change his mind as, if his son went into the Russian army, the Russians would encourage him to dislike England and could create problems. It's all very bizarre and I do not know where they got this news from.

Elsenwood, Camberley
31st March 1898

Your Majesty

I was delighted to receive Your Majesty's letter dated 18th February.

I was also pleased to receive a letter from King Alfonso and the various photographs, as I had been wondering for a while why he had not answered my letter and acknowledged the picture I sent some time ago. In fact I was rather upset, because the letter to Toonmom Toh was sent here. However, I also suspected he had probably sent it to Thailand as a result of a misunderstanding. I can now write to King Alfonso as you suggest. His letter was very nice and I am really delighted. I must tell him that Prince Damrong cannot leave at the moment, as I have learnt in your telegram about Phraya Visudh. I regret this but, if there is no benefit to the country, we should not waste any time over it.

Concerning Nai Tiem, I am also sorry not to have him along and I am afraid that Chao Khun Decho will be very upset and that it will leave a scar. However, I do think that those students who come and stay in Europe as long as he has become *farang* in their way of thinking. To coerce them into doing something that they are not wholehearted about will lead to a lot of complaining. I am concerned that Nai Tiem may incur the wrath of his father and mother on this point, but if someone is half-hearted, no amount of ticking off will work. In addition, the boy is very keen on being a British soldier and I don't think he should be discouraged from this. Nai Poum is a really good person, has a sense of responsibility and is a good student. Nowadays, he can speak a lot of Russian and the teacher praises him a great deal. I hope that Phra Visudh has sent the report which our teacher has written to Your Majesty.

My teacher has insisted that I write some Russian words and send them to you, so here they are:

Сіамъ	=	Siam
Сіамскій Кароль	=	King of Siam
Чилалонкорнъ	=	Chulalongkorn
Чакрабонъ.	=	Chakrabongse

The letters are really very strange. These days I am getting in a bit of a muddle when I write, mixing English and Russian letters.

I really hope I can go to Russia in May, for if it is any later than that I will lose a lot of time especially as this teacher has to return in June.

By the way, Prince Vudh and Prince Dilok have come to stay here now as it is the holidays. Pi Purachatra will join us next Tuesday.

I think about Your Majesty all the time

I beg to remain Your Majesty's obedient servant,
Chakrabongse

Opposite: The cricket pitch at Sandhurst.

15th April 1898

Your Majesty

It is a tradition that on the first of this month all the school children from the various schools assemble to perform gymnastics, engage in sword fights, boxing and the like in competitions held in Aldershot. An official acts as judge. All of us went to have a look. There were two Thais, namely Setsiri[1], the younger brother of Charoon, and Nai Tiem, the son of Phraya Decho. Setsiri came first out of the Harrow boys and was representing the school, while Nai Tiem was representing Malvern. The boxing looked great fun although sometimes it was rather dangerous, with blood pouring out of their noses and mouths. The boys who were boxing used up all their strength.

The Duke and Duchess of Connaught presented the prizes. The school that won the gymnastics was Dulwich. They received a shield, which they can keep for one year. Apart from that, there were prizes for the different classes.

The Duke remembered us very well. When he arrived he came straight over and called Toonmom Toh to go and sit with him, just as he had before.

Today in the evening there were conjuring tricks to celebrate the New Year[2]. Colonel Hume arranged the show and it was a lot of fun.

The holidays for Toonmom Toh and those at Camberley began on Wednesday 6th, and on the 7th Pi Purachatra came down to Camberley also. During the holidays we created a small field of dug outs just as they taught us to do in the military college. It was a lot of fun, but very exhausting at first. Some days we played war games together.

On Tuesday 12th, Mrs Werr invited us to visit them at Burnham Lodge in Slough. Colonel Hume took us to get the train and then from Camberley we cycled to Ascot and to Burnham Lodge.

After having lunch, we played a bit of tennis and came back. On that day, Somdet Chai, Prince Vudh and Prince Dilok came to London.

Prince Dilok Nabarath.

On the 14th, Toonmom Toh, Pi Purachatra, Pi Pen and I came up to London for the holidays. In the evening we went to see a play at the Haymarket called "*The Little Minister*", a play about Scotland some 40 years ago[3]. It was great fun. Today Somdet Chai, Prince Vudh and Prince Dilok are going back to Chalcott with Mr Phipps.

I have received Your Majesty's letter and am very happy. Regarding Nai Nok Yoong and Nai Poum, I am delighted that everything has been decided. I hope that the date of our departure can be determined very soon.

I am thinking of Your Majesty always.

I beg to remain Your Majesty's obedient servant,

Chakrabongse

1. HSH Prince Setsiri Kridakorn (1880-1957). Between 1903 and 1904, he trained with the Japanese army in Japan, and on returning to Thailand was first chief of the Thai Army Ordinance Department and the first director of a modern weapons factory.

2. Siamese New Year was traditionaly held for several days between 11-13 April.

3. The 1891 novel and subsequent 1897 play of the same name was by J. M. Barrie, author of *Peter Pan*.

Elsenwood, Camberley
21st April 1898

Your Majesty

I received Your Majesty's letter dated 11th March, together with a copy of Your Majesty's letter to the Russian Emperor. The latter had already been copied by Phraya Suriya and sent to me, as well as his letter to Count Muraviev. It seems that now we are just waiting for the command from the Emperor. I am virtually ready. Only my suits are not yet finished, but I am sure they can be ready quite soon. However, regarding Phraya Cholburi, I have not heard whether he has left Bangkok yet or not. Looking at the calendar it seems he must be about to.

Phraya Suriya has written to me regarding the programme during the journey. I think that I will arrange the schedule to suit myself and then Phraya Visudh can alter the parts that he thinks are wrong.

I would like to stop off in Berlin for a couple of days, as I would like to visit Toonkramom Chai before I go, as well as doing some sightseeing in Berlin, but all will depend on whether Phraya Visudh thinks it is appropriate or not.

I am thinking of Your Majesty always.

I beg to remain Your Majesty's obedient servant,

Chakrabongse

Elsenwood, Camberley
28th April 1898

Your Majesty

I have received the photographs of Your Majesty taken with Sadet Mae, in two different sizes, one large, one small. I am so pleased and thank Your Majesty very much.

On the 25th, Prince Vudh came down here from Westbury. After stopping briefly in London, he came on here. He came now because of Mr Phipps, as he is going to go to the school of Mr Litteryon where Pi Abha[1] was before in order to prepare for entry into the navy. I asked him to come down here before going to school, because when I go to Russia he will be studying and will not be able to come and see me off so we will not see each other for a long time.

On the 26th, Mr Verney invited us to go for an outing on the Thames near Reading. There were

Prince Abhakara Kiartivongse, Prince of Chumphon.

1. Pi Abha refers to Prince Abhakara Kiartivongse, Prince of Chumphon (1880-1923). Studied naval warfare in England.

Elsenwood, Camberley

5th May 1898

other Thai people apart from us, such as various *mom chao* princes and other students. We went by train to Reading. Mr and Mrs Verney came to meet us with the others and we got into the boats. I asked for a rowing boat, as I can't really scull and we went in various boats and had a race. It was a lot of fun and made me think of Bang Pa-In[2]. I have not gone rowing for two years now and at first I was not very good and rowed too fast. I got tired and stiff too quickly, but after a while I found my stroke and could row well again and did not get that tired.

We stopped for tea at an hotel some three miles from Reading. As we were 18, when we ordered tea the hotel was rather taken aback! We got back here in the early evening.

On the 27th, Prince Vudh went back to London and in the afternoon went to school. Phraya Visudh took him. Today Pi Pen also went to London to prepare his wardrobe and other things in order to go to college. He will go there on the 4th of May.

I beg to remain Your Majesty's obedient servant,

Chakrabongse

2. The summer palace of King Chulalongkorn built up river near Ayutthaya, the former capital. Boating on the river or lake was one of the major pastimes there.

Prince Chakrabongse with three of his brothers, from left to right: Prince Chakrabongse, Crown Prince Maha Vajiravudh, Prince Abhakara and Prince Benbadhana.

Your Majesty

I was pleased to hear the news that Phraya Mahibal had already left Bangkok and also that the Emperor has arranged my living accommodation. I am now just anxious about the date, as I am concerned there has been a misunderstanding with the Russian side thinking that we are going to suggest the date and us thinking that they are going to do so. Normally, as we are the ones setting out, we should set the date and then tell them. I am worried we have missed a cable from Bangkok. Anyway it seems the Emperor has arranged everything and is merely waiting for the date. Whatever the case, it seems unlikely that I can go this month, because Phraya Mahibal will not reach England in time. I am virtually ready before Phraya Mahibal arrives.

By now Pi Pen has left and gone to Wellingore school in Lincoln to study agriculture. The day before he left there was a farewell party for him at Graitney,

This evening we went to see the show at the Sandhurst Military Academy. There was singing and dancing, but it wasn't much fun. However, the children and the soldiers seemed to enjoy it a lot, clapping like mad.

I beg to remain Your Majesty's obedient servant,

Chakrabongse

Elsenwood, Camberley
17th May 1898

Your Majesty

On the 13th, Toonkramom Toh invited all of us to go and have lunch at the military academy and watch the various drills, such as the cow race which is traditionally held once a year at the school. On this day, the various cadets are allowed to invite people along. The cadets usually invite their parents and brothers and sisters. Toonkramom Toh and I complained that we were missing our parents, although we did as well as the others with regard to brothers.

The games included running races, the high jump, long jump, sack race, and the three-legged race. There were two competitions which were very good – the obstacle race and the donkey race. The obstacle race was very difficult as they had to crawl through this and over that, climb ropes and jump across water. Those who took part were exhausted and all of them could barely walk when it was finished. Indeed, some people didn't get very far before running out of energy and having to stop. Some people fell into the water and got wet and other hardships. The donkey race involved people dressing up and riding donkeys, which did all kinds of tricks which were a lot of fun. One person brought an Egyptian donkey to compete and so won easily but the judge refused to give him the prize, as he had cheated by using a donkey who was already trained in competition against others who were untrained. It is a shame that the weather was not very good and it rained quite often, forcing us to sneak off inside.

On the 18th, Mr Raleigh came down to see us and told us various items of news about Thailand. He also stayed for dinner. Dr Yarr, when he knew that you had presented him with a cigarette case, was very thrilled and said that you hadn't forgotten him and other such things.

Now the date for leaving for Russia is agreed. We will arrive on the 13th of June. Count Muraviev wrote and told Phraya Suriya that our side should make the arrangements, so that is what we have done.

I will go up to London on the 26th of this month and will most likely leave London around the 3rd of June.

I think of Your Majest always without exception.

I beg to remain Your Majesty's obedient servant,

Chakrabongse

Prince Chakrabongse photographed just before his departure for Russia.

3rd June 1898

Siamese Legation, Berlin
10th June 1898

Your Majesty

On the 1st, Prince Suriyong[1] and Phraya Mahibal arrived in London, together with Phraya Suriya. They brought Your Majesty's letter with them which I have now received. I am very pleased.

Phraya Mahibal seems to be an excellent person. Having met him these last two to three days, I like him already. He seems very keen to work and is very friendly. There are various matters he is particular about, but appropriately so, such as things to do with money.

Prince Suriyong doesn't seem that changed apart from the fact that he has undergone his tonsurate and his face is a little different. He doesn't seem much bigger. The students had heard that he was coming by boat and thus would miss seeing me.

I arrived here from Camberley on the 26th of last month and stayed in London for two days before going down to Chalcot, the home of Mr Phipps, so that I could say goodbye to him properly. Somdet Chai and Prince Dilok were very happy that I went to stay there, as during that time they did not have to study. I stayed at Chalcot until the 1st, when I came back to London. When I arrived I met up with all those who had come from Bangkok.

Yesterday I went to visit various people to whom I had planned to go and say goodbye, but I didn't get to see anyone and simply left my card.

In the evening we went to see the play at the Gaiety Theatre called "*The Runaway Girl*"[2]. It wasn't very good but had funny songs and was quite amusing.

Today Toonmom Toh and everyone else are going to come up to London in order to send me off tomorrow and in the evening Mr Verney has invited us all to dinner at his house and to see a play. I hear that Colonel Hume and many other English people are also going to see me off.

I am happy but must admit my heart is beating somewhat faster.

I am thinking of Your Majesty always.

I beg to remain Your Majesty's obedient servant,
Chakrabongse

1. HRH Prince Suriyong Prayurabandhu, Prince of Chaiya (1884-1919).

Your Majesty

Your Majesty's letter of 4th May was sent to England, when I had already left. They sent it on to me and I've received it safely. I was very pleased and will remember Your Majesty's words in this letter always.

As the time approaches to arrive in Petersburg, I feel ever more anxious. I hope it is not going to be too much, as it is something quite new. I feel that it is not just about going to study, but also about performing an important duty and I am determined to do this to the best of my ability at all times.

I left London on the 4th of this month together with Phraya Suriya, Phraya Visudh and Nai Poum. Phraya Mahibal and Nai Nok Yoong will follow later. All my brothers in England came to send me off and other people, both English and Thai, also came to the station. We crossed over and arrived in Paris in the evening. There was no wind or waves so it was a very comfortable crossing. In Paris I met Mae Oon[3] for the first time. While in Paris I visited various places, but nothing was that amazing, apart from the Salon where they show paintings. It is like the Academy show in London. However, this year they said the pictures were not as good as last and the show was huge and exhausting to walk round. It was also very hot. I went up the Eiffel Tower again. It was really to take Poum, as he had never been.

My time in Paris coincided with Russian National Day. There was a reception at the residence. The ambassador asked various things, questioning Phraya Suriya a lot about me and why I did not attend. Phraya Suriya explained that I was still young, a very useful excuse such as when I did not go and see the president this time. I am rather pleased with it.

On the 7th, Phraya Mahibal and Nai Nok Yoong arrived from London. On the 8th, in the afternoon, we all left Paris for Berlin. Phraya Visudh has now returned to London. At first Grand Duke Alexis[4], the uncle of the emperor, was going to accompany us but then he changed his mind although many people went to the station to see him off.

2. "*Runaway Girl*" was a musical comedy in two acts by Seymur Hicks and Harry Nicholls. It was produced by George Edwardes, opening 21st May 1898 and ran for 593 performances.

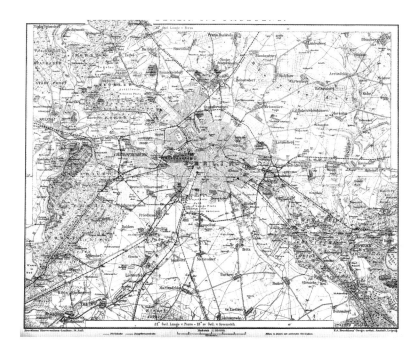

Map of Berlin in 1898.

Phraya Mahibal and his wife, Khunying Oon.

In the train there were various Russians, who seemed rather surprised to see us speaking Russian to each other. Phraya Suriya brought along my former teacher. He has promised definitely not to interfere in any way, nor to try to be a teacher in Russia.

On the morning of the 9th, we reached Berlin. Phraya Non[5] and others came to the station. I am staying at the embassy, but the others have had to stay in an hotel because there is no room here. Phraya Non has entertained me lavishly with far too much food. He has arranged everything to be as comfortable as possible and has given me as much time as possible. Yesterday morning we went to see the emperor's palace, which has just been finished, as well as the parliament in the afternoon. After which we went to a park outside the city. Toonmom Chai arrived from Boston in the afternoon but had to leave in the evening, as he had to study today. In the evening I went to an opera, which was not much fun.

This afternoon I am going to see Toonmom Chai in Potsdam and will have dinner there too. This morning I beg to end my letter now as it is the day the mail leaves.

I think about you always.

I beg to remain Your Majesty's obedient servant,
Chakrabongse

3. Mae Oon was the wife of Phraya Mahibal Boriraksha (Sawad Bhumirat).

4. Grand Duke Alexis refers to Alexei Alexandrovich (1850-1908). In 1883 he was appointed general admiral and he was allegedly Nicholas II's favourite uncle. However, he was relieved of command after the Baltic Fleet was completely defeated in the Battle of Tsushima in 1905.

Ardachev, Prince Chakrabongse's Russian tutor from England, accompanied him to St. Petersburg. His observations add colour to the prince's more formal letters to his father.

9th June 1898.
Berlin, Hotel Bristol

We have just arrived from the station and had breakfast at the hotel. We travelled from Paris to Berlin by the luxurious Nord-Express, which leaves twice a week for Petersburg. It consists of four or five enormous sleeping cars (all first class) and covers the distance of 2,500 kilometers in 46 hours, including a 6-hour stop. It takes 15 hours to get from Paris to Berlin (around 1,000 km). It's a real pleasure to travel in such a train. Cars with soft springs, no jolting or shaking, comfortable beds with clean linen, made up for the night. An excellent dining car, where we dined between Luttich (Liège) (Belgium) and Gerbestale (Germany). Thus we had breakfast in France, dined in Belgium, went to bed in Germany, near Cologne, and got up between Spandau and Berlin. Of course, I couldn't have afforded this trip myself, as the one-way ticket costs no less than 250 rubles. So the journey of our nine-person group with 50 *poods*[1] of luggage must have cost around 2,000 rubles, not counting the accommodation at the first class hotel in Berlin ("Bristol" at U.D. Linden). Most of the passengers were Russian, puzzled by our Siamese-English-French-German-Russian speaking company. I suppose only those reading the *Novoe Vremya* (New Time) will know who we are. . .

Best wishes,
Yours, Panya

15th June 1898
St. Petersburg, Winter Palace.

Hello,

I've just dropped in to the Winter Palace to see Lek. Before we had time to say hello, he was taken away for a medical examination. I made the brief acquaintance of his Russian suite, including the officer who is in charge of the Prince. He told me that he had had an opportunity to learn about the Prince beforehand through my report sent from England to Count Muraviev, the Minister of Foreign Affairs, and later handed by him to the Administration of the military educational institutions. The director of the Corps des Pages, Count Keller, also thanked me for this report that helped him gain an idea of the Prince's personality. Now I am sitting at Lek's table, waiting for him and writing this letter. We arrived at 3 p.m. yesterday by Nord-Express, together with Grand Duke Alexei Alexandrovich, who wished to get acquainted with Lek. The Grand Duke didn't know that Lek could speak Russian. On arrival in St. Petersburg, the prince and the Siamese minister were met by Russian officers and taken to the Winter Palace in the Imperial carriage. So, I went alone to my "Grand Hotel Europe" on Nevsky Prospect. From Germany we had booked by telegraph two rooms there, for me and for the Minister (with saloon). I spent the night in my 6-ruble room; the Minister's costs 22 per day. The Minister plans to move to the hotel today. He has been given an apartment in the Winter Palace, but he feels uneasy there. Yesterday Lek was taken to the islands[2].

I took a bath after 30 hours of travel and went to Fontanka to visit Count Alsufyef. Yesterday at the station I was "attacked" by a reporter, someone named Korovin. It was impossible to get rid of him and I had to invite him to my hotel. . .

The first information about the Prince in the Russian Press was my brief article, sent from Berlin. It was printed in *Novoe Vremya* on the day of our arrival. I bought this issue in Gatchina, the last station before St. Petersburg, and Lek had an opportunity to read the hearty words of the public's welcome. He was obviously impressed, as nowhere has he been received with such hospitality, neither by the English nor the French press. It is a pity, of course, that he has found himself in the company of people who are absolutely unknown to him. As for me, I am obviously not wanted here any more, although that was to be expected. Nevertheless, I am extremely happy to be the first Russian teacher of the Prince, who will be the pioneer of Russian education in Siam. I am going to stay here as long as the Siamese Minister (10 days or so) and will come back to Paris with him.

---

1. One *pood* equals 16 kilos.
2. The islands: Elagin, Krestovsky and Kamenny always were, and still are, favourite places for walks and entertainment.

St. Petersburg
6th June 1898

I've just received your letters. You, Kolya, give free rein to your imagination. As I had already said, my role is less pretentious than you think. I feel that I am not wanted here. Because of this and my disposition, I'll do my best to remain in the shadows. By the way, this accords with the wishes of those who control the Prince. . . . I saw the Prince when he came back from Tsarskoe Selo, where he had been introduced to the Tsar. He looked tired, though it's quite understandable. . . I wanted to know if the Tsar had talked to him in Russian. It turned out that he had not. Obviously, certain measures were taken to prevent this on the pretext of the prince's poor knowledge of the language, Russian court etiquette etc. I am so sorry, especially for the prince, who thereby lost his chance to make His Majesty listen to his Russian language, mastered with painstaking work far away from Russia. In snatches I try to see him everyday in the Winter Palace. I am grateful, at least, that they don't show me the door. However, it is the only favour, I get from the officials, who ignore me completely, but I don't care. . .

Winter Palace. St. Petersburg
10th June 1898

Dear Father, Mother, Kolya and all the others
I've just received my new foreign passport and leave for Paris with the Siamese envoy on Saturday 13th by Nord-Express. . . . Yesterday I was invited for dinner at the Siamese envoy's hotel. Among the guests were Count Keller, the director of the Corps des Pages, the prince's governor, Khrulov, and two other high-ranking persons. After dinner we made up a detailed program of the Prince's studies. They asked me for information and my opinion. The prince will begin his studies after settling in at Peterhof the day after tomorrow. At the moment I am writing the summary of the Corps des Pages study program in French. It will be translated into Siamese and sent to King Chulalongkorn. Today I've dropped in to see Lek, but he was out sightseeing with his companions. I am sitting at his monumental desk, waiting for him and writing to you on the Tsar's paper. Maybe this will make my letter more "impressive". I am soon leaving for Paris to finish everything (connected with the materials for my PhD) . . . it would be silly to miss this brilliant chance to go to Paris again at the expense of the Siamese.

Grand Hotel Europe, St. Petersburg
June 11th, 1898

Yesterday I talked with Lek a lot. His Russian gets better and better. He even has the typical Russian friendliness and openness. There are no traces of the recent fatigue and he looks fine – healthy, strong, happy and confident about the future. It's a pleasure for me to think that I am not the last person in the life of this very promising young man. As for Nai Poum, he looks even more Russian than I do, by which I mean that he has put on some weight here. This is certainly not my case. On my student's scholarship, I remain equally thin in Russia, England or France, and it suits me, it is easier to travel without extra fat.

Sleep well,
Yours Panya

Peterhof, June 12th.

Today the Siamese envoy and I accompanied the Prince to his new house in Peterhof. We were met at the station with honors. The charming villa, rented for the Prince, is situated near the Peterhof Palace. . . "It is even better, than the Elsenwood house" – said the Prince merrily. And this is really so, not to mention the wonderful décor and furniture in this spacious two-storied building with twenty rooms, surrounded by a garden as lovely as Eden. We arrived at 5 p.m. and had tea. Now I've taken advantage of the short break, and am writing to you, sitting at the desk in Lek's classroom to be (the lessons start tomorrow morning). The envoy and I are invited for dinner. This will be both a house warming and a farewell dinner, as we leave for Paris at 6 p.m. on Saturday by Nord-Express and will arrive in Paris at 3 p.m. on Monday. It is 5 minutes to 7, I have to go. After dinner, we (the envoy, Khrulov and me) will return to Petersburg.

Yours Panya

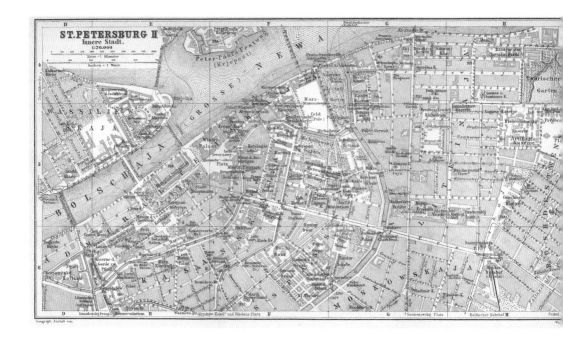

Map of St. Petersburg c. 1900.

The Winter Palace around 1905. From 1732 to 1917, the palace was the official residence of the Russian monarchs. Designed by many architects, among whom Bartolomeo Rastrelli was pre-eminent, it was largely rebuilt in 1837 after a serious fire. Tsar Nicholas II did not spend much time there as he preferred Tsarskoe Selo, or elsewhere, such as the Crimea. He arranged for Prince Chakrabongse to have a suite of rooms in the palace during his stay in Russia.

1. Count Fyodor Keller (1850-1904) was director of the Corps des Pages from 1893-1900. He was a general in the Imperial Russian Army and was later noted for his role in the Battle of Motien Pass in the Russo-Japanese War, which led to his death.

2. Corps des Pages. For details, see page 111.

3. Captain Khrulov was in the Ulan Life Guards regiment. He served as the governor of Prince Chakrabongse.

4. The Emperor and Empress. Tsar Nicholas II (1868-1918, r. 1894-forced abdication 1917) and Empress Alexandra Feordorovna (Alix of Hesse, 1872-1918).

5. Tsarskoe Selo is 24 kilometres south of the centre of St. Petersburg, the town of Tsarskoe Selo had many residences

for the Imperial family and visiting nobility. The first Russian railway was built between the city and Tsarskoe Selo in 1837.

6. Prince Peter Alexandrovich of Oldenburg (1868–1924) was the only child of Duke Alexander Petrovich of Oldenburg. He was the first husband of Grand Duchess Olga Alexandrovna of Russia, the youngest sister of Tsar Nicholas II. He was believed to be homosexual and their marriage was never consummated.

7. Grand Duchess Elizabeth Feodorovna (1864–1918) was a German princess of Hesse-Darmstadt and the wife of Grand Duke Sergei Alexandrovich, fifth son of Emperor Alexander II and Princess Marie of Hesse and by Rhine. She was the older sister of Empress Alexandra.

Tsar Nicholas II in 1898. (Photograph by A. A. Pasetti)

Grand Duchess Elizabeth.

St Petersburg
21st June 1898

Your Majesty

As last week was my first here and I did not know the exact time of the mail, I missed writing to you.

I left Berlin in the morning on the 12th of this month on the same train as Grand Duke Alexis, although we did not know that until we reached the German border. When we left Paris, we had heard that he would come, but then later someone said that he would not, so I believed that he would not be on the train. At the Russian border, there was a Captain to meet me and arrange a room for dinner. I went to pay my respects to the Grand Duke.

After dinner, we got back on the train and slept overnight. On the 13th just after 2 pm, we reached Petersburg. At the station there was an official from the royal household as well as an imperial car. I came by carriage to the Winter Palace. A second official of the royal household greeted me and took me to my quarters. Then General Count Keller[1], head of Corps des Pages[2] and the person whom the Emperor has assigned to arrange things for us, together with Captain Khrulov[3], my governor, came to see me.

On the 16th June, I went to pay my respects to the Emperor and Empress[4]. We left here at 12 and took the train to Tsarskoe Selo[5]. On arrival we took a car to the palace and had to wait in a room for a while. Prince Oldenburg[6] was there. We had to wait a for quite a while, because they took Your Majesty's letter to the Emperor first and discussed things for a long time before he granted me an audience. This took place in a small room. Both their Imperial Majesties, the Emperor and Empress, were there. The Emperor asked a lot of questions and said that he had sent Your Majesty a telegram informing Your Majesty of my arrival. He asked about Phraya Mahibal a little bit and also Nai Poum, enquiring as to whose son he was. I could hardly think what to answer, so replied that he was the son of an officer as he had heard that his father was connected with the army in some form or another. Apart from that, he asked about my uniform and other general matters before going into a larger room and asking me to introduce Phraya Mahibal, as well as Nai Nok Yoong and Nai Poum. After the audience, we went to have lunch. While walking to the dining room the Emperor insisted that I walk in front all the time and go through the door first and all that palaver, which was quite awkward and gave me a headache. At lunch there were five people: the Emperor, the Empress, Grand Duchess

Grand Duke Vladimir Alexandrovich and
his wife, Grand Duchess Marie Pavlovna.

Right: Dowager Empress Maria Feodorovna, c. 1898.

Elizabeth[7], Prince Oldenburg and myself. I sat between the Empress and the Emperor. During the meal, the Emperor chatted most agreeably and talked about Bang Pa-in among other things. The Empress seemed a bit distracted, as is normal, but I could see that she was trying to be kind because she addressed several remarks to me and smiled all the time when talking to me. After the meal I met the two imperial princesses[8]. Grand Duchess Olga could not remember me at all and asked "What's that?". Then she said, "Oh yes, that boy " and other such remarks. It was a lot of fun. The Empress told her to come over and bring me something but she refused as she was afraid. In fact she wanted to come over. She said she was going to go but didn't. It was only when I took my leave that she came over.

Leaving the palace, we went to pay our respects to other royals who were in residence but only managed to see Grand Duchess Marie Pavlovna[9], the wife of Grand Duke Vladimir[10]. Apart from that, we just left our calling cards and took the train back to Petersburg around 4 pm.

The next day on the 17th, I went to pay my respects to various nobles in Peterhof[11], but did not see them and so left my card. In the morning I went to see Count Muraviev in his office near the palace.

On the 19th, I went to pay my respects to the Dowager Empress[12] at Gatchina[13]. I had to take the train again. At the palace, Prince Mariadensky, who once came to Bangkok, met me and took me to the audience. It was the same format as visiting the Emperor. Grand Duke Michael[14] and Grand Duchess Olga[15] (his younger sister) were also there. The Dowager Empress looks very well and talked about many matters. It was similar to the audience with the Emperor, but we also talked about Prince Damrong.

8. The two imperial princesses refer to Olga Nikolaevna (1895-1918) and Tatiana Nikolaevna (1897-1918). At that time Olga was only three and Tatiana just one.

9. Grand Duchess Marie Pavlovna, formerly Duchess Marie of Mecklenburg-Schwerin, was known as Miechen or Marie Pavlovna the Elder (1854-1920). She was a prominent St. Petersburg hostess and was competitive with Empress Maria Feodorovna.

10. Grand Duke Vladimir Alexandrovich (1847-1909) was a son of Emperor Alexander II, a brother of Tsar Alexander III and uncle to Tsar Nicholas II. As Military Governor of St. Petersburg he was blamed for the events of Bloody Sunday in 1905.

11. Peterhof was a group of palaces and elaborate formal gardens with fountains laid out in St. Petersburg by Peter the Great (1672-1725). It was much used for formal entertaining and by Tsar Nicholas II and his family.

12. Maria Feodorovna (1847-1928), christened Dagmar, was a daughter of the Danish king, Christian IX, Empress of Russia as spouse of Tsar Alexander III (r. 1881-1894) and sister to Queen Alexandra of England.

13. Alexander III of Russia made Gatchina his prime residence after his father's assassination. He introduced technological modernization into the palace and parks, such as electric lights, telephone network, non-freezing water pipes and a modern sewage system. Nicholas II, his son, spent his youth there and his mother, Dowager Empress Maria Fedorovna, widow of Alexander III, continued to live there.

14. Grand Duke Michael Alexandrovich (1878-1918) was the youngest son and fifth child of Emperor Alexander III and youngest brother of Nicolas II. After 1899, when his older brother George died, he was heir presumptive to Nicholas II until the birth of Alexei in 1904.

Our chat went on for a long time before she emerged to greet various officials and gave her hand to everyone. She chatted quite a bit with Nai Poum and remarked that it was good that I had a friend to accompany me. This time the audience was after her lunch, as she ate very early because she was going to see off Grand Duchess Xenia[16] to the Caucasus where Grand Duke George is.

I have sent a telegram to Grand Duke George[17] to express my regret at not being able to pay my respects and I have laid a wreath on the tomb of Emperor Alexander III[18].

Tomorrow I will leave here for Peterhof and I will stay in a house near the palace so I can start my studies. Phraya Suriya has probably informed Your Majesty in detail about this.

I am well and happy and think of Your Majesty constantly.

I beg to remain Your Majesty's obedient servant,
Chakrabongse

Tsar Alexander III and Empress Maria Feodorvna (standing) with their family. Behind the Tsar is future Tsar Nicholas II and Grand Duchess Xenia. Front row: Grand Duke Michael, Grand Duchess Olga and Grand Duke George.

15. Grand Duchess Olga Alexandrovna (1882-1960) was the youngest child and younger daughter of Emperor Alexander III and the Dowager Empress and younger sister of Tsar Nicholas II.

16. Grand Duchess Xenia Alexandrovna (1875–1960) was the elder daughter and fourth child of Tsar Alexander III. She was to marry a first cousin once removed, Grand Duke Alexander Mikhailovich with whom she had seven children.

17. Grand Duke George Alexandrovich (1871-1899) was the third son of Emperor Alexander III and Empress Marie of Russia and heir apparent for five years. He began Nicholas II's Eastern Tour with him but fell ill and had to return. Thereafter he lived mainly in the Crimea for the sake of his health and died suddenly at the age of 28.

18. As with all the Russian monarchs, the tomb is in the St. Peter and Paul Cathedral standing within the fortress of the same name.

4th July 1898

Your Majesty

I was unable to write a letter to you for the last mail as the doctor forbade me to write. This is because of the whole falling off the horse saga. But today I can and I am fine now, although still not allowed to get out of bed. In truth, I think I should be allowed to get up now, but as it is a Monday and they are superstitious, they think it is an unlucky day to get up.

The reason I fell off was because the horse didn't know me and after I'd ridden along for a while, we came to a forest. My horse and that of Phraya Mahibal started galloping off and I couldn't control it. In the end we were trying to avoid a carriage or something I can't recall and I fell off. I can't remember anything after that. I don't know what people did and only came round when I was lying in bed. Since then there's been lots of care and attention.

On 1st July, the Emperor and the Empress came to visit me. They were going to come earlier but they were afraid that it would be awkward so they waited until I was a little better. They stayed a long time. Yesterday Count Muraviev came to see me too.

I can't write any more now because the doctor won't let me, but I imagine that Phraya Mahibal has told Your Majesty all the details already.

I beg to remain Your Majesty's obedient servant,
Chakrabongse

Villa Krassovsky, Peterhof
12th July 1898

Your Majesty

By now the whole issue of falling off the horse is almost over, but I am not completely better. The swelling on my head has not completely subsided and the doctor has not allowed me to go out. He says that tomorrow, or the day after, I can go out and all the doctors have said I don't need to stay here any more.

I got up for the first time on the 5th of this month and in the afternoon on the 6th the Emperor and Empress came to visit me for the second time. I was not aware of their visit, but before they went out I was sitting in my dressing gown. They said that when they arrived, there was no time for me to get back into bed, so I had to receive them in my untidy attire. I feel sure that there are not many people who have received the Empress dressed in a hospital gown and dressing gown. Since then they have gradually let me walk more, until now I am allowed to run around everywhere as long as I don't leave the house.

On the 10th, the Emperor and Empress came again, but it was when we were having lunch so they did not stay long and said they would come back once more. I think that, if Your Majesty agrees, as soon as the doctor allows me out, I will go and pay my respects to the Emperor and Empress to thank them for all their kindness. Furthermore, apart from coming to see me, they constantly sent fruit and flowers. My condition was reported to them morning and evening and they knew everything that was going on. I deduced this from the last time they came to see me and I was wearing the pages uniform. All they said was "So, is the uniform comfortable?" and nothing more because they knew everything already.

At the moment, the Queen of Greece is here but we have not seen her at all. On the 10th, there was a play here for charity with the money collected being given to the poor, and the Emperor and Empress attended. They sent me a ticket but I was unable to go. However, I sent some money as a contribution.

I have to say that my fall from the horse has been a big event, covered in all the newspapers and now, when I get a letter from someone or other, they all ask about it. The newspapers certainly exaggerated things and got everyone anxious. We sent a brief telegram saying everything was ok, but they did not believe it. So I will have to write to them myself in order to provide proof that I can still write and am not dead.

I learnt that that they heard about the incident in England from the British ambassador. He came and asked various questions, then reported back to London. What a lot of fuss! They are always trying to score points over the Russians. So everyone here then started going on about how they did not want people to be alarmed in Bangkok. However, Your Majesty's telegram to the Emperor reassured them.

I think about Your Majesty at all times. I believe that today the Emperor will visit again.

I beg to remain Your Majesty's obedient servant,
Chakrabongse

An account in the **Petersburgskaia Gazeta**: (translated by Maria Petrova-Desnitsky)

Siam and the Siamese Prince (from a conversation with the tutor of the Prince, Staff Captain V. N. Khrulov).

Prince Chakrabongse took up residence in New Peterhof, at one of the most elegant dachas of the place – the comfortable furnished villa of Mr Krassovsky.

It is surrounded by the venerable trees of the park, which protect the residents from the broiling sun. A tidy courtyard, covered with sand, leads to an impressive entrance; we stepped into the lobby to the accompaniment of cheerful music – the comrade of the Prince, Nai Poum, was practising the piano. The manservant had given our card to him by mistake, and only due to the courtesy of the young noble did we manage to see Staff Captain Khrulov.

Nai Poum is a sixteen-year-old handsome and graceful young man. His clever face is nice and attractive. The young nobleman is wearing the uniform of the Siamese Corps des Pages (as Mr. Khrulov told us): a short navy-blue jacket with shoulder marks representing the emblem of Siam. The uniform is extremely elegant and spectacular. The lobby is furnished with perfect refinement.

Only the white Siamese helmets take us from Europe to the south, to the country of cloudless sky and oppressive heat.

Staff Captain Khrulov, who was working in his study, welcomed us in a polite manner and answered all our questions with perfect willingness and courtesy. According to him, the Prince has not yet engaged in the study of sciences. Following local tradition, he mostly devoted his time to the scrutiny of Buddhism. In order to remember the religious rites of his native country in this faraway land the Prince is accompanied by his Siamese tutor Mr Nai Nok Yoong and the teacher Mr Sha Mook Bai.

The tuition of the Prince started only in England, where he arrived with his elder brother Prince Chira. His Highness was studying the Russian language, which he mastered almost to perfection. It is understandable that he still needs to acquire some technical skills, but this is a matter of time and practice. In Russia the Prince will enter the Corps des Pages of his Majesty the Tsar. The Prince and his comrade will be enrolled in the sixth form. Of course, the Prince will not attend all the lectures. He will live in the Winter Palace and have lessons with private tutors. The Prince will attend only the most important and interesting lectures on military science, such as fortification, strategy, war history, etc. At the same time, he will continue to study Russian and the language, history and literature of his own country.

Prince Chakrabongse is characterized by rare diligence: he spends his days reading books and takes great interest in European science. As nature has lavishly endowed him with brilliant abilities, the Prince is very quick to grasp the most complicated subjects. For example, he has never faced the difficulties our gymnasium students have to endure, when they start studying mathematics.

The Prince also demonstrates great aptitude for learning foreign languages; thus the teachers have only to develop and direct the energies of this comprehensively talented young man.

V. N. Khrulov also provided us with some interesting details about the Prince's native country. He claims that in Siam all white animals are treated with great reverence. White elephants, of course, rank first. One of the most honourable orders of Siam (the Order of the White Elephant, the second after the Maha Chakri order, granted only to representatives of the royal family) is associated with this animal, which is also featured on the national flag of Siam. White monkeys also enjoy great esteem...

In conclusion, we will write about one more curious incident: the appendix to "Novoye Vremya" published a portrait of Prince Chakrabongse. However, as Captain Khrulov states, it is not a portrait of the Prince, but of his elder brother, the heir, Prince Chira[1]. When Prince Chakrabongse saw it, he was astonished and said to the tutor: - "But it is not me, it is Chira!" The Prince so far has not had his picture taken in Russia, but plans to do so in the near future.

This is the image of the second son of King Chulalongkorn. Lavishly endowed by Almighty God with all the things other people can only dream of, the most favourable conditions have been created for the young Prince to be of great, even utmost benefit to his country.

Hopefully, his stay in Russia and studies in Russian educational institutions will imbue the young and talented soul of the Prince with those principles our fatherland has always remained faithful to: religion, peacefulness and loyalty.

1. There are quite a few mistakes in this article. Prince Chirapravati was an older half brother and not the heir.

Peterhof
20th July 1898

Your Majesty

The 15th was the first day that I was allowed to go out since I have been ill. I went to see the Emperor and both Empresses before going anywhere else. They invited me to an audience in the palace of the Dowager Empress where they all were, together with Grand Duchess Olga and the two imperial children. The Dowager Empress even asked to feel my head to see whether I was completely better. I was there for over half an hour and when I was about to leave, I thanked them deeply for all their care and attention throughout the time I was laid up.

On the 16th, there was a review of all the cadets in the Page School as well as others staying in the camp here. The senior General of this town was the person presiding over the review. I went along to watch also. This occasion was a sort of rehearsal for when the Emperor will review them soon. The cadets performed very well and were very tidy in their drills. The practice fighting was also excellent.

I was the strange creature on this occasion with people more interested in staring at me than the cadets. I was wearing my Russian uniform which also got everyone very excited. After the review was over, I asked permission to go to the barracks and talk to the cadets. They all crowded round asking this and that. All the pages seem very nice. They come from good families and can converse on many subjects. They are not at all wishy washy and were eager to encourage me to speak.

In the evening of that day, I invited the two senior doctors who had been looking after me to come and have dinner here. One of them is very close to the Emperor and often attends to him. The other one is also an Imperial doctor but not so close.

After dinner I gave them presents as a reward for looking after me. One of them received a small gold offering tray and the other a larger silver offering tray. They both seemed very pleased.

On the 18th in the evening I went to see the play performed to raise money for the poor of this town as before and about which I already informed you. The Emperor and Empress both attended, as well as some members of the Imperial family. What it was about

I don't really know, as it was all in German but the actors were all well cast.

Today the Emperor will review all the cadets and I will go and watch as before.

I am well and happy and think of Your Majesty constantly.

I beg to remain Your Majesty's obedient servant,
Chakrabongse

Peterhof
26th July 1898

Your Majesty

The 23rd was the name day of both the Grand Duchesses Olga, namely the daughters of both the Emperor and the Dowager Empress. I arranged bouquets for both of them as a token of my good wishes and congratulations.

On that day, the Emperor organised a luncheon reception for members of the Imperial family and important officials as is customary every year. I was also invited. As I am not of their religion and it was felt I might feel uncomfortable going to church, I was only asked to the lunch.

I went a bit too early and had to wait a while before they came back. At lunch the royals and the officials were intermingled, unlike the usual arrangement when the two groups are separated. There were two rooms as is customary, but the officials came and joined in where the Emperor was. The Minister of War sat at the Imperial table, whereas I was seated at another one next to Grand Duchess Olga and Grand Duke Michael. At first, a palace official told me to go and sit at a small table, but while I was walking there, Grand Duchess Olga called me over to go and sit on her left. And Grand Duke Michael sat on the other side. Apart from that, there were other royals and three ladies in waiting. The top table had the Emperor, the two Empresses, other senior nobles, the Minister of Defence and two to three other people

King Carol I of Romania, c. 1900.

The Prince of Bulgaria, Ferdinand I.

whom I could not see clearly. Apart from that, everyone else sat outside in another room.

When lunch was almost finished, we drank a toast as is traditional, then everyone stood around for a while, before the Emperor and Empresses left and we all went home.

On the 24th, I went to see horse racing at a course near Petersburg, but it was nothing special, just an ordinary race. Nevertheless, the officials there made me an honorary member and I can go along free of charge whenever I want.

Today the Emperor will review the troops at Krasnoe Selo[2] in the evening and I will go along to watch.

I have heard that the Dowager Empress will go to Denmark on the 2nd August in order to avoid seeing the King of Romania[3] who will arrive this coming Wednesday. If she was here, it could be awkward when receiving him if there were two or three empresses obstructing him. When the Prince of Bulgaria[4] came this time, she also did not appear at official functions such as the large gala dinner.

I beg to remain Your Majesty's obedient servant,
Chakrabongse

1. General Aleksey Nikolaievich Kuropatkin (1848-1925) was Minister of War from January 1898 until 1904. He was relieved of his command after the Battle of Mukden in the Russo-Japanese War.

2. Krasnoe Selo was the site of one of the summer residences for the Tsars and the summer camp for Russian soldiers based in St. Petersburg. Every year manoeuvres were held and the Tsar attended some of these, as well as the march past. As a result the town had a theatre for the officers.

3. King Charles I (Carol I) of Romania (1839–1914), born Prince Karl of Hohenzollern-Sigmaringen, ruled from 1866 to 1914. He was elected Ruling Prince (Domnitor) of the Romanian United Principalities in April 1866 after a palace coup d'état. After the defeat of the Ottoman Empire (1878) in the Russo-Turkish War, he declared Romania a sovereign nation. He was proclaimed King of Romania in March 1881. He was the first ruler of the Hohenzollern-Sigmaringen dynasty, which ruled the country until the proclamation of a republic in 1947.

4. Prince of Bulgaria. Ferdinand I (1861-1948), born Ferdinand Maximilian Karl Leopold Maria of Saxe-Coburg and Gotha, was the ruler of Bulgaria from 1887 to 1918, first as *knyaz* (prince regnant, 1887–1908) and later as tsar, 1908–1918). Tsar Alexander III had severed diplomatic relations with Bulgaria, hence the Dowager Empress's refusal to meet him.

Peterhof
2nd August 1898

Your Majesty

On the 26th, the Emperor and Empress went to review the army camps in Krasnoe Selo and towards the end the soldiers all gathered to salute the Emperor as is the tradition every year.

I went to observe the review and, while the Empress was having tea, she asked me to join her and other members of the imperial family. After tea, the ceremony began. All the soldiers who had been camping in the area came together as did all the trumpeters. They played a long fanfare to offer their congratulations. After that, they removed their hats and prayed for a while. When that was finished, three fireworks were let off as a signal for all the cannons in the camps to fire at the same time. This was the end of the ceremony. In the evening, there was a gala performance at the theatre in this town.

On that day I paid my respects to the Queen of Greece[1] who is staying in Russia at the moment.

On the 28th, the King of Romania arrived here. The Emperor went to meet him at the station with other members of the Imperial family. At midday there was a reception in the Grand Palace[2] to which I was also invited. It took place on the top floor and consisted solely of royalty, a great deal of them in fact. In the afternoon, the Dowager Empress, Grand Duke Michael and Grand Duchess Olga left for Denmark. The Emperor and Empress went to see them off as far as Kronstadt[3]. On the 29th, the King of Romania went to Petersburg and in the evening there was a large reception, but I did not go. On the 30th, there was a military review at Krasnoe Selo. I went along with the Emperor and Empress, as well as the King of Romania and the Crown Prince. We left here by train. When we reach Streslana, the Queen of Greece and her son and various other nobles joined the train.

When we reached Krasnoe Selo, the Emperor and the King of Romania mounted their horses, while the Empress went in a carriage to review the waiting troops. I went by carriage to the pavilion in the middle of the parade ground, which was set up for the review and resting. I could see the whole thing, as the regiments were arranged around the pavilion. The two kings and all the imperial family were on horseback in front of the pavilion and all the soldiers marched past. The Emperor led the entire cavalcade himself, accompanied by senior members of the royal family before taking up a position next to the King of Romania while the soldiers marched passed. The nobles attached to various regiments marched by with them. At the end, the King of Romania shook hands with the Emperor to thank him as is the convention. After the march past, there was a banquet in town. Towards the end, the Emperor drank a toast to the King of Romania, to which he replied at great length, praising the soldiers, and so forth. Then the festivities were over. I returned by carriage.

In the evening there was another banquet at the Grand Palace with a play on Olgin island in the lake. Around the pond and on the islands were various arches with hanging lights. After dinner they drove from the Grand Palace to the landing stage and went by boat to the island where the play was being performed. The performance consisted of various ballets performed in the water. It was very beautiful. After the performance was over, we went by boat to another island to drink tea and chat, before finally going home very late.

The reception for the King was very similar to when Your Majesty was here, but I could see that there was not the same intimacy and when the King and the Emperor met they did not kiss or hug.

Regarding Your Majesty's letter to the Emperor, which was sent to Phraya Mahibal, the Emperor told me to present it to him at dinner. On the 30th, I duly presented it to him as instructed, but at that time he did not read it and put it away. Until now, I have not heard any news and I have not been to see him again.

Today is very close to the name day of the Dowager Empress and Phaya Mahibal has sent a telegram from you to congratulate her as she as staying in Denmark as she usually does at this time.

I am well and happy and think of Your Majesty always.

I beg to remain Your Majesty's obedient servant,
Chakrabongse

---

1. Olga Constantinovna (1851-1926) was the wife of King George I of Greece and daughter of Grand Duke Constantine.

2. The Grand Palace was the largest of the Peterhof palaces.

3. Kronstadt is situated on Kotlin island, 30 km west of St. Petersburg proper, near the head of the Gulf of Finland. Traditionally the seat of the Russian admiralty and base for the Baltic fleet. Founded by Peter the Great, it was refortified in the 19th century.

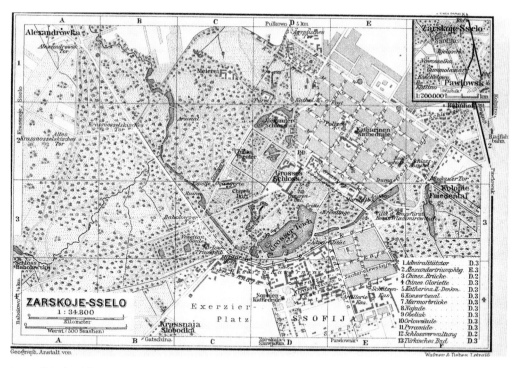

A map of Tsarskoe Selo, c. 1898.

Peterhof railway station, c. 1898.

Peterhof
7th August 1898

Your Majesty

The 3rd of this month is the equivalent of 22nd July according to the Russian calendar. It is the name day of the Dowager Empress and, as I informed Your Majesty, I arranged for the staff at the embassy to send a telegram congratulating her. I also arranged for a telegram to be sent to Grand Duke Michael in a private capacity as well.

Today I was invited to lunch in the palace as before, but it wasn't as much fun because the Empress in whose honour the lunch was held was not there.

On the 4th, I went to the grain store to see a life boat used to save those whose boats have capsized or who have fallen in the water during storms in Petersburg. It can respond very quickly to any emergency. I went down into the boat. They rowed out into the bay and, when I wasn't looking, one of them jumped into the water and everyone shouted "Man overboard!" and he was helped back into the boat. At first, I was shocked not realising it was a drill. After that, I was invited into a torpedo boat, which, together with another twin boat, always goes out in front when the Emperor goes somewhere in the royal yacht. Once in the boat, it set off at high speed as one would expect.

On the 7th, I was invited to lunch at the Palace. There was no special occasion other than that on Sundays after coming out of church, traditionally the Emperor sits down to lunch with members of the royal family and officials who are close to him. However, this time there were no other members of the family, just officials. The Emperor talked to me about Your Majesty's letter saying that it was written in mid-June and that it was a very good letter, but said no more. At first I could not work out why I had been invited and thought he would talk about official business as Phraya Mahibal had also been asked. It was only later I learned that Sunday lunch was customary.

In the evening of that day, there was horseracing at Krasnoe Selo. All the jockeys were army officers, and the Emperor and Empress went to watch. I also went along. The racing was not just along the flat but also involved various jumps. What was very remarkable was that no one fell off. The winner received a

Grand Duchess Elena Vladimirovna, c. 1898

large silver salver as well as 3,000 roubles. The racing was really good and it encourages the soldiers to ride well and practice so that they can compete.

On the 14th the Emperor and Empress will leave here to inspect the manoeuvres at Krasnoe Selo and then go on to other places. At the end of the month, he will go to Moscow and then on to the Crimea. Only in the winter will they come back to St. Petersburg.

I am well and happy and think of Your Majesty constantly.

I beg to remain Your Majesty's obedient servant,
Chakrabongse

Letter opposite
1. Grand Duchess Elena Vladimirovna of Russia (1882-1957) was the daughter of Grand Duke Vladimir Alexandrovich of Russia and Duchess Marie of Mecklenburg-Schwerin. In 1902, she became the wife of Prince Nicholas of Greece and Denmark.

2. Yelagin palace was completed in 1822 on Yelagin Island in the Neva River as a royal summer palace for Tsar Alexander I. Constructed on the site of an earlier mansion, built during the reign of Catherine the Great, the villa was designed by the architect Carlo Rossi.

Yelagin Palace, c. 1890s.

Peterhof
16th August 1898

Your Majesty

On the 14th, I went to have lunch at the palace as before, as I mentioned in my last letter. This time there were two or three other members of the Imperial family, namely the Oldenburgs and Leuchtenbergs. In addition, there was Grand Duchess Elena[1], the daughter of Grand Duke Vladimir. This time I sat at the royal table. Both the Grand Duchesses had Ladies of Honour. One of them was very old and came and praised Your Majesty to me, saying that when Your Majesty was here she spoke to Your Majesty and that she had wished Your Majesty a long life.

Today Count Muraviev also came to the palace and told me that he hoped that the differences and quarrels we are having with the French at this time would be settled shortly. I could not really ask him anything, as we were not in private and it was not appropriate to discuss affairs of state, so I remained silent. When I got back, I told Phraya Mahibal and today he went up to Petersburg to go and see Count Muraviev in order to quiz him further. I gather that nothing is really agreed, but that he has talked to the French minister and that they understand each other and the French will listen further to what the Russians have to say. I am sure Phraya Mahibal will have informed you of the details by the same mail.

This week I went to see a warship, which was blocking the wind in front of the palace here. It is rather an old, small ship and is only used for such duties but it looks reasonably good. One of the officers on the ship had been to Thailand.

By now the Emperor and Empress have left for their palace on an island in the Neva[2] near Petersburg in order to see the manoeuvres which are taking place near there. Tomorrow they have asked me to join them. They will take a boat to see the construction of a bridge across the river and soldiers crossing the bridge in order to go and fight with the northern army, which in this scenario is supposed to be attacking Petersburg.

After the manoeuvres, the Emperor and Empress will return here until the 26th when they will go to Moscow for the opening ceremony of the Monument dedicated to the memory of Emperor Alexander II. From there, they will go on to the Crimea. I am waiting to hear whether I am to follow them to Moscow or not.

Now I have started studying again as before. Classes include mathematics, Russian, target practice, drawing and accordion lessons. Then in the winter I will really start studying in earnest.

I beg to remain Your Majesty's obedient servant,
Chakrabongse

Peterhof
23rd August 1898

Your Majesty

I was delighted to receive Your Majesty's letter of 15th July. The photograph taken with Sadet Mother has been given to 12 nobles now. I took one to give to the Empress when I went to have lunch at the palace the day before yesterday. Another one I have sent to the Dowager Empress in Copenhagen, because I thought that if I were to wait until she came back for an opportunity to present it in person, it would be a very long time. I was also worried that if she knew that I had presented one to the Empress and not to her, it would not be good. So I decided to send it to Grand Duke Michael, together with a letter asking him to present them to others who had expressed a desire for one. Those whom I still have not been able to see are Grand Duke Alexander[1], Grand Duchess Xenia, Grand Duke Sergei[2] and Admiral Arseniev[3]. Grand Duchess Elisabeth is in Moscow, so I do not know when I can give one to her.

Last week there were manoeuvres here as I told you in my last letter. There were light battles between two regiments namely the enemy, the Finns, and the Petersburg regiment. The Finns attacked St. Petersburg and the Petersburg regiment defended. I only observed, as on the other days I would have had to go on horseback and they would not let me.

On the 17th, I left here at 7 am for Petersburg and went in a carriage to the port where the royal yacht was moored[4]. I went on board and met other royals who were also waiting. At 3 pm the Emperor and Empress arrived in a small boat from their palace on Yelagin island, where they stay during manoeuvres. The royal yacht left port and sailed up the Neva. At around 10 am we saw two warships fighting each other. In the imagined scenario, both regiments have the navy assisting them in their battle. The Petersburg regiment has lost and escaped to Ladoga Lake[5], before being assisted by the navy and attacking the enemy again. Having won they are in protective mode. The two army regiments are on either side of the river bank. The southern army is on the southern bank and the northern army on the north bank. The northern army could not withstand the fire from the southern army and has retreated. As a result, the southern army

The Imperial yacht, Standart.

planned a bridge across the river, but has had to wait until their navy has gone down river before starting building. We went ashore to see them building the bridge, which they did very quickly in two parts supported by a ship in the middle. They then rowed out from the two banks and joined up again. It was all very rapid and the bridge can even open in the middle if a ship needs to pass by. After seeing the bridge, there was lunch in a tent before observing the firing of torpedoes and mines, the pretence being that the southern army had laid these to prevent the northern army from attacking.

The mines were great to watch. They exploded as high as a *sen* or more, and one time they exploded six

1. Grand Duke Alexander Mikhailovich (1866-1933) was a naval officer, an author, explorer, and a brother-in-law of Emperor Nicholas II, through his marriage to Grand Duchess Xenia (his cousin's daughter), youngest sister of the Emperor. He was a close advisor to the Tsar.

2. Grand Duke Sergei Alexandrovich 1857-1905) was the fifth son and seventh child of Emperor Alexander II. He was an influential figure during the reigns of his brother Emperor Alexander III of Russia and his nephew Emperor Nicholas II, who was also his brother-in-law through Sergei's marriage to Elizabeth, the sister of Tsarina Alexandra. From 1891-1905, he was Governor General of Moscow. His conservative policies made him a polarizing figure and he was assassinated.

3. Admiral Dmitry Arseniev (1832-1915). Closely involved in naval education, in 1896 Arseniev was appointed to the Admiralty Board. In August 1900, he was promoted to full admiral and in April 1901 was made a member of the State Council. He accompanied HM King Chulalongkorn during his visit to Russia in 1897 and was awarded the Order of the White Elephant (First Class with diamonds) on July 14th by the King.

4. The Imperial Yacht Standart, built by the Danish yard of Burmeister and Wain, came into service in September 1896. She had ornate fixtures and was crewed by the Russian Imperial Navy.

5. Lake Ladoga, near St. Petersburg, is the largest lake in Europe and the 14th largest freshwater lake by area in the world.

6. Louise of Hesse-Kassel (1817-1898) was Queen of Denmark as the wife of King Christian IX of Denmark. She died a month later on 29th September.

Map of St. Petersburg and its environs, c. 1902. Tsarskoe Selo (spelt Zarskoe on the map) is in the south.

Peterhof
30th August 1898

Your Majesty

at once. It was very impressive and they even put them in a boat and exploded them. You could see the wood shattering into tiny slivers. After it was over, we went in a boat to take a look. Another explosion was also massive, with billows of smoke and the exploded earth forming a small hillock. At around 4 pm we came back to the port and from there went in a carriage to the station. From Petersburg I came back to Peterhof. I felt very tired, as we were out all day and in the sun from morning till dusk.

One interesting thing was that when we were in the yacht, the captain brought some soup as drunk by the sailors and black bread with salt to give to the Emperor and other members of the Imperial family. It was part of a special ceremony. The Emperor asked that I be given some too.

I have heard that the Queen of Denmark[6] is ill and as a result the Dowager Empress will not return for the opening of the Monument[7] in Moscow. Originally she was going to come but I fear it is serious and the Queen is elderly.

I beg to remain Your Majesty's obedient servant,

Chakrabongse

On the 26th of this month, the Emperor and Empress left here for Moscow at around 10.30 at night. I went to see them off at the station. They arrived together at almost 11 pm, along with Grand Duke Michael. The Emperor said that it was late and wasn't I yawning and sleepy. I replied that I wasn't sleepy, because I wanted to see them off. When I said goodbye, before they got on the train, the Imperial couple gave me their blessing and told me to keep well. The Ladies of Honour then all wished me well also, as I am someone they almost all like because they feel sorry for me being far away from home.

On the 28th there was a big event in Moscow, namely the opening of the monument dedicated to Alexander II within the Kremlin. It was a very grand affair and very religious. The Dowager Empress did not go because of the Queen of Denmark's illness but otherwise almost all the members of the Imperial family were in attendance. The Queen of Greece together with the Crown Prince and Crown Princess of Greece were also there. The reason why I was not invited was because I am still too young. All the young royals, i.e. those who were not yet officers, were not invited. So another prince of Greece who was actually in Moscow did not attend. Tomorrow on the 3rd, the Emperor will leave Moscow for the Crimea.

In the evening of the 28th, Phraya Cholayut[1] came to see me and took me out to dinner. He came from Denmark by boat and is staying in Petersburg. He had planned to find me in Moscow but in the end I did not go, and the Emperor being away, he did not get to see him. It has all been rather a waste of time and money for him. He asked me to lunch on his ship on 1st of September, which I shall do.

I beg to remain Your Majesty's obedient servant,

Chakrabongse

1. Phraya Cholayut *aka* Andreas du Plessis de Richelieu (1852-1932) was a Danish naval officer and businessman, who became a Siamese admiral and minister of the navy. He commanded Siamese gunboats in the Paknam Incident of July 13, 1893, that ended the Franco-Siamese War, and was the first and only foreign-born commander-in-chief of the Royal Thai Navy, from January 1900 to January 1901.

7. The Monument dedicated to Alexander II within the Kremlin was begun under Alexander III in 1893 and completed under Nicholas II. It was by sculptor Alexander Opekushin, artist Peter Zhukovsky and architect Nicholas V. Sultanov.

Peterhof
7th September 1898

Your Majesty

I have received Your Majesty's letter from Bangkok dated 22nd July and it made me very happy.

At the beginning of the letter, Your Majesty said that regarding my first letter from Russia, Your Majesty was dissatisfied because in it I did not tell you how I really felt upon my arrival in Russia, what were the people close to me like, how did it go speaking Russian and my impression of the imperial family and the nobles. I was unable to tell Your Majesty the answers to all these things straight away, because I was not sure yet. Now I feel more able to tell Your Majesty about these things point by point.

The first point was whether I will be comfortable here. Yes, I think I am very comfortable here. One thing, which is very different from England, however, is that there I felt that I did not need to think of anything apart from studying, whereas here I have to think of so many other things. I am anxious about making this or that mistake and I have to safeguard Your Majesty's honour and that of our country.

The second point is whether I like the people close to me or not. On the Thai side, they are excellent and a perfect choice. On the Russian side, all I can say, is that they all mean very well towards me.

On the third point, that of speaking Russian, it's going quite well but with those who can speak English, when we get to know each other, we mainly speak English such as with the royals, as it is easier.

On point four, I would say that my impression of the royals and the nobles is generally good. Among the royals I get on very well and I often hear it said that they are very complimentary about me and say that I am very polite. Of course, it is difficult to be objective about oneself and I might be delusional as Sadet Na[1] has said. The officials all seem very good.

Regarding all things to do with the royals, I hope that, as I said recently, Your Majesty will be satisfied. Regarding government business, Count Muraviev has talked to me, as I have told you once before.

I spoke to him about the memorandum, which he asked for from Phraya Mahibal. He said it was a good memorandum and well detailed. He asked me whether I had already read it and then commented in

Count Muraviev in 1898.

an amazed way, that I must knew a lot about government business if I could understand such a memorandum. I replied that I knew a bit about such things.

One thing I would like to have, if possible, is a copy of the letter Phraya Suriya sent you with the details of the programme, because I would like to see what is assigned for what day in case there is a mistake and I can correct it so there is no misunderstanding.

At the beginning of this week, Phraya Cholayut arrived in Petersburg from Denmark and came to see me. He came in a boat called *Siam* which goes from Denmark directly to Thailand. He invited me to have lunch on board. The ship was moored in the port and I was received very well. They flew the Thai flag and other flags as well. Numerous company directors, who had accompanied him on this trip, were also there. They were all important people. The lunch was large and very long. We sat at table for almost two hours and there were toasts to the Emperor and the King of Denmark. Phraya Cholayut also wished me well and I toasted him in reply. The ship and its company are entirely British and practically everyone on the boat spoke English. After I went home, the boat returned to Denmark.

I understand that Phraya Cholayut had intended to go to Moscow with me, but unfortunately I did

Phraya Cholayut aka Andreas du Plessis de Richelieu (1852-1932).

Above and below: Both sides of the medal struck on the occasion of the Thavidabhisek ceremony.

not go, so his plan came to naught and he came here for nothing. I noticed that he seemed very different from how he was in England. He seemed much more respectful and polite than he normally is with Thai royalty.

I was pleased to hear about the Thavidabhisek[2] and I hope there will be many more similar ceremonies. It is interesting that Your Majesty says that when dreaming Your Majesty sees me often, because for my part I have dreamt of Your Majesty very often recently and feel that I have seen Your Majesty here many times.

I beg to remain Your Majesty's obedient servant,

Chakrabongse

1. Sadet Na refers to Prince Svasti Sobhon.

2. Thavidabhisek was a ceremony celebrating the fact that King Chulalongkorn had ruled twice as long as King Rama II.

The Winter Palace
13th September 1898

Your Majesty

I received your letter dated 7th August. I understand all Your Majesty's points and am very grateful.

My fall from the horse seems to have agitated everyone a great deal both here and elsewhere. For my part, I don't see it as anything to be worried about. I didn't feel any pain. It was simply that my head swelled up in an abnormal fashion. But it didn't hurt or ache at all. Once it had got better, I found the constant questioning about it rather annoying.

The teaching in Russia is divided into two parts. The first part consists of general education and the only part that relates to military matters is how to hold a gun or a sword, how to line up for parades and shooting. It is only when one enters the 8th grade, known as the special class, that more military-related topics are taught.

On the 11th, I came to Petersburg from Peterhof, as it was almost time for classes to begin. In the palace they have arranged three rooms for me: a bedroom, a sitting room and a dining room. My Russian guardian, Luang Abhirak [also known as Nai Nok Yoong] and Nai Poum each have a room of their own. In addition, there is a classroom. Phraya Mahibal and his wife had not managed to sort out a house and so have been staying in a hotel. But tomorrow, or the day after, they can move into their house. It is not very far from the palace and is a nice house, if a little small. They are rushing to get it ready so everything is in place in time for celebrating Your Majesty's birthday.

Today is the day that the Pages school term began. Nai Poum and I went to the school early in the morning in order to report ourselves. We studied there a little and met our fellow students. First we went to present ourselves to the General Inspector and he appointed an officer to look after me and tell us which rooms to go to. When it was almost time to have a break, I went into the classroom for the 6th grade and told everyone that I was their new classmate together with Nai Poum. Once the head had gone, all the boys crowded round and pushed to shake hands. During the break we went out for a walk, and Keller, the officer in charge of all the pages, carried out an inspection. After that, we went back in

to study. Our class was Russian. The teacher said certain things and talked about various topics and we had to remember. Then he asked us about what he had said, what was it about. I could understand quite well, but if I had had to get up and answer, I think it would have been difficult because I don't know the language well enough. They must have known that, as they did not ask us anything. As for the other students, quite a few of them could not answer because they had been playing around and talking instead of listening. After the class, the doctor checked me over again and we came back to study in the palace.

I am happy to hear you do not have too much work at the moment and think that the French may have gone silent because of the discussions they are having in Paris with the Russians.

I have read in the papers that the Austrian Empress was stabbed to death in Geneva. The person who stabbed her was an Italian anarchist who has now been caught. The Empress went to Geneva incognito and no one knew she was there. For that reason the police were not guarding her as they should. I hear that the Austrian Emperor is distraught.

I beg to remain Your Majesty's obedient servant,

Chakrabongse

1. Elisabeth of Austria (1837-1898) was the wife of Emperor Franz Joseph I, and thus Empress of Austria, Queen of Hungary and Queen consort of Croatia and Bohemia. While travelling in Geneva in 1898, she was stabbed to death by an Italian anarchist named Luigi Lucheni. He chose her because he had missed his chance to assassinate Prince Philippe, Duke of Orléans, and wanted to kill the next royal personage that he saw.

2. The General Nikolai Alekseevitch Epanchin memoirs, 1931-1939, have been published in Russian. They are also on line at Columbia University Archives.

3. Prince Dr. Valapakorn Voravan (1891-1979) was the son of Prince Naradhip. After studying in the Corps, the prince entered the army medical school in St. Petersburg and served in the Russian Red Cross during the First World War. After his return to Siam, he occupied several important posts.

THE CORPS DES PAGES, ST. PETERSBURG

The Vorontsov Palace.

The Corps des Pages was founded in 1759 in St. Petersburg as an elite school for training pages and Chamber Pages for Imperial service. Then in 1802, needing well-trained officers for Guard units, the school was reorgansied as a cadet school which would accept the sons of hereditary Russian nobels and the sons of Lieutenant Generals and Vice Admirals.

The ideals of the Order of St. John lay behind a revised curriculum and in 1810 the school was moved to the palace of the Sovereign Order of St. John of Jerusalem, known as the Vorontsov Palace, designed by Bartolomeo Rastrelli around 1749. It remained there until the Revolution.

From 1885, the Corps had seven classes and two special classes, where students were taught military science and jurisprudence. It was the only military academy to prepare future officers for all sectors of the army. Indeed, graduates had the unique privilege of joining any regiment they chose. From its founding until 1917, 4,505 officers graduated from the school.

The directors during Prince Chakrabongse's period were Count Keller (1851-1904), Director, 1893-1900, and General Nikolai Alekseevich Epanchin (1857-1941), Director of the Imperial Corps of Pages (1900-1906)

Director Epanchin's recollections

In his memoirs[2] written in Paris, Epanchin recalled Prince Chakrabongse as follows: "When I took command over the Corps des Pages, Prince Chakrabongse, *the second son of the King, and two other Siamese, Nai Poum and Valapa[2] were being educated there: The Prince and Nai Poum took the special courses and Valapa the general courses, as he was much younger than his two companions. His Majesty the Tsar took care about the upbringing of these young people, and as for the Prince, he asked me to treat him as his own son. The Siamese were lodged at the Winter Palace, provided with meals and carriages from the Tsar's court, as well as servants and all other facilities. Generally speaking, they led the royal life. Their tutor was one of the officers of His Majesty's Life Guards Uhlan Regiment, Khrulov. Having looked at him closely, I finally came to the conclusion that he was not a person, suitable for this position and appointed another tutor Alexander Dmitrievich Deguy, who by that time had been the adjunct of the Corps for a few years. Deguy was a man of tact, brought up in a system of certain rules, and I hoped that he would justify my confidence, which he did absolutely. Unfortunately, his health suffered so much that he had to resign from the Corps.*

The Prince and his Siamese companions studied together with other students of the Corps des pages. Furthermore, the Prince took additional courses in French, German, English and State Law. The Prince was a person of great abilities, hard-working and inquisitive. He was on good terms with his fellow-students, always well-behaved and respectful to the teachers and authorities. From the point of view of discipline, there were no exceptions or indulgence towards the Prince, and no problems ever occurred during his stay at the Corps.

Corps des Pages from the entrance gateway.

20th September 1898

Your Majesty

Today is Your Majesty's birthday and yesterday I sent Your Majesty a congratulatory telegram. Nevertheless, allow me to profer my congratulations and good wishes one more time. May Your Majesty live a long life and be healthy, free from illness and rule over us for many more years so that the country can flourish. May our enemies stay away, or transform into allies such as is the case with Russia.

Tomorrow Admiral Arseniev will come and see me here, so I invited him to come and have lunch with me, together with all the various teachers who want to come and congratulate me on the occasion of Your Majesty's birthday. In the evening there will be a reception at the house of Phraya Mahibal. I have sent invitation cards to all those connected with me here, that is to say, those in the Royal Household and teachers from the Pages school. But I fear it will be rather a small crowd, as at the moment there are not many people in Petersburg. I have also invited Admiral Arseniev and others I know.

Now I am undertaking a full programme of study as planned, namely, mathematics, Russian language, Physics, Russian literature, natural history about various animals and trees. Apart from this, there is drawing, dancing, accordion playing, sword fighting and riding. Everyday, whether for three, two or one hours, we go to the school to join in lessons on European history and do exercises and various military drills. On Monday, I went to have lunch at the school but it wasn't very tasty. There was just one dish which was minced meat with macaroni and grated cheese on top. There was tea which tasted more like plain water than tea. It is really just eating to feel full. The dining area is a large room with long tables. Everyone eats at the same time. The head and the deputy walked around the room talking to this person and that. After the meal was finished they took a group photograph. I was made to go and sit in the middle. Once it was over, I went for a walk in the garden where there were swings and other things to play on. The boys can be divided into various groups. Some are really naughty, some are just right, while others are too quiet. All the groups, however, are very interested in me. Whenever I talked to someone for a moment, we were quickly surrounded by a group of boys which grew into a big circle. That person would ask one thing, this person something else, until I didn't know who to answer. It's good fun when I go to the school and, if on days when I don't attend, I miss it.

This week I went to see a paper factory where they also make bank notes and pictures and books. The factory is very large and the printing they do is really excellent. They impress images into the paper so that when you look one way it looks like a blank sheet, but when you hold it up to the light an image appears. The coloured pictures are very good and look like paintings. The way they make the impression is like this. First they imprint it with yellow and then with red and then blue. The last colour is brown. This creates a very good picture. They carve out the stone so it is just right and determine which part is going to take which colour. For other colours they use a mix of all these four colours on top of each other to make the colour they want. The paper factory smells really bad, as they have to get lots of rags and boil them until they fall to pieces in order to make paper, but they seem to be able to do it very quickly.

I beg to remain Your Majesty's obedient servant,
Chakrabongse

The Winter Palace
27th September 1898

Your Majesty

On the 21st of this month, all of us in St. Petersburg celebrated your birthday as is customary.

During the day I organised a lunch in the palace. Those who were invited were: Admiral Arseniev, General Count Keller, Colonel Theo Brassov (my maths teacher), M. Petrov (my Russian language teacher) and Dr Andreyev (the doctor attached to the Corps des Pages). During lunch, Admiral Arseniev invited everyone to drink a toast to the King of Thailand and the royal family.

In the evening there was a dinner at Phraya Mahibal's house. Those invited included those I have told you about already, together with officials from the royal household and some others. In all, 19 people sat down to dinner. When we were about to have dessert, I invited everyone to drink a toast to the Emperor of Russia. Then Phraya Mahibal thanked everyone who was there and invited them to drink a toast to Your Majesty. In addition, Admiral Arseniev said a few words and drank Your Majesty's health and asked me to lead the congratulations for Your Majesty and report this to Your Majesty.

After dinner, the guests played cards and other games. At that time and during dinner there was some live music. Today was the first time Admiral Arseniev came to see me and it happened to be on Your Majesty's birthday, so that is why I invited him. He seems a really good person and very kind. He said he would look after all of us in general. He said several times that he regarded himself as one of Your Majesty's close servants and that if Your Majesty desired anything to tell him.

I gave the photograph of Your Majesty together with Sadet Mother to Admiral Arseniev. He was absolutely delighted and asked me to thank Your Majesty, adding that he would also write and had not written before because he had been waiting to meet me first.

Count Keller has now agreed that I can go and stay at Phraya Mahibal's house every Saturday. At first it seemed as if he would not, but later he gave in.

Yesterday I went for dinner at Count Keller's house. I met the countess on the 25th for the first time, because she had only just come back from the country.

At the moment Petersburg is rather quiet and lonely because no one is here. It is not the season when they come to Petersburg and only those who have work are here.

I beg to remain Your Majesty's obedient servant,
Chakrabongse

4th October 1898

The Winter Palace
12th October 1898

Your Majesty

Your Majesty

As the 1st of this month is the thirtieth anniversary of Your Majesty's accession to the throne, I am delighted to beg to congratulate Your Majesty and may Your Majesty be well and happy and rule longer than any Siamese king there has ever been.

I have received the gold and silver medals struck to commemorate the Thavidabhisek ceremony. I am very pleased and thank Your Majesty very much.

On the 29th of September, the Queen of Denmark died. Her illness was really just old age, but it had been dragging on for a long time. All her children, together with other members of the royal family, are together in Denmark. I have heard that the Emperor will also go to the funeral. Here, everyone has to be in mourning for three months.

When I heard the news, I sent a telegram to the Dowager Empress to express my condolences and I received a thank you telegram in return.

On Friday and Saturday, I went to stay at Phraya Mahibal's house as Saturday and Sunday are holidays. I ate Thai food which was very delicious.

On Sunday, I invited some of my fellow student from the Corps des Pages over. At first I wanted a conjuror, but couldn't find one.

On that day I had to give out a lot of photographs. One of the guests, who is a friend, asked for a photo of me, so then everyone asked for one and I had to give them to everyone. It may become a kind of custom that anyone who comes to this place has to ask for a picture of me.

At the Corps we have now been doing artillery practice. The guns are rather heavy and we have to shoulder them for a long time which makes me stiff. Yesterday I had to run carrying a gun, which is very difficult and exhausting. The gun must not bounce about on one's shoulder, but it's very hard to stop it.

I beg to remain Your Majesty's obedient servant,

Chakrabongse

On the 9th, I went shooting rabbits and birds as is the custom here in the winter. They made me a member of the military club in order to go hunting. It is an exclusive club expressly for shooting animals and there is a small club house where you can stay.

I left here in the evening after I had finished my studies on Saturday and took the train to Krasnoe Selo. From there we took a carriage for about 20 miles until we reached the house arranged for that night.

On the morning of the 10th, we got up really early, had breakfast and set out for the place to shoot rabbits and birds. On arrival we met up with the others, such as Count Keller. Then all 15 of us lined up in a row with numbers, which were about 1 *sen* (40 metres) apart. When the beaters got the signal, they drove the animals in front of us and we shot them. When this area was finished, we went to another. The weather was very changeable going from rain to snow to sunshine.

Today it snowed for the first time this winter. Phraya Mahibal had not dressed warmly enough, so they asked him to go back because they were worried he would catch a cold. When one goes out like that, one must dress very carefully against the cold, with a thick jacket and special shoes. If not and the water seeps in, you can get a cold very quickly. I had dressed like a real Russian that day, so did not feel the cold.

Lunch was in the forest while the snow was falling, so we sheltered under a tree. If I had been wearing normal clothes, I would surely have died.

I went back to the house around dusk and had dinner, before leaving for Petersburg around 9 pm, arriving around 1 am. I shot two rabbits. They said that was very good, because it was the first time I had gone shooting. But I did not manage to shoot a bird that day as there were not many around.

Prince Chakrabongse and Nai Poum in hunting attire.

The Winter Palace, St. Petersburg
18th October 1898

Your Majesty

I have been to see a factory where they make munitions for guns. I saw where they make cannon balls and where they insert the gunpowder, etc. It looked like the place I saw when I was with you in Karlsruhe in Baden. Here, the factory is smaller and I got to see them putting in the bullets, whereas over there we only saw the casing. The insertion of gunpowder and the bullets was a secret. That we got to see it was because I was wearing a Russian uniform. The insertion of gunpowder uses people rather than a machine, because they have not designed a machine which is accurate enough. It is very tricky getting exactly the right amount.

Tonight I went to see Carmen, which I saw in Madrid when I went there with you.

The weather at the moment is very cold and it has snowed two or three times. Now when there is a snowfall it settles and doesn't melt, as the temperature is below freezing. There is still the remains of the snow from the previous snowfall. This is a bad time, as it is easy to catch a cold.

The officials here and I have bought Your Majesty a gold offering dish decorated with enamel as a birthday present, as this is the first time that there has been a celebration of Your Majesty's birthday here, and this is a significant event. The present has just been sent, as it had to be engraved on the back.

I have heard that the Emperor will arrive back from Denmark the day after tomorrow and will go to the Crimea. He will not return from there until November, a month later than previously scheduled.

I beg to remain Your Majesty's obedient servant,
Chakrabongse

The outing was great fun and if the weather had not been so bad, it would have been even better. I hope that this winter I may be able to accompany the Emperor on a hunting trip.

At this time the Emperor is in Denmark for the funeral of the Queen, and will come back together with the Dowager Empress. The latter will then go on to see Grand Duke George in the Caucasus[1].

I beg to remain Your Majesty's obedient servant,
Chakrabongse

1. After contracting tuberculosis in 1890, Grand Duke George was made to go at live in Likani in the Crimea in the hope that his health would improve. He died in 1899.

The Winter Palace, St. Petersburg
25th October 1898

Your Majesty

On the 20th of this month, I went to see a porcelain and glass factory[1]. It was not very large and is only used for Imperial china and glass. The products are not on sale. Creating porcelain is rather like lithograph printing. First a mould is created, then the clay, mixed to produce porcelain, is put inside and the design is incised. Later, it is fired and then painted and finally fired again. There are many beautiful pieces there. At present, the working day is shorter as it gets dark early and they have to stop work, as they believe working in artificial light is not good and they cannot get the colours right.

Making glass is easier in comparison. You take a long, brass, hollow tube and put one end into molten glass which is glowing red hot. Then you mould it a little and put it into a metal form. You close the metal mould and then blow down the brass tube. You wait a little while, then open the mould to release the object shaped like the form. The mouth of bottles or any other pieces not in the mould are shaped later using wooden tools. When the glass melts it can be pulled and stretched like toffee. They pulled a really long string for me to see, but getting the glass strings smooth and the same length is hard.

They also blew some glass for me to see, creating a round globe which got bigger and bigger until it broke. To make something out of glass is not hard, it gets difficult when you add decoration and is also very time consuming. In the museum attached to the factory were many diverse and beautiful things dating from the time of Empress Elizabeth, almost one hundred years ago.

Yesterday I went to Tsarskoe Selo in order to visit Admiral Arseniev, but he wasn't there. When I got back to the palace, they told me that the Admiral had come to see me here, so we were playing hide and seek and neither got to see each other.

I beg to remain Your Majesty's obedient servant,

Chakrabongse

An art nouveau style vase from the Imperial Glass and Porcelain Manufactory, c. 1900.

1. The Imperial Porcelain Factory in St. Petersburg was established by Dmitry Ivanovich Vinogradov in 1744, and was patronised by the Romanov tsars since Empress Elizabeth. It is often referred to by its well-known former name, Lomonosov Porcelain Factory.

Russia's Imperial Glass Factory was founded in 1736 by an Englishman William Elmsel, producing glass and crystal of highest quality. In 1890 it was merged with the Imperial Porcelain Factory to become the Imperial China and Glassworks.

8th November 1898

Your Majesty

On the 1st of this month, it was the anniversary of the Emperor's accession to the throne. Flags were hung in the street and lamp posts, but it was not very impressive. However, in all the theatres everyone sang the Tsar's anthem which was very grand. I sent a telegram to the Emperor in the Crimea and received a thank you in reply.

The weather is really bad here now, full of ice and snow and then suddenly warmer before getting cold again as it is now. This is not a good time to be in Petersburg, and people often get colds.

At the moment, the pupils in the school are behaving very badly. Skipping class during study times in order to play truant, and teasing the officers.

Count Keller is very angry and has meted out a lot of punishments. One student laughed when the General Inspector got in a muddle while teaching. He was punished by having his epaulettes cut off. This is the gravest punishment for a soldier and considered very shameful. The button for fastening it to the shoulder is left, so only the epaulette is cut. It looks very ugly and the person who has suffered such an indignity has to stand at the back all the time when lining up. It happens he was in a high class as well.

I beg to remain Your Majesty's obedient servant,
Chakrabongse

One of the classrooms in the Corps des Pages, 1902.

The Winter Palace
15th November 1898

Your Majesty

Tomorrow is the anniversary of Your Majesty's coronation and I am pleased to proffer my congratulations. May Your Majesty rule for a long time so Your Majesty's people can be contented and prosperous!

Yesterday I went with the other Pages, together with our guns and weaponry, to march like soldiers. We were led by two officers and drums and a bugler along the streets of Petersburg in order to train in the way that ordinary soldiers do. Along the way, people greeted us and many lined the streets, including old ladies who said that we looked very sweet. The men shouted our praises but in a soldierly fashion and made funny remarks.

We walked for about seven miles until we came to a church, where we stopped for a rest and went in to look at the graveyard. Here, they bury only rich people, as they charge a lot for the plot. In the graveyard is the tomb of a general who was so brave that it was said that no sword or gun could kill him. How true this is depends on who is telling the tale. There is also the grave of a famous doctor and other notables. Once we had looked around and were resting, Count Keller arrived and took me back with him as he feared I might be too tired. In fact I wasn't tired, it was just that my shoulder was very stiff from carrying the rifle, as was everyone else's. It is a long time to shoulder a rifle and you cannot shift it from one side to the other.

This is the first time there has been such a march, as they usually only happen when the Corps are in camp, and it is something new that Count Keller has devised. He is really strict and the cadets are frightened of him, but most also dislike him. In fact, the cadets do not like most of the officers and teachers at the school. Those they do like are those such as Captain Khrulov, my guardian. When he was in charge of boys at the school, they liked him and still do.

I beg to remain Your Majesty's obedient servant,

Chakrabongse

Count Keller, director of the Corps des Pages, 1893-1900.

The Winter Palace, St. Petersburg
5th December 1898

Your Majesty

On the 28th November, Phraya Mahibal arranged a dinner for Chao Phraya Abhaya Raja[1]. He invited Admiral Arseniev and numerous other people. Chao Phraya Abhaya was very pleased to meet the Admiral, as both had heard a lot about the other. After dinner they talked to each other a lot until the Admiral left and he said that Chao Phraya Abhaya should come back again at the end of the month, so that he would have an opportunity to see the Emperor upon his return from the Crimea. Accordingly, he has agreed to come back again.

On the 29th, Chao Phraya Abhaya Raja brought Mr de Martens[2], one of his friends in the Ministry of Foreign affairs, to come and meet me. Mr de Martens is famous for adjudicating the dispute between Holland and England, and now he is adjudicating the dispute between England and America regarding the Bering Sea. Chao Phraya Abhaya says that his voice is listened to in the Ministry of Foreign Affairs.

Gustave Rolin-Jacquemins, in full ceremonial attire.

On the evening of the 29th, Chao Phraya Abhaya left Petersburg for Berlin. This trip was very satisfactory to him with regard to Count Muraviev and all those connected with Thai affairs, and I hope that Your Majesty will be pleased with the way in which all of us here received him in a way befitting his position.

On the 2nd of this month, I left Petersburg for Krasnoe Selo and then went by carriage to Koskova Village to shoot rabbits and birds. However, this time there were very few animals and I only managed to shoot one rabbit. Count Keller and his son were also there.

I beg to remain Your Majesty's obedient servant,
Chakrabongse

The Winter Palace, St. Petersburg
27th December 1898

Your Majesty

I have heard from the telegram Your Majesty sent to Phraya Mahibal regarding my request to come back to Bangkok, that Your Majesty is concerned that I don't want Captain Khrulov to come back too and that it is a bad thing that I don't think he should come. I think that it will be rather difficult for him and it won't be of much benefit to us. All that will happen is that he will note any deficiencies we have and come back and broadcast them here. Another thing is that Your Majesty will have to give him a substantial reward. However, if Your Majesty really thinks it is bad for him not to come, then he can. It will just be a little awkward for us, that's all.

Your Majesty's telegram was difficult to decode and so we do not know whether Your Majesty will allow me to come back or not, as the main subject was concern about Captain Khrulov. I do not think this is a major problem and if Your Majesty thinks it appropriate to bring him, then, of course, he must come.

I have not had a letter from Bangkok for a long time. All I have received is a letter from Toonmom Ying[1] and one from Eeyd Lek. Neither are very informative and so I have not had any detailed news from Bangkok for over three months now. I don't know if there is any reason for this.

Next week will be a holiday. I think I will go to Moscow for about 10 days. The Emperor will arrive in Tsarskoe Selo tomorrow. The Dowager Empress is already back in Gatchina.

Last week Grand Duchess Xenia had a baby boy. His name is Feodor[2]. He is only a prince, as he is a great grandson of Emperor Nicholas I.

I beg to remain Your Majesty's obedient servant,
Chakrabongse

1. Chao Phraya Abhaya Raja was born Gustave Henri Ange Hippolyte Rolin-Jaequemyns (1835-1902). He was a Belgian lawyer, diplomat and Minister of the Interior (1878-1884). As advisor to King Rama V of Thailand (1892-1902), he played a crucial role in modernising the country and was awarded the title Chao Phraya Abhaya Raja, the highest distinction ever granted to a foreigner.

2. Friedrich Fromhold Martens (Fyodor Fyodorovich Martens in Russian) (1845-1909) was a diplomat and jurist in the service of the Russian Empire.

1. Princess Suddha Dibyaratana, Princess of Rattanakosin (1877-1922). She was the elder sister of Prince Paribatra.

2. Prince Feodor Alexandrovich was the second son and third child of Grand Duchess Xenia and Grand Duke Alexander Mikhailovich.

1899 Corps des Pages
First Trip Home

Metropole Hotel, Moscow
2nd January 1899

Your Majesty

On 30th December in the evening, I left St. Petersburg by train for Moscow. Phraya Mahibal could not come too, because Mae Oon is unwell and he could not leave her alone. In the morning at 10.10 I arrived in Moscow and went in a carriage to the hotel. At first I had thought to stay in the Kremlin palace, but, as it was very short notice, it could not be sorted out in time. Instead they arranged for me to stay here. In the afternoon I went to see the various senior officials of the city, such as the head of the royal household, the commander-in-chief of the army and other important people involved with Moscow, as well as driving around and seeing the sights.

Moscow is different from Petersburg, in being entirely Russian and unlike other cities in Europe. The houses are painted in lots of different colours. The people here seemed very interested in me, as they had not seen me before, whereas in Petersburg people are used to me. In the evening, I went and had dinner at Testof, a very good restaurant, and then went to an opera called Judith[1].

Today Grand Duke and Grand Duchess Sergei have asked me to go and have lunch at their palace outside Moscow[2]. I left here just after 12, together with Captain Khrulov, reaching the palace at 1 pm. I went to see Grand Duchess Elizabeth first. She asked after Your Majesty and said she hoped Your Majesty was well. I gave her a copy of Your Majesty's photograph taken with Sadet Mae. She asked me to thank Your Majesty and said she was very pleased to receive it. She talked to me about various things in a very friendly manner. Then when it was almost 1, the Grand Duke came in. The first thing he said was he was very pleased to see me, as he got to know Your Majesty well during the trip. At 1 pm, we had lunch together with some palace officials. The Grand Duke sat me on his right and later we talked together in his

Grand Duke Serge.

study for about half an hour before I left. Both asked me to convey their compliments to Your Majesty and said thank you again for the photograph. The Grand Duke said he would send Your Majesty a telegram.

This afternoon I went to see the church, which was built to commemorate the victory over Napoleon[3]. It is very beautiful and built all in stone. I imagine Your Majesty must have seen it, as well as the church where coronations are held[4] and where the Tsars and other nobles are married. I went up the Ivan Grozny Bell Tower[5]. In the past, this was where there was a huge bell which fell down when fire broke out. From the top of the belfry one can see the whole city. I also went to see the monument to Alexander II which was opened this September. After that, we went to a kind of market, where I was hustled to buy so much that I had to leave.

On 29th December the Emperor arrived back in Tsarskoe Selo from the Crimea and in the evening came to Petersburg in order to visit Grand Duchess Xenia. I went to meet him at the station. The Dowager Empress was also there together Grand Duke Michael and Grand Duchess Olga. The Empress is pregnant and not feeling at all well.

I beg to remain Your Majesty's obedient servant,

Chakrabongse

---

1. Judith is an opera in five acts, composed by Alexander Serov during 1861-1863. Derived from renditions of the story of Judith from the Old Testament.

2. At Ilinskoe, 40 km outside Moscow

3. The Church of Christ the Saviour was completed in 1883 and demolished by Stalin in 1933. It has since been rebuilt.

4. Dormition Cathedral, regarded as the mother church of Muscovite Russia. During the French occupation of Russia, it was looted and used as a horse stable. It was thoroughly restored in 1894-1895.

5. The Ivan the Great Bell Tower, at 81 metres high, was built in 1508 for the Russian Orthodox cathedrals in Cathedral Square, which do not have their own belfries.

Interior of the Church of Christ the Saviour.

The Great Bell.

Looking towards the Sparrow Hills from Ivan's tower.

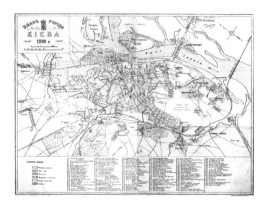

Map of Kiev in 1899.

Nikolaev Street in Kiev.

Reports on Prince Chakrabongse

Apart from the prince's letters home, the Siamese legation also wrote regular and lengthy reports to Prince Sommot in Bangkok on how the prince was doing in the Corps des Pages.

From these we learn that apart from visiting Moscow, Prince Chakrabongse also went to Kiev, where he was received by generals and city dignitaries. Although not recorded in a letter home, the report to Bangkok details some of the items given as thank you gifts – nielloware bowls, teapots and cigarette cases.

Elsewhere, it notes that once the prince was studying again, his governor Captain Khrulov was teaching him to ice skate in one of the parks, and that shortly he would learn riding again in the Imperial manege, so that when necessary he could ride out with the Emperor as Russian nobles did. (Phraya Mahibal to Prince Sommot, 30/1/1899).

Captain Khrulov to Phya Suriya

Meanwhile, the prince's governor was writing reports to Phraya Suriya in Paris as seen in the following excerpts from 28th March 1899:

"With surprise and my great pleasure, I admire the capacity, the great energy with which HRH applies Himself to study. He has made good progress in all branches of science which he is studying. He knows very well already the Russian language. He is seldom at a loss for words and it is only the turning of phrase, the

syntax and the grammar which still embarrass Him....... Not wishing to exaggerate my praise of HRH Prince Chakrabongse and to seem superfluous, yet I cannot help saying that among young men of His age, only one or two are to be found as sympathetic in every respect. H.R.H is the object of the most sincere admiration among those who know him."

His tutor then discusses the issue of his trip home for a holiday, with Count Keller being against the trip in case he forgets his Russian and the Emperor tending to agree. He also considers whether the prince should spend more time in classes at the school, or more time with private tutors. From this, it can be seen that the prince's education was taken extremely seriously by all concerned.

At the same time, Ardachev, back in Russia, kept in touch with his former pupil.

"January 5th, 1899. Petersburg.
Today at 4 o'clock I visited the Siamese. We were having tea, when Chakrabongse came; he had been on various official visits to the Palace, including the Tsar. . . I asked him, if he had seen the Grand Duke Andrei Vladimirivich (my new pupil). He said that he had, and the Grand Duke had talked about me. Chakrabongse endures the local climate unbelievably well. So far, he has not caught even a cold, just lost some of his olive complexion and become whiter . . ."

A rather damaged photograph of Prince Chakrabongse in shooting outfit, inscribed to his mother.

31st January 1899

Your Majesty

Since I wrote last, nothing exciting has happened. The Emperor is still at Tsarskoe Selo and only comes here for special events or ceremonies. I have not managed to see him and, although the Dowager Empress is here, she is still in mourning and is not going out.

My studies have started again and are going well as before and along the same lines.

What has been unusual this year is that the winter has not been cold at all and the weather has been very changeable, so that in one day it can change from 10 degrees to 15 degrees which is very strange. Snow can fall thickly and then melt straight away, making the roads very dirty and full of water turning to mud which is everywhere. It is difficult to walk about, but even in a carriage one gets sprayed with mud.

When it snows and is dry, it settles. Then one can go around in a sledge, which is very swift and smooth. Going through the streets, it is strange to see a whole lot of sledges running around without hearing anything because the snow is soft and creates no noise. The snow is sometimes ground smooth into sand and on the streets can grow black. Another thing is that the river is frozen over and they make a road across so that carriages can cross without the need for a bridge. Every year there are usually electric trams, but this year there have been none yet because the weather has been too uncertain, veering from cold to hot with no one knowing when the ice might melt. I find it very strange. Seeing the river freeze was very weird for us Thais, and if we described it to ordinary Thais they would say that we were lying.

When I say frozen, this does not mean that the whole river is solid – it is only frozen on top. Underneath the water flows as usual. Nevertheless, the ice on top is very thick at up to 2 to 3 *sog* and joining with the shore it cannot float off anywhere. Then at the start of summer, the ice breaks into lumps which float into the sea. At the beginning when it starts to freeze, lumps of ice flow down from a lake before joining together as a slab. It is said that the rivers in Russia freeze very easily because most of them flow from lakes and the water in the lake is colder than the sea water and has no salt at all. Water that has salt freezes much slower, thus the Thames in London freezes with great difficult because it is full of salt and pollution.

I have had my photograph taken in the garb of a Russian hunter as I find it so strange. It is very thick and inside is lined with fur. If I get to come home at some point, I will bring it for you to see.

I beg to remain Your Majesty's obedient servant,
Chakrabongse

Winter Palace
14th February 1899

Your Majesty

On the 7th of this month at the Corps des Pages, there was a concert. The cadets sang songs and played the accordion, which was very jolly. Those who came were almost all fathers and mothers of the cadets. Apart from that, there were military officers who once studied at the school. A very good part of the concert was when the students played together on a truly Russian instrument found nowhere else, namely the balalaika. It is a stringed instrument, which is plucked and strummed. They have been playing since they were children and were really good. In addition, there was one boy who played the accordion and sang. He was only about 10 years old, but he sang and played really well and looked very sweet. In the interval there was tea and then others played, and people came and sang from the stage, but were not very good.

On the next day, the 8th, we got into line and marched around Petersburg carrying our rifles in order to practice being soldiers. The streets at that time were really hard to march through because snow had fallen and settled like sand and was very slippery. We walked for around 4 miles to one of Victory Gates which was built to commemorate the return of the army from attacking Paris during the war with Napoleon I. And there is a memorial day to salute the soldiers who died in that war. On the way back I came in a carriage, as they were worried that it would be too much. The others had to march back, and I heard that they also got lost which wasted a lot of time and made them exhausted. For my part, I didn't feel tired at all because I just went one way.

On the 10th, Admiral Arseniev came to see me and had lunch. Recently he has been unwell and has just got better. He had received Your Majesty's letter dated 28th November, which he brought to show me. He seemed very thrilled to have received it.

On the next day he asked me, together with Phraya Mahibal and his wife, Captain Khrulov, Luang Abhirak and Nai Poum, to have tea at his house, where we met his wife. His wife is very nice, but seems not quite normal as after their son died, she became rather vacant. The admiral has to keep prompting her, but nevertheless they received us well and we were able to discuss the matter of going back to Bangkok in the holiday. The Admiral was very happy and thought it most appropriate.

Regarding the return to Bangkok, I have talked to my guardian on the Russian side. It seems that the only month we could go is May, because that is the time when there are exams in the schools and there is no studying. As I will not be able to enter the exams this year, having not managed to catch up yet, I will be free at that time. In addition, the Russians think that if I am to go, I should make it worthwhile as in other years I probably won't be able to go at all, as I will have to go to camp in the holidays at least once.

I am concerned that Your Majesty's letter in this regard will not come in time, because I have been waiting for a long time and nothing has arrived, and it is not clear whether Your Majesty has sent it yet or not. If I am to go in May, time is getting short.

I have sent you a copy of the photograph of me dressed as a Russian hunter.

I beg to remain Your Majesty's obedient servant,
Chakrabongse

The Winter Palace, St. Petersburg
26th February 1899

Your Majesty

These days nothing much that is exciting or interesting has taken place. It is really very quiet. The Empress is pregnant and feeling rather weak. She doesn't go anywhere, while the Dowager Empress is still in mourning, as is the Emperor. So there are no festivities in the palace. The Emperor also doesn't go anywhere except for when it is really necessary, such as going to inspect the various cadet schools. Around seven days ago, he came to the Corps des Pages but it happened to be a time when I was not at the school so I did not get to see him. The cadets were all very excited and when he left, ran after the carriage shouting "Hoorah" for a long way. Some of them climbed up on the springs of the carriage, others onto the horses, while some got in carriages and followed along shouting "Hoorah" in order to show their delight and their loyalty. The Emperor visits the school every year and always requests three days' holiday for the students, hence the popularity of his visits.

Yesterday I passed the imperial carriage on his way to visit the naval college. These days I have not had an opportunity to see him, as there are no Sunday lunches at Peterhof because the Empress is unwell.

At the moment the weather here is perfect, not too cold and not hot. The sky is clear and people aren't getting ill so often.

I beg to remain Your Majesty's obedient servant,
Chakrabongse

The prince's studies

(Mahibal to Prince Sommot, 1/3/99)

An argument developed between Count Keller, Director of the Corps des Pages, and Captain Khrulov as to whether Prince Chakrabongse should study in the school full time or with private tutors in the Winter Palace as before. Khrulov feared the negative influence of other boys, while Keller wanted the prince more involved. Phraya Mahibal was angry at not being consulted but anxious not to create an incident given that the Tsar was paying for the prince's education in its entirety.

The Winter Palace, St. Petersburg
7th March 1899

Your Majesty

As the 3rd was my birthday, there was a party and games for various pages at the house of Phraya Mahibal Boriraksha. I invited all the cadets who are in the same class as me, namely Class 6, apart from those who were ill or could not make it. In addition, there were some from other classes whom I had got to know and were friendly with. Including Phraya Mahibal and his wife, there were around 30 people.

At first, there were some conjuring tricks, although these were nothing special and rather ordinary. After that there was a lucky dip with everyone getting a number and going to Luang Abhirak to get their present. They got all sorts of things, some good and some bad. They seemed really pleased. Some who got rather inferior things were allowed to have another go and everyone was happy. After this was over, we all had a buffet lunch together with some wine as appropriate. Everyone was full and contented and many a toast was drunk to this person or that.

On that day, I received a wooden box painted in Russian style filled with sweets, which was a present from the pages in Class 6.

The party seemed to please everyone and the next day I received many thanks.

Recently one of the pages called Valkov died. He had a fever and was about 13 years old and was in class 4. Yesterday they took his body from his home to the church and there were prayers as is customary. I went along together with all the cadets to attend the service and walked behind the funeral carriage from his house to the church. The prayers were very long and we had to stand throughout. I was so stiff. Today they are going to take the coffin to the station and then for burial in his hometown.

I beg to remain Your Majesty's obedient servant,
Chakrabongse

The Winter Palace, Petersburg
14th March 1899

Your Majesty

Last week from Tuesday to Sunday was Carnival, a period of great fun and festivity. There are different shows in all the theatres in the morning and evening, and all the schools are shut. Such events take place every year as a tradition before Lent, when every stops eating meat and only eats fish. It is a time of prayer and penance. It is rather like our Buddhist Lent. Lent here will begin on this Monday and last for six weeks.

On Thursday the 9th, there was a play at the Corps des Pages which was performed entirely by the cadets. At first it was planned to not have it this year, as it is a period of mourning for the former director who died a short while ago. Then when it was almost time for the performance, it was decided to go ahead so everyone had to rehearse like mad for only three days. Nevertheless, it was quite good. The play was a comedy and one of the cadets was very funny indeed.

Today, the 10th, was the Fête day of the school and also the day when Emperor Alexander III ascended the throne. An argument had developed as to when the anniversary of the school was, with no one knowing for sure when the school was inaugurated as all the papers relating to this event had disappeared. Emperor Alexander thus decided that his accession date should be used for the school's Fête day and so it has been ever since.

On that day, a reception was held at the school for all the pages, past and present. Before the lunch there were prayers and an account was read out of the history of the school. After that, everyone sat down to eat. There were toasts to the Emperor and other members of the imperial family after which the celebrations were concluded.

I beg to remain Your Majesty's obedient servant,
Chakrabongse

The Winter Palace
28th March 1899

Your Majesty

Today I received Your Majesty's letters dated 16th and 21st February and I understand all Your Majesty's points now. I was very happy, as I had not heard from Your Majesty for a long time.

I am sad to learn that Your Majesty has been ill and with something new that you have never had before, but I sincerely hope that it will not endure for long.

Regarding Phraya Suriya, once I had read your letter of 16th February and seen your thoughts, I felt better, because I have no desire to create further enemies. Rather, I want to form allies and I will be delighted if, despite having long-held views in this matter, according to Your Majesty that is how it is.

Nevertheless, the fact that Phraya Suriya has come here and done various things to obstruct Phraya Mahibal is not good at all and has made work in the embassy and other things proceed slowly and with many obstacles. For me to write and explain this to Your Majesty would take a long time and perhaps not be clear. So I hope that when I see Your Majesty, I may explain things at length.

The Empress has now left here for Tsarskoe Selo. While she was here, I did not see her at all as there was no opportunity. The Emperor was here this time just for official commitments and nothing else, with no pleasurable outings at all. The Sunday lunches for the imperial family and close officials which were a feature before were also stopped. This is because of the Empress being pregnant and feeling ill, together with the period of mourning for the Queen of Denmark.

It is almost time for exams at the Corps now and someone will come separately to the palace to conduct exams for me and Nai Poum.

I beg to remain Your Majesty's obedient servant,
Chakrabongse

Letters in English

In the Spring of 1899 Prince Chakrabongse began writing some letters to his father in English. These are less formal than those in Thai. They are interspersed, however, with letters in Thai. They can be recognised by the fact that they begin "My dear father" and conclude "your affectionate son, Lek" or "your very affectionate son, Lek".

Winter Palace, St. Petersburg
April 4th 1899

My dear father

Phya Mahibal advised me to write to you in English, so that you might be able to judge whether I am forgetting my English or not.

I have received a letter from you dated 24th of February, with a copy of your letter to His Majesty the Emperor. Phya Mahibal went yesterday to Tsarskoe Selo to inform General Hesse (Head of the military household of H. M. The Emperor) of the arrival of your letter. The Emperor, after having heard of this news, gave an order that the letter be given to Aide de camp General Hesse (above mentioned) and then be brought to the Emperor by this high official. Phya Mahibal has again gone to Tsarskoe Selo today to carry out His Majesty's command.

I am very glad that my journey home seems to be now nearing a complete settlement. I shall be very glad to see you again and to see Mother, whom I have not seen for three years.

My governor, Captain Khrulov seems to be very anxious to go with us to Siam, and we could do nothing to persuade him stay here and enjoy a holiday. If the Emperor allows him to go, he will certainly accompany us. We are eagerly waiting to receive the decision of the Emperor, so that we may be able to arrange everything soon, I hope it is soon forthcoming.

With best love to you and mother, I remain your affectionate son
Lek

Winter Palace, St. Petersburg
April 17th 1899

My dear father

I received today from Uncle Sommot[1] a birthday gift from you. I thank you very much for it. I always think it is much nicer to give birthday presents in money, because then one can buy anything one would like.

I received with great joy the news from Phya Mahibal about a week ago that the Emperor has granted his permission to me to go home, accompanied by Phya Mahibal and his wife.

It was most characteristic of the Emperor such to give the decision without consulting anybody and without any delay and misunderstanding. His Majesty simply commanded his aide-camp General Hesse to inform Phya Mahibal that the Emperor grants his permission readily and with pleasure.

We shall start from here on the 22nd of May going to Berlin where we shall stop three days, because I want to see Paribatra there. Then we shall go to Paris and thence to Marseille. On the 4th of June we shall embark on a French boat and start on our sea journey. We do not want to leave before then to avoid the 31st of May.

At Singapore we don't want to stop long and want to go straight on to Bangkok, so I hope the steamer that you will send to meet us will be in readiness to start when we arrive.

Besides, I should be very glad if you could send Chira out to Singapore to meet me. I have written to ask him to come out if he is not too busy and inclined to take a holiday. If he is willing to come, do send him out, it will be very nice.

In two days' time there will be no more lessons at the Corps des Pages, but only examinations, so that I shall not have to go any more to school till the next term, which begins on the 13th of September. Then I shall be in the 7th class, that is one class higher than the present one in which I am.

I am greatly looking forward to see you again, and meanwhile I remain, your very affectionate son,
Lek

1. Prince Sommot Amornbhandu (1860-1915) was a half-brother to King Chulalongkorn, and his private secretary for many years.

TELEGRAM FROM HIS MAJESTY THE KING TO PHYA MAHIBAL BORIRAKS RECD AT ST. PETERSBURG. 23RD APRIL 1899

PLEASE COMMUNICATE TO HIS IMPERIAL MAJESTY THE EMPEROR

HAVING RECEIVED FRIENDLY VISIT OF GOVERNOR-GENERAL OF INDO-CHINA AND TAKING INTO CONSIDERATION THAT THERE IS SOME HOPE TO ARRIVE AT A FINAL SETTLE-MENT OF OUR DIFFICULTY WITH FRANCE, I APPEAL TO YOUR MAJESTY IN ORDER THAT THE RUSSIAN AMBASSADOR IN PARIS MAY BE INSTRUCTED TO SUPPORT OUR REQUEST AS A NATURAL BY CONSEQUENCE OF RESTORED MUTUAL CONFIDENCE UNCONDITIONALLY EVAC-UATION OF MUANG CHANTABURI. PLEASE ACCEPT MY GRATEFUL THANKS FOR THE GREAT KINDNESS AND MY REGARD TO THE EMPRESS. MM CHULALONGKORN

PHYA MAHIBAL BORIRAKS TO HIS MAJESTY THE KING, FROM ST. PETERSBURG, 26TH APRIL 1899

YOUR TELEGRAM HAS BEEN COMMUNICATED TO HIS IMPERIAL MAJESTY THE EMPEROR. THE EMPEROR PROMISED TO DO WHAT HE CAN.

MAHIBAL

TELEGRAM FROM HIS MAJESTY THE KING TO PHYA MAHIBAL BORIRAKS REC'D AT ST. PETERSBURG. 23RD APRIL 1899

PLEASE COMMUNICATE THE FOLLOWING TO HIS IMPERIAL MAJESTY THE EMPEROR

I AM GLAD TO HEAR THAT YOUR MAJESTY HAS GRACIOUSLY PLEASED TO HAVE INSTRUCT-ED THE RUSSIAN AMBASSADOR IN PARIS TO DO ALL THAT IS POSSIBLE TO HASTEN THE EVACUATION OF MUANG CHANTABURI. I BEG TO ASSURE YOUR MAJESTY OF MY GRATEFUL THANKS FOR YOUR MAJESTY'S EVER KIND-NESS AND READINESS TO RENDER US EFFEC-TIVE SUPPORT WITH WHICH WE WILL BE SURE TO SUCCEED FOR THE OBJECT IN VIEW. MM CHULALONGKORN

5 Grand rue des Ecuries, St. Petersburg
3rd May 1899

My dear father

During the Easter holiday, beginning on the 28th of April and ending tomorrow, I have been staying here with Phya Mahibal for a little change.

On the 25th of last month, Their Majesties the Emperor and Empress came up here from Tsarskoe Selo to spend the Easter week in the capital. The Empress Maria also returned from Denmark to Petersburg on that day. The next day, that is on the 26th, the Emperor summoned me to lunch with him in his private apartments in the Winter Palace. I went accordingly at half past twelve and both the Emperor and Empress received me first in the Salle de Malachite, adjoining the Imperial apartments, and then the Emperor called me into the Empress's private boudoir where luncheon was served.

Before lunch I submitted to His Majesty your telegram to Phya Mahibal, received on 23rd of April.

The Emperor first asked me whether I knew the content of the telegram and, after my having replied in the affirmative, read it through. His Majesty then said to me "Certainly I will do all I can". The Emperor further mentioned that he had already heard of M. Doumer[1] and that he thought him a nice and quiet man. The Emperor asked if he might keep the telegram and then locked it in the drawer of his writing table. I noticed particularly that he did not mention a word about it to the Empress and that His Majesty seemed very sincere while giving his promise. The Emperor then told me that he had received a letter from you asking him to let me go home. He further asked me when I would start. After having heard that I will start on the 20th of May, the Emperor exclaimed "Why not sooner? You are working very well and need not fear to lose your time, you ought to stay longer at home."

I thanked him for his kindness and explained that it would not be at all convenient for me to leave any earlier. The Empress also complained of such a short stay and asked whether I would meet there the hottest time of the year. I answered in the negative and men-

---

1. Joseph Athanase Gaston Paul Doumer, known as Paul Doumer (1857-1932) was Governor-General of French Indochina from 1897-1902. Later President of France 1931-1932.

The Malachite Room in the Winter Palace by Konstantin Ukhtomsky. The room, designed by Alexander Briullov, was a formal reception room for Tsarina Alexandra Feodorovna, wife of Tsar Nicholas I, after the previous room had been destroyed in the 1837 fire. It was where the Imperial family gathered in private.

tioned that the hottest time is during March and April, exactly the time when his Majesty went to Siam. The Emperor then said that he did not suffer as much from the heat as from the smell of flowers, which was too strong for him and made him feel headache. He could not do without it because the queen herself sent them to him, they were very pretty but had too strong a smell. The Empress then declared that these flowers must be very nice to have such good smell. After these conversations, we sat down to lunch, the Empress showing every kindness by asking whether I should have this or that. During the whole time, Their Majesties conversed with me most familiarly, the Emperor joking and laughing the whole time. They ask me how I amuse myself during the evening, whether many friends come to me from the Corps des Pages, how I get on with Captain Khrulov and various other questions of my concern.

The Emperor also recollected various incidents from his travel in the East eight years ago and said he remembered me quite well and that my face has not changed its character at all. His Majesty told me he had received recently a telegram from his minister in Bangkok that a mourning has befallen our family, caused by the death of Prince Prap[2] and asked what relation is this person to me. After having received my explanations according to facts, the Emperor said he could now recollect the face of "this old admiral" (according to His Majesty's own words). The Emperor then asked who will succeed Prince Prap as

Minister of Marines. I answered that I have not yet heard of the new appointment. The Emperor then asked whether Pin is too young to take the duty. I told him I thought Pin was still too young. The conversation then turned into another channel. I was asked whether I have met any of my coreligists here, because, he said, there are many Buddhists among his subjects. I told him that I have not yet met any except a Javanese, who is in the Medical Academy here. His Majesty was surprised to hear of this fact and said he did not know that before. The Emperor doesn't seem to have any sympathy with the Javanese at all.

So the conversation went on in this way on different subjects till luncheon was finished. We then sat down together beside the window, looking onto the river, which was just beginning to get free again from ice. After lunch I was surprised to have tea prepared for me without sugar and milk, while the Emperor drinks coffee always after lunch. It is my custom, however, to drink tea after meals and I don't know how the Emperor learnt of the fact. He told me after our having finished luncheon, "your tea is ready".

At twenty minutes to two o'clock, Their Majesties rose and I took leave of them. They asked me to come to them again before going back home.

Hoping you are quite well and with love
I remain your affectionate son,
Lek

2. Prince Prapborapuksha, originally called Prince Kajorn, was a son of Prince Mala. Rising in rank, his name and title changed.

The Winter Palace
St. Petersburg
May 9th 1899

My dear father

The fete of Russian Easter has just passed. It was on Sunday the 30th of April, not on the same day as Easter in other countries because they have different calendars, as you already know. This fete is considered more important than the New Year, and they pay visits to each other on this day as on New Year's Day.

I went to the Emperor to offer His Majesty and the Empress my congratulations, and was received by them both in their private apartments at the Winter Palace. The audience lasted only a few minutes because the Emperor had to receive other people.

Afterwards I went to the Empress Maria, also to offer my felicitations. She received me alone in her private sitting room and gave me a little egg made of red stone for hanging on a watch chain. It is the custom here, as well as in Europe on the whole, to give eggs during the Easter fete. The Empress was informed of my intention to go home during the holiday, and she probably thought I was taking leave of her, because she ordered me to give you her compliments and said that she will never forget your visit.

However, I will go to her again before departing to take leave of her at Gatchina. On the 3rd of May the Emperor and Empress left for Tsarskoe Selo.

On the 5th of May, was celebrated the fete of the saint patron of the Empress. I was invited to lunch at Tsarskoe Selo with the Imperial family. I accordingly went and offered Her Majesty my congratulations. There were many Grand Dukes and Grand Duchesses at the luncheon but no one else at all. That day I made the acquaintance of Grand Duchess Xenia, whom I have not been able to meet before.

Tomorrow there will be grand review of the troops by the Emperor. I will go to see it, but privately.

The Emperor ordered me every time I met him to go to him again before starting. I expect he will send a letter to you by me.

I remain your very affectionate son,

Lek

An image of the Emperor and Empress released for Easter.

Bannakom Soranee Throne Hall
21st June 1899

My dear son Lek

I just arrived back today and the date for reaching Singapore was delayed, so I arranged for someone to go and meet [you] on the 23. Chira has volunteered to go and meet you as you desire and Phraya Siharaj Decho with Jongkwa and a guard have gone too.

I have not been at all well lately. The death of Noi[1] and all the work which was the job of a person who nobody had a bad word to say about, unlike other members of the royal family, often gets forgotten. Noi was such an energetic character and would have very helpful to the country and now he is dead. In the future when receiving visitors, even if everyone is in place, I will miss the one whom no one disliked.

I am delighted that we will meet very soon. May this letter serve as my welcome. I am sure you have all the details from Chira.

Chulalongkorn

Prince Sommatiwongse Varodya, who died on 17th June, aged 17.

The MM Yarra, on which Prince Chakrabongse sailed from Marseilles. The 6,900 tonnes vessel was a mail-boat with 90 first class cabins, launched in 1883 and with a top speed of 16 knots.

1. Noi was Prince Sommatiwongse Varodaya, the Prince of Sri Dharmaraj (9 June 1882-17 June 1899). He was a son of King Chulalongkorn and Queen Savang Vadhana.

ARRIVAL BY THE MAIL.

His Royal Highness Prince Chakrabongse of Siam and Phya and Madame Mahibal, arrived on Tuesday from Europe by the M. M. Yarra. His Majesty's yacht Maha Chakrkri. arrived from Bangkok the same day for the purpose of conveying the Prince to Bangkok, and in her he resumed his voyage the same evening. Prince Chakrabongse is the next brother to the Crown Prince of Siam. He is on short leave from the Russian Regiment to which he belongs, and he returns to St. Petersburg about two months hence. During his brief stay here, on Tuesday, the Prince called on Sir Alexander Swettenham, the Deputy Governor, who returned the call at Hurricane House and also accompanied the Prince on board his yacht on his departure for Bangkok.

FIRST TRIP HOME: JULY–AUGUST 1899

Prince Chakrabongse arrived in Bangkok on 1st July 1899 and stayed till 25th August, residing in Saranrom Palace. While there he had various portraits taken. He was given the rank of Captain in the Royal Siamese Life Guards by his proud father.

Prince Chakrabongse (seated) with his entourage. Standing from left: Phraya Riddhikrai Kriangharn, Phraya Siharaj Dechochai, Phraya Mahibal, Jamuen Jongkwa, (man at right, as yet unidentified).

Bannakom Soranee Throne Hall
30th August 1899

Dear Lek

I am happy to tell you some news about Sadet Mae. After she said goodbye to you, she was sad but not too much so because she was able to control herself. I had been worried that she would decline again. The next day I invited her to the park where she saw Eeyd Lek riding and she wanted to have a go too, so I arranged for her to try. At first she was really timid, but these last few days she has become very keen and had fun. Nowadays, she rides every day and seems much stronger. She goes a long way, so the person who used to lead her, now has to ride after her. I go with her when she goes far, but if it is too cold because of the rain, I just follow her. But she is well and normal.

I think of you so much and often call Eeyd Lek, Lek by mistake. Both your mother and I are worried about the quarantine, as there is only one place where Marshal can come on. If we get stuck, it will be very crowded and it will be rough. You must apologise to the Emperor so he can see we respect his wishes very much.

I have no more news, just the same old things. Only wanted to say I am thinking of you a great deal.

Chulalongkorn Por Ror

1. In 1892 King Chulalongkorn built a summer palace, Phra Chudadhuj on Sichang island, and members of the royal family used it for rest and recuperation. In 1900 the palace was moved to Bangkok. For many years it was open to the public as Vimanmek, but it has now been closed off.
2. Prince Rangsit (1885-1951) was the second child of King Chulalongkorn and Chao Chom Manda Neung. After the death of his mother, he was adoped by Queen Savang Vadhana. At the age of 14 he was send to Germany to study. The Queen was there to see him off.
3. Aunt refers to HM Queen Savang Vadhaha.
4. Two brothers: Daeng and Rangsit. Daeng refers to Prince Mahidol Adulyadej (1892-1929), later father to King Rama VIII and King Rama IX. He also went to study in Germany, eventually being commissioned in the German Imperial Navy.
5. Jor Por Ror. These were the initials of King Chulalongkorn, which he would inscribe on certain places he visited.
6. The waterfall was called Tarn Sadet, meaning stream visited by the King.
7. The Governor was still Sir Charles Bullen Hugh Mitchell, whom Prince Chakrabongse had met before in 1896.

On board the Maha Chakri, laying off Singapore
30th August 1899

My dear Father

After you left, the ship steamed out at once from Paknam for Koh Sichang[1], where we arrived after dinner about ten o'clock. As soon as we came in to the port, we saw the "Suriya" already lying there. Rangsit[2] and I, after some preliminary inquiries, set off for the "Suriya" and was received by Aunt[3] and Uncle Svasti. Aunt seemed to have much improved in health and she sat talking with us the whole time we were on board. She was in very good humour and smiles a little from time to time. Our two little brothers[4] were already asleep so we didn't want to disturb them.

The next morning Chira came to see me on board this ship. He came from Wang Hin on board the "Nareu Bodin", which was at Bang Phra. Chira seems better, but not yet recovered from his illness. I heard he had the same kind of fits he used to have in Bangkok once a few days before that time. About ten o'clock I went on shore and was met at the pier by my two brothers, who had been enjoying the morning in the Palace grounds. Both of them look very well. Daeng has grown very fat and seemed very jolly. They are both very dark because they always play in the sun.

We lunched on board the "*Suriya*" and enjoyed Uncle Svasti's cooking. It was fairly good, considering that he is only an amateur and not a professional cook. We had some seafood too, and that made us recollect the story about a dead sea creature biting my leg a long time ago as you will remember.

The Maha Chakri left Koh Sichang at six o'clock on the 26th and directed its course to the West Coast. On the 27th, we stopped at Koh Pa-ngan and we all went up to take a bath. We mounted up to the first *Jor Por Ror*[5] and then came down to take a bath in Tarn Sadet Waterfull[6]. It was really very refreshing. We came on again that evening after the dinner and the sea has been all the time very calm.

Today at 8 o'clock in the morning, we arrived in the harbour of Singapore. We exchanged salutes with the fort as usual. At 10 o'clock we went on shore and had a drive through the town to the Botanical Garden. After lunch I went to call on the governor[7] who received me very politely and afterwards asked me to go to the drawing room to see Lady Mitchell. They both asked after you and mother, and said they had expected that you would come to Singapore as they had heard you were going to Java. I explained to them that you really thought of doing so at first, but afterwards found that you had no time as you would have to return to Bangkok for your birthday.

Sir Charles asked me and suite to dine at the government house tomorrow evening and we have accepted the invitation.

Tomorrow we think of going to Johor, we shall start very early in the morning.

I don't know for the present when the mail boat is going to leave Singapore but I hear it is very likely it will leave the day after tomorrow in the evening. The governor will only return my call on Friday as we won't be here tomorrow.

I hope you are in very good health. I miss everybody and everything I used to see in Bangkok very much.

Your affectionate son,
Lek

The Royal Yacht Maha Chakri
1st September 1889

Your Majesty

I wrote a letter to Your Majesty already on the 30th, but now I have some further news which I feel I should tell Your Majesty.

Early yesterday morning, I went to look around Johor. I left here on a bicycle. The road was very good, the only problem being that it was a bit hot. However, there were many trees along the road, so one didn't feel the sun too much. I got to the jetty on that side and took a boat across to the town of Johor. We went to have a meal. In the morning, the Sultan sent his secretary to see us and said that he would arrange a horse and carriage to take us sightseeing. Once the carriage arrived, we went off sightseeing and went to the reservoir. We also got rained on really hard, but nevertheless went to leave a card with the Sultan despite being drenched. Luckily, we didn't have to go in and see him. As a result of getting wet, we didn't go on to see anything else. We came back to the Singapore side and got a carriage back. This sight-

SIR CHARLES BULLEN HUGH MITCHELL, K.C.M.G., GOVERNOR OF FIJI.

The Governor of Singapore, Sir Charles Mitchell.

seeing trip seemed a bit of a rush, but even so one could get an idea of what Johor was like because it is extremely small. There are few people and it seems very quiet. The only thing that seemed good was the road, which was very smooth.

In the evening, I went to dinner at the Governor's residence. The dinner was just for men and included all the permanent officials. When we had almost finished, the Governor drank to their Queen as is customary and then drank to "The King of Siam, Our most friendly neighbour". I drank to the Governor and then he drank a toast to me, which was the end of the dinner. During the evening, I chatted to the Governor and we got on very well. We talked about military matters and he stressed we should quickly introduce conscription because he thought it was a good thing and very suitable for us.

Regarding a trip to Thailand, I asked him whether he would go or not, to which he replied he wasn't sure. He said he wanted to go, but was afraid there might not be time as he was about to go back to Europe. He says he is leaving this year. He said he would write to Your Majesty to say he met me.

Today the French ship will leave the port around 4.30. For that reason, I must say goodbye another time and hope that I will be able to see Your Majesty again in 3-4 years upwards.

I beg to remain Your Majesty's obedient servant,
Chakrabongse

Paquebot le Oceanien[1],
September 18th 1899

My dear Father

Allow me first of all to wish you many happy returns of the day for your birthday, as I shall not have the opportunity of writing to you on the 20th, for we shall be then in the Mediterranean.

Since we left Colombo on the 7th inst, we have had a very fair passage. The weather has been very good all along, only a little rough sometimes. However, considering that it was during the monsoon time, we were very lucky for the water never came on deck even once.

However, Rangsit and some of the boys were seasick and could not come to table, but on the whole I think we have been homesick more than sea-sick.

We arrived in Djibouti on the 14th early in the morning. Our party went on shore at once so as to escape from the coal dust, because as a rule when they are coaling, you get all black with the dust if you remain on board.

However, there was nothing much to be seen on shore. There are said to be 25 stone houses in this place, including two hotels and some café-restaurants. We went to one of the hotels called Hotel des Arcades which is supposed to be the best in this town. There was nothing much in it though: three dining rooms downstairs and about eight bedrooms above and that is all. Only one of dining rooms is properly furnished, while the others only possess a long table each and some chairs. However, we found it better to stop in this so-called hotel than to go walking in the sun, which was simply scorching.

When we came up on shore, it was only 8 o'clock in the morning but it was so hot. Oh! Much hotter than in Bangkok at 12 o'clock. We had some luncheon which was really very good, considering we were in Djibouti. The water, however, was undrinkable and we had to take mineral water, for soda water was not to be had. After lunch some of us tried to go to see something, but found out in too short a time that there was nothing to be seen and that it was much too hot for walking. No vehicles of any kind could be produced in this place, not even rickshaws. We settled down in the hotel, trying to pass the time as best one could till 2 o' clock in the afternoon we returned again to the ship.

At half past three, the ship weighed anchor and we started off again on our journey. The passage through the Red Sea was very nice and calm, too calm perhaps, for there was hardly any breath of wind, and it was terribly hot. In the night time, it is a little better than in the day time, but still we could hardly sleep. It was as if we were put into the hot room before taking a bath, like at Baden-Baden you will remember and see for yourself how one can sleep with such a temperature.

It is better to sleep on deck, but then one is awoken at 3 o'clock in the morning when it is still quite dark for they want to clean the deck and you have to go to the cabin again to be heated up and left without any sleep. However, such heat prevailed only for two days and since yesterday we have had the north wind, which has made it much cooler and pleasanter for us.

Today we shall arrive in Suez about six o'clock in the evening. The captain wants to get there before sunset because if we arrive after, the pilot might not come on board and we shall have to pass through the canal only the next morning.

All the time, I have been thinking of you, my dear father, and my pleasant stay in Bangkok, I am always wondering when I shall go back again. I hope not very long.

With best love and again best wishes,
I remain your affectionate son
Lek

1. The steamship *L'Oceanien* belonged to the French company, Messageries Martimes. She was launched in June 1884 and from 1892 to 1900 served the Far East route. She was a sister ship to the *Yarra,* on which the prince had journeyed home.

Bannakom Soranee
4th October 1899

Dear Lek

I have received two telegrams from Constantinople and I have received one from the Sultan himself as well. I have sent it on for you to see. I am delighted that the Sultan[1] received you so well and will wait to hear more details from your letter.

I have received your letter from Singapore. Sir Charles wrote me a very complimentary letter. I was uneasy when you were on the sea, but once I knew you had reached Marseilles I felt huge relief. I feel very lonely as there is only Rabi and Eeyd Lek, who seems a bit more lively and is acting very much as a substitute for Rangsit. Chira only arrived yesterday. He looks better but is not fat and his eye is still not normal. Prince Phit[2] has broken his arm falling off his bicylce in Sriracha. I was so cross I did not go and visit him until yesterday.

Defrance arrived four days ago and we have had two days of consultation, but nothing has been agreed. It seems he wants to change the things we discussed in Paris and all that Doumer said:

1. Asked to send a list of people after we have altered it or maybe discuss it before we have, but he would not agree. Wanted to say what type of people were Protégé and again would not agree. Wants us to accept all those listed, not just children and grand-children but also great grandchildren. All different from Doumer and Paris.

2. Regarding the 25 km, wants us to promise not to establish houses or villages.

3. Added stuff about shipping on Mekong river.

4. About Luang Prabang wants to inspect the border – not mentioned in agreement.

5. Has said nothing about Chantaburi.

6. Wants us to buy sessions [concessions] for the gem mines in Pailin back from the British.

7. Wants us to promise to hire French people.

I am about to write down what he said to show you. If we accept that it is correct, we will have to say enough consultation.

I have sent you another picture of the three of us which your mother does not like. I think it is OK. There is also a half portrait of me, which your mother loved and said was very fine. But when she saw the

Sultan Abdul Hamid II.

photograph was by Eym[3], she stopped being pleased. It was very funny and we all laughed. She was angry, saying I loved the six *ajariya*[4] more than her.

Tomorrow I am going to Ratchaburi, because Tan Lek[5] has gone for recuperation because of being ill. This time when he was going to be allowed to go and then couldn't, he practically cried himself to death. I am anxious about Dusit Park, but I need to go. At the moment, I am making three roads with four avenues of trees like the Vienna Ringstrasse and not like Paris. The only problem is it is very short[5].

The ministers have been changed. Phraya Thawes is agriculture minister, Naris[8] is Public Works, Prachak[9] is Minister of Defence and the navy. I think all the positions should be better. No one knew it was going to happen. I found time to talk to them individually and then proclaimed the changes that very day. Everyone was rather impressed and no one could object or disagree. It seems they were all nervous about it, but I think things will be stronger.

Your mother is having lots of fun, going out every day and refusing to stay in. She goes boating sometimes on the river and sometimes on the *khlongs* getting back around 9 pm, often after me. She looks

Ratchadamnoen Avenue shortly after its construction.

Prince Prachak, Minister of Defence 1899-1901.

better. But it's unfair as it is as if she thinks she'll live forever. I think I've solved the land problem. I was almost asleep and had to get up and tell your mother to remember. It is a really good plot 6 *sen* wide by 7 *sen* long. It is almost square and altogether fine.

Jor Por Ror

P. S. At home I have been able to buy two plots for 34 *chang*. It's not a simple as it sounds. This will be Toh's home. It is on Khlong Padung within Suan Dusit at the place that was to be the barracks. Getting through this issue was difficult. Your mother was happy to give up your plot, but I stalled which she found very amusing. I was shocked because before going for a walk made her grumble and groan and now her foot is better. If she could be like this all the time it would be good. It's very late. I must stop now.

Chulalongkorn

1. The Sultan of Turkey was then Abdul Hamid II (1842-1918), the 34th Sultan of the Ottoman Empire and the last Sultan to exert effective autocratic control. He oversaw a period of decline in the power and extent of the Ottoman Empire and was deposed shortly after the 1908 Young Turk Revolution, on 27 April 1909.

2. Prince Sonabhandit, also Bidyalabh (Phitthayalap), (1863-1913), a half-brother to King Chulalongkorn.

3. Chao Chom Eym was a consort of King Chulalongkorn. She was an amateur photographer and was also known for her traditional Thai massage skills.

4. This refers to six sages who were consulted on a Buddhist theological question in the time of the Buddha.

5. Prince Lek refers to Prince Bhanurangsi Savangwongse (1859-1928). At that time he was trying to stop drinking.

6. This refers to Ratchadamnoen Avenue, which was in three parts and linked the Grand Palace with the new Dusit Park.

7. Phraya Thewes.

8. Prince Narisara Nuwattiwong (1863-1947) was a half-brother to King Chulalongkorn. From 1894-99 he was Minster of War before becoming Minister of Public Works.

9. Prince Prachak. Refers to Maj. Gen. HRH Prince Prachak Silpakom who was Minister of Defence from October 1899-1901.

Winter Palace, Petersburg
9th October 1899

Your Majesty

I arrived back in Petersburg on the 7th at just after 10 pm. At the station was Count Keller and my old teacher, together wtih several officers from the school. As for Captain Khrulov, he had planned to meet me at Sevastopol[1] but could not get there in time. We met on the way just before I arrived in Petersburg and Nai Poum was with him too.

The next day, on the 8th, I went to see Count Keller and General Kanilovsk the inspector of the Corps des Pages.

On the 10th, I will begin my studies again.

At the moment the Emperor and Empress are in Darmstadt and will return here at the end of this month or early next. But before coming to Petersburg they will go to stay in Poland near Warsaw in order to do some shooting.

I sent a telegram informing the Emperor that I had arrived, but have not yet received a reply.

I have asked Captain Khrulov to write a letter to General Hesse, the adjutant, regarding Your Majesty's letter that I have brought. When I get an answer I will do as instructed.

The Dowager Empress is in Denmark at the moment and I don't know when she will come back.

I heard from Phraya Visudh in Marseilles that Prince Rangsit did nothing whatsoever about studying in Germany and, accordingly, I suggested to Phraya Visudh and Phraya Prasit that he come to stay in Russia first, because if he were to stay alone in the embassy in Berlin it would be very lonely and no fun for him. He wouldn't know anyone. All of my group who came to study first were never left alone straight away, but were with one or two brothers. For that reason I felt that Prince Rangsit should receive similar comfort at first. He already knew Phraya Mahibal and his wife, so staying at the embassy in Petersburg would be cosy and coming here would be quiet. Phraya Visudh agreed, but Phraya Prasit[2] argued that he could be learning German if he stayed in the embassy in Berlin. I retorted that being in the embassy in Berlin would not achieve anything as there were only Thai people there and he would talk Thai all the time. He could study just as well in the embassy here

as there are good German teachers we could find. So it was agreed and we planned the program thus while I was in Marseilles. When I left for Constantinople I entrusted Prince Rangsit to Phraya Visudh and Phraya Prasit to take to London with them. Then when I was back in Petersburg, Phraya Visudh would bring Prince Rangsit to Russia.

Now I have received a telegram from Phraya Visudh saying that he will arrive in Petersburg on the 13th of this month.

As for Thongrod[3], I have arranged for him to go to London with Prince Rangsit and then come on here with Phraya Visudh.

I have received your letter dated 30th August. I am delighted that Sadet Mother has gone riding and that this has made her better.

I beg to remain Your Majesty's obedient servant,
Chakrabongse

11th October 1899

Your Majesty

I have sent Your Majesty a report [see page 142] on my trip to Constantinople and enclose it with this mail. I had to type it, as to copy it out again would be too difficult and also I thought it would be clearer.

Regarding the decorations, the official has submitted a long list which I am sending to Your Majesty as is. It is entirely up to you as to what you present to M. Mykov Dragoman (the assistant) at the Russian embassy. He was the person who did so much regarding my visit. He is also claiming a decoration.

I have started my studies now. There are three new subjects I am studying full time, namely geography, French and cosmography which is to do with the sun, the moon and the stars.

I beg to remain Your Majesty's obedient servant,
Chakrabongse

---

1. On his way back from Thailand, Prince Chakrabongse went first to Marseilles, then to Contstantinople to visit Sultan Abdul Hamid II and finally back to Russia via the Crimea.

2. Phraya Prasit (Sa-aad Singhaseni, 1859-1931) was a royal page, then a royal guard, rising through the ranks. By 1899 he was the Siamese ambassador in London. In 1929 he was Phraya Singhaseni.

3. Thongtikayu Thongyai (Thongrod), Prince. He also studied in Russia and was later ADC to Prince Chakrabongse.

С.-Петербургъ / St. Pétersbourg

Александро-Невская Лавра. / Monastère d'Alexandro-Nevsky.

Entrance to the Alexander Nevsky Monastery c. 1900.

Prince Rangsit, shortly after he arrived from Siam.

24th October 1899

Your Majesty

On the 13th of this month, Prince Rangsit, Thongrod and Phraya Visudh arrived here from Berlin. All the Thais and I went to meet them at the station. Prince Rangsit and Thongrod are staying in the embassy. Phraya Visudh is staying in a hotel, but will probably eat and be in the embassy all the time.

I asked Captain Khrulov to take Prince Rangsit and Phraya Visudh sightseeing to various important places, there was a dinner at this palace and we went to the theatre in order to receive Phraya Visudh appropriately.

In my spare time I talked to Phraya Visudh about his trip to Thailand. It seems that he is determined to go and organise things very well. I beg to suggest that if he was head of the colleges {Minister of Military Colleges] it would be extremely good as he has really researched education to the full and is determined to do his very best. If as Minister of Education he set up a Royal Pages School as well, it would be of even greater benefit than organising ordinary schools as he is a man of great experience.

I have been to see the church of Alexander Nevsky[1]. This church is a monastery and rather like a Thai temple with priests living there. I paid a visit on the chief priest. He lives there and is a very good man. He asked me about our temples and when I told him about them, he said that it was like temples in this place. When I was leaving he gave me a picture of Alexander and a prayer book as is the custom.

In the compound there are many different buildings and in these are buried the bodies of many famous people. The body of Saint Alexander is also there, but the Thais were told not to go close.

In addition, there is a school, a hospital for the monastery and a graveyard as well.

On the 22nd, Prince Rangsit and Phraya Visudh left here for Moscow and from there will go to Berlin. In Moscow, I asked Captain Khrulov to choose a good guide to take them to the key sights.

Phraya Non has now managed to arrange things for Prince Rangsit and has found him somewhere to stay. For that reason he only stayed here for nine days. Everything went off well with no dramas.

I think of Your Majesty a great deal. Whenever I talk about Thailand, it always makes me want to go back again.

I beg to remain Your Majesty's obedient servant,
Chakrabongse

1. Alexander Nevsky Monastery is a complex of churches dating back to the city's founding with cemeteries housing the graves of some of Russia's famour figures such as Tchaikovsky, Dostoevsky and Glinka. Tsar Peter I founded the Monastery in July 1710 and it was renovated and added to over the centuries.

Excerpts from my trip to Constantinople in order to present a decoration to Sultan Abdul Hamid II

24th September. I reached Marseilles and was met by Phraya Suriya and Phraya Visudh. We decided that the best course was to go to Paris and take the Orient Express to Turkey, so we left for Paris the next day. I went to rest at the embassy with the four *mom chao* princes.

27th September. In the evening, myself, with Phraya Suriya, Phraya Mahibal and his wife, and Luang Visudh boarded the Orient Express. It stopped hardly anywhere on its way through France, Southern Germany, Austria Hungary, Serbia, Bulgaria and Turkey, allowing me a view of countries I had never seen. Austria is very beautiful and full of mountains, forests, rivers . . . . It was too dark going through Vienna which I was sad about, although I did get to stretch my legs in the station . . . We also passed through Budapest in the middle of the night. Then by morning in Belgrade, where we were the first Thais ever to reach there. The town on both sides of the Danube is no bigger than Bangkok. Here we changed trains to a small Serbian train as some tunnels had collapsed and not been repaired preventing the Express from going through . . . . after an hour we got back on the Express which was waiting at the mouth of a tunnel. Then into Bulgaria which is similar to Serbia but less mountainous... the soldiers' uniforms are very like Russian ones. . . In Sofia the ADC of the Prince of Bulgaria came to greet me and welcome us to Bulgaria and to remind me of when we met in Moscow and St. Petersburg. In fact, I had never met him so he must have confused me with Pi Chira . . .

By early morning on the 30th, we were in Turkey. When we crossed the border there was no one to meet us, but they did not know our program . . . it seemed very barren with just mountains, sand and some sparse grass. . . around 12 midday we reached Constantinople. At the station Mr Mykov, the assistant to the Russian ambassador, Colonel Sibayev, the military attaché and two naval officers came to meet us on the Russian side, while on the Turkish side was General Ahmed Ali Pasha with responsibility for foreign dignitaries . . .

From the station we went to the Russian embassy in the Sultan's carriage, where we had

Le Petit Journal
SUPPLÉMENT ILLUSTRÉ

ABDUL-HAMID KHAN
Souverain de l'Empire ottoman

lunch with the Russian officials and two Turkish officers. The Russians said they had arranged to receive me, but the Sultan refused and insisted I stay at the palace.

At 13.30 our party, except for Phraya Mahibal's wife, donned full dress uniforms to go to the palace. There was a horse guard in front and behind . . . the palace is on another hill from the Russian embassy and seemed a long way away. In front of the palace was an honour guard as well a brass band who played the royal anthem. The Sultan himself came out to meet me with high ranking officials including the foreign minister. He said he was delighted to receive me. I replied I was honoured and delighted to be able to visit . . . After introductory remarks, the Sultan invited me into a private room with Phraya Suriya Nuvat, who had Your Majesty's letter and decoration. I presented the letter . . . and then the decoration and said it was a symbol of the friendship between Turkey and Siam and also it was a thank you for receiving Prince Damrong so well. He asked about the history of the order . . . Later, I remembered it was created in the year after I was born. . . The Sultan insisted that I stay in the palace[1], so I stayed in a wing next to that of the Sultan, where Prince Damrong had stayed but since renovated for when the German Emperor visited[2].

On the first day after breakfast I strolled in the

1. Yildiz palace. Sultan Abdul Hamid moved here fearing that the Dolmabahce palace could be attacked from the sea.
2. The so-called Sale Pavilion designed to emulate a Swiss Chalet.
3. Hagia Sophia from 537-1453 AD was a Greek Orthodox. Then if became a mosque until 1931 when it was secularized.

Hagia Sophia, c. 1890-1900.

Across the Bosphorous to the Dolmabahce Palace, c. 1890-1900.

Views of Constantinople, c. 1890-1900.

The Galata Bridge in Constantinople, c. 1890-1900.

palace garden and saw the various chickens bred there. I also went to the stables and saw beautiful horses, mainly Arabs. They are not very big and are used for riding.

After lunch we went to see the Dolmabahce Palace on the river where the Sultan lived in the past ... Later he built a new palace on the hill. The carriage had to go slowly, as the road is very bad. The city is very large with many buildings and it is very lively. There are a lot of *farang* and foreign shops but the roads are narrow and dirty – worse than Bangkok ... The city is built on hills so one is always going up and down ... the palace we went to see is very beautiful with marble cladding on the walls in various patterns and furniture of the highest quality ... After this we went around the city on the Asia side as well and towards the Sea of Marmara. From here, the view is sensational as the

sea is a narrow channel with high hills on each side and many houses ... We went to two mosques. The first was being repaired. Formerly, it was a Christian church, then when the Turks came it became a mosque[3]. . . it is rather empty inside. Those who come in just sit down and pray and do nothing else. However, I did not see it when the Imam was there.

In the evening there was a full-dress banquet. Beforehand, the Sultan invited me to a private audience and the Foreign Minster brought Phraya Mahibal's wife to meet him for the first time ... The Russian ambassador[4] was also invited. At dinner at 8 pm, the Sultan sat at the head of the table with me on his right. On his left was the Russian ambassador and then the wife of Phraya Mahibal and other officials. After me, was the Viceroy then

4. Ivan Alexeevich Zinoviev was ambassador from 1897-1909.

Phraya Suriya and Phraya Mahibal. Others at the table were ministers and senior officials ... He chatted to the people on either side and was keen to behave in the *farang* way, even though you could see it wasn't that familiar for him ... He mentioned that Your Majesty had expressed regret that you had not visited during your European Tour. I replied that Your Majesty was equally disappointed and would definitely come if there was another occasion. He asked whether Your Majesty would come for the Paris exhibition. I said probably not. Then he said that he'd heard that there were a lot of Muslims in Siam, up to one million. I replied that there were a great many, but I did not know the figures and I said a lot were Thai officials. Then he said he would send his adjutant to deliver a decoration for Your Majesty. I replied that Your Majesty would be delighted to receive such a person.

Before dinner he bestowed decorations on all of us, including the wife of Phraya Mahibal. I received the Osmanieh[5] First Class with diamonds, as did Phraya Suriya but without diamonds. Phraya Mahible received the Medjidie[6] First Class, Mme Mahibal an order for Ladies of the Court Second Class, Luang Visudh Kosa, Osmanieh Fourth Class, M. Cuissard, Medjidie Fourth Class. We all expressed our deepest thanks and appreciation.

2nd October. In the morning Mr de Bunsen[7] came to see me, as arranged by telegram. He talked about Siam and asked after Your Majesty and Sadet Mother ... After lunch I went to the landing stage at the Dolmabahce Palace to go and see the palaces on the Asia side. Looking up from the sea, it was very beautiful, if small, with incredibly finely carved wood ... We also saw the pair of lions kept there.

In the Bosphorous, the water flows very fast, much more so than in Bangkok. Having returned at 4, we went to visit the Viceroy, who met us on the steps of his residence with his son. He greeted us in the Muslim way, before serving coffee and ciga-

rettes. He is very old, at least 80, and is referred to as His Highness. His son is still young and looks very intelligent. Speaking French, he acted as interpreter. We talked about the excellent reception by the Sultan and he enquired about Siam and the army....

After dinner, I had another visit to the Sultan to see a perfomance. Beforehand, in a private meeting he introduced me to four of his sons. The older one is said to be 18, but looks older. He is in the navy. The next is a cavalry officer and very smart. The third son is not very handsome, rather fat and also a cavalry officer. The fourth one is still young, around 13 or 14 – good looking, pleasant and in the navy. They all shook hands with me in the European way and seem well educated, but not speaking any foreign languages, conversation was difficult.

The theatre is in the palace and is quite private. Today it was just us Thais, the four sons and some officials. The performance was an opera called *Traviata*, one of the Sultan's favourites[8]. During the opera he chatted about this and that and asked questions such as "How long had I been in Europe? Where had I stayed? When I was in England had I seen the Queen often?" I replied that I had never met her as I was there in a private capacity. He said that in Russia I must see the Emperor often and I replied that I did. Then he asked about where I was studying and if the uniform I was wearing was my school one. ... He asked about our army and if there was a standing army and how were soldiers chosen. ... Then he praised me and said he could see I studied hard and had good manners. He said he was very well disposed towards Your Majesty and me ... He also asked how many Thai ambassadors there were in Europe and said he'd be delighted to have an embassy here ... Later he said he would give me some cigarettes and that he'd often sent some to the Emperor and asked me to tell the Emperor that he would send some more soon.

3 October. The Russian ambassador invited me to his seaside residence outside the city which is the custom here for ambassadors as the summers are so hot. ... From the Dolmabahce Palace it took about an hour by boat. On the way we passed other seaside residences and many foreign warships, including two Russian ones which had the crew lined up on deck. They blew a bugle and

5. The Order of Omanih was a military decoration of the Ottoman Empire created in 1862.

6. The Order of the Medjidie was institued in 1851.

7. Maurice William Ernest de Bunsen was Consul-General in Bangkok 1894-97, then Secretary in Constantinople 1897-1902.

8. The Sultan personally wrote the first Turkish translations of many opera classics and also composed several opera pieces, as well as hosting performances at Yildiz Palace.

The Sultan's personal steed.

Viceroy drank to the King of Siam. The performance tonight was a very funny comedy sketch.

4th October. In the morning one of the royal secretaries came to see me and brought an Arab horse, as well as two small silk carpets, one large carpet, two bolts of silk, one case of cigarettes, one case of tobacco, one large box of various sweets. Phraya Suriya and Phraya Mahibal both received two carpets each ... I asked the secretary to convey our sincere and deepest thanks.

At 11 am, we went to take our leave. The Sultan was surrounded by various officials, but it was not full dress as when we arrived. He gave us all a blessing and I said that we could not find words to express our thanks. I said I would write to Your Majesty in Bangkok and I was sure that Your Majesty would be delighted. He told me to let him know when we reached Sevastapol.

We boarded a Russian ship called Alex. It was small but clean. We stopped at the Russian ambassador's house for lunch. On the 5th by 3 pm, we were in the Crimea and at 5 pm reached Sevastopol. It is a beautiful port city. In the port were many Russian warships of the Black Sea fleet. Around 6 pm the ship docked and we were greeted by various officials. We had dinner at the station and then just after 8 pm left for St. Petersburg.

I hope Your Majesty will be satisfied with my report. If it is deficient in any way, it is because it was my first official visit and I am still young.

I beg to remain Your Majesty's obedient servant,
Chakrabongse

shouted "Hurrah" as we passed ... The ambassador introduced me to four Russian ladies, wives of embassy staff, and the wife of DeFrance who was there. She asked about Your Majesty and Sadet Mother. Then we all had lunch and after coffee and some chat, the ambassador took me to see a warship ... The ship was small – about the same size as the *Mongkut Ratchkumarn* – but with good guns and torpedoes. After the inspection, the captain took us to have champagne. The ambassador drank a toast to me and I drank one to the Emperor. Then the ambassador's steam launch took me on a tour as far as the channel leading to the Black Sea.

In the evening we went to see the Sultan again. At dinner, I drank a toast to the Sultan and the

Sevastopol station, c. 1900

29th October 1899

7th November 1899

Your Majesty

Your Majesty

Now it has been decided that Luang Abhiraksha Rachakij (Nai Nok Yoong) will go back to serve in Bangkok with Phraya Visudh, may I respectfully ask who will be coming in his place? Once he has gone, there will not be a single person who can be part of my suite on the Thai side, because Phraya Mahibal has become the ambassador. All the Russians who know that Luang Abhiraksha is leaving, have all asked who is coming in his stead. I would therefore respectfully request that an officer be sent to be my ADC, but I think he should reside in the embassy so that the Emperor does not need to bothered further. The reason that it was decided that Luang Abhiraksha should go is because he had very little to do and also tried to stop me going into the palace. Furthermore, he was better at being a teacher than anything else.

As to who is chosen, I don't think that should be a problem but don't let it be someone who is too old, because coming here will entail learning a new language, unless of course it's someone who can speak French, which would be good. I fully understand that finding a suitable person in Thailand is hard, so there is no rush, as it is not an important post. However, having someone here will be better than not having anyone.

I don't want to seem presumptious but bearing in mind Your Majesty's great generosity and the fact that Your Majesty is my father, I feel emboldened to make my wishes clear.

I am well and thinking of you always,

I beg to remain Your Majesty's obedient servant,

Chakrabongse

I received Your Majesty's letter dated 4th October, which made me very happy.

I was very saddened to learn of the problems in formal consultations with the French ambassador. It seems that they don't really want to reach an agreement and keep changing their stance and not sticking to what Doumer had said. It seems as if deFrance is jealous and doesn't want to do what Doumer has set up. Phraya Suriya had already told me some of this and how in Paris they will not agree with Doumer either.

Another thing is that I don't think the French will reduce their pressure on us at all at this time. The ministers are afraid and thinking only of their position and how everyone will say that they are weak and not strong in colonial matters. In fact, as regards colonies, the French are losing out at the moment, so to make more concessions is unlikely.

As for help from the Russians, I believe that the Emperor genuinely wants to help but Muraviev is not that convinced, being more concerned with Russian affairs. The French and the Russians are not getting on well at the moment, because the Russians did not help the French in their dispute with England over Fashoda[1]. Accordingly, the Russians are now trying to make friends with the French again and so won't want to go against them about anything,

Your Majesty's instructions that we should not discuss the proposals they have made is absolutely right. According to their proposals, we have all to lose and nothing to gain.

I think it's going to be hard to resolve this dispute with the French, because they don't really want to find a solution. They don't lose out in any way while the dispute remains unresolved. When I think about this, it makes my head spin. I don't know what to do about it. It makes me think that going in the direction of the Ministry of Defence is better than in the Ministry of Khun Naris. Strategy probably won't get any worse even if the minister is asleep.

I was delighted to learn that Sadet Mother is getting out and about and feeling better. This makes me feel much less anxious than before.

---

1. The Fashoda Incident of 1898 was the climax of imperial territorial disputes between Britain and France in Eastern Africa. A French expedition to Fashoda on the White Nile sought to gain control of the Upper Nile river basin and thereby exclude Britain from the Sudan. The two armies met on friendly terms, but in Europe it became a war scare.

Your Majesty

One other thing – regarding Phraya Visudh, whom I have praised, you may think that this is because he has praised me a lot and criticized Toonmom Toh. However, this is not the case at all. The fact that Phraya Visudh said that Toonmom Toh wasn't good in that way, I was very annoyed about. His job was to encourage Toonmom Toh in a good way and not to keep looking out for bad things to report on. If Toonmom Toh did something wrong, it was also Phraya Visudh's fault for not looking after him properly.

I have only just learnt the extent to which Phraya Visudh criticized Toonmom Toh and that he has done this behind his back rather than to his face.

I agree with Your Majesty that Phraya Visudh has not behaved according to Your Majesty's wishes.

To conclude, Phraya Visudh is not appropriate to have charge of any member of the royal family. However, in terms of education he is very knowledgeable and will execute his duties well, even if he is a little bit old.

I am thinking of Your Majesty a great deal.

I beg to remain Your Majesty's obedient servant,

Chakrabongse

I received Your Majesty's photograph and three other photographs. I think they are all very good.

I invited over Prince Ukhtomsky[1] and told him that I had received royal permission to bring a Buddha relic to present to the Russian people who are Buddhists. I asked the prince to inform the monks so they could come and collect the relic and to inform them where it should be placed.

Prince Ukhtomsky expressed his gratitude that Your Majesty has allowed the relic to brought over at the request of the Russians. He said that those who are Buddhists will undoubtedly be delighted to receive this gift. However, at the moment, none of the monks are in Petersburg and they will have to be informed by telegram, so they can come and collect the relic.

It will probably be installed in an important temple in Siberia, because that will be convenient for people coming to pay their respects either from Russia or Siberia.

The people who will come will arrange everything very well, but I think it will be quite a while before they arrive as they are coming from afar.

In the meantime, I will guard the relic here.

The Emperor will go back to Tsarskoe Selo on the 16th and I am hopeful that before too long I will be able to visit him there.

On the way back from Darmstadt, the Emperor stopped in Potsdam, where the German emperor entertained him royally. Then before returning to Russia he stopped in Poland to go hunting.

I am well and happy and thinking of Your Majesty.

I beg to remain Your Majesty's obedient servant,

Chakrabongse

Prince Esper Ukhtomsky.

1. Prince Esper Esperovich Ukhtomsky (1861-1921) was a poet, publisher and Orientalist. He was a close confidant of Tsar Nicholas II and accompanied him when Tsarevich on his Grand Tour to the East. He was a self-proclaimed Buddhist.

Legation de Siam
St Petersburg
November 27th 1899

My dear Father

On the 17th of this month, the Emperor arrived at Tsarskoe Selo back from abroad. I went down to meet him at the railway station.

The 26th being the birthday of the Empress Marie, I was invited to lunch at the Palace of Tsarskoe Selo. I went down with the other Grand Dukes and Grand Duchesses, who were also invited. When we arrived at Tsarskoe, instead of going to church like the others, I went straight to the palace and waited there.

After the religious service, Their Majesties received me separately before lunch. I gave them all Your Majesty's messages and handed the Emperor the little cup you sent for the new born Grand Duchess[1]. I also explained our custom whereby each prince or princess receives such cups a few days after their birth.

Their Majesties expressed their gratitude for the gift and said they were very touched. They both admired the enamel work very much. I also brought a gift for the Emperor of a Lao sword from Siam, which the Emperor was kind enough to accept with many words of thanks. To the Empress I presented two vases, which Her Majesty also accepted while kindly expressing her gratitude.

The Empress also asked about mother, of her health, and then I told her mother's message.

At luncheon all the Grand Dukes, Grand Duchesses and persons of the Emperor's household were invited. After lunch the Emperor had a long conversation with me. He asked about you, about my voyage and every news of Siam. He asked about Krom Damrong, Krom Prap and Admiral Richelieu.

When I asked him about the decoration, he said that the Empress will receive it with great pleasure and will be much touched by your attention to her.

His Majesty asked whether you will send the decoration afterwards or whether I have already got it here. I answered that I was ordered to inquire first because you are not sure whether she would be kind enough to receive it. The Emperor made an exclamation as if to say "Why of course she will accept it!"

The Emperor also asked me whether I have the same apartments as before in the Winter Palace, whether I am quite satisfied and if I want for anything more. I could only thank him for his kind attention.

When I mentioned to His Majesty how anxious you and mother are that both he and the Empress should pay a visit to us in Bangkok, the Emperor said "We should like to go very much but when? It is so far and takes such a long time to reach".

About two o' clock, we took leave of their Majesties and came back to Petersburg.

Phya Suriya is now staying here, waiting to have an audience with the Emperor and present his letters of recall. The Emperor mentioned to me yesterday that he will receive both Phya Suriya and Phya Mahibal in a few days.

I have received your post card sent from Ratchaburi and thank you very much for it. I should like very much to be going with you again to Ratchaburi.

Hoping you are quite well, with best love
I remain your affectionate son,
Lek

Letter opposite

1. Britian and Siam had long vied with each other for influence over the states bordering the south of Siam. In 1897, a secret convention between the two countries guaranteed the status quo. Nevertheless, problems were ongoing, with the Malay state of Perak seeking control of Raman in Yala province of Thailand.

2. The Minister Resident and Consul General at that time was George Greville.

3. Prince Henry refers to Prinz Albert Wilhelm Heinrich of Prussia (1862 -1929), younger brother of German Emperor William II and grandson of Queen Victoria. A career naval officer, he held various commands in the Imperial German Navy and eventually rose to the rank of Grand Admiral. In 1899 he was commander of the East Asiatic Squadron. It seems he was indecisive about the timing of his visit to Siam.

1. Grand Duchess Maria Nicholaievna (1899-1918) was born on 26th June. She was the third daughter of Tsar Nicholas II and Empress Alexandra.

Bannakom Soranee
9th December 1899

To my son Lek

I have received your letters dated 9th, 11th, and 24th October regarding your visit to the Sultan, which I have not yet answered. Today I received another two letters dated 29th October and 7th November. I haven't answered because it's been a bit chaotic.

I am very pleased with your trip to Turkey. Your report is excellent, there is only one mistake: *por atta jan*. Your mother said it was too formal and the word has never been used. Apart from that, whomsoever I read it to said it was perfect.

The fact that the Sultan wants his adjutant to bring me a decoration is funny in one regard, but that it has to be with Khun Suntraromlayu is very funny. He is an editor. Regarding the Muslim religion, it's a bit worrying, but the example of the ambassador from the Sultan who stayed in the east was rather effeminate and made the *farang* laugh . . . All Muslims in the end ask for money. It's really strange. I have planned to send the list [of decorations] to the Port Authority [Ministry of Foreign Affairs] to cut someone out but I fear it could be the wrong ones, so I have asked Phra Suriya to make the cuts.

I have received your telegram that the Emperor will accept the decoration. I have done the document but there is no prototype and so it will have to be like the one for the Queen of Spain. However, it isn't quite right yet. I will send it shortly. One problem is the question of Empress Marie, but, as this time they are being given separately, it should be all right to give it to the Tsarina alone.

Regarding your wish for an adjutant, I have instructed that enquiries be made. I know what kind of man Phraya Visudh is. I have been angry about the things he says twice already. He is a real show off and if you argue forcefully against him and are right, he still won't give in. The fact that he takes against people and takes umbrage is not good at all. However, once you know what someone is like, you can put up with it and just work with what you have and not complain. If one is too fussy you won't have anyone. The only unacceptable thing is swindling.

As for the French nothing seems to be better. In truth, Defrance wants things to be better than Doumer, but his manner of speaking is too much. We are open and asked for arbitration, so he refused to consult any further. This happened twice and then he offered more consultation, but nothing has improved. Just asking for this and that and posturing without seeming genuine. The consultation is just posing, with only tiny progress and we still haven't got through everything.

On the British side[1], we have managed to agree the border with Raman and Perak. They wanted to make a list of the inhabitants. On our side we have swapped and even added taxes at the end of the agreement. But whether the English will agree to this is another matter. The negotiations have been going on for ages, but the English ambassador[2] is friendly. He seems a good type and is straight talking. I am extremely pleased and feel much better. We were the ones making a fuss and in the end the British had to come and beg me to agree. I am tired but pleased to have made a fuss and succeeded.

The ministerial reshuffle seems to have had a good effect. But Prince Prachak has the fault of making trouble with everyone. It seems he doesn't like or trust anyone much, such as the investigation department which is both Thai and *farang*. Nevertheless, things are better.

Prince Henry[3] is still indecisive, but I can't change anything as it would seem rude. I will see what he's really like when he comes. The two foreign royals are coming this time for 26 days. It will make everything rather awkward. The cost of receiving them is 2,000 *chang*.

Your mother is still going to the park and is back to her old self. At the moment she's keen on tree planting in the park. It's all her ideas and I'm very pleased. If the buildings are finished, I'll send you some pictures.

I think about you a great deal. I dreamt of you once. I'm not ill though, just fine as before. This year I must say everything is much better and going along as it should. But people's laziness is a problem and everyone needs to be pushed as before.

From your most loving father,

Chulalongkorn

Grand Duke Sergei Mikhailovich, c. 1900.

1. The Mikhailovsky Artillery Academy trained officers to take the position of battery commander and serve at artillery plants and scientific institutions of artillery departments. All first-rate Russian scientists in the field of artillery and arms constructors in the 19th and early 20th centuries studied in MAA.

2. Grand Duke Michael Nikolaevich (1832-1909) was the fourth son and seventh child of Tsar Nicholas I and Charlotte of Prussia. He was the first owner of the New Michael Palace on the Palace Quay in Saint Petersburg.

3. Grand Duke Sergei Mikhailovich (1869-1918) was the fifth son and sixth child of Grand Duke Michael Nikolaievich and first cousin of Tsar Alexander III of Russia. He grew up in the Caucasus, where his father was viceroy. In 1881 the family moved to St Petersburg. He became a close friend of the then Tsarevich Nicholas. He had a long affair with Mathilde Kschessinska, former mistress of Nicholas II, recognising Mathilde's son as his own. Prince Chakrabongse also became enamoured of the ballerina over the next couple of years.

4. Grand Duke Andrei Vladimirovich (1879-1956) was a son of Grand Duke Vladimir Alexandrovich, a grandson of Emperor Alexander II and a first cousin of Nicholas II. He followed a military career and graduated from the Alexandrovskaya Military Law academy in 1905. He held various military positions during the reign of Nicholas II, but with no particular distinction.

Siamese embassy, Petersburg
10th December 1899

Your Majesty

On the 6th December, I was invited to a ball at the artillery school called the Mikhailovsky Artillery Academy[1] on the occasion of its annual fete. I arrived at around 10 pm and was invited into a room with Grand Dukes Michael Nikolaevich[2], Sergei Mikhailovich[3] and Andrei Vladimirovich[4], who were all officers of the school. All three greeted me warmly. When it was time for the dancing, I followed all the grand dukes to watch. It was a real scrum, with even the grand dukes getting pushed around and academy officials having to make a cordon around them. There were about 3,000 people there, hence the crush and it was terribly hot. After watching the dancing for a bit, we went to see the various electrical rooms. An officer explained about all the different electrical generators and took a picture of Grand Duke Michael Mikhailovich's hand using an X-ray machine. The picture was developed and the glass negative shown to him straight away. You could see the bones.

After this, the grand dukes went home. I stayed on and watched the dancing a little longer, but did not dance myself as it was so crowded and hot. After that I went and looked at the antique guns, the bedrooms and various other things. The academy is very large. There is one other ballroom. Upstairs is also spacious, but it was so crowded I couldn't get there.

The next day, the 7th, was a fete for all those who had received a decoration during fighting. Today there was a meeting of officers at the palace for those who have received the decoration and those who have the St George flag, given to those regiments which have fought well in battle.

Normally for these fetes there is a banquet for the officers and recipients of orders. However, on this occasion only the lower ranks were entertained. The banquet for the officers will be on the 10th, the fete day for the Tsarevich who died as well.

The Dowager Empress has arrived now and is at Gatchina. I have asked to see her and was told she will receive me soon, although the date is not fixed yet.

I think of Your Majesty all the time.

I beg to remain Your Majesty's obedient servant,
Chakrabongse

Winter Palace, St Petersburg
19th December 1899

Your Majesty

On the 18th, it was the Emperor's Fete. All the houses were decorated lavishly. At 8.30, I went to await him in the throne hall where he would receive guests. When he came back from church, I gave him my congratulations. I also saw the two Empresses. This was the first time I saw Empress Marie since my return. There were many other members of the imperial family who went to the church such as Grand Duke Serge and Grand Duchess Elizabeth. Empress Marie mentioned that I had requested an audience with her and said that she was pleased to see me today. She asked about affairs in Siam. I replied as Your Majesty had instructed me. She thanked me and asked after Pi Chira, as well as mentioning that Prince Valdemar was to pay a visit to Bangkok and that he was very pleased to be going there. I replied that all of us were equally delighted to receive him and were making many preparations.

Prince Valdemar of Denmark and King Chulalongkorn. It is interesting that the King chose to be photographed in exactly the same spot for both photographs.

The Emperor expressed his thanks many times that I had come to offer my congratulations and enquired after my wellbeing as usual. He said he must quickly go and put on his uniform in order to review the troops. Grand Duke Serge also asked after Siam.

On the same day there was a review of the First Regiment and there was a lavish reception in the palace for the soldiers who had been reviewed as well as members of the imperial family. The regiment in question is the Royal Guard regiment and all the members of the imperial family are in this regiment.

On the 15th, Phraya Prasit came to St. Petersburg and stayed at the embassy. Yesterday, I went for dinner there.

I saw in the telegram today that the 'indecisive one' is also visiting Bangkok. I hope that there won't be any hiccups as there were last time.

I am well and thinking of you always.

I beg to remain Your Majesty's obedient servant,
Chakrabongse

Prince Henry of Prussia and King Chulalongkorn. For some reason, the King and Prince Chakrabongse referred to him as "the indecisive one".

1900 The Crown Prince's Visits
King Umberto's Funeral
Studying Hard

1900 was to see Prince Chakrabongse well settled in St. Petersburg and receiving his brother, the Crown Prince, three times, as well as Prince Paribatra. In the summer, the Crown Prince was ill with severe appendicitis and Prince Chakrabongse went to attend him. He also represented the King at the funeral of King Umberto of Italy and later visited the Exposition Universelle in Paris. The Prince's close relationship with the Tsar and the rest of the imperial family continued and his studies went well.

The Crown Prince visited St. Petersburg three times in 1900. This photograph was taken on his second visit.

Siamese Embassy, St. Petersburg
3rd January 1900

Your Majesty

On the 29th of last month, Toonmom Toh came to visit here. I went to meet him at the station and brought him to stay at the embassy. I came to stay here too, as it was the holidays. While he was here, myself and Phraya Mahibal together looked after him and took him to see the various important sites in the city. In the evenings we took him to see plays and other things in order to provide amusement and enjoyment.

On the 1st January, there was a dinner held here on the occasion of Sadet Mother's birthday, and Toonmom Toh invited various important people such as Count Muraviev. After dinner there was a small reception to which all the people he had met were invited. Among the ambassadors were the Spanish and Brazilian ambassadors. The Spanish ambassador had met Toonmom in Madrid and had invited him to visit parliament. However, I could not remember him at all. Toonmom remembered him as a very good person and so he will be the one to send my letter to the King of Spain. He said that the 6th of this month is the Fete day of the King of Spain, and thus an appropriate time for me to write a letter. Accordingly, I will write and send my letter via the ambassador.

I have been very preoccupied arranging the program for Toonmom Toh. He has been going everywhere and I have had to accompany him at all times.

For that reason, I have hardly had time to write to Your Majesty at length. In addition, I am sure that Toonmom Toh has written to Your Majesty in detail.

I think of you always.

I beg to remain Your Majesty's obedient servant,
Chakrabongse

Letter opposite
1. Ta O was the nickname King Chulalongkorn and Chakrabongse used when talking of Alexander Olarovsky, who was appointed as Chargé d'Affaires and Consul-General of Russia to Siam on December 4th, 1897. On April 14th, 1898, the Russian Consulate-General was opened in Bangkok. Later it was upgraded into the Mission which operated till 1917. From July 1899-1909, it also took care of Danish interests in Siam.

Chakri Maha Prasat Throne Hall
12th January 1900

My dear son Lek

At the moment, I am so short of time to do my work, having both official visitors and complicated government business. It is a period when everyone is complaining and getting sick, so let me tell you how things are in stages.

1. Regarding the decoration to be given to the Empress, since I heard that she will accept it, I have had the accompanying certificate drafted, but have been hampered by the lack of a prototype and haven't been able to draft it to my satisfaction. So it's all taken rather a long time. In addition, Phra Rattana Kosa got ill with a fever in the middle. Now it is finished. I have sent it to you to present to her. Had to keep it from M. Olarovsky[1]. If he knew, he would come and take it to send himself, as he is being very frenetic at the moment.

2. This visit by Prince Henry has wiped out the anger that was there from the past. It's all gone, as he is a very pleasant man. He is high ranking and intelligent, and knows when to be grand and when not to be. He can talk seriously or joke about. All the Germans here were dancing around him like mad, but he dealt with them all. He made a fool of the German ambassador who does various stupid things, but when he needed praise he gave it, feeling sorry for him and realizing he meant well but is just slow. He did get angry one time when Phraya Cholayut made a mistake and toasted the French warships during the reception. I made him go and apologise and when he had done so, Prince Henry was in a good mood again. The fact he stayed to dinner showed we were informal together and probably will be friends in the future.

3. The visit of Prince Valdemar[2] was different. We were very informal in the past so it should have been easy, but on the contrary it was very annoying because he was rather stupid and weak and none of his people were respectful of him, so were not well organized like the Germans. Those who came with him were of three types. The first were part of the royal party. Those from the warship were slightly better as far as the adjutants were concerned, but the rest were rather poor quality officers who were somewhat coarse. Another group were traders, who had given him

spending money for the trip and were hoping to find a deal. This lot caused a lot of trouble, as they had unreasonable demands which annoyed both us and Valdemar himself. But he was so solicitous of them that it was painful to see. What has continued to be annoying is they have not left, and are waiting for the decoration to be finished. Another group were those just along for the ride, such as Blixen, the queen's nephew, a doctor and an army captain. These three were very nice and well behaved. Then the ambassador was a victim of Ta O[1] speaking rubbish which led me to say that these were not just falsehoods but complete fantasy. He tells such lies that it is incredibly annoying. Another such person is Phraya Cholayut who was also meant to receive guests. When your own people do all kinds of stupid things, it is more annoying. For all these reasons. I was much more satisfied with Prince Henry.

4. While I was looking after these royals for almost a month, the Burmese and Sri Lankans who had come to receive the Buddha relic also arrived. The Burmese are very good and worthy of admiration and pity. They didn't try to gain any advantage, but the Sri Lankans were another matter. We planned to give them three pieces but six groups came. I refused to grant them an audience and they went on and on about getting three pieces of the relic. It's all settled now, but having to receive them at the same time as the royals was not a success.

5. At this time, we are consulting regarding the agreement with the French. That is troublesome too. To try and tell you the problem is really difficult to do succinctly. Defrance has softened after we spoke conciliatory words, but there are certain things which we can't give in on. It's no different from going shopping. You let half go and then bargain about the other half. You have to act as if you're walking out of the shop and then get called back. So all in all we haven't progressed many steps, because we haven't really got

2. Prince Valdemar of Denmark (1858-1939) was the third son and youngest child of Christian IX of Denmark and his wife Louise of Hesse-Kassel. He was the younger brother of Frederik VIII of Denmark, Queen Alexandra of the United Kingdom, George I of Greece, Empress Maria Feodorovna of Russia and Crown Princess Thyra of Hanover.

down to discussions. In contrast, our talks with the British, which began later, have finished. Then there is Ta O playing a comic circus like someone who's trying to make a horse do various tricks. Things we don't say he tries to put into our mouth. Anything that is in his head just pours out of his mouth.

6. Recently the Sangkharaj[3] became ill and died last night at 2 am, so I had to come back and the opening of the railway bridge at the port is on hold.

7. Yesterday I went to see the end of the line. Left Bang Pa-In early in the morning and had something to eat at Muag Lek at 9.30. Then we got into a truck to go on. By 12.30 we had reached the end of the line north of Si Kiew village. Another 40 kilometres or 1,000 *sen* before reaching Nakhon Ratchasima. It should be finished in June including levelling the ballast. It can probably be opened in January of next year. We waited to change cars then came back down just after 1 pm reaching Muag Lek at 4.30 and had lunch at 5 pm, which was really very awkward. It was almost 9 pm before we reached Bang Pa-In. I am ill with dysentery, as have had to have so many banquets all month and having to receive the *farang* royals made it all so busy. I have hardly had a meal on my own. The other thing that complicated things was that it coincided with your mother's birthday for three days and then there was Suan Dusit also. We played from morning till night, so it took up all the time and we ate constantly. I have got over it today but still feel a bit weak.

Phraya Visudh and Luang Abhirak have arrived back, but we haven't had time to have a chat. The letter that you wrote dated 27th November was the last that arrived.

Chulalongkorn

Your Majesty

I was delighted to receive Your Majesty's letter dated 9th December.

The fact that we have reached agreement with England is excellent and I hope that it may serve as a good example to the French.

On the 10th Toonkramom Toh travelled back to England on the North Express train. His trip went smoothly in all areas and he was so happy that he said he might come again in his next holidays. I was the one who arranged his entire programme, which earned me the name "Master of Ceremonies'

The 13th was Russian New Year, which is an important holiday here. There was a big reception in the palace, with all the officials going to pay their respects, as well as the diplomatic corps. After the reception there was a family luncheon and I was invited to sit at the Imperial table.

On that day before going to see the Emperor, I went to visit the Dowager Empress in order to deliver New Year greetings, which she received graciously. But she is difficult to talk to. She asked after Toonmom Toh and talked about Prince Valdemar's trip to Bangkok. She said she had received a telegram from him that he had been very well received. Then she said that she had received a telegram from Your Majesty and that she was going to send you a photograph as a gift. I didn't quite understand why, so I didn't dare respond in any way. I didn't stay very long. Grand Duchess Olga was there too. When it was almost one o'clock, I went to await his Imperial Majesty in the dining room. Those who were waiting there with me were Princess Oldenburg[1] and the Duke of Leuchtenburg[2], who is not yet an officer and is considered somewhat junior. Princess Oldenburg asked after Your Majesty and other people with whom she was acquainted, such as Pi Chira and various other questions while we were waiting. At that time the Emperor was receiving the diplomatic corps and could not get away very easily, leading Princess Oldenburg to complain that all the ambassadors were talking too much.

3. The Sangharaja was the head of the order of Buddhist monks in Thailand. The Supreme Patriarch between 1893-1899 was Somdet Phra Ariyavangsagatayana.

22 January 1900

Your Majesty

We waited for around half an hour before the Emperor came into the dining room. He greeted me very warmly and spoke of Toonmom Toh, enquiring whether he had gone home and repeating several times: "We were very glad to receive him quite privately, you know, quite privately". The Emperor looked very tired and during the meal had to get up as if he was going to be slightly sick, but as it was in the midst of his family it didn't really matter. The Empress and female royalty were in full dress in the Russian style and looked very beautiful. The male royals wore the chain of St Andrew and were also all in full dress. Empress Marie did not attend, which must mean that she is still in mourning. Neither was Grand Duchess Xenia there, as she is pregnant again so soon after her last child.

The Emperor, Empress and Empress Marie are presently all staying in Petersburg.

During this winter there will be balls and meetings in the palace as always.

I am well and happy and thinking of Your Majesty constantly.

I beg to remain Your Majesty's obedient servant,

Chakrabongse

On the 17th of this month the Russians who are Buddhists came to see me to receive the relic, which Your Majesty so graciously gave me to bring to them. Prince Ukhtomsky was the one who got the group of 20 together and brought them along. The group included four priests and a young girl who at the moment is studying in a school in Petersburg. The monks were Lamas or Tartars, and collectively are known as Buryat[1]. There were also two Kalmyks, who came from European Russia. All were wearing full dress in their traditional style and wanted to have a large ceremony which was as follows:

When I went into the room where they were gathered, they brought a piece of dark cloth to present to me as last time and thanked me for helping them who are subjects of the white. They said that by asking you for the relic, I had done everything and that the Thai monarch was very kind and once he knew that they wanted a relic he had asked me to bring it. They took turns to come and *wai* me with their hands above their head. Once the ceremony was over, they presented me with a white cloth as another thank you.

The interpreter for all this was a Tartar, who is a Buddhist and is studying medicine in Petersburg.

I could see from their beaming faces that they were truly delighted. Prince Ukhtomsky said that throughout Siberia everyone was very happy. All of them expressed their thanks to Your Majesty and their pleasure in also having a head of state who is a king with the same religion who has been so kind to them. At that point I presented the relic to the senior monk who wrapped it in many silk cloths and then more cloths were wrapped by everyone and they said prayers in their language relating to the Chai yantoh section. After this, all the Buddhists present came to have a look.

Opposite

1. Princess Eugenia Maximilianovna of Leuchtenberg 1845-1925) was a daughter of Maximilian de Beauharnais, 3rd Duke of Leuchtenberg and his wife Grand Duchess Maria Nikolaevna of Russia. She grew up in Russia. In 1868, she married her distant cousin, Duke Alexander Petrovich of Oldenburg. The couple had an only child, Duke Peter Alexandrovich of Oldenburg.

2. Alexander Georgievich, 7th Duke of Leuchtenberg (1881-1942), also known as Prince Alexander Georgievich Romanovsky, was the only son of George Maximilianovich, 6th Duke of Leuchtenberg by his first wife Duchess Therese of Oldenburg.

1. The Buryat are the northernmost of the major Mongol peoples, living south and east of Lake Baikal. By the Treaty of Nerchinsk (1689) their land was ceded by China to the Russian Empire. They are related by language, history and habitat to various Mongol groups and the Kalmyks, who together form the principal Mongol peoples. The Buryat are among the smaller of these groups.

I am very pleased that I could accomplish this presentation and feel certain that it is a very meritorious act.

At the moment, the Duke of Coburg Gotha is staying in Petersburg on a private visit, as a guest of the Emperor. He is staying in the palace. The Duchess has not come too, which is very unusual as she is the daughter of Emperor Alexander II of Russia.

Now I have started my studies again, as it is the end of the winter holidays.

I beg to remain Your Majesty's obedient servant,
Chakrabongse

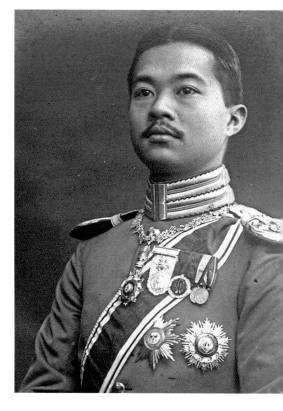

Prince Paribatra, referred to by Prince Chakrabongse as Toonmom Chai.

Winter palace
6th February 1900

Your Majesty

On the 29th of last month, I went shooting again as before. I left here in the afternoon of the 28th and went to Krasnoe Selo by train and from there took a carriage to Gochovo where we stayed the night. Early in the morning on the 19th, we went out shooting. The weather that day was very good and not too cold, nor too hot, causing the snow to melt. We went by sledge until almost at the spot, whereupon we walked through the forest. Snow had fallen snow on snow, making it very deep. It was hard going and a bit like wading through mud, although perhaps not quite so bad as snow is not as liquid as mud. It is more like sand, but not as hard so maybe somewhere between the two. In order to walk easily, you have to have planks of wood on your feet[1]. They are about 25 cm wide by 100-150 cms long. On top there is loop to insert your foot and hold it in place. However, walking on these planks is not that easy. One step sends you sliding quite far, but if you don't know how to do it, you can fall over because of a lack of balance.

This was the first time I had tried the planks, so fell over many times. However, it doesn't hurt and the soft snow breaks the fall. I managed to shoot three rabbits and the others shot both rabbits and birds, bagging about 20 rabbits in total. This is considered very little, as they used to get many more in the past.

On the 9th, Toonmom Chai will come here. I am very pleased that I will be able to see him, but I am sad that he is coming when I have classes and so I cannot make all the arrangements and look after him myself. I can only help in a small way. He will stay at the embassy, and on Saturday and Sunday I will be able to go and see him all day.

At the moment, the school is waiting for the Emperor to come and visit us, as it is the time when he usually does so. I am sure that he will come this week.

I beg to remain Your Majesty's obedient servant,
Chakrabongse

---

1. Clearly Prince Chakrabongse is referring to some type of skis.

Siamese Embassy, Petersburg
20th February 1900

Your Majesty

I received your letter dated 12th January and was very pleased. I had already thought that welcoming two European royals one after the other would cause you a lot of trouble and be very busy. I am very sorry to hear that you have been unwell, but I hope that by now you have recovered.

The decoration to be presented to the Empress has not yet arrived, only the two certificates. I am concerned that the decoration will not arrive before the Emperor leaves for the Crimea, which is scheduled for this spring.

He will probably stay on in Petersburg these next two weeks in order to observe the penances during the first two weeks of Lent before going to Tsarskoe Selo where he will remain until spring when he goes to the Crimea.

Yesterday, both the Emperor and Empress came to the Corps des Pages. I was at the school on that day and carried out rifle drill for them, together with the other students in class 7 where I am now. However, the Emperor pretended not to notice me, just as he does when the grand dukes are on parade and he pays them no special attention. The Empress smiled at me, but she was discreet, as she didn't want people to see. Yesterday it was desperately cold and it snowed as well, so the Emperor issued an instruction forbidding the cadets from running behind the imperial carriage to the Winter Palace as they usually do. Even so, when he left everyone hoorayed like mad. Before the Emperor left, he congratulated everyone and said we should all have a three-day holiday. Of course, everyone was delighted and shouted "Hooray, hooray!"

Regarding Ta O, I feel very irritated because on the whole Russians are very polite, more so than others, but those who are sent to Thailand are of a poor calibre and more like Americans than Russians. It may make our people get the wrong impression and make the British and other races in Bangkok laugh at them. People here have also said that someone like O cannot be a good man, as he has only ever been a consul, and then suddenly to be made ambassador. Muraviev has been severely criticized for choosing such a person. I am of the opinion that he should be changed. We could quite easily say, without annoying the Russians, that we love Russia very much and know what a great country it is and thus it is sad to see that the representative in Bangkok is someone who is most unsuitable and unlike most other Russians. Recently I saw in the newspaper that O is now on holiday and should be leaving fairly soon.

Recently, I have heard the news that Grand Duchess Olga is ill with cysts in her throat. This is a serious illness and very contagious. The Dowager Empress has not gone anywhere at all and, indeed, is so worried about giving it to someone else that she did not even attend the christening of the son of Grand Duchess Xenia. Now I hear that she has just gone to Gatchina, together with Grand Duchess Olga so she must be a little better.

This year has been unusual in that Empress Marie has allowed her daughter-in-law to attend functions alone and in full regalia, whereas she has kept very quiet. Even at the girls schools, it has been the Empress who has presided and not the Dowager Empress. I have even heard that she has said various items of jewellery which are crown property but which Empress Marie has been wearing, should be given to her daughter-in-law, whereas in the past she always kept them for herself.

The more I have got to know the two Empresses, the more different they appear. The Empress is much nicer than the Dowager in many ways and even the Russians are starting to feel this too.

I beg to remain Your Majesty's obedient servant,

Chakrabongse

Siamese Embassy, Petersburg
25th February 1900

Your Majesty

On the 21st, I received a letter from King Alfonso of Spain via the Spanish ambassador, together with his photograph. The letter was in answer to mine which I had sent already at the beginning of January, as I informed Your Majesty in some earlier letters. I have made a copy of his letter and am enclosing it to you.

I had written to him asking for a photograph. So it seems this is why he was slow to reply. I can see that he is much grown – he is taller and his face has changed. All in all, he has become a young man.

I have learnt that yesterday the Emperor went to the cadet school for a second time. Everyone there was very pleased, because last year he did not go. When he left, they all ran after his carriage with some climbing on, which being a sledge not a carriage was easy to board. This caused the Emperor's uniform to rip in several places. He awarded a holiday to last right to the end of Carnival, that period of festivities which takes place just before Lent. So we get four days' holiday in addition to Carnival. Adding the two chunks together, we get a whole week, which is really good as far as the cadets are concerned.

Nowadays, the weather here is better. It is much colder and the sun is shining which makes it much easier to breathe freely. When I can't see the sun, I don't feel well at all, it feels very claustrophobic.

I beg to remain Your Majesty's obedient servant,
Chakrabongse

Looking down Nevsky Prospekt, c. 1900s.

26th February 1900

Dear Lek

M. Olarovsky will leave Bangkok tomorrow and he said he could take things, so I have given him this letter and your mother has given him a book and some buttons.

I have received your letter dated 17th January and all four letters from January. In fact the 'hesitant one' only had one click [unclear]. But the fact that Phraya Cholayut made a toast to the French warships, which had come too, among the group of army officers was quite wrong. I have made him apologize, so it is all fine now to the extent of going to see them and saying thank you very politely. In summary, it seems that he asked to withdraw his words in calling him 'the hesitant one'. He has excused himself for the fact that he did not come last time, over 10 times. He swore that he really intended to come. The brother of this person is intelligent and mature. He knows how to behave, but when he jokes around, he makes a bit of a fool of himself. If one compares him with all the other European royals, he seems superior to the Crown Prince of Sweden and is at Emperor level. The only problem is he's stayed in China a long time (I thought this myself as he didn't show any signs) and seems to see the East as a bad place. Talking about Europe, he criticises some strange places such as Belgium and Osaka. It's as we see it and we say the same things about China, but that Valdemar of yours, or should I say Chira's, is really too much. He's very stupid and has a whole bunch of traders with him, who destroy his dignity to the extent that Chira won't accompany him anywhere. I was going to tell you about it in detail, but got a letter from Toh, so I have told the story once already and to tell it again … there are better things to do. Pi Chira should have taken some part in all this. Phraya Cholayut wanted to show off that he had an important position. Ramasoon to your Lek, so he's the most important person in Bangkok. It really gets on my nerves, but it also makes me laugh every day, so it is quite fun. I'm sorry I can't tell you everything, but, suffice to say, we're dealing with both of them. It's normal that Henry should see the country as rather weak.

Blessings on you for receiving our Tsarevich so well in Petersburg. Toh seemed really happy with it all.

As for the relic given to the Buddhists, that's very good. I concocted a news report for the Royal Gazette based on your letter. The Burmese and Ceylonese who came to receive it were very happy. One can certainly say that all this has increased our standing, even though as a result the Ceylonese had not even had time to get excited, before some others wanted some more and paid back everything they owed. . . . It wasted a lot of time and paper, so I stopped it and so the whole thing went away. I did not see Chao Phraya Pas collecting all the money, which he was going to pay because I know that he ordered the second level.

He who is bearing this letter wanted me to send a letter to the Emperor, but I thought this was such a piece of evidence that I delayed it. I hope you will know this from the letter to Phraya Mahibal.

I will go and stay at Dusit Park for the first time on the first of next month, but only for three days. In the middle of the month, there will be a merit-making session and the inauguration of the *bai sema*[1] at Wat Benjamabophit in the grounds of Dusit Park. At the moment, malaria is very prevalent, but I haven't been ill. However, one can say that about 50% of everyone has it. I think about you a lot.

Chulalongkorn

---

1. These are the boundary stones installed around the ordination hall (ubosot) within a Buddhist temple. Without these markers, new monks cannot be ordained.

5th March 1900

Your Majesty

On 26th February, I was invited to have lunch with the Emperor. Phraya Mahibal and Captain Khrulov were invited in their capacity as my guardians. Those who sat at the table, apart from that, were all officials and only Princess Hohenlohe, the daughter of the Duke of Coburg, was another royal.

The lunch was a private affair, just as on every Sunday after church. After lunch, the Emperor spoke to me at great length. He began by saying how sorry he was that lately he had hardly had an opportunity to meet with me, because he had had so many official engagements. In addition, the Duke of Coburg[1] had come to stay, which had added to his duties. Also, there had been frequent dances and other festivities in the palace, which had taken up a lot of time.

After that he said how he had seen me at the Corps and praised me for my rifle practice. He asked about various classmates, and said that next year I would enter the special class, and after a year or so would be appointed a Kammer Page (Page of the Chamber). I thought this was a good opportunity to say that various members of the Imperial family had asked me whose page I would be, as when you are a Kammer Page, everyone is assigned to be a permanent page to one royal or another, from the Dowager Empress and Empress downwards. As for me, some people were wondering whose page I would be, given that I was a member of a royal family myself. The Emperor replied that if I studied hard and came top of the class, I would be able to be the page to the Empress or Dowager Empress for sure.

Then he asked me whether, when I became an officer, I was thinking of the cavalry or infantry. I replied that if possible I would like to be a cavalry officer, because infantry officers have to march a lot and for a long time and it seems too tiring. The Emperor replied that for himself he was good at marching and said he found it less tiring than riding.

So I added that amongst my elder and younger brothers, who were studying in the army, no one was planning to be a cavalry officer and that that was another reason why I wanted to be in the cavalry.

During the conversation, someone else came to come and talk to him about something or other, so he talked to him for a while and then resumed talking to me, asking me whether Your Majesty was well, and that he had heard news of the reception of Prince Valdemar in Thailand. He said it looked extremely grand. I replied that Your Majesty had been determined to receive him in the best way possible and I also took the opportunity to tell him about the royal decoration which will be presented to the Empress. I informed him that the declaration had arrived, while the decoration itself had not, but that when it did I would immediately present it. I said that it took a long time to arrive, as it was such a long way.

These are all the important points that arose in the conversation the Emperor had with me today. Otherwise, there were just small inconsequential things of no importance.

I beg to remain Your Majesty's obedient servant,
Chakrabongse

1. Duke of Coburg Gotha. Alfred Ernest Albert (6 August 1844-30 July 1900) reigned as Duke of Saxe-Coburg and Gotha from 1893. He was unhappily married to Grand Duchess Maria Alexandrovna. Their only son attempted suicide in 1899 and died two weeks later.

Winter Palace, Petersburg
19th March 1900

Your Majesty

On the 13th, Toonkramom Chai left Petersburg for Berlin. I together with the Siamese officials here went to see him off at the station. Luang Visudh is accompanying him as far as Berlin.

On the 12th, the annual celebrations at the Corps des Pages were held. In truth, the 11th is the correct day but this year it is being held on the 12th in order to coincide with a Sunday. The celebrations include prayers in the chapel attached to the school and a reception for all the cadets and officers who once studied there and who come back to visit on that day. During the lunch there were toasts to the Emperor, the Empress, the Dowager Empress and the imperial family. These were followed by toasts to the cadets and the director. After the banquet, the festivites were over. I also took part in the day.

Yesterday, that is to say on the 18th, I received a visit from Adjutant General Espinosa and another adjutant of the Queen Mother of Spain, who was in his position when you went to Spain. He has recently arrived in Petersburg in order to look into cannons. He has already been to Berlin and then is going onto Vienna and Paris.

The general inquired as Your Majesty's health and asked for news of all the royal family and officials who accompanied you on your trip to Madrid.

I asked after the Queen Mother and the King of Spain, so he told me that when he left to go on this research trip and mentioned he was coming to Petersburg, the King of Spain exclaimed, "Oh! You will see my friend there", and so they realised that the two of them could come and see me here. The King of Spain told them to pass on his compliments to me.

While we were chatting, we both recalled Your Majesty's trip to Spain and the reception you received.

The King of Spain with his mother Queen Maria Christina.

The general asked about my studies and asked me to tell him all about them, as when he returned home the king would certainly ask him. I told him briefly about my studies and what I plan to do in the future. The general said that I am a favourite of the Emperor saying "I hear the Emperor has a fancy for you."

Today I went to call on them both and leave my card in return.

I beg to remain Your Majesty's obedient servant,
Chakrabongse

Opposite: The Warsaw station, St. Petersburg.

Letter Opposite
1. Libau is a port in present-day Latvia. From there the Dowager Empress would take a boat to Denmark.

Palais d' Hiver
March 26th 1900

My dear Father

On the 24th inst. the Empress Marie left Petersburg for Copenhagen via Libau[1]. I went to see her off at the station. There were a few Grand Dukes and only one Grand Duchess at the station. The Empress Marie arrived at the station with the Emperor, Empress and other children of the Empress Mother.

The latter said a few words with me. She asked me whether I was quite well and getting on well and after my having replied in the affirmative, remarked "you look blooming!" This raised a general laughter.

After the train had move off, the Emperor and Empress returned to the Palace after having hurriedly shaken hands with some of the officials who had come also to the station.

Yesterday I was invited to lunch with their Majesties. The luncheon was of the same kind as the last one that I attended about a month ago. At table, the Emperor introduced me to Countess Strogonoff, Lady Chamberlain of the Empress Dowager, who happened to sit between His Majesty and myself. The countess asked the Emperor whether I could speak Russian, to which His Majesty answered, "Oh yes! He speaks excellently." After that I noticed that while I was speaking with Countess Strogonoff, the Emperor listened to our conversation.

After lunch the Emperor conversed with me but on general subjects of no importance. He asked me once however "Do you receive letters from your father or not?", with an emphasis on the last two words. I answered His Majesty that I receive news now and then. The Empress also said a few words with me. She asked whether I received good news from home and said she thought I did very well in the gun exercises when Their Majesties visited our Corps.

I have heard that the Emperor and Empress intend to go to Moscow for Easter, that is to say in about three weeks time. They will spend about a fortnight in the old capital and will then return to Tsarskoe Selo.

The Emperor remarked in his conversation that Petersburg is not Russia, it is a cosmopolitan town and that he wants to be in real Russia during Easter. Toonkramom Toh will arrive here on the 25th. At first he thought of arriving today, but for some reason or other has postponed his departure till today instead of the 24th. Of course, we are all looking forward to his visit with joy.

Hoping you are quite well.

With best love

I remain your affectionate son,

Lek

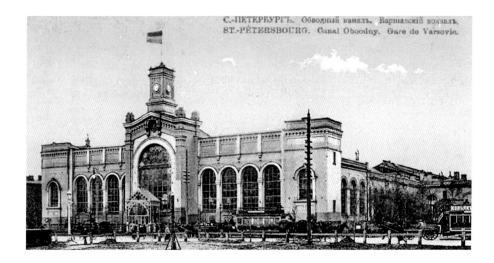

С.-ПЕТЕРБУРГЪ. Обводный каналъ. Варшавскій вокзалъ.
ST.-PÉTERSBOURG. Canal Oboodny. Gare de Varsovie.

Siamese embassy, Petersburg
3rd April 1900

Your Majesty

On 31st March, the Emperor invited Toonmom Toh and myself to have lunch in the palace. Toonkramom Toh and I went to wait at the appointed time. Apart from us, there were two Grand Dukes also waiting to see him. They were about to go to Italy and had come to say goodbye. They both asked me to introduce them to Toonmom Toh and, while we were waiting, we chatted about various things such as the war between England and the Transvaal[1]. The Emperor and Empress came out together and, after greeting us, invited us into the dining room. At the table, he asked Toonmom Toh to sit on the right of the Empress and to the left of one of the Grand Dukes. Then came the Emperor and I was on his left. During lunch he chatted in a very intimate way and it was very jolly. However, nothing of import was discussed, apart from the war, which I mentioned earlier. When this matter was discussed, the Emperor turned to me and said, "I suppose you have different opinions on this subject", implying that I think differently from Toonmom Toh. And he added that it was strange that so many soldiers had died in this conflict on the British side, adding that the British soldiers must not be brave enough to follow their officers, while the officers were too brave and attacked too strongly.

I noticed that he was very much on the side of the Transvaal, while the Grand Dukes were very direct and criticised the English a lot. I am always being asked which side I support and, when I say I am on the side of the Transvaal, they seem very pleased. One of the Grand Dukes asked me which side the Siamese supported. I answered that I had no idea and I believed that no one was very interested in the war there. Here, in comparison, there is no one who is not on the side of the Transvaal and everyone gives the war a lot of attention. In all, I have never heard the

Prince Chakrabongse and Crown Prince Maha Vajiravudh photographed in St. Petersburg in 1900.

Russians speak about politics as much as in this case. Everyone talks about it and criticises the English. In truth, on the entire continent there is no one on the British side, because in this instance they are really wrong, and aggravated them for no reason.

When lunch was finished, we had coffee and tea and chatted for another 15 minutes or so.

In the afternoon, I went and signed the book of congratulations for Grand Duke Constantine[2] who has recently been appointed as Chief of All Military Colleges. In fact he can be seen as my boss. The position of overseeing military education is very important because he is in charge of all such schools throughout the whole Russian empire.

1. The Second Boer War, otherwise known as the Second Anglo-Boer War or the South African War, between Great Britain and the Transvaal Republic and the Orange Free state started on 11 October 1899 and ended on 31 May 1902. The war ended in victory for the British and the annexation of both republics. Both would eventually be incorporated into the Union of South Africa in 1910. Russia took a close interest in the war and hoped that Britain would be defeated. Russian volunteers even went to fight for the Boers.

2. Grand Duke Constantine (Konstantin) Constantinovich (Konstantinovich) (1858-1915) was a grandson of Emperor Nicholas I of Russia, a soldier and a poet and playwright. He was both a patron of Russian art and an artist. A talented pianist, the Grand Duke was Chairman of the Russian Musical Society, and was a friend of Tchaikovsky. He was close to both Alexander III and Nicholas II. He was Chief of All Military Colleges. He and his wife were among the relatively few Romanovs who were close to Nicholas II and the Empress Alexandra.

On the 1st April, both of us went to listen to a concert at the opera. The brass bands of all the regiments came to play together as one large band. There were more than 1,000, which was very impressive. There was another group, also soldiers, who played the balalaika. The balalaika is a genuinely Russian instrument not found elsewhere. When it is played *en masse* it is very beautiful, and some church choirs also sang. They sang without accompaniment, but they did it very well and sounded like an orchestra. Once the concert was over, the audience could also sing. They sang the national anthem as the Emperor and Empress were also there. When the anthem was finished, there was a lot of hooraying and clapping. It was a demonstration of their love for the Emperor and his Empress, and was very striking and moving. Almost all the Grand Dukes were in attendance. All those who came were staying in Petersburg or nearby. This concert is extremmly important. It is an annual event to which everyone wears full dress uniform. The money raised goes to injured and retired soldiers.

Today there was a huge event at the Corps des Pages, because Grand Duke Konstantin, the new Chief of All Military Colleges, came to inspect the school for the first time in an official capacity. I was called to be in the receiving line. At first we stood in line on the veranda outside the classrooms. The pages stood in the classrooms and groups. The Grand Duke arrived and greeted the pages and inspected everywhere. When he reached the son of Count Keller, the director of the Corps, he clapped him on the shoulder and smiled to Count Keller as if to say, "I know you're the director's son". When he came to me, he cried out "Wow" and came and clapped me on the shoulder as well, asking me whether I could now speak Russian fluently. After inspecting the reception line, he went into the classrooms. All the pages went down to the bedrooms to await him. All the boarders changed from their full dress uniform into everyday wear and stood waiting for him by their beds. Those who were day boys formed up into a separate line. Once he had inspected the classrooms, he came to the dormitories and the bathrooms and went on to look at other things. All the pages who were not boarders were allowed to go home, but the other group stayed for dinner, after which he left. He gave a holiday for

Grand Duke Constantine Constantinovich, Chief of All Military Colleges.

the cadets until the morning of the 5th and that is why I am at the embassy.

This Grand Duke is one of the best. He is very hard working, very knowledgeable and intelligent, and for this reason has been given such an important job. I went to pay my respects recently, and he always talks to me in a very friendly way.

I am delighted that Your Majesty is pleased that I have presented the Buddha relic to the Russian Buddhists. My sole aim is that more people may become aware of Your Majesty's honourable deeds.

The idea that Prince Valdemar is something to do with me, I must protest about. I had nothing to do with it and all the credit should go to Pi Chira. Nevertheless, he seems very happy because the Emperor and Empress Marie are always saying that he was so well received and happy with his trip.

As for M. Olarovsky, I am sorry to say that that is to do with me, but I really do want a change.

I beg to remain Your Majesty's obedient servant,
Chakrabongse

Winter Palace, St. Petersburg
16th April 1900

Your Majesty

On the 12th, Toonkramom Toh and I received the telegram informing us of the death of Toonkramom Aa Phra Ong Yai[1], which surprised both of us and made us very sad. His illness is also rather alarming. I am anxious that his death will have made you exceptionally sad and may even make you unwell. It came very suddenly with the illness progressing rapidly, which will make the sorrow felt even greater.

Over the past two weeks, I have accompanied Toonkramom Toh to various sites in St. Petersburg and the vicinity, many of which I had not seen before.

1. On the 2nd, we went to visit the military prison in Petersburg[2]. When we first went in, the head of the prison came out to greet us and read a report to Toonmom Toh as is customary. It seems that there are 777/999 inmates in the prison, divided into those who are healthy and those who are ill. Some of the latter are in the prison hospital and others in outside hospitals. Those who are fit are divided into two groups. The first have severe sentences, are in solitary confinement, and have to work in their rooms, apart from when allowed out for exercise. The second group is allowed to be together in a particular place for work until they go back in their rooms.

First, we inspected the cruciform building where they are housed, with the small lines indicating the doors of the cells. The reason the building has this shape is to reduce the number of wardens. Thus, one man can see the doors of every cell. Apart from these doors, there is no other way of escaping.

The building has three storeys. The top floor has openwork walkways so that warden standing below can see up to the top as well. Thus, despite several floors, only one warden is needed. The stairs are in the middle and there are no other ways up.

1. Toonkramom Phra Ong Yai refers to Prince Chaturonrasmi, the Prince of Chakkrabatradipongse (1856-1900), who was a full brother of the King, and died on 11th April.

2. Designed by Antony Tomishko, the name Kresty Prison was derived from its cruciform shape. Such a layout made observation easy and it was hoped the religious significance would encourage penance among the prisoners. Construction finished in 1890. At that time it was considered the most advanced prison in the world.

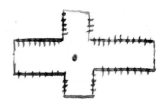

The cells are very well appointed but have no windows, apart from a small opening about 15 cm wide by 25 centimetres high to provide fresh air and light. The metal door also has an opening, so, if these apertures are open, fresh air can circulate at all times and the air inside does not become fetid. The door also has a larger opening for the warden to look through. The bed folds up against the wall and needs a key to unlock and unfold it for sleeping. This is to stop the prisoners lying down to drink their tea and not do any work. Only at bedtime is the bed released. Washing materials and other personal utensils are all provided and, though it is indelicate to mention it, the toilet box is also in the room. However, it is clean and with running water which stops it being disgusting. Most of the prisoners spin cotton or weave cloth, the latter being used to make their own clothes. They make enough so that none have to be bought. Apart from this there is a group of typesetters, with the printworks being next to the prison. All the workers are prisoners. After visiting the prison, we went to see the fan-shaped area set aside for exercise. Only one person is allowed per section and they cannot see each other as there are walls in between. The small lines represent the doors and the warden stands on the dot so as to see everyone inside each small segment.

Those who have to exercise in this way are those with heavy sentences. Those with lighter sentences are allowed to walk in single file around the perimeter of a playing field. After this we saw the bathing area and the hospital, where there were quite a lot of patients. During the visit, the prison governor took care of us and explained everything. He could speak English and so could explain things to Toonmom Toh, which made everything easier. Apart from this, we saw the laundry and the kitchens, which are staffed entirely by prisoners. Before we left, the prison governor gave us both a book on the prison.

2. On the 7th, we went to see the Deaf-Mute School[3]. I had been there once already, but not in term time unlike on this occasion. The director

received us warmly and took us to tour the school, which caters for both women and men, living in separate quarters; we started with the women.

First, we saw the women being taught to speak. It seemed very difficult. The young people could not hear anything, so when they were teaching them to make various sounds, they had to tell them how to shape their mouth, where to place their tongue, and how much breath to use on the first syllable. When we spoke, they could understand only if they saw our lips moving and guessed according to the sense. It seemed they could understand quite well, but speaking caused them a lot of difficulty and they could hardly do it. Apart from teaching the girls to speak and to read, they are taught to weave, to sew and other feminine skills. The boys are also taught to speak, as well as carpentry, ironwork and welding. Their products are quite good. There is also a printworks, where they do typesetting. One of the boys could speak really quite well and clearly. The sleeping quarters are upstairs and similar to school dormitories, namely they all sleep together with the beds arranged in two long rows. The dining room is on the ground floor next to the kitchen. The children are divided into two groups, whether boys or girls – those that are taught to speak and those that are not. Those who can't make certain sounds learn sign language instead, so they can study other subjects. I saw one pupil tell another what to write and the other wrote it very well. At the end of our tour, the director gave us tea in his room before leaving.

3. On the 11th, we went to the Pulkovo Observatory[4] near Gatchina, the home of the Dowager Empress. We left here in the evening for Gatchina by train and then took a car from Gatchina to the observatory. The director came to meet us and take us round. We looked through a large telescope and saw the moon, Venus and other planets and stars. We also took a photograph of the moon. The telescope itself is truly amazing and one sees so clearly and easily. There are many different telescopes for looking at the

A 30-inch refractor telescope was installed in 1885

stars. Once we had seen everything we went to the director's room. On the way back, we took the train from Tsarskoe Selo and got back to Petersburg around midnight.

4. The next day on the 12th in the morning, we went to see a school for training soldiers to ride really well and so train others. The director and officers of the school received us very well. First we saw the officers training on their horses and jumping practice. Then we saw the soldiers practising jumping on and off their horses to make them more nimble. After that, we saw soldiers riding horses brought from abroad in order to train them and then went to the manege and the study rooms. The classes here are only about horses. In this building there was a mess for the officers, where they relax and dine. Before leaving we went to see the privates practising sword fighting.

In this school, the officers come from various cavalry regiments to train in riding and teaching as well as everything to do with horses. They stay for two years before going back to their companies, where they are then able to teach others. Privates can also come here, but train separately from the officers.

That's all regarding what we've been to see.

On the 13th, Toonmom Toh and I went to the station to send off the Tsar and Tsarina, who were going to Moscow. The Tsar spoke to us and asked about my exams and said he was going to Moscow for two and a half weeks.

I am well and think about Your Majesty always.

I beg to remain Your Majesty's obedient servant,
Chakrabongse

3. From 1820, the Deaf-Mute School was at 18/54 Gorokhovaya Street. 1896-1901 the director was A. F. Ostrogradsky. In 1900 at the Paris Universal Exhibition the school received an honorary diploma for quality education.

4. Originally opened in 1839 under German/Russian astronomer Friedrich Georg Wilhelm von Struve. Oskar Backlung, a Swedish/Russian astronomer was director during the visit of the two Siamese princes visited.

Easter procession, c.1901-03

Siamese Legation, Petersburg
24th April 1900

Your Majesty

On the 17th in the early evening, Toonkramom Toh left Petersburg for London. We all went to see him off at the station.

The 17th saw the beginning of my Easter holidays and that is why I am staying at the legation.

On the 21st at midnight or early on the morning of the 22nd, using Western dating, everywhere here was decorated with lights and flags, as it is considered the moment when Jesus ascended into heaven. In the churches, there were prayers from 11 pm onwards. At exactly midnight, cannon were fired and all the priests came out to walk once around the church. Then they went back in to continue their service. I went and observed outside a church which was thronged with people both inside and out. The procession was similar to Chinese priests doing the *kong tek*[1]. Once the prayers are said, everyone kisses each other three times and expresses their delight in Christ's ascension. First, one says "Christ has risen!" and then the other says "Yes, truly, Christ has risen!". The kissing and exclaiming is done again when they meet the next day.

The decorations with lights are rather good this year and certainly better than any I have seen before. Although the arches have nothing more than the insignia of the Emperor and the two Empresses done in lights, the effect is impressive.

The next day I went to sign my name at various residences of the nobility who were in town, as well as visiting those with whom I am acquainted, as is the custom. This year I did not have to go to many places,

as the Emperor and two Empresses are not here and so neither are many members of the imperial family. Originally, the Dowager Empress was meant to be here, but she has stayed on in Denmark.

I sent a congratulatory telegram to the Emperor and the Dowager Empress and other important nobles, and received friendly ones in reply. I included the Empress in my telegram to the Emperor.

At the moment, there is a rumour here that the Emperor will write to Queen Victoria and the President of the South African Republic[2], asking both to cease fighting. I do not know how true this but it seems very plausible, although I don't know when this might be. If it were true, it would be excellent, as the fighting has gone on for a long time and it has caused the currency in Europe to fall greatly which has even affected the paper money here, while in England it is very hard to find large sums of capital.

As for Lord Roberts[3], there has been a letter to England, accusing the various English generals. They have all behaved outrageously. The only one who understands is Lord Roberts. However, by going to the capital of the Orange Free State for many months, he has not gone on further. I think that the English would be pleased to stop fighting, but it might look as if they have lost, so having someone ask them to stop would make it easier for the British monarchy.

I beg to remain Your Majesty's obedient servant,

Chakrabongse

1. *Kong tek* is a Chinese funerary ritual usually held about 7 weeks after the person's death. Paper replicas of valuable belongings are burnt, so the deceased can use them in their next life.

2. Paul Kruger (1825-1904).

3. Field Marshal Frederick Sleigh Roberts (1832-1914) was one of the most successful commanders of 19th century serving in India, Abysinnia and the Second Anglo-Afghan War before the Second Boer War.

The Winter Palace, Petersburg
30th April 1900

Your Majesty

I will be studying now from today onwards, but only for around 10 days before having a break because exams will start in the middle of May.

Yesterday I went to participate in the wedding of Captain Liharef and Saburof at a church that is in the Engineering School. I have known both the bride and groom since last year. Captain Liharef is in the same cavalry regiment as Captain Khrulov, my guardian. On the bride's side, her father is in charge of the Emperor's personal land holdings. The invitation stated we should arrive at 1 pm, but we had to wait for the bride for a long time. Once she had arrived and the register had been signed as is customary, the wedding began. With Your Majesty's permission, I will give an abbreviated description of the ceremony.

The groom and bride stood next to each other in front of the altar and then someone gave each of them a candle. Once these had been lit, the cross was brought for them to kiss, after which the priest said some prayers and asked them if they were certain that they wanted to get married. Having answered in the affirmative, he asked God to protect this man and this woman who are going to live together henceforth. Then he gave each of them a ring. After they had put on the rings, he asked them to stand on a special cloth and hold hands, before he made some sort of invocation which was the actual wedding ceremony. He went on for a short while and brought crowns for both of them. Then both the bride and groom kissed the picture of Jesus on the crowns. The priest held both crowns above the heads of the bride and groom. Then two of the friends of the couple came and held the crowns above the two of them, before they were replaced by another couple of friends from both the bride and groom's side, and so on. It is difficult to know how to translate this accurately into Thai. In Russian it is known as "Shaffer". Both sides ask their friends to come and perform this role at their wedding. Here, the bride had asked me to be one of her *shaffers* and so I was the first one to receive the crown. However, I did not have to hold it very long before someone came to take over. The crown is rather heavy and had to be held up high, as the bride was quite tall.

All the while the priest continued his incantations and also asked them to drink from the same cup. Then, when the prayers were finished, the priest led the bridal pair around the church three times, with those holding the crowns following on behind. Once the third round was completed, the couple are considered to be man and wife and cannot be separated, whereas before that time they can be. After the actual marriage service, there were some more prayers giving thanks to god and then the church part was over. The newly weds went out to receive good wishes in another large room, where champagne was served to them and their helpers. Everyone raised their glasses to wish them well and then people left the Engineering school and some went home. Most were invited to the house of the bride's parents and I was part of this group. During the meal there were more toasts to the newly weds. After this we went to see them off at the station, from where they were going to the country. And that concluded the wedding.

This is the first time I witnessed a wedding here and it seemed a very fine and fancy affair.

The weather here at the moment is not good at all, with cold weather followed by hot. In the sun it is very hot while in the shade it is cold. It often rains and sometimes there is snow, making it easy to catch a cold. There are very few women who are not unwell. There is a saying that sick people often die at this time.

I am well and thing about Your Majesty all the time without exception,

I beg to remain Your Majesty's obedient servant,
Chakrabongse

The Siamese Embassy, St. Petersburg
15th May 1900

Your Majesty

On 13th April, Olarovsky came to see me wearing full dress and the Crown of Siam sash. He looked very grand. He came bearing Your Majesty's letter dated 26th February. I am delighted by its contents and am grateful for Your Majesty's graciousness.

Mr. Olarovsky arrived many days ago now, but has been extremely unwell with a swollen liver because of the cold weather. He is only just recovered and, having risen from his sickbed on the 12th, he came to see me the very next day which was very kind of him. We chatted about the news in Bangkok and he told me that he had been to see Count Muraviev and Count Lamsdorf[1] in the Ministry of Foreign Affairs, but had not yet been to have an audience with the Emperor. He said that he was going to return to Bangkok soon because it was so cold here. He plans to go back around November.

I noticed that this time Mr. Olarovsky looked more presentable, but his face was thin and he looked ill. When he talked to me, he was not showing off very much. However, maybe that's just with me and he is still showing off with others.

On the 7th, the Emperor and Empress returned from Moscow. I went to meet them at the railway station. At the station the Dowager Empress, Grand Dukes and Grand Duchess Olga were also there to receive them. The Dowager Empress talked to me and also enquired after Toonmom Toh.

When the Emperor and Empress arrived, the Empress thanked me for sending her a telegram on her name day, namely the 6th.

From the station, the Emperor and Empress went to review the troops stationed in Petersburg, a major review which occurs annually in this month. The Dowager Empress did not attend, only the Grand Duke[2], who is the heir, and Grand Duchess Olga.

I went from the station to observe the review which was in a raised area at the edge of the park known as the Summer Gardens. The soldiers were lined up outside the Winter Palace and along the road as far as the large field on the east side of the park. A pavilion was constructed for the Emperor and the spectators were behind that. In front of the pavilion,

Alexander Olarovsky photographed in 1894.

the artillery soldiers formed their columns and in front of the Winter Palace were the cavalry.

The Emperor was on horseback, while the Empress was in a carriage with Grand Duchess Olga. They reviewed all the columns, beginning with the cavalry in front of the palace. At this time I could not see the inspection. Later after the inspection of the cavalry was completed, he came to review the artillery and gunners on the large field. At that point, I could see clearly. When the Emperor got close, the soldiers presented arms, the bugles played the imperial anthem and lowered the standards of each regiment in salute. The Emperor talked to every regiment and the soldiers responded vigourously, while constantly shouting "Hurrah!" Once he had inspected every column, the Empress came to the pavilion and got down from her carriage. At that point, she realized that I was there and asked me to come into the pavilion too. Meanwhile, the Emperor came and positioned himself in front of the pavilion. When he was ready the soldiers marched past to present themselves. The

1. Count Vladimir Nikolayevich Lamsdorf (1845-1907) was foreign minister between 1900-06.

2. Grand Duke Michael Alexandrovich. He was Heir Presumptive until the birth of Grand Duke Alexei in 1904.

3. The open area in front of the Grand Palace, Bangkok.

More than 27,000 men assembled for the annual military review. (Photograph by Pasetti from Burton Holmes' Travelogue to St Petersburg Moscow and the Trans-Siberian Railway).

various military cadets came first, gathered into one regiment of such cadets, then came the foot soldiers and the artillery cadets, with the artillery and gunners. Next came the cavalry cadets and the cavalry regiments and, finally, the mounted gunners. Once every regiment had passed, the Emperor thanked the soldiers and they replied "We are happy to salute your Majesty as one!"

After the march past, the cavalry regiments formed up in lines in front of the pavilion and then went to the far end of the field (which is about the same size as Sanam Luang[2]). Once they were ready, they charged at high speed, as they would do when fighting and stopped just in front of the Emperor. It was both impressive and frightening. Once they had come to a halt, they saluted for the last time and all the bugles played the imperial anthem. It was very stirring. The Emperor thanked everyone again and the response was very rousing.

At the end, the company commanders all came to present themselves to the Emperor, and the soldiers of each unit came to make a report of every company of which the Emperor is commander. An officer and a non-commissioned officer from the cavalry regiment of which he is the commander, also gave a report.

Once the review was over, the Emperor and Empress went to dine at the Prince of Oldenburg's palace, next to the parade ground. I was invited also. Those attending were only members of the imperial family. Afterwards, the Emperor and Empress went to Tsarskoe Selo and will stay there for the time being.

At the moment, I have begun my exams and will probably finish at the beginning of June. Once I have finished, I think I will go to Peterhof and then to some other cities.

I beg to remain Your Majesty's obedient servant,
Chakrabongse

The Siamese Legation, St Petersburg
28th May 1900

Your Majesty

I have presented the most illustrious Order of the Maha Chakri to the Empress, according to Your Majesty's instruction together with the two letters expressing Your Majesty's friendship towards the Emperor and the Empress.

I have been waiting for a long time, ever since these royal letters arrived, but the decorations themselves did not come until just the 25th. I had an opportunity to call on the Empress on the 24th and so told her everything that had been going on. I asked whether I could have an audience to present the decoration, as now I knew that it had arrived, could she please set a date for the presentation. The Emperor said it would be the 27th.

On the appointed day, I went by train to Tsarskoe Selo and went to wait at the Small Palace, where the Emperor is staying at the moment. The Emperor and Empress were in church, because that day was by chance the anniversary of his coronation. Once they had returned, I had an audience with the Empress. I presented the royal letters together with the decoration. The Empress declared that she was very touched and asked me to thank Your Majesty so much. Then when she opened the box and saw the order, she exclaimed that it was exquisite and wonderfully made. After that, the Emperor came and gave me an audience. I presented Your Majesty's letter and he praised the decoration saying that it was very beautiful. He said that the chain was similar to the one he had received from Your Majesty's hand during Your Majesty's visit when Your Majesty had taken it off from Your Majesty's neck to give to him. I informed His Majesty that the decoration was the same order.

On that day, the Emperor held a private lunch for his close officials. There were four members of the imperial family. I was honoured to sit at the same table. Once the lunch was over, he chatted with the officials for a while and left. He asked me about my exams and whether I would stay on in Peterhof, and in the same house, as well as other incidental remarks. The Empress asked in detail as to how the decoration should be worn.

I had thought that the presentation of the decoration should be low key, because I agree with you that neither the Emperor nor the Empress are keen on large formal ceremonies. If I had asked for such a thing, it would have been an imposition. I do hope Your Majesty will approve of the way I have handled it.

On the 17th, it was the Emperor's birthday. He invited me down to Tsarskoe Selo, so I could deliver my congratulatory wishes. I went down early in the morning and went to wait at the Large Palace while the Emperor and members of the Imperial family were in church. When they came to have a rest and a snack before going in to the ceremony, I was able to convey my congratulations. The other royals also came to rest. Then the Emperor and Empress granted an audience to the officials who were gathered to present their birthday wishes. Only senior officials were there, together with those delegated by the regiments of which the Emperor is commanding officer. Afterwards there was a large banquet in full dress, during which there were many congratulatory toasts. After lunch the Emperor and both Empresses greeted and chatted with the officials for around 30 minutes and then left.

On the 24th, there was the launch of a new warship at the Admiralty Shipyard. Grand Duke Alexis, who has overall command of the navy, invited me to come along. At 5 pm the Emperor and both Empresses arrived at the naval dockyard. Grand Duke Alexis and other royals and officials received him. Once he had inspected the honour guard and the regiment, only recently created on the 17th, the Emperor went into the docks and went on board the ship. He hammered in a tenon, affixed an icon and the plaque with the ship's name as part of the ceremony for beginning the building of that ship. He also asked the two Empresses, Grand Duke Alexis and Grand Duchess Olga to hammer in nails. The overseer of the naval yard and the person in charge of building also hammered some. After this he inspected the boat, which was to be launched, named "Aurora". Once he had inspected everything, he went to sit in the pavilion at the river's edge and instructed the workers to launch the ship. The ship entered the water in magnificent fashion with no hiccups. When she hit the water, spray went up and it looked most impressive. At that moment, the imperial anthem struck up, the warships fired a salute and everyone who was there took off their hats and offered a prayer in blessing for the ship. After the ceremony, the Emperor and the imperial family went into a small steamer and went to the Baltic shipyard[2], which is on the gulf near the sea. Here he hammered in the tenon for another new warship which he named "Imperator Alexander III".

The Emperor requested that Empress Marie install the icon and the nameplate. Here another warship was also launched, named the "Chaiya Chumna". There was a similar ceremony as before. After that he went by steamer to an older warship, which had just returned from the east. He inspected it thoroughly before getting back in the steamship and traveling to the landing stage of Grand Duke Alexis. Here he sat at table with members of the royal family and senior officials. The Grand Duke was entertaining him as a thank you. After lunch he came

out to greet people in the garden and that was the end of the festivities. I accompanied their Imperial Majesties throughout the day.

At the moment, I have exams all the time. It is very hot and all the leaves have come out, making everything look beautiful and joyful.

On the 27th, Olarovsky brought M. Barbrov who is to be the new secretary in Bangkok to meet me. He seems very well behaved and polite. He can talk English, but not very well as probably he has not had much practice. He asked a lot about Bangkok and says he's going to learn Thai. Olarovsky says he will return in October and has speeded his departure up, because he cannot stand the cold. It is a bit strange that he still has not been to pay his respects to the Emperor. He also said the Emperor must be very keen to see him.

I beg to remain Your Majesty's obedient servant,
Chakrabongse

Aurora in 1903.

Baltic Shipyard.

Imperator Alexander III.

Russian Naval Power in the 1900s

1. Russia's large-scale military development program of the 1880s and 1890s made it the world's third-largest naval power after Britain and France.

The cruiser *Aurora* was laid on 23 May 1897 and launched on May 11. She served in the Far East between 1902-1906, but is most famous for participating in the October 1917 revolution.

2. The Baltic Shipyard was founded in 1856 by St. Petersburg merchant M. Carr and the Scotsman M. L. MacPherson. In 1874 it was sold to Prince Ochtomski. The Baltic Shipyard made a huge contribution to Russian naval development, and it was here that the largest and most powerful battleships of the time, including the Victory-class cruisers, were built. It is situated on Vasilievsky island and is still active today.

3. *Imperator Alexander III*. The design of the Borodino class was derived from the French-designed battleship *Tsesarevich*. The ship was completed just before the start of the Russo-Japanese War in February 1904 and was sent to the Far East to break the blockade of Port Arthur. En route, her destination was changed to Vladivostok. During the Battle of Tsushima in May 1905, the ship was sunk with the loss of all her crew.

Randolph Hotel, Oxford
7th June 1900

Dear Father

On the 1st in the morning, I received a telegram from Phraya Prasit[1] with the news that Toonmom Toh was ill with peretiflitis and had been operated on successfully. I was very shocked, as I thought it must be something serious but was not sure what it was exactly. So I had to get Captain Khrulov to write to the doctors and find out what it was. The doctor explained that it was caused by a swollen caecum, the junction between the small and large intestine. The doctor said this small pouch serves no purpose. Its inflammation is a dangerous condition, but if it is operated on straight away it is not critical at all. However, if not operated in time, it can cause death. Having heard this I was even more upset, although I felt slightly better knowing that he had been operated on at once. That afternoon by chance the Emperor's personal physician, Dr. Hirsch[2], came to the embassy and explained all the details of this illness to me. It was as the doctor in England had described, as I am sure you already know.

So the next day when I had finished my last exam, I, together with Phraya Mahibal, decided to go to England as we felt that being closer was better for sure, even if we might be of little use. In this way we could observe his condition more closely and immediately, which would make us feel better and at least help us, if no one else. Then in the early evening of the 2nd, myself, Phraya Mahibal and his wife left Petersburg by train straight for London. Early on the 4th, we reached the border and had a brief rest. I wrote a letter informing the Emperor as to why I had had to leave for England and apologizing for not calling on him beforehand. Today I received his reply by telegram which I have copied to you below.

I wrote to the Emperor in Russian but I have sent you a translation.

1. Phraya Prasit refers here to M. R. Siddhi Suthat, ADC to the Crown Prince. It is confusing as the ambassador in London was also Phraya Prasit.

2. Dr. Gustave Reinhold Hirsch was in fact the personal physician to the Tsarina. He died in 1907.

3. Toonmom Toh had gone up to Oxford in 1899 to study law and history at Christ Church but his illness prevented him from graduating.

At 11 pm on the third day, the train reached Berlin. We had a short rest. Toonmom Chai came to see us and I learnt that Phraya Non had also gone to England.

The next day we crossed the Channel from Ostend to Dover very easily and reached London just after 7 pm. During the day I decided that I would stay in London that night because if I left for Oxford, it would only cause inconvenience, as I would not arrive until after 11 pm. Then when it was dinner time, Phraya Prasit sent a telegram saying we should stay in London and that Luang Sorasit would come up to London first. So we sat waiting for news from the latter, while at the same time having decided we would go down to Oxford[3] early the next day.

When Luang Sorasit arrived at the embassy, he said that the doctor requested that I stay in London, because he could not allow me to visit Toonmom Toh. He said that his patient was at a critical juncture where he could either get better or decline again, as his scar was still fresh and needs to be drained through a rubber tube. Accordingly, he needs to be still both in body and mind, with no excitement of any kind. Any kind of movement or pressure could cause the drainage pipe to pierce his intestine. The doctor has forbidden anyone to visit, apart from those who have been in attendance already. No one is to encourage him to speak and should spend as little time with him as possible. As for seeing me, I might be the worst thing, as he would be too excited. Phraya Prasit had countered by saying that if I couldn't see him, surely I could stay in his residence. To which the doctor said "No", as he might hear me or whatever. All this has made me miss him and want to see him even more than before. I said that I didn't know what to do. The doctor replied that I should believe him. To contradict him does not seem right, as all I want is for Toonmom Toh to get better. If going to see him would make him worse or even endanger him, I don't think I should go. However, I have refused to stay in London and insisted on going down to Oxford. If I can't see him, so be it, but let me hear the news and let me be as close to him as possible. So the doctor

RANDOLPH HOTEL, OXFORD.   TELEPHONE 290.

allowed me to go down, but forbade me from going to his residence or for anyone to tell him that I had arrived. On the 5th in the afternoon, I went down to Oxford. Phraya Prasit met me at the station and brought me to this hotel. Listening to his health report, it seemed as if he was getting better as I am sure you have heard from other quarters.

On the 6th, yesterday, Dr Manson, Toonmom Toh's personal physician, came to see me and explained why he had forbidden me from seeing Toonmom Toh. In this regard, everyone seems a bit scared that I might be stubborn and not do as I was told. I asked Dr Manson whether this illness could recur as the caesum has not been removed, although surely normally it was. The doctor explained that it was generally removed if the illness was not that advanced, but when it was acute, as in this case, and was septic, it could not be removed. However, it would not reoccur as the caesum would wither away when the abscess burst. Hearing this I was reassured, as I had been worried that it might happen again. To be operated on two or three times would be difficult.[4]

The doctor said that quite soon Toonmom Toh will be much better and, when it is certain there is no danger, I can see him and stay at his residence.

Toonmom Toh's illness has been really frightening. Being such a long way away, I am sure that it must have made Your Majesy very anxious.

I beg to remain Your Majesty's obedient servant,
Chakrabongse

PS The letter to the Emperor I have sent to you in translation, whereas his telegram to me was in English.

My letter to His Majesty the Emperor of Russia:

Your Imperial Majesty
Having received the sudden news of my brother's illness, I am obliged to leave for England today after the end of the examinations.

I humbly beg your Imperial Majesty to kindly pardon me for not having gone to take leave of you personally.
Your Imperial Majesty's Most faithful
Page Chakrabongse

This letter was written according to the Russian military form.

Telegram from His Majesty the Emperor of Russia to me, received 7th of June:

Hope your brother better, thanks for letter before you left.

Nicholas

4. In fact it did reoccur. Crown prince (later King) Maha Vajiravudh had to be operated on again and the condition caused him much pain and discomfort throughout his life.

Cartrev, Oxford
21st June 1900

Your Majesty

After informing Your Majesty in my last letter that initially the doctor would not let me see Toonmom Toh, on the 11th he finally agreed that I could see him for the first time. I noticed that his face looked well and unaltered, but that he had lost weight. On that day, I moved to stay at his residence and have seen him every day and had long chats to stop him being bored. From that day on, his health has improved rapidly every day, to the extent that he can now come downstairs and go out in the garden for long periods of time. When he comes downstairs, someone has to carry him which is rather awkward. The first time he was carried down, he wasn't very happy because he didn't know the person, but afterwards, when he had carried him down a few times, he was fine about it. He reminisced to me about the people who carry the royal palanquin in Bangkok and said that if he had some people like that carrying him, he would be much happier. During this time, many people have come to see him, such as Mr and Mrs Verney. Yesterday was the first time that he went out in the park in a wheelchair with an attendant, as well as me and a nurse. My job was to chat with him, while the nurse was there to keep watchful eye. Today, we were to go out again, but, unfortunately, it has rained all day. Tomorrow, the doctor has said he can come out in the car.

In truth, Toonmom Toh has recovered very quickly when compared with other people. It is planned that around the beginning of next month, he can move from Oxford. We are thinking that he should go to the seaside, so he can breathe the sea air and regain his strength.

While staying in England, I have gone up to London sometimes to see my other brothers. Now I have seen everyone, except Prince Dilok. Prince Vudijaya and Prince Suriyong came up to see me in London on the 9th and 11th. I went to see Somdet Chai and Pi Purachatra at Harrow, and after that met with Pi Pen, when Somdet Chai and Pi Purachatra also came up to London.

I am very pleased to be with my brothers, as we have not seen each other for two years.

I have decided to stay on with Toonmom Toh as long as possible, because I think it will make him feel happier. I think about Your Majesty such a lot in this time of difficulty. I imagine how upsetting it must be for Your Majesty to be so far away and the news received must seem insufficient and not like seeing things personally. Toonmom Toh has said that as soon as he can write a letter, he will do so at once to reassure Your Majesty.

I beg to remain Your Majesty's obedient servant,
Chakrabongse

Letter opposite
1. See box.
2. Extra territorial subjects. Refers to the system whereby those who declared themselves to be under British or French rule or citizenship, for example, were not subject to the laws of Siam.
3. Jek. Slang for Chinese. Equivalent to Chink.
4. Mystery words which have not yet been deciphered.
5. This refers to Empress Dowager Cixi (1835-1908).
6. Today called Sriracha.
7. Mae Klang. Queen Savang Vadhana.
8. Rachanat. Refers to Rachanattayanuhan (Phas Bunnag), one of the royal secretaries.

Bannakom Soranee Throne Hall
28th June 1900

To my son Lek

I haven't written to you for a long time. If I were to answer you letter by letter, it would take a long time, so I'm just going to write whatever I can think of and they'll probably be new thoughts, which may well be better than answering your letters directly.

Let me talk about the Transvaal, about which you told the Emperor, you suspected people weren't very interested in Bangkok. That is mainly true, but those of us who like to read have been interested in the matter. We have had to study it, because in the past we haven't paid much attention to Africa. If I were to ask two or three people their opinion, they would answer unanimously that they are on the side of the Transvaal, that they want them to win, but don't think they will. They also hope that gold won't be found in Thailand. We don't want it. So you could say that our views are not any different from Russia's. What is true, is that however interested we are, we do not give it the same importance as the events which have arisen in China[1]. Both men and women talk about this all the time and people feel sorry that the *farang* are treating them very badly. Partly they are thinking about our country, while another part is to do with fearing that if China fell more under the influence of the *farang*, we would suffer negative consequences with more extra territorial subjects[2]. On the other hand, however, they cry out "Jek"[3]. We have a lot and people are frightened they will copy them and become Boxers as has been the case here when asking about the Kimtung language. It is understood, they are the same lot as the Kimtung which are known as Kiwliwsamka[4]. No one dislikes the Chinese Empress[5] more than your mother, but at the same time she is angry with the *farang* who are exploiting them to such an extent. We are anxious that China may fall into a major revolt.

My trip to the seaside this time was no fun at all as it was so hot. There was not even the hint of a breeze. But no day was as bad as the last day. I got back to Bangkok and my stomach was bad, but I'd agreed to go to Sri Maha Racha[6] to see Mae Klang[7]. I felt terrible. I went there at 10 am, then at 11 am Rachanat[8] sent a telegram saying that Toh was ill.

Events in China 1899-1900

This refers to the Boxer Rebellion, a violent anti-foreign and anti-Christian uprising that took place in China between 1899 and 1901. It was initiated by the Militia United in Righteousness (Yihetuan), known in English as the "Boxers", and was motivated by nationalist sentiments and opposition to imperialist expansion and Christian missionary activity. Boxer bands were active in the countryside around the capital Beijing.

In early June 1900, an international relief force of some 2,100 men was dispatched from the northern port of Tianjin to Beijing. On June 13th, the empress dowager ordered imperial forces to block the advance of the foreign troops, and the small relief column was turned back. In Beijing the Boxers burned churches and foreign residences, and killed suspected Chinese Christians on sight. On June 17th the foreign powers seized the Dagu forts on the coast in order to restore access from Beijing to Tianjin. The next day the empress dowager ordered that all foreigners be killed. The German minister was murdered, and the other foreign ministers and their families and staff, together with hundreds of Chinese Christians, were besieged in their legation quarters and in the Roman Catholic cathedral in Beijing.

Imperial viceroys in the central Yangtze River (Chang Jiang) valley and in South China ignored government orders and suppressed anti-foreign outbreaks. Meanwhile, the foreign powers assembled an international force of 19,000 to relieve the capital and rescue the Christians besieged there. It was not until September 1901, however, that a Protocal was signed ending the hostilities and determining reparations.

Above: Dowager Empress Cixi (1835-1908).

The worse thing was that only half was translated, with the first half saying he was ill but stable, while the untranscribed bit was not clear as to how bad it was until I got hold of Doctor Reytter[9] to explain things. However, I was still anxious because the day of the operation was 30th June [day of Queen Sunanta's death] and so I could not relax until I had been to Koh Sichang and returned to Bangkok, which I did not reach until 9 pm. I wanted to arrive earlier so I could send another telegram, but the drunken captain put the boat on the Bar[10] and it was clear it couldn't be shifted. The admiral, who had not seen the sea for 30 years, had the nerve to insist that in half an hour we would get off (in fact, the boat was stuck for another two days and only got off by having a steamer pull us). I wouldn't listen and got in the rowing boat to go to the boat Murta at Deep Hole. Getting onto that boat was also hard with high steps and strong waves. The women had to be lifted on board, I almost died. Then, when half way back, I began worrying that the train, which I'd sent a telegram to come and meet us, would have stopped as it was too late. But thank goodness, Phraya Bumreupakdi (Jerm)[11] went down to await us. Krom Naret had thought to cancel it. We got to the train at 2 am and got back to Bangkok at 3 am. Imagine how difficult this has all been. It was lucky that Krom Luang[11] sent a telegram to await me at Paknam, saying that he'd been operated on and was out of danger. This made me feel a lot better.

As to your wanting to be a cavalry officer, it seems as if the Emperor wants you to be an infantryman. Your mother is rather afraid of the cavalry, because falling off is so painful, but all this is up to the Emperor.

For the person who will join you, I have come up with two. Originally I chose Nai Cheon[13], who is a lieutenant. He is the son of Phraya Phitakphutorn, an old family like that of Phraya Mahibal. Chira is full of praise for him and said he came top in his class. He is 26, but doesn't know any foreign languages.

However, Phraya Mahibal wants it to be a mature person, so I chose another, namely Luang Sorasakdi Prasit. He is someone from the school as well and once took the payroll to the army when they were still in Luang Prabang. He received a medal for dealing with the Haw[14]. He is the son of Phra Saton and grandson of Chao Phraya Phuttarapai, another old family. But he is married and is 29 years old. Chira

says both of them are better than Luang Sorasit. The only problem again is he doesn't speak a foreign language. If one wants a better mature person, there is Luang Pittayut (Mom Ratchawongse Chai), the son of Mom Chao Klang but he is an important officer in the school. Another possibility is Phra Rittichak, but he is an old type of soldier who has not gone through the officer school. In which case, it could be Phraya Ratchawallop as he is a royal bodyguard and has a civilian job to do. So I think that the two I have mentioned could be possible. The reason I haven't sent them yet, is that I am waiting for the ambassador who will change with Phraya Non, as the two who don't have any language skills cannot travel alone.

As for the house, I have been able to buy only one large plot. The smaller plots won't agree a price, as they are trying to cheat by being too expensive, as they are excited. So I've decided to leave it for now, as I don't think anyone else will buy it and, when things calm down, I'll be able to.

I went and stayed in Dusit Park for a while and it seemed rather comfortable, but at the moment it's been raining a lot, so staying in the palace is better. I planned to take some photos to show you the changes, but as I see it all the time it doesn't seem that different. So I am waiting until it's dramatically different to send them. The teak trees I planted are more than 8 sok high and are shooting up really fast, almost a sok a month.

The discussions with the French haven't had any results, as they intended to stop and use it as an excuse. After the exhibition, I don't know about consultations and an agreement. They shouldn't have ceased, as we were almost in agreement. I'll write about this to the Emperor and send you a copy.

You have probably met with Nai Busmahindra, who has gone abroad to be in a lakhon [play]. This is a major thing which almost didn't come off, but seeing that his heart is like Phra Lor, who agrees to leave his position and sacrifice everything, Ta O organised things and has been so forceful that the Emperor said that they must find a theatre for the show.

The Nakhon Ratchasima railway line will be open for freight in October. I had thought that it would open as far as Khorat, but, as October still isn't a suitable time, I think it should be delayed until November. Many people are saying that going as far as Khorat will be a mistake and much worse than

*King Chulalongkorn at the opening ceremony of the
Khorat station in December 1900.*

Jaggards, Corsham, Wilts
29th June 1900

Your Majesty

Since I wrote to Your Majesty last, Toonmom Toh is
very much better. He has been coming downstairs
every day and also is fully dressed. He has been practising walking again. At first it seemed rather hard
and he had to have someone supporting him, but ever
since it has got better and better in stages, until now
he can let go and has even tried going upstairs. He
thumped about a bit and had to stop half way up.

On the 24th, he came downstairs and dined with
all of us for the first time, while in the afternoon he
always goes out for a drive, unless it is raining.

On the 25th, I went up to London to meet with
some old friends and relax a bit. Pi Pen is also in
London at this time.

Mr and Mrs Fuller asked me to stay with them in
Corsham. Mrs Fuller is the second daughter of
Mr Phipps, with whom I stayed three years ago. She
married Mr Fuller when I first went to Russia. Mr
Fuller is an important person in the district and
people love and respect him very much, so he is
thinking of standing as an MP. In England they are
going to change their members of parliament very
shortly, and have what is known as a general election.
It will be next month.

I came down here on the 26th and it is very
comfortable, as both husband and wife have received
me very well and in a relaxed manner. This evening,
I have to go back up to London because Mr and Mrs
Verney have invited me to dinner. Tomorrow I will
come back down again as Mr and Mrs Fuller have
invited me until the 30th.

I beg to remain Your Majesty's obedient servant,

Chakrabongse

everyone has said. It's arranged that in January we can
organise cremations at Wat Bavornsathan[15]. However,
the monks have abandoned it ages ago and no one
believes it will happen, so that I am also somewhat
disbelieving.

I hope that this letter will arrive punctually, while
you are still in England and that you are well and
happy. I feel I would rather like to see the
Exposition[16], but I'm feeling a bit chagrined with
Paris, as it was so entertaining last time that I almost
died and they forced us to go so many places, that I
might as well have given up sleeping altogether.

This year there is a lot of rain in Bangkok. I think
we'll be richer than last year.

Siamindra[17]

9. Dr E. Reytter, physician to His Majesty the King of Siam, was
Belgian. Born in 1860, he was educated at Brussels University,
graduating in 1885. Practice in Brussels was followed by service
as a military surgeon. In 1886 he received an appointment in the
Congo State, and was Chief Government Surgeon until 1895,
when he moved to Siam.

10. This refers to the sand bar at the mouth of the river upon
which many ships had got stuck. It was one of the reasons for
the importance of Koh Si Chang, where heavy boats were off
loaded.

11. Jerm Amatykul.

12. Krom Luang refers to HRH Prince Devawongse Vorapakarn
(1858-1923). He was a half-brother of the King and full brother
to Queen Saovabha. He was Minister of Foreign affairs for 38
years and one of the most influential figures in Siam.

13. Choen Pakdikun.

14. This refers to the so-called Haw wars in which the Siamese
attempted to suppress the Chinese "flag gangs", which in the late
19th century were ravaging large areas of northern Laos.

15. The King decreed that a *meru* should be built in the grounds
of the temple for a series of royal cremations to be held in
January and February 1901.

16. The Exposition Universelle, which Prince Chakrabongse was
to visit that summer.

17. *Siamindra*, meaning King of Siam, was how the King signed
letters when he had dictated rather than written them himself.

Grand Hotel, Broadstairs
5th July 1900

The Grand Hotel, situated on a precipitous chalk cliff above the beach at Broadstairs.

Your Majesty

Last month Mr and Mrs Werr invited me to a dinner party at their home, so I came up to town from Corsham on the afternoon of that day. Dinner was at 8 o' clock. Mr Verney has only just recovered from an illness and is not fully better, because two or three days ago he fell off his bicycle. He had to have stitches to many cuts on his face, and, on his ankle there was a very deep cut, so he can't walk properly. By the time of the dinner, the cuts on his face had healed, but his foot was still painful and he walked with difficulty.

For the dinner, he invited some friends as well as the deputy Japanese ambassador. He also invited the Chinese ambassador, who at first said he could come and then later something happened, which meant he would have to go to China and he had to cancel various European meetings and go into hiding and not appear. The dinner was a private affair and passed off well. Those whom I had known from the past, were Mr and Mrs Karnack and Mrs Hume. Apart from that, there were the other Thai guests.

On the next day, the 29th, I went back down to Corsham to Mr and Mrs Fuller. Then in the afternoon of that day, I said goodbye to the Fullers and returned to London and decided to stay there until Toonkramom Toh came up from Oxford. While I was in London, I went to see various things which made me happy as I was on holiday.

Then on the 3rd in the afternoon, Toonmom Toh came from Oxford. I could see that he seemed much better and he walked well, if rather slowly. He had to stay at Bailey's Hotel because they had a room on the ground floor, so no stairs were involved. If he had gone to the embassy, he would have had to go up many flights of stairs, as the lowest bedrooms are on the third floor as Your Majesty knows.

On that evening, Mr and Mrs Karnack invited me to dinner at the Windsor Hotel in London. After dinner they took me to a play called "*School for Scandal*" at the Haymarket. The play is an old one and shows very well how English people lived some 100 years or so ago. It's also very amusing. The costumes are of the period and were very sumptuous. Mr and Mrs Karnack were very polite and praised Your Majesty and our country extensively. They talked about the treasury and also that I was great and so forth as is customary. They also talked a lot about Suan Dusit.

The next day, on the 4th, Toonmom Toh came to this town and all of us came down too. He chose this hotel and it seems clean and comfortable. This is a small town standing on a hill, which falls in a cliff to the sea. It is very steep. The hotel is very close to the sea, but very high up. There is hardly any beach, as at high tide the water covers it completely and when the tide goes out, it is rocky. The sand is rather black. The doctor thinks he should stay here for around three weeks, so that the sea air will restore his strength and energy. In fact he is much stronger already and can walk well, he just can't run about because if he fell over it could be very dangerous.

I feel well and the sea air will probably also be good for me, as I notice that I can eat more than before. Normally, I eat a lot and sleep a lot, but here I yawn and feel sleepier than usual.

I am thinking of Your Majesty all the time and remember when I went to visit Your Majesty last year, as the 1st marked exactly a year since that time.

I beg to remain Your Majesty's obedient servant,
Chakrabongse

17th July 1900

Your Majesty

On the 11th of this month, I went up to London in the morning. When I arrived, Toonmom Chai had come to meet me at the station, which made me very surprised, as I did not know that he had already arrived in London, but rather thought that he was about to arrive. I understand that he only arrived in London from Germany that very day.

That evening Phraya Prasit organised a dinner in my honour to celebrate the one year anniversary of my commision into the Royal Guards regiment. He invited all the officers who were studying in England. During dinner, he asked everyone to propose a toast and after that there were many speeches. All the officers were in full dress uniform and it looked a very grand affair.

The next day, the 12th, in the afternoon, I accompanied Toonmom Chai back down to this town. Staying here is really rather comfortable, but there is nothing much to do, apart from playing various games. I am not so fond of that, so I mainly read books and talked. Toonmom Toh is so much better. He can walk really well now, but still cannot run at full tilt. If he runs very fast, his scar hurts. However, in a short while, he will be completely recovered.

On the 16th, we went by car to Deal, which is about 15 miles away. We left in the morning and arrived in time for lunch. After lunch we went to see Walmer Castle, which is near the town. This castle was formerly a defensive fort and the exterior still very much as the appearance of that. However, inside there are comfortable living quarters. The owner of this castle is known as the Lord Warrant of the Cinque Ports and he is charge of the ports in the area. The Queen can appoint whomsoever she likes, although usually it is the prime minister. Currently, Lord Salisbury is the owner. We went to see it because in the past it belonged to Lord Wellington, one of England's most famous soldiers who beat Napoleon. Lord Wellington lived here a long time and actually died here. The room where he died has been left just as it was. The Queen has also stayed there two or three times. They pointed out where she had slept. The castle is not large, but it seems comfortable. The rooms are a strange shape, because the castle itself is round. so the rooms are partitioned in a very strange way. The walls are so thick that one can carve a room out of them. Nowadays, the moat is planted with trees as a garden and nearby there is another large garden full of flowers, which is very magnificent. It is amazing to see rose bushes that are much taller than a grown man.

Walmer Castle in Deal, c. 1890s.

Today Chao Phraya Abhaya Raja came down to visit Toonmom Toh, arriving early in the morning and having lunch here. He left in the evening. He looks well and said he would return to Bangkok shortly, leaving Europe in October.

Toonmom Toh will most likely not stay here much longer, as the doctor thinks he should go to Scotland, so as to breathe some cool air which will make him better. Mr Olivier has gone to find him somewhere to stay already. He will probably go there in August. I will probably accompany him and stay there for a while, before going to Paris and back to Petersburg.

I beg to remain Your Majesty's obedient servant,
Chakrabongse

The Siamese Legation
23 Ashburn Place
London SW
27th July 119

Your Majesty

On the 20th, I accompanied Toonkramom Toh from Broadstairs to London for a dinner for the Royal Guards which the officers in the regiment had arranged for that evening. The idea for the dinner arose because they realised that all the royal guards members in Europe, both old and new, when added up came to seven, a remarkable occurrence. At that time, all were gathered together in England, except

for Phraya Non. So it was decided to organise a convivial dinner to celebrate the regiment. Phraya Non was also invited to come from Berlin. Everyone was asked to contribute to the party, so everyone who was a royal guard paid. It was organised at Bailey's Hotel near the Legation and was for soldiers who were serving Your Majesty or were studying in England. The civilians were just Pi Pen and Phraya Mahibal. Altogether we were were 14. At 7.30 we all met up, wearing half dress and our decorations. Once we were all ready, we went to have our dinner. During dinner, Phraya Wallapa, the Chairman, made a long toast to Your Majesty in which he referred to Your Majesty's benevolence to the Royal Guard regiment from the past until the present, which gave us all much pleasure. After that we drank to the Queen, my mother, Toonmom Toh and the royal family, as well as the Commander-in-Chief of the army. Everyone took it turns to make a speech and show their loyalty to the army and the need for such an army in Siam.

After dinner was finished, we chatted most enjoyably until, at the appropriate time, the party broke up.

All of us contributed money to send a telegram to Your Majesty and when we got a reply, we were all delighted and touched.

I sent a letter to Toonmom Aa and Pi Chira, as well as sending my good wishes and congratulations to both of them. Phraya Wallapa wrote them for us and all of us signed our names in order of our army ranks.

On the 21st in the afternoon, Toonmom Toh went to the wedding of Mr Smythe who works at the Legation here. I did not go as I was not invited.

On the 23rd, Phraya Prasit had a dinner for Toonmom Toh at the embassy to celebrate his recovery from illness.

Four brothers: Prince Benbadhana, Prince Paribatra, Crown Prince Maha Vajiravudh and Prince Chakrabongse.

On the morning of the 24th, Toonmom Chai left London for Paris in order to see the Exhibition.

In the afternoon, Toonmom Toh went back to Broadstairs. I said goodbye and remained in London.

I am well and think about Your Majesty always.

I beg to remain Your Majesty's obedient servant,
Chakrabongse

Back row from left to right: Luang Siddhi, the Crown Prince, Prince Chakrabongse, Prince Paribatra.
Front row from left to right: Phraya Krai Kosa, Siamese ambassador in London, Phraya Wallapa and Phraya Prasit.
Apart from the ambassador, the non-royals were all part of the Crown Prince's entourage.

Queen Margherita of Italy. She was first cousin to King Umberto

Bannakom Suranaree Throne Hall
25th July 1900

Dear Lek

I received your letter dated 28th May reporting that you had presented the royal decoration to the Empress and various other matters. The subject of Ta O being finished, I had already heard about from Phraya Mahibal and how it is linked to inappropriate behaviour, just like when he went to see you.

Then I received the letters dated 7th and 20th June with the copy of the letter to the Emperor and his return telegram.

The fact that Toh has borne this illness well is due to his nature, which is well known already. When the doctor forbade him most strictly, he said to your mother, if Lek had been forbidden in such a way, it would probably have been more difficult.

I have sent a copy of my letter to the Emperor in the same envelope. Please tell Phraya Mahibal about it too. No special formality is required in order to present it to him, just do it when you can. I know you have performed this well in the past.

The reason why I have only just written the letter is because I felt it was difficult to explain things succinctly. If I were to write a lot, it would be boring and someone would have to read it in a shortened form. So I asked Phraya Abhaya Raja to draft it, as I thought it was important, but he wrote something incredibly long, using language that was very legalistic. I was anxious that the Emperor might say, "Who's been putting words into your father's mouth?" So I had to give up on that one and then Krom Luang [Devawongse] took it away to redraft, and held onto it for ages. Then, of course, it was in Krom Luang's language and he sent various versions. I didn't like these either, but both of them had offered to draft the letter and each kept it for far too long, so a lot of time got wasted. Finally, I had to do it myself, so that it would sound like me, as I imagine the Emperor can remember the way I express myself. To so blatantly ask him for his help, makes me feel rather uncomfortable, so I presented it more as a report and I hope that he will help.

We have been impressed by the Chinese question. Some of the *farang* here are anxious that the Chinese in Siam will rise up too. They are so fearful. The newspapers are inviting people to consider volunteering to fight the Chinese. If they really did this, there would be clashes. In truth, the Chinese here are of a lower class and don't know the upper class ones. They feel that, while they may well be fighting in China, here they are fine. The Chinese in Bangkok are from southern China. As all the troubles are in the north, so they are not that bothered. Trade is beginning to decline on the China side. If it continues, I imagine we'll also be affected. But it's hard to know anything for certain, because the *farang* don't understand the Chinese character, and on the whole just speculate randomly .

Both of us are well.

I think of you a great deal.

Chulalongkorn

Bannakom Soranee Throne Hall.
7th August 1900

To Lek,

I am sending this letter to introduce Nai Choen, Luang Surayudh Yothaharn, who is coming to be your aide-de-camp. This Nai Choen, according to Tan Lek and Chira, is someone who likes to study. In the officer school he came top of the class, he will be a true friend, and is better educated than Luang Sorasit. But whatever the case, he has to be your superior, just as Luang Sorasit is for Toh. He doesn't know the language and how to be in a *farang* meeting, but they think he will be easy to train.

Another thing, today it was decided that you will attend the funeral of King Umberto for sure. I hope it will all pass off well and there won't be any trouble. I feel so sorry for Queen Margaret. When I was in Rome, she asked me to tell him to look after himself better, because the *farang* Boxers were waiting to kill him (before I arrived someone climbed onto his carriage to try and stab him). He said: "I think it's the duty of European royalty to come out and try and lure these people into the open. I can't not do it. If they see that, they'll be even more dangerous."

Thus taking Luang Sorasit, please do as I have planned. I haven't put it into the telegram because I see that it has to be thus.

I think about you a great deal.

Chulalongkorn

Special edition of Le Petit Parisien *for 12th August 1900 with King Umberto (also Humbert) on the cover.*

1. Umberto I (1844-29 July 1900) was King of Italy from 9th January 1878 until his assassination on 29th July 1900. He had survived two previous assassination attempts by stabbing. This time, the king was shot four times by an Italo-American anarchist Gaetano Bresci, claiming to avenge those killed in Milan during the suppression of the riots of May 1898.

Grand Hotel de Rome, Rome
10th August 1900

Your Majesty

I beg to present my report on the occasion when Your Majesty graciously instructed me to attend the funeral of King Umberto of Italy.

On the 4th, I received Your Majesty's telegram instructing me to come to Rome. I immediately began making my preparations and the next morning, on the 5th, I left London for Paris. Before leaving London, I received another telegram stating that if no other royals were travelling to Rome for the funeral, I need not go. I then checked the newspapers and saw that the Crown Prince of Denmark and Prince Henry of Prussia were going. Accordingly, I decided that I should go to Rome.

On the 5th in the evening, I reached Paris and went to stay in the embassy for one night.

On the 6th at 8 pm, I, together with Phraya Suriya Nuvat, Phraya Mahibal Borrirak, Luang Sorasit Yanukarn and M. Dorallie, left Paris for Rome. Phraya Mahibal came in his capacity as my tutor and Luang Sorasit as my ADC, as I requested in my telegram. As for Phraya Suriya and M. Dorallie, they were in their diplomatic roles.

The journey was uneventful in every way and we reached Rome just after 7 on the 8th. The welcome was formal with an honour guard of soldiers at the station, as well as ministers and various officials. From the station, we went by official car led by cavalry officers and police to the Roma Hotel, used by the city council. The hotel is where Your Majesty once came to dinner with the Duke of Genoa when you were in Rome last time before leaving for Bangkok. The municipal council arranged for a royal guard to be stationed there with me, namely Colonel Baron Coporandy Dovarae.

On the 8th, there were no official duties. The King, together with the Queen and Dowager Queen, arrived in Rome from Monza today. In the afternoon I went to call on various royals who had come for the funeral, but, not seeing anyone, merely left my card. As for the Crown Prince of Denmark[1], I met him at the hotel entrance when I was waiting to see other royals. When he caught sight of me, he came and gave me his hand and greeted me warmly. He asked after

Toonmom and expressed his pleasure that Prince Valdemar was so well received when he visited Bangkok. The day after I met with him, he said that if I was writing to Your Majesty at any point, I should convey his respectful good wishes. Throughout the funeral ceremonies, he was always very friendly to me and would enquire whether I was tired or not, as well as asking about my studies in a very cordial manner.

The royals who have come this time include the Crown Prince of Denmark and Greece, Prince Henry of Prussia, Grand Duke Peter[2], Archduke Ranieri, The Duke of Oporto, The Prince of Montenegro and Bulgaria[3] and the Prince of Bavaria[4]. Apart from this there were just special ambassadors.

Prince Henry and the Archduke of Austria[5] shook hands with me on the next day, the day of the funeral, but there was no time for them to talk to me. Prince Henry seemed very friendly and I was sad not to be able to talk with him, while the royals whom I had met before greeted and chatted to me as is customary.

The 9th was the day for the funeral procession and burial. At daybreak I went to the station in full dress uniform. All the royals and officials were gathered there. Around half an hour after dawn, the king arrived[6]. He shook hands with all the royals and ambassadorial representatives. He shook hands with me and said "Good Morning". I could see that he clearly remembered me at once, as he spoke in French to the others, but switched to English when he came to me. Later, when we were waiting for the body, the King called me over for a chat. He asked me where I

1. Crown Prince Frederick became King Frederick VIII in 1906, having been Crown Prince for 42 years.

2. Probably Grand Duke Peter Nicholaievich (1864-1931) who was married to Princess Milica of Montenegro.

3. Nikola I Petrović-Njegoš (1841-March 1921) was the ruler of Montenegro from 1860 to 1918, reigning as sovereign prince from 1860 to 1910 and as king from 1910 to 1918. One of his daughters was married to Victor Emmanuel III and so became Queen of Italy, while two others became Russian Grand Duchesses.

4. Rupprecht or Rupert, Crown Prince of Bavaria (1869-1955) was the last Bavarian Crown Prince.

5. Archduke of Austria. This could be either Franz Ferdinand or Leopold Ferdinand.

6. King Victor Emmanuel III (1869-1947), r. 1900-1946.

was at the moment, was I in London? So I told him that I was in Petersburg. Then he asked about Your Majesty, to which I replied that Your Majesty was well, but was deeply sorry that such a tragic event had occurred in Italy and within the Savoy royal family. The king replied "Of course" and said that Your Majesty was always so kind towards his family and he was truly grateful that Your Majesty had allowed me to attend the funeral.

When it was almost 7, the funeral carriage arrived and the king, the royals and the officials all stood to attention and bowed. Once the train had stopped, the coffin was brought down and placed on a gun carriage drawn by artillery officers. Once everything was in place, the procession left the station for the Pantheon, where the body of Victor Emmanuel II is. The funeral procession was only soldiers, whether cavalry officers or artillery officers, together with cadets from all the military academies. In front of the coffin was his sword and behind his horse. On either side were royals and royal guards. The king walked behind, together with members of the Italian royal family and foreign dignitories representing their monarchs, as well as many other officials. On either side of the king were royal guards and local police. The route from the station to the church was around 2-3 miles, but it took a long time as we walked incredibly slowly and stopped frequently. On either side were crowds of onlookers, but also soldiers standing shoulder to shoulder to prevent any disturbances. The onlookers did not seem to see it as a sorrowful occasion, but rather the procession of a new king. They were chatting away to each other and did not doff their caps, which seemed disrespectful. However, I noticed they were interested in the new King and he seemed very brave and upright.

During the procession, an event occurred which was very sad. Suddenly there was a loud hubbub toward the back of the procession, with people running amok and seeming as if to run towards the king. Everyone who was following thought that something had happened and maybe someone was going to harm the king. The soldiers all ran to surround him, without thinking about anyone else. Both royals and officials were barged into without exception. The Persian ambassador even fell to the ground. I was able to step aside in time and didn't get pushed around much. The commotion went on for a while, until it

Panic in the crowd during the funeral of King Umberto I of Italy. From Le Petit Journal.

transpired that nothing had happened. The crowd had simply decided that, the procession having passed, they could leave their positions and go home, which led to much pushing and shoving. This made others think something had happened and they started running amok. It may also have been that the horses got excited and ran along the road, trampling people, which created a panic. Once things had calmed, the procession continued but everyone was a bit anxious, because they thought something bad had happened and feared anarchists might attack the new king. It was related later, that the Prince of Montenegro had even drawn his sword and had had to be calmed down by the king. In truth, it was very frightening because the king was walking along the street and the road was narrow. If anyone had thrown a bomb down from a window, they would have been successful. There was no way in which the police could check every house and, in certain instances, the owners would not let them in.

Before reaching the church, there was another similar incident, but no one was unduly alarmed and the people were brought under control. The fact that such incidents occurred was most upsetting and people clapped their hands in a derisive fashion. We processed for almost two hours, before reaching the church. The coffin was brought in and those in the procession took their places. The dowager queen, the queen and the female members of the Italian royal family were already in the church and when we walked by, we all bowed in respect. Once the coffin was in position, there were Catholic prayers, which seemed closer to those of the Chinese *kong tek* than anything else. The king and officials stood throughout. After the prayers were over, at around 5 pm, the two queens left first, followed by the king, after which we all left and the funeral was over.

On the 9th, throughout the day, people went *en masse* to the church and laid many wreaths, but I noticed that crowds of people were strolling about looking happy, with the funeral seeming rather as something strange. When I went out for a drive, it appeared that many people knew me and shouted out "Siam, Siam!" In addition, many people doffed their hats as a sign of respect.

On the 10th, I had an audience with the king at 2 pm. When it was almost time, we all changed into full-dress uniform and went to the palace. Soldiers formed a guard of honour both inside and outside the palace. When I arrived, I had an audience straight away. The king received me most graciously. I beg to proffer my report on our conversation in English, as it is a more accurate transcription. If I were to translate it into Thai, it would not be so clear. I saw him for around 35 minutes, before getting in the car to come back. And that was the end of the formalities.

This evening I will leave Rome for London, as I agree with you that to stay longer in this time of mourning would not be appropriate.

The fact that I came this time meant I met Druhan Pasha, who had formerly received me in Turkey, and is now the ambassador for the Sultan. This reminded me that the decoration that Your Majesty wishes to present to the Turkish Sultan still has not arrived, and I wonder why this should be.

I beg to remain Your Majesty's obedient servant,

Chakrabongse

PS Phraya Suriya will make a list of the decorations that should be presented to the Italian officials and will send it to Your Majesty shortly.

King Victor Emmanuel III of Italy, as portrayed by Vanity Fair artist Libero Prospero in 1902.

Report of the audience graciously granted by H M the King of Italy

As soon as I entered the antechamber and was being-told to wait at the door of the audience room, His Majesty saw me and said at once, "Oh! Come in, please come in." Phya Suriya and my suite followed. The king greeted Phya Suriya, after which I had the honour of presenting my suite to His Majesty. After the introduction and greetings the King turned to me and said " I am very sorry to have to receive you under such painful circumstances." I assured His Majesty that we all feel this very much too and sym-pathised with His Majesty's sorrow. I informed the king again that Your Majesty was deeply pained by this event and ordered me to express to him Your Majesty's sorrow and to offer Your Majesty's sincerest condolences. The king asked me to thank Your Majesty and continued to say "His Majesty has been always so kind to us all and we shall never forget it. I still remember how kind he was during his visit to Italy and it is very nice of him to have sent you here, nothing he could do would touch me more." I then made haste to inform the king that what Your Majesty had done was simply out of gratitude to His Majesty and the Royal Family for their kindness dur-ing your visit to Italy, and that you will never forget it. His Majesty seemed pleased and continued to question me as to where I am staying now. I informed him briefly as to the facts. The king then said that he remembered having seen me in Naples and that the queen also remembered. I then took the opportunity of asking after the health of Their Majesties the Queens and offered them condolences on the part of mother. His Majesty was interested in the medals I had on my breast and questioned me closely about them. Being satisfied by my explanation, he went on to say "I am very sorry not to have put on your deco-ration, I should have put it on." This was really very kind of the king, because everyone knows that today he has been receiving various princes and deputations the whole time and cannot possibly think of decora-tions. I, however, seized the opportunity of thanking His Majesty for having given me the Order of St. Moritz. The king then said, "Oh for God's sake don't mention it, it is only natural."

The Duomo in Milan, c. 1900.

13 Chalcot, Westbury, Wiltshire
16th August 1900

Your Majesty

On the 10th in the evening, I left Rome by train for Paris. Early in the morning of the 11th, we arrived in Milan. The train stopped for a long time, so all of us went off to have some breakfast at an hotel and did a bit of sightseeing in the time available. I had seen many photographs of the cathedral in the city, but never the real thing. It is truly beautiful with so much incredible detail.

A little while after leaving Milan, we entered Switzerland and went through the St. Gotthard tun-nel and could see the magnificent scenery. At dawn on the 12th, we reached Paris. I went to rest at the embassy until 5 pm, before leaving Paris to cross over to England.

In Paris, Ong Dilok has come down with scarlet fever. On the first day it was rather alarming, but after that he started to get better. Phraya Suriya and his wife took charge of his care to the best of their abili-ty. This illness is contagious, but I hope that everyone at the embassy will not catch it.

I went to stay at the embassy in London for two nights and then, on the 14th, came down here to stay with Mr Phipps, my former guardian. He invited me to stay for some six days before returning to Russia.

When I arrived in Paris, I received a telegram from Your Majesty, which made me very happy.

Regarding my ADC, I have heard that he has left Bangkok. I am waiting to see what he is like.

I met Nai Bus in Paris [the son of Chao Phraya Mahindra of the Prince Theatre]. He told me that the play is being performed in Vienna and that the takings are good. I noticed that his way of speaking is not as extravagant as in the past. He was kind in explaining how difficult it was and he seemed very cautious. How far the tour will go is not known. I learned that they will go to America later. Before going to Rome, I went to see the exhibition, but only went round once. In other words, it was a fleeting visit and not a thorough examination. I just went to see the Thai pavilion, which was really very bad and seemed to be aimed at selling stuff, rather than displaying beautiful objects. It was really very inappropriate. The actual pavilion was good and in the form of a *prasat*. I only saw the exterior of the other pavilions and, of these, the Italian one seemed the best. I didn't manage to go inside.

I beg to remain Your Majesty's obedient servant,

Chakrabongse

The Exposition Universelle was held in Paris from 14th April to November 12th to celebrate the achievements of the 19th century and to look forward to the next. In the foreground is the Thai pavilion.

Your Majesty

I am truly sorry not to have written to Your Majesty last week, but I was so occupied with visiting the Paris exhibition. I also thought that it would be better to write to Your Majesty once I had viewed the exhibition completely, rather than writing when I was half way through and so part of it would be missing.

In the Paris embassy, Prince Dilok still has scarlet fever and, because it is very contagious, I stayed in London until the 16th August before crossing over to Paris. Somdet Chai and Pi Purachatra came with me. When we arrived at the embassy in Paris, we learnt that the youngest son of Phraya Suriya had caught scarlet fever from Prince Dilok. After consultation, and not wishing to catch scarlet fever ourselves, we decided to stay in a hotel near the embassy.

As for the exhibition, I saw as much as I possibly could in the few days that I was in Paris. I think I can say that I saw just about everything of importance. Those things which were not that important or I was not very interested in, I went by rather quickly. The exhibition is truly massive, with so much to see. If one were really to look at everything, one or two months would not be enough. I went in from early morning, so had lunch within the grounds and then went on looking round until the late afternoon. However, for dinner I went to the embassy, before shortly thereafter going back to the exhibition again. This was the pattern every day and so I managed to see rather a lot. In the evening, in truth, one couldn't see very much apart from the dancing shows and various plays of which there were many. There was one street, called Rue de Paris, which was lined on either side with theatres and dance halls. However, on the whole, the shows were rather bad in the French way and the halls were small and not very good. By now, some of them are rather squalid. Of the shows, only the Japanese one was unusual and performed indigenous material, with strange gestures and postures a bit like Chinese opera, *ngiw*, but portraying ordinary people. It was actually a *farang* play, which made it even more amusing. Another play was *farang* imitating Khmer. In other words, dressing up as in Thai theatre and

EXPOSITION UNIVERSELLE 1900.

Champ de Mars.

dancing in imitation. It was really very funny, as their dancing was not at all like ours. Their bodies and hands were so stiff. The orchestra was Vietnamese, with a bamboo xylaphone and a *khong* in Thai style too, but with no one who could play it.

The things I saw in the daytime were so diverse and various, that I would like to tell you about them in stages, according to the days on which I went to see them.

First of all, I started with the Thai pavilion, as was to be expected. The actual pavilion looks extremely fine and, for the *farang*, appeared to be truly Thai in every way. The son of the consul was the architect. He worked from a photograph and did an excellent job. However, the exhibits that were sent out are really rather bad. The nielloware, gold and silver pieces are very poor and exhibit appalling craftsmanship. Other items, such as agricultural products or wood carvings, were not shown. Such things are important and should have been sent, as our country is above all an agricultural one and it is only natural that our manufactured items are bound to be inferior to theirs. The choice of objects seemed much more governed by selling considerations than display. Such as sending 300 cradles for children to play with – things that are of

no use at all. If one has seen the other displays and then comes to the Thai pavilion, it makes one sad, as it is so much worse than the others and could have been much better than that. From the Thai pavilion, I went to see the other Asian ones, as they were nearby. I began with the pavilion of Russia in the East, which was truly magnificent. The building was modelled on the Kremlin in Moscow, and was large and impressive. Here I saw the train which will be used to go to Siberia. You can go in and see inside the train, which is very luxurious and comfortable. There is a bedroom, a bathroom and a room for exercising on a bicycle. Outside the train, they had drawn a panorama of views along the route, all the way from Moscow to Peking, and, by using a machine, the picture moves continuously giving the impression that the train itself is passing through various towns. It's such a clever idea. Apart from the train, there were exhibits of items from Siberia and many other towns in Asiatic Russia

From the Russian pavilion, I went to see the Chinese. Their exhibit was in a garden set about with real Chinese buildings and exhibits on display inside, such as Chinese silk and blue and white porcelain. There were some good pieces, but, apart from that,

Russia in the East pavilion at the Exposition Universelle.

Japanese pavilion at the Exposition Universelle.

Chinese pavilion at the Exposition Universelle.

there was nothing much. There was also a small inn, which was serving Chinese food, so I went and had some and was served by Chinese waiters.

Next was the Japanese pavilion, which was very well done. The arrangement of the buildings was similar to the Chinese, but, in the important pavilion, various antiques were on show, such as sculptures in stone, brass and bronze, each piece being said to be 1,000 or 2,000 years old. There were also ancient paintings. But apart from that, they were also on show all around in other countries too, as I will explain later. In their own section, there was also a shop with Japanese products. There were beautiful glazed items, which looked like enamel and displayed exquisite workmanship. The *farang* were full of praise.

In the Asian section were pavilions for the various colonies – the French, English and Dutch, but I went by quickly and I didn't examine these closely, as I dislike them. In the Cambodian Pavilion, there was an image of Angkor Wat and lots of ancient artefacts from the temple, as well as many pictures of Thailand.

The Transvaal pavilion was also in this group, with items from that region, as well as a stone sculpture of President Kruger. People had laid flowers in front of the statue with cards attached, showing their support for him. Next to the pavilion was a typical Transvaal hut, and one could go inside. It was very authentic and dirty. Seeing it made me sad, but also amazed that people like that have been fighting a war against a large country like England for almost a year now and it still is not over. It really is very amazing.

That was the end of my first day. On the next day, I went to see the pavilions of many different nations in Europe, which were next to each other in a row. Each one built a pavilion in the diverse architectural styles of their nations. It was impressive. The Italian pavilion was the most beautiful and large. Inside were items from various cities throughout the country, chosen for being unique to that particular city. Some cities had a lot of products, others few. The Italian pavilion was very full, because they had sculptures, paintings and art objects, which other countries did not have. America had nothing like that at all, as they have no old or unusual things and had to display ordinary items with which to compete with other places. The English pavilion was like an old English house. Inside it was fully furnished as a home, with furniture of the best quality and well arranged. The Germans were very clever, with many academic books and prints, while Austria had many good paintings by local artists. There was no Russian pavilion in this section, as they had done one in the Asian section. All these pavilions were on the edge of the water so that looking across the river one saw a collection of diverse pavilions, which looked unusual and picturesque.

I spent a long time on these pavilions as there were so many, and thus another day was over.

On the following day, I went to the Palais des Beaux Arts, which is where various paintings and sculptures from every country were on display. This building is extremely large and walking round it just once is very exhausting. There were so many paintings, that it became too much. Many of them were beautiful, with Italy being the best as one might expect. There were also many French paintings and they got so many prizes that people were angry and said the French got all the prizes.

Here the Japanese were also surprising. They had lots of painting on show and were very accomplished. It was good that their works did not follow the *farang* style, but went their own way. The *farang* really liked their works and felt that some were better than theirs, so they won a lot of prizes. Their sculptures were also good. America was really hopeless as they have no art of their own and can only copy Europe rather poorly.

On that day I felt extremely tired, as I walked such a lot, and so I had to rest and didn't see anything else. The next day I went to the Palais des Invalides, where there was an exhibition of fine craftsmanship. It consisted of jewellery and other adornments, or small *objets de vertue*. It was arranged by country within the same building. In this regard, Russia excelled, with very beautiful jewellery. Some of the Empress's jewellery was also on show. There was also enamelware and jade, all chosen for their beauty and

English pavilion at the Exposition Universelle.

all of the highest craftsmanship. There was a map of France, made of different stones from the Ural mountains, with gems for the various cities, as I told Your Majesty before when I saw it in Petersburg, and now I saw it again in Paris. People were very excited by this map and a dense crowd surrounded it.

There were many beautiful items from other countries, but nothing that unusual. There was a pearl necklace in the British shop, which was particularly stunning but the price was extremely high also. The people in the shop knew us and said that this necklace should be bought by Your Majesty. The shop is a gold and silversmiths, which was very famous at the time when Your Majesty visited London.

From here we went to see the weapons and items for warfare, both on land and sea. All the countries were divided into groups. There were dummies wearing uniforms from the past to the present, which was fascinating. The weaponry was similarly historical and modern and by various manufacturers from many countries. Russia was also strong in this area and not inferior to the others. England did not display any army material, just models of naval vessels.

On the next day, we went to the Champs de Mars, where there were enormous pavilions with many different things inside. Machines and engines to generate electricity and other manufactured goods filled the place to such extent, it was impossible to see everything. So we had to pass through quickly, as we did not have enough time to stop and study each exhibit. Here, I was very taken with the Japanese embroidery, which was truly impressive. On the whole it is embroidered on silk and is so skilful that it looks like a painting. The *farang* cannot possibly match them. Almost every piece had won a prize. I asked the prices and they were on the high side, so I had to pass.

And that was the end of looking at things. There were some other details, but they are not important or worth relating.

For the exhibition as a whole, it wasn't as good as people made out, as the arrangement was not that impressive. There were crowds of people, various other problems and so much walking. True, there was an electric train, but it only ran around the perimeter. To look inside, one had to walk. Nor was the food very good and it was very expensive. I gather that the venture has lost money because it is so large, and there

A painting giving a panoramic view of the Exposition Universelle by Lucien Baylac, 1900.

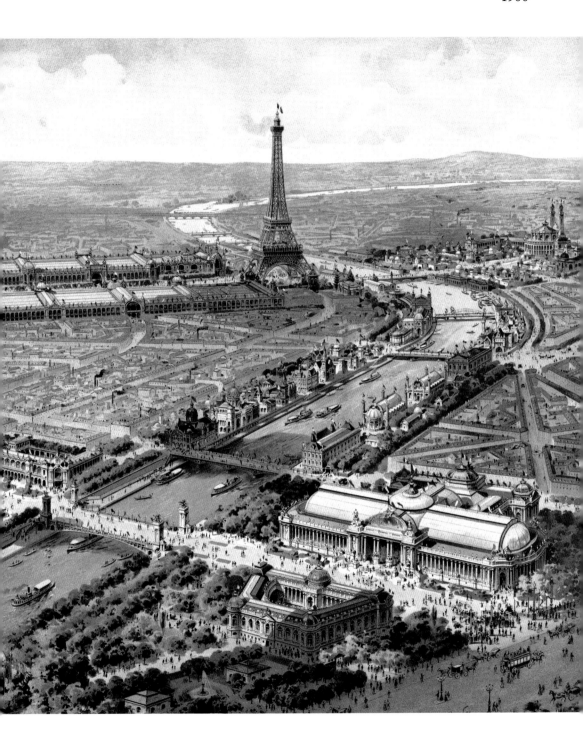

have been various accidents which have made people alarmed and not wanting to visit. The entrance ticket, which was meant to be 1 franc, has now been reduced to 30 centimes or 40 at best. They are hoping that this month there will be more people, as it is not so hot, as before it was very hot indeed.

The day before I left Paris, the Siamese Consul invited me to dine at the restaurant in the Thai pavilion. It was very lavish and he drank a toast to Your Majesty and Sadet Mother, which he asked me to tell you.

On the 31st August, I left Paris for Berlin. I left hurriedly as I wanted to see Toonkramom Chai in Berlin. It happened to be the time when he was there for a review, before going back immediately for manoeuvres.

On the 1st September in the evening, I arrived in Berlin and also saw Prince Rangsit, which made me very happy. Toonmom Chai stayed in Berlin until the 3rd morning, when he had to go back on manoeuvres with his regiment.

On the 2nd, I went to see him at his quarters which seemed comfortable and the room was well arranged. Prince Rangsit is very much taller. In fact, now he is taller than me, but he is not any fatter and I think this is because he has grown so quickly. He is in school in Halberstadt and had to return on the 3rd as well, as he was worried he would miss too much school.

I will leave Berlin tomorrow for Petersburg. I should arrive many days before studies start, as the due date is the 15th.

Last night, the lower floor of the embassy caught fire. It was very frightening. However, thanks to Your Majesty's protective powers, the embassy was not under threat at all. There were just lumps of soot everywhere, which turned many things black. When the fire happened, I was out at a play, as was Phraya Non, and no one told us until we were going to leave. When we got back, the fire was out so it wasn't frightening at all.

Prince Rangsit while studying in Heidelberg.

The people who were there said it was very alarming. That room is all charred now and I am sure it is thanks to Your Majesty that the embassy did not burn down. If it had occurred in Bangkok, it would have burnt to the ground for sure and spread to other houses. Here, it just burned on the ground floor.

I beg to remain Your Majesty's obedient servant,
Chakrabongse

The Siamese Legation, Petersburg
12th September 1900

Your Majesty

I received Your Majesty's letter dated 25th July, together with a copy of the letter to the Emperor and I thank Your Majesty sincerely. At present the Emperor is in Poland, and I am not certain where he is exactly. In approximately another 15 days, he will go to stay in the Crimea. Phraya Mahibal will take Your Majesty's letter to present when they have arrived in the Crimea, as it will be more certain to reach him. Waiting until he returns to Tsarskoe Selo or Petersburg would be too long.

I left Berlin on the 6th in the morning and arrived in Petersburg in the afternoon of the following day after an uneventful journey. I arrived to very cold weather and constant rain, making it colder still because of the damp.

I will not start my studies until the 14th, when the school is scheduled to open, so I can rest for a good time before starting. I think my classes this year will be very different from before. I will be in class 8, known as the special class, where the students are sponsored by the Tsar with only a few civilians. All those who enter this class, go on to a commission in a regiment, with the rank of private in the royal guards. We have to perform guard duty and, if there is a war, can be called to fight by joining with the senior students from other military colleges to form one regiment. Those who enter this class have to swear an oath of allegiance. However, Nai Poum and I will not do this, as it is tantamount to changing one's nationality. I have enquired about this, as I feared it would look bad not to join with the others, but I have learned that this has already happened with the Bulgarians and other foreign nationals studying here, none of whom had to swear the oath. So it won't seem odd if we do not swear.

I am delighted that I will be able to serve in the Emperor's army and that I will be pursuing genuine military studies from this moment on.

I beg to remain Your Majesty's obedient servant,
Chakrabongse

Siamese Legation, Petersburg
17th September 1900

Your Majesty

I have received Your Majesty's letter, which you sent with Luang Surayudh Yotaharn. I was truly delighted that you have allowed him to come and be my ADC. I feel very honoured and grateful. Luang Surayudh arrived safely in Petersburg on the 12th, having come straight from Genoa after staying in Berlin for two days.

I have observed that Luang Surayudh conducts himself very well. He is very polite and dedicated to his work. I am sure he will continue to be a good man. As for the language, he is determined to master it, although the cost is a slight problem as he does not have enough money to find a good teacher. Phraya Mahibal has written to you about this, so I hope it can be resolved. For the moment, he has agreed to use his own money, so as not to waste time before he has your agreement to use government funds.

Since being back in Petersburg, I have not started studying, but now it has been decided that I will start tomorrow. There is rather a lot to study this year and I will have to start at 7.30 am and continue until 7 pm, with a break in the afternoon as usual.

Phraya Mahibal has undoubtedly told you of my timetable and the subjects in detail.

This afternoon I went to the school for the first time since my return. The classrooms and dormitories are completely new, because I have changed class and also changed company. In this new company, the discipline is very strict and I noticed something today which was very strange, namely that all the students who were together before and used to misbehave, ignore orders and make a noise in class and training, have stopped completely. Now we cannot talk during training at all. As I have informed you before, this new class is fully integrated into the army and, for that reason, the commander behaves as if in a real military company and is strict and a disciplinarian. Today Grand Duke Constantine, Head of the Military education department, came to watch training also.

I beg to remain Your Majesty's obedient servant,
Chakrabongse

18th September 1900

Your Majesty

In my last letter dated 17th, which I had already sent, I forgot to mention about the Buddhist Tartar monk who came to see me, so I am obliged to write to Your Majesty again.

This Tartar monk is an important person, who knows Russian well and knows his studies too. To put it concisely, he is very civilised. He comes from Abudaria[1], which is the centre of Russian Buddhists, and asked M. Olarovsky to bring him to meet me.

On the 16th at the appointed time, M. Olarovsky brought the priest to meet me. He brought a Chinese-style Buddha image to present to me, together with a dark blue scarf, as is the tradition. He expressed his delight and gratitude for the relic from Your Majesty, which has now been sent to Abudaria. The Buddhist community is very thrilled. This monk has come from there and he is going on to Paris to see the exhibition, before travelling to Bangkok in order to be able to thank you in person and on behalf of the Buddhist community.

I thanked him and said I was delighted to hear he was going to go to Thailand and said that I was certain all of us would be so happy to welcome him, as we were all Buddhists together.

After that, we chatted about this and that, and he explained how happy he was to be under the rule of the Emperor. He also explained that there were many Buddhists both in European and Asian Russia. The monk plans to travel to Bangkok around December.

I beg to remain Your Majesty's obedient servant,

Chakrabongse

P. S. The monk said he would bring a large Buddha image and some *dhamma* texts in his language for Your Majesty.

Winter Palace, Petersburg
7th October 1900

Your Majesty

The new director, replacing Count Keller, who left at the beginning of the year as I told you, is called Epanchin and is a Colonel attached to the Chief-of-Staff. Some people have said that he is straight down the line and very strict, a stickler for the rules. I can see that must be true, as he is only a colonel but has taken up an important position normally reserved for generals. Some others have said that he won't be director for long, before being promoted to assist Grand Duke Constantine who is Head of All the Military Colleges.

Today I went to see Colonel Epanchin at the Corps. I observed that he seemed a serious person and was probably very strict, which will be very good for the school.

My studies are progressing well. I trust that Phraya Mahibal has sent you the timetable already. This year we will study all aspects of soldiering and as for general studies, the important additions are German and law. At the moment we are studing the history of law from the past until the present. Later we will study criminal and common law, as well as international law. Our law studies are at the same level as university students. It is strange that the Corps des Pages study law only superficially, so I have asked to study it in greater depth in line with your desire that I should also study civilian subjects. I hope that Pi Rabi will also be happy.

There is no particular news here, as no one is here at the moment and it is a bit lonely. The Emperor is still in Crimea and he will not come back for around another month and a half. I hear that the ministers of the Foreign Office, War Office and Treasury have also gone to the Crimea, as the problem in China is rather acute at the moment.

The newspapers have reported a strange thing, which perhaps no one has told you about, namely that a Khmer prince, who is heir to King Norodom, travelled to Europe and came to Paris to see the exhibition at the invitation of the French who wanted to show him off. When he arrived, he went crazy and wrote to the papers berating the French for the way they govern Cambodia, saying they have done

---

1. It is not entirely clear what Prince Chakrabongse is referring to by Abudaria. It could be Buryatia or Amudarya meaning the Amu River.

nothing for the country, except plunder its riches for their own gain. They have destroyed the power of the king and no one respects the Resident but simply mocks him. He spoke very well and intelligently. The only bad thing he said, was that giving up gambling was a mistake and meant that the king had made a large loss and gained nothing.

The newspapers made a huge furore about this throughout the country, both those that agreed with him and those that did not, to the extent that it was rumoured that the government would fall from a vote in parliament because of this. The government was naturally very annoyed and threatened Norodom in various ways, so that now I hear that the king has cut off this son and instructed that he be sent back. The Khmer prince has fled Paris for Belgium and there is no news as to where he is now. The English press say that the Belgians will probably ask him to leave and so he will probably go to England. What will happen next is impossible to say.

I thought this was an unusual story, so I have informed Your Majesty just in case no one else had told Your Majesty about it.

I beg to remain Your Majesty's obedient servant,
Chakrabongse

From time to time Prince Chakrabongse would have a new portrait taken in uniform to give away as a carte-de-visite when calling on dignitaries. This one is dated October 1900.

Colonel Epanchin in his study at the Corps des Pages.

The Winter Palace, Petersburg
October 14th 1900

My dear father

Everything is so quiet here at the present moment that I have hardly anything of interest to tell Your Majesty. All the same, I must write to show that I always think of Your Majesty, and to say that I am in good health and getting on with my studies.

Yesterday the pages of the Senior special class (the last class and one higher than mine) were appointed by order of the Emperor to be pages of the chamber. The latters [sic] are ordered to be attached to the person of the Emperor, the Empresses, and the Grand Duchesses accordingly. As a result of the appointment, there was a general rejoicing at the Corps. We of the junior class, showed our sympathy and good will by throwing the newly appointed cadets up into the air and catching them just before they reached the ground. This is how we always show our affection to our comrades or sometimes even to the officers.

Our new director, Colonel Epanchin, is a very nice man indeed. He and I have exchanged private visits and I am very pleased with him. He is serious and strict as a superior officer, but at the same time is pleasant and friendly as an ordinary man.

I really don't know when the Emperor and Empress will be coming back here. They seem to be enjoying their stay at the Crimea very much.

Hoping you are quite well and best love
I remain your affectionate son
Lek

The Winter Palace, Petersburg
20th November 1900

Your Majesty

I am sorry to have to inform you in this letter that the Emperor has been ill.

At first, I heard that he was ill with influenza and that it was not very serious. For that reason, the newspapers were forbidden from reporting the news any further, but simply put a notice in the *Imperial Gazette*. Then, about a week later, there was a big news story that the Emperor was no better and, in fact, had typhoid fever which is a very serious illness in Europe. From then on, his condition was reported in the newspapers daily, although it did not seem very serious and his condition was stable but not better. It is said that with this illness, one has to let it reach its peak and, if there is no danger at that time, one can recover and be stronger than before.

The Emperor has quite a mild form of typhoid, caused from a disease in the intestine, so that when he has a fever he must be very careful about what he eats until his intestine is back to normal.

Everyone has been very surprised that the Emperor got ill and some have been worried and wondered why he got such an illness, which can only come from a catching a chill or eating something very unwholesome. This latter fact, has caused some people to rumour that his food was poisoned and that many people in his palace in Livadia have been locked up. What the truth of this may be I have no idea, as all the officials are stony silent on the subject. I tend to think it is not true, as the Emperor always eats with the Empress, so why is she not ill as well. So I think the illness has another cause.

Meanwhile, in churches throughout the land, everyone prays for the Emperor's recovery. As the 16th of this month was the anniversary of the Emperor's coronation and the birthday of Grand Duchess Olga, the Emperor's elder daughter, I used the occasion to send a telegram to the Empress to present my congratulations and to express my regret about the Emperor's health and to wish him a speedy recovery. The Empress replied, as I have informed Your Majesty.

Livadia in the Crimea was the summer residence of the Tsars. Nicholas had his father's palaces demolished and rebuilt.

On the 2nd of this month, it was the anniversary of the Emperor's accession to the throne. I sent him a congratulatory telegram and also informed him that I had now entered the Junior Special Class in the Corps des Pages. I said how delighted I was to be now fully in the Emperor's military service and wanted to express my loyalty and devotion to him. He telegrammed in reply and I have translated this and sent a copy to Your Majesty, together with this letter.

I beg to remain Your Majesty's obedient servant,
Chakrabongse

Nicholas II recovering from typhoid in Livadia.

Winter Palace, Petersburg
27th November 1900

Your Majesty

On the 23rd of this month, your telegram regarding the Emperor's illness arrived at the embassy. It was written in English to Lek Siamaduts Petersburg. The embassy staff saw the words embassy and didn't check properly, so opened it and then saw it was Your Majesty's royal telegram and immediately translated the code. Phraya Mahibal then rushed to send a telegram back. Then on the 24th, a Satuday, I came to the embassy and saw the telegram was to me as I have answered Your Majesty already.

Ever since I knew about this, until I received your telegram back, I have been very anxious that you would be angry that I had not replied, or that you might have been worried as to my disappearance.

Between the 21st to the 23rd, the Emperor's condition worsened. He could not sleep and his temperature was very high, but then on the 24th his temperature started to come down and he is now sleeping well and his temperature is normal or below normal. His condition has been reported in the newspapers every day.

In truth, his illness is not that serious, but the fact that it happened now, when the situation in the country is rather unstable and there is the China problem, has led to the newspapers covering it more than they might have. In newspapers all over Europe, there have expressions of concern over the Emperor's illness and all have praised him and expressed hope

for his speedy recovery. From this, it could be seen that the Europeans love and respect the Emperor, with no one criticizing him.

One story told by someone who came back from the Crimea, suggests that he fell ill for the following reasons: On the first day there was a storm and a big and strange fish was washed up on the shore by the Emperor's palace. One of the royal guards informed His Majesty. At that time he was doing paperwork and only wearing loose, white clothes. He immediately grabbed his hat and rushed out to see the fish, without wearing a proper coat, at a time when the wind was strong and the weather was becoming cold. He caught a chill and became ill. Something which started as influenza, later became typhoid fever. This rumour seems closer to the truth than the others and the person recounting it had come from the Crimea.

I have also heard another rumour that the Empress is pregnant again. I do hope that this time it will be a Grand Duke.

The Grand Duke Heir Apparent has come back from Denmark and was in Petersburg for only two days before going to Gatchina. I think that the Emperor asked him to return, but not to go to the Crimeas as it would make everyone too anxious.

I beg to remain Your Majesty's obedient servant,
Chakrabongse

Winter Palace, Petersburg
December 11th 1900

Your Majesty

On the 7th, I was on duty at the Corps all day, as it was my turn in the First Company of the school. It is decreed that students in the senior class must also be on guard duty, with one in Company I and one in the hospital; from the lower classes there are two on duty, one with group 2 and the other with a different group 2. The guard duties are decided depending on where your name comes in the alphabet. Many are given guard duty as a punishment when their initial has not been reached. For that reason, those who are on duty because it is their turn, don't have to do it too often.

On the 7th, I was on duty for the first time, and had to begin at 9 o' clock in the morning and stay until 9 o' clock the next day. I had to sleep and eat at the Corps. Those on duty from the senior class are responsible for the behaviour of the company, while those from the two lower classes take orders from the senior officer. The duties include telling the students to go to their classes at the appointed time and, once in place, to await the teacher. When the teacher arrives, he must tell the teacher how many are in the class and keep discipline during the lesson. During breaks, one must keep a watch on the students and tell them to get back to class. Once classes are over, the students need to be taken back down and then taken to training or other physical activity at the appropriate time. In the evening, they tell them to eat their food and then prepare them for the next day's classes. At bedtime, they have to be seen to bed and one must report to the head before one can sleep oneself, by which time it is around 10.30 at night.

In the morning, one gets up at dawn before the other students and, at half past six, wakes all the others and makes sure they are washed and dressed in time. We then study until 9, when the guard changes.

If the head student has to leave the company, he must appoint one of the guards from a lower class to replace him. That student is not allowed to leave at all and must keep an eye out for the head when he is inspecting the class, or, if the Director comes to inspect the company, he must report how many are absent or ill, or on punishment. Those two on duty from the lower classes cannot both leave at the same time.

The duties as outlined above are not very taxing, but they are tiring as one has to stand practically all day and call out orders constantly. If an officer comes in or something else occurs, one must call out for the students to stand. My time on duty went very well and, luckily, the officer in charge was very kind and told me what to do in a friendly manner, rather than trying to find fault as some others do.

On the 10th, I marched with my fellow class mates on an exercise. We marched to the regiment, holding our weapons, and then around the town for about two hours with a bugler in front. It was all rather grand. People were impressed and there were onlookers all along the route. Lots of people who saw me cried out, "The Thai Prince! The Thai Prince!" Some ordinary people thought we were real soldiers and exclaimed "Fancy taking such young men on a march", and various other remarks. Before the march, the director came to inspect us.

By the way, the Thai play organised by Nai Bus is being performed here on the 10th and 11th in two Imperial theatres[1]. The Emperor has generously granted free entry and so it has been full on both days. The audience enjoyed the shows a great deal and, on the first night, there were many members of the aristocracy. The Director of the Imperial Theatres invited me to his box on both evenings.

I have not received a letter from Your Majesty for a very long time, so I imagine Your Majesty must have been very busy.

I beg to remain Your Majesty's obedient servant,
Chakrabongse

---

1. An Imperial theatre troupe was established early in the 19th century.
The Mariinsky is an historic theatre of opera and ballet in Saint Petersburg. Opened in 1860 as the Imperial Mariinsky Theatre, it was named in honour of the wife of Tsar Alexander II, and became the pre-eminent music theatre of late 19th century Russia, where many of the stage masterpieces of Tchaikovsky, Mussorgsky, and Rimsky-Korsakov received their premieres.

The dancers and orchestra of the Mahindra Theatre Troupe, photographed before leaving for their European tour in 1900.

The Alexandrinsky Theatre[2] in the late 19th century.

2. Alexandrinksy Theatre. Since 1832, the theatre has occupied an Empire-style building designed by Carlo Rossi. It was built in 1828-1832 on Alexandrinsky Square (now Ostrovsky Square), which is situated on Nevsky Prospekt between the National Library of Russia and the Anichkov Palace. The theatre and the square were named after Empress consort Alexandra Feodorovna.

Winter Palace, Petersburg
8th December 1900

Your Majesty

On the 29th, I received a letter from Toonkramom Toh, asking me to enquire about the Emperor's illness. Accordingly, I wrote to the Empress and added your name to the telegram as well. The telegram read: "My father and brother are greatly concerned with His Majesty's illness. They both wish for a speedy recovery."

The following day, I received a telegram in reply from the Empress, stating: "The Emperor begs you to send his heartfelt thanks to your father and brother for their kind inquiry. Thank God he is getting on very well." I hope that I did the right thing in sending the telegram and that it accorded with Your Majesty's wishes.

The Emperor's health improves every day and his temperature does not go above normal. He can eat more and sleeps very well, so is getting stronger daily. Today, I heard that yesterday he could get up. I believe that very shortly, he will be back to normal.

There is no other news here, apart from his illness, and government continues as normal, but anything very important has had to put aside at this time and must wait until the Emperor is better.

It is very cold here now and the river has frozen over, with sledges being used in the streets. During the Christmas holidays, Toonmom Toh will come to Petersburg. I hope it will be as successful as his last visit.

I beg to remain Your Majesty's obedient servant,
Chakrabongse

11 December 1900

Your Majesty

This week, the condition of the Emperor has continued to improve a great deal every day. He is eating and sleeping very well with the resultant return in strength, and he will shortly be fully recovered.

I have heard that in about 15 days he will return from the Crimea to Tsarskoe Selo.

I have also heard that the weather in Crimea is not good at all and lots of people have fallen ill. Two of the sons and daughters of Grand Duchess Xenia have had the same illness as the Emperor. I imagine they are both better now, as I have not heard any more bad news about them.

Empress Marie has returned from Denmark and is staying in Gatchina and not going to the Crimea, as the Emperor might be worried if she went there.

There has been a rumour that, while the Emperor was ill, something happened which led to the Head of the Royal Household having to resign his position. When the Emperor was still very ill, the Empress had ordered that if there was to be a telegram sent to Empress Marie regarding his health, she must see it first and otherwise no such telegram should be sent. The reason she did this was to prevent any dissemination of alarmist news and she was always playing down his condition as she feared that Empress Marie would be over anxious and would come from Denmark to Livadiam which would create more problems all round. Also, she did not want Empress Marie to be made anxious.

Whether the Head of the Royal Household thought it was his duty or perogative is not clear, but he did not obey her order and sent a telegram in his own name, saying that the Emperor's condition was very grave. The Empress sent her own telegram as usual saying he was not too ill.

The next day the Empress received a telegram from Empress Marie asking what was going on, as the two telegrams were quite different and signing off with the words, "I am coming!"

In this way, the Empress realised that the Head of the Royal Household had disobeyed her orders and was very angry. So now it is said that the Head will resign. Meanwhile, Empress Marie has come back here, as I informed Your Majesty at the beginning of this letter.

I cannot vouch for the validity or otherwise of this matter, but it is widely talked about and I suspect it is probably very close to the truth.

I beg to remain Your Majesty's obedient servant,

Chakrabongse

December 19th 1900

My Dear Father

Some days ago, Phya Mahibal showed me your letter, recently received, in which you said that Phya Suriya had been ordered to arrange special programs for Thoonkramom Toh and other brothers, so that they might spend their holidays in a useful and wholesome manner. From your letter, I understood that I was not concerned in this new order of things, as I am under the supervision of the minister in London.

However, two or three days later, I was surprised to hear that Phya Mahibal had received a letter from Phya Suriya, asking for complete details concerning my holidays, as the latter was going to arrange a program suitable to the circumstances.

I became rather perplexed. I was sure I had interpreted your letter quite correctly, but at the same time I could not suppose that Phya Suriya would have been mistaken, as he must have received a clear instruction and could not have misunderstood.

To make sure of the fact, I sent you a telegram, to which I received an answer confirming my view of the matter.

I thank you for the reply and hope I did not cause trouble in telegraphing. As you know, I am always very impatient and I sincerely hope you will pardon me for having caused so much trouble.

His Majesty the Emperor is now quite well. No further bulletins are issued. I have heard that His Majesty goes out in the open air already and intends to come back to Petersburg at the beginning of next month.

Toonkramom Toh will arrive here on the 24th with Yugala, who has asked to come too. I hope they will both enjoy themselves well.

My holiday for the winter will soon begin. I shall spend it here, of course, as brothers are coming. Hoping you are quite well, I send you my best love and remain,

Your very affectionate son,

Lek

Prince Chakrabongse and Nai Poum, together with their teachers at the Corps des Pages.

1901

Exams at the Corps
Kschessinska Affair
King's Trip to Java
Page to the Empress

15th January 1901

Your Majesty

I haven't written to Your Majesty for quite a while and left a longer gap than usual. I am very sorry and am worried that Your Majesty must be very angry. However, I hope I can be forgiven this one time.

Around 15 days ago, I received Your Majesty's letter, together with a map of Bangkok which included a plan of Suan Dusit. I was so happy to see the placement of all the palaces of my brother and relatives near to Dusit Palace, and it appears that it will be very convenient in the future when we are all living there, working for Your Majesty. I hope this plan will come about in the near future.

Seeing the plans for Bangkok and thinking of all the changes taking place has made me want to come and see you very much, but I do not know when I might be able to return again. I hope that when Toonmom Toh goes back might be a good opportunity to come too, as it would be a lot of fun.

On the 28th December, Toonkramom Toh arrived in Petersburg together with Somdet Chai, Phraya Wallapa Nusit and Mom Sit. All of us here went to meet them at the station.

On this visit, there was no opportunity for him to see the Emperor, as he still has not returned to Petersburg, but he was able to visit Grand Duchess Elizabeth, the wife of Grand Duke Constantine. On the day I went to the school for the end of year concert, the Grand Duke and Duchess were there and asked to see me before departing, as they couldn't see me in the crowd of students. They talked to me very kindly and said that as my brother was here, they would like to meet him. When I told Toonmom Toh about it, he agreed to go and call on them.

On the 30th December the Grand Duchess received Toonmom Toh in her palace. I went along too. The Grand Duke had some other business to attend to so was not there. The Grand Duchess received us in an informal manner and asked after Your Majesty and Pi Chira, as well as enquiring about Toonmom Toh's education in England. She also asked whether he met with members of the English royal family. He told her that he saw a few, compared with in the past when there were none at all. The other things we talked about were unimportant.

On 8th January, the royal brothers performed in a play as seen in the programme opposite. Prince Chakrabongse played Maria and signed himself in Russian accordingly.

In the second half, Prince Chakrabongse played Captain Absolute. He sent this photograph to his mother, Queen Saovabha.

Crown Prince Maha Vajiravudha and Prince Chakrabongse during the former's visit to St. Petersburg in January 1901.

The theatre programme for the plays performed during the Crown Prince's visit to St. Petersburg in January 1901.

The 1st of January was the birthday of my mother and Toonmom Toh so there was a party among us Thais and we drank a toast as is customary.

On the 8th January, we performed at play at the embassy as we had planned last time. For this, Phraya Mahibal invited the ambassadors, deputies and officials from various other embassies in Petersburg, as well as some Russian officials.

The performance went really well and the audience had a very good time and were very complimentary. During supper, all the cast came out to the invited guests, who expressed their delight and were full of praise. The wife of the American ambassador seemed to enjoy it more than anyone and, in the sad bits, even cried. The different nationalities seemed very impressed by Toonmom Toh and the other Thai princes. They crowded around to talk to us and were very polite and respectful. The English ambassador was rather strange because Toonmom Toh had come from England and the play was also in English, so the English were rather shocked. I have sent a copy of the programme to Your Majesty with this letter.

On the 9th, in the early evening, Toonmom Toh, Somedet Chai and their entourage left Petersburg for London.

The 14th was Russian New Year and the city was bedecked with flags as is the custom. However, New Year this year was quieter than usual, as the Emperor was not here in Petersburg, which is rather like

Bangkok when Your Majesty is not there. In the afternoon of that day, I went to sign the book of good wishes for the Imperial family and visited officials as is customary each year, but it was less than usual as many of them were away and many of the officials were in Livadia.

I sent New Year telegrams to the Emperor, the Empress and the Heir and received kind replies from all three of them.

The director of the Corps des Pages, Colonel Epanchin, has now been promoted to Major General which is appropriate for his position.

Some 15 days or more now, I have heard from Phraya Mahibal that Your Majesty has graciously presented me with the Most Illustrious Order of Chula Chom Klao First Class. I am so delighted and honoured by Your Majesty's great kindness. I have received the decoration and will look after it with the utmost care and will do nothing to dishonour Your Majesty and Your Majesty's great goodness in bestowing it upon me. I am more determined than ever to repay Your Majesty's beneficence in the future. If I have a son and grandson in the future, I will teach them to respect this order, and be good people, and rise to the honour of this decoration, which they will inherit in due course.

I beg to remain Your Majesty's obedient servant,
Chakrabongse

January 29th, 1901

My dear father

At last Their Majesties the Emperor and Empress have arrived back in Petersburg. In view of the fact that His Majesty had passed through a rather serious illness and that this was the first return to the capital since his recovery, there was a grand reception.

Already before the day of the arrival, which was the 26th, preparations were made for the reception. The houses were profusely decorated everywhere and there were preparations for illumination. From early in the morning on the day, fixed troops lined the streets along the whole route from the station to the Palace. The whole garrison of Petersburg turned out for the occasion. They did not carry rifles as they were not on duty, but only came to greet Their Majesties.

All the pages, cadets and scholars also turned out to greet the sovereigns, even the girls belonging to different schools. There was an enormous crowd along the whole route. I was ordered to go with the pages. We had our stand just in front of Kazan Cathedral.

The Emperor and Empress arrived at the station at nine o'clock in the morning. Long before we saw their carriage, we heard loud cheers coming nearer and nearer. As soon as the Imperial carriage passed by

us, we of course raised a most enthusiastic cheering. The carriage stopped before the cathedral of Kazan and Their Majesties went in. Here they were welcomed by the Metropolitan of Petersburg and a short thanksgiving service was held. When it was finished they came out and, before entering their carriage, the Emperor said to us "Good Morning, Gentlemen!" and we answered, "We wish you good health, Your Imperial Majesty!", according to custom. Loud cheers resounded again as soon as Their Majesties started on their way to the Palace. The Emperor looked very well and even fatter than before, which is most satisfactory to everyone. The Empress also seemed well if rather sad on account of the death of Queen Victoria [22.1.1901]. She was dressed in deep mourning. Both the Emperor and Empress saw me, but they did not give any sign of recognition as I was in the line with other pages.

In the evening there was to be an illumination, but it was given up, I think, by His Majesty's order on account of the mourning.

While we were waiting for the Imperial arrival, the Minister of War[1] came to inspect us and said "Good Morning!". When he saw me he said "Good Morning", to me personally, and asked a few questions. He seemed rather surprised that I should be already in the First Company of the pages, as I have

February 5th 1901

My dear father

Alexei Nikolayevich Kuropatkin (1848-1925).

The Emperor and Empress kindly invited me to lunch yesterday. His Majesty received me alone first and, speaking in Russian, asked after my health and whether I did not catch cold while standing to receive him in Kazansky Square. Shortly after the Empress came and the conversation turned to English, with Her Majesty having begun it by asking about news from home. The Emperor expressed his thanks and pleasure for having received so many telegrams from you during the period of his illness. I then assured the Empress again how glad we all are now that he is so well recovered and how anxious we were during his illness. His Majesty said that it was a very light attack of typhoid and that he was feeling fairly well the whole time. "I got very thin, however", added the Emperor, "but now I am very well and quite sound in health, while my face is rounder than before. I had a very good rest after the illness; a moral rest, you know, not physical rest." I was asked how I had spent my holiday, to which I answered that I stayed mostly in England during that time with my brother. Their Majesties then asked after Thoonkramom To's health and what kind of illness did he have. The Emperor seemed to have an idea that he had some illness in the brain, but I informed them both of the real nature of the illness, having previously asked the excuses of the Empress. The Emperor asked repeatedly whether Thoonkramom Toh was quite well now and that there was no danger now. I assured His Majesty that he was perfectly well and also told him that Thoonkramom Toh had come to Petersburg during the Christmas holiday and that he was very sorry not to have been able to pay his respects to both of Their Majesties personally.

been here only for such a short time. The Minister also spoke to one of my comrades, who is the son of General Linevitch[2], a distinguished person, who led the Russian forces to Peking.

I have not yet been received by Their Majesties since their arrival. I have been told that His Majesty will summon me to lunch on Sunday, as he does not wish to interfere with my work on weekdays.

The Grand Duke and Grand Duchess of Hesse-Darmstadt are now staying here, but whether in the Palace or with one of the Grand Dukes I do not precisely know.

With best love

I remain, Your affectionate son,

Lek

The Emperor asked when I began my work again this term and, after having answered that it was from the 1st of September, said he was very glad I am now in his company. I answered that I was delighted to be in His Majesty's service. "Yes, real service now", the Emperor added and continued to say that he was very pleased of my successes in sciences. I must explain that the 1st company of the Pages' corps is called His Majesty's company, as is the 1st company in every regiment of which the Emperor is chief. His Majesty

Opposite: Kazan Cathedral, 1900s. Construction of the cathedral began in 1801 and ended in 1811. The architect, Andrey Varonikhin, took his inspiration from St. Peter's in Rome.

1. Alexei Nikolayevich Kuropatkin (1848-1925) was Minister of War from 1898-1904. He was largely blamed for Russia's defeat in the Russo-Japanese War. In fact, he had not supported the conflict from the outset.

2. Nikolai Petrovich Linevich (1838-1908) was a career soldier and became General of Infantry in 1903 and Adjutant General in the Imperial Russian army in the Far East, during the latter part of the Russo-Japanese war.

is also chief of the Pages' Corps. I am now, as you know, in the 1st company of our corps and that explains the Emperor's expression, "I am very glad you are now in my company."

Before lunch I was presented to the Grand Duchess of Hesse, who is staying now in this Palace, while her husband is in England attending Queen Victoria's funeral. I reminded Her Royal Highness that we had previously met at Darmstadt and then she recollected the fact.

Before sitting down to table, the Emperor asked me whether I had been in Paris to see the Exhibition and after my answer to the affirmative. His Majesty asked about the Siamese section, and said that the pavilion was very well done judging from photographs that he had seen of it (see page 192).

When we were settled down at table, the Emperor turned to the Grand Duchess of Hesse with the following words: "Now you must begin by being familiar at once. He is called Lek and when he first came, he fell from a horse and gave us such a fright." The conversation then turned to the subject of my falling from horseback, in which the Empress joined. After that, I was asked by both of Their Majesties on many matters, such as the school and the life there, after which the general conversation turned to military and naval matters in general, during which the Emperor consulted me many times to see whether I was well up on things.

The Empress asked about Chira and the Emperor wished to know in which branch of the service he was. I informed His Majesty that he was in the Staff. The Emperor recollected that I would finish the Corps very soon and asked whether I would like to go into the infantry or cavalry. I said I would prefer to enter the cavalry.

Both of their Majesties conversed with me in the most kind and familiar manner the whole time, the Emperor calling me by name now and then. The different subjects mentioned are not of any importance or special interest, so that I need not relate them all. His Majesty asked about the railway in Siam and expressed his wish to know how far it had gone. I answered that it has now reached Khorat itself, and

The Grand Duchess of Hesse.

to this the Emperor expressed his pleasure. Our Siamese *lakhon* was also discussed and the Emperor said he thought they were coming again in the spring. His Majesty related to me how he had seen the Mahindra Theatre troupe in Bangkok and said he was told by the Minister of the Imperial Court that the troupe was now in Europe and wanted to play before His Majesty very much, but that he was ill at that time and could not see it.

After lunch, one of the little Grand Duchesses came out and looked at me with the utmost curiosity. That was the third child and the Emperor jokingly said, "third edition". I was with Their Majesties for about an hour and a half: from one o'clock to half past two. After having accorded me leave to go, the Emperor added: "I am very glad to have seen you."

His Majesty seemed on the whole in the best of health and spirits, while the Empress was also perfectly well and most kind. Another child of Her Majesty will probably be born about May or June, according to my own judgement. I have not heard for certain. I hope and expect it will be a boy as I am sure everyone does.

Hoping you are quite well and with best love,
I remain your affectionate son,
Lek

The three daughters of Tsar Nicholas II in 1901. Olga (b.1895) is at the back, Tatiana (b. 1897) on the left, and Maria (b. 1899) on the right.

1. The Grand Duchess of Hesse was Princess Victoria Melita of Saxe-Coburg and Gotha and Edinburgh (1876-1936), the third child and second daughter of Alfred, Duke of Saxe-Coburg and Gotha and Grand Duchess Maria Alexandrovna of Russia. In 1894, she married a paternal first cousin, Ernest Louis, Grand Duke of Hesse, on the wishes of their shared grandmother, Queen Victoria. Their marriage was a failure and she scandalized the royal families of Europe by divorcing her husband in 1901.

2. This refers to Grand Duchess Maria (June 1899-1918).

23rd February 1901

Your Majesty

On the 18th of this month, I was on duty in the palace together with the other pages in Company No. 1, comprising 24 students in all. There was a captain in charge and a sergeant chosen from among the students themselves. Normally, all the Royal Guards regiments take it in turn to send companies of guards to be on duty in the palace every day, with one large company outside and three inside. Students in the senior classes, namely those who are considered to be already in military service, are included in this process so they become accustomed to military duties.

On that day, my fellow students and I, together with two other colleges, making three in all, were called to guard duty inside the palace at 12 midday. We left the Corps at 10 am and marched in line to the palace. Once there, we went up to a room reserved for the students. Inside, we took off our thick outer garments and rested. Then when it was almost time, we formed into a line again and went down to the big room on the middle floor, near to the room where I used to stay. Here, the students from the three schools formed into lines and waited. At 12, Grand Duke Vladimir, the Commander of the Petersburg region, came to inspect us. He greeted the students as is customary. Then when he went along the line and saw me, he stopped and inclined his head and bowed, as well as greeting me individually. He said, "So you're in the First Company now then", and, upon noticing Nai Poum, said "You've both come".

Once he had inspected us, he told us to go to our duties. When one group takes over from another, there is a drill similar to that used in Bangkok. We had to take up four positions. In one, we stood as a pair. Those who stand can change over three times. And these shifts are demarcated, as to who stands where and when he will change. Poum and I were together in the third shift, so did not have to go on duty straight away. When one is not on duty, one must stay in the guard room and cannot leave it without permission from the captain. Nor can one take off one's jacket or lie around in that room, but must be ready for duty at any time. One cannot even remove one's cap without permission from the captain. Food is provided by the palace, and is very good. We took it in turns to go and eat in the changing room.

I was on duty from 3 pm until 5 pm the first time. When you are standing, you cannot move from your place or sit down at all. If anyone orders you to do something else, you cannot obey unless it is the express command of the Emperor, or the captain in command, or his sergeant. During the period 3 pm to 5 pm, Grand Duke Constantine, the commander of the Education department, came to inspect everything. He quizzed the students as to the duties of being on guard duty in great detail and questioned me in just the same way, questions which I could answer satisfactorily. The guards stand on duty for two hours, before changing, and then rest for four hours, before going on duty again.

I went on duty again at 9 pm until 11 pm. At around 10.30, the Emperor came to inspect the Guard together with the Empress, the Grand Duke and Grand Duchess of Hesse, Grand Duke Serge, Grand Duchess Elizabeth and Grand Duke George, who was the ADC on duty that day. The Emperor inspected the guard and greeted all those who were on duty. When he came to me, he smiled, as did the Empress and other members of the Imperial family. He asked me if I was tired, to which I replied that I was not. The Emperor spoke to me in Russian.

After that I was on duty again from 3 am-5 am and I was yawning and very sleepy. Then in the morning, I was on duty again from 9 am-11 am, before it was over. At 12, others took over and it was the end of our duties and we walked back to the Corps.

I must say I was really very tired as I hardly slept all night. There was only two hours when I could go up to sleep, between 1 and 3 am, but had to sleep like a real soldier without taking off my uniform and lying on chairs in a row instead of a bed. So I did not sleep very deeply at all.

On the 21st, the director of the Alexandrovsky Cadet School, invited me to visit the school, which was holding a concert performed by the students. This is the school which Thongrod has recently entered. Grand Duke Constantine also attended the concert, together with his wife Grand Duchess Elizabeth. Both of them talked to me in a very friendly manner throughout and, during the concert, the Grand Duchess asked me to sit beside her.

The concert was performed entirely by the

Grand Duke Constantine Constrantinovich.

students, playing, among other instruments, the accordion, the violin and the trumpet. The standard was very high and, in addition, there were poetry readings, which were excellent. After the concert, there was dancing. The Grand Duchess danced with the students and Grand Duke Constantine was very informal with the students, talking with almost everyone and asking how they were getting on. He seems to perform his role as Director of All Military Colleges extremely well. The students of all the colleges love him and his wife.

On the 22nd, the students of the royal civilian school[1] invited me to their school to watch a play. The Dowager Empress, together with Grand Duchess Xenia, also attended. The play was performed by the students themselves. Some of them were quite good. During the interval, the Empress went to rest in a private room and took some tea and other refreshments. She invited me to come and join her. She asked how I was getting on, as well as inquiring whether Your Majesty was in good health. So I told her Your Majesty was very well.

The students welcomed me warmly and looked after me, as well as taking me round their museum, which had some artefacts which belonged to Pushkin, a famous writer in this country.

I beg to remain Your Majesty's obedient servant,
Chakrabongse

P.S. On the 13th, I received a telegram from Phraya

8 March 1901

The Princess of Asturias, Maria de las Mercedes.

Your Majesty

Following my letter to Your Majesty reporting that I had written a letter to the Princess of Asturias regarding her wedding, I have now had a reply via the Spanish embassy here. I have copied her letter and sent it to you.

Here in Petersburg, something very tragic has happened, namely the Minister of Enlightenment[1] has been shot and is gravely ill, although not in danger. The facts, as reported by the newspapers, are as follows: On the day in question, the Minister went to the ministry as usual and, at a certain time, came to the reception room to see the various people waiting for him. There were many people as usual and they all presented requests to the minister one after another. At that moment, a young man came into the room and said his name was Karpovich and he had a request to present to the minister. So the official in charge let him come in. He came and stood near the line of citizens from Chernikov. The Minister came to stand at the head of this line of citizens and, after talking for a long time, he turned to go to Karpovich, at which point, Karpovich pulled out a gun and shot him. The bullet passed by the ear of the citizen mentioned and entered the minister's neck near his right artery. He collapsed and everyone was shocked and rushed to support him, while others went to catch the assassin. The latter made no kind of fuss and allowed himself to be captured. It happened that there were two doctors present who quickly administered first aid before calling other doctors and arranging for him to be taken home. Since then, his condition has been very serious, but not to the extent that his life is in danger. The bullet exited at the back and now it is near his intestine, but did not catch his windpipe. At the moment, he is much better.

I gather that the person who shot him is a student who was formerly in Moscow University, but was sent down and later went to university in Yuriev. He was then expelled from there. Before coming to Russia this time, he had studied in Berlin. When he went into the Ministry of Education, he was holding a request to enter a new college here. At the moment it is not certain whether he shot him of his own accord,

Suriya, telling me that the Princess of Asturias[2] had asked after me and he thought I should write to her to congratulate her on her marriage. Accordingly, I immediately wrote a letter, sent it to Phraya Suriya and asked him to deliver it to the Princess.

This wedding made me think of the news I heard that Pi Abha will shortly marry Ying Thip. This is a surprise to everyone in Europe as, before he left to return to Bangkok, he had agreed to marry the eldest daughter of Phraya Suriya, and Phraya Suriya and Mae Jee had begun preparations. The fact that Pi Abha has changed his mind in this way has caused the young lady in Paris great distress. My brothers are all rather keen on the girls in Paris, because they are Thai but also behave in a *farang* way. I have heard a rumour that Prince Suriyong will be engaged to one of the girls there soon. However, this is only a rumour and may well be untrue.

1. The Tsarskoe Selo Lyceum where Pushkin was a student.
2. María de las Mercedes, Princess of Asturias (1880-1904), was the eldest child of King Alfonso XII of Spain and his second wife, Maria Christina of Austria. She was heir presumptive all her life. She married a second cousin, Carlos Bourbon-Two Scicilies in February 1901 and died giving birth to their third child.

Opposite
1. The Minister of Enlightenment (The Minister of Education), Nikolay Pavlovich Bogolepov (1846-1901), was assasinated by Socialist Revolutionary activist, P.V. Karpovich, but did not die at once. He had had to suppress student rioting, while his assassin had been expelled from Moscow University.

March 12th 1901

*Nikolay Pavlovich Bogolepov (1846-March 1901),
Minister of Education.*

My dear father

Today being the fete day of our Corps, I was ordered to go to the school very early in the morning, but in reality it was unnecessary. The other pages had to go early for the purpose of rehearsing their singing in church. As I did not understand anything in the least, I had simply to stand and listen to them. At 10 o'clock we formed in line and marched to church, where a service was held. The Grand Duke Constantine, Head of All Military Establishments, arrived soon after the beginning of the service.

Henceforth, people began to fill up the church. A great many officers, from generals downward, who were educated in the Pages' Corps, came to attend the service. Towards the end, the Grand Duchess Elizabeth, wife of the Grand Duke Constantine, also arrived.

After the service was over, we went out from the church and formed lines in a hall. The Grand Duke presently came to inspect us, said good morning and congratulated us on our fete day.

Then a lecture on the history of the Corps was given by an officer of our school. Unfortunately, I was standing too far to hear distinctly what was said and therefore was unable to understand anything.

After the lecture was over, we went to luncheon. The Grand Duke and Grand Duchess sat down to table with us and talked with the pages near them all the time. The other guests sat at separate tables.

Many toasts were proposed and drunk: for the Emperor, the Empresses, the Heir Presumptive, the Grand Duke Constantine and his wife etc., etc.

After lunch the Grand Ducal couple left the Corps, and the formal proceedings ended.

or whether it was a plot by a group of students. Nor is it known whether he was forced into the assassination or volunteered.

The issue of students[2] in Russian universities at the moment is a real problem. The students are not happy at all with how the universities are run and so organise various protests. However, no one knows exactly what their demands are, so I am unable to tell you. But they are showing their strength and even fighting with guards and the army in a major way. Those carrying out these actions are all bad students and not typical of the majority at all.

At the Corps, the captain of Company 1 has changed. Colonel Bawer has a new position and so has left the school, and Captain Maxsmantan has taken over from him. Colonel Bawer had been in the school for a very long time and was greatly loved by the cadets. Today, he was given a send off and all the students showed their affection and sadness that he was leaving.

I beg to remain Your Majesty's obedient servant,

Chakrabongse

2. In February and March 1901, mass actions by students and workers took place in many cities including St. Petersburg, Moscow, Kiev, Kharkov, Kazan, etc. The immediate cause of the demonstrations was the drafting of 183 Kiev University student into the army as a punishment for participating in a student meeting. On March 4th 1901, the demonstrations in the square in front of Kazan Cathedral was broken up with great brutality.

Prince Chakrabongse seems either to have been somewhat oblivious of the true seriousness of these events, or deliberately downplayed such incidents, so as not to worry his father. In fact, between 1899-1902, students formed the principal mass protest movement in Russia.

Engagement photograph of Grand Duchess Olga Alexandrovna and Prince Peter of Oldenburg.

I have heard today the Grand Duchess Olga, sister of the Emperor, is engaged to be married to Prince Peter of Oldenburg. The engagement has not been officially announced, but it is already confirmed by everyone and by the Grand Duke Constantine too.

Prince Peter of Oldenburg is staying in Russia and serves in a Russian regiment. He is besides His Majesty's aide-de-camp, as are all the other Grand Dukes and Princes here. The Oldenburg family is related with the Imperial house, being descendants of one of the Grand Duchesses, who in her time married one of the Grand Dukes of Oldenburg. The family is considered here as belonging to the Imperial Family. Prince Peter is only a "Highness", but I suppose that the Grand Duchess will retain her full title which she now has.

Hoping you are quite well and with best love
I remain yours affectionately
Lek

18th March 1901

Your Majesty

The engagement between Grand Duchess Olga and the Prince of Oldenburg, which I informed Your Majesty of in a previous letter, is now confirmed and the news has been widely circulated. The date of the wedding is not certain, but there are reports that it will be in July of this year.

Today, the Emperor and Empress left Petersburg for Tsarskoe Selo, while Empress Marie has also left for Denmark.

The Russian Minister of Education, who was shot and about whom I wrote previously, has died. In the beginning, it seemed as if his condition was not that bad, but as time passed he developed a fever and they could not operate to remove the bullet, since it was in his intestine and the entry wound was so close to his spine that it was impossible to operate as they feared they would cut a major artery. Given that the bullet could not be removed, it gradually moved down his throat and lodged near his spine which caused a lot of pain and meant that his legs and arms could no longer move. I heard that when he was close to dying, he begged many times for them to operate, but the doctor felt that there was no longer any point.

This whole affair is most upsetting and depressing and it is terrible that the person who has now left us had to suffer most dreadfully, all because he tried to devote himself to serving his country to the best of his ability. Mr Bogolepov was Minister of Education for three years. He started changing many aspects of education and was planning to do more, before his life was cut short in such a cruel way.

Meanwhile, the students are showing their power and causing disturbances. Yesterday they planned a gathering to cause trouble and at 11 am started their activities. The main road, namely Nevsky Prospekt, was thronged with both male and female students and their supporters, as well as those who had just gone along to have a look. The police and army were also there to make sure there was no violence. Although it went on all day, it was not clear what the students will do next or what they are doing. They just seem to be marching and shouting out various slogans, while the soldiers chase them here and there. I have heard that one of the soldiers was killed and one of the officers was hit on the head by a stone. Some students were also injured and some killed apparently. The police asked me not to go along that street, so I did not see anything and just heard stories, which means that even now I don't really know what went on. The protests did not end until late at night, but early today it is all calm with nothing going on.

Today is the funeral of the education minister and it is feared that there could be more disturbances, but until now have not heard anything.

The whole student thing is very strange, as no one knows exactly what they want and what methods they will use. There is also anxiety that other ordinary people will join with the students, as well as from abroad. So everyone is waiting to see and not taking any real action, which is the worst possible thing, as the matter cannot be brought to a conclusion.

I read from the *Royal Gazette* that Your Majesty has been unwell and could not attend the reception for the Austrian ambassador as planned. I hope with all my heart that this was just a minor ailment. Also, I heard from Your Majesty's telegram sent to me for my birthday that Your Majesty had been to the seaside which I am sure will have made Your Majesty feel better. I have been worried that the various cremation ceremonies, one after another, has been too tiring and made Your Majesty unwell.

I think of Your Majesty all the time and hope that Your Majesty is in good spirits and free of any illnesses.

I beg to remain Your Majesty's obedient servant,
Chakrabongse

April 2nd 1901

My dear Father

Allow me once more to send you my very best wishes for the New Year. May it bring you every happiness and glory.

Last night we attended a concert given by a big band, composed of all the military musicians from every regiment of the district of Petersburg. The concert was given to collect money for the benefit of the invalids and veteran soldiers.

His Majesty the Emperor was present with many Grand Dukes and Grand Duchesses, and also the two Princesses of Montenegro, who are now staying here.

Over one thousand soldiers took part in the concert, some playing on brass instruments and some on the balalaikas (purely Russian instruments). There was also some singing by the choir of the court church and others.

There was a great deal of cheering for the Emperor when he entered the Imperial box, as well as at the end of the concert. The whole theatre was filled with officers of the guards and lines regiments, while many boxes were occupied by ladies. The sight on the whole was a very pretty one.

His Majesty came up from Tsarskoe Selo for this concert and went back the same night, I believe. The Empress did not come owing to her position[1].

The students are now more or less quiet. Many of them were arrested during the disorder last time, up to seven hundred persons, half of which were women receiving their education in the high schools or universities for women. The latter are very dangerous and very difficult to be dealt with, as they are women. One cannot do anything with them as one can with men.

After the last disorder, there was a cabinet council, held under the presidency of the Emperor himself, during which, as far as I can guess, resolutions were taken to suppress all these riots in the most energetic manner. Anyhow, soon after that, the Minister of Interior[2] published a most energetic circular to all the governors and heads of the police of every town in the empire. In his circular, the Minister urges the authorities to prevent the possibility of a riot taking place in every way and, in cases of non success, to suppress it by every possible means. A great deal of power is given to all the heads of the police, who alone are responsible for the good order in their respective districts.

This circular has produced good effects it seems, as since that time there have been no more disorders anywhere.

As a consequence of the last riot in Petersburg, a member of the Council of the Empire has been excluded from the list of the said members.

---

1. The Empress was pregnant with what would be her fourth daughter, Anastasia, born on June 18th, 1901.

2. At that time the interior minister was Dmitry Sergeyevich Sipyagin (1853–April 1902). He was interior minister from 20 October 1899 to 2 April 1902, when he was assassinated.

3. Probably Prince Yasensky not Yiasemsky.

That gentleman, a certain Prince Yiasemsky[3], tried to criticise the conduct of the Head of the Police here during the disorder. Besides, he is said to have a great deal of sympathy for the students and their ideas and, in consequence of all this, he has been punished as already mentioned.

Today I have finished all my lessons for this term. From this day onward, we shall have only the examinations.

On all the military subjects, I shall be examined in the corps with others, while some examinations will be done here I hope.

Hoping you are quite well and with best love
I remain your affectionate son
Lek

10th April 1901

Dear Father

On the 6th of this month, Nai Poum and I had our first exams, which were held in the palace. We were examined on the literature of various countries in Europe about which we had studied this year. We haven't quite finished the course and must study further in this subject next year. The rest of the class have already finished this course, as they started studying it from class three, that is three years before I started studying.

During the exams, the director of the school and the inspector of studies came to look round the palace. They and the teacher were the people examining us. When it was over, I got full marks, namely 12 and Nai Poum 11.

On the 11th, which is today, there were more exams at the school. It was the first time myself and Nai Poum took our exams with the other boys in our class. The subject was rules for soldiers and the small arms currently used in the Russian army. I got full marks of 12 and Nai Poum received 11.

From today onwards the school is closed for the holidays, but Nai Poum and I will have other tests on the 13th. We will be examined in geography in the palace, as the class has finished studying geography as they began it earlier.

On the 9th, the officials organised for all the army cadets in Petersburg to go and see a play in a theatre called Theatre in the name of Emperor Nicholas II for the citizens[1]. This is a brand new theatre, which is excellent, and is for ordinary people to go and see plays at a cheap price. There are places to eat and it is all very well arranged. As for the plays that are performed, they all have a moral message to instruct the people how to be better citizens. On the day we all went, they were performing Peter the Great based on the history. It was very good and informed people as to why that emperor was great and the good deeds he performed for the nation.

The theatre was full of soldiers on that day, with no women or ordinary citizens – only army cadets and their officers, together with those working in the military academies. Grand Duke Constantine, the Head of the Military Academies, was also in attendance and greeted the cadets by shouting out from his box. All the cadets replied in unison and the noise resounded through the hall. The Minister of Defence was also there. When he met me, he shook my hand and greeted me in a very cordial manner. I also paid my respects to the Grand Duke who chatted to me as was appropriate.

By the way, the post of Minister of Military Education, which was empty, has now been appointed. General of the Royal Guards, Vanovsky[2], is in charge. This man was formerly Minister of Defence for 17 years, only resigning a few years ago.

When there was a problem of the students causing trouble two years ago, he was the one who sorted things out and investigated everything. As a result, he knows everything very thoroughly, and so the Emperor asked him to take over this position so as to reform the education system and remove any problems.

Your affectionate son,
Lek

1. The Emperor Nicholas II National Theatre was built in the Alexandrovsky Park. At first the Hall was used as an Opera House, performed in by the Mariinsky troupe. Renowned entertainers performed on its stage (such as the bass Fyodor Chalyapin), lectures were held with demonstrations of "hazy pictures" (slides), and films were also shown. It is now the St. Petersburg Music Hall Theatre.
2. General Peter Semenovich Vanovsky (1822-1904) fought in the Russian-Turkish war of 1878-1879. From 1882 to 1898 he was Minister of Defence, before in 1901 becoming Minister of National Education.

23rd April 1901

My dear Father

During the last week, I had a few days rest owing to the Easter holiday. After I wrote to you last time, we had another examination here in the Palace. The subject was geography of Europe. It passed off well and I also received full marks, that is 12.

On the 14th of April, Russian Easter day, I had the honour of being received by the Emperor and Empress in order to bring their Majesties my congratulations. The Emperor very kindly thanked me and the Empress spoke some kind words. After that, a most interesting ceremony, to which I was a witness, took place. Their Majesties received a great number of people, including the Palace clergy, the choirs, the court orchestra, the Palace attendants, the servants, the Palace guardians, the officers of His Majesty's convoy, the drivers of the Imperial carriages, the footmen, the cooks, the policemen, etc., in fact all those who daily serve Their Majesties. The Emperor kissed each of them three times, without exception, while the Empress gave them each an egg made of porcelain with her monogram. It is the custom here in Russia that on Easter day, one must kiss everyone three times, saying "God has arisen!", in spite of any difference in rank. It is therefore a traditional custom that the Emperor kisses all these people every year on Easter day. Furthermore, a deputation comes from each regiment of which His Majesty is chief, to be honoured in the same way by the Emperor. This time, however, they did not come on that day, but on the next, I believe, so that I did not see them.

After the ceremony was over, Their Majesties kindly invited me to stay for lunch with them. The Emperor said that it must have seemed most strange to see him kissing with all those people. His Majesty had to go to wash his face before going to lunch. Both the Emperor and Empress asked about you, about mother, and also about Toonkramom Toh. Whether you were quite well and what news I had from you. I informed Their Majesties that I recently received a telegram from you, and it seemed that you were quite well and cruising in your yacht. The Empress gave me a nice egg made of stone for making, according to her own words, the head of a walking stick. There was nobody at lunch except Their Majesties and myself.

The conversation was animated and both the Emperor and Empress showed great kindness and cordiality as usual. We talked chiefly about the examinations, about the Corps and my comrades in general. I told Her Majesty that I was working hard to receive good marks in order to become her chamber page, to which she kindly replied that I was too grand for that. The Emperor once more expressed the hope that I would receive good enough marks to become Her Majesty's page.

On the whole, I must say I am getting more and more enchanted with the kind, cordial and familiar conduct of both of Their Majesties towards me. My gratitude towards them increases more and more and with it my respectful affection. I think I can say also, without boasting, that Their Majesties also have some slight affection for me.

While allowing me to take leave of the Empress and himself, the Emperor said to me, "I wish you every success in your examinations and remember number 12!" (the full mark).

From here I went to the palace of the Empress Marie, to whom I also had the honour of offering my congratulations. Her Majesty received me graciously, and also give me an egg. She asked about you and also about Chira. She also asked about myself and on the whole was very kind. There I also saw the Grand Duke Michael and the Grand Duchess Olga with her fiancé, Prince Peter of Oldenburg. The Empress said that she had received a most charming telegram from you on the occasion of the betrothal of "those young persons", according to Her Majesty's own words.

From the Empress Mother, I went to pay a great many visits to all the Grand Dukes, Grand Duchesses, Generals and friends.

On the whole, I had about five days' rest and after that I had to begin my preparation for the next exam. This morning, the exam I was preparing for took place at the Corps. The subject was military tactics. It also went well and I received 12.

I am now preparing for another exam, which will take place on the 28th, the day after tomorrow. The subject is Russian language.

Hoping you are quite well
With best love
I remain your affectionate son
Lek

May 7th 1901

My dear Father

Since I wrote to you last time, we have had three more examinations at the Corps.

On the 28th of last month was the exam on the Russian language, on the 30th on mechanics, and on the 4th on artillery. I am glad to be able to say that I received full marks in all subjects.

Today we ought to have had a parade of all the troops in the military district of Petersburg, in which we also take part. However, the review has been postponed owing to the very bad weather we are now having. Two days ago, it was quite warm with the sun shining as bright as ever, but the day before yesterday the weather suddenly changed and we have been having three days (including today) of rain, snow and everything possible.

We had been rehearsing a great deal for the parade. All the cadets take part in it and they form a regiment. The first battalion is composed of the cadets of the Pavlovsky college[1], the second consists of our company and three companies of the cadets of the Engineers' college[2]. Four companies from the cadet corps with the Second Company of the Pages form the third battalion, while the fourth consists of the naval cadets.

First, we had rehearsals at the corps and then we went to join the Engineers at their college and rehearsed with them. The last day we had a general rehearsal of all four battalions together on the Champ de Mars, where the parade takes place. That day we had to march past four times and with such quick and long steps that I had to run often. It was fairly tiring.

Yesterday was the fete day of the Empress. I was invited to lunch at the palace at Tsarskoe Selo with other members of the imperial family. Before luncheon, I had the honour of offering Her Majesty my congratulations.

The luncheon was a private one and nobody besides the members of the imperial family and the princes staying here were invited. After lunch, the Emperor had a short conversation with me, asking about the examinations and about the time when we shall go to camp.

All the Grand Dukes were nice and kind to me; the young ones were very friendly as usual.

I have forgotten to write to you that a Cossack officer came to see me not very long ago. He is a Buddhist and, having learnt before that I was staying here, took the opportunity to come to see me as soon as he found himself in Petersburg. He expressed great delight in seeing a Buddhist prince, and said he had learnt that you have given the Russian Buddhists some Holy Relics of Buddha. I asked how many Cossacks profess our religion, and learnt that there were about a million in European Russia. I also learnt from him that in reality their religion is very distant from ours in all forms, but that the chief dogmas are the same. They never become priests for example, and the officer told me that there were very few monasteries and very few priests. He asked me to give him my photograph in order that he might be able to show it to his co-religionists. I, of course, acceded to his request. When taking leave of me, the officer took my hand up to his forehead and overall expressed such respect that I was moved. I wished him every happiness and prayed him to express to his people my joy at knowing that there are so many co-religionists of mine in this country.

Hoping you are quite well and with best love
I remain your very affectionate son,

Lek

---

1. Pavlovsk Military College, named after Emperor Paul (Pavel) was a military school in St. Petersburg, established in 1863 and closed in November 1917.

2. Probably the Nikolaevsky Army Engineering College founded in 1810 and today known as the Military Engineering-Technical University.

Part of the meru *for Crown Prince Maha Vajirunhis (1878-1895).*

The royal urn being transported to the meru.

8th May 1901

To my son Lek

The fact that I have not written to you for a long time is not because I was angry or annoyed with you, even though it might seem so. However, until I have investigated I will not be angry. Rather the reason I have not written is because I haven't had a spare moment and it's been a period when we've been occupied with the Meru[1], which has never gone on as long as this. In addition, it has been modified and redesigned with great sorrow and sadness. Also, I haven't been well, with real asthma right up until the funeral of Somdet Yai[2], and on the day of the procession I could hardly attend. From then on, I've been feeling weak. After the ceremonies I went to sea for 10 days, but could only go ashore three days as I felt so feeble. Nevertheless, it did bring some benefit and when I got home, I got through all my work apart from the less important matters. Now I have come away to try and escape the beginning of the rainy season. However, I couldn't breathe very well one day because it was raining so hard.

When Dilok came back this time, I must admit that I have been rather sad, as he does not seem to have improved as much as he should have. But we have had little time to meet as he is occupied in nursing his mother. Then when his mother was better, he got sick. So he has come back and seen everyone, but nevertheless his studies are not going as well as they should.

Now I have to criticise you. I have heard that you are infatuated with a showgirl[3], although there is nothing definite between you. Nevertheless, this news has made your mother very anxious. I, on the other hand, still have great faith in your good sense, but fear that you may throw yourself into something, feeling that you are handsome and it is smart to have a woman in love with you. Phraya Mahibal himself is

1. The *meru* is a special funerary building for performing royal cremations and symbolising Mount Meru of Hindu mythology. In May 1901, a group of royal cremations took place. The *meru* was built next to the front palace and not on Sanam Luang. Those cremated were one of the King's younger brothers, Prince Chakkrapat, his Aunt (see below), the Supreme Patriarch and two of his sons with Queen Savang Vadhana: former crown prince HRH Prince Maha Vajirunhis and HRH Prince Sommati-wongse Varodaya.

2. Somdet Yai refers to HRH Princess Sudaratana Ratchaprayoon, an aunt of King Chulalongkorn.

3. Mathilde Kschessinska, see box opposite.

worried about this and if that were to be the case, it could be bad for your reputation. The fact that I know all this is not because somebody or another is trying to defame you. Please think about how the world works and don't exempt anybody from the possibility of suffering from loss of reputation.

It is part of the human condition to love oneself above all others. If people behave well, it is because they love themselves, or if they behave badly, it is for the same reason. The reason why people love themselves but behave badly can be because of desire for something, anger about something, or stupidity. Of these three causes, the last is the most serious and often controls one's thoughts and makes one see things wrongly, to the extent that, even when one knows something is wrong, one goes ahead and does it.

No one is going to be jealous of someone like you and have bad intentions towards you. If there was to be something that affected you, it would be from someone wanting to advance themselves and thus allowing you to do things you want, so as to get some benefit for themselves. Or it could be that one deludes oneself into thinking that someone is an enemy or dislikes one, to justify doing what one wants. The ability to be free of earthly desires of this kind is impossible. However, the right course is to see clearly that those who let one have one's way and those who prevent one, may both be thinking of themselves and deciding which course will benefit themselves and which won't. In addition, one must examine whether such benefits and disbenefits are morally right or wrong, will they be of long-lasting benefit or just a short-term gain. I have really thought about this and when I say that I believe that Phraya Mahibal is intending to get something from you through your desires, I haven't just come up with this idea suddenly. He allows you some leeway. Phraya Suriya is also looking for some benefit by being ordered to investigate. So he has investigated enough to find out what was going on, but has not added anything as he thought that just daring to tell the truth was already good enough. Thai people find it hard to be courageous enough to tell the truth. Just getting by without being told off is what they aim for. In all this, Mr Verney was also looking out for himself, but because he was a *farang* he didn't need to

Mathilde Kschessinska (1872-1971)

Mathilde Kschessinska was born at Ligovo, near Peterhof, of Polish heritage. She trained as a ballet dancer and performed at the Imperial Mariinsky Theatre of St. Petersburg with the renowned Imperial Ballet. She made her début aged 17 in a pas de deux from *La Fille Mal Gardée*, a graduation performance in 1890 which led to her catching the eye of the future Nicholas II. At the post-performance supper, Tsar Alexander III sought out the young dancer and told her to "Be the glory and adornment of our ballet."

She was the mistress of the Tsarevich for three years and later had relationships with two Grand Dukes: Sergei Mikhailovich and his cousin Andrei Vladimirovich. In 1902, she gave birth to a son, Vladimir, who was accepted by Grand Duke Andrei. Prince Chakrabongse was enamoured of her. For his part in the play performed at the embassy in January 1901, she showed him how to faint in a feminine way.

After the revolution, she had a ballet school in Paris, where, among others, she taught Dame Margot Fonteyn and Alicia Markova.

In the Pharaoh's Daughter *1898 by Petipa.*

be scared. Once he was no longer being employed, he became someone else. Why did I listen to his reasons? Well, because he had good intentions to himself and also was of benefit to us in a moral way. But I didn't think that everything he said was gospel truth, simply that he was worth investigating and protecting.

So please examine things carefully. Nowadays, you are not that much of a child. You must act like an adult, which is a good thing, and take trouble to examine the motives of those involved with you, without being vengeful. In this way, your displeasure will not cause you to lose your goodness and the respect and fear of others.

I am pleased that the Emperor has recovered from his illness and is feeling better and that the Empress is pregnant again. This time, I believe it will be a boy and have prepared an appropriate gift. As soon as I hear news of the birth, I will send it straight away.

By the way, the Siberians have come to Bangkok and brought me a Buddha image and some scriptures. I gave them a silver Buddha image and an abridged *Tripitaka* wrapped in silk brocade. I also gave them lunch. I gather that the relic that I gave them has led to conflict with another sect who also wants some. I said that if a new lot wanted a relic, they must ask again. I also gave them a picture of you and me in the uniform of the royal guard.

As for the affair regarding Bus Mahindra, it seems it will cause many more problems. The fact that Nai Bus agreed everything secretly, and then took great advantage, has caused many female members of the royal family to lose money. In this affair it is very sad for those who were stupid enough to part with their money.

Grand Duchess Olga really should not have married Prince of Oldenberg. He looks so shabby, but I suppose they want to keep her in Russia. I am pleased to see that the Princess of Spain is still friendly. The Queen must need a lot of help in this matter.

It's good that you are on duty and being a soldier, but the fact that you want to be a cavalry officer makes me a bit uneasy. I feel like that, because when you fell off before, it gave your parents so much grief. In truth, I think in our country the cavalry are not of much use and all they do is wear a fancy uniform. But

this issue is for the future. The important thing, at the moment, is that the Emperor takes an interest in you and asks you things and praises your studies. I am so pleased about this. All you have to do is not get exhausted at any point.

Regarding going on holiday, which you asked Phraya Suriya to enquire about urgently so as to know before the budget, it is an important point as applied to the coming and going of my children. Toh had thought to separate it out, because, as he is coming back to Bangkok, he has to pay visits to many courts and is worried that there won't be enough money. However, now we think there is enough to go first class without increasing the budget.

Regarding the marriage of Prince Abhakara, I can't tell you why they agreed to it. I had intended not to have anything to do with it, but merely to do my duty as a father. They had already decided and told me to ask, so I did and, in fact, I was quite happy about it in the end. Whatever happens, I just ask that it is not a *farang* who is brought in. If it is a *farang*, that child will be finished and encounter so many problems. Don't forget the promise you gave your mother and forget yourself. Even if you don't bring her here, but start a relationship, please understand that you are deliberately killing your mother and father. That I say this is more to do with your mother's anxieties than mine, because I still think that you can control yourself.

My trip here this time has been to escape the rainy season, as I am worried about asthma. I think I will stay here for more than 30 days, while Bangkok is very rainy. I will go to Singapore for a bit but won't go on shore. I am thinking about you very much, because I am thinking about the last time.

In conclusion, I just want to say that you must think correctly. Don't think you are too handsome or clever to escape falling for someone. Please don't become a victim of intoxication, by letting your heart lead you into a situation where you can't see the right path. Please think about the love of your father and mother. Just keep in mind that you must behave, so as to be the loved one of your father and mother. This is very important and please do not forget this.

From your loving father,
Chulalongkorn

While Prince Chakrabongse was berated by his father, the mother of his governor, Captain Khrulov, wrote to the Tsar to allege that the prince's entourage had led her son into bad ways. Later, on the Thai side, letters reveal allegations that Captain Khrulov had borrowed money from the Thais and that the prince had helped clear his debts, which made the Tsar very angy.

Nadzhda Khrulov's letter to the Tsar

Your Majesty,

My son, Captain Khrulov, is so depressed by the fact that he had been defamed in the face of Your Majesty that I worry a lot about his health.

Only Your kind words could cheer him up, relieve his sorrow and bring him back to life. Being aware of Your boundless mercy, I take the liberty of assuring Your Majesty, that my son has done nothing to dishonor himself. Being the governor of the Prince, he took care not only of him, but of his awful staff as well, who abused his kindness without ceremony. He tried to direct, protect and indulge them, and was unaware that they had been weaving plots against him. This disagreement with the Siamese has nothing to do with the upbringing of the Prince, which was always excellent.

My son did his best to justify your Highest confidence and didn't spare himself. In spite of all the problems, obstacles and knocks from the Siamese, he organized the upbringing and education of the Prince in such a good way, that now anyone can continue with it.

The Siamese, always displeased, despising Russia and all Russians, pursued their objects. They incited the Prince, who is rather neutral by nature, against his governor. Being keen on ballet, the Prince, encouraged by the Siamese, started annoying Madam Kshessinskaya with his childish visits. The Prince protested against his governor and his exacting requirements. The Siamese made use of this and talked the Prince into complaining against the governor, who watched over his behavior.

Moreover, the avarice and indelicacy of the Siamese often provoked conflicts, and my son had to settle them, making enemies. My son never complained and always tried to shield and protect them, often spending his own money to enhance their prestige and high status. But the Siamese preferred not to notice this. He spent more money on them than he could afford, and, consequently, got in to debt. And this how he has been repaid!

My son has been working tirelessly for three years. He did his best to make gentle people out of these wild folk, and they have turned him out, as if he is a miserable slave. However, he was serving not them, but his beloved Monarch. Indeed, he served devotedly and selflessly, with all his heart, sparing neither his strength nor his health, which has been undermined by the Siamese. He served honestly, trying to justify your Highest confidence. He served with enthusiasm and delight, but has fallen a victim to the Siamese conspiracy.

They have separated me from my only son, plunging me into despair. Both broken-hearted by our family misfortune, my son and I supported and consoled each other. The kind sympathy of Your Majesty brought us back to life, but malice and envy have ruined everything[1]. Again we are alone, stricken with grief!

Unable to stand the suffering of my son, caused by these exaggerated, unjust accusations, I have dared to tell the truth to your Majesty. I know my son will submit to his fate [sentence?], but I beg for a kind word from your Majesty. Only this can ease his pain.

Throwing myself at your Majesty's feet, I humbly apologize for having bothered you with this letter.

Your devoted servant
Nadezhda Khrulov
The widow of Lieutenant General Khrulov
January 11th 1900.

1. Clearly something must have happened to the family in the past – perhaps the death of General Khulov – whereupon the Tsar had rendered assistance.

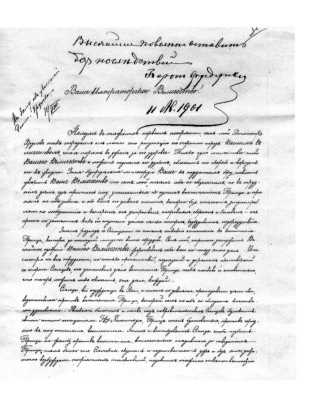

Part of the letter from Mme Khrulov to Tsar Nicholas II.

May 21st 1901

My dear father

Since I wrote to you last we have had many examinations. On the 11th we had chemistry, for which I received 12 marks. On the 13th we had the German language, for which unfortunately I only received 10. The fact is that we had no time to prepare for that examination at all. Our teacher told us that we would not be examined on this subject and, only on the night before the day appointed for the exam, we received news that it will take place.

On the 15th there was an exam of natural history for which I received 12. On the 17th there was an examination of the French language for which I also received full marks (12).

At last today there has been an exam of topography for which I received 11. There remains now only one more and this will take place on the 25th. It will be on jurisprudence. After this, all the exams will be finished. 14 altogether.

On the 14th of this month, His Majesty the Emperor reviewed the troops of the military district of St. Petersburg. About 30,000 soldiers took part in the parade. Our company went from the corps about half past nine to the Champs de Mars, where we formed lines at the place indicated to us among other military colleges and cadet corps. We were waiting for the Emperor's arrival for a fairly long time during which the Grand Duke Constantine, head of all military schools, came to inspect us. His Imperial Highness remained with the cadets' regiments till His Majesty's arrival. The Grand Duke Paul, who commanded all the infantry on parade, also came to inspect us. The Emperor arrived in front of us on horseback at about half past eleven, while both of the Empresses drove in a state carriage with the Grand Duchess Olga. The scene was a most thrilling one, when, on command, we all saluted His Majesty, while the drums and flutes played together, and the standards bowed before the Emperor.

His Majesty said "Good morning!" to us and our answers were followed with cheers for Their Majesties. Thus, all along five lines of troops on the Champs de Mars, Their Majesties went by and were saluted by every regiment in the same manner. I must not omit to mention that the cavalry was standing on the Palace Square and along the quay and that His Majesty had already reviewed them before coming to us. The foot artillery was with us in the fifth line, while the horse-artillery was with the cavalry.

When the Emperor had finished passing the line, the march past began. The two Empresses took their places in the Imperial tent while the Emperor remained on horseback before the tent. First, all marched past His Majesty's convoy, after them the gendarmes of the guard. Then came the cadet's regiment, at the head of which was a battalion of the Pavlovsky College. The second battalion was composed of one company of His Majesty's Pages Corps and three companies of the Engineers college. Then came a mixed battalion of five cadet corps, including the second company of His Majesty's Pages Corps. The last battalion was composed of the naval cadets. At the head of the regiment marched the Grand Duke Constantine. When our company passed the Imperial tent, Empress Alexandra recognised me, made a bow and smiled. The Emperor also saw me also, but did not show any sign as is His Majesty's custom.

The empress's cavalcade at the annual review.

After the cadet's regiment went the infantry, then the foot artillery and with them the artillery colleges. The cavalry was led by the cavalry college, after which came all other regiments. Last of all, came the horse artillery. The marines also took part in the review and they marched past after the infantry. When the march past was finished, there was an attack made by all the cavalry together. The moment was a very interesting one, when all the regiments came at full gallop and then stopped just before the Emperor, to whom they made a salute. The whole proceedings were wound up with the reports to His Majesty from every company of which the Emperor is chief. Reports were also given to both of the Empresses from their respective regiments.

After the parade, the Prince of Oldenburg entertained Their Majesties and all members of the Imperial Family at lunch to which I was also invited.

The 19th of May being the birthday of the Emperor, I was invited to lunch at the Grand Palace of Tsarskoe Selo. I went accordingly by train and arrived at the Palace where I waited. After the service in church was finished, His Majesty with the Empress Marie came to the room, where I waited and I had the honour of offering my congratulations to the Emperor. Here Their Majesties with all members of the Imperial Family took hors d'oeuvre, after which the Emperor received congratulations from different persons and deputations. Then a state luncheon took place. At luncheon besides the members of the Imperial Family, were many ministers, generals, other dignitaries and ladies of the court. After luncheon Their Majesties conversed with different persons and then left for the Small Palace.

The Empress was not present at lunch, owing to her interesting position.

I came back to Petersburg with other members of the Imperial Family. At the station I met the Queen of Greece, who had arrived on that same day in Petersburg.

The Emperor and Empress will move to Peterhof tomorrow, the 22nd, and will probably stay there all through the summer. We are all waiting for an addition to Her Majesty's children and hope that we shall have the Cesarevich this time[1].

Hoping you are quite well and with best love I remain your very affectionate son

Lek

---

1. In fact, Grand Duchess Anastasia born 18th June 1901.

3rd June 1901

Your Majesty

I was very concerned to receive the letter from Phraya Prasit telling me the news that I had had from your telegram that Eeyd Lek[1] was very ill and with an illness that is dangerous. I was very worried but then having heard nothing further, I assume that he must be getting better every day.

Phraya Prasit also told me that the volcanic eruption on Java was not dangerous, even though you were on the island at the time. I felt very relieved.

On 25th May, I had my last exam, which was law. Again I got 12 points. In all, I took 14 exams.

On the 27th in the evening, I went with all the other pages by train to Peterhof in order to do mapping. On arrival we drove to the first barracks arranged for the students. I slept in the same room with the other students and we all ate together too. The whole time we were at Peterhof, there was nothing else to do except mapping. We had to leave early every day and got back at dusk. We woke at dawn and left at 7.30. We mapped all day until our return in the evening. After dinner there was nothing we had to do, so we could do what we liked but were not allowed to leave the premises. At 9, there was supper and, at 10, we had to go to bed. The bedding was straw and so was not very comfortable. In fact, the first night I found it hard to sleep. Also, when you sleep in a large group, if one person wants to chat and doesn't want to sleep, it is difficult for all the others.

Living like a real soldier is rather lacking in creature comforts and we have to do mapping all day in the full sun, so are all sun burnt. My face is now so dark that lots of people do not recognise me. My forehead, however, remains white as it is protected by my hat. I am darker than when I came to see you two years ago in Bangok.

Mapping is not that difficult and we are allowed to do it in pairs. I was working with Poum. I was sent special food, but only in the evening. Otherwise, all

Prince Asdang Dejavudh, Prince of Nakhon Ratchasima, in 1901 on the trip to Java.

the students had to pool their money and buy food to eat. We did this in groups of 10 or 14, depending on what we decided. I joined in and my group had 15 people and so we had a lot of money to buy good food.

On Saturday, we were allowed to leave Peterhof and go and stay with our families. Then, on Sunday evening, we had to return.

On Saturday, Phraya Mahibal came to take me back to Petersburg and I will stay until tomorrow, as today is a holiday according to the Christian calendar.

I beg to remain Your Majesty's obedient servant,
Chakrabongse

1. Eeyd Lek was the nickname of Prince Asdang Dejavudh, Prince of Nakhon Ratchasima (1889-1924), younger brother of Prince Chakrabongse.

17th June 1901

My dear Father

You cannot imagine how glad I was to get your letter of the 8th of May, after such a long period of silence. Your reproach is so sweet and I heartily thank you for it, especially for the kind way by which you let me know of your displeasure. I cannot express to you how very thankful and glad I am that I have you as father, you who are always so sweet and condescending to your sons.

I will now endeavour to explain in the most exact manner about the matter which has caused so much trouble to your mind and that of mother. It is perfectly true, of course, that I am acquainted with an actress and went to see her at her house, in all about ten times over the period of one year. As I was pleased to hear that you were aware, our relations did not go further than an ordinary acquaintance, to this I can swear before everything that is held sacred by me.

I will now try to explain why I became acquainted with this woman. Please believe me that what I am going to say now, I do not intend to say to plead myself unguilty. I only want to let you know all the facts in every detail. In the first place, she is a very pretty woman, and you know that when one is young, one is always desirous to be acquainted with pretty women. Besides, I learnt that she is acquainted with nearly all the Grand Dukes and is regarded by everyone not as an actress but as a lady. She used to be also the favourite of the Emperor, while he was still Crown Prince, and even now she is living on pay from His Majesty and is living in a fine house, given to her by the Emperor. One of the Grand Dukes is known to be her husband, but privately, of course, without marriage. Being aware of all this, I could not have any other intention besides making her acquaintance, which I did following fashion more than anything else.

As to Phya Suriya's intention towards me in reporting the fact to you, I must of course bow to your wisdom. I deem it necessary, however, to tell you certain things, which make me doubt very much the sincerity of Phya Suriya's good intentions.

In the first place, the minister did not inform you of all the facts I have just been relating above. That he is aware of them I am quite sure, so it seems to me

that he kept silence on that point on purpose, because the facts rather tend to minimise my fault.

In the second place, the whole inquiry of my conduct was made under the strictest secrecy from me. I was never asked a word about it. Phya Suriya got hold of Captain Khrulov and the latter told him all that he knew about my conduct. After that, Madame Suriya wrote to Thoonkramom Chai to ask for more details, but the latter as a good and faithful brother wrote to me first to ask my permission before saying anything. The letter was forwarded to Paris, while I was in Rome. Madame Suriya saw the letter, recognized the handwriting and telegraphed to Thoonkramom Chai to ask whether there was anything concerning this matter in the letter. Having received an answer in the affirmative, Madame Suriya sent the letter back to my brother, asking him not to mention a word about all this to me.

Now, why all this secrecy? As far as I am concerned, Phya Suriya having heard of my conduct ought to have given me a word of advice and tried to correct me before troubling you. That would have been friendly and fitting for a minister trusted by the Sovereign to look after his sons. What he has done is simply like acting as spy, which is a most dishonourable act possible for a man of his position. I am not alone in this opinion, on the contrary many agree with me.

Now, I have said all this, only because I ought to be quite frank with you in all my thoughts and I hope you will try to get into my position and see things in the true light. Be assured, my dear father, that I have not the least wish to be Phya Suriya's enemy. In fact, I used to regard him as a friend and used to like him very much.

Only by degrees did I come to know that he was [not] wishing me well and was acting towards me as only an enemy could do. Even now I have no intention to do anything against Phya Suriya, but only have to defend myself in case he tries to ruin me. Thoonkramom Chai used to assure me also that Phya Suriya was not my enemy as I seemed to imagine, but now he fully agrees with me that Phya Suriya cannot be my friend. He even wrote to me thus: "[how can]

Corps de Page camp, Krasnoe Selo
25th June, 1901

Your Majesty

I continue to be a friend of the Suriyas anymore, because it is not natural to have the enemies of one's friends as friends." You cannot imagine how glad I was to get this letter. It showed me that the tie between brothers is stronger than everything else.

I hope you will believe what I have been telling you in this letter. I shall never be able to bear the fact that you do not believe me. However, in case you want a witness, I can bring forward Thoonkramom Chai, who will be ready to confirm every word I say.

I have heard, I do say it is true, that Phya Suriya told you not to believe a word of what we, your sons, tell you. I wonder if such thing can be true; if it is, I should regard Phya Suriya as a most daring villain in the whole world, going so far as to make father mistrust his sons, and charging all of us of being liars.

In the end, I ask you to rest assured that I will never do anything unworthy of being your son and of the name of Siam. Thank you, my dear father, for your kind love for me. I am proud of it and consoled by it. It will, however, never make me do bad things and will only make me try to be worthy of it.

Never cease to trust me and your trust will make me hold myself upright. Pardon me for having caused such trouble to you and mother. I am deeply sorry.

Your very affectionate son,
Lek

Regarding your recent letter, there is one thing I want to answer in detail. On the matter of becoming a Hussar, which you are concerned about it, it is really rather essential. Being an infantryman is even more difficult than being a cavalryman. You have to march for a long time and the soldiers here walk fast and I can scarcely keep up with them. I have had to do a lot of marching already and it was really hard. So, for that reason, I decided to join the cavalry. Your point that in Thailand there is scarcely any cavalry is true, but it doesn't mean that it is something that is not good or is not required. It's simply that it has not been established yet. In truth, the cavalry are very necessary. During a battle, infantry without the cavalry is like a person missing one leg and being short sighted. The fighting between the British and the Transvaal (the Boers) showed exactly how vital the cavalry was. In addition, the cavalry here are not just trained as such, but are also taught to descend and fight just like infantry. Thus, they are very useful and can be used in two different ways, i.e. both as cavalry and as infantry.

I am sorry to have to tell you that the Empress has given birth to another daughter[1]. It is such a shame. No one believed it for a long time until in the end the Royal Household issued a proclamation and we realised it was true. It seems that everyone was sad but the Emperor apparently declared that he felt that daughters really belonged to him and so it was a good thing. A son, on the other hand, would belong to the nation and not to him. Grand Duchess Marie, the wife of Grand Duke George Michaelovich, also gave birth recently and it was another girl. Apparently Grand Duchess Xenia is also pregnant.

On the 17th of this month, the royal pages have set up camp at Krasnoe Selo. Before leaving Petersburg, we all went to the school together and there were prayers for good luck. We then marched out of the school to the railway station to travel here,

1. Anastasia (June 1901 – July 17, 1918) was the youngest daughter of Nicolas and Alexandra and sister to Grand Duchess Olga, Grand Duchess Tatiana, Grand Duchess Maria, and Alexei Nikolaevich, Tsarevich of Russia.

arriving in the early evening. Our accommodation is a large wooden building, which is nice and wide with beds in four rows. I am sent separate food. Around the house are fields for exercising. And behind are houses for the officers, stables for the horses and a manege. The camp of the Royal army of the left flank is close to the Finnish army. In all, at Krasnoe Selo, there are three regiments who have set up camps. As I already mentioned, the Royal regiment, a cavalry regiment to the northeast and the forward regiment to the northwest. The exercises, which take place every day, consist of many different things, such as aiming and firing guns, learning to judge distances, riding practice and fighting by enlarging the ranks and attacking. The exercises change every day and go on for around eight hours. In addition, there is target practice but only once a week.

On Saturdays and Sundays, we are allowed to leave the camp, but apart from that we don't go anywhere at all. On Saturday, we can go home, but we have to be back in the evening as there is shooting on Sunday, after which we are free again until Monday evening. During my free time, I have been going to stay in a house in Duderhof near the camp, which Phraya Mahibal has rented for me on the recommendation of General Epanchin.

Living here is quite convenient, but on some days I get really tired when we have to exercise a lot. However, all this is very good for the physique and I feel much fitter over all.

The Grand Duke of Mecklenburg[1] is visiting Petersburg at the moment. He was received with full ceremonies when he arrived, even though he is on a private visit. He is staying in the palace of Grand Duke Michael Nikolaevich, who is his grandfather on his mother's side. His mother also came.

I hope you are in good spirits.

I beg to remains Your Majesty's obedient servant,
Chakrabongse

1. Frederick William, Grand Duke of Mecklenburg, KG (1819-May 1904) was a German sovereign who ruled over the state of Mecklenburg-Strelitz from 1860 until his death. Married to his first cousin, Princess Augusta of Cambridge, a member of the British Royal Family and a granddaughter of King George III.

Bandung, Java
26th June, 1901

Dear Lek

Since my arrival here, I have received two letters from you, but I haven't been able to reply. I feel like a diver who has just managed to surface. You probably know that your younger brother Eeyd Lek has been ill, even though we can't work out what is wrong with him. It was much worse than the occasion on Koh Sichang, to the extent that we thought that he would die at any moment, three or four times a day over a two-week period. In fact, we were so prepared, we had a coffin ready. It was really strange and a time of great suffering and exhaustion. We had to think about getting a machine to make his blood dry. While we were ordering it, I fainted at least three times. His illness began before reaching Singapore. He was playing on deck when rain and a storm came. He got a bit wet and we thought it was nothing much, but did not let him go ashore in Singapore. We continued our trip. Then he was better and went ashore at Buitenzorg, to go to the park with your mother. There he got quite a lot of sun, but was still fine until in the afternoon he went in a carriage and got rained on. This time he had a fever once again, although no one thought it was very serious. We stayed at Buitenzorg for six days before coming here. On the second night just before dawn, I heard the sound of him being sick and screaming out for a long time. I lay there thinking he was angry about something. I then thought it sounded out of the ordinary and got up to have a look and just saw Jam hugging him. Eeyd Noy was lying there in the room with two maids, but no one woke up. Your mother was in the room next door, but did not wake either. I went around waking people. The doctor came in a sleepy state and kept saying there was nothing much wrong and got everyone to agree that I was overreacting. I kept on, however, so they checked further and found it was a kidney problem. He has always been short of breath and it has got worse like Chai Yai. His pulse was almost disappearing, it was so fast. The doctor tried to get his temperature down by covering him with a sarong and putting ice on until it was damp, something which had never been done before. Both the Thai doctors said he would not survive, and

people were crying and wailing. I begged everyone that if he only had a few hours left, could they do something that might save him. When we did what the doctor said, his temperature came down at once by two degrees and he felt better briefly, before the temperature went up again. Then it came down again and there was the worry of it being too low, and he had to go on a drip, and he almost died. No one could agree what to do . . . I got most people out of the room. After he had been on the drip for a while, he got better and we had got through another crisis. However, now he could not pee and was in such pain, he was going to expire and was screaming, so he had to have a catheter inserted. Afterwards I could see that he should have tried to pee before inserting it, but no one would agree. Then his condition did improve, so that is one of the good things about *farang*, and he got through it. The food is terrible. They forced him to drink three bottles of cow's milk a day. He couldn't stomach it, as he was about to die. When he came round, he drank it all and it wouldn't digest, so he was all bloated and had a fit. He also had cramps and cried out, almost dying several times. It was the food and everytime he ate it, he had a reaction. Only after eating rice porridge, did he get back to normal.

This is the third time Eeyd Lek has been very ill. The question of his having a weak heart and his kidneys have become unimportant. It is all because of malaria. Now he can sit up, if he is leaning back, but he has recovered very quickly. So on this trip we haven't been able to do any sightseeing. It's been expensive and wasted a lot of time. I feel extremely run down and am very thin and my feet are cold. My ribs are swollen. The weather is very unusual with lots of rain out of season, so not at all pleasant. All that's wrong with your mother is that she fainted, when she knew about her son but she was not bruised. When he was very ill, I did not let her nurse him – only when his condition improved, so at least I didn't have to worry about another person

I asked the Phra Rattana Kosa to cable you, because I did not leave the sick room. He combined it with one to Toh. Now his symptoms have gone and he is better, I have a bit of time. Having asked, I find that in those 15 days I managed to have only about 2-3 two-hour stretches of uninterrupted sleep. So in fact, no more than four hours sleep a day. The members of the royal family and the accompanying officials helped as much as they could. Those who were nursing took it in turns to be on duty for three

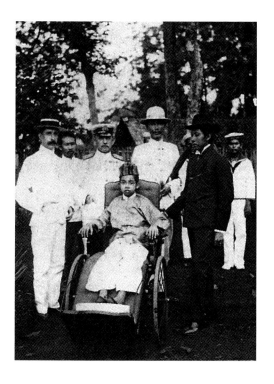

Above: Eeyd Lek, in a wheelchair with members of the Siamese entourage while convalescing from his illness.

Opposite: King Chulalongkorn on his third trip to Java, 1901. He is standing with Susuhunan, who is bedecked with medals as before. Slightly behind the king on his right is Prince Damrong and next to him, Princess Suddha Dibbyarattana, the daughter of Queen Sukumala Marasi, who is hiding behind the king.

hours at a time. Those who weren't very healthy, like Rabi, got very run down. Until now, none of us have got over our pain and exhaustion at what we have gone through. We are meant to leave on the 13th of next month, arriving in Bangkok on the 24th.

I think of you a great deal and am made very anxious by the fact that Eeyd Lek is often ill like this. If he were to go to Europe, I think it would cause me a lot of anxiety, so we'll have to wait and see.

Chulalongkorn

Letter at right:
1. Between 1809 and 1917, Finland was an autonomous part of the Russian Empire as the Grand Duchy of Finland. Between 1881 and 1901, the Grand Duchy had its own army.

3rd July 1901

Dear Father

My studies at the camp continue. Apart from the exercises I have told you about, an additional thing is the construction of a lookout for the camp and also we are going on exercises with the Finnish army[1].

The 28th of June was the first day that we marched with them. On that day, the entire regiment went on exercise outside their regiment, which is referred to as training the regiment. The pages were assigned to various companies, some 4-5 per company. I was placed at the head of the column of the first company. Thus, I was the head of the entire rank. It was quite amusing to see little me standing at the front of a line full of much taller soldiers.

The companies of soldiers assembled in lines in front of the camp of the four battalions. Major General Rudanovsky, the commander-in-chief, came to inspect the ranks and talk to the soldiers. When he saw me, he stopped his horse and saluted and said how pleased he was to see me and was honoured to receive me into these ranks.

Once he had completed his inspection, he led all the colours of the companies out at the same time. Once the flags had come to the front of Company No. 1, they were marched to the parade ground. It was a long march and took around one hour. Once there, there was a brief rest and then exercises began. The whole regiment marched together in various directions. We marched forward and then reversed, left right, angle right, angle left, etc. After the marching, we had fighting exercises, attacking a fort which wasn't that far away from where we were. At first, we had to gradually fire into the fort ending with running in and launching a full scale attack. At that point the band played and drummed, which was very dramatic. After this, everything was finished and we marched back a different way, reaching the camp at around 8 pm. So in all, we were out for four hours.

I didn't feel tired at all, as I found it very exciting to be with real soldiers for the first time and to take part in actual exercises, as well as firing weapons even though the rounds were not live. The soldiers seemed very interested in me, asking all sorts of questions.

Yesterday there were more exercises with soldiers, but this was a grander affair, with senior officers coming to inspect the manoeuvres. The format was similar to the previous time, except that we marched past the generals inspecting us twice, and the fighting was more extended also. The inspection passed off well and the inspectors thanked the soldiers. Afterwards, the company commanders also praised everyone and thanked them. In addition, they praised the students and thanked them and said that, as a reward, any more training for that day should be cancelled.

The weather today is cold, dark and windy. No fun at all.

I beg to remain Your Majesty's obedient servant,
Chakrabongse

Royal Yacht Maha Chakri
22nd July 1901

To my son Lek

On the trip, the officials have sent out many letters, but I hear that in Bangkok they are all just lazing about. The letters sent via the Harbour Department[1] are really bad. I gave them a strong lecture, but I will probably receive them in Java after about a month. Others get them three times as fast. I have received your letter dated 7th before the third June and got your letter dated 17th yesterday.

Eeyd Lek, since going on board, has got noticeably better every day, so that now he is almost normal. The only thing is that his thighs are not back to normal size, so that when he walks on his own, he is a bit wobbly. However, if you just saw his face and was told he was ill, you would hardly believe it. As to the question of whether he has a weak heart or not, I got two doctors to come and check him and they said they could not find anything wrong. They said that after such an illness, if he had a weak heart he would not have survived more than seven days. If I can make a comparison so that you could understand, Eeyd Lek was many times worse than when you had pneumonia and his illness went on much longer too. The only thing showing he was still alive was his shallow breathing. The doctor thinks he will not be sickly in the future. I am not worried about Eeyd Lek, except if he were to go to Europe, which would be far from my care. If he were to get ill and I could not take

care of him, I fear that I would die, before I heard that he was better. Simply looking after him here, even the doctor said he was so sad that he was almost crazy. When I think about him leaving me for abroad, I feel an instant fever course through my body. On the other hand, if he doesn't go, I fear he will be stupider than the others. So, at the moment, when I think about it, I push the thought away as it's not yet time.

I received your letter regarding the truth of your infatuation with the show girl and I am happy that you have come to your senses and remain aware at all times. I am pleased you will take care and also that you take notice of what your father says, because you love him and not out of fear. However, your view that Phraya Suriya has bad intentions towards you and has told me that I should not believe anything you say, has no truth in it whatsoever. Phraya Suriya could certainly not tell me what to do and even someone stupider than him would not try either. Only a lowlife sort of person would try such a thing. Usually, those who want to complain about a child to the father must imagine that the two speak to each other. Thus, the act of telling on the child has to be dressed up with an aura of good intentions. Surely no one could imagine that, having told tales about the child, the father and child would then not discuss it. That would be most unusual. Another thing is that when telling tales, they have to say as little as possible, so as to show they only want to indicate that some reprimand is necessary. Why Phraya Suriya did not ask you directly or reprimand you, is difficult to say, nor can I say how your relationship will be in the future. I can see, from previous letters that you have written, that Phraya Suriya might have been fearful and thought that there was no point [in reprimanding you]. One could accept that Phraya Suriya does not like you, but that he would wish you ill is going too far. One can see that the whole furore arose because two women want to be the best in the world of Siam. Having a husband should be enough. They also have to take responsiblity. The wife says go this way and that's what they do. Whoever doesn't like their wives is finished. This is what started the whole thing off.

I do not argue that Phraya Suriya is not close to Phraya Mahibal and I firmly believe that Phraya Mahibal dislikes Phraya Suriya. This hatred may be

---

1. The Harbour Department was later the Ministry of Foreign Affairs.

King Chulalongkorn and his entourage outside a factory making panama hats, on 18th May 1901. In the front from left to right: Prince Chirapravati, Prince Chaiyantamongkol (Chaiyan), Queen Saovabha, the King, Prince Prajadhipok and Prince Damrong. Prince Asdang, who became so ill, was presumably still recuperating.

why their bosses see them acting in a demented fashion. By seeking to say bad things about each other, it may impact on their royal charges. Or trying to curry favour in a way that goes over the top. And you have got involved in this quarrel. I have discussed this issue with Krom Luang Devawongse and Krom Luang Damrong, and we feel that this unfortunate behaviour may cause a rift which could impact on the royal family, as everyone knows what is going on abroad. The reason why I did not think it important and did nothing for a while was because I thought it would open a can of worms. I would rather let things calm down before writing. But I was very pleased to get your answer this time. I am pleased that you trust and love Prince Paribatra and this has soothed my anxiety. And those who mean ill towards our royal family should be careful. It will probably continue, because they want to use us to further their interests.

Let me speak frankly and say that, as far as I am concerned, Phraya Mahibal in his ideas, his knowledge and his character shows all the traits of a Wang Na person. He thinks only of himself and is full of tricks and doubts. He flatters a little, praises a little, all the while planning things just like those palace officials . . . all of which I have seen before. Although they make trouble, they don't really do anything. I am sure he won't really do anything either, because he is stupider than Lek. In the end, there will just be Phraya Mahibal on his own. The fact that I have focused on Phraya Mahibal is not because I am angry or given up trusting him. No, I knew his character before he went abroad and I believed that he could do

his job. However, I knew that his nature was like this. If you know how to handle him, he will serve you well, because there is no question mark over his loyalty to both me and to you. He will do everything he can in a good way. I am telling you this, so that you can be aware of his former vices, which might lead him down a certain path from time to time, rather than saying he is a bad person. As for Phraya Suriya, if he has such an intention in order to further his own gain, I would ask you to see that Phraya Mahibal lets you do whatever you want and isn't cautious. I have to say that the fact he told me about all this was good, but how we proceed is another thing. Probably better than leaving it or turning a blind eye. I would like you to consider all this and collect your senses as per my words. I have been in many more difficult situations than you, when there was no father or mother to give advice. If I had been impetuous and decisive, rather than considering all the angles, by now I would have been finished, and you would never had the chance to be my son.

I have written a very messy letter, which must be because there are waves, but I don't feel sick at all and want to go home quickly. The day after tomorrow I'll reach Bangkok. I have sent you a photograph taken in Java by a photographer who wanted to show off his skills in taking colour photographs.

From your loving father
Chulalongkorn

Right: Grand Duke Vladimir and Nicholas II during military manoeuvres, c. 1900s

24th July 1901

Your Majesty

On the 18th, Grand Duke Vladimir[1], the Military Governor of St. Petersburg, came to inspect the camp and went everywhere. All the soldiers came out to line up and receive him in front of their respective camps. On that day I was on sentry duty, and so stood to greet him in the sentry position. The Grand Duke saw me and said hello as usual, and later asked the director how I was faring living in the camp. During the inspection, the Grand Duke was on horseback with many aides. The Grand Duchess and their daughter followed on in a horse carriage. The Grand Duchess also said hello to me.

Early on the 19th, the page students went to carry out exercises together with the Finnish regiment, distributed among the various companies as before. The military exercises this time were very realistic, with the Finnish company fighting another one called Pavlovsky. Both companies had heavy artillery and cavalry. The Finnish contingent had to march for about 6 miles from Trasnoe Selo towards Tsarskoe Selo and wait there in order to attack Krasnoe Selo. The Pavlovsky company were on the receiving end. The company of heavy artillery had also taken up positions there, while the cavalry had to make sure the enemy could not make a sudden attack.

The soldiers had set up small tents, which they had had to carry with them for sleeping in. Tents were also provided for the cadets and we slept on the

ground in the same way, with just a little straw in between. In the middle of the night, it was very cold indeed, as the fog came down and the ground was very damp. We had breakfast at 9 in the morning. Then we marched off towards the enemy, beginning with a fast march which turned into a run towards the end, as they were worried we would not get there in time. The distance was around $1^{1}/_{2}$ to 2 miles from Krasnoe Selo. We met the enemy and began firing, which lasted for half an hour. Both sides attacked and, as is usual in these practice skirmishes, it was difficult to tell who had won as both sides shouted that they had.

The same mock battles were also held yesterday, but in a different direction and, this time, the Finns were awaiting the assault from the others. We had to spend the night as before and the place was not good, being near a lake and very cold. Luckily a few, including me, had brought blankets, which made it a bit better. In the battle we were lucky, as we didn't have to march and just waited. When we saw the enemy, we began firing, so much that my ears ached. Then when the enemy got really close, we stood up and attacked. This time I am certain that the Finns won, because the enemy marched straight in and did not stop firing and were in a group, so we could fire

1. Grand Duke Vladimir Alexandrovich (1847–1909) was a son of Emperor Alexander II of Russia, a brother of Tsar Alexander III and the senior Grand Duke during the reign of his nephew, Tsar Nicholas II. He became a member of the Council of Ministers, Commander of the Imperial Guards Corps and Military Governor of Saint Petersburg. Later, the events of Bloody Sunday in 1905 were to tarnish his reputation.

at them easily. If it had been for real, they would all have been dead for sure.

Yesterday, the older cadets left the camp to go and get experience in the regiments, where they will be posted in the future, so only the lower classes remained.

I went to Tsarskoe Selo on the 21st to see the Director as he had invited me. I went by car as the train is awkward and I would have had to go to Petersburg first. When I got to the Director's house, General Epanchin and his wife and children received me graciously. They gave me tea and took me to see the sites of Tsarskoe Selo. We went on the lake and went to see a palace, which has a very unusual feature in one room, where the dining table can descend into the floor so that nothing is visible above. Then it comes up when you want to eat. There is no need for waiters, as the plates are filled up from down below. It's good not to have people stomping about.

He told me how when the Emperor of Persia came, he was invited here and at first just saw an empty room. Then he was taken into another salon for a moment. Walking back in, he was amazed to see a fully laid large dining table and four smaller ones.

I also had dinner at the Director's house and then went to see the elephant, which the Tsar had received from Bangkok. It is very large now, but doesn't look well. It's probably because during the winter it has to stay in and hasn't been out at all. Now it's the summer, it is allowed out and can have a bath.

I beg to remain Your Majesty's obedient servant,
Chakrabongse

General Nikolai Alkseivich Epanchin (1857-1941) was Director of the Imperial Corps des Pages (1900-06).

31st July 1901

Your Majesty

Our stay at the camp ended as of yesterday, the 30th. The last three days were very jolly, with the Emperor turning up too.

The Emperor arrived on the 27th in the evening, and from the station came to inspect the camp. All the soldiers stood to attention to receive him in front of all the camps. And those whose camps were not on his route came and lined the road in order to see him. The Emperor also passed the camp of the Imperial pages and all of us stood in front of our camp, as did the others. The Emperor and both Empresses rode by on horseback, together with the princesses and male members of the imperial family. In addition, there were many followers also on horseback.

When the Empress rode by our camp, she saw me and nodded her head and smiled. When the Emperor had passed by, I got in a carriage and went to the imperial tent to receive him there, when he had finished his tour of inspection. He listened to the reports from the different companies of which he was commander-in-chief. The Empresses then received the reports of their regiments. After that, they had tea and the military band played. Once the concert was over, three flares were fired and all the heavy guns fired. The sound was impressive and reverberating. Then the band played an evening hymn and the soldiers prayed, as is customary. After that, the Emperor and Empresses left the tent for the palace. All the officers were invited as was I. After dinner the Emperor and Empresses talked to me, enquiring as to how life was in the camp and about other things. Then everyone watched a play.

On the 28th, it was the name day of Grand Duke Vladimir, the Military Governor of St. Petersburg. I went to his palace to wish him good health and happiness. At 11 am, there were prayers in the church, but I did not attend the service. The Emperor and the two Empresses and almost all the members of the nobility were there. After the service, there was a large banquet. Apart from members of the Imperial family, there were the commanders of the various regiments. I was also invited and the Emperor and two Empresses also attended. During the luncheon, the Emperor drank the Grand Duke's health.

On the 29th in the morning, the Emperor reviewed the various military schools, but the Corps was not involved. In the evening, there was horse racing between the soldiers and officers. It is a way of encouraging cavalrymen to look after and train their horses well. The Emperor and Empress came and presented the prizes to the winners.

On the 30th morning, there was a big review. All the soldiers, who were in the camp and in the nearby area were on duty. In all, there were over 50,000. The pages joined the ranks of the Finns as before.

The companies had to leave their barracks at dawn and, on the way, we practised marching past to present ourselves to the Emperor. All the regiments gathered on the open battlefield. The infantry were in five lines, with the cavalry opposite, and, in between, the heavy artillery. At 9 o clock, the Emperor arrived and inspected every row from the beginning to the end. He talked to every regiment. Both Empresses also carried out an inspection. Once the inspection was complete, the Empresses sat in the pavilion with the Emperor remaining on his horse in front. Every regiment marched past and presented themselves to him. He then thanked the soldiers. When we marched past, I was at the head of my column. The people were staring, because I looked odd amongst the other soldiers. The Emperor also noticed me.

Today the Empress left Krasnoe Selo for Petersburg. Once all of us had come back to the camp, we prepared to return home as our stay there was over. The director of the school came to wish us well and the company commander congratulated me on doing a good job, saying there was nothing with which he could find fault.

The cadets were extremely pleased to be going home. I will probably stay in the embassy at Duderhof. On the 3rd of next month, I plan to go to London to see Toonmom Toh.

I beg to remain Your Majesty's obedient servant,
Chakrabongse

Emperor Nicholas II in the uniform of the Hussars.

6th August 1901
Bannakom Suranee

Dear Lek

I am more upset than I can possibly tell you that I did not send a telegram to the Emperor to congratulate him on the birth of Grand Duchess Anastasia. When the King of Italy had a daughter almost at the same time, I managed to send one, but I knew nothing about the other, until I received your letter. I felt as if I had been stabbed. I couldn't resist exclaiming, as to what I should do. So I sent a telegram while I was still angry and can't blame anyone for the fact that I did so. It's like the Kim Ting law, if you are a committee member, it is your duty to know what happens, so whatever I say that's how it is. Nevertheless, I can't help grumbling that going to Java has been like being in a black hole, as I couldn't read the newspapers as there were none in another language. In addition, the Reuters news service assumed everyone was Dutch, and so just sent news about the fighting in Africa, as they don't want to hear about anything else. As for news from Bangkok, this time Tan Lek was very good and always sent personal letters recounting things that

were not in government missives, such as illnesses. Government letters, however, because I was abroad, were sent via the Foreign Ministry who have been asleep these two months and sent nothing on at all, so all I had were telegrams. Those sent by Prince Lek came via the Port Authority, and I received every one, apart from the one telling me that the Emperor had had a baby. I made enquiries but to no avail. At first I was going to complain that I had appointed Phraya Sathiern [to deal with such matters], but when he did not accept, I had no proof of anyone seeing the prince about to post the letters but then forgetting. The government offices are like that, they think I have died already. I was so angry that I had to laugh.

That isn't all, however. Once I heard the news, I told them to find the gift which I had ordered when the Empress was five months pregnant. When you told me about it, it still wasn't finished and they asked for another 8 days. Then, when the 8 days were almost up, they said it would be 10, then when the 10th day came, it changed to 12. Today it has been 13 days and they have asked for another 3 to finish it. This is driving me crazy. Nowadays, Dook is nothing to do with it and never comes to the palace. I only go to Suan Dusit in the evenings, or some days not at all, if I'm feeling lazy. Sometimes I have a fever and have to be begged not to get ill. If someone talks amusingly to me till dawn, then the fever does not take hold. These days, illnesses become braver as I get older.

I have sent a copy of the letter to the Emperor with this letter. I did not know how to make excuses, so I wrote a letter just like that. However, when I will get the gift I don't know. When it arrives, please present it to the Emperor.

Eeyd Lek is better, but is not as strong as normal. It has been raining a lot, so he hasn't been out walking, but he is improving. Since my return, my stomach has not been very good and I feel overwhelmed with all the work that has piled up. I hardly have any free time. I think of you very much.

Chulalongkorn

15th August 1901

Your Majesty

As I told you in my last letter, after the camp was over, I stayed on Duderhof until the 2nd of this month, before returning to Petersburg in order to get ready to come to England. Then the next day, on the 3rd, I took the train direct to London arriving on the 5th just after 10 pm. It was very late because the train was delayed in Berlin, as there was something wrong with the engine, which we didn't know about.

At the station, several of my brothers came to meet me, as well as many officials. Toonmom Toh had also come, but, as the train was so late, he got too hungry and went back earlier. I am very pleased to be able to come and see Toonkramom Toh and my other brothers again. All the brothers in England were there, except for Pi Pen, who has gone to Germany, and Prince Vudh, who is in the middle of exams and so could not come. I hope that I will see him a bit later.

On the 10th, I accompanied Toonkramom Toh to the wedding of the daughter of Mr Phipps, with whom I stayed in the past. The wedding took place in the church near his house and went off well. Everyone paid their respects to Toonkramom Toh, as was appropriate to his rank. On the 12th, we performed a play at the embassy as we have often done before and it was a lot of fun. Everyone took part and all the students came to watch, so we all had a good meeting. Nowadays, I only know about half the students in England, but from what I can see and hear, things are going much better than last year, as those who were no good have been sent home. Their studies seem to be progressing well. In this regard, I can say that Mom Anuwat has been very important as he has disseminated many good ideas to the students. Mom Luang Sai Yud is also very good. He is an excellent student, has a degree both in engineering and law, and is also a good person. He has not become a *farang*, even though he has been in England a very long time. I gather that he will return to Bangkok shortly. I beg to suggest he should be taken into government service. I am very pleased to see how the students have improved, as last year they weren't up to much. By a bit of rearrangement among the princes, Danai and Traidos are now doing well. In fact,

Danai's results are very good after he failed one time, but now is fine. Traidos is also doing very well and now has passed into Cambridge, so I hope that he will be another success story.

On the 14th, I accompanied Toonkramom Toh to Delton to stay with Mr and Mrs Verney. Somdet Chai also came down, with Phraya Prasit and Phraya Rat. Chao Phraya Abhai Racha came across to London and was also invited. Phraya Suriya was there too, but the latter two have returned already and are going back to the continent.

On the 20th Toonkramom Toh will visit the Glasgow Exhibition[1] in Scotland and I will accompany him. I will tell you all about it in my next letter.

I beg to remain Your Majesty's obedient servant,
Chakrabongse

The Glasgow International Exhibition, held in Kelvingrove Park, was the second of four international exhibitions held in Glasgow during the late 19th and early 20th centuries. It ran from 2nd May to 4th November 1901.

Windsor Hotel, Glasgow   V. & S., Ltd., D. 53776

The Russian Pavilion in the Glasgow Exhibition 1901.

29th August 1901

Your Majesty

Since I wrote to you last, I have accompanied Toonkramom Toh to Glasgow in order to visit the exhibition being held there. We left London in the evening of the 20th and reached Glasgow in the early morning. We went to stay at the Windsor Hotel. The head of the town council came to receive Toonkramom Toh and pay his respects.

In the afternoon, we went to see the exhibition for the first time. The head of the town council came to meet us at the entrance and took us to the VIP room. He suggested what we should and should not see. In addition, he provided a guide for us. That day we saw a lot of different types of machinery and these were the star pieces of the exhibition. After seeing the engineering display, we saw various paintings. Among the foreign pavilions, we visited the Japanese one. There are very few foreign pavilions, namely only the Russian, French and Japanese pavilions. Apart from that, there were exhibits of the various English colonies. Other countries just sent items to display in the main hall and there wasn't that much. They were mainly items for sale, or for trade. The Japanese pavilion was in essence a big shop.

The next day on the 22nd in the afternoon, I accompanied Toonmom Toh in a boat for a trip around the port on the river. There were many ships at anchor and numerous docks, both for mooring and repair. I saw a Japanese mail boat and we wanted to see that ship come in to dock, but unfortunately the tide was too low and it could not enter. An officer of the port authority showed us around. The port is administered by a large committee known as the Clyde Trust, with the receipts from the mooring fees used for upkeep of the port and its improvement. Today, there was no time for the exhibition because we were at the port.

On the 23rd we went to see the exhibition, but before going there went to see a bicycle race and other competitions. We met the Duchess of Montrose and her two sons. The elder one, The Marquess of Graham, took us out at lunch time to see Scottish dancing. It looked very fast and neat.

Then, we went around all the things at the exhibition we had not seen the day before. The Russian pavilion was very large, but the items on show were from the Paris exhibition of the year before. Most things were linked to trade. I talked to the organiser of the Russian pavilion. He complained that this exhhibiton was strange as there were no prizes, and sales were poor. They had to pay for their stand, and the crowds were rather sparse as there were no performances of any kind, only three brass bands and a concert hall. There was also one Russian band.

On the 24th in the morning, we left Glasgow for London, arriving in the evening.

At the moment, I am staying with Mr Phipps, as his wife invited me to stay for around four days. The weather is glorious – not like in London and I am feeling very well.

I beg to remain Your Majesty's obedient servant,
Chakrabongse

Bannakom Soranee
7th September 1901

To my son Lek

I received your letters dated 25th June, 3rd and 24th July. Firstly, I have to express my regret at the Emperor's child being another girl, and I must also answer about the question of the cavalry. Nowadays, we do have cavalry in our country and it's not that I don't know that they are important – what I am complaining about is that the horses are so large and we are small, and I am worried you are going to fall off and hurt yourself. My pain about your last fall has not gone away. All this is only because of my love, which makes me grumble and such like. There is something Krom Luang told me, which he heard from Ta O and Mr Barbarov. They told Phraya Piphad that Phraya Mahibal is someone who people in Petersburg don't like, because he suggested you go take the money, which Captain Krulov borrowed, to pay back the official from the Tsar's treasury. This made the Emperor so angry, that he removed Captain Khrulov from being your guardian. Everyone thinks Phraya Mahibal should not have you involved you in this negative affair, even though no one thought badly about you, as you were a child.

I didn't really believe him and said that I didn't think it would be true as Captain Khrulov had to leave for other reasons, which are well known. Also he is a soldier and must get a soldier's pay, so why would he take money from the treasury. The issue of borrowing money is true. Mr O must have heard something. I agreed to ask you about this and so, if there is any truth about this, please let me know.

By the way, Krom Luang has been rather angry with Phraya Mahibal about the strongly worded telegram he sent. I have asked to stop the action to replace him, because if that were to happen, it would seem to be unsympathetic to the lady, and a bad thing.

At the moment, my back is hurting a lot and I can hardly write, so I will stop now. Your brother Eeyd Lek's hair is falling out, and I've collected almost as much as the top knot. At the bottom there is a white streak. Took teases him a lot. He is better, but his skin is pale and he looks not as healthy as before.

Chulalongkorn Por Ror

Winter Palace, Petersburg
17th September 1901

Your Majesty

I haven't written to Your Majesty for three mail drops now, because I have been travelling to and from various places and, when I should have been mailing the letters, I have been in the train.

I left London on the 7th of this month, crossed from Dover to Ostend and took the train to Frankfurt, reaching there late on the same day. Stayed the night and, early the next day, had a look around the town, which is rather fine. Frankfurt is a large city, and is clean and orderly. Many people live there because the weather is good and it is near to the various spas such as Wiesden [probably Wiesbaden] and Homburg.

In the evening of that day, I took the train for Kronburg, which is where Empress Frederick lived and died. From there, I went to the hospital near the town. This is where Oon, the wife of Phraya Mahibal, is receiving treatment and I went to visit her. The hospital is really good and stands on a hill with excellent fresh air. It is clean, tidy and very comfortable. It specialises in internal cysts, or what is referred to in English as lung diseases. They treat them in a new way, using air, as the doctors have discovered this new method, which does not require drugs. Simply, the strength of the patient is boosted,

Opposite above: Prince Rangsit photographed in Berlin.   *Above: Belle Alliance Platz, Berlin, 1900.*

so they can fight the disease themselves. Everyone believes this now, and the person who built the hospital is a good example, as previously he suffered from a severe lung disease, but after treatment here was completely cured. As a result, he established the hospital and has cured a lot of people, although it is true they only take those where the disease is not over developed.

I stayed in a hotel near the hospital for one night, before returning to Frankfurt and from there went to Berlin, reaching there in the early morning. I went to the embassy. This time, Prince Vudh came too which made it more fun. In Berlin, I met Prince Rangsit, who is really tall – much more so than me. He is also good at his studies and the teachers are very complimentary. From talking with him, it seems to me that he knows more than Prince Dilok and Prince Suriyong, who preceded him.

I am really sorry I did not see Toonkramom Chai this time, as he was engaged in military manoeuvres.

While I was in Berlin, I saw the Chinese prince[1], who has come as ambassador to try and apologise to the German emperor about the German ambassador being killed. The ambassador is very young, being only 19. He has a very pleasant face, and I gather that the Europeans have rather taken to him.

I stayed in Berlin for only two nights and left for Petersburg on the 12th, arriving on the 13th in the afternoon. I brought Prince Vudh with me, as I agree that it was a good opportunity for him to see the city.

On the 14th, I began studying again. I go to every class with the other cadets. I have to leave for class at 8 am and get back around 4.30. In certain subjects, where I am still deficient and really can't keep up, a teacher comes to the palace, or in free periods at the school, such as when the others are studying religion.

My new tutor[2], whom the Emperor has appointed for me, as a result of the incident about which Phraya Mahibal has already informed Your Majesty in detail, has begun his duties satisfactorily. And he seems much better than the previous one.

In Berlin, I received Your Majesty's letter discussing the question to do with Phraya Suriya. I am very grateful. I believe in Your Majesty's judgement and will do as Your Majesty says at all times.

I beg to remain Your Majesty's obedient servant,

Chakrabongse

s1. This was Tschang, Yin. The German Minister who was assassinated was Clemens von Ketteler..

2. Prince Chakrabongse's new tutor was Colonel Alexander Dmitrievich Deguy.

Winter Palace,
25th September 1901

Your Majesty

I have received Your Majesty's letter dated 6th August and thank Your Majesty very much. The letter, which I am to take to the Emperor has arrived, but the gift for the Grand Duchess has not. In addition, at present the Emperor is staying far away from here, being in Spala[1] in Poland, and I'm not sure when he will return. I think I should wait until he gets back before I present the letter, as I agree that it is not terribly important or urgent.

The Emperor's trip to France this time was very grand and impressive. The French received him very well and they excel at this sort of thing[2]. My studies are going well. I have to go to the Corps every day from 8 am to 16.30, while, in the evening, there are more classes in the palace. The additional lessons include Military administration, Military law, History of wars, Hippology (to do with horses) and International law. All these new subjects seem very

Spala, Bialowieza, Poland. The hunting lodge of Nicholas II.

useful. As to the timetable of my studies, I am sure Phra Sri has informed you.

On the 11th, at the embassy there was a party for the Thais in order to celebrate your birthday [20th September] and we all drank your health. On the 23rd, Prince Vudh and Phraya Mahibal left Petersburg for Germany.

I beg to remain Your Majesty's obedient servant,

Chakrabongse

1. Spala was the site of a hunting lodge owned by Nicholas II

2. Despite Chakrabongse's positive spin on the visit, in some quarters the reception of the Russian Tsar was judged to be less cordial than on the Emperor's previous visit in 1896 and he was criticized for not visiting Paris.

The Empreror and Empress near Bethune, France, 1901.

Opposite: Two details from the panorama commemorating the Tsar's French trip by Pavel Yakovlevich Pyastesky. At the top the Emperor and Empress in a carriage; below, the Imperial Yacht Standard mored at Dunkirk.

Opposite below: Poster released by Bon Marché to promote the alliance between Russia and France.

Royal Pages School, Petersburg
7th October 1901

Dear Father

Last week my German teacher died which is very sad because this teacher was an excellent person who died suddenly of a heart attack. I went to help with the funeral and made a contribution of 200 roubles, as the teacher was not a rich man, depending only on his salary. On his death, his widow has been left with nothing.

Last week I came and stayed at the school full time, as I had various duties to attend to, and was in sole charge with two younger cadets as my assistants. I am lucky that one of them is good, so it is not too hard. Usually, at the beginning of the school year, the assistants don't really know what they are doing and make lots of mistakes, for which the person in charge has to take responsibility.

This week we have begun to have mock exams. During the year, there are a series of mock exams across all the subjects that we study.

Apart from my studies, there is nothing much going on. It is very quiet and no one is in Petersburg at the moment. The Emperor is still in Spala, but I hear that he will come back slightly earlier than expected, within the next 20 days or so the rumours say.

I have heard that Your Majesty is going to travel north. I am sad I cannot accompany Your Majesty.

I beg to remain Your Majesty's obedient servant,
Chakrabongse

30th October 1901

Your Majesty

I have received Your Majesty's letter dated 7th September and understand everything now.

Concerning Mr Olarovsky and Mr Barbrov talking about Phraya Mahibal with regard to Captain Khrulov, the story is rather strange. I can tell you the truth of the matter to the best of my ability. Phraya Mahibal lent the captain money on many occasions, as Your Majesty knows. And the captain used the money as he pleased, with no one knowing what he spent it on. It seems that Captain Khrulov also had debts with the royal treasury and, when he got money from Phraya Mahibal, he may have used it to pay off this debt. It seems very likely, because the captain is a real scoundrel, running up debts everywhere, whether in connection with his work or privately. He was wont to use money, that should be for his duties as tutor, for his own private use and asks for money from everyone, while promising to pay it back.

However, because Captain Khrulov has used money from Phraya Mahibal to pay back the treasury, it does not mean that the Phraya gave it to him for that purpose. He lent it to him for general expenses and whatever the captain did with it nobody knows.

In my opinion, it is true that the Emperor seemed angry with Phraya Mahibal, because someone probably told him that Phraya Mahibal gave Captain Khrulov the money to repay the Imperial treasury. When he repaid the debt, no doubt one of the officials asked where he had got the money from and he probably replied that it was my money. Anyway, the Emperor asked the treasury to repay Phraya Mahibal on behalf of Captain Khrulov immediately. This shows that the Emperor felt he had lost face in that I, a foreigner staying in Russia as his guest, had had to use my money to clear a debt with his treasury run up by one of his officials. He was displeased that Phraya Mahibal got involved between his officials and the treasury, which was incorrect behaviour. This is what I am guessing. So then Phraya Mahibal got told off, despite having done nothing wrong in giving Captain Khrulov money to use in a general way, instead of continuing to pay him a salary. Rather it was Captain Khrulov who used the money incorrectly, and there was nothing Phraya Mahibal

could do about it, if that is, he even knew about it.

Regarding who should replace Phraya Mahibal is another difficult question. I am very surprised that Luang Visudh's name would come again because when he returned last year he went back for a reason, which was serious enough to make him unlikely to return. When it was known that Luang Visudh was coming again, no one believed it. Then, when he arrived, those who met him were shocked and amazed. The appointment of Luang Visudh as a government official, I agree is not a good idea for many reasons. As a person, he is a good man and he understands his job and how to do it. However, nowadays he likes having a good time and spends a lot of money, saving nothing. Then when his own money is finished, he makes use of government funds. There is no difference between Luang Visudh and Captain Khrulov. The fact he is going to take over from the ambassador is one thing, but that he will also be my guardian is something else.

This point is extremely important. Luang Visudh has a character, about which I have already informed Your Majesty, and he is a bad example for me. The Russian guardian does not trust him, as he is rather young and likes having too much of a good time. He will probably not allow me to come to the Thai embassy, which will make everything much more complicated. I tried talking to Phra Sri and he was grumbling in an awkward way. It was for all these reasons that I sent you a telegram, asking that Phra Sri take charge of this matter, because otherwise government business will not go smoothly. For example, this winter Toonkramom Toh is going to come and will stay at the embassy. To have Luang Visudh in charge of receiving him and looking after him is rather unsatisfactory. Everyone will be able to gossip and criticize.

I received Your Majesty's telegram from Phitsanulok. I was very pleased, but really sad that I could not accompany Your Majesty. I wanted to see my town, but I hope that I will be able to do so another time.

On the 26th, I was appointed as a Chamber Page, which is equivalent to the military rank of cornet. I was appointed to the Empress. Being appointed in this way is part of being in the Corps des Pages and

1. The identity of Mr Barbrov has not yet been determined.

Corps des Pages School,
20th November 1901

Your Majesty

nothing to do with the army, but of course it is a great honour. In order to be appointed a page of the chamber, you have to get good marks, that is to say at least 9 points out of 12. This year, 25 pages were appointed. Being appointed to an Imperial personage is determined according to the rank of the royalty. The person who is top of the class is appointed to the Emperor, second and third are appointed to the Dowager Empress, fourth and fifth to the Empress, sixth to the first ranking Grand Duchess, and so on down the imperial hierarchy. In fact, I should have been appointed to the Dowager Empress because I came first, but the Emperor decided I would be appointed to the Empress and that is what I wanted too. I did not want to be appointed to the Dowager Empress. Nai Poum has also been appointed to the Empress as my pair, as he came fourth, and the fifth best cadet has been appointed to the Dowager Empress.

I have heard that the Emperor will come back to Tsarskoe Selo around the 18th of November. I am concerned that the gift I am to present for the birth of the new Grand Duchess has still not arrived. I am worried it will not be here in time.

I beg to remain Your Majesty's obedient servant,
Chakrabongse

On the 18th, the Emperor and Empress returned to Tsarskoe Selo. Since their return from France, they have been staying in Poland in Spala and in Skranewitz. At the latter site, the Emperor shot huge numbers of different animals together with members of the imperial family and high officials. He shot so many, that it was a shocking thing and extremely cruel. According to the news on the first day, 1,600 animals were killed, which is really deplorable.

From now on, the Emperor will probably stay at Tsarskoe Selo until January, with trips to St. Petersburg from time to time, as is customary.

I have asked for an audience, in order to present your letter and the vase which you have sent for the baby Grand Duchess. I am sure I shall be granted one soon. I held back the letter and did not send it earlier, as I agree with you that there was no urgency, and I was waiting for the gift. The vase only arrived around 2-3 days ago, which is good timing.

On the 16th November, the anniversary of Your Majesty's coronation, the officials of the Page school, led by the director and all my teachers and friends, came to congratulate me and asked me to pass on their good wishes to you.

These officials and teachers come to every celebration to do with Thailand, such as Your Majesty's birthday and the coronation, as this time.

The weather here is now very cold and the river has frozen over which is unusual for mid November. Normally it freezes at the end of November or early December.

I beg to remain Your Majesty's obedient servant,
Chakrabongse

The Tsar and one of the stags killed at Spala in Poland

Corps de Pages, Petersburg,
10th December 1901

Your Majesty

The 9th of this month was the fete day of St George
and a very important day in the Russian calendar
because one of the Russian decorations is named after
this saint[1]. It is given to officers and those who show
bravery in battle and is seen as an award, which is
dedicated to true soldiers. As a result, this day is a
holiday for all those who have received the award and
there is a large ceremony at the palace.

I attended the ceremony in my capacity as page to
the Empress, together with the other chamber pages
and their charges.

We all left the school for the palace at 10 am. After
we arrived, we had a brief rest and then at 10.30 went
to wait near the balcony, where the Emperor appeared
at around 11.30. The Emperor came out alone at first
and inspected the serving soldiers assembled in the
palace. In that group, there was a page who had
received the award for gallantry during the war with
China two year's ago[2].

When it was almost 12, the two Empresses came
out with the female members of the imperial family.
We all bowed and went to carry their trains, as is our
duty. For the train of the two Empresses, there are two
pages, and for the male members of the family one.
The trains are very long and are separate from their
gowns, rather than being all of a piece. In order to carry
the trains, much practicing is required at the page
school. The two Empresses went to the throne hall,

Representatives of the 8-nation alliance in China.

which is known as the golden throne hall, where they
waited for the Emperor for a while. He then arrived
with the male nobles. Then a procession began, which
included officials from the Imperial palace and many
others who had received the aforementioned
decoration. The Emperor walked leading the Dowager
Empress and a Grand Duke took the arm of the
Empress, followed by other members of the imperial
family in pairs. They were followed by other officials
from the government and the palace. The pages
followed closely behind, carrying the trains through
the various throne halls. Along the way were
government officials and courtiers, tightly packed on
both sides. Eventually we reached the church within
the grounds of the palace. Here priests were waiting for
the royal party. They kissed the crucifix and the priests
gave them holy water. The procession went on, with
pairs of chanting priests in front, followed by more
priests, the Emperor, Empress and members of the
imperial family. They went past the veteran soldiers,
the police and others who had received the medal for
valour, at some point or another, and had all gathered
together at the palace today. The procession went on,
until it reached the St. George's Throne Hall, named
after the saint of the same name.

Within the throne hall, all the soldiers who were
still serving and had received the medal were lined up,
together with the company flags presented to the
regiments for valour during fighting. These are known
as the flags of St. George and had been brought into
the throne hall. Grand Duke Constantine was
commanding all the soldiers in the throne hall. When
the Emperor arrived, the soldiers all presented arms in
salutation and the trumpets played the imperial
anthem. The Emperor and Empresses inspected the

---

1. The Order of St. George was originally established in
November 1769 as the highest military decoration of the
Russian Empire by Empress Catherine the Great. It was
bestowed until the 1917 Russian Revolution and was only
awarded for extreme bravery in the face of the enemy. There
were four classes and the order was to be worn at all times.

2. This refers to the Boxer Rebellion which took place between
1899-1901. An 8-nation alliance sent 20,000 troops to China
and, in the Relief of Peking (14-15 August 1900), broke the siege,
begun in June, in which diplomats, foreigners and soldiers were
being held in their legations.

Russia used the opportunity to send 200,000 troops into
Manchuria, which by October 1900 was completely occupied.
Under the so-called Boxer Protocol, the Russian forces were to
withdraw, but they did not, and this was one of the factors leading to the Russo-Japanese war.

St. George's Hall, the principal throne room in the Winter Palace. Painting by Konstantin Ukhtomsky, 1862.

soldiers and came to sit in the middle of the room. All the priests assembled in the centre of the room, where there was an altar, and prayed for those soldiers who had been killed serving their regiments. This was followed by a blessing for the Emperor and the two Empresses. The nobles kissed the crucifix again and the priests gave them more holy water. They also sprinkled holy water on the various flags and the soldiers in the room. After this, everyone filed out and the Emperor, Empresses and members of the imperial family sprinkled holy water on the retired soldiers and others who had received the medal. Then, the two Empresses and female members of the imperial family went back the same way and withdrew. The Emperor stayed on to witness the flags being taken back. I did not see this ceremony because I accompanied the Empress back. After the ceremony, the Emperor went to see the soldiers having their banquet, provided by the government. After the Empress went up, the daytime part was over. When the ordinary soldiers had eaten, they were given the knives, forks and the plates used

today as a souvenir. As for all the pages, after our duties were over, we went to a room to rest and have some food.

At 4 .30 pm, we got ready again and went down to perform further duties. At dusk, there was a full dress banquet for all those officials who had received the St. George decoration. Everyone who lived in Petersburg, or nearby, was invited. As a result, there was all ranks, from generals to captains, both old and young. There were also civilians of high and low rank. One person didn't even have a uniform.

Once all the officials were in place, the Emperor, the Empresses and other members of the imperial family came out. The male members were all royal and had received the St. George medal. All the female royals sat at table. The two Empresses sat next to each other in the middle of the table. To the right of the Dowager Empress was the Grand Duke heir presumptive, and on either side were the Grand Dukes and Duchesses in order of precedence, followed by officials. The Emperor sat in the middle of the table on

Grand Duke Michael Alexandrovich (1878-1918), the youngest brother of Nicholas II and heir presumptive. Painted by Ilya Repin in 1900.

Corps de Pages, Petersburg,
25th December 1901

Your Majesty

The 19th was the Emperor's nameday, an important and joyous festival in this country. On that day the Emperor and Empress came to Petersburg and in the morning there were prayers in the palace, and high-ranking officials and close colleagues visited to present their congratulations.

Only those pages attached to the Emperor and Empress were instructed to attend, so I was in that group. Our duties this time were not very onerous. All we had to do was follow them to the church and stand waiting outside. Then, when they emerged from the church and had received the good wishes of the various officials, we followed them back to the palace. Before the Empress went up, she thanked her pages and gave us her hand as usual.

After this, the Emperor received congratulations from the sergeants of the various regiments of which he is head, and then he inspected the companies which were celebrating that day.

In the afternoon, I had an audience with the King of Montenegro[1], who is staying in Petersburg at the moment. He received me very well. He asked me how

the other side. On his right was Grand Duke Michael, who has received the order of St. George First Class. He is the only one. On his left was General Vanovsky, Minister of Military Strategy, followed by other officials. During the dinner, the pages stood behind the chairs, as custom dictates. When the meal was almost over, the Emperor drank a toast to the most senior person who had received the order, namely Grand Duke Michael, and then all those who had received the order. He kissed the Grand Duke, who then drank a toast to the Emperor.

After the dinner, everyone lined up to pay their respects to the Emperor. The Empresses came out to talk with everyone. The pages followed. At that time, I noticed that the Emperor spoke in Russian to all those who could not speak French. At 9 pm, the royals withdrew.

The Empress gave me her hand and thanked me very much, asking me if I felt tired or not.

That was the end of proceedings. The Empress gave me the menu and the musical programme as a souvenir. Today was the first day the pages really had to perform their duties, but everything went off well.

I beg to remain Your Majesty's obedient servant,

Chakrabongse

The King of Montenegro.

Царское-Село — Tzarskoé-Sélo
Вокзалъ — La gare.

long I had been in the Corps des Pages and said he had seen me performing my duties in the morning. He said that Thailand must be a beautiful country and said that he had heard from the Emperor that Your Majesty had received him really well. He also asked whether Your Majesty was in good health and he said that he remembered Pi Chira, and asked me to tell him that he remembered him well and that, "I have an affectionate souvenir of him".

I gave him my congratulations as, having the same name as the Emperor, today is his name day as well. When I said goodbye, he came out to see me off on the steps of the palace.

The 22nd was the day when all those who had been appointed pages of the chamber were to present themselves to the Emperor and the Empress, according to a tradition that takes place every year.

All of us went from Petersburg to Tsarskoe Selo in order to see the Emperor in the palace, when he came out from church. All the pages were waiting for him. When he came out, he chatted with us and the director presented us by calling out our names in order. The Empress came after the Emperor and the Commander of the First Company called out the names to be presented in the same way. Both the

Emperor and Empress spoke to every page and asked after their fathers and mothers, and which regiment they were intending to enter. With me, both the Emperor and Empress spoke about Toonmom Toh's impending visit here, and they also mentioned that they had heard he was about to return to Bangkok. I replied that he would be returning in the summer and thus, before leaving for good, he would come and say goodbye to both of them. The Empress asked for news from Bangkok and how things were, and the Emperor said that he had written to Your Majesty.

When he had talked to every page, the Emperor gave his blessing to the cadets and hoped that we would all study hard and have success. Having said goodbye, he then left. All of us were given lunch and then we took the train back to Petersburg.

The next day on the 23rd, I went to perform my duties again on the occasion of the Empress receiving the wives of those officials who were bringing their daughters, or relatives, to be presented so that they could work at court in some capacity or another. All I had to do was walk behind her as before.

Concerning Toonmom Toh's visit this time, it has been decided that he will stay in the palace and there will probably be an official assigned to him in line with his rank. He will arrive here on the 6th of January.

I beg to remain Your Majesty's obedient servant,
Chakrabongse

1. Nikola I Petrović-Njegoš (1841–1921) was the ruler of Montenegro from 1860 to 1918, reigning as sovereign prince from 1860 to 1910 and as king from 1910 to 1918.

The graduating class of 1902.

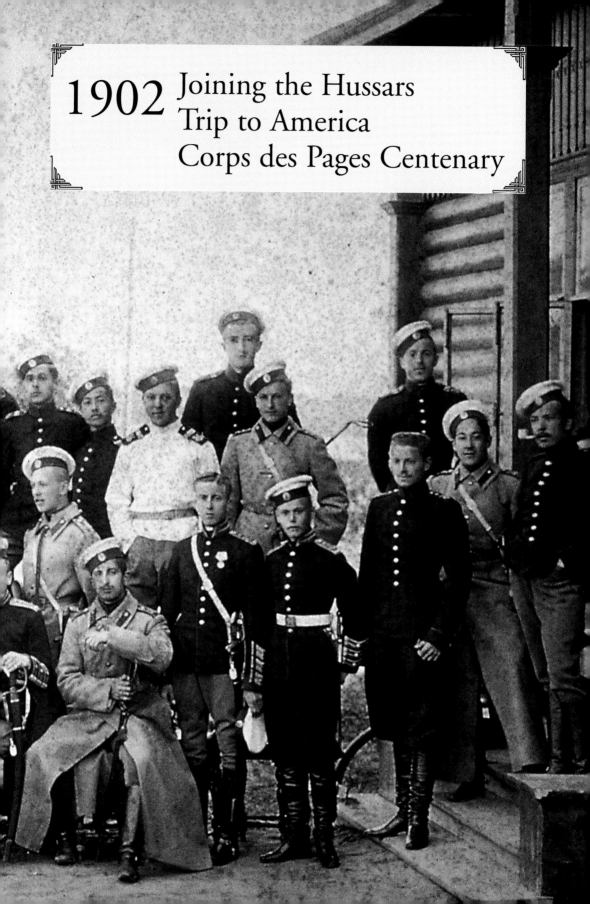

1902 Joining the Hussars
Trip to America
Corps des Pages Centenary

Siamese embassy, Petersburg
1st January 1902

Your Majesty

I have heard that Your Majesty has decided to remove Phraya Mahibal from the post of ambassador here and that Your Majesty is recalling him to Bangkok. I am very surprised and do not clearly understand the reason. I am aware of the fact that Phraya Mahibal had requested a sabbatical from his official duties, which according to the rules of the Foreign Ministry is allowed, and for which he had a good reason as his wife was very unwell and there was no one to take care of her. It is normal that any man would go and help look after his wife to the best of his ability. Now, she is much better and should be completely cured quite soon. Indeed, her condition is so much improved that Phraya Mahibal came back here in order to serve Your Majesty once more, only to be ordered to return. Everyone here is very surprised as to why the ambassador is being changed. The Minister of Foreign Affairs[1] expressed his astonishment and sent a telegram to the Russian ambassador in Bangkok, which Your Majesty probably knows about.

Despite what M. Olarovsky has been saying in Bangkok and what Your Majesty has probably heard concerning the Emperor being furious with Phraya Mahibal, I now know that there is no truth to this rumour whatsoever. The personal doctor to the Emperor, who is very close and sees him every day, has confirmed that it is not true. This doctor has also said this to the Head of the Royal Household and the foreign ministry. Both these people want to meet with Phraya Mahibal, in order to explain that he has been falsely accused with no basis whatsoever. Now that the Minister of Foreign Affairs has heard that Phraya Mahibal is to leave, he understands that it is because Bangkok has been listening to M. Olarovsky and is worried that the Russians dislike Phraya Mahibal. They even thought of writing a letter explaining everything and showing that there is no truth to the allegations. To sum up, here it seems extraordinary that Phraya Mahibal is going back and everyone will be very upset, if it is because of the misunderstanding I have told you about.

As for M. Olarovsky, he will probably be withdrawn as ambassador to Bangkok quite shortly

Count Vladimir Nikolaivich Lamsdorf.

because Count Lamsdorf has seen clearly that he is not acting in Russia's best interests. Count Muraviev made a bad choice, or did not make a choice at all, because he was sent straight from China and he had not even met him before he was sent to Thailand.

Regarding Count Lamsdorf, I have listened to the views of Phraya Suriya, who holds that Count Lamsdorf does not like, or actively dislikes Siam, while always praising Count Muraviev as being so excellent. In this matter, I am very uneasy. Count Muraviev is not good at all, but very cunning and babbles a lot for show. In reality, he does nothing. When he was minister, it was Count Lamsdorf who did everything, while Count Muraviev just showed off. Count Lamsdorf is a serious person who does things himself and works 14 hours a day. He talks little and does a lot. All the ambassadors here praise him, including the Japanese ambassador and usually the Japanese don't like the Russians much. Another thing is that the Emperor is very fond of Count Lamsdorf, as they have the same attitude of not bothering people and of walking a very straight path. In contrast, the Emperor did not much like Count

1. Count Vladimir Nikolayevich Lamsdorf (1845-1907) of Baltic German descent, served as Foreign Minister from 1900-1906, a critical period which included the Russo-Japanese War and the 1905 Revolution.

Poum and Prince Chakrabongse at the end of 1901.

Muraviev because they did not agree on things. Count Muraviev likes flashy things, while the Emperor is rather quiet and restrained. I have told Your Majesty all this, so Your Majesty can see how these two differ from each other. On the question of whether Count Lamsdorf dislikes or loves Thailand, I cannot comment. However, my view is that Count Lamsdorf is someone who talks little and only does something when the opportunity arises. In general, he has to look out for Russia's interests overall, and it is usual that all countries think about themselves more than others.

I am informing Your Majesty of all this, based on what I have heard from those close to him. I would not like the government in Bangkok to take against Count Lamsdorf for no reason. And as for M. Olarovsky, he has done everything on his own initiative and not according to the wishes of the minister at all. For that reason, he cannot be held up as an example, and I will be pleased if a new person takes over.

I beg to remain Your Majesty's obedient servant,
Chakrabongse

21st January 1902

Your Majesty

On the 10th of this month, Toonmom Toh came to Petersburg. Originally he was going to leave [London] on the 6th, but he was ill with a cold and the doctor forbade him to travel, so his departure had to be delayed. It was very awkward, as we had to inform officials in the various departments who were waiting to receive him, some of whom had left Petersburg to meet him at the border.

On the day before he was to arrive, I went to await him. I went quite a long time in advance, but did not get there in time for Grand Duke Michael. Later, I learnt that he had come from Gatchina, and so waited at the station. The Grand Duke talked to me the entire time that we were waiting and asked me to introduce Thongrod and Luang Surayudh, as he had not yet met them. He asked whose son Thongrod was and when had he arrived.

On the Russian side, those who came to meet him were the Mayor of Petersburg, the Commandant of Petersburg, and the Head of Police, as well as Colonel Dutchkov who is detailed to look after the royal family.

Once the train arrived, the Grand Duke went in to meet Toonmom Toh in the train and escorted him out. He introduced all those who had come to meet him and Toonmom Toh introduced Phra Sri Thammasan, M. Cuissard to the Grand Duke, as well as Luang Sorasidh who had also accompanied him. Prince Oblensky, the royal guard, had gone to meet him at the border and accompanied him here, and will stay with him throughout.

The Grand Duke invited Toonmom Toh to go in his carriage to the Winter Palace. Awaiting to receive him there, were officials of the Royal Household, Baron Frederick, a senior protocol officer, Prince Kodaruk, the deputy protocol officer, Count Beckendorf, General Drisprenesky, in overall charge of the palace, and the assistants to the various Grand Dukes who introduced all these august people to Toonmom Toh. After that, they led him up to his quarters, showing him all the various rooms and chatting for a while before taking their leave.

The next day, the 11th, Toonmom Toh went to lay a wreath at the tomb of Emperor Alexander III and went to leave his card with various members of the imperial family. He also went to see Grand Duke Michael in the Emperor's apartment in the Winter Palace.

In the evening he went to see a play and the Emperor graciously arranged for him to sit in the imperial box the entire time he is staying in the palace.

On the 12th, we went to visit the Emperor. Apart from Toonmom Toh and the officials accompanying him, the Emperor invited me too. We left Petersburg for Tsarskoe Selo just after 11 am, reaching the palace at 12. Toonmom Toh went in to see the Emperor and Empress on his own first and I waited with Grand Duchess Marie, who chatted with me until the Emperor and Empress emerged for lunch. Today there were many government officials in half-dress uniform. The Emperor was in half-dress uniform and wearing the Chakri sash. There were few members of the imperial family, apart from Grand Duke George, the royal equerry on duty, and Grand Duchess Marie, his wife.

At lunch, Toonmom Toh sat on the right of the Emperor and I, on his left. The Emperor sat opposite the Empress. During lunch the Empress chatted with me about holding her train and explained how to hold it in a way that was comfortable for her. I told her how we had to practice. She laughed a lot and said she would love to see us doing that. I asked after her daughters. She said they were only just feeling better, as all of them had been unwell. She also talked of many other matters.

The Emperor raised his glass to drink with Toonmom Toh and then with me. I stood up and the Emperor said loudly, "Sit down, sit down!" I drained my glass and he smiled. I said that when drinking to the Emperor, one must drain one's glass and he bowed deeply.

After lunch, I asked the Emperor which regiment I should join. He asked me which regiment I would like to join. I replied that I would like to join the Hussars[1]. He replied that he must think about the matter further. The first time that Grand Duke Constantine had raised the matter with him, he had not had time to discuss it fully, and then the Grand Duke had left Petersburg.

He asked whether I had written to Your Majesty about this. I replied that I had not, as I knew Your Majesty had the utmost confidence in his judgement and desire that he should choose and that whatever he chose would be good. The Emperor said that was correct and, therefor, he needed to think carefully. He promised

that on the 17th, he would definitely give me an answer.

The Emperor enquired further as to whether I wished to enter the Academy, to which I replied in the affirmative. He said that I should serve for two years as an officer first and explained why serving in the regiment was beneficial for a young man, who was just establishing himself, adding that he had experienced this himself. In the regiment, the officers have to train the young soldiers who come into the army every year. They have to be trained not only to shoot, throw and carry their guns, but also to train others. They have to be educated in various things and learn to be polite and a good person, much in the way that parents train their children. In order to be able to train others, one has to train oneself to be good first. Thus, it is good for officers to have to train raw recruits. The Emperor said that he felt sorry for civilians, that they did not get such a training. And explained that for this reason, soldiers could go and take jobs in various ministries and do a good job. The only exception was the Ministry of Finance, as that required specialist training.

After that, he praised the Russian lower classes, such as those who came to be soldiers and said that they were excellent and good hearted. He also said they were the only good people in the country.

I told him that I agreed with him wholeheartedly and that I had seen such qualities for myself when I was with the Finnish regiment during the summer camp.

Then the Emperor asked about that regiment and which company I was in and who was the captain. He said it was an excellent regiment.

After that, the Emperor talked about the Hussars. He said it was a very good regiment and that, together with the infantry regiment, the Preobrazhensky regiment[2], these were the two that he regarded as 'my own private regiments'. He said that he liked both equally. The Emperor asked me whether I had seen the Hussars during military manoeuvres. I replied that I had, and that I had heard a great deal as to how it was an excellent regiment and how the officers of other

1. After reforms to the cavalry in 1882, there were two Hussar Regiments. Of these, Prince Chakrabongse wanted to be in The Lifeguards of His Majesty

2. The Lifeguard Preobrazhensky Regiment was one of the oldest, elite guard regiments of the Imperial Russian Army.

3. Thongrod was the nickname of Prince Thongthikayu Thongyai. One year after Prince Chakrabongse arrived at St. Petersburg, he also enrolled in the Corps des Pages. Later in 1908 he joined the Cossack regiment and trained in the elite Cavalry School.

regiments, if they know the Hussars were backing them up, would exclaim that they felt relieved and certain of victory. The Emperor explained that in the regiment, the officers all got on very well, even though they came from different cadet schools and there was never any friction.

The Emperor talked about Thongrod[3] and asked if he had entered the Pages School now, and the Empress also enquired as to whose son he was. I answered the enquiries appropriately. He asked about Poum and whether he could keep up well with me, to which I replied he could keep up well. The Emperor replied, "I am glad that it is going so well." He also asked if the new tutor was working out well. I said he was fine and the Emperor said he was a good man. All in all, the Emperor talked to me for about 10-20 minutes, before going to chat with some officers.

At around 1.30, the Emperor said we could all take our leave, having invited Toonmom Toh to come and join in the New Year's celebrations in two days' time.

On the 14th, which here is considered to be the 1st and thus New Year's Day, there are grand celebrations at the palace. I had to go and attend in my capacity as a chamber page. I had to go to the school in the early morning and then go to the palace at 10 am and wait as instructed. Toonmom Toh came along and both Phraya Rat and Luang Sorasit were also invited. At 11 o clock, the Emperor emerged with Empress Marie on his arm. The Empress graciously asked Toonmom Toh to lead her out. Other members of the imperial family followed behind and they processed as a group through the various rooms in the palace, where officials were waiting to pay their repects. The procession continued as far as the Imperial chapel in the palace. In the chapel, there were the traditional prayers for around one hour, after which they processed back. They then received the ambassadors and consuls who had come to present their good wishes for New Year. They talked to everyone in order of rank. The Emperor came first, followed by Empress Marie and the Empress. All the ambassadors were rather impressed that I was a page to the Empress. Toonmom Toh came and led the Empress. The French Secretary General remarked to Phra Sri Thammasan, "Today you lot are certainly very grand!"

The reception for the ambassadors and consuls went on rather a long time, over an hour, as there were so many of them. From there, the Empress went back to her rooms and had lunch, together with the imperial

The chapel within the Winter Palace.

Prince Chakrabongse, in Hussar uniform, and Thongrod, in the uniform of the Corps des Pages, 1902.

The Finland station in St. Petersburg.

The fort in Vyborg.

family. When lunch was almost finished, the two Empresses came out again. Before emerging, she called the pages to come in and support her train. She asked me whether I had had anything to eat or not. When I said no, she was shocked and said I must be very hungry. This time both Empresses came out to receive the female officials and the wives and children of the officials. All these ladies lined up and kissed their hands. After this, she withdrew and that was the end of proceedings for today.

On the 15th, the Emperor gave a luncheon in honour of Toonmom Toh. I was also invited, as were the officials accompanying him from England and the embassy staff. On the Russian side, apart from the Emperor and Empress, there were various Grand Dukes and close officials. During the luncheon, the Emperor drank a toast to Toonmom and Sadet Mother. The trumpets played a fanfare. During the meal he talked to all those in attendance. I saw the young Grand Duchesses, whom I had not seen for a while. They were much grown, in particular the oldest one and she conducts herself in a very grown up and polite fashion.

Today Toonmom Toh took his leave of the Emperor and Empress and, in the evening, left Petersburg to go to Vyborg in Finland. This was the end of the state visit.

I accompanied Toonmom Toh on his trip to Finland, as did Phraya Rat, Luang Sorasit, Phra Sri Thammasan, Nai Poum, Luang Surayudh and Colonel Deguy, my tutor, who was in charge of all the arrangements for the trip.

At around 10 pm we reached Vyborg. The mayor of that city came to receive us, together with many officials. Actually, we had not told them of the trip, as it

was a private one. However, they came anyway. From the station we went to the hotel. On the next day, 16th, the mayor came early in the morning and asked to accompany us on the trip to Imatra. We begged him not to, as it was a genuinely private visit and it was quite unnecessary, but in the end we had to let him come. In the afternoon, we went to see the fort in the middle of the town. This fort is around 600 years old. Nowadays, it used as the HQ for the commander of the regiment stationed in Vyborg. The fort has a high tower. I went up and from the top had a good view, but as it was the winter, all I could see was mainly snow and ice. If it was the summer, it would have been very beautiful. This fort was attacked by Peter the Great 200 years ago.

In the evening of the 16th, we left Vyborg for Imatra. In this township there are famous rapids[1], which are very impressive and visited by many tourists. The train reached there around 9 pm. We stayed in a hotel that night. We went by sledge to see the rapids. But unfortunately the electricity, which used to illuminate them, was off. Although we couldn't see the falls that clearly, we could discern their power and magnificence.

On the 17th in the morning, we went to see the rapids again and could see how impressive they were. The water flows very strongly indeed and it is said that the power of the water could provide electricity for the whole of Finland. From here we went to see another waterfall, known as the Small Imatra falls. The route was completely snowbound and we passed through beautiful forested mountains. The waterfall is also very dramatic and can be seen at the very edge close up.

In the afternoon, we left Amatra to return to Petersburg, and Toonmom Toh stayed on at the

The Amatra Falls c. 1900. (Library of Congress)

embassy in a private capacity. The 19th was a Russian Fete day as it is considered to be the date on which Jesus was baptized. There was a big ceremony in the palace, which I had to attend in my role as royal page.

There was a procession from the royal quarters to the chapel, just as at New Year, but in the various rooms there was half a regiment composed of all the regiments in the Petersburg county, together with their regimental colours. Before going to the chapel, the Emperor made an inspection and talked to the soldiers. This time, we had to stand in the chapel for a very long time. Then from the chapel, the priests were carried in procession to the podium, which had been set up on the edge of the river. The Emperor was presiding, but the two Empresses remained inside and observed from the

gallery. For that reason I did not have to go outside, which was extremely lucky, as it was exceptionally cold and everyone had to remove their hats. At the pavilion, they made holy water in the river and sprinkled this on the Emperor and the various flags. Once the ceremony was over, the Emperor went back inside. Before going up, he came over to me and said that I should enter the Hussar regiment, so that is decided. After the ceremony was over, the Emperor and Empresses had lunch with the nobles and various officials, as well as the ambassadors who were invited to observe, but were not received by the Emperor.

I am well and thinking of Your Majesty constantly,
I beg to remain Your Majesty's obedient servant,
Chakrabongse

1. The Imatrankoski Rapids are Imatra's most famous site and have been a tourist attraction for hundreds of years. At the turn of the century, the rapids had Imatra's historical and still famous hotel, the Valtion hotelli, standing on its banks.

*Charlemagne Tower Jnr, American ambassador
to St. Petersburg, c. 1900.*

Gustave Lannes de Montebello in his study in St. Petersburg.

*Auguste Pavie (left) and Pierre Antonin Lefèvre-Pontalis
(right) in 1893.*

1. Pierre Antonin Lefèvre-Pontalis (November 1864-1938) was attaché at the embassy for the special mission to Indochina in 1889 and member of the commission determining the border from the Red River to the Mekong. He was secretary at the embassy in St. Petersburg in 1899. He and Prince Chakrabongse were to meet again between 1912-1918 when he was Minister Plenipotentiary in Bangkok.

2. Gustave Lannes de Montebello was French ambassador in St. Petersburg from 1891 until November 1902. Nicholas II was godfather to his oldest grandson and attended the christening on his visit to France in September 1902. However, the ambassador was withdrawn from his post after his wife turned up to a luncheon wearing a hat, when all the other ladies were bare headed. This was considered a sign of arrogance.

3. Charlemagne Tower Jnr was ambassador to Russia from January 1899-November 1902.

Corps de Pages, Petersburg
5th February 1902

Your Majesty

On the 26th January, Toonkramom Toh left Petersburg in the evening to go to Vienna and then go on to Egypt.

On the 27th, I was invited to go to a meeting at the American embassy. There were quite a lot of people, consisting mainly of ambassadors. On that day, I met with the Secretary General of France, M. Pontalis[1], who went to Bangkok at one time. We got on quite well together and discussed how I hoped he could be ambassador in Bangkok. He said he had always wanted to go there, but that the government kept him here. He told me that the French embassy here always got news direct from Bangkok and he invited the ambassador here to come and meet me. The ambassador[2] is rather grand and haughty, as is normal, but I behaved in a very polite and conciliatory manner. He praised me, saying that I could speak many languages and that my French was also good, although he said that I had an English accent.

The American ambassador here is very good and gets on well with me. The Americans are very pleased that now there is a Thai ambassador in the USA.

On the 28th, there was a State Ball in the palace. All the officials were invited. In all, there were about 3,500 people, including ambassadors, deputy ambassadors, first secretaries – everyone. I attended as a page.

The palace was decorated beautifully. The ballroom was massive, indeed the largest room in the palace, but even so it was crammed with people and there was hardly any room to walk. The Emperor and Empress attended, with officials following on behind. They processed through the room and back again. The Empress danced with the various ambassadors, one after another. She danced for almost half an hour, before going up to take tea with the imperial family, and the ambassadors were also invited.

After tea, the Empress came out to receive the wives and daughters of all the officials who had come today. There were a great number of people, almost 200, and the reception took a long time. She must have been very tired. After this, she danced a little more and then sat down to dine. All 3,500 guests were seated, with the Empress sitting in the middle and the Turkish ambassador on her right and the French ambassador on her left. Also at the table were Grand Duchesses and other ambassadors, as well as two or three senior officials both male and female. Everyone else sat at other tables, both in the same room and throughout the palace. The Emperor walked around to every table, as the custom in Russia requires the host to go to every table, seeing that everyone is well taken care of. After he had made his rounds, he then goes to sit in an empty place somewhere. Today he went and sat next to the Duchess of Sutherland, who is visiting Petersburg at the moment and was thus invited too.

After dinner there was a ballet performance, which went on until 2 am. This was the end of the evening.

On the 1st February, a play was performed at the Pages School. All the pages took part and many people, who were either relatives of those performing or former students of the school, came to watch,

This time, the Dowager Empress came also, and so the whole event became very grand, as various other members of the imperial family were also in attendance.

As I have now completed my studies in the Pages School, I have asked Phra Sri to send a list of those who should receive royal decorations for Your Majesty's perusal. After their names, I have added the decoration, which I feel is appropriate. I hope Your Majesty will agree with my suggestions. Another thing is that I would like to ask if these decorations and the accompanying certificates could arrive here around August, or at the latest by October.

Previously, I had thought that before I became a soldier here, I would ask Your Majesty's permission to come home again, but now something has intervened which makes this difficult. In the winter, the Page School will celebrate its centenary. Originally, the commemoration was planned for October and I thought I could leave after that, but now I understand that it has been postponed until December, as in October the Emperor will not be staying near the capital. Therefore it is difficult for me to come home this winter, as it would look bad if I were not part of these celebrations and how often will there be an event that is so important in the history of the school? For this reason, I am thinking I should serve here until around September 1904 and then come and visit Your Majesty. I am sad that events have intervened which prevent me from seeing Your Majesty shortly, but later this year Toonmom Toh will be returning home and, therefore, Your Majesty won't be needing to talk about me that much and I might get in the way of all the receptions planned for him.

When I am an officer, I will have some spare time for a rest before entering the regiment. The appointments will be made around the end of August. For that reason, the break period will be suitable for Toonmom Toh to go to America. I would like to ask Your Majesty's permission to follow him on the trip. If that could be agreed, I would be so delighted. At the end of the holiday, I will then come back to enter army service. The period off will be about one month. In this matter, if Your Majesty agrees or disagrees, it would be very good if Your Majesty could send a telegram, so that I can make arrangements with Toonkramom Toh in good time.

By the way, I am delighted to be able to tell Your Majesty that, adding together all the marks obtained in retaking certain exams from September until now, namely half of the total period of my studies, I have received the most points so far. I am determined to continue to study hard and to graduate top of the class and have my name carved on the marble panel. Whether I will succeed I don't know, as the students who are my competitors are intelligent and have very good memories, making them very hard to beat. Their language skills are better also.

I beg to remain Your Majesty's obedient servant,
Chakrabongse

Royal Pages School, Petersburg
17th February 1902

Your Majesty

On the 9th of this month, we went to see an exhibition of fishing equipment[1], which is on display here at the moment and to which our country has contributed. The curators of the exhibition received us very well and took us to see everything. In the show, apart from Russian fishing gear, there is material from many other countries, including Germany, France, Japan, Sweden and Norway. That provided by Germany was nothing much, with just a few fish and models of equipment for preventing the fish from going bad. The French section was very large, with lots of things on show, such as fishing equipment and actual fish, as well as oysters and other things. Their fishing equipment has many good features. The French officials gave me a book about fishing, which is very large and has many beautiful plates. The Japanese exhibit was also excellent, like that which they have in Tokyo, as well as information about the school for teaching fishing methods and also breeding. The officials said it was an excellent school. The Thai pavilion looked very good and reasonably authentic, but there was not much to see inside. The exhibition officials liked our nets and said they were among the best. They said that when Russian fishermen saw our nets, they praised them more than any others. The reason they admire them so much is that they have a small chain around the perimeter of the net to weigh it down, whereas here they use lumps of lead tied at intervals, which are not so effective.

In the Russian section, there were many fish which can be bred by collecting the eggs. This is very useful, as fish stocks in the rivers are declining every day because of steamships and various factories, sited on the riverbank, releasing polluted water into the rivers and causing many fish deaths. In addition, they also over fish. So fish stocks are getting less all the time, hence the need for breeding, so that people can still eat fish in the future. I think that this would be a very good thing to do in our country as well, if not now but in the future, as fish stocks in Siam will also decline. In the exhibition, there was an aquarium with live fish. There were many species, including our fighting fish. Visitors found the fighting fish very bizarre, as well as

the unusual way in which they are kept. I told them how in Thailand they are very common and that people use them to gamble heavily. The official found it so intriguing, that he wrote about it in the newspaper.

Once we had looked round the entire exhibition, the official asked me to go to a reception room, which had been beautifully decorated in order to welcome the Tsar. They had laid on some refreshments. General Lerin, chairman of the exhibition committee, sent his good wishes for Your Majesty and Siam as well. After that Mr Grimm, head of the management committee, drank a toast to Siam. I thanked them and drank a toast in return.

With reference to my request for royal decorations for various officials here, there is still one missing, namely for Colonel Barochin, who is also in the Corps des Pages. He was responsible for training me in sword fighting. I agree that he should receive the Order of the Crown of Siam 3rd Class. In this regard, I imagine Phraya Sri Thammasan has already added his name to the list.

I beg to remain Your Majesty's obedient servant,
Chakrabongse

17th February 1902

Your Majesty

On the 15th of this month, one of the Kalmyks[1], who are Buddhists, Major Ulyanov, came to seem me with various books written in their language, concerning Buddhism, the priests and the Kalmyk people and their costumes, including drawings of the Kalmyks and Buddha images. He wanted me to send these to Your Majesty. They look very interesting. One of the books is in Russian, while the rest were in Kalmyk, although one had a French translation. All these things I have arranged to be sent to Your Majesty. I asked M. Olarovsky, who is going to return shortly, to bring them with him, as I think this is easier than sending them off on their own. I think they will be safe like this. These things are rare and very valuable.

1. This was the International Industrial Fishing Exhibition 1902, in which Siam took part. Afterwards, the items exhibited were donated to the the Indochinese collections of the MAE (Peter the Great Museum of Anthropology and Ethnography). The museum was begun from gifts donated to Tsarevich Nikolai Alexandrovich (later Tsar Nicholas II) during his Eastern Voyage. to the exhibition to the Museum.

They are all catalogued and described in French. The explanations have the names of the priests and the officers in detail.

The reason the Kalmyks came to see me was to beg me to ask Your Majesty to give them a Buddha relic that you received from India, as you had already given one to the Buryat people. However, the Buryats are next to Siberia and far from the Kalmyks, who are unable to go and worship the relic, as they would like. For this reason, they would like to receive one for themselves. The Kalmyks live in European Russia in the river county [?], among the southern Russians near the Black Sea. In one of the books written in Russian, there is a history of the Kalmyk people and an account of the existence of Buddhism in great detail. I am sure M. Olarovsky, or the First Secretary of the Russian embassy, would be delighted to translate this for Your Majesty.

I replied that I would be delighted to inform Your Majesty of their request, but that I was unable to predict how Your Majesty might respond. I thanked them in advance on Your Majesty's behalf and for myself too for their bringing such valuable items as gifts. I'm sure Your Majesty will be delighted with them.

At the moment there is dancing in the palace and various plays two times a week and I am always invited. The Emperor and both Empresses are well, but the other members of the royal family are rather prone to illness. One minute, one is ill and the next minute another, taking it in turns without cease.

People fall ill here rather frequently, generally with influenza. I have not been that well for 2-3 days, but I am quite recovered now and back to normal.

It has been decided that Mr Olarovsky is going to return again and will be promoted to ambassador. He is extremely pleased. I have asked him to bring with him photographs of me in my Hussar uniform for you, Sadet Mae, Somdet Aunt and my younger brothers. The photo shows me in full dress and in other uniforms, and wearing a cap as well as a group photograph of me, Nai Poum and Colonel Deguy, who will continue to my adjutant.

I think of Your Majesty always and I hope that Your Majesty is happy.

I beg to remain Your Majesty's obedient servant,
Chakrabongse

Bannakom Soranee
3rd March 1902

Dear Lek

I have received many letters from you, which I have not answered, as this year my asthma, which I have had for three years, has got much worse because the weather in Bangkok has been colder than before and gone on for longer. The water is always rising. Many people without exception, whether noble or commoner, young or old, have been unwell with serious illnesses. Government business has also been heavy, with nothing around being calm or normal.

Now I want to answer you regarding Phraya Mahibal, as it is something you want to know about first. Before Phraya Mahibal took leave, there was an exchange of telegrams between him and Prince Devawongse. The prince did not like the language used by Phraya Mahibal and wanted to withdraw him straight away. However, I thought that his desire to tell him off, for not thinking of his work, was not the only thing, but was rather Thai so I coaxed him into allowing it and suggested he choose Phra Sri who was going to come back in his stead. Later, Krom Luang arranged for Luang Visudh to go. When I went north, I was anxious about this and talked to your mother, who said that Luang Visudh was impressive, but nevertheless was still young and did not know anything about interior affairs. So I sent a telegram to the prince, saying that I and your mother wanted Phra Sri Thammasan to stay on. For that reason Prince Devawongse telegrammed in line with my instruction. On the same day, or two days later, I received your telegram asking to come home so that was how it ended.

Then when the French affair happened, Prince Devawongse telegrammed the ambassador in Paris to ask Phra Sri to find out whether Russia's policy had changed or not. Phra Sri received an answer today. In addition, the ambassador here received an order by telegram to be friendly, because Toh was about to go to Russia and, at that point, Phraya Mahibal decided to

1. The name Kalmyk was given to the Oirats, western Mongols in Russia, whose ancestors migrated from Dzhungaria in 1607. From 1630-1724 the Kalmyk Khanate existed in Russia's North Caucasus territory. Today, they are the majority in the autonomous Republic of Kalmykia on the western shore of the Caspian Sea. Kalmykia has Europe's only Buddhist government.

return to work again, before the date he had requested and which Phra Sri had already given to the Russian government, based on my previous order. In addition, there was a telegram reinforcing my instruction regarding the matter on which the Russian ambassador is working now, namely to bring Siam under Russian protection. This is going too far and I do not agree with it. Even if it were true, to send a telegram like this which Russia might see before us. Prince Devawongse thinks he is someone who has lost his head and his judgement. He thinks only of himself and what he can get, and acts accordingly. Even though he has not been definitively removed, I can't let him return to his former position. He has shown his hand so clearly, it could cause a rift with Russia. That is why I sent a telegram to change ambassador immediately, in order to show that we still believed in and were steadfast with Russia and did not listen to such scandalous talk. If I had wanted to change anything, I would have, but, in fact, I, and the meeting, agreed that the order of Prince Devawongse should not be countermanded.

The fact that the Russian government has come to check has happened, but nothing more has developed.

That all the senior people feel dissatisfied with Phraya Mahibal's behaviour is not just based on this occasion, nor is it that they have heard it from someone or other. Rather, they have heard it from his own mouth, which shows what sort of person he is. Those who can think, cannot agree. Those who are wise think that he is someone who thinks very little and only of his own benefit. I have received warnings to this effect from the Prince, and others are anxious that he is close to you, because you are someone who is intelligent, but not yet wise. When you listen to the ideas of Phraya Mahibal, who has shown that he is narrow minded and short sighted, thinking only of himself, it might negatively affect your thoughts and behaviour, or it might affect you badly without you even being aware.

Therefore please reflect carefully upon all the things you thought you knew about Phraya Mahibal and his intentions. He uses his emotions as a basis, then constructs his thoughts. If you take the words and

thoughts of Phraya Mahibal as correct, that can only lead to bad things in the future. Those who follow their suppositions rather than carefully considered reason, mostly make mistakes. Furthermore, those who believe things too easily, tend to make others mistrust them or lose their love for them. If someone is no longer trusted by two or three people and this fact gets around, then this mistrust will only increase. Accordingly, it is very important to understand that once people think someone's character is not to be trusted, such an impression is very hard to correct. So, if you want to have an important position in the future, please think carefully about this and behave accordingly. My teaching to you in this matter comes from love and not a desire to tell you off.

The fact that Prince Devawongse sent a telegram to ask the Russian government was not because of any real suspicion, but so they would tick off Mr O. It seems they understand this now and don't mention it.

Eeyd Lek has had his tonsurate now. I was so happy, I almost cried. I was so happy because I never thought it would happen. In the end, it was performed in the Amorn Phiman Mani throne hall. The five monks chanting were also pleased. To think he was ill and then got better. I will send you a photo.

From your loving father,

Chulalongkorn Por Ror

Kng Chulalongkorn mounting the steps to the pavilion for one part of the tonsurate ceremony for Prince Asdang Dejavudh.

Prince Asdang Dejavudh, wearing the full apparel of a Chao Fa prince and with the appropriate regalia on either side. (Photograph by Robert Lenz)

The actual date of Prince Asdang Dejavudh's tonsurate was 26 January 1902.

Lying off Singapore
March 1902

Dear Lek

I am here on government matters, caused by aggravation from the British. But I haven't got the energy to tell you about it, as I have been unwell all the time. Since having asthma, I keep feeling I have a fever. I wasn't really over it and then coming in the boat with the waves made me incapable of doing anything. The tonsurate of Eeyd Lek passed off well. I felt as happy, as if I had never performed a tonsurate before. But I'm too tired to tell you the details. Prince Paribatra is going to come back, so I've given him a photograph and asked him to send it. Eeyd Lek is very fat now. I have things to do, so I must stop now.

Chulalongkorn Por Ror

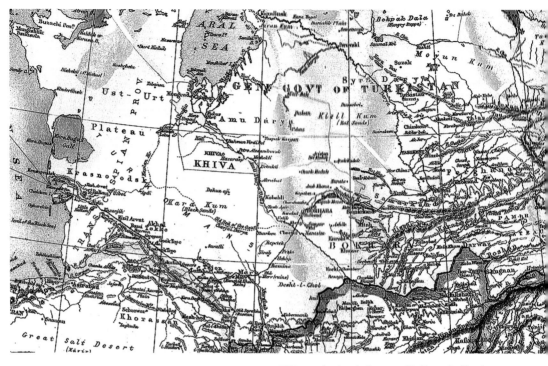

1903 map showing the location of Bokhara (Bukhara).
(From John Bartholemew's XXth century Citizens' Atlas)

5th March 1902

Your Majesty

On the 26th February, I went to visit the Emir of Bukhara[1], which is a *khaek*[2] country. It is in the centre of the Near East to the north of India. It is a protectorate of Russia. The ruler of this country is in Petersburg at the moment and is staying in the Winter Palace, only a few steps from my quarters. The Emir received me very warmly. The interpreter was a Russian officer. He said, "I am delighted to welcome a friend". After he invited me to be seated, he asked me how many years I had been here and wasn't I studying in the Corps de Pages and would become an officer this coming August. He said that was very quick and asked whether I had gone home

in these three years, how long it took and other such matters. He asked whether I had any brothers and sisters, to which I gave the appropriate answers, as well as telling him that Toonmom Toh had only recently visited here and had stayed in the very room that the Emir was now occupying. When I said goodbye, the Emir thanked me and, perhaps because he considered I had visited him as a result of Your Majesty's request or permission, he conveyed his thanks to Your Majesty, asking me to also convey his respects.

Then on the 3rd, the Emir paid a return visit to me, dressed in full dress uniform and bringing his crown prince with him. The crown prince[3] had studied in the cadet school. However, it is said that he was a very poor student. Nowadays, he is a Russian officer and has the rank of Serene Highness.

The rank of the Emir is His Highness and he is a full general in the Russian army. In addition, he is a general in the Imperial Guards and has received the decoration of St. Vladimir, High Class, which is only given to monarchs. The Emperor only has St. Vladimir 4th Class.

1. Abdul-Ahad bin Muzaffar al-Din (1886-1910), known as Manghit Khan, was educated at a Russian military school and was an adjutant-general in the Russian army. He brought more Russian influence into Bukharan life. In 1868 the Emirate had lost a war with Russia and In 1873 it became a Russian protectorate.

2. Thais use *khaek* as a general term for people from the Middle East and India.

The Emir of Bukhara, c. 1899.

The Emir has been received unusually well, in view of the fact that in reality he is no more than our Ruler of Chiang Mai. However, here he has been received as a veritable king, staying in the palace and using a royal carriage, wearing a crown and being given a gala dinner by the Emperor. In addition, all the members of the Imperial family have had to come and call. It's all a bit much. The Emir has brought so many gifts for the Emperor and Empress – it's almost like tribute, but he has received a great deal in return. He certainly understands European ways and manners very well – much more so than the Shah of Persia.

On the 20th February, I went to see the barracks of the Royal Guards 1st Company. When I arrived there, the commanding officer, Major General Ragochin, and other officers came out to welcome me and take me round everywhere. The barracks are large and impressive and the soldiers live in comfortable, light conditions. While I was there, I saw this year's new recruits doing their drills. There were firing

3. The Crown Prince, Alim Khan, had been sent by his father, aged 13, to Saint Petersburg for three years to study government and modern military techniques. In 1896, having received formal confirmation as Crown Prince of Bukhara by the Russian government, he returned home.

drills, and aiming and stabbing with the bayonet at the end of the gun. It is strange that these soldiers are recruited for two months only. They already looked strong and accurate. After this, I went to see the illiterate soldiers learning to read and write. Those who can read, then learn to write. Many had beautiful handwriting. Others are studying other subjects. For example, they might be asked what are the duties of a soldier, why is there a regimental flag, how many nobles there are and what are their names, what are their duties and other things. In all these drills and subjects, there is an officer assigned for each subject.

Next, we went to see the place where the soldiers buy their food. Before alcohol was sold, but now it is strictly forbidden. Near here, there were rooms for the sargeants. Then we saw the kitchens, which are clean and tidy with no smell, and tasted some of the dishes. We went to the drill hall and saw them practising artillery drills, lining up and marching. It all looks very orderly and well run. How they load their muskets and prepare to fire is excellent. Within less than half a second, the soldiers can prepare to fire, having loaded five bullets.

I also watched some gymnastics, which were very good with everyone being at the same level. After they have been in the gym, they are allowed to play other games, such as pulling the snake's tail and the like.

Then we went to see target shooting and where they keep their uniforms and battle gear. Infantry regiments in Russia in peacetime are only at half strength, being brought to full strength only in times of war. For that reason, they have to prepare uniforms and store them well, so they can be given out at a moment's notice. All these uniforms are brand new and have not been used. They have all been kept like this until there is a war. In other words, once the uniforms have been made, they might be kept for a year, or two or three, depending on the situation. After this, we went to the armory, which again is full of weapons to be handed out in time of war.

Finally, we went to see the school for the soldiers' children. It is extremely well appointed and very comfortable. The children wear uniforms from a very young age and look very sweet. After looking round everything, the Commanding Officer invited me to eat lunch in the mess hall, together with all the officers, who numbered over 70. During the lunch, the Commanding Officer drank a toast to me and

I drank one to the regiment and the Commanding Officer. After lunch, I chatted with all the officers in a relaxed way, before taking my leave.

After seeing this barracks, I could not help but wonder when our army might attain a similar level. In Russia, there are a hundred or two hundred such regiments. The strange thing here is that a regiment is 1,600 men during peacetime and 3,200 during wartime.

On 25th February, the Emperor and Empress came to the Corps des Pages. They arrived at the school at just after 9 am and inspected everywhere, entering every classroom. I had to answer questions about cannons, and the teacher asked me to draw pictures of various cannons and be prepared to answer any questions when the Emperor came to the classroom.

When the Emperor came to my classroom, he talked to the teacher and then asked me if I was nervous. I replied that I wasn't unduly so. Then he asked whether I had drawn all the cannons myself. I replied that I had. Then the Emperor asked about Nai Poum and how he was feeling. I replied that he was slightly better. Nai Poum has had measles for about one month and is in hospital in the Corps des Pages.

After the Emperor had gone round the entire school, he came to the assembly hall where all the students were waiting and those who were musicians played for him. He listened for a while and then he appointed four pages as Pages of the Chamber. Those students had not gained enough points initially to receive this rank, but now they had attained them and could be promoted.

Before leaving, the Emperor and Empress inspected the chapel in the grounds of the school. Before going outside, I and the empress's other page, gave her her coat. She looked at me and smiled, inclining her head in a friendly way.

After looking round the chapel, they returned to the palace in their carriage. All the pages ran after the carriage shouting, "Hurrah!", until they were exhausted. The Emperor gave us three days' holiday.

I have not had a letter from Your Majesty for a long time and am feeling rather neglected and lonely.

I think of you all the time.

I beg to remain Your Majesty's obedient servant,

Chakrabongse

Corps des Pages, Petersburg
12th March 1902

Your Majesty

On the 5th of this month, the Emir of Bukhara sent Colonel Gestdet and a civilian official, M. Lods, to tell me that the Emir asked me to receive a decoration from him, to commemorate our meeting and friendship. He also asked me to send a decoration for Your Majesty, together with a letter. I expressed my pleasure, conveyed my thanks to the Emir and said that I would send the decoration and letter to Your Majesty with all haste.

When I received Your Majesty's telegram, asking me to thank the Emir, I went to see him again and told him that I had had a telegram from Your Majesty and that Your Majesty wished me to thank him sincerely. I also thanked him for my decoration. The Emir said that he was delighted that, through the kindness of the Emperor, he had been able to know the King of Siam and me. I replied that Your Majesty was also delighted to have cordial relations with another country in Asia. After that, we chatted some more. He wished me well and I answered in kind and said that I hoped he would have a safe trip home.

The next day on the 6th, the Emir went to take his leave of the Emperor and Empress. I was in attendance, in my role as the Empress's page.

The order presented to Your Majesty is called Iskander Salis[1]. Iskandar means Alexander and it was created to commemorate Tsar Alexander III. It is the highest order, with the sash worn from the right shoulder to the left. I have arranged to send the decoration and letter to Your Majesty.

I humbly hope that Your Majesty will be kind enough to present a decoration to the Emir and the crown prince as well, as it was he who presented the decoration. I humbly suggest that the Emir should be presented with the Chula Chom Klao First Class, while the Crown Prince should receive the Crown of Siam First Class. For the latter, this will be adequate, as he only received the lowest order of decoration from here. I will send the names to Krom Khun Sommot.

I think of Your Majesty always.

I beg to remain Your Majesty's obedient servant,

Chakrabongse

25th March 1902

Your Majesty

I have received Your Majesty's letter dated 3rd March. I am very pleased and thank Your Majesty for the advice as to how I should conduct myself in accordance with Your Majesty's wishes. I am always endeavouring to do this and strive to do Your Majesty's bidding to the best of my ability.

As for Eeyd Lek's tonsurate, I am also very pleased and can scarcely believe it either, that Eeyd Lek has grown up so much as to have a tonsurate ceremony.

Now, however, there is something on which I must ask for Your Majesty's goodness once more. Mr Cuissart, who has been allowed to come here from Paris to work in the embassy, has informed me that he would like to have a wife, but is unable to do so because his salary is insufficient. The cost of living in Petersburg is very high and, if one has a wife to support, it can only be more. I told him that I would bring the matter to Your Majesty's attention and said that maybe more money could be forthcoming, as Thai staff who are accompanied by their wives, do receive more money than those who are single.

I agree with Your Majesty that Mr Cuissart is very able, knows his job and has good manners. He is very diligent and wishes to serve Your Majesty to the best of his ability. If he were to have a wife and bring her here, this would not only be good for him, but would also bring great benefit to the embassy.

On the whole, looking after oneself in a home, without a woman to take care of one, is very difficult. Men tend not to know about decorating a home, or other household matters. Receiving and visiting other people, if there is no mistress of the household, is also very awkward. This is why the Thai embassy is not capable of visiting other ambassadors or the Russian upper classes. I agree with Your Majesty that an important part of having a Thai embassy in Petersburg is to make us better known and well liked in order to foster good relations. In this way, Russia will respect the Siamese in the same way as they do other nations, and from here we can expand elsewhere. In this regard, all of us who are here are doing our best and have been rather successful in fostering close relations, based on the foundations created by Your Majesty and the Emperor. However, if we are to proceed forward, wives are needed. I am here all the time and I can see how the embassy this year is very different from how it was last year. Nowadays, nobody comes to the embassy and nobody gets to meet anyone, nor have proper chats. It means that we miss out on a lot of the news and gossip. In addition, people are less aware of Thailand than they were before. All this is because there is no mistress of the embassy. If we leave things too long, it will doubtless be like the Berlin embassy during the time of Phraya Non. It is strange that, in Europe, having a wife is so important. For all the above reasons, I feel emboldened to request that Your Majesty raise the salary of Mr Cuissart. At the moment he receives 400 pounds per annum, but he has requested an increase to 700 or 800 pounds. Of course, this is all up to Your Majesty's gracious decision.

Today is my last day of study in the Corps des Pages. From tomorrow we will start exams in order to become officers.

I beg to remain Your Majesty's obedient servant,

Chakrabongse

Letter opposite
1. Order of the Sun of Alexander (Iskander Salis). Established in 1898 in memory of Emperor Alexander III of Russia. Displayed on a blue ribbon.

1. Georges Charles Cuissart de Grelle Rogier (c.1847-1910) began working for the Siamese Ministry of Foreign Affairs in Paris, before being part of the Legation in Petersburg for many years, first as an interpreter and later as First Secretary.

8th April 1902

Your Majesty

I received Your Majesty's letter, graciously sent with Toonkramom Chai, together with the photograph of Eeyd Lek on the day of his tonsurate. Your Majesty's goodness is greater than I can possibly say. As for the tonsurate on this occasion, I followed it with interest in the court circular and it seemed quite unusual.

In my last letter, I went on at such length about Mr. Cuissart, that I neglected to tell you about various other things that I should have reported on.

By now, I have finished my classes at the Corps des Pages, with all that is left being the exams. They started already on the 25th March and will finish on the 19th May. The reason why the exams go on so long, is there are various holidays in between. Thus, from the 21st onwards, the students must observe Lent according to their religion. Then that is followed by the Easter holiday, with normal service only being resumed at the beginning of May. However, during this period, I have not stopped and have had to take other exams in subjects, which I have been studying on my own apart from the Corps. I am having the following exams until the 17th:

1. Military rules. 28th March. Completed
2. Tactics. 1st April. Completed
3. Military history. 5th April. Completed
4. Military laws. 8th April. Completed
5. Hippology. The study and care of horses. 11th April. But this is not of concern in any way.
6. Military administration. 12th April.
7. German. 17th April.
8. Artillery. 8th May
9. French. 5th May
10. Topography. 12th May
11. Fortifications. 12th May
12. Russian. 17th May

Separate exams I am taking on my own:
1. Geography. 22nd April.
2. International law. 26th April
3. Literature. 1st May
4. English. 19th April

Once the exams are over, I have to go to the Corps des Pages camp to practice shooting and map making until the 14th, after which I have to go and join the Hussar regiment where I will be an officer. The Hussars are based at Tsarskoe Selo and so I will have to go and stay there. The Emperor has been so gracious as to let me stay in the palace there, as well as allowing me to keep the room I am staying in at this palace at the moment. On the 28th June, the Hussars will move to their camp Kaporskoe, some 10 *versts* or seven miles from Tsarskoe Selo. Here they carry out their summer exercises, until manoeuvres are over at the end of August. When the manoeuvres are completed, I will receive the rank of lieutenant. When one gets a promotion, one is allowed one month's holiday, but I am going to ask for longer until the 14th November, in order to accompany Toonkramom Toh to America, as Your Majesty has already granted permission. On my return, I can then take up my duties in the regiment, when I will have to be based at Tsarskoe Selo. While I undertake my military service, I will be able to study various civilian subjects, such as continuing international law, as well as political economy, financial law and other subjects, so that in no way will this be a waste of my time.

As for the exams which have taken place already, they passed off well and I obtained full marks all the time, although I don't know what will happen with the rest. I have to study a lot and read up on all the subjects I have studied from beginning to end. Also, some exams deal with topics I studied in the previous year. So I am sitting reading my textbooks from morning till night, apart from in the afternoon when I have to go to the Corps for various exercises.

Regarding the accommodation at Kaporskoe, I will have to get a new house. Phraya Sri Thammasan has requested this from the Tsar, complete with all the details. In addition, I will have to buy two good horses, which together with doing up the house and buying the uniform will cost quite a lot.

When I go to America, I do not yet know whether it is Your Majesty's wish that Phraya Sri Thammasan should accompany me or not. That is entirely up to Your Majesty. However, I would ask that Luang Surayud and Nai Poum can come with me because it is their job to accompany me, and if they don't people will think it odd. Nai Poum is my travelling companion, while Luang Surayud is my ADC. Whenever he does not accompany, people find it strange. On the other hand, Phraya Sri Thammasan is the ambassador and if he were to go there would be no one to replace him. Thus, if Your Majesty decides it is unnecessary, I do not think it is necessary either. However, in this regard I must ask that Your Majesty does not let him know I have discussed this, so he does not think that I am trying to prevent him from going. I am sure he wants to go, but I am suggesting

this so that Your Majesty does not have to spend too much money. If Your Majesty is so kind as to let him go, I will be delighted. Last time Phraya Mahibal sent a telegram to Sadet Lung [Prince Devawongse], asking whether he wanted him to go to England with me or to return to his duties here. And he received the answer, that if I desired it then he should stay on, that's why I am writing to ask Your Majesty's opinion, so it can be clear and it does not seem that I am trying to cut across or prevent him in any way.

I am well and happy. I think of Your Majesty constantly.

I beg to remain Your Majesty's obedient servant,
Chakrabongse

Prince Chakrabongse and Nai Poum, with their teachers from the Corps des Pages.

23rd April 1902

Your Majesty

I believe Your Majesty may have heard that a tragic thing happened on the 14th, namely that the Minister of the Interior, Dmitry Sipyagin[1], was assassinated. The assassin[2] disguised himself as an aid to the grand duke[3] and drove to the meeting of the ministers. The guard at the gate was reluctant to let him in, but he insisted he was the grand duke's ADC and had a personal letter from the grand duke for the interior minister. The guard, seeing him formally dressed in a soldier's uniform, did not dare protest in any way and had to let him wait. Then, when the minister arrived and took off his coat, the assassin went up to him and said, "Are you the minister? I have a letter for you from the grand duke." When the minister extended his hand to receive the letter, the villain shot him twice with a colt pistol. The muzzle was almost against his body. There was nobody close by, except the minister's servant, who came and gave battle straight away and he also got shot. The minister was then shot twice more, at which point, the guard and others who came to help apprehended the assassin. The minister died an hour later.

The villain claimed to be a former university student from Kiev, who had been punished because he caused trouble with other students, and later was a private soldier. Despite the Emperor pardoning him, he decided to take revenge and planned this until he succeeded.

This minister was a favourite of the Emperor, although many did not like him, because he was not strict enough, and he was criticised for not dealing with troublesome students, or, if he was harsh, it was in the wrong areas. For those reasons, there had been talk of replacing him for a long time.

A new minister has been appointed. He is called Plehve[4]. He is very strong and harsh, so it is thought that the situation will be better than before.

Regarding all the upheavals, one cannot believe the foreign press, as they enjoy inflating everything, as if the whole of Russia is in a state of anarchy and will soon become a republic or something similar. Thus, while in Bangkok, the English are no doubt pleased with this turn of events, the reality is that all the troubles are caused by a group of people, who want to

Dmitry Sipyagin and Vyacheslav Konstantinovich von Plehve. Both these Ministers of the Interior served for only two years before being assassinated.

bring about a change of regime, so that power is in their hands and then they can do whatever they want for their benefit alone. They do not think about anyone else or the country. An example is the French revolution, when this type of people created everything. Here, such people represent less than one thousandth of the total population, but they cause a great deal of disturbance. Among the students, there are many who do not side with the troublemakers and who want to study. Then, when those who are trying to disrupt the studies close the classrooms, those who want to study, fight back against the troublemakers and drive them off. Such actions are not reported in the English press. To summarise, I agree with you that there is long way to go before there could be a revolution here. Those who are alive now are surely unlikely to see it happen.

As for my part, the exams went well. Now I am taking some individual exams, as the school is closed now and the students are observing Lent.

I am well and thinking of Your Majesty constantly.

I beg to remain Your Majesty's obedient servant,

Chakrabongse

1. Dmitry Sergeyevich Sipyagin (1853-15th April1902) was Minister of Interior (1900-1902). He was assassinated in the Mariinsky Palace by Socialist-Revolutionary Stepan Balmashov. Shortly before he died, Count Witte had warned him about such an eventuality.

2. Stepan Balmashov had been a student at Kiev university, where he was arrested for joining in the strike of 1901. He was a member of the Socialist Revolutionary Party.

3. Grand Duke Sergei Alexandrovich.

4. Vyacheslav Konstantinovich von Plehve (1846-July1904) was Director of Police and later Minister of the Interior. He was also assassinated.

30 April 1902

Your Majesty

The 29th of this month was an important day in this country, because it is the anniversary of the day on which Jesus ascended into heaven, three days after having been crucified[1]. For seven days before the crucifixion, Jesus underwent various tortures. As a result, people observe penances. They cannot eat meat. Then on the day he ascended into heaven, the austerities end and everyone can celebrate to the full. On that day, everyone goes up to their friends and acquaintances and kisses each other three times, saying: "Christ is risen."

On the evening of the 26th, or counting in the *farang* way, from midnight onwards on the 27th, there was a big do at the palace. All the officials, both governmental and from the royal household, gathered together. I had to go, in my capacity as page to the Empress. At 12 midnight, the Emperor and the two Empresses, together with members of the imperial family and the officials, went in procession from their quarters to the church, passing through rooms, where officials and dignatories were waiting to attend them. At the church, they were met by the priests and prayers connected with Christ's ascension began according to their rituals. When it was over, the Emperor and Empresses kissed the crucifix and various icons of different saints, after which they kissed each other, as is customary. After that, all the nobles kissed the Emperor and Empresses and the senior officials. Ministers and commanding officers waited in order of seniority to greet the Emperor and kiss him three times before kissing the Empresses' hands. After everyone had paid their respects, there were more prayers, as is customary every Sunday. It was not over until around 3 am. The Empress had to go and rest, because she had had to stand so long. After the prayers were over, there was a supper party in the palace until 3.30 am. My job was to carry the Empress's train as usual and I had to stand in the church all the time, which made me very stiff.

The next day, on the morning of the 27th, I went to call on the Dowager Empress in order to present my good wishes on this important day. I had to wait a long time, because they said that she had not yet

Empress Alexandra in Russian Court Dress.

come out of her boudoir. While waiting, I met with the Minister of War[2], who invited me to kiss him according to the Russian tradition. This I did and he gave me his blessing and praised me, saying that he had heard only good things of me and that he hoped that when I went back to my own country, I would not forget Russia. He added that, even though the weather was very cold here, the Russians knew how to love and were warm hearted just like those in hot countries.

Then, when I was received by the Empress, she greeted me with great cordiality and asked after Your Majesty, saying she hoped I always had good news from Your Majesty. The Empress gave me an egg, as per the tradition whereby everyone gives each other eggs. The egg she gave me was made of porcelain and bore her initials. She then had to go out and receive many other people who had come to see her and so I took my leave. On that day, I also went to visit all the other nobles, as well as many senior officials who have

1. This is Easter, which Prince Chakrabongse had already described to his father the previous year.

2. Alexei Nikolayevich Kuropatkin (1848-1925) was the Russian Imperial Minister of War (1898–1904). He is often held responsible for major Russian drawbacks in the Russian-Japanese War, notably the Battle of Mukden and the Battle of Liaoyang.

had something to do with me, such as officials in the imperial household.

The 28th was the day on which I went to see the Emperor and Empress, in order to present my good wishes. I went together with others in my capacity as the Empress's page. Many officers came to pay their respects, in particular the commanding officers and also sergeants, as well as two or three ordinary soldiers from every regiment of which the Emperor is head. In addition, there were representatives from all the military academies. The Emperor had to kiss all the people assembled here, who all lined up. It looked very exhausting. The Empress on the other hand gave out eggs and those who received them kissed her hand. I lined up with the others. When the Emperor saw me he smiled and, when I got to him, he extended his hand and asked if I was well, saying nothing to do with religion.

The Emperor has many cares at the moment, because one minister has been killed and another has resigned. The new minister is called Sanger[1] and he has a lot knowledge and is a philosopher.

Then, in the south, there are also problems with the workers causing trouble[2], but it's not clear what they are up to. Now the minister of interior has gone to see the situation for himself, so things should be sorted out quickly.

As for me, I have exams all the time. On the 26th there was one on international law and I got full marks again. Tomorrow there is an exam on European history.

I beg to remain Your Majesty's obedient servant,

Chakrabongse

Phraya Sri Thammasan in 1899.

12th May 1902

Your Majesty

I learn from Phraya Sri Thammasan that Your Majesty has said that you fear that the level of the decorations I have proposed giving to the various teachers is too high. In choosing the entry level, I compared them with the various Russian decorations they had already received. I felt, as did Your Majesty, that it was inappropriate to give them a decoration at a lower level than the domestic ones they had received. In the list I sent, there were many who recorded that they had received the Order of St Vladimir 4th or 3rd Class. And if I set all the orders at 2nd Class, it would be odd. In truth, it is because this Order is a high one anyway and those who have it at 4th class, will also have two other decorations at second class. Once they move up to the 3rd level, the next time is a sash. It is for that reason, that I decided to award the decoration at 2nd class. I did ask Phraya Sri Thammasan to explain all this, but he obviously didn't and so it all must seem a bit strange. It is true that some people have decorations only of the third class, but I set our decoration at 2nd class, because those in question are colonels and would it be right to give them the same class as a captain might receive?

---

1. This was Grigory Sanger, who was Deputy Minister of National Education.

2. At the turn of the century, discontent with the Tsar's rule was manifested not only through the growth of political parties dedicated to the overthrow of the monarchy, but also through industrial strikes for better wages and working conditions, protests and riots among peasants, university demonstrations, and the assassination of government officials, often by Socialist Revolutionaries. There were strikes in Ukraine and later in the year, a significant strike in Vladikavkaz and Rostov-on-Don.

Prince Chakrabongse was sheltered from much of this and also probably did not want to worry his father. Furthermore, as the son of an absolute monarch, he was unlikely to be sympathetic to demands for workers' rights.

С. Петербургъ — St. Pétersbourg

Дворецъ Вел. Княз. Владиміра Александровича
Palais du Grand Duc Vladimir

Edition „Richard", St. Pétersbourg No. 215

Palace of Grand Duke Vladimir.

In all this, I did try and give the lowest level possible, as I am very protective of our Thai royal orders and don't want them to become commonplace.

On the 6th of this month, it was the Empress's name day. I was instructed to go and present my birthday greetings, in my role as her personal page, together with one other page.

Last week, on the 8th, there was to be the annual review of the army, but the weather was not good enough, raining and cold, so it was postponed until the next day. Then, as the weather did not improve, it was cancelled and will be held on the 20th when President Loubet[1] comes. After the review, it had been planned that Grand Duke Vladimir would give a luncheon banquet in his palace and, although the review was cancelled, the luncheon went ahead. I was invited. The Emperor and the two Empresses attended, as well as all members of the royal family who were here. I spoke to many of them, from the highest downwards, but did not get a chance to speak with the Emperor or Empress. However, both of them smiled at me in a friendly manner. The difference in the Empress's manner was most

apparent. During the time that I have been at the Corps, she has become much more friendly and relaxed.

My exams went well. Only two more subjects and they will be over. They finish on the 17th.

I am well and happy and think of Your Majesty always.

I beg to remain Your Majesty's obedient servant,

Chakrabongse

Emile Loubet in 1900, photographed by Paul Nadar.

1. Émile François Loubet (1838-1929) was the eighth President of France. He inaugurated the Paris Exhibition of 1900, received Tsar Nicholas II of Russia in September 1901 and paid a visit to Russia in May 1902, staying at Tsarskoe Selo.

Duderhof, near Krasnoe Selo
17th June 1902

Your Majesty

I have received Your Majesty's letters dated 2nd and 8th May, for which I am truly grateful. The matter of M. Cuissard is entirely at Your Majesty's discretion.

Regarding the Emir of Bukhara, the Harbour Ministry has sent Your Majesty's letter to Phraya Sri Thammasan and he passed it on to me, to deal with as I see fit. However, the decorations have not yet arrived. The Emir has now returned home and, accordingly, I have asked Phraya Sri Thammasan to send Your Majesty's letter and the decorations when they arrive to the Minister of Foreign Affairs here to send on via the correct channels. It seems this will be the best thing to do. The Emir will probably be thrilled to get a high-ranking decoration and it is his first foreign award.

In Your Majesty's second letter, there is the issue of spending too much money. I am trying my hardest not to be extravagant, but it is unfortunate that this is a time when a lot of money is needed. Joining the regiment requires purchasing a horse, ordering the uniform and doing up accommodation. But this is just a temporary situation, not a permanent one. I was very unfortunate in the matter of buying a horse, as I found a really fine-looking one, which everyone said was so hard to find. Sadly, after only a short while, the horse fell and the money was wasted. I was going to have to buy another one, as according to regimental regulations one must have two horses, but the matter came to the attention of the Emperor, who gave me a horse from the royal stables, so I did not need to buy another one after all. His Majesty said it was very regrettable that my fine horse fell.

As for the annoyance that has occurred in Bangkok, I know a bit about it as a result of what Phraya Sri Thammasan learnt from Bangkok, or from other ambassadors and this affair has concerned and preoccupied me. I have given Phraya Sri Thammasan some advice from time to time, based on my knowledge. I also contemplated telling the Emperor about the matter, when I had the opportunity to visit him, but feared that I might be overstepping the mark and the Emperor might think I was causing trouble, so I stopped myself.

Prince (later Tsar) Ferdinand of Bulgaria.

From the 9th to the 14th of this month, the Prince of Bulgaria[1] has been here and has been received officially, but not in the way accorded to a true monarch. Thus, the Emperor did not go to meet him at the station. It was strange that no other relatives went either, apart from Grand Duke Vladimir. One day there was a gala dinner and I was on duty in my capacity as a page. The Emperor talked to me then, asking about my stay in camp and when the map making would be completed as well as other things.

On the 14th, the Prince of Bulgaria came to inspect the various camps at Krasnoe Selo, together with Grand Duke Vladimir. In addition, Grand Duke Paul came to inspect the Corps des Pages camp. Grand Duke Vladimir called me to go and talk to him and teased me by saying, "Let me take your hand, you terrible soldier!" He introduced me to the Prince of Bulgaria, who also shook hands and said he knew my older brother. I told him that he had, in fact, also met me in Rome during the funeral of King Umberto.

The Prince of Bulgaria has come to Russia this

1. Ferdinand I (1861-1948) was born Ferdinand Maximilian Karl Leopold Maria of Saxe-Coburg and Gotha. He ruled Bulgaria from 1887 to 1918; firstly as *knyaz* (ruling prince, 1887-1908) and later as tsar (1908–18). He was also an author, botanist, entomologist and philatelist.

time in order to show his appreciation on behalf of the Bulgarian people for Russian help in gaining independence from Turkey 25 years ago.

The map making and placement of soldiers carried out by class 9 of the Corps des Pages students was all finished by the 14th of this month, and signals the true end of my studies in the Corps. On that day, all the teachers met to decide who had got what marks and who was to be placed in what position. It was decided that I had graduated top of the class, with 11.82 points, these marks being closer to a full 12 than anyone else. My name will be engraved in gold on a stone plaque within the school according to tradition. Nai Poum came second with 11.53 marks.

Thus, out of the 40 students who will now become officers, the two Thais came higher than anyone else. I am extremely pleased about this as I feel it greatly enhances the profile of our country.

At the moment, I have had five days' rest. Then on the 20th, everyone will go to the various regiments they have chosen. I am staying in the embassy in Duderhof, but on the 19th will go to Tsarskoe Selo, in order to go to the regiment early the next day. The Hussar regiment will remain at Tsarskoe Selo until the 25th, before coming to Kaporskoe, so as to camp near Krasnoe Selo at Tsarskoe Selo. The Emperor has assigned a room in the palace for me.

I am well and thinking of Your Majesty always.

I beg to remain Your Majesty's obedient servant,

Chakrabongse

Kaporskoe Village, Hussar regiment
22nd July RS 121

Your Majesty

In my last letter to you, I did not finish recounting the visit of the King of Italy, so I beg to continue.

On the 14th of this month in the morning the King of Italy arrived in Petersburg. Then in the evening the King, together with both the Emperor and Empress and other nobles came to Krasnoe Selo in order to inspect the camps. The Emperor and the King were on horseback, while the Empress and other female members of the nobility went in carriages around all the camps. I went with the regiment to receive the royal party as instructed. The King of Italy saw me and bowed. The Empress also bowed and smiled. Once the camp inspection was over, they went to the royal tent, but before that it rained heavily and everyone got drenched. Within the tent, there were trumpeters from all the regiments playing music, followed by prayers and gun salutes as is customary. In the royal tent, I was able to pay my respects to the Emperor and various other nobles, as well as the King of Italy. He said he had not met me for a long time and asked how I was. He also referred to Your Majesty, remarking that you were always very kind to him and his wife.

On the 15th there was a major review in honour of the King of Italy. It started at 11 am. I was in the

Arch erected for the state visit by King Victor Emmanuel III of Italy (r.1900–abdication 1946) in July 1902.

The King of Italy, Victor Emmanuel III, drives in an open carriage through St. Petersburg.

Tsar Nicholas II and the King of Italy inspect the troops at a major review held in his honour, July 1902.

line up of the First Company, the Hussar regiment. The Emperor and the King were on horseback. Both the Empresses were in carriages. The Emperor talked to the soldiers as he went by. When she passed me, the Empress inclined her head and smiled as usual.

The King of Italy also bowed. Once the inspection was over, the regiment marched passed the stand. The Emperor then led the soldiers past the King of Italy and they all saluted. After the march past, there was a reception in the royal tent and then back to Peterhof. On the 16th, the Emperor and the King of Italy went to inspect the Italian ships, which had moored at Kronstadt. In the evening there was a banquet at the palace of Grand Duke Peter[1]. On the 17th there was a reception at the palace, after which the King of Italy left Peterhof and went home.

This is the first time that a King of Italy has come to Russia. He had come here several times as crown prince, but not once he had ascended the throne. Furthermore, this King has only begun to visit various royal families and the fact that he came to Russia first has pleased everyone greatly.

There are exercises at the camp all the time. At the moment there are brigade exercises, namely of two companies together, as well as division exercises, consisting of four companies. Grand Duke Nicholas[2], the overall Inspector of the Cavalry, always comes to watch the manoeuvres himself. We practised many different manoeuvres and tomorrow there will be war games for the first time.

I have received Your Majesty's letter dated 11th June and am extremely grateful for the decision regarding Pi Chira coming to Europe. I think I can guess the purpose of his visit, but it is certainly not to cure his illness.

I beg to remain Your Majesty's obedient servant,

Chakrabongse

1. Grand Duke Peter Nikolaevich (1864-1931) was the second son of Grand Duke Nicholas Nicholaievich the Elder (1831–1891) and Duchess Alexandra of Oldenburg (1838-1900). He served in the army as a Lt. Gen. and Adjutant General. In 1889, he married Princess Militza of Montenegro. His elder brother married Militza's sister Princess Anastasia. Both sisters were interested in the occult and had links with Rasputin.

2. Grand Duke Nicholas Nicholaevich was a general, as well as grandson of Nicholas I of Russia. He was first cousin, once removed, of Tsar Nicholas II. Between 1895-1905, he was Inspector-general of the Cavalry. His led reforms in training, cavalry schools, cavalry reserves and the remount services.

The King of Italy departed from Peterhof Station, July 1902.

Duderhof, near Krasnoe Selo
28th July 1902

Your Majesty

Today is the name day of Grand Duke Vladimir. I went to pay my good wishes to him early in the morning. Both the Grand Duke and Grand Duchess said that Your Majesty's reception of Grand Duke Boris had been extremely lavish. Grand Duke Boris[1] was thrilled and made the programme of events public. I replied that I had had a letter about this also and that Your Majesty was delighted to receive him.

To celebrate his name day, there was a grand reception at the palace of the Emperor. Empress Marie and all the nobility were in attendance. The Empress did not come because she is heavily pregnant. The Queen of Greece, who is on a visit here at the moment, was also there and I was invited too.

Once the dinner was over, I chose an opportune moment to inform the Emperor that Pi Chira had arrived in Europe and that he would like to know when he could pay a visit. Pi Chira had sent a telegram to Phraya Sri Thammasan, asking for some information on this point and so I volunteered to obtain the information, as I knew I would see the Emperor today. The Emperor was surprised when I informed him and said, "Really? Where is he?". I replied that he was in Germany. The Emperor said "Surely there's nothing important to do in Germany!" and continued by saying that he could come here whenever he wanted. He told me to write and tell Pi Chira to arrive here by the 9th of August. By that time he would be back from Reval, where he is meeting the German emperor. He said he was happy that he would see Pi Chira again and asked whether he had come to Europe alone, or with someone else. I replied that he had come with some officials, who were going to be working in France, but that he was travelling in a private capacity and was simply in the same party. The Emperor repeated many times that he would be delighted to see Pi Chira again.

After that, the Emperor enquired as to whether I was happy in the Hussar regiment and he reminisced about when he was in the regiment and was stationed in Karposkoe as well, a place he liked very much. He

---

1. Grand Duke Boris Vladimirovich (1877-1943) was a son of Grand Duke Vladimir and first cousin to Nicholas II. In 1896, he graduated from Nikolaievsky Cavalry School with rank of cornet of the Life Guards Hussar Regiment and was ADC to the Emperor. Later as a Major General in the Russian army, he took part in the Russo-Japanese war. He was a playboy and a spendthrift, who in 1901 had a son with a French woman Jeanne Aumont-Lacroix. To break the relationship he was sent on a world tour, including to Thailand. In 1911, he represented the Tsar at the coronation of King Vajiravudh of Siam.

Nicholas II in 1902, photographed when he went to meet his third cousin, Wilhelm, at Reval in the summer.

Kaiser Wilhelm II in 1902. Photographed by T. H. Voigt of Frankfurt, a court photographer.

also asked if Nai Poum was in the same company as me, as he recalled seeing him when the King of Italy came to review the troops. I was in front of the first group and Nai Poum was in front of the third. Empress Marie also enquired as to my overall well-being and said she had admired me during the review.

On the 4th of August, the German emperor will come to the city of Reval[1] on the Baltic coast. The Emperor will go and meet him there, and there will be naval manoeuvres. He will stay there until around the 8th and will not go to Petersburg.

Originally, it had been planned that the Shah of Persia would come here, but that trip has been been aborted.

At the end of August, the King of Greece will come here for the saint day of Prince Nicholas of Greece and Grand Duchess Helen, the daughter of Grand Duke Vladimir.

The exercises over the last week have been arduous with four companies practising together and Grand Duke Nicholas observing everything constantly. There were also military manoeuvres.

I beg to remain Your Majesty's obedient servant,

Chakrabongse

Revel, or Reval c. 1900. Present-day Tallin, capital of Estonia, was ruled by Russia between 1721-1918 and was known as the Governate of Estonia. Until the late 19th century, the governate was administered independently by German-Baltic nobility.

Annual military manoeuvres at Krasnoe Selo, c. 1900s.

Karposkoe village, Hussar regiment

11th August 1902

Your Majesty

On the 8th, Pi Chira arrived from Denmark. Phraya Sri Thammasan and Luang Surayudh went to meet him at the border and I went to meet him at Gatchina, which the train passes through about one hour before reaching Petersburg. The train was late today, so I had to wait around. Once Pi Chira arrived, I conveyed him to Duderhof and the embassy.

I am so happy to see Pi Chira and it has been a great opportunity to catch up with news from Thailand. Luckily, at the moment I have some free time, with not much happening in the regiment, so I was able to be with my brother constantly. On the 9th, I accompanied Pi Chira to Petersburg to do some shopping.

On the 10th, he was able to visit the Emperor at the Krasnoe Selo racecourse. The Emperor has just come back from Reval, where he was receiving the German Kaiser on the 9th of this month. Then, on the 10th, he came to Krasnoe Selo to see the races between the various army regiments, an annual event.

Later, the Emperor asked Pi Chira to come and see him again so he could give him a letter. Today the various regimental halls have been inspected – all the military colleges, whether the infantry, the cavalry or artillery. The Corps des Pages were not involved, as the more senior classes were all dispersed among various regiments and the younger classes have all gone home. The Emperor did not stay at Krasnoe Selo and, when the races were over, he went back to Peterhof, coming back again today in the morning to inspect the military schools. After lunch, he went back to Peterhof.

From the 13th August onwards, the Hussars will leave here to perform manoeuvres and will move from place to place, not returning here at all. The manoeuvres will probably continue until the 23rd. Once they are over, the regiment will go directly to Tsarskoe Selo, their home for the winter months. The 23rd is the day when the officer appointments will be made for the cadets who graduated from the corps this year.

I beg to remain Your Majesty's obedient servant,
Chakrabongse

The Thai embassy in Berlin
4th September 1902

Your Majesty

I haven't written to you for a long time, as I have been very busy and hectic.

From the 13th August, I was involved in military manoeuvres and it was impossible to write, as I had none of the necessary tools with me. This series of military manoeuvres was rather unusual, consisting of marching to a spot and waiting, with hardly any fighting at all.

In the 10 days devoted to military manoeuvres, my company only fought properly twice. Apart from that, we marched about and waited around. The weather was terrible this year, too, raining constantly without a break. It was very damp and soggy, as well as very cold. Even though it is summer, it was colder than the cool season in Thailand. This made everything difficult and we suffered hardships, with the NCOs having to sleep on the ground, with only a tent to protect them from the rain and dew. The officers slept in small tents, two to a tent, but we had a bed, so it wasn't too uncomfortable. The first fight took place at Shlisselburg, some 40 miles from Petersburg. This meant that after marching from Krasnoye Selo and then attacking, it was in total around 70-80 miles. The fighting was also strange, as the cavalry fought with the infantry. In the plan, the enemy were coming from the east of Petersburg to attack the city, while the infantry, who were to defend the city, were not ready and the cavalry had to be called on. In all, eight regiments had to take on the enemy and prevent them advancing further, until the infantry were ready. In the fighting, the cavalry had to dismount and stand shooting, just like infantrymen. If there was an opportunity to fight on horseback, one got back on and fought. My regiment all dismounted, fired and advanced just like infantrymen. Then when we had delayed their advance enough, and they were not coming forward, the cavalrymen got back on their horses and went home. This showed the benefit of using the cavalry. If they had used the infantry here, they would not have got there in time, as they march too slowly. Such situations are common in wars, which is why the cavalry are so vital. Today, they are also useful for intelligence gathering and quick manoeuvres such as this.

Another battle, in which my company took part, was on the last day, when there was a big battle. Two regiments, commanded by generals, fought a regiment of the enemy who were going to attack Petersburg. We were in the attacking regiment and we won. In these manoeuvres, the Emperor came to observe and stayed at a village called Feodorovsky Pasad, a high point with a view all around. Over the 10 days of manoeuvres, the Emperor visited many different sites for observation purposes, but we weren't involved. In the last few days, when he was about to arrive, all the cadets gathered at Feodorovsky Pasad in order to receive their officer ranks. Once the Emperor had given the order to cease fighting, all the cadet school students lined up forming a large square. Once everything was ready, the Emperor, the Dowager Empress and other nobles arrived. The Emperor inspected all the cadets and greeted the students in every company. He then took his place in the centre of the square and said: "I am sure that all of you will serve with strength and honour, just as your forefathers have done before you. May you all enjoy good health and flourish in the tasks which lie ahead of you. I bless you all, my new officers." All the cadets shouted their thanks and gave cheers for the Emperor. Grand Duke Constantine, head of the strategy department, then called the pages of the Dowager Empress, namely Nai Poum and another, to go and attend her and she gave them their letters of appointment. According to tradition, the creation of officers does not involve a contract, but is simply recorded in a royal decree which is printed later in the government newspaper. Royal decrees come out every day and the Minister of Defence signs them, recording on the front where the Emperor was on such and such a day.

Once the Dowager Empress had given her orders, Grand Duke Constantine called the pages of the Empress, namely myself and another to attend the Emperor, as the she was not there owing to her pregnancy[1]. The Emperor congratulated me particularly and gave me my orders, which he said were from the Empress. He said that she had asked him to tell me, that she was sad she had not been able to come in person and gave me her blessings. Once that was over, I planned to go back to my line, but the Dowager

---

1. In fact this was a phantom pregnancy.

Prince Chakrabongse in his Hussar officer uniform.

Grand Duchess of Mecklenburg-Schwerin, also Grand Duchess Marie Pavlovna of Russia.

Empress asked to see me and she gave me her congratulations, even using the term 'dear' which was rather exciting.

After that, I went to pay my respects to the Queen of Greece and Grand Duchess of Mecklenburg-Schwerin[2], who both congratulated me. The Emperor also invited me to meet the King of Greece, who had recently arrived in Russia and was attending the ceremony. The king is here on a private visit for the marriage of his son.

Those pages who had been attached to the various grand duchesses, received their commissions from their respective former patrons. After the various officers had been appointed, there was a banquet in a tent on site. I sat at the royal table. All the nobles who were there congratulated me and wished me all the best in hearty fashion, with Grand Duke Constantine going so far as to kiss me! The Minister of Defence was also very fulsome in his congratulations, even asking me to go and sit beside him. It seems that everyone was delighted. During the dinner, all the members of the nobility drank my health from the royal family downwards. After dinner, I returned by carriage to Tsarskoe Selo to change into my Hussar uniform. Along the way, we passed many companies

of soldiers and all of them cheered and shouted congratulations. Then when we reached our own companies, everyone dismounted to receive congratulations. Once Tsarskoe Selo was reached, I got dressed in my full dress uniform at the palace and went to present myself to the commander in my new position of an officer. Over the following days, I was occupied in visiting various people as a newly commissioned officer. For example, I had to pay a visit to all the officers in the regiment, obliging me to run from Petersburg to Tsarskoe Selo every day.

Then, on the 27th, I went to pay a visit to the Emperor again as a new officer. He received me warmly and immediately expressed his pleasure at seeing me in the uniform of an officer, inspecting me from head to toe and making me turn around. He commented that the uniform was very well cut. Then he talked about my stay at Tsarskoe Selo and hoped that the accommodation would be satisfactory. He said that we would probably see each other often and that I would most likely be with the guards, as he had been in the command of the guards when he was in the Hussars. He also said he had written to Your Majesty and would send it via Pi Chira. Finally he said that the Empress was keen to see me too.

2. Duchess Marie of Mecklenburg-Schwerin (1854-1920), later Grand Duchess Maria Pavlovna, was born Marie Alexandrine Elisabeth Eleonore of Mecklenburg-Schwerin. A prominent hostess in St Petersburg following her marriage to the Grand Duke Vladimir Alexandrovich, she had an open rivalry with the Empress Maria Feodorovna.

Prince George of Greece in 1902,
when he was Governor of Crete.

Prince Nicholas of Greece and Grand Duchess Elena of Russia.

Then he talked about other things of less interest and finally congratulated me again and said that he hoped I would fulfil my duties as an officer, as well as I had when I was a page. I bowed and took my leave. He suggested I went to pay my respects to the Empress. Accordingly, I asked an official to present my request and after a few moments, I went to call on her. I was really thrilled to see her, because at the moment she is not receiving anyone, which made this very special. The Empress received me very warmly, expressing her pleasure that I had become an officer and her regret that she had not attended the inauguration ceremony in person. I thanked her for always being so kind to me when I was on duty as her page. She replied that she had been delighted to have me as her page, as it was pleasantly informal. She asked if my new uniform was comfortable and not too heavy. She said it looked very good and that it was her favourite uniform. After that, she talked about my accommodation at Tsarskoe Selo and where I was going to go in my holidays. When I said I was going to go to America, she said that that was very far, but that as I was used to long journeys, such a distance would not seem too bad to me. She also talked about another of her pages and which regiment he had joined, as well as wondering who her next page might be, whether he would be good or not, and whose son he was. After that, she asked about Pi Chira and said how pleased she had been to see him, but that he was much changed – older and thinner, as well as wearing glasses and not looking so well. Various nobles here

have been much concerned with Pi Chira's glasses. I don't know why. In addition, the Empress said his teeth had deteriorated. In fact, she could barely remember him. She also talked about many other things and promised to give me a photograph. She then indicated I should leave, but while I was walking out of the door, she shouted out, "I am so glad to see you a Hussar".

The 29th of August was the wedding of Prince Nicholas of Greece and Grand Duchess Elena (Helen), the daughter of Grand Duke Vladimir. There were big celebrations, to which I was invited. The party was held in the large palace at Tsarskoe Selo. All the nobility were inside and Grand Duchess Helen came in, so the female nobles and high-ranking officials could help her put on the crown and grand robe, befitting her station. The ceremony was attended by many members of the royal family – all the Russian nobles and all the Greek royal family, from the king and queen downwards. The crown

Opposite

1. Frederick Francis IV (1882-1945) was the last Grand Duke of Mecklenburg-Schwerin and regent of Mecklenburg-Strelitz. He inherited the throne when he was fifteen years old in 1897 and was forced to renounce it in 1918.

2. Grand Duchess Anastasia Mikhailovna (1860-1922) was a daughter of Grand Duke Michael Nicholaevich and a granddaughter of Tsar Nicholas I.

3. Prince George of Greece and Denmark (1869–1957) was the second son of George I of Greece and Olga Constantinovna of Russia. He saved the life of the future Nicholas II in 1891, during their visit to Japan together.

princess was also there as was Grand Duke Mecklenburg-Schwerin[1] and another Mecklenburg royal, as well as those who were already in Russia, such as the Dowager Duchess of Mecklenburg-Schwerin[2] and her daughter, and Duchess Saxe-Coburg-Gotha with her daughter. I got to meet Prince George of Greece for the first time, since coming to Europe. We talked about his trip to Siam 11 years ago and he teased me that at that time I was just a tiny boy. There's also one prince I forgot – Prince Christian of Denmark[4] and his consort also attended. Prince Christian chatted with me in an informal manner. He asked after Your Majesty and Pi Chira and inquired about governmental matters in Bangkok. I thought he was wasting time a bit, so I answered rather generally. Within the Russian court they do not like official matters to be discussed on social occasions such as this ball. The King of Greece also talked to me, asking me how many years I had been in Russia and how long I was going to stay.

As for the wedding, once the Grand Duchess was dressed, the procession got in place and went to the church in the grounds of the palace. In the church there was a service by a Russian priest in Russian, followed by a blessing from a Greek Orthodox priest. After the ceremony was over, we processed back and rested. In the evening, there was a huge and very grand banquet in full dress uniform. I was invited as well. It was most impressive. Staff of the Imperial household stood behind the chairs of the Emperor and Empress and all the imperial family, as well as the royal pages. I was very amused to see the pages standing there, all people I knew and with whom I had attended school, albeit in a different year. After the toasts were drunk to the Emperor and Empress and other nobles, a salute was fired. Finally there were toasts to the priest and the officials. The Dowager Empress bowed first towards the priests, then to the left and right towards the officials. It looked strange.

The Empress did not attend the banquet, so the Dowager Empress took her place.

After the banquet, there was a reception for all the officials. The Emperor and Empress, together with the imperial family, processed up and down three times. After that, all the imperial family went to the palace of Grand Duke Vladimir to wait for the return of the newly weds. Beautiful lanterns hung all along the route. Then when the time was due, the Emperor and Empress led in the newly weds to the palace of their mother and father. All the imperial family were waiting and it was an informal gathering of relatives. It was all most enjoyable with singing and everything in a very relaxed atmosphere,

On 1st September, there was a gala theatrical performance to which I was invited, but I did not attend because I would have had to come from Petersburg and that day there was a well wishing at the palace of Grand Duke Vladimir.

On the 30th, I left Petersburg for Berlin in order to see Toonmom Chai. I arrived safely on the same day. Toonmom Chai and his equerry met me at the station and came to the embassy.

I was very pleased to see Toonmom Chai because I had not seen him for a long time. Indeed, this was the first time since leaving Bangkok together. I asked him a great deal of questions about everything.

At the moment, I am thinking of going to Vienna and Budapest to have a look around. I have never been there and will then return to wait for Toonmom Toh to come from Denmark. He is coming via Berlin and then we can go on to Paris and then America.

I beg to remain Your Majesty's obedient servant,
Chakrabongse

4. Prince Christian of Schleswig-Holstein (1831-1917) was a minor Danish-born German prince, who became a member of the British Royal Family through his marriage to Princess Helena of the United Kingdom (1846-1923), the fifth child and third daughter of Queen Victoria and Prince Albert of Saxe-Coburg-Gotha.

5. The wedding on 29th August was between Prince Nicholas of Greece & Denmark, 3rd son of King George of the Hellenes, and Grand Duchess Elena Vladimirovna, only daughter of Grand Duke Vladimir Alexandrovitch of Russia and Grand Duchess Marie of Mecklenburg-Schwerin.

7TH SEPTEMBER 1902

HM KING TO PRINCE CHAKRABONGSE
I VERY MUCH REGRET TO HEAR THAT THE EMPRESS OF RUSSIA HAD MISCARRIAGE BUT I DOUBT WHETHER I OUGHT TO TELEGRAPH OR NOT. IF YOU HAVE GOOD OPPORTUNITY AND IF YOU THINK THAT IT IS QUITE RIGHT YOU MAY EXPRESS MY REGRETS BUT IF YOU THINK THAT I SHOULD SEND TELEGRAM TELL ME SO IMMEDIATELY.

Hotel Kaiserhof, Berlin
18th September 1902

Your Majesty

As I informed Your Majesty in my last letter, I have been to Vienna and Budapest. I left Berlin on the 7th of this month in the morning and reached Vienna the same day, but late in the evening. As it was very late, I couldn't see anything and went to the hotel. On the next day, the 8th, I went to look around the city, visit the palace and go to the museums, parliament and other sights. It is all very beautiful. The houses here are very elaborate and large. The paintings in the museum are very good. In the evening I planned to go to the opera, which has a reputation for incredible singing, the best in Europe. However, on that day the opera was not very good and so I did not go. The next day was the anniversary of the death of Empress Elizabeth, so the opera was closed, and then the next day I went to Budapest. In the afternoon, I went to Schoenbrun palace, but only managed to see outside and the grounds because they would not let me in as the Emperor was in residence. The gardens of Schoenbrun are really magnificent, being very extensive, and I admired the trees which have been trained into walls. I imagine that if Your Majesty saw them, Your Majesty must have liked them very much. I also went to see the royal zoo and wanted to see the Thai elephant, but I was told that the Thai elephant had been sent to Budapest, because it got very angry and bit the other elephants, necessitating its transfer to somewhere it could be on its own.

On the 9th, I took the train up onto a high hill near Vienna, from where you can have a panoramic view of the whole city.

On the 10th, I went shopping and went to the shop selling leatherware where Your Majesty went on the trip to Europe. The shop is really well arranged and all the items are of great quality. I bought a cigarette case and lots of other things. In the afternoon, I left Vienna for Budapest. The route just before reaching our destination was very beautiful, with views of the river and the mountains, which seemed very high. There were also castles on the tops of the mountains and it was a delightful view.

The Hungaria Hotel, Budapest, c. 1900.

The Stephanskirche, Vienna, 1902.

On arrival we drove to the Hotel Hungaria, where Your Majesty stayed on Your Majesty's European tour. The owner of the hotel received me in style and arranged an excellent room, as well laying on a carriage and footman to take me around.

On the 11th, we went around the town and up to see the palace in the castle, which is in a fantastic position. However, the palace doesn't seem quite finished and work is still going on. Inside it is very impressive with one room which is decorated in true Hungarian style. Then I went up onto the highest hill, where there is a fort and a view over the city and the surrounding countryside. Mr Albert, who accompanied me, explained that Your Majesty did not come

up here but only to the palace. I really like Budapest and think it is one of the finest cities I have been to.

Today, late in the evening, Pi Pen arrived here and is staying in the same hotel.

On the 12th, I went to Margaret island in the middle of the Danube river. It was very beautiful and has been made into a park, so is easy to walk about. We walked around the island and saw the hot spring waterfall, which is apparently the only one in Europe. The water is indeed hot and is supposed to be good for treating various ailments. Many people come to take a cure in the hotel near by. They say it is very good for rheumatism.

On the 13th, we did not go anywhere in particular, but simply walked about and did some shopping. In the evening, Budapest is really rather hot. I have never felt as hot all summer as I have here. It is so hot, that wearing a wool suit is not at all comfortable. On the 14th, we left Budapest to return to Berlin via Vienna, but did not stop. We reached Berlin on the 15th in the evening. In the middle of that night, Somdet Chai arrived in Berlin and came to stay at the same hotel. It is a shame that Toonmom Chai is not here still, but he has gone on manoeuvres.

Today Toonmom Toh is coming back from Denmark and is going to stay for a couple of hours, before going on to Paris. Somdet Chai and I will accompany him.

Concerning the miscarriage of the Empress, it's still very confusing. There are many rumours circulating, but it is not yet clear what really occurred. I have written to the Emperor's personal doctor, with whom I get on very well, asking him to tell me what really happened, but he has not replied yet. Yesterday, a bulletin appeared in the newspapers, signed by the royal accoucheur Professor Ott and the royal surgeon Girsh[1].

I am unable to tell Your Majesty any more about this at present. I will have to wait and see. Perhaps the doctor has accompanied the Emperor on manoeuvres in Kursky and has not received my letter. When I find something out, I will let Your Majesty know.

I beg to remain Your Majesty's obedient servant,

Chakrabongse

Panorama of Budapest, c. 1900.

1. A newspaper bulletin, dated 20th August 1902, signed by the royal obstetrician, Professor Ott, and the royal surgeon, Girsh, suggested a miscarriage.

Hotel Arlington[1], Washington
13th October 1902.

Your Majesty

I have now arrived in America and I beg to address Your Majesty from the New World, which is almost opposite Siam. May I also show off that I have finally come somewhere new, where Your Majesty has not yet gone.

We left England on the 3rd of this month, and were on the sea for seven days, arriving on the 10th in New York. During the crossing, there were strong winds and high seas, as it was a bad time to travel, but we were fine and not as bad as we might have been in such conditions. Nevertheless, the boat was very much delayed and the naval vessel and the officials, which were to meet us, had to wait the entire day until 10 o'clock at night, before the boat arrived.

The President sent Mr Purse, the third assistant to the Port Minister (here there are three assistants with equal rank), to meet Toonmom Toh on his behalf together with a Mr Morgan. These two were to accompany us at all times and look after us officially. In addition, the Siamese ambassador[2] also came to meet us, together with other people who knew Toonmom. As the ship was so delayed, we had to take the train to Washington immediately as the program was arranged thus. That night, we slept in the train.

On the morning of the 11th, we arrived in Washington and were met by the presidential car and another soldier. We came to stay in this hotel, where the Siamese embassy is also based. At 11 o'clock, we went to see the President[3] wearing full-dress uniform. We were proceeded by cavalry officers. The president was still unwell and should not have seen us. He has been ill ever since his fall and had to receive us sitting down, as he was unable to stand. He was very pleasant and apologized several times for being unwell, as well as expressing regret that he could not receive us appropriately and that he had had to ask

the Port Minister, Mr Hay, to arrange things for him. He said that nowadays America was turning towards Asia and, for that reason, was always interested in the well being and development of Siam and hoped that it would continue to prosper. He asked Toonmom Toh about his studies and what he was going to visit. He said he should go and see the cavalry who were stationed near here. In all, he received us for about 10 minutes and said this was the first time he had received visitors since being ill.

In the evening, the Port Authority gave a dinner for us at their building. There were other ministers and important people. The Minister of the Port Authority is a very good man, being polite and well spoken. I can see that Americans are very friendly and informal. They look genuinely pleased to see us and have no pretence. They asked when Your Majesty might pay a visit. That day I went to see the Russian ambassador[4], as I thought this was an appropriate thing to do, given my connection. The visit went well and he asked me to dinner.

On the 12th, in the morning, we went to see the house, which the government provides for former soldiers[5]. It is a really beautiful and clean place and very inviting. There is also a large garden. In the afternoon, we visited a military cemetery[6]. All those who died in action are buried here and it is like a beautiful park.

In the evening, the Siamese ambassador gave a dinner for the Port Authority Minister. Other ministers also came, as well as those Americans who have connections with Siam, such as those who had been consuls or ambassadors in Siam. The dinner went off well and everyone seemed content.

Today, in the morning, we went to see the Capitol, where parliament meets. It is very impressive being built entirely of marble. We also went to the National Library, which is enormous and very well arranged. In the afternoon, we took the train to Annapolis to see the naval academy. The officials received us very well and the cadets all lined up for us. When Toonmom Toh arrived, they all saluted and

---

1. Hotel Arlington was one of the best hotels in Washington in 1902, being only a block from the White House. The Siamese embassy was actually in the hotel.

2. The Siamese Ambassador in the US was Phraya Akharaj Varathorn, 1901-1911.

3. President Theodore Roosevelt (in office 1901-1909).

4. Count Arthur Cassini was ambassador from 1898-1905.

5. The Armed Forces Retirement Home was established in March 1851. As well as being a home for Veterans, at that time it was also a park for Washington residents.

6. Arlington Cemetery was established in 1864.

7. Annapolis US Naval Academy was founded in 1845. After the Spanish-American war of 1898, the campus was almost wholly rebuilt and much enlarged between 1899-1906.

President Roosevelt, c. 1902.

The Capitol, c. 1902.

Arlington Cemetery, c.1900.

The Library of Congress, c. 1902

Washington DC, c. 1902

played the national anthem. He then watched the cadets march past, which they did very well. After that, Toonmom looked at various buildings, but there was nothing special distinguishing this academy from any others we have seen. In the school there are around 400 cadets, who study for four years in four classes. They study hard, whether on land or sea, with only one month's holiday. At the moment, they are planning to enlarge the school greatly, because the navy is increasing in size, there are not enough officers and they need to increase the intake of cadets. At the end of today, I am going to have dinner with the Russian ambassador.

I am well and happy and thinking of Your Majesty always.

I beg to remain Your Majesty's obedient servant,

Chakrabongse

Count Arthur Cassini, Russian ambassador to the US (1898-1905).

PS One thing I forgot to tell Your Majesty is regarding the Empress. I received a letter from the Emperor's personal physician stating that the rumours that she will not be able to have another child are not true at all. However, he said nothing more, so it seems the miscarriage is true.

Rain tonight and Sunday; increasing easterly winds.

The Evening Times

Number 2248.   WASHINGTON, SATURDAY, OCTOBER 11, 1902.

CROWN PRINCE OF SIAM RECEIVED BY PRESIDENT

His Royal Highness Pays a Brief Visit to the Temporary White House and Is Cordially Greeted.

THE CROWN PRINCE OF SIAM.

The Prince and His Suite Then Repair to the Siamese Legation, Where They Received Many Callers.

Chawfa Maha Vajiravudh, Crown Prince of Siam, arrived in Washington this morning and called upon President Roosevelt, to whom he extended greetings from Chulalongkorn I, King of Siam. The visit at the White House occupied not more than ten minutes, after which the prince and his suite repaired to the Siamese legation, where he received a number of distinguished callers.

This afternoon the prince remained quietly at the legation. Tonight he will be the guest of Secretary and Mrs. Hay at dinner at the Hay residence.

It was originally intended that the prince should go to Annapolis late this afternoon, but the plans have been altered and he probably will not go there until Monday.

Arrived at 8 o'Clock.

The special train bearing the royal party arrived from New York at the Pennsylvania station at 8 o'clock this morning. On the train, besides the crown prince, were Prince Chakrabongse, brother of the crown prince; the Siamese minister; Colonel Rajavallobh, first aide-de-camp to the crown prince; Major Sarasiddhi, second aide-de-camp; Mom Anuvatra, private secretary; Luang Surayudh, first aide-de-camp to Prince Chakrabongse; Lieut. Nai Poun, second aide-de-camp; E. H. Loftus, secretary of the Siamese legation. The United States officials on the train were Third Assistant Secretary of State Peirce, representing the President, and Edwin Morgan, secretary to the President's representative.

retary of War; Hon. Henry C. Payne, Postmaster General; Hon. James Wilson, Secretary of Agriculture; Admiral George Dewey, United States Navy; Brig. Gen. G. L. Gillespie, United States Army; Hon. David J. Hill, Assistant Secretary of State; Hon. Alvey A. Adee, Second Assistant Secretary of State; Hon. Herbert H. D. Peirce, Third Assistant Secretary of State; Hon. George B. Cortelyou, secretary to the President; Hon. W. W. Rockhill, director of the Bureau of American Republics; Henry White, E. V. Morgan, and Col. T. A. Bingham, United States Army.

Tomorrow will be spent in sightseeing and at 8 o'clock the Siamese minister

will dine the Prince and members of the Cabinet at the Arlington. On Monday a visit will be made to Annapolis where his royal highness will be received with full honors.

To Visit Mount Vernon.

On Tuesday at 1 o'clock the royal visitor will be taken on the Sylph, the President's yacht, for a trip to Mount Vernon and at night he will be entertained at a private dinner by Prof. Gore, of the Columbia University, who is a special friend of the Siamese legation. On Wednesday morning the Prince will leave Washington for Wilmington to carry out his public itinerary.

SECRETARY ROOT MEETS MORGAN

Conference Held Aboard the Financier's Private Yacht Corsair, Lying at Anchor in North River.

HE DECLINES TO TALK

It Is Supposed the Appointment Was Made by the Two Parties Over the Long Distance Telephone Friday.

NEW YORK, Oct. 11.—Elihu Root, Secretary of War, came to this city this morning and had a conference with J. P. Morgan on board the yacht Corsair, lying at anchor in the North River off West Thirty-fifth Street. Mr. Root's departure from Washington was a companied and preceded by reports to the effect that his trip to this city was concerned with the coal strike. The last time Mr. Root was here, nearly two weeks ago, his visit preceded the invitation extended by President Roosevelt to the anthracite operators and the heads of the miners' union, which resulted in the fruitless meeting at Washington a week ago yesterday.

Dispatches from Washington reported this morning that yesterday afternoon Mr. Root had a long distance telephone conversation with Mr. Morgan. This, and the fact that Labor Commissioner Wright returned hurriedly to Washington seemed to give importance to the conference which President Roosevelt had yesterday afternoon with Mr. Root. Mr. Wright, and Attorney General Knox. Mr. Root left Washington last midnight. He gave as the only reason of his visit to New York, his desire to register for the forthcoming elections.

WRIGHT CONFERS WITH PRESIDENT ON STRIKE

WANT DISTRICT LOCAL SELF-G

WHY THE PRESENT FORM OF GOVERNMENT IS W

Whereas the people of the District of Columbia were, in trarily and unjustly deprived of their inalienable right of local ment, and an unrepublican, un-American form of government them without their consent; and

Whereas the present form of government in the Capital of —the political heart of the Nation—is contrary to the most principle of American liberty to establish which our Revolu fathers pledged their lives, their fortunes and their sacred hono a successful seven years' war, and for the maintenance of whi tens of thousands of brave and patriotic men sacrificed their the War of the Rebellion; and

Whereas the ballot in the people's most effective weapon, which they are powerless to peaceably redress their grievance

Resolved, That it is the sense of the Union Veteran Unio gress should re-establish in the National Capital a governmen in form and in harmony with the spirit and institutions of o "a government of the people, by the people, and for the people suffrage, limited only by a reasonable educational test, under th system of voting.

Resolved, That the commander-in-chief is hereby directed copies of these resolutions to the President of the United States request that he recommend to Congress the advisability of re government in the District of Columbia, to the President of and to the Speaker of the House of Representatives.

BEAUMONT OIL TO HE THE CAPITOL BUIL

Experiments With the Substitute Fuel Succ Machinery Ready.

It is announced that the Capitol will be kept at a pleasant temperature all winter, regardless of the strike, and the fact that the coal supply is exhausted the building will be heated and lighted by oil from the Beaumont fields.

Experiments with oil as a material for heating and lighting have been made with success and the boilers for the oil are nearly completed and will be in readiness by November 1.

ling it for their own use strike continues.

Large quantities of h are coming into Washing the anti-smoke law, are factories, restaurant and tors and apartment hous Prices continue at the sags. Anthracite is sellin $21, and bituminous at $ $12. The wood supply is

18th November 1902

Your Majesty

While I have been accompanying Toonmom Toh on his American tour, it has been very hard to find time to write letters. We have to go and see this and that, or be invited by someone all the time. It is very hectic and there is hardly any time to rest. For that reason, I have not been able to write to Your Majesty. When there is some spare time, such as in the boat or train, it is very hard to write because of the movement. I have only been able to write on my return to Petersburg. It may also be better to recount all the things we saw and did in America in one go.

I did write one letter from Washington, which spoke only about our visit to the President and dinner with the Minister of the Port Authority. Now I can continue. We stayed in Washington from the 11th October until the 15th in the Arlington Hotel, where the Siamese embassy is. The city of Washington is completely new and was built expressly to be the capital. One can see that it has been built to a plan as all the roads are straight, the houses are not very tall but are made to be comfortable. Most houses look very much like the villas found in the countryside around Peterhof, with trees and gardens everywhere. For that reason, the city seems like a very pleasant place to live. Almost all the people who live here, work for the government, or else are ambassadors and consuls. Thus, all the people that one gets to meet are decent people.

Nevertheless, while we were in Washington, we were well guarded at all times. Two detectives took it in turns to accompany us. These two policemen were real gentlemen, very polite and reliable. Wherever we went, the two policemen went with us, without exception, even going in the same car. One of them was assigned to Toonmom Toh and the other to me. The two followed us everywhere we went in the United States. In Washington, apart from the detectives, there were also uniformed police on bicycles following the carriages, four to a carriage. So wherever we went, it was like a small procession.

While we were in Washington, we saw various sites such as the Capitol, where congress meets to run the government. The Capitol is a huge building, entirely in marble, and is very imposing. It must have cost a lot of money. Inside, it is very extensive with meeting chambers both for the Senate and the House of Representatives. There is also a High court chamber, as well as offices, canteens and the like.

The National Library is also another massive building, even more lavish than the Capitol. The large dome is clad in gold and the interior is extremely luxuriously decorated. A multitude of books is arranged in the most up-to-date manner, with a machine which collects the books from the various cabinets and sends them to the central reading room. In this way, no one has to carry books about and waste time. There is a printing works inside, as well as room for blind people to read using books with raised type which they can feel.

The military cemetery is slightly outside the centre and has been created in the form of a large park. Here are buried all the officers and soldiers who died in battle for their country. It is very impressive and, being in the park, one almost feels it is worth dying just to be buried there.

The home for retired soldiers outside the city has a similar feel. There are many buildings, both large and small, in an expansive, shaded park. It is for long-serving soldiers and veterans, who are injured and can no longer serve. The government provides for them to come here and pays them an allowance, so they can live in comfort. In the grounds, there are some allotments, where they can do some gardening and keep occupied. Everyone is allowed to do what they want. I think it is very impressive to have such an institution. In this way, the soldiers know that if they serve well, when they are old, they will not starve and can see a future. Otherwise, on the whole, soldiers who have served for a long time encounter problems when they can no longer continue. When they retire, they cannot find enough to support themselves, as all they know is soldiering, and to earn a living is difficult.

One day while we were in Washington, we took a boat on the river to see George Washington's former home, Mount Vernon, and pay our respects at his tomb. Toonmom Toh and I laid a wreath, as is the custom. The house is small but comfortable. It is arranged just as it was during the time of George Washington, in almost every detail. The setting is very good, being on a hill beside the water and with a fine view. We also visited the naval academy, which is in Annapolis, a 40-minute train ride from Washington. The academy received us in great style,

Mount Vernon, the former home of George Washington, c. 1902.

Right: Independence Hall, Philadelphia, c. 1902.

firing a salute, and with a guard of honour at the station. At the college, the cadets were in line to receive us and performed a march past. The students look strong and march very well for naval cadets. Once we had inspected them, we looked around the college. There is a chemistry lab, a gym, classrooms and the usual. It was unusual, however, that they did not show us the cadets' dormitories. The course seems very thorough, taking four years and having four classes. They stay at the academy all the time and hardly go home at all. During the summer, they have to go and train on warships. After graduation, they then have to spend two years at sea before becoming a naval officer. I do not know enough about the navy to evaluate how good the college is, but I could see that the organization is very comprehensive.

On the 15th October, we left Washington for Wilmington, the capital of Delaware state. We stayed in the home of Major General Wilson, whom Toonmom Toh already knew. I was invited too and we were there in a private capacity. Wilmington is a small town, but there are various types of manufacturing there. One we went to see was a factory making wool and other fabrics using water power. It was rather hot and smelly, so not much fun. General Wilson is a very good type and very straightforward in the American way. He does not respect tradition, but is very kind.

On the 16th, we left Wilmington for Philadelphia where we stayed outside the town with Mr Potter[1], another former acquaintance of Toonmom Toh's. He also invited us in a private capacity. This

Mr Potter was formerly an ambassador to Rome where he was much liked by the former king [King Umberto I] and the royal family. He is an excellent man. He understands all the conventions and, however friendly he was, he never overstepped the mark. He is one of the best Americans we met. While we were at his home, he did everything to make the trip enjoyable. In addition, Mr Potter is very interested in, and admiring of, Siam. It is he who found Mr Stroebel. He is full of admiration for Toonmom Toh and I also count him as a close friend. He also knows the Minister of the Port Authority very well and can be useful in the future.

While we were staying here, we went into Philadelphia two or three times. It is a large city with over 1 million inhabitants and was the capital of the United States before the creation of Washington. We went to see the Independence Hall[2], the building where they came and met to declare independence from England. It is an old building and has many mementoes relating to that time. It is not a commercial museum, simply a museum. It also has offices for trade with trading companies throughout the world, who want to trade with the US. Or it helps arrange for US companies to find out about selling abroad

1. Mr William Potter was envoy to the legation in Rome, 1892-1894.

2. The Independence Hall is where both the United States Declaration of Independence and the United States Constitution were debated and adopted. The building was completed in 1753, as the colonial legislature (later Pennsylvania State House) for the Province of Pennsylvania.

Cramp Shipyard, c. 1900.

435 PHILADELPHIA— BALDWIN LOCOMOTIVE WORKS

and whom they should contact. It seems a huge organization and very well set up. The objects in the museum were all related to trade and showed what products could be obtained where.

The shipyard belonging to Mr Cramp[3] is enormous and known throughout the world. All kinds of ships are built there – warships both for the US government and other countries, including Russia. When I went there, I had hoped to see a Russian warship, but unfortunately it had just left and there was only a Turkish one. This shipyard is so large that just walking around it makes one exhausted. It was also very hot that day, so we got very tired.

The Baldwin Locomotives Works is another huge manufacturing plant. All they make is locomotives, producing several a day, or around 30 engines per week. However, I have be honest with Your Majesty and admit that looking around factories is something I don't really understand, as I haven't studied it. They explained everything and I just nodded, as it was difficult for me to discuss anything or go into details about the manufacturing. All I could ask was how many people worked there, how many hours they worked, and such like. In truth, these are not very useful facts for anyone to know. People who look round factories should at least have some basic knowledge.

On 22 October, we left Philadelphia to go to New York. This is a really strange place. It is enormous and has a population of over 3 million. The houses are very unusual, as they are very high, most being 20 stories up. It looks so strange. However, I can't say that they are beautiful. In fact, I would say they are rather ugly. If anything, this city is closer to

3. William Cramp & Sons Shipbuilding Company of Philadelphia was founded in 1830 by William Cramp, and was the premier U.S. iron shipbuilder of the late 19th century.

4. The Baldwin Locomotive Works was founded in Philadelphia in 1825 by Matthias W. Baldwin. By 1900 the company used the Vauclain Compound engine with two pistons, one for high pressure and one for low pressure steam, leading to lower fuel and water consumption. By 1906 the firm were producing 2,500 engines per annum.

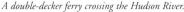

A double-decker ferry crossing the Hudson River.

Seth Low, Mayor of New York.

London than anywhere else. Furthermore, when I was there they were having to use a weak coal, because coal at that time was very expensive, so it was dark and smoky. In New York, I saw one thing which I beg to suggest we could use in Bangkok, namely the ferry crossing the Hudson River. The city of New York is situated on a very wide river difficult to bridge. There are two to three bridges, which are very well built, but we would not be able to do them. Therefore, we need a ferry. They have ones which take carriages and people, as the boats are large with two floors. On the top are the people and on the lower deck the carriages. The sides are filled in on the bottom, so the horses are not scared. They have many such ferries and, if you go in a carriage, you drive straight on without any fuss. I think it is rather convenient. On the day we arrived, the Mayor[5] came to see Toonmom Toh and we returned the visit. This mayor is a good man and, unusually, is very ordinary. Normally, mayors are just people with a lot of money, but this one is very nice and polite. While we were in New York, we went to see various places such as the Insurance Office. It was nothing special, simply a large company with a lot of money.

The Stock Exchange is a very remarkable place, as people can become millionaires in one day, or they can lose all their money in one day also. Here, the

officials received us in style, with a welcome speech and taking Toonmom Toh out onto the balcony to look down into the hall where the trading takes place. It was really crowded and everyone was shouting at each other. We went to see the building, which will be the new exchange. It is very impressive and has a vault to store all the money, with doors that are impossible to open. The day we saw all these things was the day we went into the heart of New York, referred to as the city. Everyone is in business and it is very frenetic. There were people running in front and behind, and it was all a bit much.

The tomb of General Grant[6], which is near New York is very fine. We went to pay our respects and laid a wreath. General Grant came to see Your Majesty in Bangkok some time ago. Columbia University is unusual in having a very fine library, which Mr Low built using his own money.

The underground railway is still being built. It is unusually difficult, as New York stands on rock and drilling is arduous and expensive. Only the Americans could undertake such a feat.

The Fire stations and Fire brigades in America are among the best in the world in terms of their speed. The station is all ready and when the signal comes, the horses come out of the stable, the doors opening automatically, and run under their traces, which then descend on to them. Meanwhile the men come down from the upper floor via a pole. In just a few moments, everything is ready. It takes about 15 seconds. They showed us how to place the ladder and run up it too most efficiently.

Outside New York we went to see the army college at West Point. It is about a two-hour train ride from New York, or 4-5 hours by boat on the Hudson

5. The Mayor of New York, Seth Low (1850–1916), was an American educator and political figure, who served as Mayor of Brooklyn, as President of Columbia University, as diplomatic representative of the United States, and as the 92nd Mayor of New York City.

6. General Ulysses S. Grant (1822-1885) came to Bangkok in 1877, when King Chulalongkorn was just 25. The tomb was completed in 1897.

7. Library belonging to Mr. Low. Now the Low Memorial Library.

Tomb of General Grant.

Columbia University.

New York firemen's drill, 1900.

West Point during centennial year, 1902.

River. All of us went on a small military vessel laid on by the government. There was a lot of saluting. The military vessel saluted 3-5 times, and at the school there were also salutes. I have noticed that Americans love saluting. If there is a moment when they can salute, they do so. The boat trip along the Hudson River went through beautiful scenery. All along the bank, there are fine properties with people living in country houses, of greater or lesser size, but all very comfortable looking.

At the college, they received us very well. At the landing stage were the Commander and other officers, together with some cavalry who accompanied our carriage. At the academy one battalion of cadets lined up, divided into six companies. They had been trained to look and march past saluting, as is customary the first time, and then run past another time. Having seen the cadets, I was very impressed by their strength, their training, and how in time they were. I have never seen such a smooth performance. Once they had done their training, I exclaimed that I had never seen such a fine and smooth battalion as I had seen here. The grounds of the academy are very extensive. We got to see everything: the classrooms, the mess hall, the gym, the manege, the club house – all very tidy, clean and impressive. The bedrooms were all small and they slept two or three to a room. The rooms are bare with just beds, a basin and a wardrobe. The cadets have to keep their rooms tidy. Their riding is so good, that I was amazed. They don't just do normal riding, but do various jumping exercises on horseback in a similar way to the Cossacks. All did the tricks equally well. At other academies, there are always a few who can do riding tricks, but not everyone like here. It made me think that maybe it is something we could try in Bangkok. Another thing is the way they carry their supplies and essentials into areas where a carriage cannot go. I think it is an excellent method, because it is much quicker than putting it in a cart or carriage.

Their studies are also very thorough. There are four years, each corresponding to a class. During the year, they have one month off, but must spend the rest of the time in the academy. What they study is as elsewhere. They learn French and Spanish, but their training is most comprehensive, which is why they are so orderly, as I have already informed Your Majesty. I was truly amazed by this school, as I had not imagined that it would be so good. I used to rather look down on American soldiers and, although I don't know what the ordinary soldiers are like, I can see that they really train their officers well. I think that we could send Thai students here and in that way they would not have to learn another language first before being able to enter, apart from English, thereby making things much easier for them. I made some enquiries and it seems the government will be only too pleased.

We also saw another American regiment, while we were in Washington, but I forgot to tell Your Majesty about it. We went to see the cavalry regiment stationed in Washington. They showed us some training. I could see that their precision was not equal to the Germans, but in terms of fighting I doubt they would be defeated. We were shown their uniforms, saddles and all their kit. It is all very practical, with little thought for aesthetics. Both the officers and men ride their horses in a very brave way. The way the regiment is arranged and the exercises are all totally different from in Europe, although I had to study it for quite a time before it was discernable. Their way is rather unusual, but I haven't examined it closely enough to be able to tell Your Majesty, whether their methods are better or not. However, I believe that they will be just as agile and efficient as in Europe.

In New York, we went to lots of different places and there were numerous receptions with many anxious to see us. On the whole we had to decline most of the invitations, as we were rushing around and barely had time to rest.

One dinner was given by the Mayor and another at the Lotos Club[8] was given by the Presbyterian Missionaries. The Presbyterians invited us as a thank you for Your Majesty's kindness towards them in Siam and the fact that they have never had any problems. During dinner, Mr Brown, who went to Bangkok about a year ago, drank a toast for the well being of Siam and wished Your Majesty well at great length, as well as thanking Your Majesty in various ways. It was a very good speech and the dinner showed how sincere they were in wanting to truly thank us.

One day, Toonmom Toh gave a dinner for all those who had welcomed us and arranged the trip. It included the Mayor and everyone was appreciative.

On the 27th, we left New York for Boston, arriving in the evening. Representatives of the Governor for the State of Massachusetts[9] and the Mayor of Boston came to meet us. On that very evening, the Governor invited us to dinner. The mayor was there together with other officials. The Governor seems rather strange and uncouth and wanted to show off his rank, but didn't quite know how. Then, when he spoke, he wasn't very eloquent and forgot things, having to discuss with his aides. In fact, he kept having discussions with them, with no concern for others. During dinner, he got everyone running around discussing what we should visit, while at the end he was probably discussing government business during dinner. It all looked rather rude.

Boston is an old town, rather like one in England, and the people are also rather like the English. We went to Harvard University, which is near Boston. It does not seem anything special, but looks comfortable and pleasant. This university is where Mr Stroebel was a teacher. We went to see a watch-making factory, a shoe factory and an electricity generating plant situated in two towns near Boston, about half an hour's train ride away. The watch making factory was very good. They have excellent machines, so that they only employ very few people and everything is beautifully laid out. We rather rushed through the electricity generating plant and scarcely saw anything, as time was short.

While we were there, we went to see the governor and the mayor in their office and we were shown the parliament building for the State of Massachusetts.

The day before we left for Boston, Mr Purse, his ADC, gave a leaving dinner, as from Boston on, the visit is truly private with no government involvement.

8. The Lotos Club was founded as a gentleman's club in New York and had a strong literary and artistic bent. In 1893, the Club moved to 556-558 Fifth Avenue at 46th Street, purchasing their first clubhouse.

9. Governor Winthrop Murray Crane (1853-1920) was in office from 1900-1903.

On the 2nd November, Toonmom Toh continued his trip, but I was unable to accompany him, as it was time to return. I was really sad, as I only got to see a few sites. We only visited four cities and I did not see Niagara falls. I felt a real wrench saying goodbye to Toonmom Toh because we will be far apart, and it is difficult to write to each other and even harder to meet. In the past, whatever the situation, we could speak to each other easily.

On that day, I returned to New York and stayed quietly until the 4th, when I took the boat back to Europe.

I noticed during my stay that Americans are good people, unlike Europeans. They are kind and straightforward. If they love someone, it is sincere. They are good listeners, from the boss downwards. They have good intentions towards Thailand. Toonmom Toh's trip here aroused a lot of interest among the general public. They wish to trade with Thailand. America is flourishing, because it is getting better and better every day in trade, and is almost overtaking Europe. In addition, it is a large country and, if they are truly interested in our country, they will be a great support in maintaining our independence. I think that Toonmom Toh's trip here was of the utmost important in raising awareness of Thailand in the minds of the people of such a large and important nation.

Americans are really good, as I have told Your Majesty already. Sometimes they made so much fuss in wanting to receive us, that it became annoying, but in truth it came from the goodness of their hearts. Their warmth and generosity is very different from that of the Europeans. I really would like Your Majesty to visit. It is rumoured that Your Majesty will for sure, with many people coming to talk to me about this. I pushed the question aside, but I am sure that were Your Majesty to come here, there would be a reception unlike any that Your Majesty has received elsewhere. However, I also fear that some things would drive Your Majesty crazy, as there would be too many people fussing around. In addition, the newspapers, which are the worst in the world, would also not leave Your Majesty alone.

The country itself is very beautiful and different from Europe. It is worth visiting and studying. I am still upset that I did not see very much, as I had so little time. But, nevertheless, my trip this time has allowed me to learn a lot and been a real eye opener. I hope that one day Your Majesty may allow me to make at least one further trip, so I can see the whole country. In this letter, it has been my intention to inform Your Majesty about our reception and all the new things we saw and my impressions. I am sure there will be many errors, but I imagine that Toonmom Toh will have written a much more comprehensive report.

I left by boat on the 4th, reaching England on the 10th. There were massive waves throughout. The ship was large, but nevertheless rolled about. But thank goodness, I felt well throughout and did not get ill or seasick.

On the 14th November, I reached Petersburg and returned to Tsarskoe Selo to be with the regiment. On the 16th, I presented the decoration which Your Majesty had graciously agreed to bestow on Grand Duke Constantine. The Grand Duke thanked Your Majesty from the bottom of his heart and will write a letter shortly. I also took the tray and silver coffee set, which Sadet Mother had ordered, and said that it was a present from both of Your Majesties for the Grand Duke and Grand Duchess. He was delighted and thanked you both.

Regarding the other decoration, it is for the assistant to the Grand Duke, General Kurbatsky. Originally I had cut him out, as I thought that he had nothing to do with me and, in fact, didn't even know me. But later the Director of the Corps des Pages told me that he must be given a decoration, otherwise they would be very upset. For that reason, I had to send Your Majesty a telegram to that effect.

The Emperor and Empress are in the Crimea. I sent a telegram to the Emperor when I arrived back and I received a very cordial one back.

I beg to remain Your Majesty's obedient servant,
Chakrabongse

25th November 1902

Opposite: Pages line up to greet the Tsar.
Far right: Program commemorating the
centenary of the Corps des Pages.

Your Majesty

Since I returned to Russia, I have been serving in the Hussar regiment. At first there was not much work, apart from practising for the review on the annual fete day for the regiment.

On the 19th of this month, it was the annual regimental day. In the morning, there were officers from this regiment, while before that both former officers and others came in great numbers and the regiment lined up in the manège in order to receive Grand Duke Vladimir, the Commanding officer of Petersburg and representative of the Emperor. Today, various other nobles turned up, such as Grand Duke Nicholas who used to be commander-in-chief of this regiment.

At 11 o clock, Grand Duke Vladimir arrived. He inspected the regiment and there were the usual prayers, after which the soldiers marched past the Grand Duke twice, before going to the banqueting hall. Here the Grand Duke drank a toast to the Emperor, the Empress, the Imperial family and the regiment.

After this, there was a reception in the main hall. The Grand Duke sat at table with the Grand Duchess and all the guests, both men and women, ate together.

Later in the evening, there was supper and various entertainments. Grand Duke Nicholas was there, together with other officers who had served in the Hussars. It was great fun and very informal, with just the regiment and former Hussars.

The carousing went on all night, until at around 4.30 am, Grand Duke Nicholas ordered two companies to get ready for battle immediately. This was a drill and everyone ran around like mad, but succeeded in being ready. Within around eight minutes, the two companies were lined up for inspection. The Grand Duke was full of praise.

After these celebrations were over, life in the regiment went back to normal. I was ordered to go and observe everything that the soldiers had to do in First Company. Work begins around 8.30 am. There is a break for lunch and then work continues until 3 or 4 pm. The things we have to do, include training, gym practice and the duties of the soldiers. The men are divided into groups and one officer has charge of

one group. Officers also have specific duties, such as training the new recruits for this year, or training the intelligence section, training in gymnastics or teaching. I have been assigned to the intelligence gathering department.

I beg to remain Your Majesty's obedient servant,
Chakrabongse

Bust of the Tsar, presented to the Corps des Pages
by Prince Chakrabongse.

Siamese embassy, St. Petersburg
30th December 1902

Your Majesty

On the 24th of this month, the Emperor returned from the Crimea to Tsarskoe Selo, in order to celebrate the centenary of the Corps des Pages.

The period from when the school was transformed into a real school for soldiers, during the reign of Alexander I until the 24th October this year, is exactly 100 years. As a result, the Emperor set up a committee to ensure that the celebrations would reflect the school's illustrious history. However, the event has been postponed until this month because he is not in the capital in October. The celebrations have been very grand and began on the 25th.

On that day in the morning, there were prayers in the church where the Tsars are buried[1]. This was to honour Emperor Alexander I and the other emperors down to Alexander III. All the officers who had studied in the school and all the pages were in attendance.

In the afternoon, at the Winter Palace, nails were driven into the flag, which will be presented to the school in commemoration of the anniversary. The Emperor and both Empresses were there, together with all the members of the imperial family. After the

1. The St. Peter and St. Paul Fortress.

ceremony, the pages took the flag back to the school.

In the evening there were prayers at the school and a meeting of all the pages, past and present, so that they could chat. There was also music and refreshments. As part of the celebrations, I managed to find a portrait bust of the Emperor for the school and it will stand there in the future. Many people praised me for presenting this.

On the 26th, there was a ceremony to present the flag to the school. The cadets lined up and, behind the current pupils, were all the former members now officers. They stood in lines, regardless of age or rank, but simply according to when they left the school. So it went from all of my year, who left this year, to one general who left the school in 1838. The line of officers was incredibly impressive, as it was made up of all kinds of people, who had worked all over. High and low ranks were all mingled together.

At 11 am, the Emperor arrived. The soldiers saluted and he inspected the cadets. He gave his blessing on this important day and walked along the lines of all the officers. After he had finished his inspection and the prayers had taken place, the Emperor asked Grand Duke Constantine, the Chief of All Military Colleges, to read the speech which he had prepared for the centenary. It praised the school for training people to serve so well and gave words of advice to the current students and those to come, to follow the good example of their predecessors. The speech was very eloquent and both former and current pages were moved. After that, General Epanchin announced his gift of the standard to the school, and there was a ceremony in which the pages pledged allegiance to the flag in front of the director. The director received the flag and then gave it to the standard bearer, who paraded it past all the students and officers and then stood at the front of the line, whereupon everyone including the Emperor saluted at the same time.

After that, the pages marched past twice and bowed. Then, the Emperor talked to the General who was the oldest living page. He praised all those who had left the school and gave advice to the current intake from his own lips. He said that he had decreed that his Heir, his younger brother, and three other grand dukes had been appointed to be officers in the school, in order to show how much he admired the school. After these words, he said goodbye and left.

In the evening of the same day, the Emperor hosted a banquet in the Winter Palace for those who had been pages and the current students. It was a true gala dinner, with around 1,200 people. I was invited in my capacity as a former page, but was seated with the nobility and went with the other members of the imperial family. The Emperor talked to me very warmly and gave his blessing in connection with this event. The two Empresses and other members of the nobility also wished me well. The Empress recalled when I was her Chamber Page. During the dinner the Emperor said: "I drink to the health of my dear guests, those who used to be pages and those who are now pages, those who served in the Corps and those who serve now, to your health Gentlemen!" After the banquet, we all moved to the large hall. The Emperor and Empress talked to everyone. And all the officers who had once been pages to the two Empresses divided into two groups and came forward with bouquets for each of them. Both Empresses were very pleased.

On the 27th at the Corps, there was another lot of prayers. This time the Chief Priest himself officiated at the ceremony, attended by both the Emperor and the Empresses. After the prayers and before leaving, they went around the school, which was beautifully decorated by the pupils themselves.

After that, there were congratulations from other schools, regiments and societies. All of them came with an address and there were a great deal, totalling over 70. The German Kaiser sent a General and another officer, with four cadets to help as well.

Phraya Sri Thammasan and I got it slightly wrong by not letting Your Majesty know soon enough for a congratulatory telegram to be sent, which would have given the Emperor a lot of pleasure. I only thought of it when it was too late. I hope Your Majesty is not too angry with me.

On the evening of the 27th, the Emperor ordered that a play be performed in the Imperial Theatre for the pages, old and new. It was another gala and the Emperor and both Empresses came with other members of the imperial family. During the interval and before the next act, the imperial anthem was played nine times in total. The audience shouted, "Hooray!" very vigorously, as they were touched and grateful that the Emperor had been so beneficent to the school and made it so apparent on this occasion.

The Director of the Corps received the honour of being made a Royal Guard, as well as receiving a sash, while the pages received the Emperor's initials to be affixed to their shoulder. For those who had already left, there was a medal to be affixed to their chest showing they had been in the corps. This will doubtless continue for all future cadets who graduate from the school.

On the 28th, in the evening, all those who had graduated from the school gathered for our own celebration, which was like old school friends getting together. It was very lavish, but I was rather tired, as there have been activities from morning till night.

On the same day, I was fortunate enough to receive an invitation to join the Emperor for lunch in the palace at Tsarskoe Selo. It was a Sunday and thus it was the customary Sunday lunch for the imperial family. Both the Emperor and Empress talked to me warmly, as usual, but I did not have an opportunity to talk with them at length, as there were many other people there. The Emperor said that soon he would send for me for a proper chat. On that day, I talked with Grand Duke Serge and the Grand Duchess. Both asked after Your Majesty.

Also, on the 28th, Somdet Chai and Prince Suriyong arrived to see me during the holidays.

I was very happy to see some members of my family.

I beg to remain Your Majesty's obedient servant,
Chakrabongse

CENTENNIAL CELEBRATIONS - CORPS DES PAGES

Above left and right: Programmes for the concert performed as part of the celebrations for the Corps des Pages.

Centre: Menu for supper on the 13th December (o/s)

Reunion of past pages during the Centennial celebration.

All photographs page 301 (right) and this page are courtesy of the Bakhmeteff Archive of Russian and East European History and Culture, Rare Book and Manuscript Library, Columbia University in the city of New York.

1903
Life in the Hussars
The Great Ball
Second Trip Home

Siamese embassy, St. Petersburg
7th January 1903

Your Majesty

Ever since the Emperor and Empress returned to
Tsarskoe Selo, I have been to see them often. I have
been to lunch every Sunday, as members of the imperial family customarily do after having been to church
with the Emperor and Empress. Also invited are close
officials and commanders of the various regiments.
The 4th was a Sunday, so I was there and today is
Christmas so I was invited again.

The Emperor looks very well and has got slightly
fatter. The Empress is as well as ever.

I have heard that very soon the German Crown
Prince[1] will come here on an official visit.

There is a holiday at the moment with no work,
as it is European new year. I have come to stay at the
embassy with two of my younger brothers.

On the 1st of January, it was the birthday of Sadet
Mother and Toonmom Toh, so the ambassador invited
various high-ranking military officials involved with
me, as well M. Olarovsky and some other people. It
was good fun and went off well. M Olarovsky is full
of talk about going back to Bangkok again, but I have
heard rumours that the ambassador will be changed
ere long. But in any event, he will come to present his
credentials and say goodbye to Your Majesty. M.
Lisakovsky, the deputy ambassador at one time, has
now returned here and met up with me. He greeted
me in Thai straightaway, as far as his limited knowledge allowed. He seems to be a very pleasant person.

Grand Duke Boris is still full of praise for his trip
to Thailand and talks of it constantly to me. He is
very friendly and informal, as we are in the same regiment. He understands that now he has received the
Chakri sash, he can also wear a special uniform
appropriate to that order. He is desperate to get one
and has asked me to order one for him from
Bangkok. In this matter, I need to ask Your Majesty's
opinion and will abide by Your Majesty's wishes.

I beg to remain Your Majesty's obedient servant,
Chakrabongse

*Boris Vladimirovich (1877-1943),
first cousin of Nicholas II.*

German Crown Prince Wilhelm c. 1901.

1. Prince Wilhelm (1882-1951), full name Friedrich Wilhelm
Victor August Ernst, was the last Crown Prince of the Kingdom
of Prussia and the German Empire. He was the eldest child of
the future German Emperor Wilhelm II and his wife Empress
Augusta Victoria. When his father became Kaiser, Wilhelm
became Crown Prince at the age of six, retaining that title
until the fall of the empire in November 1918.

4th March 1903

Your Majesty

In the past week, there have been many events in the palace, which have been a lot of fun as it is the last week before the period of Lent, when all festivities must come to an end. The last week before Lent is known as Carnival.

On the 24th February, there was a play in the palace and everyone in the entire audience was dressed in the fashion of Tsar Alexis[1], the father of Peter the Great. Tsar Alexis ruled during the 1600s. And the clothes in those times were very archaic, not like today. They were also very different from other European countries, looking rather Middle Eastern, or Indian mixed with Chinese.

The outfits were very diverse and everyone competed to see who could look the best. They were covered in diamonds and precious jewels. The Emperor was also in period costume and in fact was dressed exactly like Tsar Alexis himself. The Empress was dressed as the consort of that Tsar. They both looked magnificent. The archaic dress really suited him. The Grand Dukes and Grand Duchesses were also all impressively attired.

All the shows performed were linked with that period. The theatre itself looked very unusual as the audience was so dressed up that they seemed as much a part of the spectacle as the performers. After the show, there was supper followed by dancing. During the dancing, 16 couples from the civil servant class came out and danced in true Russian style in front of the Emperor. It had been specially arranged for this occasion and they danced extremely well. Everyone had a great time. Then, on the 26th, there was a ball[2] with everyone dressed in period costume as before. The first evening the crown prince [of Germany] was

1. Aleksey Mikhailovich (1629-1676). On the eve of his death in 1676, the Tsardom of Russia spanned almost 8,100,000 km2. Peter I, known as Peter the Great, was his son by his second marriage to Nataliya Kyrillovna Naryshkina (1651-1694).

2. The 1903 Ball in the Winter Palace was extremely luxurious and was held in two stages, on February 11 and 13. It commemorated 290 years of the Romanov dynasty. All wore bejeweled 17th-century style costumes, made from designs by the artist Sergey Solomko in collaboration with historical experts. It is often referred to as the last grand ball held by the Romanovs.

Tsar Nicholas II and Empress Alexandra in archaic Russian dress at the 1903 ball.

Princess Maria of Greece and Denmark at the 1903 ball.

Grand Duke Sergei Alexandrovich at the 1903 ball.

*Prince Chakrabongse dressed for the costume
ball in the Winter Palace, 1903.*

ill and unable to attend. On the second evening, he did attend, as did the Dowager Empress, although she was not in costume as before.

On the 1st of this month, which is considered the last day of carnival, there was a dinner at the palace, followed by dancing and supper. It was very lively and a grand end to the carnival. The 2nd onwards is the beginning of Lent and all frivolity is at an end.

On the 2nd, in the morning, I left Tsarskoe Selo with another six officers and some soldiers in the intelligence corps to practice long-distance marching. On that day we walked about 28 *versts*, reaching the village of Lisino. We stopped for a rest and decided to stay the night. On the 3rd, we left Lisino and went via a roundabout route to Sablina and Yamisor. We stopped there for lunch and then walked on back to Masarskoe. We journeyed all day and covered around 50 *versts*[1], making a total for the two days of 78 *versts*. It was very lucky that the weather was good, it was not cold and there was constant sunshine. Being on horseback and being shaken about made my bottom hot, and I almost thought that it was summer rather than winter.

The group sent for training comprised those undergoing special instruction, in order to be intelligence officers. In each company, there are 16 such soldiers with an officer to train and command them. The group that went were 16 men from six companies and an officer from each company, together with a colonel overseeing the exercise. There will be other such exercises in the future.

I beg to remain Your Majesty's obedient servant,
Chakrabongse

18th March 1903

Your Majesty

I have received Your Majesty's letter dated 30th of January, for which I was very happy and grateful.

I am happy to hear that Toonkramom Toh arrived safely, but I am sorry to hear that he is feeling rather awkward. I had rather feared that this might be the case, as it is in his character to be like that and it is very difficult to change. I think it is a very good thing that Your Majesty has talked to him about this. It is very important that he is close to you, otherwise people who love themselves more than the country, could try and cause trouble.

As for the matter of the Crown Princess[1], it is something I find rather difficult to talk about because I am not clear as to why she likes me. In this way, I must admit that I am being very Western in my ideas and I feel we should wait for evidence.

As to whether she could be Princess Chakrabongse, I thank you deeply for saying that you would have no objection, but this is a very complex and delicate matter, and perhaps you will have no reason to sigh about it at all.

There is not much news as this is Lent and so everything is quiet.

Yesterday the Dowager Empress left Petersburg for Denmark. I went to see her off at the station. The Emperor and Empress will go to Tsarskoe Selo shortly. The Emperor will visit Rome next November.

I beg to remain Your Majesty's obedient servant,
Chakrabongse

---

1. One *verst* is equivalent to 1.0668 km or 0.6629 miles.

1. Frustratingly, it is not clear at all who this so-called Crown Princess might be.

Prince Chakrabongse with the Hussar regiment.

Legation de Siam
24th March 1903

Your Majesty

I had planned that, once I had become an officer here, I would ask Your Majesty's permission to come home again. However, during the last holiday, there was no suitable time or long-enough break. I agree with Your Majesty that the period when the annual manoeuvres are over would be a good time to come back to Bangkok again. So, may I now formally request Your Majesty's permission to come home.

I would like to arrive in time to celebrate Your Majesty's 50th birthday [20th September], which should be a wonderful time. The details I will work out in due course, if Your Majesty is in agreement with the plan. If Your Majesty could write a letter to the Emperor as before, it would make everything much easier. I am sure he will not have any objection.

At the moment, there is a lot going on in my regiment as it is the time when the commanding officer comes to inspect all the training. Today he was observing riding drills, sword fighting and other things. Everything went smoothly. All the soldiers in 1st company, trained by myself and Nai Poum, performed better than any others in the regiment.

I am thinking of Your Majesty so much and I hope that I will be able to come back quite soon. As to where to stay, that is very easy, as I can stay with Toonmom Toh. No new quarters are necessary and would be a waste of money. I would be very happy with such an arrangement.

I beg to remain Your Majesty's obedient servant,

Chakrabongse

2nd June 1903

Your Majesty

I have received Your Majesty's letter dated 23rd April. I am delighted to hear about the Buddha relic. As soon as I receive it, I will hand it over. Grand Duke Boris is thrilled with the Chakri uniform and is eternally grateful to Your Majesty.

I am so pleased that I have permission to return and see Your Majesty again. I plan, with Your Majesty's agreement, to leave here at the beginning of August. I am still checking the departure times of the boats, so I cannot give an exact date at this time. The only slight problem is that I would have to leave here before the manoeuvres, which will probably annoy my superiors, but if I wait until they are completed I won't be there in time for Your Majesty's 50th birthday, a time when I would really like to be in Bangkok. In this regard, if Your Majesty could write to the Emperor, I am sure everything would be fine.

At this time, there have been a lot of events one after the other. On 22nd May, the Emperor and

Empress came to dine at the Hussar Regiment, of which I am a part at this time. It was to celebrate the 36th anniversary of the Emperor becoming an officer in the regiment [he received a position in the Hussars from birth]. The officers received him with great pomp and all those who had ever served in the regiment participated. Apart from the banquet, there was singing and dancing until dawn. The Emperor left at 7 am, which is so late as to be unheard of. This was also the first time that the Empress ever went to dine in the regimental mess hall and so was a great honour for the Hussars.

The 28th was the fete day of the Uhlan Life Guards of which the Empress is the Colonel-in-Chief and this year they were celebrating their 250th anniversary. The Emperor and Empress came. The latter wore the Uhlan uniform and rode out at the front of the regiment and past the Emperor. It was very impressive. There was also dancing, but I did not go. I hear it was very well organized.

On the 29th, there was a celebration for the bi-centenary of St Petersburg. A new bridge across the river was opened. The event was not much fun and rather tiring. The Emperor complained that it was somewhat annoying, although there were various games and activities laid on by the municipality rather than the government.

At present, I have seen the Emperor and Empress very often, without missing a week and sometimes even two or three times a week. I have lunched and dined at the palace frequently.

Currently, the regiment is training the various companies. All are involved and we are on horseback

Empress Alexandra in the uniform of the Uhlan Life Guards.

for two hours every day. It is very hot and we wear our thin summer uniform. It is like being in Thailand. In three weeks or so, the regiment will go to camp at Krasnoe Selo

I beg to remain Your Majesty's obedient servant,
Chakrabongse

Above: Painting of Trinity bridge by Mstislav Dobuzhinsky.

Left: The opening of Trinity Bridge. At 582 metres, the new Art Nouveau-style bridge was the second longest in the city.

4TH JUNE 1903
PRINCE CHAKRABONGSE TO HM THE KING

IF YOU PERMIT I WILL LEAVE BY THE
GERMAN MAIL 19TH AUGUST ARRIVE
SINGAPORE 10TH SEPTEMBER. WILL YOU
ALLOW LUANG SURAYUDH AND POUM TO
ACCOMPANY, LEK

27TH JUNE 1903
PRINCE CHAKRABONGSE TO HM THE KING

HAVE SENT YOUR LETTER FOR THE
EMPEROR ABOUT LEAVE, LEK

29TH JUNE 1903
HM THE KING TO PRINCE CHAKRABONGSE

PLEASE INFORM ME BY TELEGRAPH IMMEDI-
ATELY HOW LONG YOU INTEND TO BE ON
LEAVE SO THAT I MAY PUT IN MY LETTER TO
EMPEROR. M.R.

10TH JULY 1903
PRINCE CHAKRABONGSE TO HM THE KING

IT IS THE WISH OF THE COMMANDER OF MY
REGIMENT THAT I SHOULD RETURN TO ST.
PETERSBURG IN TIME FOR 19TH NOVEMBER
FETE OF OUR REGIMENT – IF YOU PERMIT IN
ORDER TO LEAVE GERMAN MAIL ARRIVE
SINGAPORE 5TH AUGUST IN ORDER TO
RETURN SOON ENOUGH YOUR LETTER WILL
NOT ARRIVE IN TIME. IF YOU CONSENT
PLEASE TELEGRAPH AS SOON AS POSSIBLE
TO THE EMPEROR FOR PERMISSION. I WILL
DO MY BEST TO CLEAR MATTERS TO HIS
MAJESTY MYSELF, LEK

12 JULY 1903
TO H.I.M. THE EMPEROR OF RUSSIA

IN CASE YOUR MAJESTY SEES NO OBJEC-
TIONS I WOULD BEG YOUR MAJESTY'S GRA-
CIOUS PERMISSION FOR LEK TO VISIT HOME
ON A SHORT LEAVE OF ABSENCE. M. R.

15TH JULY 1903
TO HIS MAJESTY THE KING OF SIAM

CERTAINLY SEE NO OBJECTIONS THAT LEK

SHOULD LEAVE ON A VISIT HOME HOPE YOUR
MAJESTY FEELS WELL.

NICOLAS

16/7/03
TO EMPEROR NICOLAS II

VERY PLEASED TO RECEIVE YOUR MAJESTY'S
TELEGRAM. I THANK YOUR MAJESTY FOR
GRACIOUS CONCURRENCE TO LEK'S VISIT
HOME AND ALSO FOR KIND ENQUIRY AFTER
MY HEALTH.

M. R.

16TH JULY 1903
HM THE KING TO PRINCE CHAKRABONGSE

I HAVE RECEIVED A TELEGRAM FROM THE
EMPEROR GIVING YOUR LEAVE TO VISIT
HOME. M. R.

15TH JULY
PRINCE CHAKRABONGSE TO HM THE KING

I WAS RECEIVED BY THE EMPEROR IN CONSE-
QUENCE OF A MISTAKE IN MY NAME YOUR
TELEGRAM WAS NOT CLEAR. I HAVE
EXPLAINED THE MATTER TO THE EMPEROR
HE CONSENTED AND TELEGRAPHED TO YOU
AND WILL SEND A LETTER WITH ME, LEK

NO SOONER WAS HE HOME THAN HIS PARENTS
WANTED HIM TO STAY LONGER.

30TH AUGUST 1903
TO H.I. M. THE EMPEROR OF RUSSIA

AM MOST HAPPY TO SEE LEK SAFELY
ARRIVED TODAY. WOULD BE EXTREMELY
GRATEFUL IF YOUR MAJESTY WILL GRANT
HIM EXTENSION OF LEAVE IN ORDER TO BE
PRESENT ON MY FETE DAY 15TH NOVEMBER.

30TH AUGUST 1903
TO HIS MAJESTY THE KING

HAPPY TO LEARN LEK'S SAFE ARRIVAL. HE
CAN CERTAINLY EXTEND HIS LEAVE IN ORDER
TO REMAIN LONGER WITH YOUR MAJESTY.

NICOLAS

After an intense telegraphic exchange Phraya Sridhamasan and Prince Chakrabongse left St. Petersburg on 30th July by train to Berlin and then, on 2nd August, left Berlin for Genoa where they boarded the German Mail. This arrived in Singapore on 26th August where King Chulalongkorn had sent his royal yacht *Maha Chakri* to pick him up. The royal party left immediately and the consul in Singapore reported by telegram to Bangkok that the boat should reach the Bar at the mouth of the Chao Phraya river at 3 pm on 30th August.

Altogether the Prince stayed in Bangkok for four months.

Prince Chakrabongse on his second trip home. Photographed after receiving his new rank of Captain in the Siamese Royal Guards Regiment and the Maha Chakri Order.

During his trip home, Prince Chakrabongse's younger brother below him, Prince Asdang, was ordained as a novice monk. The photograph shows all the Chao Fa princes with King Chulalongkorn. Back row from left to right: Crown Prince Maha Vajiravudh, King Chulalongkorn, Prince Chakrabongse (half visible), Prince Paribatra. Front row: Prince Chudadhuj, Prince Prajadhipok, Prince Asdang (in monk's robes), Prince Mahidol and Prince Yugala.

17th October 1903

Your Majesty

I beg to come and see Your Majesty on my own when convenient, as there is a private and personal matter I want to discuss with Your Majesty. I hope Your Majesty will have time tomorrow, or the day after.

I beg to remain Your Majesty's obedient servant,
Chakrabongse

22 October 1903

Your Majesty

I would beg Your Majesty to decide once and for all, whether I should go and study for another four years or not. In this regard, Pi Chira does not agree at all and has said so several times, beginning with when he came to Europe this last time. Then, when I came back here, he said again that he cannot allow me to go and study for so long as the government needs

people urgently. He even went so far as to say that my wishing to study for so long was selfish, as all I wanted was to obtain knowledge for myself, with no thought for my country. He complained that he had not had a chance to tell Your Majesty all his reasons in detail.

Having listened to all this, I have considered the matter at great length and looked around to see whether there is such an urgent need as he has said. I can now see that there is such a need and, so that it cannot be said that I am selfish with no concern for the country, I have decided to do what Pi Chira has said in every way. I have telegraphed the legation, for them to send the progam of study at the Academy to me, so I will take only those subjects which are really necessary.

Thus, the opportunity to wear the eagle insignia on the chest, as a sign of prestige for the country, will have to be given to one of my younger brothers, who can then come back and fill this need.

In this matter, I await your decision.

I beg to remain Your Majesty's obedient servant,
Chakrabongse

Prince Chirapravati in 1904.

Above left: The opening of the Makawan bridge on 1st November 1903. The King is under the umbrella, with Prince Chakrabongse behind him and to the left. Further to the left, in the front, is Crown Prince Maha Vajiravudh and on his left, Prince Prajadhipok.

9TH DECEMBER 1903
TO HIS MAJESTY THE EMPEROR
HAVING ONCE OBTAINED YOUR MAJESTY'S KIND PERMISSION I HAVE WITH GREAT RELUCTANCE TO SUBMIT BEFORE YOUR MAJESTY THE QUEEN'S REQUEST FOR YOUR GRACIOUS PERMISSION THAT THE LEAVE GRANTED TO OUR SON LEK MAY EXTEND TO JANUARY NEXT WHEN SHE MAY HAVE TO HER GREAT DELIGHT & COMFORT ALL HER CHILDREN TOGETHER AT THE TIME OF HER NEXT BIRTHDAY.
THE QUEEN FELT SURE OF YOUR MAJESTY'S GRACIOUSNESS THAT WHEN THESE CIRCUMSTANCES WERE PLACED BEFORE YOU, YOUR MAJESTY WOULD BE PLEASED TO FAVOUR HER WISHES.
WITH OUR HIGHEST ESTEEM AND SINCERE REGARDS TO YOUR MAJESTY AND THE EMPRESS.
(MANU REGIA)

18TH DECEMBER 1903
HIS MAJESTY THE KING, BANGKOK
I ACCEPT WITH PLEASURE THE QUEEN'S REQUEST LEK MAY CERTAINLY EXTEND HIS LEAVE TO JANUARY NEXT THE EMPRESS AND I SEND YOU MAJESTIES OUR HEARTY RESPECTS.
NICOLAS

8th December 1903

Your Majesty

I have received Your Majesty's letter and understood all Your Majesty's points.

The fact that Sadet Mae has asked for me to delay my departure date, I only knew about tonight, when I came back from my audience with her. But she had mentioned it before several times. I told her that if I were to postpone the date again, I would be wasting too much time. Or to come back again would be losing a lot of time. Now, however, I understand the reasons clearly and after receiving this last letter, I agree that I should postpone my return.

As to whether there should be a telegram, I agree that there should be and, if it were to come from Your Majesty, it would be the best thing.

The mail can certainly be delayed for another two sessions. The mail will probably leave Bangkok on 6th January.

I beg to remain Your Majesty's obedient servant,
Chakrabongse

Before Prince Chakrabongse left for Russia again, Queen Saovabha decided to have a photograph taken with her five sons.

From left to right: Prince Asdang, Crown Prince Maha Vajiravudh, Prince Chakrabongse, Queen Saovabha, Prince Prajadhipok and Prince Chudadhuj.

Tsar blessing the troops.

1904

Return to Russia
Russo-Japanese War
Military Academy

2nd January 1904

Your Majesty

I have received the ivory box[1], which Your Majesty has been so kind to give me yesterday and I can't express my thanks enough. I have arranged a training ritual so that it will be smooth from here on.

Regarding Your Majesty's letter to the Emperor, I must beg to remind Your Majesty about this, as it is near the time when I am about to leave, namely the 6th of January.

I hope that Your Majesty's illness is not too bad and that the symptoms have abated.

I beg to remain Your Majesty's obedient servant,
Chakrabongse

The Royal Yacht Maha Chakri, Samut Prakarn
6th January 1904

Your Majesty

I have received Your Majesty's letter, together with the photograph which Your Majesty's page has brought me. I can hardly thank Your Majesty enough for the good wishes bestowed on me and the words which I will remember and follow in every way.

Saying goodbye to Your Majesty this time, I felt very sad indeed, as it is the third time now that I have had to take leave and go far away. If I include the time when Your Majesty returned from Europe as well, it is in fact the fourth time. My sorrow cannot but increase each time we part, as I do not want to be away from Your Majesty and want to be close and repay Your Majesty's kindness at all times. However, it is genuinely necessary for me to go away to study those subjects, which I cannot find at home. I comfort myself with the fact that I am gaining knowledge and will be able to serve Your Majesty better than if I had not gone. I will do my utmost to study to the best of my ability, so that it will not reflect badly on Your Majesty and no one will be able to say that one of Your Majesty's sons is inconsistent, or did well before but has let things slide. I will also endeavour to study as fast as possible, so that I can quickly come back to serve and be a benefit to my country and my heritage.

Leaving this time, I was very concerned about Sadet Mae, as I can see that the illness she is suffering from at the moment is unusual and seems to be a chronic one. It is worrying and something should be done to make her stronger than she is at present.

I will present Your Majesty's letter to the Emperor as soon as I have an opportunity and I will hear any government news from Phraya Suriya.

I beg to kiss Your Majesty's feet one more time and say goodbye again. I hope that it will not be too long before I will be able to see Your Majesty again.

This letter is full of mistakes, but it is because I am feeling very emotional and I beg Your Majesty's forgiveness.

I beg to remain Your Majesty's obedient servant,
Chakrabongse

1. The fashion of collecting small ivory boxes began in Bangkok around 1902. It was believed that rubbing them daily would bring out the grain in the ivory.

Royal Yacht Maha Chakri, Singapore
10th January 1904

Your Majesty

I arrived in Singapore today at 1 pm. En route we were buffeted by strong waves, but thankfully we arrived safely and everyone is well. When the ship had dropped anchor, Mr Anderson[1], the consul, came to inform us that the governor of Singapore was absent at this time, so that was a lucky escape and we didn't have to have anything to do with officialdom. The fort fired a salute for the royal standard. Apart from answering the salute, I asked the captain to pay the fort a visit and thank them, as is customary. At first we were startled, as we were just sitting around when the fort started firing. Our answering salute is also over now. Later, I learnt that saluting the flag signifies seeing a flag which they do not recognise. They had to look in their manuals before they fired another salute.

In this town it rains heavily all the time and is noticeably much hotter than in Bangkok. However, there is a strong wind and some small waves, so that the boat rolls slightly while in harbour.

I did not go ashore, because I knew that on the morrow I would be going to take a car to the other ship. Prince Nara was very impressed [by the salutes], as he had never received one. However, when he went ashore, he said that he was disappointed and thought it would be much better than it was.

There is a lot of fuss here about the war, which is rumoured to be about to occur between Russia and Japan. The consul could hardly talk of anything else and brought me the paper and telegrams to read. I tend to agree with Your Majesty that they will not go to war, but I could be wrong as I have been away for a long time.

I am thinking about Your Majesty a great deal and am feeling very depressed at having to leave my country yet again. Going away several times makes me even more reluctant each time. The first time was exciting, wondering what it was going to be like, now it has lost its flavour. I hope Your Majesty is happy and that the illness Your Majesty had when I was going to say goodbye has cleared up completely.

I beg to remain Your Majesty's obedient servant,

Chakrabongse

1. The Hon. Mr John Anderson was born in 1852 at Rothesay, Isle of Bute, and came to Singapore aged 7. He entered the Straits Civil Service for a while, before becoming a businessman and head of the firm of Guthrie & Co., Ltd. He was Siamese Consul-General for Singapore at this time and had a seat on the Singapore Legislative Council.

The ship *Kiautschou*
11th January 1904

Your Majesty

I left Singapore in the Mail ship Kiautschou[1] at 1 pm today. The ship is very large and seems comfortable. There are not too many passengers and so it is not crowded. Tomorrow we are scheduled to reach Koh Mak[2] in Malaysia and we will stay there until evening. At the moment, the sea and the winds are calm, but it is raining almost constantly and has hardly stopped at all. Even now we are en route, the rain has followed us. It is really damp and if you were to come this way, I'm sure Your Majesty's condition would worsen.

Mr Anderson came and talked to me today about the town of Sai[3] and said he was worried. He gave me his opinion in writing and asked me to present his thoughts to Your Majesty in a private capacity. He complained that his thoughts and advice, which he sends via official channels may not be reaching Your Majesty, or that what he says may be being twisted in various ways. Accordingly, he asked me to tell Your Majesty the truth, at least once. I said that I would and that I would transmit his opinions. I said that whatever he heard, he could tell Your Majesty and that to hear diverse views was no bad thing. I have copied his thoughts and am sending them to Your Majesty with this letter.

The thing is that in Saiburi, at the moment, the financial situation is very bad because Yahiwanla, whom Chao Phraya Sai appointed to be Chao Muang Saiburi and who now has been removed, has taken all the official money and spent it on partying in Penang. He has bought horses, a house, had clothes made and many more things. Once the money was gone, he borrowed more in the name of Saiburi. As a result, he

---

1. The German ship *Kiautschou* was launched in 1900. It weighed 10,900 tons and was named after the German colony in China.

2. Koh Mak refers to Penang.

3. Sai refers to Saiburi, now Kedah. At the end of the 18th century, the Sultan handed it and Penang to the British, but Siam invaded in 1821. In 1896, it was combined with Perlis and Satun into the province of Syburi until transferred to the British after the Anglo-Siamese Treaty of 1909.

4. This refers to a naval blockade, from December 1902 to February 1903, imposed on Venezuela by Britain, Germany and Italy over President Cipriano Castro's refusal to pay foreign debts and damages suffered by European citizens in the recent Venezuelan civil war.

THE Siamese Royal yacht *Maha Chakkri* arrived from Bangkok at noon yesterday with H. R. H. Prince Chakrabongs on board. The Prince and suite transhipped from the yacht to the German mail steamer *Kiautschou* this morning and were saluted by the yacht on leaving.

As announced in the Straits Times, February 12th 1904.

has run up huge debts, which cannot be paid off to the extent that Yahiwanla cannot show his face in Penang, as he is afraid his creditors will seize him. In fact, the debt is owed by Saiburi. Then, when Prince Damrong asked for an account of expenses in Saiburi, Raja Muda was the one preparing them, but after a long time he was not successful. However, when Chao Phraya Sai came to see Your Majesty in Bangkok this time, he made as if everything was fine, that the private expenses of Chao Phraya Sai were sorted out. The money that was left would be used to pay off other debts as well as this one and everyone agreed to sign off on it. Yahiwanla also signed. Then, when Chao Phraya Sai came back, he saw the name of Yahiwanla and went into a rage. He said that the debts of Yahiwanla were run up by cheating the government and therefore Yahiwanla should pay them back. It was quite wrong to use government money to pay them off. They had a quarrel and the problem of the budget is still not finalised. The people of Saiburi are divided into two groups – those who side with Phraya Sai and those who take the part of Raja Muda. It has turned into a terrible business.

The British government is happy to see all this confusion. Mr Anderson said himself that the English are delighted and the government of Malaya even more so. Now there is a warship off Saiburi, and the Governor has gone to stay on Penang to monitor the situation from there. Furthermore, all the debts have been run up with English people, which would give them an easy excuse to cause trouble. They could behave as they did with Venezuela[4]. In this matter, the British could allege that they were owed so much by Saiburi, and that it was so badly governed that there was no hope of getting their money back and they had to intervene. I think the situation is very perilous. I have also heard the opinion of Nai Lek Phra Saja, who is close to the situation. He says the same and agrees that things are extremely worrying. In his view, the Thai government should pay the debts and have done with it. Things will then settle down again and a more competent person from the budget bureau can come down and implement a system. He says that English people from Penang are always going to Saiburi sniffing around. They say that they are tourists, but this may or may not be true.

He added that in Satun the situation is little better, as there is no Chao Muang at the moment. He heard this from relatives in the town. A relative of Phraya Satun himself said, that if a good Thai official could be found to be in charge of the city and could sort things out, he would be much happier than if Muang Sai was in charge.

The things I am venturing to tell Your Majesty are simply the views of two people, who are close to events and should be able to see things clearly. However, I do not know the whole story and I cannot vouchsafe that these two people are telling the truth, nor that they have analysed the situation correctly, as I have just listened to their opinions. I have not had an opportunity to study things in detail. Nevertheless, as they are on the ground, I did not think there was anything to lose in informing Your Majesty. Nai Lek said that, if an official were appointed to come and inspect things, it would be little different from his account. I don't know what the truth of the matter is, but I think it is quite clear why a gunboat has been sent there. I read in the Singapore newspaper that the boat is called *Algerine*. It was about to go back to England,

The ruler of Saiburi, Yahiwanla.

but received an order to go to Saiburi and stay there. The newspaper did not know why.

Having listened to all this, I cannot help but be anxious, and have thus informed Your Majesty of everything immediately. I feel it is my duty, if I learn anything relating to the country or government, to report it, even if it is just the opinion of certain people. I'm sorry if I have overstepped the mark, or been presumptuous.

I beg to remain Your Majesty's obedient servant,
Chakrabongse

A Chinese merchant's house, Penang, late 1890s.

Penang
12th January 1904

Your Majesty

I arrived in Penang at 2.30 pm today. Among the people coming to meet me at the boat and take me ashore were Phraya Damrong Sujarid, Phraya Luang Suan, Phraya Rasada, the Raja Muda of Saiburi[1] and another Sai official, the Consul in Penang and various Western officials such as Mr. Giles[2]. I officiated at the housewarming of Phraya Damrong. The old house has been sold and the new house moved to the edge of the sea. It was only just finished and the housewarming is today. He asked if he could call it Chakrabongse House.

I quizzed Phraya Rasada about Saiburi and told him what I had heard from Nai Lek Phra Saja and Mr Anderson. Phraya Rasada said he had not heard anything like that, but that the budget had not been satisfactorily sorted out. He said it was because Phraya Sai would not agree to it and said that, from the time of his grandfathers, there had never been a situation where the ruler had had to stick to a fixed budget, but could spend money as he saw fit. So they did not know what to do. Phraya Rasada takes the side of Raja Muda and is in his camp, while the people who told me everything before are the people of Chao Phraya Sai, and so put all the blame in a different direction. For me to question Raja Muda seems incorrect, as I have no role in asking about government matters. It would seem to be going too far and could cause offence. The conversations I have had earlier took place in a private capacity. I don't know Raja Muda well enough to talk to him in such a way. Phraya Rasada said that Raja Muda has complained to him a lot about these problems and feels that the only solution is to elevate the son of Phraya Sai to be the state ruler. Chao Phraya Sai could be the senior person and the new ruler should not have so much

Phraya Rasada.

Raja Muda of Saiburi

Phraya Damrong Sujarid

1. Sultan Abdul Hamid Halim Shah (1864-1943) was the 26th Sultan of Kedah. He reigned from 1881 to 1943. During his reign, the Sultan asked for a $2,500,000 loan from Siam during a state financial crisis in 1905. Presumably, this is a continuation of the financial problems discussed in the letters.

2. Mr Francis Henry Giles was an Englishman in the service of Siam, who in the next reign received the Thai title of Phraya Intharamontri.

power. There should be a consultative group of officials, who would have the last word. However, if this were proposed, Phraya Rasada and I feel that Phraya Sai will not agree. Trying to put pressure on him is also difficult, as he might jump into the arms of the British, and there are rumours that the government is preparing a Resident and that they will ask the Siamese government to install him in Saiburi. Mr Giles[2] from the tax department of the Interior Ministry, who came from Saiburi two or three days ago, expressed the opinion that this matter should be addressed urgently, otherwise it will get very serious. Phraya Rasada also thinks that the Siamese government should settle the debts and use this as an opportunity to request going in to rearrange their budget department as a quid pro quo. We can quite easily say that we have allowed Muang Sai to manage their own financial affairs for a long time, but it has not been successful. In all this, I am just telling Your Majesty so that Your Majesty is informed.

I asked Raja Muda about Chao Phraya Sai. He said he was very well and that, when he went to Bangkok last time, he had a great time and was very taken with a certain dish, even bringing some to make in Muang Sai, which he managed to do. Chao Phraya Sai went to play every day and Raja Muda went several times and said it was great fun.

I am staying at the house of Phraya Damrong and having dinner there.

I beg to remain Your Majesty's obedient servant,
Chakrabongse

Your Majesty

I arrived in Colombo this afternoon. On the way from Penang, the sea and the winds were so calm, that it was almost uncanny. The ship did not roll at all the entire route. It must be because the boat is so large, as in fact there were a few waves. However, the ship showed no sign of being affected by them. A smaller ship, or even the royal yacht, would definitely have rolled a bit.

The ship is to be in harbour for over 24 hours and, accordingly, I have come ashore and am staying in a seaside hotel. It is comfortable, but I can't go and see anything, as we got there in the late afternoon on a Saturday. Everything is closed and tomorrow is Sunday. Originally, I had thought that I might go up to Kandy once again, but I had to change my plans as on a Sunday there are fewer trains. En route there has been nothing to do either and it is really boring. All one can do is sit about, or sleep. If I read all day until evening, I would have finished my books by now.

I have heard that Lady Curzon, the wife of the Viceroy of India, will go back to England on the same ship and will board here in Colombo. However, I doubt I will be able to make her acquaintance, as I hear she is very proud and conscious of her position because she is an American[1]. Once she became the Vicereine, it is quite natural that she would become very grand. But I will see what happens. If I do get to meet her, I will ask her about lots of interesting things.

Regarding the flat, ivory, pocket-watch box[2], which I received from Your Majesty the day before I left, I have been unable to find another. Can I ask that someone buys another? It is such a lovely case and easy to handle. Now the red has come up and the design is very beautiful. The 'Busaba Chan' is one I have touched many times. It is completely yellow with a few red touches, but the pattern is a bit messy. However, with 'Baht Thammarat', no matter how much I handle it, the ivory grain does not come up. The one I received from Your Majesty before leaving is much better than all the others.

I am thinking of Your Majesty a great deal.

I beg to remain Your Majesty's obedient servant,
Chakrabongse

1. Mary Victoria Curzon, Baroness Curzon of Kedleston (1870–1906), was a British-American peeress who was Vicereine of India as the wife of Lord Curzon of Kedleston, Viceroy of India.

2. The ivory boxes were given names.

The ship *Kiautschou*
27th January 1904

Your Majesty

Ever since the ship left Colombo, one can say that it has kept going constantly, as we stopped in Aden for only four hours. No coal was taken on and the stop was simply to send letters and other small things. From there we entered the Red Sea, followed by the Gulf of Suez and tomorrow we should reach Suez town and enter the Canal.

Fortunately, since leaving Colombo until now, there have been no waves. It is always calm, but with a cool breeze, so it did not feel hot at all. Even Aden, which is known to be blisteringly hot, was not so at all, with a refreshingly comfortable breeze. I felt pleased for all those who have to stay there all year long. They must have really enjoyed it, as having to live in Aden must truly be very uncomfortable. I once heard a trader recount having to spend four months in Aden, during one of the hottest times of the year. He had to go out in a boat into the middle of the sea in order to cool down. Despite that, the heat almost drove him crazy. The Red Sea was also not hot, with a cooling north wind. By the time we got near Suez, it was becoming cold. Yesterday and today, it was really cold. In Aden I saw something very unusual, namely that it rained. It is rumoured that sometimes it does

not rain for five years at a time, so it was amazing to be there for only four hours and see rain.

This is my fourth trip to Aden, but the first time I have seen rain. I am sure that among the princes and people travelling to Europe, most of them will not have seen rain, so it is something I can boast about.

During the journey at sea, I have not heard any news at all. I am anxious about the possibility of war between Russia and Japan. I saw many battleships going by. Before reaching Aden, I saw a British naval vessel. I understand that it was the newest cruiser, *Edward VII*, waiting to anchor. We also passed numerous Japanese ships but as it was night time we couldn't see them, just heard word of them. Apparently, they are crewed by English sailors, hired by Japan for their new ships bought from the Argentine. Some of them went a bit crazy and resigned, refusing to go any further. They got off in Aden and travelled back on our ship. It's rather strange that Japan has had to hire western crews. The reason is that the new ships have been bought for the war and need to be got back to Japan as quickly as possible. Sending Japanese crews would take too long, but hiring Western crews has resulted in incidents such as this. Not all resigned - only 15 or thereabouts.

HMS Edward VII battleship. It was built in the Devonport Dockyard and was launched in 1903. It was the Royal Navy's lead battleship.

The Suez Canal in 1904.

In the Red Sea, I saw some Russian naval vessels. There were two large warships and many torpedo boats, perhaps up to 10 all together. We saw them at night, but when they shone a searchlight on our ship, we decided to have a look and could judge with almost certainty that they were Russian ships, because I know that Russian ships passed through the Suez Canal on the 25th, the day we saw them.

Looking at the telegraph traffic, it seems that there is no war. I am greatly relieved, because, if there is a war, it will be very hard for me to bother the Emperor. And the whole issue of my new studies, based on the subjects determined by Pi Chira, needs to be discussed with the Emperor for them to go ahead.

Coming back this time has made me understand that this is the best season to travel to Europe, because there are neither waves nor winds. In addition, it is not hot in the Red Sea, which normally can be very wearing. The only problem is that one then hits the winter in Europe straightaway. For those who are used to the cold, such as me, it is definitely the best. I have never encountered such calm seas.

I do hope Your Majesty is in good spirits with no illnesses. I think of Your Majesty all the time without exception. When I sleep, I dream only of Bangkok. Recently, I dreamt that Your Majesty was angry with me and punished me with a switch. I awoke with a start, but afterwards was amused. According to dream manuals, such dreams are good. In particular, being punished by Your Majesty in person is very auspicious. I hope that it will be as the manual suggests.

I beg to remain Your Majesty's obedient servant,
Chakrabongse

Russian ships sailing through the Suez canal, 1904.

The Russo-Japanese War – 1904-1905

The war, which had been much anticipated after the failure to engage in fruitful negotiations in 1903, began on 8th February 1904, and was to last almost a year and a half, until September 1905. It has been described as the "first great war of the 20th century". Its roots lay in the rival imperial ambitions of the Russian Empire and Japan over Manchuria and Korea.

It began when the Japanese fleet attacked the Russian fleet anchored at Port Arthur, without a declaration of war. Ever since his Eastern Voyage as Tsarevich, Nicholas II had been keen to expand the empire to the east, and sought an all-year warm water port at Port Arthur. In 1902, Japan and Britain had signed an alliance, which effectively meant neither France nor Germany supported Russia. Nevertheless, despite this and several defeats to the Japanese, the Tsar was certain of victory. At first, Prince Chakrabongse was also convinced that the war would go in Russia's favour. Thailand, meanwhile, remained strictly neutral. The victory of the Japanese in 1905 was suprising to world observers and changed the balance of power in the east.

Battlefields in the Russo-Japanese war.

Japanese political cartoon, c. 1904.

Russian cruiser Pallada *being hit by a torpedo, December 1904.*

Russian political cartoon, c. 1904.

Genoa
3rd February 1904

Your Majesty

I arrived in Genoa this afternoon. Phraya Suriya had ordered Mr Rickman, the attaché from the embassy in Paris, to come and meet me and take me to an hotel. I will stay here for one night and then take the train to Berlin.

Travelling from Port Said to Naples, the waves were rather strong, and most people were seasick. It was also very cold, with a very strong northerly wind. The ship reached Naples on the 2nd. In fact, it arrived late in the evening on the 1st, but could not enter the port, because it was too late and we had to wait until the morning. On arrival, a doctor came to check us for fear of sexual and infectious diseases. He did not touch us, but carried out a cursory inspection. After that, we could go ashore. I went and had a look around, but Naples at the moment is very dirty because it has been raining a lot and there is a lot of fog. It is very damp and the streets are full of mud.

I got back to the boat too late, because of a misunderstanding. I thought that we would leave again at 5 pm, but in fact it was meant to be 2 pm. Fortunately, while driving past the office of the mail boats, I popped in to ask and found out it was leaving at 2. I was really worried and rushed back, but the captain was waiting and I got on safely. If he had not waited, I would have had to take the train.

The weather in Genoa is also appalling, with rain, fog and an overall darkness. It is incredibly damp.

I have written to Phraya Suriya, asking him to tell me government news regarding the situation between Siam and the French government, so that I can know what Your Majesty's wishes are. If I were to go to Paris, it would take more time. I want to get to Petersburg as quickly as possible.

Another thing is I have heard that the Empress is pregnant again. This is good news, as, when she miscarried last time, there were rumours that she would be unable to get pregnant. Those who were close to her said it was not true, as I informed you at the time. Nevertheless, this is one in the face, for all those know-alls. I do hope that this time it will be a boy.

I beg to remain Your Majesty's obedient servant,
Chakrabongse

7TH FEBRUARY 1904
PRINCE CHAKRABONGSE TO H.M. THE KING
WITH REGARD TO CRISIS BETWEEN RUSSIA AND JAPAN DO YOU THINK IT STILL ADVISABLE TO PRESENT YOUR LETTER TO THE EMPEROR. PLEASE SEND YOU ANSWER TO BERLIN. LEK

8TH FEBUARY 1904
H. M. THE KING TO PRINCE CHAKRABONGSE
I HAVE RECEIVED YOUR TELEGRAM 7TH FEBRUARY. MY LETTER TO THE EMPEROR IS PARTICULARLY TO EXPRESS MY THANKS FOR HIS INVARIABLE KINDNESS TO YOU AND CASUALLY REFERRED TO OUR AFFAIRS WITH FRANCE LEAVING TO HIS MAJESTY ANY STEP HE THINKS FIT FOR THE GOOD OF THOSE RELATIONS AND NOTHING WILL INTERFERE WITH PRESENT CRISIS. YOU WILL THEREFORE SEE IF YOU HAVE ANY OPPORTUNITY YOU CAN PRESENT IT.

9TH FEBRUARY 1904
PRINCE CHAKRABONGSE TO H.M. THE KING
I HAVE RECEIVED YOUR TELEGRAM IF I HAD KNOWN THE CONTENTS OF YOUR LETTER I WOULD NOT HAVE TELEGRAPHED. I WAS AFRAID IT WOULD SEEM THAT YOU TROUBLED THE EMPEROR INOPPORTUNELY. I WILL ARRIVE ST. PETERSBURG 12TH FEBRUARY. I HAVE HEARD THAT THE EMPEROR HAS GONE TO MOSCOW. HE WILL GIVE A PROCLAMATION. MATTERS LOOK VERY SERIOUS. I DO NOT KNOW IF I WILL BE ABLE TO ARRANGE FOR MY EDUCATION. LEK [THERE WERE SOME MISSING OR MISSPELT WORDS SO TELEGRAM WAS SENT AGAIN]

Hotel der Reichshof, Berlin
10th February 1904

Your Majesty

I left Genoa on the 4th in the morning and took the train via Milan, and then Switzerland. We went via the St. Gotthard tunnel out of Switzerland. It is good that I came to Basle, or as it is also called Basel. In the Alps it was pretty chilly, but not too cold as at the time there was a southerly wind blowing. This reduced the cold, but led to rain and continued damp. As we went higher, the rain changed to snow, which was heavy. It was dark with low hanging clouds, so that it was hard to tell which were mountains and which were clouds. It all looked very strange. From Basle, I got onto the sleeper and entered Germany. At 5 pm on the 5th, the train reached Berlin. The embassy folk came to meet me as usual and I came to stay in this hotel. Phra Visudh Kosa has not yet arrived from London.

When I reached Berlin, I heard the news about Russia and Japan and how [the Russian reply] had not reached the hands of the Japanese government. It was meant to get there on the 6th, so the Russian ambassador sent it on the 5th. The Japanese ambassador in Russia went to tell the Foreign Minister that his government were ceasing diplomatic relations, and he asked for time to leave Petersburg. Everyone is very surprised and all have said the same thing, namely that Japan must take responsibility for the war this time, because they are the ones starting it, not Russia. Russia has tried its hardest not to have any fighting. But how can a large country like Russia agree to the Japanese order? A line must be drawn, beyond which one does not go. If Russia agreed, other countries would laugh and it would look as if Russia was frightened of Japan. In Germany, they like Russia on the whole, while the people who are completely in with the Japanese are the Americans. They want Japan to win, as this would be good for them and represent a lessening of Russian power. America could then go in and exert their influence in Asia. Even if Japan loses, it doesn't matter. England is staying very quiet, as they are frightened that they will have to fight as well, as a result of the alliance they signed. This guarantees that if Japan loses, England has to take on Russia and tell her to stop and if not there would be more fighting.

A war with Russia is something that England fears more than anything in the world. All the countries, as is normal, think only of themselves and nothing else. It is quite comical really.

The Emperor has had to go to Moscow, in order to proclaim the war to the people. This is because Moscow is the old capital and the centre of the Russia, being referred to as the heart of the nation.

I am worried that I will not arrive in time to see the Emperor before he goes. And even getting to see him will be difficult, because at the moment he must have an incredible amount of work. The newspapers say that his face appeared very strained and that he was not saying much to anyone. On the 9th, there was a meeting in the Winter Palace with the officers who are in Petersburg and the neighbouring towns, in order to pray to god regarding the war. I notice that all the news is very over excited and anxiety producing. I am incredibly worried and fear that I will not be able to organise anything regarding my studies, as to rearrange things as Pi Chira has instructed requires consulting the Emperor, otherwise it will be hard to make it happen. However, as soon as I get to Russia, I will be able to see how things stand more clearly. Anything I tell you at the moment is more or less said with my eyes closed, so I will stop for now.

As for the war itself, it is very strange that suddenly Japan has become all warlike, as a result of the answer sent by Russia on the 4th. Everything has got more strained all the time. When I was in the boat and reached Genoa, everyone was still saying that there would be no fighting. Everyone believed that there wouldn't be a war, to such an extent, that several Grand Dukes were holidaying in France. But what was happening was that Japan was awaiting an answer from Russia. Then, suddenly, on the evening of the 7th, there was news that Japan had ordered the withdrawal of their ambassador to Russia and the end of diplomatic relations. Everyone was really shocked and, looking at the news, no one was as surprised as those in Russia. Count Lamsdorf could not believe his eyes when he saw the letter withdrawing the ambassador. I am also really anxious that I will not be able to present Your Majesty's letter to the Emperor and that to try and talk to him at this time is extremely inappropriate. Accordingly I have sent a telegram informing him. I also don't know what is in Your Majesty's letter and so am worried about that too.

PORT ARTHUR. Drawn by a Japanese Artist.

Then when I got a telegram back, I felt a bit better, but when I will get an opportunity to see him is not clear at all. According to the newspapers, the Emperor will go to Moscow to make the war proclamation, as is the royal custom in Russia when something grave occurs.

In Berlin, I met with Prince Dilok and Prince Rangsit, as well as almost all the military students in Germany. Prince Dilok continues studying in Munich and he still seems somewhat crazy, although a bit better. We got on very well together and much better than before. I also got on very well with Prince Rangsit, so I don't think there is anything wrong there, although he does have some rather strange opinions.

The latter is very tall and still seems to be growing. He is a good student and will finish his schooling very shortly and then go on to university.

I was very happy to see my two cousins again. They also seemed very pleased, as they could ask lots about Thailand. Naturally, this was what they wanted to discuss most and I told them everything I could.

All the students seemed to be in good order and have no problems with their studies. Two more have finished their schooling, namely Dossiriwongse[1] and Nai Phet[2]. I can see that the German students are very good and wish to maintain their Thainess. They have not forgotten their Thai at all, because they are together a lot. In England, it is generally believed that, if students spend too much time together, they will acquire the English language more slowly, as they are always speaking Thai. In fact, it isn't like that at all. Being with people who have been in the country already is a very good thing, as those who came earlier can explain to those who are following on. However, if everyone comes at the same time and stays together in a group, then that isn't so good.

I have to apologise that I always said that Russia and Japan would not go to war. Now,o arrogant as to go to war. The war this time is purely of Japan's making, as Russia did not want to fight at all. If she had wanted to, they could have fought long ago. Russia has been very forebearing, while Japan has waited around until the warships from Europe reached the South China Sea and then cut off diplomatic relations without waiting for the answer from Russia, which was on its way. It's rather bad form. I don't dislike Japan at all and, in fact, I rather like the country, but in the matter of the war, I see them as the aggressors.

I am well and thinking of you,

I beg to remain Your Majesty's obedient servant,

Chakrabongse

1. M. R. Dossiriwongse was the son of Prince Chaturonrasmi, the Prince of Chakrapadibongse (1884-1950).

2. Nai Phet Bunyarattapun (1882-unknown) studied at the cadet school in Bangkok, before going to Engers College in Germany. He served in the German army from 1905-1907, before coming home and progressing through the ranks in Siam.

Tsarskoe Selo
16th February 1904

Your Majesty

On the 11th of this month at 7.30, I took the train from Berlin to Petersburg. On the train were Grand Duke Alexander Michaelovich and Grand Duchess Xenia. After we had left Berlin for a while, the Grand Duke came past my compartment and, seeing me, popped in for a chat. He asked whether I had just arrived, enquired about my journey and talked about the fighting. He is furious with the Japanese for sneaking in and attacking the Russian fleet, on a day when war had not yet been declared and the Russians were not prepared. So they hid in a dark place and attacked them when they were not expecting it. It's not good at all. He is incandescent with rage and expounded at length on the arrogance of the Japanese. They will probably get their comeuppance. Indeed, the fact that the Japanese attacked first, before declaring war, has been greatly criticised. In Germany, almost everyone was critical, as was almost every newspaper. It is both a violation of international law and a breaking of relations, before receiving the last letter from Russia. By attacking the Russian warships immediately, it has shown everyone that the Japanese are those seeking a fight. And, as is the way of the world, he who challenges the other to fight, is the one who must take the blame for causing a war. Russia can say that it did everything in its power to prevent war from breaking out, but rather the Japanese were spoiling for a fight.

I arrived in Petersburg on the 12th in the afternoon. Officials from the embassy and Colonel Deguy came to meet me at Gatchina, while at the Petersburg station some friends came to meet me.

On the 13th, in the morning, I went to the Hussar regiment to present myself to the commander and the company commander. My brother officers and friends received me with great pleasure, which was clearly manifest by practically everyone embracing me. So now I am beginning my career in the regiment.

On the 14th, the Emperor asked me to go and call on him at 12 noon. I wore my full-dress uniform, as this was a special audience, namely when first returning, I needed to present myself in my role as a prince. The Emperor and Empress received me very warmly and chatted in a most informal manner. They expressed their pleasure at my return. After a suitable interval, I presented your letter. The Emperor received it and, putting it aside for the moment, asked me to join them for lunch. Apart from The Emperor, Empress and myself, there were only two of their daughters and no one else. After lunch was finished, I was invited to the Empress's boudoir, where I chatted a while longer before taking my leave. I have written a summary report of the important topics of our conversation and sent it to you.

From the 13th to the 16th, there has been a holiday, so I stayed in Petersburg and caught up with my old friends.

Petersburg these days is very caught up with the war. Hardly anyone talks about anything else and, among the young officers, there is a great desire to go and join the fighting. Because the various life guard regiments are all here and have not gone to war yet, those officers who are desperate to fight have to get transfers to other regiments. Grand Duke Cyril and Grand Duke Boris, sons of Grand Duke Vladimir, are both going to join the war. Meanwhile, the women are busying themselves with the Red Cross, making clothes and other things for the soldiers. Both Empresses, as head of the Red Cross, have taken charge themselves, and wives and daughters of imperial officials come and meet every day in the palace. The Empress comes and chairs the meeting all the time. A great deal of money has been donated and continues to pour in. It goes into the Red Cross, in order to help the wounded. A great many noble-born young ladies have also volunteered to be nurses. Among those I know, many have studied nursing and, if the fighting continues, will be sent off. They all seem very ready. And all the soldiers want to go into battle also. Nowadays, it's a matter of preventing them from going, rather than finding volunteers, while those who are unable to fight want to assist in other ways.

Everyone, including the ordinary people, are excited and demonstrate their loyalty to the Tsar and their country. The streets are always thronged with people cheering and shouting and, whenever they come across an officer, they shout 'Hurrah'. The square in front of the palace is thronged with people coming to show their loyalty to the Emperor, and the

Emperor has to come out and bow from his balcony very often, whereupon the people shout 'Hooray' and other blessings. Those who used to abuse the government and, sometimes even the Emperor, such as the university students, have now turned into the most loyal supporters, constantly seeking to demonstrate their devotion to the Emperor and Russia. Such demonstrations are not confined to Petersburg, but are occurring in towns and cities across Russia. All the Emperor needs to do is thank the mayors of the various towns, but it takes a lot of time and is rather boring.

Everyone agrees that Russia did not want to fight and that the Emperor, who believes that peace between nations is the most important thing, has done everything he could to prevent the war. Japan has wanted to show off and challenge Russia and will get what it deserves. Another negative side effect is that everyone hates England, which has helped Japan in various ways. Among the soldiers, there is a call to go to India and, in Turkey, the army has been mobilised, as Turkey adjoins India. Thus, if England helps Japan and disobeys international law further, there were will probably be war.

Although we Thais are on the right side, we are seen as siding with the Japanese and when we walk in the streets, people think we are Japanese and stare at us intently. It is rather frightening and dangerous. However, I wear Russian uniform, which helps, as there is no chance that a Japanese would be wearing one. The newspapers have reported that we are allied with the Japanese and that in Thailand the Japanese have a great deal of influence. They also reported that we clashed with the French, leading to rumours that we are going to fight the French at this time and are thus allied with the Japanese, who are fighting the Russians and the French. People say to me many times, that we are going to fight the French, aren't we? To which I reply no, we are not intending to fight and that, on the contrary, we have recently signed a treaty with France, so why would we be planning to fight them? Regarding the treaty, once it was signed, it was reported in the papers that very evening and everyone knows about it.

There has been so much talk of us being allies with Japan, that it reached the ears of the Emperor, and the Empress talked to me about this, as I have informed you in my telegram.

If people ask me what Thailand's opinion is on the war, I am going to say that when I left no one imagined that war would break out and that the journey has taken a month and so I have had no news. In fact, this is very close to the truth, so I do not feel I am even telling a lie.

I have a slight cold on account of the cooler weather but it is not serious.

I beg to remain Your Majesty's obedient servant,
Chakrabongse

17TH FEBUARY 1904

H. M. THE KING TO PRINCE CHAKRABONGSE
I HAVE RECEIVED YOUR TELEGRAM 14TH FEBRUARY. I AM GLAD TO HEAR THE EMPEROR AND THE EMPRESS ARE BOTH WELL. I ALWAYS FEEL VERY GRATEFUL FOR THE EXTREME KINDNESS THEIR MAJESTIES HAVE INVARIABLY SHOWN TO YOU. YOU ARE RIGHT IN INFORMING THE EMPEROR OF OUR SITUATION AND THE VERY STRICT NEUTRALITY WE HOLD OURSELVES. I DO NOT DOUBT THAT OUR SETTLEMENT WITH FRANCE, WHICH HAS BEEN JUST CONCLUDED MUST HAVE BEEN GREATLY INFLUENCED BY THE EMPEROR. M. R.

FRANCO-SIAMESE TREATY.

SIAM YIELDS.

LONDON, Feb. 14.

Siam has granted the concessions demanded by M. Delcasse, the French Minister for Foreign Affairs, at the instigation of the colonial party in France.

France will not evacuate Chantabun until she assumes possession of Kra.

The treaty has been signed.

By the Convention of 1902 the frontier between Siam and Cambodia was defined, and the frontier between Luangpratong and the provinces of Muang Phechai and Muang Nan. At the same time it was provided that simultaneously with the handing over by the Siamese Government to the French authorities of the provinces of Meluprey and Bassak the French should evacuate the town of Chantabun, occupied by them provisionally since 1893. The Convention was objected to by the Colonial Party of France as not being favourable enough to French interests, although the nation gained a great strip of territory. The cession of Kra, which joins Siam to the Malay Peninsula, has apparently placated the Colonial Party.

News of the Franco-Siamese Treaty, as reported in the Sydney Morning Herald *of 15th February 1904.*

Tsarskoe Selo
23rd February 1904

Your Majesty

Over the past week, I have been carrying out my soldierly duties as before and everything is going well. In fact, there hasn't been much to do because it's been a long period of rest before entering Lent.

As for my new studies, they have now been sorted out and, in two to three days, I will probably get started. I am going to go back and stay in the Winter Palace as before, because staying at Tsarskoe Selo is very hard for the teachers. They have to take a train here, which takes half an hour and then another half an hour back, which wastes a lot of time, and all the teachers have other affairs they have to attend to or are civil servants.

I will probably serve in the regiment as well, but only for two days a week. On the other four, I will study. Sunday is a rest day, but in the summer I will probably take part in manoeuvres and go to camp with the regiment, as I have done in the past. In this way, my studies will go well and my training won't suffer either.

I have found the best teachers and all are colonels or generals. They teach at the Academy, or used to but have left, and are all pre-eminent in their fields. I feel I will gain excellent knowledge, which will be extremely useful. Colonel Deguy, my tutor, has shown that arranging things this way is much better than via the Academy, as one can chose the teachers one really wants and are the best. And the teachers can tailor their lessons to suit, adding this and cutting that. It is not necessary to follow the programme of the academy, which is tailored for Russians who will then serve only in Russia.

My teaching has been organised extremely well and much better than I had anticipated. All this is due to the great kindness of the Emperor and the determination of Colonel Deguy, who has arranged everything so well and rapidly. In addition, all the teachers have been most kind and willing to come and teach me, even though they all have a great deal of work already. Thus, two generals who have stopped teaching in the Academy, or to anyone else, have agreed to come and teach me. All this shows that the Russians have a very good attitude towards us and a special relationship, based on the close friendship between Your Majesty and the Tsar.

Regarding the war, these last two or three days have been somewhat quiet with little news. There is a lot of news in the English language press, but it is hard to uncover the truth. The Japanese are playing games, in terms of releasing news – only reporting that which is good for them and suppressing the times when things did not go their way. In deciding who is right or wrong, I can't comment, as both have the best interests of their countries at heart and both want the same thing. However, in this war the Japanese have contravened international law on many counts. They attacked the boats at Port Arthur, fired on the battery there before declaring war and sent a large contingent of ships to attack two Russian ships

Colonel Deguy, Poum (standing) and Prince Chakrabongse.

Your Majesty

at Chelumpo in Korea, which in fact is a neutral port. It is a great shame that Japan behaved in this way, as it has only recently entered the group of major nations and only just come to be recognised as a civilised country equal wth those in Europe. However, by behaving in this inappropriate way, it makes everyone think that Japan is uncivilised and there has been much talk of evicting Japan from the international group of nations. In some ways, this conflict has turned into a fight between Europe and Asia, with divisions into two groups. It's made the '*farang*' hate the Asians and given them the urge to quash them comprehensively. As a result, I think this puts us at a disadvantage too. It may lead to consulates being closed and other such things. The Europeans will all say: "They're all like the Japanese who just want to pick a fight." And in addition, the informality between Asia and Europe will also decline. I can feel it myself. In the past, it seemed to me that no one regarded me as an Asian or a foreigner. In fact, they generally treated me as a Russian. But now people are always saying to me, "Oh you must be siding with the Japanese", or "You must be on the side of the British", which in fact means siding with the Japanese. All the officers here are obsessed with going to war, to the extent of changing their regiments to those which are going east to fight. It is very admirable. And a great deal of money and clothes has been obtained to help the wounded. Everyone is united in giving. There is also a collection to build a new battleship. It seems as if everyone is finding something they can do to help the country. It is most amazing to witness and very impressive. They have already raised many millions of roubles, with Moscow alone raising over four million. One senior official donated one million roubles on his own.

Grand Duke Cyril and Grand Duke Boris are also going to war.

I am well and thinking of Your Majesty always.

I beg to remain Your Majesty's obedient servant,

Chakrabongse

Today I started my studies according to my new timetable and have moved back into the Winter Palace as before, because, as I told Your Majesty previously, staying at Tsarskoe Selo is too inconvenient for the teachers, who would have to take the train. Today, I began studying tactics and French. Tomorrow, I will start more new subjects. I hope that my studies will progress smoothly from now on.

At the moment, there is not much news about the war. The army have not engaged in battle yet, but are establishing their positions. All that is known for certain is that the Japanese navy have lost more ships and men than the Russians, but they cover up their losses very well and do not let anyone know about them, merely announcing good news. However, the truth will out nevertheless.

The excitement here has greatly abated. Processions on the street and large gatherings in front of the palace have stopped and everything is calm in the city as before. Many, many soldiers have volunteered to fight. From my regiment alone, at least 10 or more are going, with two having left already.

Tomorrow Grand Duke Boris is leaving and Grand Duke Cyril has gone already.

General Kuropatkin, the Commander-in-Chief, will remain here for another week or two. There are many diverging views about the war. Some say it will last for many years, while others think it will be over soon.

Japan probably does not have the necessary finances for a long war, but, on the whole, people think it will endure for at least a year. However, most do not think there will be another five points incident and that Russia will surely win.

I am well and thinking of Your Majesty constantly,

I beg to remain Your Majesty's obedient servant,

Chakrabongse

13th April 1904

Your Majesty

Today I went to see the Emperor to deliver my greetings for the Easter Fete. In Russia one gives good wishes for Easter in the same way one does for New Year. On Easter day in the palace, there are prayers in the chapel and the officials are all in attendance. I did not go, however, as the Emperor said it was unnecessary, as I did not have the same religion and would be tired for no reason. The prayers go on for over two hours, during which time one has to stand throughout.

When I paid my respects today, the Emperor received me very well. He asked about my studies, and how I was, as well as asking after Your Majesty, saying that he had heard that Your Majesty was well. He went on to say that Your Majesty must be following the progress of the war, adding it was a good thing that it was not too near to Thailand, but, nevertheless, it was closer than to us here. I replied that in Thailand there was a lot of interest in the war. After that, the Emperor talked about the officers in my company, many of whom had gone to war and other military matters. Before leaving, he asked me to send his compliments to Your Majesty and Sadet Mae.

There isn't so much news of the war at the moment. Everyone is waiting for the fighting on land to begin, but so far only a few skirmishes have taken-

place. The Japanese navy has attacked Port Arthur several times with little effect and their attempt to sink boats and block the entrance has proved futile. On the contrary, the Russian navy has become stronger and goes steaming outside Port Arthur constantly, preventing the Japanese from transporting their soldiers to Basily Bay. Ever since Admiral Makarov arrived, the Russian navy has been greatly strengthened. This admiral is full of passion and is very brave and strong.

Here, the fears and excitements so evident at the beginning have subsided. Now it is believed that we won't lose to the Japanese for sure. More soldiers are being sent all the time and the Siberian railway is running well with no problems. Before, it was difficult because the section along Lake Baikal to Manchuria did not have enough engines and carriages. It was very difficult to supply them, as the line had a break at the lake. A route to circumnavigate the lake could not be found and people arriving there had to get into a horse carriage and cross the frozen lake, before boarding the train again. To solve these difficulties, the first step was to build a railway line over the ice, which was very difficult. However, this has been

Japanese troops shelling Port Arthur in 1904.

achieved, and now the locomotives and carriages can be transported in sufficient numbers. That it was successful is largely due to the efforts of the Minister of Public Works, who went to supervise the work in person and has stayed on site all the time.

The collection of money to finance the construction of a new battleship has raised a huge amount of money and the Emperor has set up a committee with his relative as chairman and Grand Duke Alexander Michaelovich as President in administering the money. However, what it will be spent on is not entirely clear.

There has been a scandal at the Red Cross, of which the Dowager Empress is the head, because a great deal of money has gone missing. It seems that the staff have put a lot of the money in their own pockets. It's been a real drama and it is rumoured that Empress Marie has been in tears, because she does not know what to do. Of course, no one has donated any more money since the news got out that so much money has gone missing. Until now, it is not known how the matter will be solved.

The British press are changing their tune somewhat and behaving more circumspectly. I heard that this is because the King of England was furious that they were spreading false rumours and lies. *The Times* was a major culprit, because the editor is Jewish and normally they hate Russia. The American press has also quietened down, because the President has forbidden the paper to take sides and insisted it must stay neutral.

For the above reasons, I hope there won't be any further escalation, with other countries joining in the fray as was greatly feared initially.

I agree with you that Thailand has undoubtedly heard a great deal of misleading and incorrect news, because news there is entirely in the hands of the British and most people read the English-language press.

My studies are proceeding smoothly and I think of Your Majesty constantly,

I beg to remain Your Majesty's obedient servant,

Chakrabongse

The Winter Palace, Petersburg
3rd May 1904

Your Majesty

The 27th April was the day on which the officers and sailors from the ships, *Varyag* (a cruiser) and *Koreets* (a gunboat), which went out on their own to engage the Japanese navy in Chemulpo Bay, were due to arrive and a large welcome was organised for them. The sailors came by sea to Sevastopol and then on by train. All along the route, local people came out to welcome them, as everyone admires them for doing their duty with no concern for their own lives. They engaged the enemy who far outnumbered them so that the good name of the navy should not be diminished. The reception here was as follows:

At the station, Grand Duke Alexei, The Commander of the Navy, went to meet them, together with other senior naval officers and other officials. From the station, the sailors marched to the palace, preceded by a military band. The whole route was lined by soldiers, with all the regiments in Petersburg represented wearing their full dress uniform. On the square in front of the palace, all the sailors lined up and the Emperor came out to inspect them together with other high officials and members of the imperial family. He talked to the sailors and expressed his delight that they had come home safely. He told the sailors to march past the palace in the square. The area was absolutely packed and everyone shouted, "Hooray!" with great fervour. People pushed forward to try and be as close as possible and the police had a headache controlling the crowd.

After the inspection in the square, the Emperor went into the palace and together with the two Empresses received the officers, talking to each one in person. Meanwhile, the ordinary ranks marched into a large room in the palace, where a banquet had been laid out. They stood around the various tables. When the Emperor and Empress had finished talking to the officers, they retired to a room reserved for the imperial family for a short while and then came into the banqueting hall. The Emperor congratulated every-

---

1. Stepan Osipovich Makarov (1849-13 April 1904) was a Russian vice-admiral and a highly accomplished and decorated commander of the Imperial Russian Navy. In command of the battle fleet in Port Arthur from 24 February, with the battleship *Petropavlovsk* as his flagship, he pursued a much more aggressive approach, forcing the Japanese to withdraw. Unfortunately for the Russians, he was drowned when the *Petropavlovsk* hit a mine on 13th April 1904.

one and drank their health. The words which he spoke were beautiful and most touching, making one feel that, even if one had to die, one's life would not have been in vain. After that, he circulated round all the tables and talked individually to many sailors. In addition, he presented the Order of St George for bravery to the captain of the *Koreets*, who had not received it yet. After that, he sat down at the top, together with the officers who had returned from the front, members of the imperial family and high officials. He also blessed the officers and told them that he had ordered the creation of a medal to commemorate the battle of the *Varyag* and the *Koreets* with the Japanese navy.

Once the dinner was over, the Emperor, Empress and imperial family chatted with the officers for about an hour before leaving. The sailors went by boat across the river to a large theatre, where a play was performed for them, followed by supper. They were also given many diverse things. In addition, they were allowed to keep the dishes and plates, on which they had been served the imperial banquet in the Winter Palace, as a souvenir. The officers went to the Hotel de Ville to hear an address and receive gifts from the city.

The reception was so large and impressive, that everyone could see that, if one performs one's duty to the full, it will be acknowledged by everyone, from the Emperor down to ordinary citizens.

Now the Emperor and Empress have gone back to Tsarskoe Selo. They are both in good spirits, but the Empress is with child again, as can be clearly seen, disproving earlier rumours that she could not get pregnant again. The question of whether it will be a girl or a boy is a very pressing one.

The significant news from the war is that the *Petropavlosk* ship has sunk and the commander-in-chief of the navy, Admiral Makarov, has died with her. Grand Duke Kirill (Cyril)[1] was incredibly lucky to survive and was not that severely injured. However, he will get back here fairly soon. The fact that the Grand Duke is coming back is not very good, as it makes him look weak. On the other hand, one can understand that, having being blown up and immersed in icy water, would shake most people.

I am well and thinking of Your Majesty constantly,

I beg to remain Your Majesty's obedient servant,

Chakrabongse

LE · PETROPAVLOSK · TORPILLÉ
Mort de l'amiral Makharoff et de 600 marins russes

12TH AUGUST 1904
PRINCE CHAKRABONGSE TO H.M. THE KING
HEIR TO THE THRONE BORN EARLY MORNING
AT PETERHOF NAME ALEXIS. LEK

1. Grand Duke Kirill (Cyril) Vladimirovich (1876-1938) was first cousin to Tsar Nicholas II. He served for 20 years in the navy, just surviving the sinking of the Petropavlovsk. During World War I, he was made Commander of the Naval Depot of the Guards in 1915 and, in 1916, he achieved the rank of rear Admiral in the Imperial Navy.

It is not clear why there was a three-month gap with no letters. Most likely they have been lost. The letters to King Chulalongkorn were presumably kept in the palace after the king's death in 1910, unless Prince Chakrabongse requested their return? Then, when Prince Chakrabongse died in 1920, Prince Chula was only 12 and was shortly sent off to England, so would not have been able to deal with such things. Overall, it is remarkable that so many letters have survived.

Biarritz
21st September 1904

Your Majesty

On the 16th of this month, I went for a break to San Sebastian, which is not far from where I am now. I went by car with a few friends. The drive is spectacular, as the road passes through the Pyrenees and then along the sea. The city is very large and beautiful and much cleaner than other cities in Spain. It is where the king of Spain spends his annual summer holidays.

This afternoon there was a competition, which involved riding horses over fences and other things. Officers from Spain, Belgium, France and Austria took part. I went along and by chance met the king. Alfonso remembered me well and so we had a chat and I met the Prince and Princess of Asturias[1]. The Queen was not there. Everyone talked to me in a friendly and informal manner. They asked whether Your Majesty was in good health and also enquired after Sadet Mae. When I was taking my leave, they invited me to visit them in their palace[2] and have lunch. Alfonso is very grown up and very tall. On this same day, I met Duke Santo Mauro and chatted with him as appropriate.

On the 17th, when I was invited, I left here early in the morning by train to go to San Sebastien. The Duke of Santo Mauro came to meet me at the station with an official car. I went to the hotel to get changed, and then, at the appointed time, went to the palace, which is small and in country house style. It is about the size of Phra Thinang Uttayan[3]. It stands on a cliff and has a wonderful sea view. After I had been there a short while, an official took me in to see the King. In fact, he was still in a meeting with a minister, but

King Alfonso XIII of Spain.

he dismissed him. When I went in, he invited me to sit down and said that we had known each other for seven years. After that, we talked in a relaxed fashion as young people do[4]. I felt that although Alfonso was the King, he was also still a boy and had not really changed, but simply got taller. His ideas and his reading are still that of a child. He seems much younger than me, which made me laugh. After we'd talked for a while, the Queen came in and we chatted informally as before. We talked about the time I went to Madrid and they asked after Your Majesty, the Queen, Toonmom Toh and other princes that they knew. The Queen took me into another room, to allow Alfonso to finish his work, and I met Marie Teresa[5], who talked to me like an old friend. She is

1. Prince Chakrabongse met the Spanish royal family when he accompanied King Chulalongkorn on his European tour in 1897.

2. The Miramar Palace, set on a hill overlooking the bay.

3. A small wooden palace in Swiss-chalet style, built within the grounds of Bang Pa-in palace. Nicholas II stayed there when Tsarevich on his Eastern Tour. It burned down in 1938.

4. By then King Alfonso XIII was 18 and Prince Chakrabongse, 21.

5. Infanta Marie Teresa of Spain (1882-1912). Her elder sister was Infanta Mercedes.

not much bigger, but chats in a vivacious and amusing manner, which is better than her elder sister.

At lunchtime, the Queen asked me to take her in and we all conversed most enjoyably. The Queen chided me as to why I had been in Biarritz, right next to San Sebastian, for a long time and had not thought to come and see them. At this, I was speechless, as there was no excuse I could give. If I had said that I was worried that she might not remember me or that I didn't want to bother them, she would have said: "Are you suggesting I can't remember things?".

When the lunch was over, Alfonso made me run up to the top of the palace to see the view, his bedroom and other things, just like a child. And the things we talked about are not suitable for Your Majesty's ears, which shows that not only is he still a child but a naughty one at that.

After that, Alfonso took me in his carriage to see the jumping, which was being held again as before. He insisted I sat on the right and, despite my protestations, would not budge. Everyone who saw us thought it was rather odd. When we arrived and went up to the Palanola, he again made me sit on the right, but his behaviour changed to that of a grown up.

When it was almost four pm, I took my leave and came back to the hotel, before leaving for the station and taking the train to Biarritz. The Duke of Santa Mauro and the royal carriage came to see me off and I recalled being with Your Majesty in Madrid.

The Queen and two other members of the Royal family send their wishes to Your Majesty, as did the Duke.

I beg to remain Your Majesty's obedient servant,
Chakrabongse

23RD SEPTEMBER 1904
HM TO CHAKRABONGSE
GLAD TO RECEIVE YOUR TELEGRAM FROM
ROYAL RESIDENCE WHERE I HAD BEEN SO
WELL AND INTIMATELY RECEIVED. CONVEY TO
KING AND ROYAL FAMILY MY SINCERE
THANKS FOR KIND MESSAGE. ALSO FOR KIND-
NESS TO YOU, MY RESPECTS TO THE QUEEN
WHOSE GOODNESS TO ME I HAVE NEVER FOR-
GOTTEN. REMEMBER ME TO THE KING AND
ACCEPT BEST THANKS AND LOVE FOR YOUR-
SELF. M. R.

Winter Palace, Petersburg
23rd November 1904

Your Majesty

I have been back in St. Petersburg since the 14th of this month, having left Paris on the 11th and gone on to Berlin. I stayed there for one day and met with Prince Dilok and Prince Rangsit, who came from Munich and Leipzig to see me. During my holiday from Russia this time, I have met up with all my brothers and spent time together. Biarritz also gave us the chance to chat. I am happy to report that everyone is applying themselves to their studies, are well and happy, and there have been no untoward incidents.

I got back in good time, as it was the day on which my regiment holds its annual celebration. However, as this year is wartime there was very little in the way of festivities. There were just prayers and the Emperor came to inspect the regiment, followed by lunch. The Emperor and the two Empresses both came to lunch at the regiment.

On the 20th, I went to call on the Emperor and Empress at Tsarskoe Selo. I took the enamel water beaker, which Your Majesty had sent for the Tsarevich [born on 12th August] and put it into the hands of the Empress herself. They were both very pleased and said how beautiful it was and asked me to tell you that they were both very grateful.

One problem that has arisen recently is that, because of the war, many officers in my regiment have left to volunteer. Thus, there are very few officers left and not enough to carry out training properly. In my company, there are none left apart from the commander, myself and Nai Poum. For that reason, the commanding officer has decided that I should take charge of training the soldiers who are new this year. However, I still have a full programme of studies and it would be more than I can manage to train the soldiers as well. On the other hand, to take leave and refuse, or leave the regiment and only study, also seems wrong and looks bad. I have received their patronage and been looked after by Russia for a long time and learnt so much from Russia also. If, when the country is in a time of need and has a shortage of officers and I am asked to help out, I reject them, it seems most ungrateful. When I went to see the Emperor, I told him about my dilemma and asked him what he would like me to do. The Emperor replied that it was an unusual situation and Russia was in a very difficult spot, because of the war and the lack of officers, such as in my own regiment. He said that if he were in my shoes, he would undoubtedly agree to do the training, according to the wishes of the company commander. He then asked me what I thought. I replied that I was very keen to repay the debt of gratitude I owed to Russia for all the special treatment I had received. And thus when the country was in a difficult situation because of the war, I would be happy to even go and fight. But if that was not possible, I would like to do something else to the best of my ability. On the other hand, I did have my studies and all the teachers think that in order to finish my studies well and quickly, I should leave the regiment. I said I had no idea what to do for the best and therefore needed his decision. Once I had said that, I could see that the Emperor and Empresses were very pleased. All three smiled and the Emperor said that it was very simple. I should go and tell my teachers to reduce my studies so that I could continue in the regiment and train the new recruits, as there were not enough officers.

So it has been decided that I will train the new recruits. My studies in the academy will not be completely abandoned, but will be significantly less and I will have to study in the evenings whenever I can. The teachers will have to confer as to how to arrange the lessons for the best.

For this reason, my studies will take longer and will not be completed as quickly as I had planned. However, I really feel that I owe the country a great deal and I should repay their kindness and show my gratitude. Any other course would seem quite wrong. I hope that my views will not differ too much from those of Your Majesty.

I am well and thinking of Your Majesty constantly.

I beg to remain Your Majesty's obedient servant,

Chakrabongse

1. The French had already seized Chanthaburi in 1893 and from there had moved on to Trat. Subsequently, in 1907, the Thais were to sign an agreement with the French, giving them Battambang, Siem Reap and Srisophon in return for Trat. At this point, discussions and problems were still dragging on.

2. *Tiew ton* were the king's incognito trips to the countryside.

3. Nong Lek refers to Eeyd Lek, Prince Asdang. He moved into a traditional Thai house with woven rattan walls (*faa krachaeng*). It was customary in Siam to have a ceremony when moving into a new house, hence the prayers.

Ruen Ton, Dusit Park
26th December 1904

Lek

I haven't written to you for I would say around a year. The main reason is asthma and all the phlegm got very bad. It was bad for a whole month. In addition, I was so upset about the French[1] harassing us again, and lots of small things. The country is getting smaller all the time, one can't go anywhere on either side. In addition, all year my body has got much worse. When the Trat affair occurred, I got so upset that I felt faint and lacked all energy. My blood was weak and I was worried my old illness would return. It had to be cured using drastic measures. So I left all government matters and went off in a small boat, travelling both on the river and down to the sea for one month. When I came back, I had recovered. I call it *tiew ton*[2], a holiday in a Thai way. I decided to build a small house. So my illness was nothing more than to do with the *farang*. When I hear or plan to see them, my pulse weakens. It's not that I am frightened of them, but I hate them more than I can say. But after I had gone away and relaxed for a month, I found that when I came back I could stomach them again. I have been born to deal with such things and can't escape, but I must look after myself a bit more.

Today I almost started wheezing, but managed to ward it off successfully.

The letter in which you said you are going to actually serve in the Hussars made me very happy. If you had taken any other decision, it would have been wrong. I am happy that you think things through so thoroughly.

Sadet Mae has somewhat resigned herself to being in a decline. She has various side effects and often can't walk. Dr Reytter speculates that it is because she is taking too much medicine, but at the moment she has revived a bit.

Nong Lek[3] is going to move into the Ruen Faa Krachaeng, with various designs that he really wanted. The prayers will be tomorrow. Because I am not very well, I will stop writing now.

Thinking of you a lot.

From your loving Father

Dining with the Hussars. Note the paintings of Hussars on horse-back in the alcoves. Prince Chakrabongse is fourth from the left.

1905
Training Recruits
Representing the King
Revolution

Father Georgy Appollonovich Gapon (1870-1906) was not injured in the shooting on Bloody Sunday. However, he was murdered a year later for being a police informer.

A crowd of petitioners led by Father Gapon near Narva Gate, St. Petersburg.

Bloody Sunday is so named after the events of Sunday 22nd February 1905, when unarmed protestors led by Father Georgy Gapon marched towards the Winter Palace to present a petition to Tsar Nicholas II. Father Gapon was head of the "Assembly of the Russian Factory and Mill Workers of the City of St. Petersburg" formed to represent the rights of workers and those in need. Although sponsored by the police, it was in effect a workers' union.

In December 1904, four workers at the Putilov Ironworks in St Petersburg were fired because of their membership of the Assembly, although the plant manager insisted they were fired for unrelated reasons. Virtually the entire workforce of the Ironworks went on strike, when the plant manager refused to rehire the workers. Sympathy strikes raised the number of strikers to 150,000 workers in 382 factories. By 21st January 1905, the city had no electricity and no newspapers whatsoever and all public areas were declared closed.

The petition, outlined the problems and wishes of the workers and called for improved working conditions, fairer wages, a working day of eight hours, an end to the Russo-Japanese War and the introduction of universal suffrage. The marchers felt that if the Tsar knew their problems, he would help them. The Tsar, however, decided to leave for Tsarskoe Selo.

Despite portrayals in films and paintings, there was not one single violent incident, but various shootings, one involving innocent pedestrians on Nevsky Prospekt. Overall, the Imperial Guards and Cossacks were disorganised and unsure of their orders. The total casualties are not known, with the Tsar's side recording around 93 dead and 333 wounded and the protesters around 4,000. Although absent, the Tsar was blamed for the way the march was handled and foreign governments and media were uniformly negative.

The short-term consequence was that strikes spread to many other cities, with over 400,000 off work during January. The longer term consequence was that the age-old social contract between the people and the Tsar was broken and he was no longer seen as having a divine right to rule. His subsequent vacillation between conciliation (establishment of the Duma) and repression did nothing to heal the situation.

24TH JANUARY 1905

FROM H.E. PHYA SRIDHAMASANA TO HRH
PRINCE SOMMOT, BANGKOK. ST PETERSBURG,
24TH JANUARY 1905

OWING TO THE STATE OF DISORDER PREVAILING
IN ST PETERSBURG ON ACCOUNT OF THE STRIKE
OF WORKINGMEN I HAVE ARRANGED THAT
HRH THE PRINCE OF PHITSANULOK TO STAY
AT TSARSKOE NEAR EMPEROR UNTIL PERFECT
ORDER HAS BEEN RESTORED. SRIDAMASAN.

24TH JANUARY 1905

TO KROMLUANG DEVAWONGSE FROM
SIRDAMASAN.

YOUR TELEGRAM RECEIVED: IN REPLY I HAVE
TO SAY THAT UP TO THE PRESENT TIME THERE
IS NO REVOLUTION; IT IS ONLY A GENERAL
STRIKE. LEK STAYS WITH THE REGIMENT AT
TSARSKOE, WHERE THE EMPEROR IS STAYING
WHICH I THINK WILL BE QUITE SAFE. BESIDES
UPON INQUIRY IT WAS FOUND THAT THE SITUA-
TION IS MUCH BETTER TODAY.

*Still from the Soviet movie Devyatoe Yanvarya
("9th of January"), 1925.*

25TH JANUARY 1905

FROM PRINCE DEVAWONGSE TO PHYA SURIYA
PARIS.

REUTER'S AGENCY TELEGRAMS OF LAST TWO
DAYS REGARDING THE DISTURBANCES IN ST
PETERSBURG ARE RATHER ALARMING. PLEASE
HAVE LEK IN MIND. M. R

25TH JANUARY 1905

TO PHYA SRIDHAMASASNA.

PLEASE COMMUNICATE THE FOLLOWING MES-
SAGE OF HIS MAJESTY TO HIS ROYAL
HIGHNESS THE PRINCE OF PITSANULOK:

THAT DURING THE TIMES OF GRAVE DANGER IN
THE INTERNAL SITUATION OF RUSSIA, IN CASE
THE EMPEROR WOULD DEEM THE PRINCE'S
PRESENCE A TEST OF OUR DEVOTION AND
INCLINES FOR THE PRINCE TO STAY WITH HIM,
THEN BY ALL MEANS STAY. BUT IN CASE OF
THE PRINCE'S EVALUATION THAT IF ONE STAYS
AT GREAT RISK ONLY FOR SAKE OF DOING DUTY
TO THE EMPEROR WHO WOULD NEVER ATTACH
ANY VALUE TO SUCH DOING, THEN THE PRINCE
OUGHT TO OBTAIN PERMISSION OF THE
EMPEROR TO FREE HIMSELF FROM THIS
TUMULTUOUS TIME.

Ruen Ton, Dusit Park
25th January 1905

Dear Lek

The account in the Reuters telegraph two days ago described the events in St Petersburg as being very violent. Sadet Mae and Krom Luang [Devawongse] have been anxious from the beginning, but I have kept my counsel. Now, I, too, have become concerned at your being in a place where there are riots, or where, if there were bombs in somewhere such as the Winter Palace, you would be in danger. When I got the telegram from Phraya Sri Thammasan that you were not in Petersburg, I felt relieved and stopped the telegram I was about to send. Instead, I am sending this letter.

I would never force you, unlike some other people, such as your mother and your uncle, because I believe that those who are on the spot know better what is really going on. Another consideration is my love for the Emperor and a strong feeling of shame. I also think that it would be a noble thing and karmically right to show goodness instead of criticism, which could be interpreted as cowardice. So, all I want to say, is this.

Consider the fact that you are serving in the army, as a volunteer in a time when they are in need. It is something that a good person, a loyal person and someone who understands shame must do. It has nothing to do with the Emperor forcing you, nor is it a question that if you neglected your duty you would be lost.

Now, I would like you to consider carefully whether this action will please the Emperor briefly but will not be an act of goodness that is always associated with you, or whether it is a good deed which the Emperor will see as being done out of sympathy. If it is not a whim, but a genuinely good deed then you should endure it to the end. However, if the Emperor merely sees it as quite a nice gesture, but then forgets about it, or if it simply makes you happy

Prince Chudadhuj Dharadilok, referred to in the family as Tiw, before his tonsurate.

that you have repaid him and don't have to feel ashamed, you should avoid any danger as far as you can, while still doing your work as well as possible.

I am speaking this way out of the sincere love of a father and mother for their son. Of course, we are anxious for you and we cannot stop our hearts from being fearful. All we can do is control our words to a greater or lesser extent. I have been silent for a long time, but I am speaking now because it is someone else's country. There are many important things to do here. They don't lack people as we do. We must look after our people so they can benefit our country. I hope that by saying simply this, you will understand everything and, when you are in a difficult situation, you will find a good way of dealing with it.

The younger boy Tiw[1], has had his tonsurate. I took lots of pictures and will send them to you later. In the middle of next month, we will have the cremation of Pi Nu[2] at Bang Pa-In.

---

1. Tiw refers to Prince Chudadhuj (1892-1923), the second youngest of Prince Chakrabongse's full brothers who was nine years younger than him. The tonsurate was on 18th January 1905.

2. Pi Nu refers to HRH Princess Srivilailaksana, Princess of Suphan Bhakavadi (1868-October 1904), who was cremated on the 17th February 1905.

8th February 1905

Prince Chudadhuj Dharadilok after his tonsurate.

Your Majesty

I received Your Majesty's letter dated 25th December with great pleasure. I was thrilled, because I have not had a letter from Your Majesty for such a long time.

I am pleased to learn that Your Majesty is happy for me to train the new recruits in the Hussar regiment. Frankly, it seemed very clear to me that there was no other course of action possible and, for that reason, I was brave enough to go ahead without having heard Your Majesty's opinion.

The fact of serving in the army and studying difficult subjects on my own, means that I have a lot of work and am rather exhausted. The regiment is in Tsarskoe Selo and I have to take the train from Petersburg. My studies are here, as all the teachers are here and they all have other things to do and can't go back and forth. Accordingly, I have to take the train every day, which is somewhat difficult and wastes time. I don't get enough sleep, which makes my body rather tired.

The bloody French really have left Chantaburi. They have gone to Trat instead. I am keeping quiet, as fighting with them only makes them want to stake out the border. It's always the same.

I think about you, Lek, more than I can say and now am anxious about you too

Your loving father

I have heard some news that Your Majesty is not in very good spirits and has various ailments, which is very worrying. However, I hope that now the French crisis has calmed down, there is less to cause stress and Your Majesty will soon be feeling much better.

I would like to give Your Majesty my thoughts on one matter, which is simply a personal view based on my somewhat childlike experience and please correct me for any mistakes. However, I feel that now we

Part of the ceremonies for Princess Srivilailaksana's cremation, held in the lake at Bang Pa-In.

have dealt with the French crisis and it has subsided, we must prepare ourselves and be ready to fight if necessary. We must make sure we have enough troops to fight the French troops in the colony, so we can be successful and achieve our aims. Transporting troops from Europe is very difficult and, in that sense, we have already won. They have to be transported by boat and we have two or three small warships to harass them and cause them enough trouble. Japan is a very clear example. The Japanese just needed enough troops to deal with the Russian forces in Siberia and enough ships to fight the Russian ships in the region. As soon as they were ready, they declared war at once. The results are self evident. What Japan can do, we can too. All we need, is to be as industrious as the Japanese. Even if we accept that the Japanese are cleverer and better than us, for us to fight the French is easier. For a start, we don't need to move our troops across the sea. In addition, the French are not like the Russians. This is important. When they lost in their own country, they immediately surrendered and got rid of all their ministers. Or else they had a revolution. This is their nature, which we should not forget. If it were the English, then I would not be so bold, but with the French, yes. However, we must set our mind to it and persevere. If we are brave and not frightened of this or that, or compromise, I am sure we would succeed. I am not saying this from arrogance, but I am convinced that if we committed to doing this and had enough money, in 20 years or less, I would be happy to command the troops to attack the French. If we did not succeed, I would give Your Majesty my head. The important thing is to be determined to succeed. The Japanese are an example. I don't want to think that we are so much weaker than the Japanese, or that we cannot succeed at something that is easier and for which we can prepare longer. The things I am proposing are simply ideas in my head and if they are right or wrong Your Majesty must criticise me.

I have heard from Bangkok that several civil servants of various levels are collecting money for the Japanese Red Cross and signing their names. If this news reaches the Emperor, I am sure there will be hard feelings. Of course, it is always good to give, but if they are to make donations, they should give to both sides. The government is neutral, so the officials must be the same. In France, there have been prob-

lems because of this. A government official started raising money and had to be stopped. I would not like similar hard feelings to arise with the Emperor. As for the Russian people in general, there is no problem. I think there has been a lack of communication on the part of the government, which has allowed the officials to think just in the short term. Also, even if we do take the Japanese part, I don't think we should entirely. Anyone who is to close to the Japanese will be accused of preparing to fight and such like. If we don't want people to know what is going one, we should let them think that we are sleeping. So no one will think that we are preparing to wage a war. We must be able to prepare, without them being prepared. Only then can we succeed. The war that is taking place now, has made me think about many things, many of which should not have happened. Things are all right in Petersburg, but elsewhere there is a lot of dissatisfaction for various reasons. There are various discussions, but few decisions. Here, there is a lack of someone to push things along. The Emperor takes decisions all the time, but these do not impact on the ministers, who are making a mess of things. Many things here are similar to with us, but when it's a big country, things are more complicated. We are a small country, so things can stay calm. If we were larger, it would also be a matter for concern. I can't go into great detail about this, because it would take too long, but what has happened here has taught me a lot and made me aware that we must be sure to solve problems, before they can really develop.

I think of Your Majesty constantly,

I beg to remain Your Majesty's obedient servant,

Chakrabongse

25TH FEBRUARY 1905
CHAKRABONGSE TO THE KING
EXTREMELY UPSET DEATH ANOTHER SISTER
SO SOON ACCEPT DEEPEST CONDOLENCES HOPE
YOUR HEALTH GOOD. BEST LOVE LEK

St. Petersburg,
Ist March 1905

Your Majesty

I was extremely sorry to learn of the death of my elder sister, Somdet Ying Yai[1], and it is even more upsetting that it comes so soon after Pi Nu and during her funeral. I am worried that Your Majesty must be very depressed which is only natural but I hope it doesn't make Your Majesty too unhappy.

On the 19th February, an event took place which was very tragic, namely Grand Duke Sergei was assassinated on the way to his office. A bomb was thown into his carriage, when it came out of the Kremlin in Moscow, and exploded violently. The carriage which was closed was completely shattered, leaving only smoke and the four wheels, which the terrified horses ran off with. The Grand Duke died immediately and his body was in so many pieces, that they could barely be called pieces. His head was completely obliterated and his brain was spread over a wide area. People went and picked up his remains later. The largest piece was just one hand. It is absolutely tragic. The person who threw the bomb was arrested straight away and is a Russian anarchist but we don't know very much more about him yet[2], as he has said nothing apart from showing off and saying that he had fulfilled his mission and other such things.

All that remained of the Grand Duke's carriage.

1. This was Princess Chandra Saradavara, Princess of Phichit, (1873-February 1905). She died during her half-sister's funeral at Bang Pa-In.

2. Ivan Kalyayev, a member of the Socialist Revolutionary party.

Princess Chandra Saradavara.

When the incident happened, Grand Duchess Elisabeth, his wife, was in the Kremlin. When she heard the bomb, she guessed straight away what had happened and ran out without wearing her headdress or her outer wear. She knelt down by the remains and tried to find his head but could not find it. Of course, by then many people had arrived on the scene and they all knelt down. There was no one who was not crying and some sobbed loudly. Later, the remains were taken into the palace and the usual ceremonies were performed. The Grand Duchess is greatly to be pitied and also to be admired. Thus, in the midst of her great sorrow, she managed to do everything correctly and even went to see the Grand Duke's driver who was badly injured. Then two or three days later, the driver also succumbed to his injuries and the Grand Duchess went to his funeral and walked behind the coffin all the way from the hospital to the station, a distance of many 100s of yards without showing any fear.

She then arranged a meal for a great many of the poor in Moscow, in order to make merit, as is the Russian custom. This is similar to the Thai tradition. After that, she went to visit her husband's assassin in

Ivan Kalyayev, shortly after the assassination.

prison. She asked him why he had done this. He replied that he had to do it, because he was in an anarchist group and if one was chosen, then one had to perform one's duty. The Grand Duchess listened to his explanation and asked him whether he was religious. He replied that he was, so she gave him a small picture of a saint and told him that God would have to chose between the Grand Duke and the assassin. For her part, she had forgiven him for the great pain he had brought her and had begged the Emperor not to execute him, even though he was an evil man. When he heard this, the anarchist bowed his head and burst into tears. What the Grand Duchess did is most admirable and worthy of her position as a lady of high birth.

The funeral took place in Moscow. The coffin lay in state for a while. If the body had been brought here at this time, it was feared that it would have been an excuse for more dangerous acts. If the burial were to be here, the Emperor would of course attend, but if he were to walk along the roads in Petersburg at the moment, it is considered too dangerous, hence the decision to choose Moscow. The Emperor did not attend and he forbade other members of the imperial family to travel to Moscow. Grand Duke and Grand

Duchess of Hesse, Grand Duchess Maria, the daughter of Emperor Alexander II, who is Duchess of Coburg-Gotha, Princess of Battenburg, the elder sister of Grand Duchess Elizabeth and Grand Duke Paul were allowed to attend the funeral. Originally Prince Henry was also going to come and the German Emperor was going to ask him to represent him and was going to send other military officers. But the advice from here was not to come, as I informed you in my telegram. Given that Grand Duke Sergei was someone whom Your Majesty liked and was one of your friends, I wondered if you would like me to go to Moscow, as your representative, or do something to show our sorrow. That's why I sent a telegram to ascertain your wishes. Then, after I heard that it was to be a low-key funeral and that the Emperor was not keen for representatives of foreign heads of state to attend, I sent you another telegram telling you what I thought was the right thing to do. On the same day as the Moscow funeral, prayers were held at Tsarskoe Selo and all the members of the imperial family and high officials were invited, together with the ambassadors. After the prayers, there was a reception at the Alexandrovsky Palace, the small palace where the Emperor is staying at the moment, although the one for the ambassadors and officials was held in the big palace. I talked with the Emperor and told him of Your Majesty's desire to send me as his representative to the funeral in Moscow, as Your Majesty regarded him as a very special royal friend, but I agreed with him that it would not be appropriate and it would be difficult for the Russian government. And as there were representatives from other countries, I told you that I would not go. The Emperor thanked Your Majesty and said he had received Your Majesty's telegram and that my decision not to go to Moscow was the correct one, because I need to help out here and he invited me to Tsarskoe Selo.

I did not find that the Emperor was changed in any way. He seemed calm, despite this event that has bought so much grief and concern.

The assassination of Grand Duke Serge has made every one very sad and depressed, but no one was surprised, as the Grand Duke was rather reactionary with beliefs akin to those of Alexander III. He used force as a basis and was extremely fierce. People really hated him and he had great influence with the Emperor, as he was related to the Emperor through his wife as well[1]. Those who are more forward thinking and those who want to revolt, consider that he made the Emperor stubborn in refusing to grant a parliament or make any other changes. They saw him as a threat to the good of the country and felt he should be removed. Nowadays, the revolutionaries have a program to assassinate many other royals such as Grand Duke Alexis, Grand Duke Vladimir and Empress Marie, as they see these three as preventing change and being very influential on the Emperor. If they were dead and the Emperor continued to be stubborn, they would then assassinate the Emperor. These plans by the revolutionaries are causing serious problems, as it is difficult to run the country. Various mistakes have been made, which the war has made very clear. The reason why Russia has been losing to the Japanese is not because the soldiers are no good or anything like that, but because the higher echelons haven't organised things properly, are asleep, and haven't seen what was coming with poor tactics. So, idiocies have arisen all the time. When this is so, there is much talk that the officials in charge at the moment are no good at all and think only of themselves, doing exactly as they please with no one overseeing or checking up on them. Everything is really in a mess and it is clear that other people, who are not in the various ministries, should have a voice in governing the country.

However, once they had evaluated the situation and expressed an opinion saying this is what should be done to improve things, the government has prevaricated and refused to agree to their demands, which has led to the various riots and disturbances. Workers have gone on strike. The railway workers have stopped running the trains and the students have stopped attending university. To put it simply, the upper classes, or those whom *farang* call the intelligentsia, can be divided into two groups. One group consists of the officials, who are in the ministries and who do everything and have full power. The other group do other things and have nothing to do with government. They have no power. There is a third group, who are ordinary citizens and the workers and real peasants. The first group mentioned run the country, according to the wishes of the Emperor, but

things are not going smoothly and there are hundreds of bad mistakes, which cause hardship to the third group in various ways. The second group state that the mistakes are because the first group works in isolation, with no one checking up or overseeing them in any way, as all the power is in their hands. The Emperor can't do anything either and whatever his wishes, they change or subvert them. For this reason, the second group wants to cut the power of the first and ensure that they can also be involved. Then, everything would go well, because the second group are very clever. But the first group won't agree at all, so there have been riots. The third group who make up the majority and have suffered the most, say nothing and are quiet. This means it is the two groups in the intelligentsia, who are fighting each other. These people cannot be compared with the ordinary, average citizen. When the situation is thus, it is difficult to come to a speedy resolution. If the second group become involved in running the country, they might also be hopeless and misuse power just like the first. Or they might be so busy with infighting, that nothing would get done and the country would likely not improve. The third group would be no better off. If things are reorganised, so that the second group can have the power they have been calling for, there is no way of saying whether things will be better or not. These matters are very difficult to judge, as the gap between the intelligentsia and the ordinary people is very great. The intelligentsia want to be western liberals and to have a parliament and grandiose reforms. However, the peasants don't even understand what a parliament is. As an observer, I can see that the intelligentisia are thinking mainly of themselves, but use the good of the country and other fine words to make them seem and sound better.

As for the Emperor, it is difficult to tell exactly what he thinks. Does he want change or not? Hence the great confusion and unrest. The Emperor is too good natured and wants to please everybody, but ends up satisfying no one. With two groups who are so opposed, he cannot please both.

I am well and thinking of you constantly,

I beg to remain Your Majesty's obedient servant,

Chakrabongse

1. Grand Duchess Elizabeth was the elder sister of Empress Alexandra.

8th March 1905

Your Majesty

I received Your Majesty's letter dated 25th January and am more touched and grateful than I can adequately express. The letter was music to my ears and touched my heart. I am pleased and delighted to hear that Your Majesty trusts me to find the best way to avoid danger and stay alive to serve my country in the future.

To be frank, the Reuters cable service and the British Press do exaggerate the situation. In this country, it is hard to get at the truth. Newspapers get closed down and then when they are closed, they fabricate stories. Their reports on the riots here are mainly fabricated. For example, the statement that up to 20,000 people were killed has been published in all the papers. In fact, that number is a long way from the truth. There are one million people in Petersburg so if 10,000 died that would be 20 percent[1] and one would see a difference. In fact, Petersburg has hardly changed. Another thing is that many of the British newspapers are taking bribes from the Japanese, so when they say something about Russia it should not be believed as everything they say is negative.

The possibility of a revolution here seems difficult, as I respectfully told you already. The population of ordinary Russians, numbering 130 million, are still quiet and still respect the Emperor as their leader. Those who are causing the trouble at the moment are some groups of upper class people who lack power. They are not government officials, but students or merchants. There are not as many as a million people. Then there are labourers, who are very active, but again not many millions. Then there are the anarchists. Added all together, they are fewer than those who are indifferent or are opposed to a revolution. In such circumstances, how can there be a revolution? Furthermore, in Russia there is an army of over 1 million with many tens of thousands in Petersburg. The army are still loyal, so how can a revolution succeed? It definitely can't take place.

The fact that Grand Duke Sergei was assassinated, does also not automatically imply revolution. The Empress of Austria is the same, as is the King of Italy[2]. Even in America, presidents get assassinated without things turning into revolution. As far as the anarchists are concerned, nothing that is done will satisfy them.

At the moment, the English newspapers want there to be a revolution, so are always proclaiming that there is one already. The newspapers just write what they want. If they want it to be so, they fabricate it to be so. I am here, so if I saw anything really dangerous and frightening I would certainly have told Your Majesty, but because I haven't seen anything, I have kept quiet and just communicated by letter. What I do know is that it is very different from the news on the Reuters telegraph for sure.

Now the Emperor has announced that soon he will call the peoples' representatives from all over to a meeting, so they can give their views and participate in drawing up new laws and reforming the government, in other words have some sort of basic constitution. The riots at the moment are because the officials are not handling things well. They follow the wishes of certain groups and then others say that things should be done in another way, because there is no parliament. In fact, the Emperor would definitely be happy for there to be a parliament. Why does he want to have the whole weight of power on his shoulders? I can't see that it is fun in any way. But he can't give a parliament, because a parliament must be for the people as a whole, all 140 million of them. But at the moment the people of Russia don't yet know what a parliament or a constitution is. And they will not be able to vote or chose representatives. There is one group of people or maybe several groups who have joined together – it's difficult to judge – perhaps 10 million people, but probably not as many as that. They are calling loudly for a parliament. On the other side, are 130 million people who don't want it at all, because they don't understand what a parliament is. The Emperor must think about this. Normally, one follows the wishes of the majority, but now they are going to change and follow the wishes of

---

1. Prince Chakrabongse's maths is rather suspect. If 10,000 died out of a million, it would represent 1% not 20%.
2. These two were assassinated in 1898 and 1900 respectively.

the minority. The reason for all the riots is because in Russia there are two groups who are very far apart: those who are referred to as the 'intelligentsia' and the other group, who are the indigenous Russians who can't even read. For the first group, they should be governed in the European way, for the other group the only way is to go on as before. Those who have to govern are the Emperor and the government and they have to think what to do. It is not an easy matter to be joked about. Many people like to compare Russia, at this time, with France before the revolution. In fact, that isn't right at all. In France, the king and the government oppressed the people for over 200 years, while philosophers expressed their views on how to solve the problem and wrote numerous books. As a result, in the end the people knew there was a way to solve the problem and there was a massive uprising. But this took a long time, while the populace understood nothing. Those who understand what's what in Russia are very few and far between. And it's not as if the government has done nothing and has always been oppressing the populace. They have improved certain things. Now they want to take things slowly, but those who are unhappy want things to move faster. But to do something immediately is not a good idea at all. England is now the freest county, but did this take place in one year or two? No, it happened gradually over 1,000s of years.

This matter needs a great deal of consideration. If someone doesn't think things through, but does something sudden, the country might collapse tomorrow. I can't see what there would be to stop that happening.

I know that with far greater insight, Your Majesty will have understood that being a long way away, it is difficult to know what is happening. Those who are closer know things in greater detail.

Can I ask Your Majesty to most kindly show this letter and others like it, dealing with the situation, to my mother, Sadet Lung and anyone else who is worried about things, so they can understand everything more clearly. I would also like to say once again that I have been born and received Your Majesty's beneficence in order to serve the country and repay Your Majesty's goodness. That I would risk my life through carelessness in the service of another, is not going to happen. But while taking every precaution, I cannot behave like a coward. Behaving in a cowardly fashion is not worthy of being Your Majesty's son. If I were to behave in such a way, it would damage Your Majesty's high standing. No one can know when death may come. If I were to get sick and die, I could not be accused of not fulfilling my duty. For that reason, death has no rules, if your time has come, you can't escape. It's as simple as that.

I beg to remain Your Majesty's obedient servant, *Chakrabongse*

PS Regarding the reason for the shooting in Petersburg[1], I explained in my previous letter and I am sure Your Majesty can see the extent of the riots.

1. This is a reference to Bloody Sunday, see page 344-45.

Ruen Ton,
9th April 1905

Dear Lek

I haven't written to you for a while, despite having asked you to help out in the matter of the Crown Prince, which I hope will be of benefit to you too, as we are in credit with Adalbert at the moment.

The fact that Russia has lost to Japan this time has made me ponder things a lot. I am genuinely sad, but I did not desperately want Russia to beat Japan either. The result will probably signal a change that allows Japan to go forward further, rather than remaining stationary as before. How this will manifest, I cannot guess.

Relations between us and the French seem better. with no aggressive talk. They have a lot on their plate at the moment and their fighting this time will keep them quiet[1]. So we can breathe more freely. At the moment, I am free, as I have a bit of a temperature but it's probably because I have an upset stomach. I have taken some medicine as a way of overkill, but I think it will keep it in check.

There is one important thing, which has made me write to you urgently, so that you know what's going on. As you know your mother has had various illnesses and taken certain medicines from time to time, but they seem not to be doing any good.

She is rather moody and lethargic. She likes to sit and chat in one place from morning till night, and this could be one of the reasons why she is unwell. Another problem is that she self-medicates. When the medicines don't have any effect, she gets very upset. This behaviour has become habitual now.

I have discussed this matter with Toh. He says that she does not want to worry him, so if he goes and sits with her, she hardly asks for anything. But who can go and sit with her all the time? So we think that the only solution is for you to come home. You are her favourite and intelligent (I did not say this), so perhaps you could work some magic on her. I am not that certain that you would be successful. Eeyd Lek

The interior of Ruen Ton.

The exterior of Ruen Ton, where the king spent much of his time.

managed to entice her out in a motorcar for a bit, but then she gave up. If you were able to get her out, she would probably soon give up again. The reason we can't solve the problem as before is that, if I can be frank with you, she is quite old now. She should be independent. She is clearly intelligent, as everyone knows, and has even been the Regent.

I think she has become overconfident in herself, so that if anyone tries to say anything, she gets upset or angry. To try and force her to take the middle way is difficult, because she is independent and rather distant with me. When she was ill this time, she sent a telegram saying that it was because Eeyd Lek was going abroad, but, in fact, it started about one month earlier. It was due to getting angry among her inner circle, which was nothing to do with anyone else or any politics or intrigues. The issue of Eeyd Lek going away got mixed in and made the matter worse.

The decision to request Dr Kaiser[2] to write to you asking you to return was made by Toh, as he didn't know what to do and used it to try and cheer her up and encourage her to get better.

I am also fed up and want you to come back. It doesn't seem as if much else will happen with the war and no one can say you abandoned them in a difficult period. Do read this and think about it. Here, Phra Satid[3] is in full swing. He is involved with everything, from palaces downwards, changing this and fiddling with that. He keeps saying it will be finished soon, but he could be telling fibs.

Phra Satid has been in his element at Toh's place, which gets so waterlogged. The building isn't affected because the grounds have been filled in.

I think of you, but the reason I haven't written for a long time is because there is a lot of government business. I also have to be honest and confess that before, when I had free time, I wrote letters, now when I have a moment, I take photographs and relax a bit.

Your loving father
Chulalongkorn

1. In Spring 1905 the French were preoccupied with the so-called First Moroccan crisis and so had difficulties of their own (slowly swallowing as the king says in Thai)

2. Dr. Kaiser was one of a team of royal doctors.

3. Phra Satid Nimanakan was in the Public Works department and was the architect in charge of the various palaces.

4. Toh's house was the Chitralada building in the grounds of Paruskawan palace, which he later swapped with Prince Chakrabongse.

26th April 1905

Your Majesty

I have received Your Majesty's request for me to represent Your Majesty on the occasion of the marriage of the Crown Prince of Germany. I informed Phraya Visudh Kosa, the ambassador in Berlin, so that he can arrange things according to Your Majesty's wishes. I have also considered who should accompany me on this occasion. One person who is certain is Luang Surayudh, my ADC, and perhaps Phraya Sri Thammasan, who is my guardian. However, Phraya Sri Thammasan is acting as ambassador here and, if he were to accompany me, it might be awkward for the ambassador in Berlin and look strange as to why there were several ambassadors. Accordingly, I asked Phraya Sri Thammasan to telegraph Your Majesty asking for permission to wear the uniform of a palace official and to accompany me in that capacity. In that case, everything would be fine and there would be no awkwardness. Phraya Sri Thammasan will be there simply as my guardian and not as an ambassador. I am very grateful that Your Majesty has acceded to my request in this matter. Phraya Sri Thammasan will call himself Chamberlain to His Majesty the King of Siam attached to the person of HRH Prince Chakrabongse.

The fact that Phraya Sri Thammasan has been granted the right to wear this attire on this occasion, is a great honour and very generous of Your Majesty. But I would like to say that Phraya Sri Thammasan has performed his duties as my guardian for many years with discretion and great care, and has never caused me any difficulty whatsoever. It is, therefore, appropriate that he has received the honour of being in the royal household and should continue in that department as a reward in the future. This would please me and Phraya Sri Thammasan more than we can express. But I am really sorry if Your Majesty thinks I am overstepping the mark here.

I do hope that the gift, which I am to give to the Crown Prince of Germany will arrive in time together with Krom Luang Sarnphasart tomorrow.

On the 21st of this month in the Hussar regiment, there was an inspection of those who were admitted this year. There was a test of their general knowledge and their ability following their two months of training. Every aspect of their knowledge was tested and it is an important day for the officer, who has trained the new recruits, as it demonstrates whether he has taught them properly or not. Those soldiers whom I trained passed their test satisfactorily with good marks. The commander was full of praise, and said in front of all the other officers that he knew that I had applied myself truly to the task and he wanted to thank me especially. This was most unusual as the commander has never singled out one particular officer to say anything like this before, especially in front of all the others. Later, in private, the commanding officer told me that when he had a chance, he would inform the Emperor and praised me again fulsomely. He said he would remember for the rest of his life that I had volunteered to train the new soldiers, a difficult task but a vital one. It requires a lot of intelligence and skill to take rough recruits and turn them into useful soldiers in a short period. I am telling Your Majesty all this, so it can be seen that what I have been engaged in has not been a waste of time and has shown everyone that Your Majesty's son is not a wastrel, sitting around doing nothing in the manner of princes here and *farang* nobles in general.

Here, at the moment, everyone thinks only about the Russian navy, which is in the China sea. It is both the subject of hope and great concern. Many people ask me if I have any special news, as they think that Thailand is quite close. I have to keep reiterating that we are nothing to do with this at all and that the Russian navy has not, nor would have, passed by at all. We are 3-5 sailing days away and we can't see anything that is going on.

Domestically, things are calmer with the main question being whether to have a parliament or not. The power of the Emperor will not be removed. It is all very interesting, but I don't know how to explain it all in a letter without it being too long. All I can say is that in the past year I have heard a lot of very strange things, which have given me much cause for thought and I have learned a lot both in terms of waging war and internal affairs. For an observer, it is a very valuable time. I have thought about many things and have many ideas, which I hope to tell Your Majesty in detail when I have the opportunity of seeing Your Majesty again.

I beg to remain Your Majesty's obedient servant,
Chakrabongse

Battle of Tsushima. 27th-28th May, 1905. Japanese print.

31st May 1905

Your Majesty

On 26th of this month, I went to see the Emperor to inform him about going to Berlin for the marriage of the Crown Prince. The Emperor invited me to stay for a private lunch. Apart from me, there were just his daughters and Grand Duke Andrew, who today was his adjutant. The Empress talked to me in an informal manner just as before. I observed that the Emperor looks well and was unchanged. He talked about cheerful subjects and seemed no different from normal. After lunch, the Emperor took me into his office and I told him that Your Majesty wanted me to be Your Majesty's representative at the wedding. I asked permission to take Nai Poum with me. He gave his permission and asked in detail about when I was going and when I was coming back. He said, with a smile, that I would meet the Japanese prince. He asked me whether we knew each other and I replied not yet.

After that, I asked to have a rest this summer, as in the winter I had worked very hard, both training recruits in the regiment and studying on my own and that I was exhausted. I also said that in the summer I wouldn't be able to study, as all the teachers were on holiday. For that reason, leaving Petersburg would not affect my studies. If I did not go in the summer, but went in the autumn, as last year, it would take time out of studying. The Emperor agreed to everything and gave his permission. He added that he would inform the commanding officer to that effect.

During lunch and afterwards, the Emperor asked me about my studies in detail, demanding to know how they were going, when there would be exams and other things. I told him how things were.

Before saying goodbye, the Tsar took me to see his new bathroom. It has a large marble bath. The water can come over one's head, so it is possible to swim. He said it was most enjoyable.

The Emperor and Empress asked after Your Majesty, Toonmom Toh and Pi Chira in detail, and I told them the news as far as I could. The Emperor and Empress remarked how greatly Pi Chira had changed when he came to see them after not having seen him for two years. They said they could hardly

Admiral Togo on the deck of the Mikasa before the Battle of Tsushima.

Sinking of the Borodino in the Battle of Tsushima.

remember him and wondered why he had changed so much.

The situation in Russia has calmed down a great deal, although there are still some disturbances in the countryside. In the city, all is quiet and the Emperor will be able to go and stay in Petersburg as usual.

Today, there was bad news that the Russian navy has been defeated in Japan again[1]. Everyone is very upset, but no one is surprised, as they knew that the navy sent out there was not as robust as that of the Japanese. And the Japanese being on their own territory, can do what they want. The Russians have come from afar and have nowhere to stay, which is a telling difference. The fact that the Russian army, had such difficulties is beyond the imagination. That they could fight at all with the Japanese, at such long distance, is extraordinary. It has never happened before, that a navy had been sent so far with no ports in which to shelter en route. No one believed that they would succeed. Those who had studied naval strategy, said it was quite impossible. The fact that they could fight at all is most unusual, but nevertheless it was not successful, which is most disappointing. But one should not despise or look down on the Russian navy. One can only regret that the Russian navy was so much weaker than the Japanese and was not sent before the Russian navy in Port Arthur had been destroyed. If it had been sent at that time, there might have been a window for success, as the ships in Port Arthur could have come out to help.

Trying to guess what the Russians will do next is

very difficult and it is still not known how many ships reached Vladivostok.

Tomorrow at 12 midday, I will leave here for Berlin. Phraya Sri Thammasan, Luang Surayudh, my adjutant, and Nai Poum will accompany me. Our reception will be inferior, but there is nothing we can do as we are a small country. The Japanese prince will be impressively received and the Kaiser will come and meet him at the station.

After the ceremony, I will come back here straightaway, as at this time I should not be outside Russia for long. While I am here, I am an officer in the Russian army and must behave like everyone else and realise that our country is in a difficult situation. So it would be wrong to go gallivanting anywhere else.

In the summer when I will have a rest, I think I will stay in Russia and holiday here. When the Emperor asked me where I would go, I said I thought I would stay in Russia. The Emperor said he was delighted and thought that was the right thing to do.

I beg to remain Your Majesty's obedient servant,

Chakrabongse

1. The Battle of Tsushima was a major naval battle between Russia and Japan. It was naval history's only decisive sea battle fought by modern steel battleship fleets, and the first naval battle in which wireless telegraphy (radio) played a critically important role. In this battle the Japanese fleet, under Admiral Togo Heihachiro, destroyed two-thirds of the Russian fleet, under Admiral Zinovy Rozhestvensky. The destruction of the Russian navy caused a bitter reaction from the Russian public, which led to the Treaty of Portsmouth, being signed on 5 September 1905 without any further battles.

1st June 1905

Your Majesty

I beg to report to Your Majesty on the task assigned to me, namely to represent Your Majesty at the wedding of the German Crown Prince in Berlin[1].

To start with, I am very sorry to have to tell you very candidly that the German Kaiser behaved in a way that belittled Your Majesty the entire time, by almost failing to greet or talk with me at all. More importantly, he did not ask after Your Majesty, or proffer thanks for sending me in any way. I find this extremely rude and a most unbecoming way to treat the monarch of a country, which is independent like his own. I feel very bitter about the whole affair. I am not upset, because he did not talk to me. As a person in my own right, I am no one special in any way and there is no reason for me to go and see him or talk to him, but on this occasion I went as Your Majesty's representative and I am one of Your Majesty's sons. The fact that the German Kaiser had the cheek to behave in this way, is a grave insult to Your Majesty.

I have had the honour to visit the kings of many countries and have never encountered such a thing. Without fail, the first question that is asked is concerning Your Majesty's wellbeing. It isn't even the case that there is nothing to talk about, there's plenty. First of all, good manners dictate that if you ask someone to come and join in a celebration, you should thank them for coming and Your Majesty received Prince Adalbert[2], his son extremely well just recently, but the Kaiser did not think it worth a mention.

On the other hand, all the other royals who were there, almost 100 of them, were very pleasant and grateful for having visited Your Majesty, or received Your Majesty's kindness in some form or another. They would ask about Your Majesty and express their

Kaiser Wilhelm II.

Poum, Prince Chakrabongse, Mr Cuissard and Luang Surayudh Yotaharn.

1. The wedding of Duchess Cecilie of Mecklenburg-Schwerin and the German Crown Prince Wilhelm, 6th June 1905. Kaiser Wilhelm II invited over 50 guests from different European royal houses awaited them, including Grand Duke Michael Alexandrovich, for his brother, Tsar Nicholas II, Archduke Franz Ferdinand, representing the Austrian Emperor Franz Josef, as well as representatives from Denmark, Italy, Belgium, Portugal and the Netherlands. The wedding ceremony took place in the Royal Chapel and the nearby Berlin Cathedral.

2. Prince Adalbert of Prussia (1884-1948) was a son of Kaiser Wilhelm by his first wife Princess August Victoria. He visited Siam in November 1904.

3. Frederick I, Grand Duke of Baden (1826-1907) was married to Princess Louise of Prussia.

4. Grand Duke of Hesse. Ernst Louis Karl Albrecht (1868-1937, r. 1892-1918) was the last Grand Duke of Hesse and by Rhine.

5. Prince Henry of Prussia (1862-1929), younger brother of Kaiser Wilhelm II, had visited Siam in December 1899.

thanks at great length. For example, when the Grand Duke and Duchess of Baden[3] saw me, they remembered me at once and talked at length about Your Majesty and asked to be remembered. They were full of good wishes, expressed most fulsomely. Whenever I encountered them, they reiterated such remarks again. The Grand Duke of Hesse[4] was also very nice and volunteered to be my guide during the ceremonies, saying that whatever I needed help with, I should tell him. He also invited me to Hesse again, having remembered that I followed you there before. In addition, I had two other 'nannies', namely Prince Henry[5] who behaved very cordially to me immediately, as a result of having visited Your Majesty. He made it his business to look after me and took me to meet the Kaiserin and other royals, as well as telling me what I should do and where I should go. He was always chatting to me at great length, as we usually sat together at the various functions. My third guardian was Duke Johann Albrecht of Mecklenburg-Schwerin[6], who had also been to see Your Majesty and had received a letter from Your Majesty as a result of seeing Your Majesty in Berlin. His Duchess also talked to me at length and was very informal. Other members of the royal family whom I met, were the two princess sisters[7] of the Kaiser, whom I led into dinner two or three times and they too were very cordial. Others, who I knew had visited Your Majesty during the European tour, were the Crown Prince of Sweden, Prince Christian of Denmark, Duke Uberto of Portugal, and the Duke and Duchess of Aosta, Italy. Then there were nobles who knew Toonmom Toh, such as the Prince of the Netherlands. All were very friendly and, on the whole, asked me to send their respects to Your Majesty. From Russia, Grand Duke Michael came as the representative of the Emperor and there was also Grand Duke Nicholas Michaelovich[8], as he is the uncle of Princess Cecilie who was getting married. The two Grand Dukes were incredibly friendly to me, as they regarded me as coming from the same country. We were always together and could gossip in Russian about the others. The

Prince Arisugawa Takehito (1862-1913).

Japanese royal[9] who came to the wedding was a very strange person among this group. Were it not for the fact that everyone is excited by Japan at the moment, he might have been a laughing stock. Even so, he was the object of some mirth, albeit kept under control. He was very clumsy and uncouth, having never seen anything like this before. He was also tiny, being several inches shorter than me. He looked like his hand was itching, and seened always ill, with a strange face. All in all, he did not look suitable to be the lord of a capable and intelligent people such as the Japanese. He is also ignorant of any customs or norms. He is messy and arrogant. The Kaiser might be talking to someone else and he would go up and tap him on the arm. The princess is not beautiful either and is very thin, as well as having no manners. They are rather comical, but the Kaiser and other senior nobles make a fuss of them. The reason is they are doing well at the moment and want to be their allies, instead of the British. The Kaiser's head seems to be full of politics and nothing else. He received the Japanese prince so well and was so excessive towards him, that everyone could see he was sucking up to them because they are successful.

The running of the Prussian court appears very complicated and not like in Russia. There is a lot of

6. Duke Johann Albrecht (1857-1920) was married to Princess Elizbeth Sybille of Saxe-Weimar-Eisenach.

7. This could refer to any of the four sisters: Princess Charlotte, Princess Viktoria, Princess Sophia and Princess Margret.

8. Grand Duke Nicholas Michaelovich (1859-1919) was the eldest son of Grand Duke Michael Nikolaevich and a first cousin of Tsar Alexander III.

9. Prince Arisugawa Takehito (1862-1913) was an Admiral in the Japanese navy and an officer who had had two stints of studying in Britain. He also represented the Meiji Emperor at the Golden Jubilee of Queen Victoria. Prince Chakrabongse's evaluation of him was clearly biased by his Russian affiliation.

etiquette and ceremonial between the members of the family. In Russia, it is much freer and more informal. Here, there is bowing and scraping from dawn till dusk. However, between the royals and the civil servants, the protocol is not strict and everyone mingles together and pushes themselves forward, so that it is a real scrum and difficult to walk around. Such behaviour would never happen in Russia, where the royals are treated with more respect. Another thing is that in Prussia, there has never been such a large gathering of foreign royals, as there is no coronation. This is the first such event and so it is a bit of a muddle. The staff of the royal household seemed to be a bit frenetic. But, nevertheless, for such a large event, on the whole things passed off very well.

The programme overall was as follows. I left Petersburg on the 1st June by train. From the German border, the government sent a special carriage, which took me all the way to Berlin. On the 2nd at 7.30 pm we reached Berlin. There was a full-dress reception at the station. Prince Adalbert was there, as well as some military and police officials, a guard of honour, a brass band and a flag. When I got out of the train, Prince Adalbert came and greeted me and said that he was here to receive me in the name of the Emperor. He then introduced me to General Hubfner and Captain Auer, whom the Kaiser had arranged to attend to me while I was in Berlin. He also introduced the senior officers, who came to meet me, as well as his adjutant. I introduced him Phraya Sri Thammasan, Luang Surayudh Yotaharn, my adjutant, and the captain who was with me. Then he took me to inspect the guard of honour and the company marched past as is usual. The niceties completed, he led me to my carriage in a very formal way and took me to the Hotel Heiselhof and up to the room, which the government had provided for me. Along the road there were many people standing waiting and they shouted "Hooray!" as we came along. Prince Adalbert said he had just received a letter and a photograph from Your Majesty two or three days ago. He was delighted and thanked Your Majesty very much. He asked if Your Majesty was well and talked about when he visited Your Majesty in Bangkok. He was most complimentary and told me that Sadet Mae had given him a sapphire ring. Telling me that it was a special memento for him and that he never took it off, he showed me the ring. He said Your

Crown Princess Cecilie.

Majesty was extremely kind while he was in Bangkok. I asked whether the Kaiser and Kaiserin were well, and enquired about her fall and whether she had recovered. When he was leaving, I thanked him very much for meeting me and bringing me to the hotel.

The 3rd was the first day of the festivities, beginning in the afternoon. In the morning I went around delivering my card to the various royals who had come to attend. Crowds thronged the streets, and as soon as they saw an Imperial carriage they shouted "Hooray!" It was rather tiring and made me feel I was an actor on stage all the time. The streets were decorated with leaves and flowers, and looked very magnificent.

In the afternoon, Princess Cecilie came in procession into Berlin. The Princess had actually arrived in the area already, but had gone to Bellevue Palace which is outside the city. The Kaiser, Kaiserin and the royal children went to receive her there during the day. It was family only, with no other people. At 5 pm all the guests, both royal and official, went to the palace to welcome the Princess. I went along as instructed, and that was the first time that I met all the nobles. There were so many, that I was dazzled and could not make out who was who. However, there were some to whom I had paid my respects in

The wedding procession.

the past such as the Grand Duke and Grand Duchess of Baden, so I went to say hello and we chatted, as I have already informed you. There were a huge number of royals, as they had come from every country and in Germany itself from every city. It was all rather crowded. The Kaiser came out and said hello to everyone. He saw me and gave me his hand, but did not say anything. I had planned to say that it was kind of him to invite me and I was delighted, but when he said nothing, I felt I could not say anything either, the custom being that the senior person must initiate the conversation. As he was silent, that was it, as there was no other opportunity.

Princess Cecilie got into the carriage with the Kaiser, and there was a large procession with many cavalrymen, leading both in front and taking the rear. They travelled from Bellevue to the Inner Palace [the Berlin Royal Palace]. When they arrived, the Kaiser took her hand and led her to meet various royals. With me, as with other lowly royals, he just passed me by. Princess Cecilie had met me a long time ago when she was still a child, because she used to come to Petersburg every year with Grand Duchess Anastasia, her mother, and the Dowager Empress. For that reason, she came over to see me herself and said she

was delighted to see me again. She didn't say anything to the other royals.

After that, there was the signing of the marriage agreement between the Royal House of Hohenzollern and Mecklenburg-Schwerin. This was followed by a dinner for all the royals. The seating was arranged by country. Large countries with a crown prince in attendance went first, followed by those who were closest to the Kaiser. Among the smaller countries, it was a muddle. If the Kaiser respected a certain country, they

Princess Sophia of Prussia, who was married to the Crown Prince of Greece, Prince Constantine.

were given precedence. Then the German royals came after everyone else. It was all rather strange. Thus, the Crown Prince of Romania, notwithstanding being a crown rince, was down as low as me, while the Crown Prince of Greece, a small country, was right up with the large countries, even preceding the grand dukes. This was because his wife was the younger sister of the Emperor. It is strange here like this and difficult to see which custom they are following. They just seem to please themselves.

After dinner, I asked Prince Henry to take me to pay my respects to the Kaiserin, as I had not done so yet and she had never met me. She talked to me in a friendly manner, asking me where I was from and talking about Prince Adalbert and Prince Henry's trips to Thailand. She also asked me how many times I had been to Berlin. It was all a bit superficial, but fine. The end of the dinner, was the end of the day's events.

The 4th was a Sunday, and so in the morning everyone went to church. The Kaiser, Kaiserin and the royals, the Crown Prince and Princess Cecilie all went and the foreign royals were also invited. I forgot to tell Your Majesty that yesterday I saw the Crown Prince and he was very friendly, remembering that we had met before in Petersburg. The Crown Prince and Princess Cecilie also chatted to me for a short time at the dinner, but were then called away somewhere else.

In the evening there was another dinner with nothing special. However, there were even more royals, as some of them had only arrived that day. Before the dinner, General Hoepfner came to present me with the Order of the Red Eagle[1] from the Kaiser. I wore it in the evening for the dinner. This decoration is a low one, but, among non-German royalty, I was the only one to receive it. Everyone else got the Order of the Black Eagle, which is a bit embarrassing, but there is nothing I can do. Toonmom Toh has also not received one. I thanked the Kaiser, as was appropriate. He said he was pleased to be able to give me this decoration, but then said no more and walked on.

On the 5th, in the daytime, nothing was going on so I went around leaving my card on those who had arrived later. I also took the opportunity to take Your Majesty's gift and present it to the Crown Prince in the palace. This was the day that he was receiving various deputations, but he saw me first. I took in Your Majesty's present and said it had been sent from Thailand along with warm wishes for his happiness. I

The bride and groom, the Crown Prince and Crown Princess of Prussia and the German Empire.

said that Your Majesty was most interested in the Crown Prince's welfare and happiness. The Crown Prince replied that he was more grateful than he could express and would never forget Your Majesty. He begged me to convey his sentiments and also said how pleased he was to see me again here, having already met me in Petersburg.

In the evening, there was a so-called Family Dinner, but everyone was in full dress, as afterwards there was a gala performance at the Opera. The dinner in the palace was unremarkable and was only for the royals. After that, we went to the Opera, where everyone was invited, and it was very glamourous. They performed one act of Lohengrin before the interval, during which everyone squeezed forward to try and greet the Kaiser. The Crown Prince was kind enough to ask a member of the Royal Household to run around trying to find me. Once he had, he came over to chat and it seemed to me that he was doing this deliberately to make up for the behaviour of his father. The Crown Prince is very nice, polite and not full of himself.

1. The Order of the Red Eagle (*Roter Adlerorden*) was an order of chivalry of the Kingdom of Prussia, awarded to both military personnel and civilians.

One of the many souvenirs of the wedding.

The second half of the Opera was cancelled, because it was so hot. The Kaiser stayed until everyone had left. I stayed until the end, when there were only two or three people left. Nevertheless, the Kaiser did not talk to any of us. It looked very odd, and almost as if he was doing it on purpose.

The 6th was the day of the wedding. At 4 pm everyone arrived at the palace, and a civil marriage was performed. Then we walked in procession to the church. We walked in threes, with sometimes a princess in the middle and two princes on either side, or other times with the man in the middle and a woman on either side. It was a very large procession. We all went into the church in the grounds of the palace. Here, a protestant ceremony was performed, after which we all walked back in procession to rest and give our congratulations. I gave my congratulations and on Your Majesty's behalf to the Crown Prince. He thanked me effusively and asked me to thank Your Majesty again. He also thanked Your Majesty for the present, which he said was very beautiful. I told the Kaiser that Your Majesty sent your congratulations and was very delighted. He simply replied "Very kind", and then said no more.

From there, he went out into the throne hall. All the officials were there and came by in procession to bow. It took rather a long time. The members of the royal family had to stand there as well. When it was over, there was what they call a State Supper to make it sound very grand. Various generals and senior officials in the ministry had to help serve at table, as an honour. The Kaiser made a speech conferring his blessing on the couple, which went on for a long time and was in German. I could not understand a word. During the dinner, the Crown Prince and Princess drank a toast to me personally.

After the dinner, we went into the throne hall again. There was dancing, but it was very strange and only among the royals. It is known as Dancing Under the Candles. 12 pages carried candelabra in front, followed first by the Kaiser and then the Crown Princess and the Kaiserin. The latter two held hands and all three went once round the room. Then the Crown Prince did the same with all the female members of the Imperial family and the Crown Princess with all the male members of the family. And that was the end of the dancing. It derives from the idea that before the bride and groom give up their single status and leave their friends and family, they get to have a last goodbye. Then the bride and groom are delivered to their room, as weddings always take place in the evening. It is an old German custom which has continued in the palace.

After this dance, the events were over. On the next morning, the bridal couple went on honeymoon.

I left Berlin for Petersburg on the 9th. I was exhausted, as there was one event after another. It was always full dress, and the weather was very hot. It was as hot as Bangkok and, although I shouldn't say such things to you, my jackets were wet through to the outside every day. Other princes teased me and said I should have felt at home with such heat.

My trip this time went off well, except for the Emperor's behaviour, which was insulting to Your Majesty and about which I have already informed Your Majesty. It was beyond me to know how to alter this, and all I could do was feel extremely bitter. When he said nothing, there was nothing I could do. I waited for this opportunity or that, but it never came.

I beg to remain Your Majesty's obedient servant,
Chakrabongse

12th June 1905

To Lek

I have received your letter dated 26th April. I was happy that you were praised for your ability to train the recruits. Importantly, when you return, I hope you will get a good reference from the Emperor, which will allow me to boast about you.

In the previous letter, which you've probably received by now, I mentioned the report from Toh saying that he was certain that you were no longer studying and that many officers had left the academy and therefore it was not necessary for you to stay on.

Regarding your staying on in Russia, it is only me who thinks it is a good thing, while your mother, your uncle [Sadet Lung] and Toh always make a disbelieving face at me. It is not in my thoughts to bring you back, no matter who thinks you're mad. Although there is some truth in this, I know what I really think. I feel that if one starts something, one should stay with it to the best of one's ability. I know you are the only one to have inherited this crazy approach from me. But I feel that if I have been able to save the country and regain the power of the monarchy, it is because of this strong belief in not giving in, so I can't accuse you of being stubborn because

I know that even if you want to come back, you are not going to give in. At the same time, saying this doesn't mean you have to overdo things.

As for coming back to look after your mother, I am sure she might get better, but you cannot stay on indefinitely. When you get to Bangkok, I will tell you about it.

It seems a good juncture to leave now, as the truce will mean that things quieten down, as there are not enough troops nearby, apart from holding on to Vladivostok. If you wait until everything is over, it will be too long.

I am having so much trouble with the Department of the Royal Household. Prince Phit has been awful for three years now, and this year he has become impossible. I have removed him and replaced him with Prince Naris. While in Bangkok, Phraya Suriya is acting Minister of Public Works, but he will have to leave to negotiate settlements for the tax rates for a couple of years. So I've left it at that. I hope we will have time to see each other. Eeyd Lek still seems to have very little knowledge. No one seems to look favourably on Russia. If Eeyd Lek were to go, your mother would probably become worse. Ever since Toh arrived, your mother has become pro Japanese, although she already was before the truce.

I think about you a great deal, but I understand you, so will have to bear our separation a bit longer.

Chulalongkorn

HRH Prince Narisara Nuwattiwongse (1863-1947) was a younger brother of King Chulalongkorn and a minister in various departments. Apart from his government posts, he was well known for his artistic talent.

Prince Narisara Nuwattiwongse was appointed as Head of the Royal Household instead of Prince Phit.

6TH JUNE 1905
CHAKRABONGSE TO THE KING
IF MOTHER IS NOT IN IMMEDIATE DANGER
BUT IN CASE YOU WOULD LIKE TO RECALL ME,
I BEG TO SUBMIT THAT IT WOULD BE MORE
PROPER TO TELL EMPEROR BY LETTER. IT
SEEMS TO BE MORE POLITE TO THANK HIM
IN THAT WAY FOR ALL HE HAS DONE FOR ME.
SURELY THE DECISION OF RECALLING ME
OUGHT TO RENDER MOTHER HAPPY ENOUGH
TO BE ABLE TO WAIT A MONTH LONGER, LEK

20TH JUNE 1905
HM THE KING TO CHAKRABONGSE
AS YOUR MOTHER IS NOT IN IMMEDIATE DAN-
GER THERE IS NO CAUSE OF ALARM. IT IS ONLY
ANXIETY FOR THE FUTURE AND IT IS THE WISH
OF HER THAT THE DOCTOR ADVISED WHAT IS
IN MY LETTER WHICH WILL REACH IN THREE
WEEKS WHICH WILL EXPLAIN ALL CIRCUM-
STANCES. YOUR ADVICE TO TELL EMPEROR BY
LETTER MEETS MY INTENTION BUT AS THERE
WAS AN IDEA THAT TELEGRAM SHOULD BE
SENT I AGREED ACCORDINGLY BUT NONE HAS
BEEN SENT TO EMPEROR. I AM OF OPINION
THAT IT WOULD NOT BE PROPER AT PRESENT.

26th June 1905

Your Majesty

I received a telegram from Toonkramom Toh that Mother was ill and the doctors think that I should come home, so that the illness would not get any worse which could be dangerous. Toonkramom has asked me to give my opinion as to whether there should be a telegram to the Emperor calling me back. This telegram has created a huge dilemma for me, because, of course, there are problems in leaving Russia now and so suddenly. At this very moment, when the Russian navy has just been sunk, it could be interpreted as demonstrating that as soon as Russia has less strength, Thailand immediately recalls their prince because there is no point in having him stay on any longer. Or it could be seen as sending a message that Russia is in such a mess, I should not stay. Such an implication would hurt the Russians for sure and,

in particular, the Emperor. I feel that my stay in Russia is not the same as that of the other princes studying abroad. Staying in other countries is paid for by us and we make the arrangements. In other words, we are buying an education and are under no obligation. I, on the other hand, have stayed here for nine years. I have eaten at the Emperor's expense, stayed in the Emperor's palace and used the Emperor's carriage. We have not paid for my studies at all and not bought even a single pencil. For that reason, I owe him a huge debt of gratitude, and how can it be right to behave in an uncouth way and satisfy myself without thinking to repay such a debt in one way or another? Just taking and not giving would look really bad. For me to leave Russia now is like abandoning a friend's house where I have been staying as soon as a fire broke out. It seems that in Bangkok, no one can understand. I am at my wits' end and don't know how to explain any more. The crux of the problem is the severity of my mother's illness. If it is very serious and by not coming back, it were to be more dangerous, I don't need to think about the damage done here, as the life of my mother is far more important. If that is really the case, I should leave at once. However, I cannot make that decision as to how things are. Only someone who is on the spot can choose. If she is as seriously ill as stated, then I should be called back straight away. However, if the situation is not so serious as to outweigh the loss of leaving here, this course of action should be stopped. These two things have to be weighed up and it is a problem I cannot solve. I ask Your Majesty to make the decision, and transmit it so others can understand your point of view and my heavy heart.

I am not very well at the moment, with very low energy levels. The doctor has given me mineral waters to drink. It's a performance and I have to rest and can't do anything. The problem with this illness is that if not looked after it can turn into kidney disease, but if dealt with straight away it can be completely cured.

I must also tell Your Majesty that in Russia there is a rumour that, when the Japanese navy defeated the Russian one, Your Majesty sent a telegram to the Japanese emperor expressing your pleasure. The Russians have all asked me about this. I replied that it was certainly not true, but no one seems to believe me and my friends keep asking me whether I am leaving, with all thinking it very likely that I will be recalled. They say nowadays Russia isn't important and Thailand will have to suck up to the Japanese. I have told Your Majesty this, so you can see how sorry for themselves the Russians are feeling at the moment.

I beg to remain Your Majesty's obedient servant,
Chakrabongse

4TH JULY 1905
HM THE KING TO CHAKRABONGSE

JUST RECEIVED YOUR LETTER OF 26TH JUNE. YOUR MOTHER IS STAYING PHRAPATHOM. SHE HERSELF SAYS SHE HAS RECOVERED FROM ILLNESS BUT SHE IS STILL IN A STATE OF CONVALESCENCE. SHE CAN WALK LONG DISTANCES NOW. YOU NEED NOT BE ANXIOUS RUMOURS ABOUT MY SENDING TELEGRAM MENTIONED AT THE END OF YOUR LETTER ARE ABSOLUTELY FALSE. M. R.

21st July 1905

Your Majesty

I have received Your Majesty's letter dated 9th June giving Your Majesty's view on mother's illness. It is a great shame that things have got to such a pass . . .

The question of leaving hurriedly, when I think about it, has many bad points, as I have told Your Majesty many times already. It will hurt the Emperor and I do not think that is a good idea and quite wrong, as the Emperor has been so good to me. When I received the telegram from Toonmom Toh informing me that he was going to send a telegram to the Emperor, summoning me back, it was exactly the time when news reached Petersburg that the Russian navy had been sunk, which caused great anguish everywhere. If, at the very same time, there was a telegram to the Emperor recalling me, what the result would have been I simply dread to think. It would be what the diplomats call a political statement on a large scale. And, at that time, the Emperor would naturally be very depressed. To upset him in any way would be most indelicate. For that reason, I immediately sent a strong telegram to Toonmom.

For me to leave now would undoubtedly be damaging. I have a study timetable, which I want to finish. It is planned that by December this year everything should be completed. If I am recalled halfway through, everyone will wonder why I am being called back and abandoning my studies, which I came here to pursue and which they have worked so hard to plan for me. When they try and find the reason, they will come up with one obvious one – that Thailand is fearful of Japan, but no longer feels any obligation or love for Russia. They will think that straight away and this will hurt the Emperor and the Russian people for sure.

As for the impact on me of having to leave my studies halfway through, I will not get all the knowledge that Pi Chira received and that he told me that I must obtain so that I can serve Your Majesty in the future. If that is so, there will be damage to the country as well.

Thinking about all the negatives that will accrue to the government and Your Majesty's interests, and weighing them against the need or benefit that will arise, if I were to leave at once, it seems that the cons outweigh the pros. But in this matter I must defer to Your Majesty's judgement. If Your Majesty rules that I should return, I am very happy to obey Your Majesty's wishes. As Your Majesty knows, I am totally loyal and will always accede to Your Majesty.

As far as I am concerned, I feel I should leave after my studies are finished in December, which isn't very long. And leaving then will not cause any damage. My studies will be completed, I will have learnt everything and my leaving will not seem strange in any way. It's natural that I would leave at that point, as there was never any question of me staying here all my life. Everyone will be happy and there will be no other emotions. It will be appropriate to Your Majesty's position and the close friendship which exists between Your Majesty and the Emperor.

Apart from the above reasons, leaving now would also be difficult for me personally, as I am still recuperating, and summer in the Red Sea – through which the boat must pass – is unbearably hot, but, of course, this latter point is not really important.

Naturally, I would be happy to see Your Majesty, my brothers and sisters and my homeland as soon as possible. However, I am most anxious to return having obtained all the knowledge I can, so that I can

25th July 1905

Your Majesty

serve Your Majesty and the country to the best of my albility and be of true benefit. Knowledge is so important and, especially in military matters, knowledge and tactics are vital. For that reason, the more you know the better it is. I am determined to make the Thai army into an important one, which is feared by other countries. For that reason, I have applied myself to my studies to the best of my ability. Apart from my books, I have always kept abreast of events, followed the news in the papers and read other books so that I can glean as much information as possible. That is why to have to cut my studies short in any way would make me extremely sad. Of course, I love my mother more than words can say, but, if it is not truly vital, I find it very hard to leave my studies halfway through and also hurt the feelings of the Emperor, who has been kind to me in ways that words cannot express.

I do hope that Your Majesty will see my point of view to a certain extent.

I beg to remain Your Majesty's obedient servant,

Chakrabongse

I have received Your Majesty's letter of 12th June and am honoured that Your Majesty has praised me and my endurance and ability to not give up on something before I have completed it, a quality Your Majesty compared to Yourself. This gave me great pleasure, in fact more than I can say, but I'm sure it won't go to my head, as I am becoming more responsible and have learnt that I must continue to behave correctly so as to be worthy of Your Majesty's praise. When I receive praise from Your Majesty or an important person, I always remember that one has to try harder all the time. One small decline in behaviour is much more noticeable than with people who have behaved badly already.

I agree with Your Majesty that I should stay on, as otherwise my studies would have been abandoned halfway through and I would like to finish. The question of causing distress to the Emperor is not linked to the conduct of the war. He would be more distressed if I were recalled suddenly and abandoned my studies. On the other hand, if I had finished, no matter what sort of state Russia was in, if it was time to leave, it would be time to go. I have never thought to spend my life here. It seems that no one understands me in Bangkok. I beg for Your Majesty's understanding in this matter. I was very surprised to hear that Toonmom Toh had submitted a report stating that I am not studying at all and I wonder where he got his information from. I studied throughout the autumn and winter, and carried out training from 8 in the morning until 10 o'clock at night every day without fail. If he does not believe this, he can look at the report by Phraya Sri Thammasan. I am sure there is a copy in the secretary's room. To make such a report highlighting my fecklessness, is extremely strange. To say that I am hanging around here doing nothing, not studying, receiving money from you and avoiding work in Bangkok, is not something one should accuse anyone of lightly. I am very upset that Toonkramom Toh has submitted such a report about his own brother. To speak in a more vulgar fashion, I would ask, "What is he playing at?". As it is a holiday period now, I suppose I could be accused of doing nothing. However, I cannot study at the moment

Inside the Siamese Embassy at the lustral water ceremony for King Chulalongkorn's birthday in September. From left to right: Luang Surayudh, a Siamese embassy official, Monsieur Cuissart, Phraya Sri Thammasan (the ambassador), Prince Valapakorn Voravan, Prince Thongthikayu and Prince Chakrabongse. All are in full-dress uniform for the occasion.

because there are no teachers to teach me. They are all on holiday and, for myself, I'm not feeling very well and I have to rest and recuperate, as I have already informed Your Majesty. But soon I will begin my studies again and, until that time, will be reading my books without a break. If one wants to level accusations in this way, I could tell Your Majesty how those who are at university in England have no less than six months holiday and study for no more than eight weeks before having a week off all the time. Everyone knows that this is the case, but I don't see anyone saying that these people are just having fun and wasting their time for six months of the year. If we were to discuss who studies more or less, I am happy to explain how studies work in England and how very different it is in Russia, but that would simply be a waste of time and paper. Let's see later who will serve the country better.

Further to my taking the liberty to comment on Eeyd Lek's education in England and arguing with Phraya Raja Nuprabandhu, I have now received a letter from him and Your Majesty's permission to make changes. Phraya Raja arranged everything and then consulted me. Even though it couldn't be changed, I had to tell him my opinion. Before, I said nothing, as Your Majesty had entrusted Phraya Raja with the arrangements. But when he did consult me, I used the opportunity to write to Your Majesty, bearing in mind that I have only the best interests of my younger brother at heart.

Now Phraya Raja has sent me a copy of his letter to Prince Sommot with the budget for Eeyd Lek's studies in the sum of £4,000 or more, as they have to rent a house. If he stayed with a family, it would not cost so much and it would be better for his English, as I have already written to Your Majesty. Accordingly, I would beg your permission to protest strongly.

I beg to remain Your Majesty's obedient servant,
Chakrabongse

4th August 1905

Your Majesty

I have received a letter from Eeyd Lek complaining that Phraya Raja Nuprabandhu has arranged for him to stay in his own house and other matters, as Your Majesty knows. Eeyd Lek doesn't think it will be a good idea at all, as he knows that Phraya Raja can't look after a house in any way. He says that the embassy is so dirty that walking about makes his feet, hands and face absolutely black. So if Phraya Raja is going to be looking after Eeyd Lek's house, he thinks it will be quite revolting. Phraya Raja just likes having a good time and won't do anything for Eeyd Lek at all. I am copying part of Eeyd Lek's letter for Your Majesty as evidence.

Apart from that, Somedej Chai has complained that Phraya Raja's plan won't work well for sure. It means that he will take his family to live with Eeyd Lek, ie his wife and his children and the Japanese servants. And all these people will take money from Eeyd Lek. This means that Phraya Raja won't have to pay for any of these people any more. That's why he's set the amount of money needed for Eeyd Lek at £4,000. Phraya Raja is very profligate. The £3,000 he has received from Your Majesty is not enough for his clothes, his outings. Seeing as this is the case, can I respectfully ask Your Majesty once again to tell Phraya Raja to arrange things according to the opinions of various other people and send Eeyd Lek to live with a family. The boy himself agrees to this and wants it to happen. If you send such an instruction there will be no embarrassment to Phraya Raja. Your Majesty can simply say you have decided on a different plan.

Somdet Chai has said that Eeyd Lek staying at the embassy in London is very lonely. He stays at home sometimes for two days at a time without going out at all. This is not good for his health, as in Europe sitting in a stuffy room is very bad. Eeyd Lek cannot go out, because Phraya Raja has forbidden him to go out except with him. However, Phraya Raja does not take him anywhere.

I have asked Phraya Raja to bring my three younger brothers (Prince Asdang, Prince Mahidol and Prince Chudadhuj) to Petersburg in September as I don't think I can go to London. I am not particu-larly well and the doctor wants me to rest here. And at the moment, Russian soldiers are forbidden to go on holiday abroad. I would be very grateful if Your Majesty could telegram Phraya Raja asking him to arrange for the boys to come here. I really want to see them and, if there were not various obstacles to this, would have gone to England myself.

As to the point that Petersburg is dangerous in any way, I can guarantee that the weather in September is not cold at all and is still hot[1].

I beg to remain Your Majesty's obedient servant,
Chakrabongse

14TH SEPTEMBER 1905
CHAKRABONGSE TO HM THE KING
I HAVE RECEIVED A TELEGRAM FROM THE CROWN PRINCE OF SIAM TELL ME THAT HE WANTS ME TO GO HOME TO REPLACE HIM BESIDES MOTHER. I AM AWAITING YOUR MAJESTY'S COMMANDS DIRECT WHAT AM I TO DO. I BEG RESPECTFULLY TO REMIND YOUR MAJESTY HOWEVER THAT MY EDUCATION IS NOT FINISHED THERE REMAINS 3 MONTHS MORE BUT IF YOUR MAJESTY JUDGES THAT I NEED NOT FINISH IT AND SHOULD GO BACK, I AM READY TO OBEY YOUR MAJESTY'S COMMANDS. IN THIS CASE I BEG YOUR MAJESTY TO SEND A LETTER TO THE EMPEROR. ONLY AFTER HAVING RECEIVED THAT LETTER AND TRANSMITTED IT TO THE EMPEROR CAN I LEAVE AND THEREFORE WILL NOT BE HOME BEFORE 2 MONTHS ANYHOW ACCORDING TO ORDINARY COURSE I SHALL BE HOME IN 4 MONTHS. LEK

---

1. Prince Chakrabongse is being disingenuous here, as the danger being alluded to is unlikely to be from the weather, but rather from on-going political disturbances and protests.

17th September 1905

Your Majesty

On the 14th of this month, I arrived back in Petersburg from my holiday, taken at the doctor's insistence and about which I have already informed Your Majesty. I have started my studies again and am also working in the regiment. I hope that my studies will completed at the beginning of January, or the end of December as per the Russian calendar.

When I got back here yesterday, I received a telegram from Toonkramom Toh[1] regarding his need to go and inspect work in the northern counties, but he does not want to leave Sadet Mother as she has said she needs to have at least one of her sons at her side. Accordingly, he has asked me to come back and take his place, as it is impossible for him not to go.

I have told Your Majesty about this in a telegram, asking for a decision on this matter and have been glad to receive Your Majesty's answer allowing me to stay on and complete my studies.

I think it's extremely odd why Toonkramom Toh has telegrammed asking me to come back, before asking me whether I thought I could come back or not. It implies that whether I stay or go is entirely up to me and that I don't have to listen to Your Majesty's decision. I find it really strange. I left to come here as a result of Your Majesty decision for me to study military matters until completed and, when these studies are not finished, how can I think about coming back on my own without asking Your Majesty's permission? And why did Toonkramom Toh not ask Your Majesty directly, so Your Majesty could agree and then ask me to come back? If such were the case, I would come back straight away. When he contacted me, I wrote to Your Majesty as I saw fit. That Your Majesty's decision did not agree with Toonkramom Toh's wishes is surely not my fault. Nevertheless, I can see that in Bangkok, I am regarded as stubborn and refusing to come back which is quite strange.

I have received a letter from Phraya Raja, the ambassador in London, saying that Your Majesty now desires that Eeyd Lek's education should be arranged along the lines I have suggested. However, he has asked my opinion yet again, as if I had not already said what I think. I said what I thought again, but I can't help wondering why he needs to ask again? Did Phraya Raja take my first letter and throw it into the fire or what? I really don't know. But then to say that he has to ask my opinion again and telling Sadet Lung that he couldn't do anything, because I had not replied! I would like to ask him, "Well, what about my last letter? Where have you thrown it?".

Now I have had a telegram to the effect that he will cease arranging anything until he has met with me here and he says he is bring my younger brothers here within the week.

I am delighted to be able to meet with my three brothers, as I have wanted to see them for a long time. I am sure that their agreeing to come is because Your Majesty was good enough to tell Phraya Raja, and for that I am extremely grateful.

This letter is already long, so I beg Your Majesty to allow me to leave out one letter in the week and then I will tell you about the end of the war and the reasons behind it[2]. There is going to be a parliament here, which I will also tell you about in detail. Both are very unusual things and worthy of study.

I beg to remain Your Majesty's obedient servant,
Chakrabongse

1. After being extremely close when both brothers were studying in Europe, one senses here the beginning of an estrangement which only increased over time.
2. Sadly, this letter about the war and the Duma is missing.

26TH SEPTEMBER 1905
CHAKRABONGSE TO HM THE KING
AS ASDANG IS COMING HERE AND THAT
FACT WILL BE UNAVOIDABLY KNOWN TO THE
EMPEROR, I THINK THAT IT WILL BE WELL
TO PRESENT HIM TO THE EMPEROR. BESIDES
AFTER MY RETURN ASDANG WILL HAVE TO
REPRESENT YOU AT VARIOUS COURTS TO COME
IN CONTACT WITH DIFFERENT SOVEREIGNS. I
THINK IT MOST FITTING TO BEGIN HERE. I CAN
ARRANGE IT QUITE PRIVATELY MYSELF WITH
HIM SO THERE WILL BE NO INCONVENIENCE IN
THE MATTER OF LANGUAGE OR OTHERWISE.
I BEG RESPECTFULLY TO SUBMIT THIS SUGGES-
TION TO YOUR MAJESTY'S WISDOM. LEK

28TH SEPTEMBER 1905
HM THE KING TO CHAKRABONGSE
IN REPLY TO YOUR TELEGRAM I APPROVE. YOU
MAY PRESENT HIM TO THE EMPEROR. ASDANG
IS NOT LIKE YOU. HE IS VERY SHY. HE DOES
NOT LIKE TO MEET PEOPLE OR TO SPEAK WITH
THEM SO DO ALL THAT IS POSSIBLE TO CURE
HIM OF IT NOT ONLY FOR THIS OCCASION BUT
FOR THE FUTURE. M. R.

3rd October 1905

Your Majesty

Yesterday I went to meet Eeyd Lek, Daeng and Tiw at the station, together with the ambassador to London, Nai Bua and Mister Batman. I arranged for them to stay at the embassy, as it is comfortable and secure. Phraya Sri Thammasan and Luang Surayudh, my ADC, went to meet them at the border.

The three seem unchanged over the year and a half that has passed, since I saw them in Bangkok. I had thought that Eeyd Lek would be taller than me by now, as we were the same height in Bangkok, but he is not.

I took them to see all the major sights around town as appropriate.

The Emperor has only just come back from the seaside and I haven't been to pay my respects yet. I am going to ask permission to bring Eeyd Lek to see him.

Eeyd Lek is not that shy and awkward. He talks well, but he doesn't push himself. He finds it hard to find things to talk about and so is quiet. If he can get over this, I think he will be fine. I force him to say hello to this person and that person, and don't let him sit there silently.

I talked to Phraya Raja and discussed making some changes to Eeyd Lek's studies. Phraya Raja seemed to accept everything and did not argue on any point. The problem with the house that has been rented is that we may lose money on the prepaid rental, as it is the winter and difficult to find a tenant. However, it won't be that much and the new arrange-ments for Eeyd Lek will only be around 500 pounds. In other words, his rent and his guardian will be much less than before. Phraya Raja will arrange every thing with Mr Wims.

I think that Eeyd Lek should study French, so that he can speak it fluently and thus go to court in various countries and not lose out, because he sits there silently being unable to speak the language. In the holidays, he should go and stay in France or a French-speaking country such as Belgium. He should stay with a French family, so that he can learn to speak fast and fluently. I have consulted Phraya Raja who agrees. There are three months in the sum-mer holidays, which are more than adequate to find a family. France is considered unsuitable as they are so horrible, so Belgium is the chosen country. Phraya Raja suggested the Siamese consul in Ostend, Monsieur Doma. He has just recently received a dec-oration from you, is a respectable person and well-known in the highest circles, to the extent of asking the Belgian crown prince to dine at this home. He has a large house in Ostend and a wife and son. He should be suitable. I agreed with this suggestion and I expect Phraya Raja will inform you of all the details.

I am studying at the Academy satisfactorily. Some subjects have been completed and, in a short while, there will probably be exams.

I beg to remain Your Majesty's obedient servant,
Chakrabongse

Seated left to right: the Siamese ambassador in London, Phraya Raja Nuprabandhu, Prince Asdang, Prince Chakrabongse, Prince Chudadhuj, Prince Mahidol and Phra

Lipikorn Koson. Standing: Nai Bua, a Siamese official, Phraya Sri Thammasan (Siamese ambassador in Russia), Luang Surayudh, Phraya Sudharm Maitri and Nai Poum.

By October 1905, the situation in the Russian Empire was very serious. It is extraordinary that the Emperor still had time to receive Prince Chakrabongse and his brother. The calm attitude of the Siamese embassy is also very remarkable.

11TH OCTOBER 1905
CHAKRABONGSE TO HM THE KING

THEIR MAJESTIES THE EMPEROR AND EMPRESS RECEIVED ASDANG AND MYSELF TODAY. THEY WERE EXTREMELY KIND AS USUAL. I HAVE TALKED THE MATTER OVER WITH THE SIAMESE MINISTER IN LONDON ABOUT THE ARRANGEMENTS CONCERNING ASDANG. THE SIAMESE MINISTER IN LONDON WILL PROCEED TO LOOK FOR SUITABLE FAMILY AND A TUTOR. THERE ARE CERTAIN DETAILS REQUIRE YOUR MAJESTY'S SANCTION. I WILL WRITE IMMEDI-ATELY AND WHEN YOU HAVE RECEIVED ANY LET-TER AND APPROVE OF IT, PLEASE TELEGRAPH TO THE SIAMESE MINISTER IN LONDON AS SOON AS POSSIBLE. PENDING THE COMPLETION OF ALL ARRANGEMENTS ASDANG HAS NOTHING TO DO

BUT TO WAIT FOR THE FAMILY AND HOUSE. CANNOT BE ARRANGED BEFORE WEEKS THERE-FORE HE WISHES TO REMAIN WITH ME HERE DURING THIS TIME AND I HAVE DECIDED IT IS POSSIBLE TO CONCUR WITH HIS WISH AND LET HIM REMAIN HERE BUT I BEG FOR YOUR MAJESTY'S SANCTION. LEK

30TH OCTOBER 1905
SRIDAMASAN TO HM THE KING

I BEG TO INFORM YOU THAT THERE IS A GENERAL SYSTEMATIC STRIKE IN THIS COUNTRY BEGUN LAST WEDNESDAY. EVERY PRECAUTION IS BEING TAKEN BY THE EMPEROR AND THE AUTHORITIES THOUGH NO VIOLENCE OF A SERIOUS CHARACTER ANTICIPATED. P. CHAKRABONGSE IS STAYING AT WINTER PLACE. ASDANG AT THE LEGATION. BOTH WILL BE QUITE SAFE. TRAVELLING AT PRESENT IMPOSSIBLE OWING TO THE INTERRUP-TION OF RAILWAY COMMUNICATION. UP TO THE PRESENT TIME EVERYTHING IS VERY QUIET HERE AND THERE IS EVERY APPEARANCE OF THE TROU-BLE COMING TO AN END SOON. SRIDAMASAN.

8th November 1905

Your Majesty

At the moment, there is much unrest here and many massive changes, which could almost be called a revolution. However, it is a new sort of revolution of a civilised nature, not like the French one, one hundred years ago.

I had written a little bit in an earlier letter that the situation had arisen because of the intellectuals complaining that things were not running properly here as the officials are no good and can do exactly what they like. Thus, all the decrees and laws are enacted as they wish, with no oversight or control. They have been demanding a parliament and causing various disturbances, such as calling on other intellectuals to stop work. The government has not wanted to accede to their demands, because the general populace doesn't want a parliament, far outnumbers the intellectuals, and furthermore doesn't listen to them. However, the latter group have not given in and have become more forceful by the day. The government does not have enough power to suppress them, as most people support the intellectuals, accusing the government of losing control. In the end, a parliament was granted on 19th the August, but it is composed solely of those whom the government trusts, namely those who are very rich and are genuine citizens. There are two laws – one for those who are rich and another for those who are middle class such as professors, doctors, and university students. The workers have no right to vote for parliamentary representatives because they don't have enough money as laid down in the new law or are not citizens. Most of those who could vote are intellectuals, and so the government did not trust them and it didn't go ahead.

These people were, of course, most displeased and more riots ensued, with calls for everyone to be allowed to vote. They also called for various guarantees such as exist everywhere in Europe. These included guarantees of personal freedom, freedom of speech, freedom of conscience, freedom of meeting, and freedom of the press. They want people to be able to say what they want, or, in other words, criticise the government as much as they like. Printed matter must be the same, and people should be able to meet where they want, and say anything they like. Any religion is to be permitted and can be changed at will and they are not disadvantaged as a result and no one can be imprisoned without trial. The government rejected all these demands, but the intellectuals were determined to get them. So they planned that all the trains throughout the empire should go on strike, as well as all the other workers. Everyone would be inconvenienced and unable to go anywhere, buy anything, or find food. Even the bakers and abattoirs would join in. This plan was carried out on 23rd October. Everyone, whether commoner or noble, was affected, as some things are essential. Those who went on strike attacked those who didn't, so the whole country came to a standstill. People were hungry and in difficulties. The government had no response and didn't know what to do, so they had to give in and there was an announcement by the Emperor agreeing to all their demands. He asked Count Witte to be Prime Minister in order to carry out his wishes. So, Russia will become a constitutional monarchy and not an absolute one.

However, despite granting these concessions, things have not calmed down. The peasants who are free don't plan to do anything except to beat up the students and the intellectuals. They are beating up the students because they have received hardship as result of them. The peasants don't want the things the students are calling for and say they are seeking on the peasants' behalf. They have called on the peasants to do various things such as go on strike. It's fine for them to stop working because they still have food to eat. But for the workers, if they stop working, they have no food. There are many other issues as well and so, when the peasants became free, they have started beating up the students and the intellectuals. In the city and all over, two factions have arisen. One group is composed of citizens with the national flag and pictures of the Emperor, who march about singing hymns in his praise or praying for the Emperor. The other faction is made up of students and workers, who march about, waving red flags (the socialist flag), criticising the government, and calling for a republic and other demands. When the two groups meet, they start fighting, and really fighting, to the extent that people have been killed and the government has had to send troops out to control both parties.

The intellectuals are most unhappy. They have many other demands and are claiming that when they

17th October, 1905 by Ilya Repin.

Count Witte, former Finance Minister and co-author of the "October Manifesto".

It is impossible to summarize the events leading to the 1905 revolution in the space of a few lines. The remarkable aspect in connection with Prince Chakrabongse is how little he reported – perhaps out of fear of worrying his father, or anxiety that telling the truth might lead to him being called home. Interestingly, his analysis seems to put the blame on the intellectuals (he writes the word in English) for fomenting everything.

In March 1905, all higher academic institutions were closed for the rest of the year. Later, a railway workers' strike on 21st October led to a general strike and, by 26th October, more than 2 million were on strike. The army was also restive after their defeat in the Russo-Japanese War,

confirmed by the Treaty of Portsmouth, signed on 5th September. Nevertheless, the army remained loyal enough to be used to supress the uprisings. On 30th October, the so-called October Manifesto drawn up by Count Witte and Alexis Obolenskii, was signed by the Tsar. This granted basic civil rights, allowed political parties, extended the franchise to a certain extent, and established the Duma as the central legislative body. Nevertheless, more strikes in December were only ended by the army.

In 1906, various measures weakened the powers of the Duma, while state suppression and lack of support by the Zemstvos meant it was doomed before it ever got going.

get beaten up, it is because the government has incited the peasants. The government soldiers have shot workers and killed or wounded them, which is something that should not happen. The army should not be involved. Those who are neutral should be protected and also the womenfolk, wives and children of the soldiers. Otherwise, there really will be revolution. The government doesn't know what to do. You can see clearly that the country is being controlled by the intellectuals, who say that the government is oppressive and that they are calling for freedom for the people. Even though the peasants are more than pleased, the intellectuals are asking for more.

For the government to support one side or another is difficult. The peasants are far more numerous, to be sure, but the intellectuals have more power because all the workers are in their hands. If the workers go on strike, there will be riots. If they side with the intellectuals, the peasants will rise up. Thus, the government is in a very difficult position. It seems to me that virtually no one can deal with the situation. Because the two groups want opposing things and both are determined to get their way.

This matter is very interesting, but I can't put all the details into a letter.

I beg to remain Your Majesty's obedient servant,
Chakrabongse

Prince Chakrabongse and Poum with the staff from the Military Academy. Colonel Deguy is at the far left.

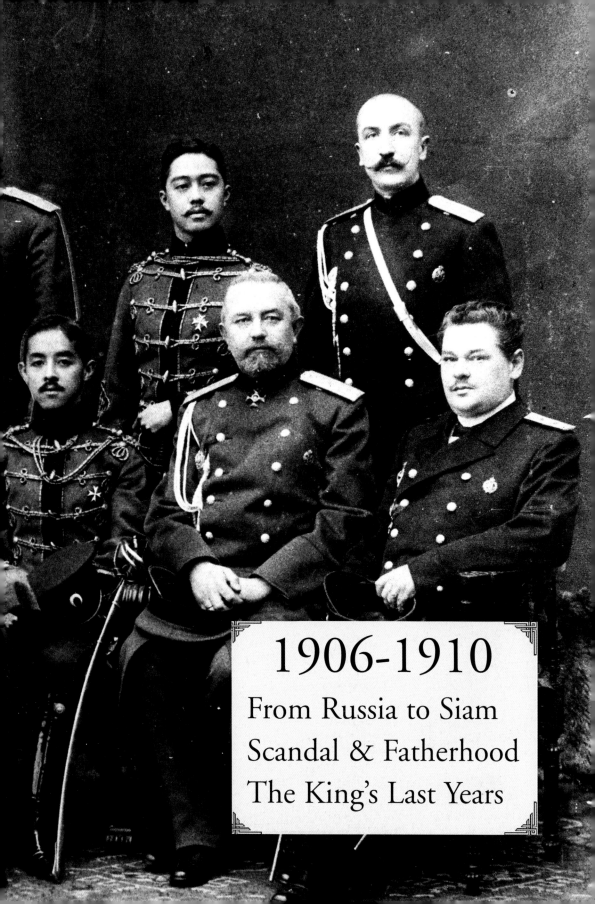

1906-1910

From Russia to Siam
Scandal & Fatherhood
The King's Last Years

Letters from Chakrabongse to Katya – Late 1905-early 1906

As the time drew near for Prince Chakrabongse to leave Russia, these 10 letters from him to Katya (Ekaterina Ivanovna Desnitskaya), whom he had met at Mohovaya Street, the home of Elizaveta Ivanovna Chrapovitskaya in 1905, reveal his true plans. They had fallen in love and were determined to be together. Without a word to either his father or the Tsar, he planned to leave St. Petersburg with his fiancé secretly and marry in Constantinople. The only thing that might thwart their plans was the possibility of having to attend the funeral of King Christian IX of Denmark, who had died on 29th January 1906. In the letters, Chakrabongse refers to leaving on the 25th, a difference in dates arising from the use of the Julian calendar in Russia at that time.

Dear Sister

Today in the afternoon I've been terribly busy, and can't send you a telegram so that's why I'm writing. Please come to Elizaveta Ivanovna for dinner. She will be happy as she keeps asking me when my little sister is coming. As for me, you already know how much I enjoy your company. In fact, it is an urgent desire. But this all depends on your good will. If you are not bored by my company and feel comfortable at Elizaveta Ivanovna's, if your heart suggests you do a kind thing, please come. If you can't for one reason or another, well then nothing can be done. I am very persistent but everything depends on your good will.
I look forward to seeing you tonight.
Your brother

My dear soulmate Katya

The wedding thing has taken a nasty turn. Firstly, the King of Denmark has died. Of course, God Rest His Soul, but he has chosen an inopportune moment to die. The point is, that my father will have to send a representative to the funeral. Usually it is my duty. Of course, I am not eager to go to Denmark now, but if I have to go, our plan about Constantinople will be ruined. It is impossible to manage Denmark and then Constantinople in 8-9 days . . . I've sent a telegram to my father today, asking him to appoint my younger brother (who is now in England) as his representative, for I am very busy getting ready for the departure to Siam and it is inconvenient for me to go.

The point is how my father will react. My brother is still very young, inexperienced and can't speak foreign languages. Probably father will say, "I can't send him, it should be you". Then, I'll have to go. On the other hand, my father is such a sensitive man and loves me so much, that probably he will heed my request and send my brother instead. Anyway, the issue remains open, and we should wait for my father's reply. The trip to Denmark, won't foil our departure, as I'll go there and come back. After that, we will leave together, but unfortunately without Constantinople. I know you will say, "Your damned position again!". Yes, it is not easy to be this stupid Royal Highness.

Moreover, I am constantly being asked to postpone my departure till February. There are several reasons, they have to prepare some things (presents), a letter for my father, a decoration for my mother, etc. I am supposed to take all these things and they worry they won't be done on time by the 25th, as is necessary for the wedding in Constantinople. So it seems we should forget about Constantinople and think of converting to Lutheranism instead. I've made inquiries about this. One pastor here says that he has a brother in Germany who probably can do this. But they would like to see you first, i.e. the pastor here wants to talk to you, to know why you want to convert to Lutheranism, and how firm your decision is. If you decide to do this, the meeting will be tomorrow at 2 pm. You should say that you intend to convert because you don't agree with some aspects of the Orthodox doctrine, for example, its intolerance of other religions, its bureaucratic hierarchy, or whatever comes into your mind. Say nothing about getting married. Tell him that you are leaving Russia for good, going abroad somewhere, to the east possibly. You are in a hurry and wish to do everything in one or two days. Ask him if that is possible. If the answer is positive, ask him to wire to his brother at once in order to get him reply.

What do you think? If he says that nothing can be done, then so be it. But we must try. I thought of this Lutheran plan, only because Constantinople seems problematic. If we fail with Lutheranism, I will try to go to Constantinople at any cost. The question is whether I have to go to Denmark or not. If not, then we could leave on the 25th.

Your Lek

My dear Katya

I've just returned from the Tsar. I've been afforded the honour to wear the Hussar uniform for life. I am very happy, as it would have been hard for me to take it off. I am proud of it and wear it as an ordinary man, not your friend Prince Chakrabongse. The Tsar and Tsarina were very kind and chatty, asking me about my life, etc.

I know nothing about Denmark so far, but our plan remains in force, the tickets have been bought and everything seems to be in order. I'll be very busy these days, saying goodbye to Grand Dukes. On Sunday I am dining with Grand Duke Constantine Constantinovich in Pavlovsk, on Tuesday there is the farewell dinner with the regiment.

Please come to Mohovaya tomorrow, otherwise we probably won't see each other before the departure. By the way, we are leaving on Wednesday, not Thursday (it was my mistake). The train leaves on the 25th at 9.15 pm. So come to Mohovaya and then go to the station. We will discuss the departure later, as it is necessary to check all the details in order to avoid misunderstanding.

You should certainly come tomorrow, for I will get the fateful news about Denmark at last. I hope you slept well last night, instead of pacing about the room. This Denmark business bothers me, as I am afraid I will have to go. Everyone says I will, but let's wait until tomorrow.

Your Lek

My soulmate

I am exhausted, as there is still no telegram about Denmark – I wonder why. If there is no answer at all, it's all right, but if it comes at the last minute, it could ruin our plan. I have no idea why they don't wire. Today I am in a terrible rush. In the morning went to Tsarskoe Selo to have breakfast with Vladimir Alexandrovich, then visited Michael Alexandrovich, then Olga Alexandrovna. When I came back to the city, I hurried upstairs, looking for the telegram. But it was not there. I am absolutely worn out.

In an hour and a half, I have to go to Pavlovsk to dine with Constantine Constantinovich. That's how my day looks. The same thing tomorrow and the day after tomorrow. What hell! How are you? Feeling better? Please take care, your foolish behaviour drives me to despair.

On Wednesday, you should do the following: take someone with your luggage to the station at 8 pm and order them to wait for Alfred. When Alfred comes, your man should give the luggage to him and leave. At 8.30 you go to the station with the ticket that I will give you, find the carriage and the compartment and wait for me. Don't worry. If anybody says this is Prince Chakrabongse's compartment, pay no attention. At the worst, show your ticket and sit there until I come.

See you at Mohovaya tomorrow.

Have you got the portrait?

Your Lek

My dear soulmate

I am going mad. You can't imagine what is going on at Mohovaya. Poum[1] says he will shoot himself, while Elizaveta Ivanovna threatens to take poison. Marusya is worried that she might do it. If she kills herself, Popov will be the next. It's a madhouse in fact. I rush about, listening to each of them and they all blame me.

What can I do? Only Katya could save me, but she is not coming, leaving me alone with this lot.

Now I am being dragged to the restaurant and I can't refuse, as they all take turns to fall in love with Elizaveta Ivanovna. It is so foolish. She can't return their feelings for various reasons, but they all insist they are going to shoot themselves. Can this be called love?

I love Russia and it is hard to leave, but I just can't stand it any more. It is time to go, go, go. You are coming with me to our real motherland to live there for each other's sake. It is true, Katya, and you will

---

1. Poum did fall in love with Mme Chrapovitskaya and confided in Prince Chakrabongse, later giving this as a reason why he did not want to leave Russia.

agree with me. You say unpleasant things (but you don't mean them).

Everything seems to be OK so far. My father's letter has been received, the permission for your passport will come soon. That is the most important thing, all the rest doesn't matter. Thank God, we are leaving in a week. How I long to see you! So, use all means come back on Wednesday. This is only the first letter, I'll write more in the afternoon.

Your Lek

My dear soulmate Katya

We have to leave on January 25th at 9 pm. On the 27th in the evening, we will arrive in Odessa and take a ship to Constantinople on the 28th. On the 29th, we arrive in Constantinople and remain there until January 31st.

On the 1st or 2nd February, we will arrive in Greece, at any rate before Maslennitsa (pancake week), but the ship will dock only for a few hours. On the 4th, it arrives in Alexandria. So it is possible to organise a wedding in Greece, but we must do it quickly and not waste time searching for a priest. We must choose the church and the priest beforehand. Maybe your brother could make inquiries. But please don't tell him that we are in such a hurry. Just ask him about the church and that is all. If you are tired of talking and thinking, send him to me and I'll ask him.

As for the conversian to Lutheranism, we will find out tomorrow. Have you heard any news from the patron (curator of the community)? I'll come to the community tomorrow at 3 o' clock. Will that suit you?

Please cheer up. Nothing is achieved without effort. If you really love your Lek so much, don't give up, we will manage.

Your Lek

Dear soulmate Katya

I'll be very glad to meet your brother. If he can come to the Siamese embassy at 3 pm, I'll be there waiting for him. Here is the address of the embassy: Admiralteyskaya Naberezhnaya (embankment) 6. I'll leave orders that he will be let in and brought to me immediately. It is better than coming to the palace, as now they regard all students with great suspicion and his visit might give rise to a lot of talk.

By the way, I'd like to know how much your brother knows of our secret. Have you told him everything? Please let me know what you have told him tomorrow before 3 pm. Then I will know how to handle him.

Your Lek

I am in a rush now. I hope the girl will not die – at least not today.

Dear soulmate Katya

I've just talked to your brother. He is sure that everything can be settled in Constantinople. I even confessed my fears, but he showed no hesitancy. So don't worry about him. It seems to me that he strongly objects to converting to Lutheranism, so we can agree upon going to Constantinople and having a wedding there. If we fail, it will not be our fault.

Only two problems remain, so far we haven't got your uncle's permission for the passport and my father's letter to the Tsar. With God's help, everything will be settled in time and we will leave on the 25th. I look forward to this happy moment. Nothing else matters, the most important thing is to leave together.

It was unbelievably boring yesterday at Mohovaya, so many people were hanging around. A lady was singing, rather well I would say, but her face was so ugly! Your godmother was also present, she is delighted with you.

Today I have to dine at the General Headquarters. It won't be much fun, but Thank God I can discuss serious military matters there, instead of talking rubbish. There will be some competent people there.

After dinner, I will go to Elizaveta Ivanovna. She also invites you, but it seems to me that you would rather come tomorrow, when I will be able to stay all evening and see more of you. If you come today, you won't come tomorrow, will you? If you can manage both days, it will be great. You can come as usual and I'll join you later. But, at any rate, please promise to come tomorrow. How is the Lyceum pupil doing? He hasn't tried to kiss you, has he?

I beg my darling Katya to cheer up. We are leaving soon and to hell with all the rest. From now on, we will live for the sake of each other.

Your Lek

Dear soulmate Katya

Hooray! We are not going to Denmark. This is great news. As for your request, I am glad to fulfil it immediately. I admire your delicacy and that you feel embarrassed to borrow money from me. But soon we will finish with all this. After the 25th, all my fortune becomes yours. So not a word of this, you will only take. I don't accept any other kind of relationship between husband and wife. We will share everything – money, fortune and our life. Remember, after the 25th, nothing will belong to me, only to us. I beg you, I want it to be that way. Please, never think with a frown that you need to ask me for something. If you need anything, you must just take it. If you save money, save it not for me but for yourself. Don't forget this. I've seen cases were people keep thinking "this is mine, this is his", and as a result become estranged.

I am glad that your brother also shares my opinion that it is unwise to tell your aunt about our departure. As for the picture, you should follow my advice and say you would like to make a copy.

So dearest, there are only two days left and you will be my Katya, only mine and the most beloved forever.

Your Lek
And hateful Prince Chakrabongse as well

My dear soulmate Katya

Have you heard anything from your brother? This uncertainty is awful. I was in Tsarskoe Selo today and have already returned. Everything seems normal, no strikes. I hope you haven't been to any funerals lately.

On Thursday I have to organise a dinner for the regiment – a farewell dinner, boring but necessary. I've been very busy, writing invitations, and some

people visited me, including the Prince of Serbia, who had studied at the Corps des Pages. I'm only just free.

How strange, really, that I'm not doing anything special, but am busy all the time. Tomorrow I am invited to breakfast, on Thursday I have this dinner, on Saturday I will probably have to go somewhere else. I can't stand this.

When will we resolve our problem? It is unbearable when our happiness hangs by a thread. I am so sorry that I won't see you today. You should come to Mohovaya tomorrow.

You are on duty today, aren't you? I hope this girl will not die during your nursing hours, but probably she has died already, poor soul.

I hope you are OK and in good spirits.

Your Lek

More information about Katya, and her life before this and in Siam, can be found in *Katya and the Prince of Siam.*

19th January 1906

Your Majesty

As I told you by telegram, on the 7th of this month, I took my last exam at the Academy and this is the end of my exams in this institution. I received a mark of 12, which is full marks and the highest score in all subjects. Adding all my results together, I got the highest score that anyone could achieve. In the almost 100 years of the Academy's existence, such high marks as these have only been achieved twice before.

Today I went to pay my respects to the Emperor on the occasion of passing these exams. I went to see him, together with Colonel Deguy, my tutor, myself and Nai Poum. The Emperor received us very well. He praised me and showed his great pleasure in the fact that I got full marks in every subject. He presented me with the Order of Saint Vladimir 4th Class, which is never given to non-Russians and, in Russia, is only given for special services or after long government service. It is rather like the Dusadee Mala medal in Thailand. The various Grand Dukes all get the 4th class and above. The Emperor still only has the 4th class to this day. The Emperor explained that he was giving me this medal as he considered me to be a Russian officer, and told me himself that this medal was not awarded to foreigners. It was for that reason that he had chosen to give it to me. After that, the Emperor thanked my tutor, who had supervised my studies and looked after me. He said: "You and I, we were responsible before the King for his welfare (at this moment he pointed at me). Now I think we can say we have done our duty well, I hope His Majesty will be content with us". These were the Emperor's very words. After that, he reminisced about the time when I fell off my horse when I was first in Russia. He explained that it caused him a lot of anxiety. He felt guilty and didn't want to telegram Your Majesty in Bangkok, although he felt that he should. He sat at his desk for several hours debating whether he should send a telegram or not.

Nai Poum was given a gold cigarette case, with a diamond encrusted eagle on the cover, as a reward.

After seeing him in an official capacity, I was invited to have lunch together with the Empress and the imperial children. The Empress praised me and gave her congratulations and also expressed her sor-row that I would be leaving in a short while. After lunch was over, the Tsarevich came in. He is chubby and tall and can walk and run. He is very sweet.

As for the matter of Eeyd Lek, I have arranged everything satisfactorily. I have found a good family with a large house in a very comfortable town in England. He can study to get into university as quickly as possible. As to university, I think he should go to Oxford to study history and get a degree. Afterwards, he can really work. If he were to go to university and not study for a degree, there is no point and it will make him lazy and not study, as he would not have to take an exam.

Nai Bua is someone who is not correct at all, and has some very strange ideas. He wants to keep in control, have Eeyd Lek in the palm of his hand and not let anyone else get close to him. Anyone who is close to him, Nai Bua will find fault with and is always digging for dirt on them. His head is full of envy and stopping anyone from getting close. He only thinks about himself and not Eeyd Lek at all. He may be bad for Eeyd Lek, because he is always trying to manipulate him, telling him to dislike people and not to believe anyone apart from him.

When I was instructed by you to sort out Eeyd Lek's education, Nai Bua listened, and seeing that I would not organise things according to his wishes, he said that everyone was trying to interfere. Everyone thought they could have a hand in things, when in fact it was solely his prerogative. I knew he would say something like that, so I asked him what evidence he could provide to prove he had sole power. Did he have an instruction from Your Majesty, or something else? Of course, he did not, and I was able to produce Your Majesty's telegram to show him. To this, he said anyone could write such a telegram and Your Majesty had not written it yourself. In other words, he was suggesting that I had made the telegram up. I didn't want to escalate matters, so I simply threatened him and said, if he did not want to listen to me, I could ask for him to be recalled, and eventually he shut up. But he is still trying to cause problems. Anything I try and organise, Nai Bua always has a counter argument and makes things difficult. No one in England can stand him. If Your Majesty could recall him, it would be a very good thing.

I beg to remain Your Majesty's obedient servant,

Chakrabongse

8TH JANUARY 1906
PHYA SRIDAMASAN TO PRINCE SOMMOT

I BEG TO INFORM YOU THAT HRH PRINCE OF
PHITSANULOK HAS PASSED THE FINAL EXAMINA-
TION TODAY. HE HAS OBTAINED THE HIGHEST
MARKS IN EVERY SUBJECT. POUM WAS SECOND.

WRITTEN ON THE TELEGRAM TO BE SENT ON:
MOST HAPPY TO LEARN YOU HAVE PASSED FINAL
EXAMINATION WITH HIGHEST MARKS. ACCEPT
AFFECTIONATE CONGRATULATIONS AND BLESSINGS
FROM YOUR FATHER AND MOTHER.
M. R.

15TH JANUARY 1906
CHAKRABONGSE TO HM THE KING

IN CONSEQUENCE OF MY DEPARTURE FROM ST.
PETERSBURG THE RUSSIAN OFFICER ATTACHED
TO ME WHO WAS BEFORE MY PERSONAL TUTOR AS
COLONEL HUME WAS TO THE CROWN PRINCE OF
SIAM, WILL BE LEFT WITHOUT EMPLOYMENT FOR
SOME TIME. HE HAS DONE MOST SPLENDID SERV-
ICE, BEING CONSTANTLY WITH ME ARRANGING
EVERY THING CONCERNING MY EDUCATION. HE
HAS RECEIVED ABSOLUTELY NO PAY FROM YOUR
MAJESTY. I THINK IT ADVISABLE THAT YOUR
MAJESTY SHOULD GRANT HIM NOW THE SUM OF
5,000 ROUBLES AS THE VERY BEST FAVOUR.
IN CASE YOUR MAJESTY FINDS NO OBJECTION
I BEG THAT THE MONEY TO BE REMITTED NOW
(BY) TELEGRAPH. I ALSO BEG YOUR MAJESTY
TO TELEGRAPH TO THE EMPEROR SAYING YOU
ARE GREATLY SATISFIED WITH HIS SERVICE.
THIS WILL HAVE A GREAT MEANING FOR HIM.
LEK

HM THE KING TO HM THE EMPEROR
TO HIS MAJESTY THE EMPEROR

I AM MOST GRATIFIED AT THE SUCCESSFUL EXAMI-
NATION MY SON LEK HAS PASSED IN THE RUSSIAN
ARMY WHICH I CANNOT BUT THINK THAT IT WAS
DUE TO YOUR MAJESTY'S GRACIOUS COMMAND
FOR ALL THE ARRANGEMENTS FOR HIS EDUCATION
WHICH HE HAS COMPLETED AND IS NOW ABLE TO
RETURN TO SIAM AND I FEEL MOST DEEPLY

THANKFUL TO YOUR MAJESTY FOR ALL THAT HAS
BEEN DONE BY YOUR MAJESTY'S ORDERS AND
FOR KINDEST TREATMENT AND HONOUR YOUR
MAJESTY HAS BEEN GRACIOUSLY PLEASED TO
BESTOW ON MY SON, ESPECIALLY THE MOST TOUCH-
ING MANNER WITH WHICH YOU RECEIVED HIM IN
THE LAST AUDIENCE. YOUR MAJESTY IS PERFECTLY
RIGHT IN THINKING THAT I AM THOROUGHLY SATIS-
FIED AND I BEG ALSO TO MENTION THAT I AM THOR-
OUGHLY SATISFIED WITH THE SERVICE OF COLONEL
DEHAY [DEGUY], THE RUSSIAN OFFICER WHO WAS
ATTACHED TO MY SON BY YOUR MAJESTY'S COM-
MAND. WITH BEST REGARDS TO YOUR MAJESTY
AND THE EMPRESS AND BEST WISHES FOR THE
HAPPINESS OF YOU BOTH.

CHAKRABONGSE TO HM THE KING

I WAS RECEIVED BY THE EMPEROR TODAY. HE
WAS EXTREMELY KIND. GAVE ME ORDER OF ST.
VLADIMIR WHICH HAD NEVER BEEN GIVEN TO
FOREIGNERS BEFORE AND GIVEN FOR SPECIAL
MERIT. ONLY YOU WILL REMEMBER SEEING THE
EMPEROR WEARING THIS ORDER ALL THE TIME. THE
EMPEROR WAS PLEASED TO SAY I HAVE FINISHED
EXAMINATIONS IN A BRILLIANT MANNER. HE
EXPRESSED THE HOPE THAT YOU ARE SATISFIED AND
THAT HE FELT RESPONSIBILITY TOWARDS YOU, HAV-
ING TAKEN YOUR SON TO EDUCATE. HE HOPES YOU
WILL SAY HE HAS DONE WELL AND THAT YOU WILL
BE PLEASED WITH HIM. HIS KIND WORDS WERE
MOST TOUCHING.

LEK

28TH JANUARY 1906
THE EMPEROR TO KING CHULALONGKORN

I THANK YOUR MAJESTY FOR YOUR GRACIOUS
TELEGRAM. YOUR SON LEK PASSED ALL HIS EXAMI-
NATIONS BRILLIANTLY. IN RECOGNITION OF HIS
EXCELLENT SERVICE AND CONDUCT I AM READY TO
LEAVE HIM IN THE LISTS OF MY GUARD HUSSARDS
WITH YOU MAJESTY'S KIND PERMISSION. THIS WILL
ENABLE HIM TO FEEL ALWAYS AT HOME WHENEVER
HE COMES BACK TO RUSSIA. WITH MY BEST
REGARDS TO YOUR MAJESTY AND THE QUEEN.

NICOLAS

Back row, left to right: Phraya Samosorn Samprakarn, Prince Purachatra, Prince Chakrabongse, rest unidentified. Front row, l to r: Mom Chart Dedudom (M. R. Sataan Snidwongse), Prince Chirapravati, the Crown Prince, Phraya Siharaj Dechochai (M. R. Arun Chatrakul). The rest are unidentified.

21st May 1906

19th April 1906

Dear Lek

I have received the letter regarding the King of Serbia[1] presenting me with the Order of the White Eagle.

So I suppose we have to give him something in return, or can we just not worry about this? It pains me to give the Chakri as I am very protective of it.

Siamindra

4th May 1906

Dear Lek

Luang Rattana Napadi has sent me a telegram informing me that Nai Poum will not return to Bangkok and has resigned from the civil service. What's this all about?

In addition, what is the meaning of the report in a newspaper about your personal life and someone calling herself Madame de Phitsanulok?[2]

Siamindra

1. Peter I of Serbai (1844-1921) reigned as the last King of Serbia, 1903-1918, and as King of Serbs, Croats and Slovenes 1918-1921.
2. This refers to Katya who used Phitsanulok as her surname as Prince Chakrabongse was Prince of Phitsanulok. She stayed in Singapore at first while Prince Chakrabongse went on to Bangkok.

Letter opposite
1. This refers to Elizaveta Nikolaevna Chrapovitskaya, the estranged wife of a wealthy colonel in the Hussars, who built a French-style chateau in Muromtseva (see p. 387) some 200 km from Moscow near Vladimir. Designed by Petr Boytsov, the main house had 80 rooms, there was a cascade of ponds, a stable, a lodge, a steward's house, music and boat pavilions, a wharf at the pond, a water tower and a theatre. However, the most unusual thing was the building of a theatre which was a miniature copy of the Maly Theatre in Moscow

Your Majesty

I have heard the news from the Ministry of Foreign Affairs that Luang Rattana Napadi has reported to Sadej Lung that I told him that Nai Poum had fallen in love with a Russian woman, who is already married[1], and for this reason is refusing to return to Bangkok and wants to stay on. This report was to be presented to Your Majesty. I have been thinking about this and feel that when Your Majesty sees the report and compares it with what I have said, the two will not accord with each other. Your Majesty will say that I am making things up. The truth is difficult to determine. Before I left Petersburg, Nai Poum came to beg me to request of Your Majesty that he be allowed to stay on, so that he could study, and he also told me that he was in love with a woman. He said that the woman would suffer greatly and that she might kill herself if he left. At the time, I did not particularly believe his story, because I knew other reasons why Nai Poum did not want to leave, such as he had been so comfortable here and other officers were encouraging him to stay, as I told Your Majesty in my previous letters.

The reason I suggested he stay on was that I feared, that, if he was forced to return, he would make a fuss and cause a scandal. Also, I thought that Phraya Sri Thammasan agreed he should stay. So I told Luang Rattana Napadi, as he was staying on too. I asked him to keep an eye on Nai Poum and then send him back. I explained that he was in love with a woman, as I needed to tell him enough for him to understand the situation. At that point, I was about to go to the train to leave and so did not explain everything, only the part about the woman. That is why Luang Rattana Napadi talked only about the woman.

In fact, I made further enquiries and found that the matter of the woman was not the main issue. It is most unlikely that Poum has fallen in love with her to the extent of wanting to change his nationality and make a scandal. The woman is over 12 years older than Nai Poum, is already married and also unwell which makes any sexual relations inappropriate. I have found all this out and have observed that Poum does not want to return, thinking that life in Europe is more comfortable than it really is. Another thing is

Nai Poum in the uniform of the Hussars.

Elizaveta Nikolaevna Chrapovitskaya taken during the First World War.

that Nai Poum begged me not to tell everyone, as the news would get abroad about the woman. Instead, he asked me to say simply that he wished to study further. I agreed and once I had given my word, I felt obliged to keep it. He had told me a secret and believed he could trust me, so to go and spread the story seemed wrong. In his report, Luang Rattna Napadi says it is a secret, but tells it all the same, which is strange. For my part, if someone says something is a secret, I treat it as such and don't tell anyone. Thus, when Pi Chira asked me what was going on, I did not tell him. Only when he suggested that it must be something to do with a woman, did I say it probably was. Then when he asked me further, I told him that it was to do with a woman, but I did not give any details because I felt they were not key and that other factors were more important. I think Nai Poum has focused on the woman aspect, because how could he say to me that he didn't want to come home and wanted to stay there? I might have managed to force him to come. That's why he brought other factors into the discussion, so I would let the matter go

until I had left. At that point, Nai Poum decided to change his nationality. It was pure trickery.

I am sorry if this report bothers Your Majesty with petty details, but it is because the report will suggest that I have been telling falsehoods, that I have felt it necessary to explain things.

I beg to remain Your Majesty's obedient servant, ***Chakrabongse***

The French-style chateau built by Vladimir Chrapovitsky.

Once the truth of Prince Chakrabongse's marriage became clear, the letters between king and son became angry and infrequent. The responses of Prince Chakrabongse to his father's hurt and disappointed letters have not been preserved.

16th June 1906

Dear Lek

I received your letter and read it with a beating heart. The reason for this was not only because I was angry. In fact, I was sad and upset more than angry because the love I feel for you is absent at the moment. You know all this only too well. Normally love means that one wishes only the best for those we love. When one sees someone one loves making a fool of himself, it makes one feel very uncomfortable on their behalf. One wants them to be liked and respected. Everyone had confidence in you, but now they see you in a situation, which is not respected and they feel you have thought only of yourself. You have not stopped to consider whether the consequences will be good or bad. You have lacked any discretion. You have failed to consider all the angles carefully, you have not shown any endurance. You lack perseverance and the ability to control your desires and this will not be helpful to you establishing yourself and being successful in the future. You have given in to your infatuation and allowed yourself to be brought down from a good position. In sum, I can't hope to rely on you any more and you can't be trusted to do the work you need to do. Self-control is essential for people in important positions and they should not be ruled by their heart in difficult situations. You have selfishly put your own desires above all others and behaved badly in ways too numerous to mention.

When someone like me, desiring so much for you to be in as secure and good position as possible, sees you creating these obtacles, how do you think I feel? Of course, I am going to feel desolate. This is what makes me feel so sad. So, despite the fact that my love for you has not lessened, I cannot rejoice in your happiness and I cannot feel joyful.

The reason why I have not said anything and seemed to be sulking was because I could see you did not want to listen. I am a man too, and I have been crazy about women in my time. It is normal to feel sad and unhappy. This is why I stayed calm, waiting until you realised that you were going the wrong way, achieving no benefit to yourself apart from a brief satisfaction. It is a desire that will not endure in your heart in the future. Better to realise how it is and to understand that this one mistake will affect you for the rest of your life. It is normal that young people fall in love and are taken with desire once, or even twice. But when you come to your senses, you can come back to where you were. As a human being, you will not love someone physically all your life and, if you see that you are entrapped, then you should be able to free yourself.

I feel sorry for the woman, truly sorry for her, so my aim is not that you should abandon her, as this would endanger her. But I want you to free yourself from her and compensate her for the damage you have caused as appropriate.

What I have said is already too much, but I want you to understand that I am so consumed by anger that I am unable to see the happiness or unhappiness of others, or that I can't sympathise with those who are in love. But the sorrow that arises from my love for you cannot be exchanged for mercy, as I do not love the other party. I only love one side and wish the best for that party. When I think it is the wrong path, I am full of sorrow and I can't force a smile. If you want me to cry at any point, that would be much easier. This is what is in my heart, so what other punishment could I exact? If you want me to be cheerful as before, it would come from seeing there are no obstacles to your future success.

All that I have said is just a start. There are other issues, that might make me breathe less easily in the future, but they are complex and better not spoken about yet. For now, please just think about what I have said.

[Unsigned]

Katya in 1906.

17th June 1906

Dear Lek

I have received your response and I can see that you have understood some of the points in my letter, although you have mis-evaluated your position and can't see all the implications. So I want to add a few more words.

You say that you can see the obstacles to your success and faith in you. However, I was not referring just to you, but have put myself and you in the same place. I have taken the views of other royals, officials and ordinary people into account as well. It's not just that I don't approve or trust the situation, everyone from Thais to foreigners feel the same.

Another misconception is that your analysis is based on you being like an official and me being the king, so that if you work well, I will be fair to you and

reward you. But that is wrong, you are my son, and so how I behave to you is as a father to his son. Thus, whether you please me or not, it is as a child will please or displease his father. For others, you are in a position of being close to me and therefore someone whom people look to. No one cares what that wretched Poum does, but you are someone on whom people have pinned their hopes and trust. If you are in a bad position, then, of course, you are the object of gossip and conjecture.

The question of obstacles to your success lies in the fact that if people look down on you or are anxious, it will make it difficult to progress. If you work hard, you will get success to a certain extent, but obtaining success as a member of the royal family earns greater respect than being an ordinary official. If that aspect has been damaged, you'll just have the respect due to an ordinary person who has worked hard and, in fact, less as they will know that you have behaved badly.

In addition, if you want to look at it in the *farang* way, that this is a personal matter, don't think that such behaviour is tolerated either. Rulers have to prohibit such things. In fact, the Thai way is better – if something is not completely in opposition, one accepts it. In this case, it is not just Thais who will criticise you. *Farang* will also gossip about you and respect you less. Accordingly, when you think just of changing my mind, it won't improve things that much. When you are in a high position, you are the object of scrutiny. If you make a mess, you will be observed and be the object of dislike. And, however much you are lifted up, it won't do much good. Please consider thoroughly what I have said previously and this time. It is the truth, and is spoken frankly. Don't let pre-existing ideas cloud your vision. Once you have seen clearly, then you can consider what you can do next, and only then make a decision.

Chulalongkorn

From 1907 there are only two surviving, short and factual letters from Prince Chakrabongse to his father. To date, no letters from his father to him have been found from that year.

The most likely explanation must be that during his second trip to Europe (27th March until 17th November 1907), King Chulalongkorn no longer felt the need to write to his grown-up son.

13th February 1907

Your Majesty

The Defence Minister[1] has instructed me to take the military cadets to perform manoeuvres in Ratchaburi, with the cadets departing on 15th February and staying there until the 12th March[2].

For this reason, I beg Your Majesty's leave to take the said students to Ratchaburi, leaving the military college at 11 pm on the 14th and taking the train.

Then, on the 17th at midday, I will return to Bangkok in order to celebrate Your Majesty taking up residence in the new throne hall[3]. Once the ceremony is over, I beg leave to return to Ratchaburi until the military students are due to return, namely 12th March.

I beg to remain Your Majesty's obedient servant,
Chakrabongse

23rd December 1907

Your Majesty

The first company of Sappers will go to Ratchaburi to test exploding a fort, a camp, a field and various other things using gunpowder which has recently been sent to us according to a special recipe. The Ministry of Defence has authorised me to take some officer cadets to go and study the exercise. For this reason, I ask for Your Majesty's leave to go to Ratchaburi on the 27th of December and I will come back to see Your Majesty on the 30th of the same month.

I beg to remain Your Majesty's obedient servant,
Chakrabongse

1. The minister of defence was Prince Chirapravati.
2. Prince Chakrabongse was appointed Commandant of the Army Cadet School when he first returned to Siam.
3. This was the Amporn Sathan Throne Hall, completed that year.

Paruskavan Palace shortly after its completion.

On March 28th 1908, Prince Chakrabongse and Katya had a baby boy. Replying to a letter informing him (missing), the king wrote a harsh reply to Prince Chakrabongse that he would not allow the boy to be a royal. This was later changed by the Prince's brother, on his accession to the throne as King Vajiravudh, and Chula was made a *mom chao* and later elevated to the *phra ong chao* level of prince.

2nd April 1908

To Lek

I received your letter of 29th March but, as it was a holiday, I was very busy and unable to reply.

Now I will answer the last section of your letter first. The things that I said to your mother are things I said in anger overall and the sort of thing that husbands and wives discuss in private, when they are speaking openly. Inheritance in Thailand is in the control of the King. I have appointed a crown prince, but have not gone any further than that. No one can think that they will be the heir after that. All those children who are *chao fa* or *phra ong chao* princes, or younger brother princes, could be chosen as the next heir, but there is no certainty when that might happen. Anyone who gives an oath of allegiance, but behaves in such a way when he has not yet been chosen or elevated, seems to be acting without foundation. Also, I refer you to your earlier letter in which, when you did not yet have a child, you said you did not care whether any child would be a member of the royal family. Now that you have one, you feel sorry for him and want him to be a royal. This is an example of saying something and not meaning it. When it was not a reality, you said one thing, then when it became an actuality you regret it and ask to be allowed to choose again. Speaking just for the sake of eloquence, without considering the consequences and changing your mind, will not lead people to respect you and I am not referring just to this matter.

In this case, Thai and *farang* traditions do not differ – the King has the right to choose if someone is to be royal or not. They can confer position and remove it. Those who are royal are so because the King appointed them.

You say it reflects badly on the position of your mother. Believe me, it reflects badly on me too, so why would you try and separate us? I consider that allowing him to be a royal would reflect worse on my honour, than not allowing him to be. I have many other children. If I were to agree in this case, it would set a precedent, and they would have children with no matter whom all over the place. I would have to accept them all as royal and it would look very bad. Having gone off and found a foreign woman, you must abide by *farang* customs and nowhere would consider this child a royal. Before saying I have no compassion, just consider the numerous cases of foreign royals who have wives of whom the king does not approve. So let me say one final time – I will not allow him to be royal.

Siamindra

Prince Chakrabongse and his son, shortly after he was born. At first, Queen Saovabha gave him the name Pongchak, later changed to Chula. His nickname was Nou, meaning mouse.

With his nanny Chom in Paruskavan Palace.

Prince Chakrabongse, Chula and Katya.

Chula and Katya.

6th April 1908

Your Majesty

Headteacher Khun Inthara Prasat of the Military Academy has edited a volume of writings, which has now been published. He has asked me to present a copy to Your Majesty and I now beg to do this along with a letter that he has written.

I beg to remain Your Majesty's obedient servant,
Chakrabongse

19th July 1908

Your Majesty

In the matter of my house, having heard Your Majesty say that at this time it is impossible to find a place by the river, and if there was anywhere it would be near the sawmill and therefore inconvenient, I agreed with Your Majesty and had accepted that I would settle for some land elsewhere in a place Your Majesty saw fit. However, I remained concerned about a landing stage and a boat house. Having looked into the matter, I have found a place belonging to Sadet Mae, between the palace of Pi Pen and Phraya Angkaraj[1].

This was formerly the site of the Saovabha School which has now been moved, and so it has been left vacant and is not used for anything. Accordingly, I asked my mother for this land and she has given it to me. And there is enough room for a boat house and a landing stage. One problem is that it abuts the city wall and the gate there, which is in fact very small, through which vehicles cannot pass. I have noticed that Pi Pen's palace has taken down the wall and made a new palace wall, so I am thinking that if a little more was demolished, it would not be a problem. Accordingly I am requesting to take down the city wall in that area, from the walls of Pi Pen's palace to those of Phraya Angkaraj's house. If I receive Your Majesty's gracious permission, I can organise this myself, although I would like Your Majesty's authority to use the bricks from this wall to landfill the site.

I beg to remain Your Majesty's obedient servant,
Chakrabongse

24th August 1908

Your Majesty

As in September the Cadet school will be closed and the students on holiday, the Ministry of Defence has given permission for me to go and investigate the case of the quartermaster student in Nakhon Sawan, and from there go on to Phitsanulok province.

Accordingly, I am writing to request Your Majesty's permission to visit these two provinces from the 30th August until the 19th September.

I beg to remain Your Majesty's obedient servant,
Chakrabongse

1. This later became Chakrabongse House. While Paruskavan Palace was taken by the government in 1932, the Ta Tien land was private property and so remained in the family.

A class from the Military Cadet School.

1909 saw a softening in the King Chulalong-korn's attitude to Prince Chakrabongse. No doubt, favourable reports from Queen Saovabha regarding her grandson and daughter-in-law (see *Katya and the Prince of Siam*) began to placate him. In addition, the king asked his son for help with various matters – from banquets for foreign royals to the education of Prince Asdang and security matters. By 1910, the king was very depressed about various ministers and their lack of input, ongoing problems in the Ministry of Justice, and a three-day strike by the Chinese in China-town. The only cheerful news was progress on the building of the Ananta Samakom throne hall and Baan Puen Palace in Petchaburi.

26th February 1909

Lek

Even though we've been angry with each other from time to time, I haven't seen you for a long time. I'm missing you. If you are free on Saturdays, do come and have dinner with me once a week, as this will make me feel better.

Siamindra

The interior of the Amporn Sathan Throne Hall was a treasure trove of objects bought or ordered in Europe.

10th March 1909

Dear Lek

I have received the catalogues and have decided to draw a plan and send it to Charoon[1] to find the items I need, as the rattan stuff is mainly for use on the terrace. Then there are two rooms inside – one is a dining room, the other a reception room. I am thinking of making the dining room into a room where one can sit as well, just like the rooms in ordinary people's homes. France is cheaper than England.

As for eating together on Saturday, it should be as we discussed, except for when there is other business. We can miss some from time to time and we don't need to say why.

Siamindra

15th March 1909

Lek

Tomorrow, I have to have a cabinet meeting unfortunately, so we will have to postpone the date for having dinner. I hear that Prince Nara[2] is going to perform a play . . . So I would like you to come on Tuesday.

Siamindra

18th April 1909

Dear Lek

Chira has told me about Medi Khan applying to join government service and wishing to change his nationality. I would like to know more about this extraordinary happening and whether you knew him or not. How old is he? And can we check him out, apart from Petersburg or Berlin, regarding his behaviour in the past.

Siamindra

1. Prince Charoonsakdi Kritakara was ambassador in Paris from 1906 to 1909, and again from 1912-1928.
2. Prince Narathip had a theatre troupe known as the Neramitr troupe.

The Military Cadet School, Bangkok.

17th May 1909

Your Majesty

I know that Your Majesty has become aware that I have said that I planned to become a monk during this Rains Retreat period. However, now something urgent has occurred which means that I need to postpone this plan, even though I had not yet presented the said plan to Your Majesty. When I heard the news had reached Your Majesty's ears through others, I was anxious that Your Majesty would criticise me for pretending to say I would enter the monkhood, but when it came to it, I would find an excuse not to. Accordingly, I beg this opportunity to explain everything to Your Majesty.

I have long wanted to enter the monkhood, but I waited, as I wanted first to serve Your Majesty and prove myself in government work. This year, having established the Cadet School on a firm footing, I planned to ask your permission to become a monk.

I consulted Pi Chira about this but he did not agree. He said that my work would suffer, to which I replied that this juncture seemed rather suitable, as my duties in the the school are those that anyone could take on, provided they followed the system. And to find someone to replace me for four months should not be very difficult.

However, Pi Chira still did not approve and, after arguing about this at length, I decided that I would present the matter to Your Majesty and ask Your

Majesty to decide. I wrote this letter on Saturday 12th, but before I could send it, I received a telegram from Pi Chira, asking me to go and see him in Ratchaburi on the 16th. I, of course, went as instructed and returned to Bangkok on the same day. Pi Chira told me that he had ordered Mom Chart Dej-udom[1] to be Deputy Minister of Agriculture and the position of Chief of Staff of the Army is thus vacant. You have instructed that Bavoradej should go to be ambassador in Paris, leaving no one to become Chief of the General Staff and the army is also short of two generals. If I were to become a monk in this year, that shortfall would rise to three and, at this time, it is not possible to find anyone capable of this position, as those who will have the ability in the future are still too junior. Pi Chira wants me to take on the role of Chief of the General Staff[3] together with my current position as Director of the Cadet School. He said otherwise Mom Narend would have to come down from Nakhon Ratchasima, but then there would be no one to replace him there. Pi Chira asked me if in my opinion there were any officers ready to be promoted to general, and I had to say that there were none.

This being the case, Pi Chira said that my desire to enter the monkhood this year would adversely

1. Mom Chart Dej-udom (M. R. Sathanklang Snidwongse), 1866-1940, studied in Denmark and became an army general before moving to the Department of Agriculture.
2. Prince Bavoradej (1877-1947) was one of the sons of Prince Naret, who was famous later for leading the eponymous rebellion.
3. Prince Chakrabongse was Chief of the General Staff from January 1909 until his death in 1920.

17th May 1909

Prince Chakrabongse when he was commandant of the Military Cadet School, Bangkok.

Lek

I have received your letter telling me that you have accepted the position of Chief of the General Staff and that accordingly will not be entering the monkhood.

I am more delighted that you are undertaking this work than by anything else. When I saw that two generals were being removed out of necessity, I was worried, but this is an important post and I beg you to do it to the best of your ability. Why do you have to become a monk anyway? You can do that whenever you have some spare time.

Siamindra

6th July 1909

To my son Lek

affect the government. All that would happen if I were to take over is that I would be at the Academy less, which is not a major problem. The problem of the lack of generals is a more serious one.

I have to agree with him on this point and, for this reason, I have abandoned my monkhood plans until there is a more suitable moment, as it is really a personal matter and work is more important. All that I have told Your Majesty is completely true and Pi Chira can testify to that.

I am very sorry that I cannot be a monk as I had wished, and I understand it will give people the opportunity to mock me, as they see me as a sort of *farang* and say why would I want to enter the monkhood. But I don't care what other people say, I am only concerned that Your Majesty knows the truth and, accordingly, I have written this long letter and I am sorry if I have overstepped the mark.

I beg to remain Your Majesty's obedient servant,

Chakrabongse

I have heard from your mother that you will take Eeyd Lek to study at the Military Cadet School. That is a good thing. Monsieur Ramlay[1], who has been hired to teach English, receives his salary from the Royal Household, but if you want to borrow him, Chameun Sri is the person at the palace who is involved in his duties. In fact, he is the person who receives all the reports. Now that Eeyd Lek is going to be at the Cadet School, take that Ramlay to help out, so that there is more time to study and divide up the work as appropriate. It's not that I want Ramlay to be a soldier, but to be a private teacher. His salary can come from the palace and you would just have to oversee him. He could come to you for advice and discuss how and what he should teach. Tell Phra Nai Sri what you want. I have told him to send him already.

Siamindra

1. Monsieur Carmel Ramlay (or Ramlet) was hired as a private tutor to Prince Asdang. Unfortunately, it has proved impossible to find any further information on him.

7th July 1909

Your Majesty

I have received Your Majesty's letter dated 6th July in which Your Majesty has asked me to look after the education of my younger brother Eeyd Lek. I feel very honoured. I am extremely pleased that I can repay some of Your Majesty's goodness to me in a personal capacity and I will organise things as Your Majesty suggests, so that everthing is as successful as it can be to the best of my ability.

Having reflected on this at length, I feel that trying to organise things as between two brothers might not be the best way. It is true that I am his older brother, but I have no authority to tell Eeyd Lek what to do. All I can really do is give him advice and if he ignores it, I cannot punish him to make him respect me. Accordingly, I wonder whether if I had the authority which came from his being in the army as well, things might be easier?

May I therefore respectfully request that, if Your Majesty agrees, the Minister of Defence could issue an order that Eeyd Lek be loaned to the command department of the Army Cadet School. That would be most suitable, as for the Ministry of Defence to issue this order is not wrong in any way, as Eeyd Lek is already a Lieutenant unattached to a regiment in the First Infantry Guards regiment. Once Your Majesty has given your permission, the commander of the Ministry of Defence will be happy to order the transfer of Eeyd Lek from the Royal Guards Regiment to be with the command centre of the Military Academy. I will then have authority over him, in my capacity as commandant of the Cadet School, to give Eeyd Lek any orders as appropriate.

Eeyd Lek's studies, based on the timetable I intend to implement, will include him fulfiling the duties of a lieutenant in the Senior Cadet School, as well as arranging particular studies for him as well.

For his first day, his program will be as follows:

At 6 am until 7.30 am, he will come and train the cadets and other solders. Then from 9 till 12, a special tutor will instruct him in soldiering and how to command.

In the afternoon, M. Ramlay will come and teach him Western disciplines, such as foreign languages, literature, etc.

In the evening he should report to Your Majesty in case he is needed for something. This it how it will be on weekdays and Saturdays, with a full day off on Sundays.

I think that if the program goes like this, Eeyd Lek will receive instruction both in specific subjects and in how to train and lead people, which will be very important when he enters government service in whatever role. In addition, he will have had experience in a lowly role as well, rather than simply turning up as the boss. Being a soldier is a strict discipline and he can't play up. I think it will be a very good thing, as, at the moment, the thing that is lacking in Eeyd Lek is any discipline.

I beg to venture that in a year or two, Eeyd Lek will have been trained to take on any government position Your Majesty sees fit.

In that which concerns Monsieur Ramlay, Chameun Sri Sorarak has consulted with me and we have decided that after the new program has been implemented, he will bring Monsieur Ramlay to see me and I will be in charge of him from then on.

I am undertaking this task with the intention of repaying Your Majesty's great goodness and hope that it will be of benefit in the future to my younger brother, but if I do something wrong, please forgive me.

I beg to remain Your Majesty's obedient servant,
Chakrabongse

8th July 1909

Dear Lek

I received your reply regarding the plans for Eeyd Lek and am very satisfied. I have written to Chira for him to issue the order for Eeyd Lek to enter government service in the Headquarters of the Cadet School.

The problem with Eeyd Lek is that he has not learned to think for himself and is easily influenced. The important thing is to teach him to stand on his own two feet. I am giving you authority to organise his studies, as you see fit, including the foreign studies and military matters.

Siamindra

Amporn Sathan Throne Hall
10th August 1909

To Prince Chakrabongse Bhuvanath

I received your letter dated 9th of this month regarding the military studies of Eeyd Lek and that he is studying hard and with understanding. I have also received the report from Mr Ramlay regarding his general studies. I am happy that his education is on a firm basis, that he is trying hard and is coming to see me in the evening from time to time. If he wants to go with you on a trip, this time there is no particular work or necessity for him to stay.

Siamindra

28th August 1909

Your Majesty

Following Your Majesty's letter asking me to tell Mr Peel[1], about Eeyd Noi meeting with Lady Gage on the wishes of Mr Peel, I only met him yesterday for the first time since coming back from Petchaburi and told him of Your Majesty's wishes. He was very pleased, thanked Your Majesty profusely, and told me that he had also received a letter from his younger sister saying that Eeyd Noi had gone to see her.

I am awaiting a telegram from Prince Damrong, as to whether the water in the Petchaburi River is high enough to use the steam launch to come and see Your Majesty, but I still haven't heard, so I don't know when I can come, although I am very anxious to, as I am thinking of Your Majesty and Sadet Mae very much.

I beg to remain Your Majesty's obedient servant,
Chakrabongse

2nd November 1909

To my son Lek

I have had the letter with the report from Mr Ramlay. Truly, I am very sad about Eeyd Lek and his lackadaisical approach. He lacks a sense of direction, and just wants to have a good time. I'm worried that he's in the habit of starting something and then becoming bored. He'll be a soldier for a while and then give up. What can we do? I suppose we have to persevere.

We need to keep Mr Ramlay. If we ask him to stop half way through, that would be even worse. But I want Eeyd Lek to promise one thing – he must stay in government service. Why should he be placed in a job where there are already plenty of people? If another was added it would be a waste of money. I don't really understand his character and have only come across someone like that once. To try and praise him to Prince Devawongse, I wouldn't know what to say. You have seen him more and may undertand him better, so perhaps you can talk to the prince [Devawongse] and persuade him. Maybe he can teach him and use him. He needn't promise to take him into the foreign service and appoint him to an embassy, but if he turned out well and was employable, I would not be against that, but would see it as a good thing.

Siamindra

10th December 1909

To Lek

Your mother has a very bad pain in her ear and I am worried she might have a cyst. Professor Berger is an ear, nose and throat specialist. If he could have a look, it would be a good thing. Even if he did not treat her, it would be good to know what's wrong. However, that chap can't speak Thai and his English is limited. If Prince Naris acts as interpreter, it should be more or less all right, but if you could bring him along and ask him everything, it could be even clearer.

Siamindra

20th December 1909

To Lek

Grand Duke Michael[2] has died. Should I ask the Emperor for news or not? I used to know Grand Duke Alexander and I think I should enquire.

Siamindra

1. Arthur Peel (1861-1952) was British ambassador in Bangkok between 1909-1915. His sister's son was at Eton with Eeyd Noi.
2. Grand Duke Michael Nicholaevich (1832-18 December 1909) was the fourth son and seventh child of Tsar Nicholas I.

Visit of Duke Johann Albrecht of Mecklenburg (from 1907, Regent of Brunswick). Front from left to right: Prince Marupong Siriphat[1], Prince Paribatra, the Duchess of Mecklenburg (Princess Elizabeth), the King, the Duke, Princess Prasong Som.

In the back, second from the left, Nai Tiem (formerly a candidate to go to Russia with Prince Chakrabongse), together with the entourage of the Duke. Photographed in front of the Utthayan Bhumi Sathien Throne Hall.

24th December 1909

To Lek

The list for the banquet[2] as proposed seems in order. The other thing, which hasn't been thought about, is the play at Pridalai. The members of the royal family who are going are Chira and his wife, but couldn't there be some more? It's no good some going to watch it from somewhere else, they must be in the same room. With the play there is supper and those having supper should be determined. Anyway, I'm sure you'll understand and have sent you the list.

Siamindra

1. Prince Marupong Siriphat was at that time the governor of Ayutthaya province, then known as Monton Krung Kao.

2. The banquet was held for Duke Johann Albrecht of Mecklenburg (1857-1920) and his second wife, Duchess-Consort Princess Elisabeth zu Stolberg-Rossla, who visited Siam between 26th January and 9th February 1910. The couple had married on 19th December and were on their honeymoon.

Duke and Duchess of Mecklenburg about to board the train at Ayutthaya Station.

30th December 1909

30th December 1909

Your Majesty

To Lek

I beg to send you the list of those who will attend the play at Pridalai and have supper with Your Majesty, as well as those who will have lunch at the Utthayan Throne Hall and attend the evening reception at the Varobhas Throne Hall, Bang Pa-In Palace, on the 8th January[1]. Those going to Pridalai are the same as those who went to the banquet on that day, with the addition of four people. Having inspected the venue, I think that 12 is a good number for supper as the room is very small. More than that will not look good. I have added Toonmom Toh, as originally he was only going to the banquet with no informal occasions for him to attend. I also added Prince Rabi Bhadanasakdi and Prince Vudhijaya and Ying Prom[2], who have not been included in any Bangkok events.

Maybe you can add a few people to the farewell banquet. If they are soldiers fine, and if they are civilians, check with the Ministry of Interior as to who should come. If you don't have to get some people from Bangkok so much the better.

Siamindra

The luncheon at the Utthayan Throne Hall is truly intimate, so I have arranged it for those who came with the Duke, or who were involved in meeting him. However, if there were no royals it would be a bit strange, but just to have a royal there for the sake of it is not right either, so I arranged for Toonkramom Chai and Ying Prasong[3] to attend, as they are particularly closely connected. In addition, there is Prince Marupong, who is responsible for receiving them in the Ancient City. I wanted him to come in the early evening, but he said he could not, as he must have a lot to do in organising the garden party.

31st December 1909

Your Majesty

I beg to send Your Majesty the lists, amended according to Your Majesty's instructions, of those who will be part of the entourage to see the play at Pridalai and have supper there, the list of those having lunch at the Utthayan Throne Hall and those having dinner at the Varobhas Throne Hall.

For the play, I have added Toonmom Aa [Prince Bhanurangsi], instead of the Prince of Rajaburi, as he has only attended the banquet, together with Toonkramom Toh.

The luncheon is set for 18, as I understand that the dining room at the Utthayan can hold that many and, if less, it will look a bit empty.

In the evening reception at the Varobhas Throne Hall, apart from those in the Ducal entourage, I have organised some officials from Ayutthaya province, as well as some Department heads from Bangkok, who did not attend the banquet at the Chakri Maha Prasat Throne Hall, where only the Ministers and Chao Phraya Surasak, Phraya Suriya and his wife were at the table. As for the royals, I chose those who were not invited to Bang Pa-In Palace.

For the reception at Varobhas Throne Hall, I have added some provincial officials, except for the governor of Saraburi, as the Ministry of Interior said that he was busy with an event at the Buddha footprint and could not easily leave at this time. Instead, I will keep a minister, as that day there is a garden party and he will have to go to Bang Pa-In in any case.

I beg to remain Your Majesty's obedient servant,
Chakrabongse

I beg to remain Your Majesty's obedient servant,
Chakrabongse

1. In fact the ducal couple did not arrive until 26 January so, Prince Chakrabongse has made a mistake with the month.

2. Ying Prom refers to Princess Prom Braobarn Vudijaya (1888-1924), the wife of Prince Vudhijaya (formerly of the Diskul family) and daughter of Prince Damrong.

3. Ying Prasong refers to Princess Prasongsom Paribatra (formerly of the Jayandta family), the wife of Prince Paribatra.

4. It must have been strange for Prince Chakrabongse to compile all these lists, but be excluded himself by virtue of his marriage.

Duke Johann Albrecht and his wife, Duchess Consort Elisabeth.

2nd January 1910

Your Majesty

I beg to request a leave of absence to go and inspect the soldiers who are preparing for manoeuvres in front of Duke Johann Albrect during his visit. The schedule is as follows:

On the 4th: Stay in Phra Phrathom
On the 5th: Stay in Rajaburi
On the 8th: Stay in Chachoengsao
On the 10th: Stay in Nakhon Sawan
I beg to remain Your Majesty's obedient servant,
Chakrabongse

4th January 1910

Your Majesty

I have received Your Majesty's letter of yesterday, concerning Pi Rabi and have noted everything.

In truth, I planned for Pi Rabi to only attend one reception on the 4th day, namely the last one, as I know that he doesn't like public occasions. But I cannot leave him out entirely. Pi Rabi came and talked to me about this and I expressed my opinion, which made him very angry to the extent that he bothered Your Majesty.

Now Your Majesty has requested that his name be removed from all the reception lists and I have told Pi Chira accordingly.

I beg to remain Your Majesty's obedient servant,
Chakrabongse

Prince Chakrabongse inspecting preparations for military manoeuvres, during the visit of Duke Johann Albrecht of Mecklenburg.

12th May 1910

My son Lek

I have read your letter regarding more building works at your house, and building a pavilion in the garden at Paruskavan. You should do it, and I have ordered Prince Sommot to pay the money for this.

Siamindra

30th May 1910

Your Majesty

Monsieur Ramlay, Eeyd Lek's tutor, came to report that he had tested his knowledge by asking him to write essays in the following three subjects: history, international law and physics. He showed me the answers, so I could present them for Your Majesty to judge whether his knowledge is good or bad.

Accordingly, with this letter I am sending Your Majesty all three papers, which Monsieur Ramlay would like returned in order to show Eeyd Lek where he went wrong.

I beg to remain Your Majesty's obedient servant,
Chakrabongse

3rd June 1910

Lek

Regarding the Chamber of Commerce, I have thought about how to change it, but just haven't got round to it. I want there to be no possibility of the Chinese complaining.

Regarding the transportation of goods, I have thought about it, but it's not necessary yet. I have worked well, there is just a little left. I will probably keep it with me as before.

Siamindra

Private
4th June 1910

Lek

I have just received a letter from Chao Phraya Yommarat[1] that the French embassy wants us to hand over the Chinese man, Tan Cheo Seng Fatinsieng, the leader of the troubles caused by the Chinese and the one who published that proclamation to the embassy at 3 pm. We have known about this for several days now and are about to send a boat to apprehend him. We have been worried he will take a boat to Saigon, and have had him surrounded for many days. So it is a good thing that they want him.

Siamindra

6th June 1910

Lek

I did not answer your letter sent yesterday, as I had only just asked Prince Damrong to investigate the rumours in Nan, which do not seem to have any basis. The French seem to be trying to please the Chinese and also keep good relations with Siam. So they have been rather cool about this matter.

Prince of Prachak[3] is probably there, but he can't control things and he makes up a lot of things which are untrue. Anyone who listens and takes him seriously will come a cropper.

Siamindra

1. Chao Phraya Yommarat (1862-1940) was formerly Pun Sukum. After being a novice monk, he entered government service and progressed up the ranks with many changes of title. He occupied several ministerial posts and was an influential figure from the reign of King Chulalongkorn to that of King Prajadhipok.

2. A group of Chinese living in Siam led by Tan Cheo Seng Fatinsieng were angry that they would be taxed on a per capita basis, just like Siamese nationals, and so went on strike for three days. Other Chinese opposed them, and fighting broke out. Some 31 Chinese were expelled on 19th June.

3. Prince Prachak Silpakom (1856-1924) was the governor of the northern *monton* at that time, with a residence in Udorn Thani. One of the sons of King Mongkut, he had studied English with Anna Leonowens.

9th June 1910

Lek

Regarding the letter with news about the Chinese, although things have calmed down now, I do not feel it is over. It is rather like a boil that gets reabsorbed, but does not burst and can re-emerge at any time.

Many things show that the Chinese man named Hong[1] was involved in this, and one can see his desire to be a leader and spokesperson. He wants to be important and so we have to take notice. Being important, he will get benefits and money, but in order to satisfy them will also take money. Maybe they can organise it with their work. They like destroying things and I cannot see what that achieves. Another thing is their claim to have collected almost a million can't possibly be true, as it would take a lot of work to get such a lot of money. It seems they can't escape our hearing.

A new development with the Ang Yi[2] is that they won't set up a shrine, they will be low key and will integrate as Thais. It is called Meng. I know about it but can't quite make it out. As for weapons, they just have that tunnel. It seems that the house is not particularly keen.

Another thing to be careful of is the rumour floating around among them a lot. Perhaps it has been talked about too much. It must be caught in time. They should not close their ears to this. Encouraging them to go on strike is in order to take over the lottery. The fact that the army is ready and can be ordered in at any time is very important. Don't be complacent. If you hear anything else, let me know.

Siamindra

1. Hong most likely refers to Yi Ko Hong, aka Hong Techawanit and later Phraya Anuwat Rachaniyom (1851-1936). He was the founder, with other influential Chinese, of the Por Tek Tung Foundation.

2. *Ang Yi* or *angyi* is a Teochiu word referring to Chinese secret societies, which were established in Thailand since the early 19th century (or probably earlier), as a side effect of Chinese immigration to Siam (which has the largest Chinese diaspora in the world). The societies helped their members and controlled labour, but also engaged in some criminal activities.

Private
15th June 1910

Lek

There is one matter, which the French ambassador[1] has written about, namely that there is a Vietnamese, who is an old friend of Dedindard or Guidard whom we expelled from Bangkok. Before that, he was in Bangkok. He was the one sending letters between the coup plotters in Vietnam[2], and was the one who thought to send weapons to Laos. Please catch him and expel him.

IN ENGLISH *"Tu Hua, whose complete name is Dang Thuc Hua, and whose borrowed name is Nao Sinh, is by origin from the village of Luong Dieu, hugen of Thanh Chuong, province of Nyhe-An, son of the former Tri Huyen, he left Annam for Japan in 1907 and left that country for China and Siam some time ago.*

"The description of his appearance is as follows: Age: thirty years; height: medium; Complexion: rather dark. Visage: slightly pockmarked. Beard: none."

When I read this, it made me think of the man who gave news to the army that time. It is likely the same person. I felt very sorry for him. We have an obligation to help the French this time, because they handed over that person and did not raise any objection when we wanted to expel him. For that reason, if it is him and the soldiers think that he could be helped, he could be told to escape to Singapore or somewhere else. But if it is just a rumour passed on, don't repeat it. Don't talk about it too openly, just give an indication that he should slip away. I hope that the regiment will arrange things satisfactorily. Don't let the news escape and keep this letter top secret.

Siamindra

15th June 1910

Lek

I am happy with the letter you wrote. So I can show that we think along the same lines, I will show you the letter I sent to the Department of Education[3], in reply to their letter requesting more money. I wrote to them last year, then about four or five months later received a letter from the Capital Department of the Interior Ministry, the Department of Education, stating that they did not agree with the setting up of a commission to examine education. If we debated this I might win, but then who would the commission consist of – those very people who don't agree we should have one. They don't agree with it because they don't have a single thought in their head. When they are sent to inspect, they just want to see how the others are dressed, or how smart they look. It's a waste of money. They just want to prove that my suggestion is wrong. I am so discouraged and heavy hearted. Now, in particular, I am sad and despondent, as I have come to believe that Thailand is incapable of improvement – like a patient who refuses food and water and whose condition gets worse all the time, until the doctor does not have the skill to save them. It is not just the junior people, as the senior government officials are all the same. I seem to be the only one dancing about and I can't find anyone who thinks like me.

This letter is written when I am depressed and angry. Maybe my feelings may change later, as I have never given in to despair before. So I'll stop for now and continue when I'm out of this mood.

Siamindra

---

1. The French ambassador was Jules Lefaivre. He was in this post from the end of July 1909 to January 1912.

2. In 1908 there had been various protests in Vietnam against the French, such as the protest by farmers against tax rises which began in Hue and were put down with great ferocity. In June there was an abortive Hanoi uprising and a poison plot.

3. The Department of Education was established in 1887 and for a while was grouped under the Ministry of Religious Affairs, until, under King Rama VI, a separate Ministry of Education was established.

Letter opposite

1. The British ambassador was Arthur Peel.

2. Beri-beri refers to a cluster of symptoms caused mainly by thiamine (vitamin B1) deficiency. The rice grain husk is a good source of thiamine, but polished white rice has none left. This link was only discovered in the late 19th century.

Three brothers: Prince Damrong, King Chulalongkorn and Prince Devawongse.

15th June 1910

Lek

I had to end the last letter, because it was time to go outside. If I did not go out, they would say that I am scared of the Chinese. Please let me complain a bit more. Our difficulties seem very complex. To put it bluntly, I lack people to help me think, people with endurance and a sense of direction. Even those on whom I rely are not my equal. And this is even true of the senior princes, such as Prince Devawongse and Prince Damrong. In fact, their knowledge is greater than mine and they are better at meeting people, but their endurance and determination to do their best and do it properly is very different from mine, in fact probably half of mine. If I try and encourage them by various means to think more progressively, this lasts only a little while. It's as if I have to push all the time and they still don't become perceptive as part of their nature. I don't want to show off, I just want to tell you how I am really feeling. I am very far from liking to show off, as I am seeing everything rather negatively and feel there is nothing to show off about. When someone praises me, I feel embarrassed. The difference I can illustrate from something that I heard today. The English ambassador wrote to the Harbour Department that the Governor of Singapore had asked him to inform the government that various doctors had tested polished white rice and were certain that it causes beri-beri[2]. Could the government find a way, whereby the owners of the rice mills could be persuaded to change their methods, otherwise Singapore would prohibit the buying rice from us, or would buy as little as possible. He sent a report of the tests, based not just on our rice, but also on rice from Burma and Indochina. Of course, nowhere were the findings as bad as in Thailand.

This letter arrived on February 15th. Prince Devawongse replied on the 20th of the same month, saying it was an important matter and he would consult with his fellow ministers.

But from then on, nothing happened until the 12th of April, when Phraya Pipattana wrote to Chao Phraya Yommarat expressing no opinion whatsoever. Chao Phraya Yommarat then did nothing.

Then on 26th May, the English ambassador sent the letter to various other people as well. The original letter came from Hong Kong and had also asked for this matter to be looked into and asked to know what the Siamese government intended to do.

On the 30th of May, Phraya Pipattana wrote a letter to the Capital Department and to the Farm Ministry. And that's as far as the matter got.

Now it is almost the date by which they warned us to have looked into things.

You probably heard Prince Devawongse say today that he did not think this matter was of any importance and so had not said anything to me. I am grateful for that in a way, but he should have been more active and consulted with the others as to what to do. At least he should have said that we are not going to do anything, which would be better than no reply. But no, the whole thing was left hanging in the air and then at the last minute, the matter was thrown over to me.

The Markwand rice mill which was situated on the Chao Phraya River.

I imagine that Berli Commercial[3] will be unable to get an agreement with the mill owners. Whether it is a commerical or official matter, it is the job of the government to take care of this, because the rice trade is the life blood of Thailand. Instead, however, it is seen as nothing to do with the government, but just a commerical matter. I could go on endlessly!

I also consulted the Capital Department and it seems this matter is outside the control of the Ministry of Foreign Affairs, while the Capital Department feel that they have no jurisdiction over trade. The matter was then sent to the Ministry of Agriculture, who said they had never exerted any control over the rice mills and that they felt it was nothing to with them. However, they did write to the Ministry of Foreign Affairs saying that not answering was not an option. So what I want to know is, who is the government in the understanding of the term "government of Siam" as used by *farang*? No one seems to feel that they are. Could you say that I am the government? But then why did I not inform them as they wished? When this is how it is, I can see that there are absolutely no principles or structure on which the government is based. The fact that it is thus, is because there is no unity. The feeling of gain or loss, good or bad, is only felt in an individual way.

No one wants the best in a collective fashion, they want just good enough. Everyone is happy when that is the case. Someone who tries very hard like me will simply destroy himself. I can't find anyone to help me in anything. When a country has only one person thinking, how can it get anywhere? I have only given you one example, just to show you where this sense of discouragement in my heart has come from. The fact that the people involved in the example I chose are better than the general show-offs or the selfish people and yet are still like this is depressing. How many people like this are there? And for those who are far behind them, how many indeed? I can see all the time that the results of my work over 43 years are only two parts done, with still another 8 parts to go. Where will I get the years and time to do this? I lack a partner to help me think and persevere. Even if I think of something, I don't see how it can come to fruition. In this way, I feel a heavy weight in my heart and I don't know where I can put it down. I am in despair, as it seems that our country won't survive, as good people are not coming through in the way that they do in more developed lands.

Siamindra

3. The Jucker company was taken over by Albert Berli in 1889 and, in 1901, the sons of Albert Jucker, the original founder, returned to Siam and became partners in the company, whose main activities were rice milling, mining, timber and shipping.

18th June 1910

Lek

This list is of all those people on whom I have had my eye for a while, but the problem is that they lack experience in their new tasks, something that weighs heavily on me. Being in government service has become something which is no longer for the benefit of the country. Whoever is boss can easily order people around. It's creating new people which is hard, respecting one's boss as a teacher. Some of the employees form cliques and groups. Those who go in and have ideas and think carefully should be kept. If the boss makes a single mistake, he will be hated, so he has to support everyone. Once someone is secure, then they become lazy. It's all very depressing.

Your favourite Charoon[1] has made a huge mistake. We had already discussed that Nai Thiem[2] should be dismissed and then not allowed to represent cases in court. If he were to preside, he would request a fee higher than his wage. He thinks he is smart and we are stupid. If we are quiet, he will go to court again. The foreigners didn't know that he had been dismissed, until they saw the newspapers. I inquired and it seems that he has been allowed to practice again. When I wanted to forbid this, I learned that the French ambassador had gone to his home with Hong the Chinese and paid the fee. There was nothing I could do as, if I were to order his dismissal, I feared the consequences. Such being the case, the only way was to let the ministry fall apart. It could be said that the forest was out of order. This is one of the problems of trying to use new people. Let me ask you what you would do in my situation.

Siamindra

1. Prince Charoon, having been ambassador in Paris (see footnote p. 394), came back to Bangkok to serve as Director-General of the Justice Ministry, when Prince Rabi resigned.
2. Nai Thiem Bunnag (1871-1911) studied law and rose quickly in the Ministry of Justice. On 8th June he was dismissed as a judge for siding with Prince Rabi, see below. Thiem was Director of the Foreign Court, hence reference to the French.
3. The ministry was established in 1891 and the courts and judicial system were centralized, with sixteen courts combined into seven. When a group of 28 'Young Turk' Thai lawyers took sides with Prince Rabi Badhanasakdi over a case involving another member of the royal family, the Ministry of Justice was in chaos and the king became very upset. The matter continued to bother him till his death in October of that year.

Prince Rabibadhana, Minister of Justice from 1897 to 1910.

19th June 1910

Lek

Your accurate and to the point remarks pleased me greatly. The fact that Charoon has fallen into this position has upset me a lot. When appointing him, I waited for Rabi to suggest it and promised that I would not bully him. But choosing Charoon was really my choice, as I thought him intelligent enough to be a minister and he was well aware of the problems within the Ministry of Justice[3]. However, sometimes I can choose a bad egg and I can't blame anyone else. Rabi is rather inconsistent. One minute he thinks one thing, another minute another. Then he says something and forgets he's said it and changes to something else. One can't be certain with him. His heart is not really democratic, nor is it republican.

For that reason I brought Charoon in to replace him and to play one off against the other, as the main palace and the front palace used to do. Some people just do not understand that the laws of the country are something we have to protect together. All they do is sign up to be servants to the British.

Some of the 28 lawyers who resigned in support of Prince Rabi. Nai Thiem Bunnag, the ringleader of the group, is seated third from the left. He was Director of the Foreign Court at that time.

The fact that I have been angry with those crazy people has been widely reported, but they probably misunderstand. I have seen the copy of the reply to Chao Phraya Yommarat, telling him not to let me see it. He wanted to know. He sent a copy to Prince Prachak to trap me into saying something, but I was silent, so they were angry with me for splitting up the Ministry of Justice and getting rid of Nai Thiem. Other people resigned. They can't come back yet. The letters were written in a rage, which Toh said were like bad essays, full of misspellings. The truth is they got above themselves. I believe that they wanted to show that whoever took them on would lose, the whole ministry would be in chaos and they would have to be invited back to calm things down. Then when I put my foot down, it was not what they wanted, so they decided to take me on in another way.

However fantastical the letter was, it made people criticise them. It is a shame that they did not just resign. So, in the end, they are not coming back and they are going to wait and fight it out. They must be planning more intrigues. They don't work for the government any more. What I mean is that the case of Nai Thiem is a ruse.

I have also heard that the permanent secretary[1] has been annoyed by Charoon for two days. This morning Rabi came back, but did not let me know. I don't know if this is true or not. The whole thing comes down to a question of doing a favour and meeting with those sorts of people. I doubt he can change. It's like you thought.

As for Nai Thiem, I will ensure he goes away. But if the minister does not resign, and jumps in to destroy the court and sides with Nai Thiem, it will be a huge scandal. The foreigners in Thailand will see it as a serious matter.

Wait, and you will see that I haven't done anything wrong. Pure ingratitude, and he wants to take me on for no reason.

Siamindra

20th June 1910

Lek

I'm writing to you about the agent of the Vietnamese. I forgot to tell you about the huge quantity of weapons that they managed to bring in. Now there is a real witness. There is a Hakka Chinese, who has cut off his queue, behind it all. Around 18 mercenaries, who have been undergoing military training in the jungle between Phrae and Uttaradit, are behind it all. Their arrest was ordered and all 18 were caught at Phrae, together with around 100 military uniforms, caps and water bottles. However, the guns had already been sent on ahead to Nakhon Lampang and are still being pursued. Someone saw some long boxes. These people call themselves Kekmeng[1].

1. Chao Phraya Mahitorn (La-or Krairiksh, 1874-) studied law and became a judge and, in 1903, permanent secretary in the Ministry of Justice.

They are in revolt against the Manchu dynasty, but I understand that this is just a front. They intend to enter China through the north. Their route seems to be via Chiang Rai and Chiang Saen, before crossing the Mekong at Pan or Chiang Tung and then going towards Muang Singh and down to harass the northern Vietnamese. The thought that they would go up to Nong Sae, Chiang Rung and into Yunnan seems implausible. If they really want to enter Yunnan, they have to get on a French train. If the French would let them, then why come in via Bangkok? Why not go straight to Tonkin? I don't believe the Kekmeng are planning something against China, but there are Kekmeng that sympathise with the Vietnamese revolt. Their base is in Japan. The Kekmeng in our country definitely have the Japanese behind them.

The agent of the Vietnamese asked us to help supply weapons, or, in other words, turn a blind eye so those going to Phrae could easily do so by boat.

Taking weapons through our country is an arrestable offence, and we have them, but if the agent has contacts in the army, then I think it's best to let them go, so we can get favours and benefits in return. The agent should slip away. If it is nothing to do with us and we have no ties, there is no need to get involved.

Siamindra

20th June 1910

Lek

I was very pleased with your letter concerning the French ambassador and the consul. It is probably as the consul says, but it is all part of the problems relating to Nai Thiem, which the French ambassador needs to make clear. How hard is that? Because the ambassador is having fun, he's misbehaving a little, while both of our sides are afraid. I hear from Prince Devawongse that the plaintiff is going to object to Nai Thiem, while the minister has ruled that he cannot object. That we should intervene at this stage would not be good, because the judge, despite being in prison, could by this means still be involved. The fact that foreign lawyers have to have our permission

1. *Kekmeng* is a Tiachiu dialect word meaning revolt.

to plead a case, while Thai lawyers do not, is a loophole by which he can get the better of Charoon, when he did not give an order. If an order were to be given now, it would look like a punishment. The French seem to have quietened down. I think I should deal with this via decree, like that of King Rama IV forbidding corrupt officials. Better to remove him.

....

Making personal enquiries as you have been doing is very helpful. Please keep your eyes and ears open.

Siamindra

21st June 1910

Lek

The story of the Chinese who cut his queue, taking arms up north mystifies me. It transpires it was a huge quantity and consisted of genuine army supplies. We have them now: 915 grey uniforms, front fastening with a turn-down collar and holes for shoulder marks, 952 pairs of navy trousers, 62 water bottles in army style, 105 water bottle straps, 920 puttees in dark brown. How can we ignore such a large quantity of material? Someone must have seen it. However, we failed with the guns and only managed to seize five. There were shotguns as well. I suspect they must have stolen them from our soldiers, which is why the whole thing has been hushed up. Prince Damrong hasn't done anything about this, as he still believes everything is destined for China. Almost all the orders that he gives have to be corrected. It seems as if Prince Damrong is on the side of Phra Nikorn[2] (the son a woman called Sap). However, it is impossible for Phra Nikorn to get the truth out of these Chinese. So first we should prosecute them. Phra Nikorn did not know that he had the authority to arrest them. Once this was pointed out, he did catch them, despite still be afraid of the Chinese getting together and revolting in the provinces. In the end, he continues to believe that the material was for Szechuan which is impossible. Prince Damrong is still not sorting it out.

Siamindra

2. Phra Nikorn Kittikarn (1878-1948). After studying at Suan Kularb school, he entered the Ministry of Interior. In 1907 he was appointed governor of Phrae province.

21st June 1910

Lek

Prince Devawongse got a letter from Nai Thiem to me. I have made a copy and am sending it on to you. I would like it back, as I want to study it further.

Siamindra

Why Prince Devawongse wants to appoint Prince Svasti Sobhon[1], I do not know.

24th June 1910

Lek

Prince Devawongse asking the French ambassador to send in a report went well. I have sent it to you to have a look. You can see he was lying in wait for us.

Siamindra

Once you've read it, send it back. The matter of the Chinese wanting to have a voice, he heard from the person himself. It is not how it was imagined. I asked Luang Sophon[2] to come and introduce the new members of the Capital Department. Luang Sophon was grumpy and I was so cross that I thumped the table and, accidentally, spat some betel nut juice onto Luang Sophon's jacket.

The king relaxing in his study. At this period, he sometimes wrote to Prince Chakrabongse twice a day. In addition, he wrote to several other sons and ministers, meaning he must have written at least 20-30 letters every day.

1st July 1910

Your Majesty

I have asked Pi Chira to appoint Eeyd Lek as commander of a company in the Senior Cadet School, as this will give him a chance to do a job, really take responsibility and make his own decisions. If he does nothing, he will fail and feel ashamed. I believe this is a good way to stop him being a child and learn to be a leader.

However, it will be difficult for him to do this well, as he is still not used to the discipline of the army and has only finished one year's study. I think that if he was able to see and study the way things are done in the various regiments, taking examples to use himself, it will be very valuable and easier than studying from books. Accordingly, I would like him to visit some provinces and cities where the soldiers are based in order to observe the various regiments.

The program I am proposing is as follows:

8 July – Eeyd Lek to accompany Your Majesty to Petchaburi and stay there for around two days, observing the duties carried out by the regiment, before leaving for Ratchaburi. After that, he will come through Bangkok and go to Chachoengsao to the army camp there, before returning to Bangkok.

1. Presumably the king was referring to a possible appointment as Minister of Justice. Prince Svasti in fact became Minister of Justice only in 1912, a post he held until 1918.

2. Luang Sophon Petcharat worked in the Harbour Department i.e. the Ministry of Foreign Affairs.

Next, in October, when the school is shut for the cadets to go home, he can observe the regiments in Nakhon Ratchasima, Nakhon Sawan and Phitsanulok.

On these trips, I will send Dossiriwongse[1], the assistant director of the Cadet School, to accompany him and suggest various activities.

I have proposed this program as I think it will beneficial, not only from a military point of view, but also it will be a chance for him to see more of Siam.

Despite having approved the program verbally, I beg to have Your Majesty's permission again.

I beg to remain Your Majesty's obedient servant
Chakrabongse

P. S. Your Majesty asked me once before why Eeyd Lek has not become a monk. In this, I have no objection, as I think it is a good idea, but as he has not mentioned it, I have gone ahead and arranged a program that I think will be of benefit. If he does wish to become a monk, the program can be postponed.

1. Prince Dossiriwongse Chakrabandhu (1884-1950) was Assistant Director at the Military Cadet school. Later he became a general and commander of the Fourth Army.

Prince Asdang in 1910. At that time, he was a lieutenant and is shown wearing the full-dress uniform of the Royal Guards.

1st July 1910

Lek

I approve of the plan to send Eeyd Lek to go and observe army bases in the provinces. Regarding becoming a monk, it is not essential this year, as it would be too rushed. If he becomes more grown up after this trip, it will be a good thing . . .

Siamindra

5th July 1910

Your Majesty

Regarding the big guns that Your Majesty wishes to acquire, I have consulted with Pi Chira, who has said that he will come and see Your Majesty today to discuss this, after which the two of us will choose the appropriate guns together.

The French consul in Bangkok has told me that the French embassy has received a letter from the consul in Nan, saying that there is widespread rumour in Nan that Thailand and France have been fighting each other in Cambodia. The consul in Bangkok was concerned and complained that it was clear that someone, or a group of people, were trying to create a rift between Thailand and France.

I replied that as long as we both knew that someone was trying to do this, all we had to do was not have a rift.

The consul continued that Monsier de Mayerie had send a telegram from Peking, enquiring about the Chinese strike and what had happened. And what the Chinese we had captured had done. The government wanted to know informally and so he had asked.

These things aren't important, but I thought they were quite interesting and so have informed Your Majesty accordingly.

I have heard, from someone who went to see Pi Rabi, that he said that when Your Majesty goes to

Petchaburi, he will go to his country house. That he cannot stay in Bangkok, otherwise someone will tell you that he is using the opportunity of Your Majesty's absence to interfere in the Justice Ministry. That he should say this shows that Pi Rabi is being incited, or rather still being incited, to think in the wrong way. I believe that Prince Prachak is another case. If Pi Rabi had gone the wrong way on his own, it would not have mattered that much, but now it has started a trend. It is almost as if someone wants to damage Pi Rabi and so is consequently feeding him misinformation. Accordingly, I think that if Pi Rabi asks Your Majesty for leave to visit his rice fields, Your Majesty should refuse and say that in view of his illness, it would be better to stay in Bangkok. In this way, he will see that you are unconcerned at the thought of him staying in Bangkok. Toonmom Toh could also answer in similar fashion.

If my suggestions to Your Majesty outlined above are wrong in any way, please forgive me.

I beg to remain Your Majesty's obedient servant,

Chakrabongse

15th July 1910

Lek

I have received your letter with the orders for the officers to go to Japan. The orders are well detailed and satisfactory. It is a shame that only one person knows Japanese. It makes our position weaker, but it is important. If we did not set up a commission to really go and have a look, it would not be good. The people creating the commission have a difficult task. If they do not know what they hope to achieve, it's impossible to get anything out of it. I am obsessed with education. That's what I want them to go and see. However, it is not enough just to understand each other, but also whether they can understand each other when there is no one to receive the report. To be successful, it's no good rushing off but getting no tangible benefit.

The Chinese affair is still not over. It was in the newspapers again and I've sent a translation for you.

Siamindra

Translated from the Hau Siem Sin Po, 18th July 1910. The leaflet from the Love Our Homes in Kie Eng Society regarding the fact that Chinese in . . . are being abused.

Having seen the Dong Hua Po newspaper, let me tell you all what is going on. Because the government has decided to increase taxes and the Chinese have no possibility to pay, they have decided to go on strike and stop trading. This is simply because they have lost all incentive and ability, and so have had no choice but to take this action. It is very sad but the government has not observed international law. They have seized 700-800 Chinese people who have done nothing wrong, imprisoned them and beaten them up most harshly. They have suffered in an inhuman manner. This harsh treatment has not only abused our traders but is an insult to our country. Our countrymen in this place who have been working in . . . are not insignificant in number. It is vital that we think of how we can protect ourselves according to our strength. Accordingly, we are announcing to all and sundry that we Chinese should get together and make our point of view heard. Please present your thoughts to the society within 10 days from the receipt of this leaflet, so it can be decided what should be done next.

Announced on 12th by Love Kia Eng City Society

Chinatown, c. 1900s.

21st July 1910

Your Majesty

I received Your Majesty's letter dated 19th of this month for which I am more grateful than I can say.

I forgot to tell Your Majesty that in the matter of the Ministry of Defence sending a commission to Japan, the aim is for all the officers to be fully qualified in every way. However, they lack a wider vision as they have never been abroad and this will be a good opportunity for them. I have chosen three people who do not know any foreign languages and one who has been abroad and can speak a foreign language to be their mouthpiece. I want them to receive some personal benefit as well, apart from the positive effects on their work. The methods which are used abroad will be very helpful so there will a double benefit.

However, if the only benefit the government desires is to send the commission abroad in order for them to come back and revise things here, then people should be chosen who speak a foreign language.

Your Majesty's remarks, that the importance lies in those who appointed the commission getting a good or bad report and revisions can be done later, are very true. If the initiators of the commission cannot state their aims, there is no point in sending one.

I see it as vital to ensure that education in our country is really good, as it is the root of everything. It is something that will have results in the future and should not be subject to time limits. But we must hurry up and arrange things.

I think that if Your Majesty is not fully confident that those in charge of education at present can establish the commission, perhaps one person that Your Majesty does trust should be appointed specifically to arrange it – to determine where they will go and how they will inspect things. Once the commission has gone, returned and completed its study, then will be the time to change the head of education. The fact that the commission will have done its research, is one way to clear any problems in this matter that are of concern.

Another way is to change the minister at the Thammakarn Ministry (Ministry of Education), as I believe that if the current staff in the ministry had a strong minister things will go much better.

Sending a commission to inspect education is easy and more convenient than inspecting military matters, as there is no secrecy involved and furthermore education is something that *farang* respect – all governments support it. Education is one of the key things about which foreigners show great feeling and about which everyone is in agreement. As Your Majesty has remarked, some Thai people love proposing things which will accord well with the *farang* viewpoint and want to get involved whether it is appropriate for the country or not in order to be popular. . . .

If what I have said has caused offence or has overstepped the mark, I beg Your Majesty's forgiveness.

I beg to remain Your Majesty's obedient servant,
Chakrabongse

P.S. Regarding the Chinese, I think they are very vociferous, because they are angry that they did not achieve what they wanted. The question of the six *baht* is given as the ostensible reason, but it is surely not the real one.

As for Your Majesty's concern that a French warship visiting Bangkok at this time might incite the Chinese further, I have had an informal chat with the French. The ambassador has talked to his government and it has been decided that the warship will not come.

21st July 1910

Lek

I have received your letter expressing your views about the commission. The education commission is not difficult, but to use it well and implement its findings will be. Our education system has started out wrong just like the Royal Survey Department . . .

It was begun without knowing any background to do with education and was more a matter of guesswork which was then adapted as necessary. It's similar to building a house without any knowledge or without an architect. It is built and then redone and redone until it becomes a total mess. Examples can be seen in the throne halls in the Suan Dusit compound and the Chakri Maha Prasat Throne Hall. However much it is altered, it is impossible to put right and cannot be fixed apart from starting from scratch again. To be successful, one needs an idea, care, and skill, as can be seen in the Ananta Samakom Throne Hall. Only then is there the basis for a smooth conclusion. In the education department there are good craftsmen and workers – all it lacks is a good minister, who has ideas, is a good speaker, and is respected by other ministers. Education does not take place just in that Ministry, it needs the Interior Ministry and the Capital Department as well. The whole problem stems from not having that good leader.

Siamindra

The Ananta Samakom Throne Hall under construction, 1910.

13th August 1910

My son Lek

I received you letter and the books by Mom Narendra.

I know about Prince Thong and the bad Vietnamese. He told the French himself concerning their plan to rob Pak Hin Bon city. Today I heard that the French caught Prince Thong because he crossed over to the other side. We kept in touch with the embassy at all times.

I don't know the location of the place that Mom Narendra calls Tambon Pak Panang. I have never heard that name used in this area, but only Pakse and Pak Moon. Pak Panang I've heard about only in connection with Nakhon. We should try and find out which district he is talking about.

The French boast that merchandise landed in Saigon is cheaper than in Khorat may be true, but if Monsieur Cobultas raises taxes as he is planning, it will not be cheaper any more.

Mom Narendra is thinking about the train only now, whereas we have been thinking about this for a long time. We have the train to Khorat, to Ubol and Nong Khai. The reason the French fought with us in 1893 was from fear of the train, knowing full well that if we pushed ahead that way and pumped water from the Mekong River into other rivers, the French

aim to navigate the Mekong would be over. For that reason, they seized the Mekong River with everything at their disposal and forbade us from taking the train further and pumping the water from the Mekong into other rivers. They allowed us one line which would have come straight from Mukdahan down to Saigon. This would have made it easier to take merchandise there and so for that reason we did not do it. We could not raise money from elsewhere, only from ourselves or by taking a loan from the French. The users would only have been the Thais or the French, so nothing would have come of it. It was just a way of playing around. If we had built that long line joined with the other too, the French would have been finished. They did not dare do it themselves. If at any time Mom Narendra's ideas had got to the French, they would have been furious as there is no fairness there at all. Just the Ubol line could have killed their trade immediately, whether we would have lost money or not. Even if we did not get railway traffic, we would make a lot of money in Bangkok as the topography of the area along the Mekong needs to be developed from Thailand not from Vietnam or Laos. Because the geography is such, the French cannot make any money in Laos. If we had enough strength

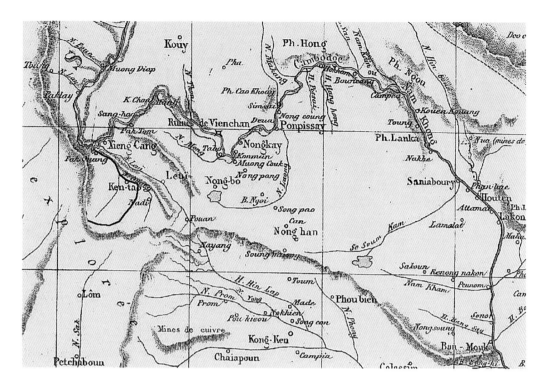

Part of a French map of Indochina by Francis Garnier.

19th August 1910

to fight the French we should do it tomorrow. . . .

Whether we would make money or lose it, if we could do it, we should take them on once more. Their attempt to bring boats up to trade, despite having an agreement that we should put markers in the water, done a while ago, was a failure and they lost a lot of money and left their buildings to go to ruin three months ago. They have asked for a new license as before regarding those five boats. . . .

Please explain to Mom Narendra that we are always at a disadvantage versus a larger country and they have both the east and west sides [of the Mekong]. I have returned his letter.

Siamindra

1. Mom Narendra refers to Mom Rajawongse Siddhi Sudhasa, who studied at Sandhurst and was mentioned by Prince Chakrabongse when he was in England.

2. Lady Gage, née Leila Peel, was the sister of Arthur Peel, British ambassador in Bangkok. She was married to the 5th Viscount, Henry Charles Gage. The Gage family had lived at Firle Place for hundreds of years.

My son Lek

I have something with which to reward Mr Peel for going to investigate Nai Thiem that time. When he first arrived, he said that either his younger or older sister called Lady Gage[2] wanted to meet Eeyd Noi. I said I would be delighted. Then later she asked that I instruct the governor of Eeyd Noi to give permission, as she was worried he would not agree. I wrote to Bavoradej. It happened that he was on holiday in Spain and Portugal at that time and only received the letter on the 15th of last month, saying that Eeyd Noi had met with Lady Gage's son who is at Eton. Lady Gage sent an invitation to Mr Arthur and it is agreed that in the first week of the next holiday, Eeyd Noi will go to Firle Place. Bavoradej will enjoy it more and it is a way for them to meet more people.

If you see Mr Peel, tell him I've sent him something and the news in my letter.

Siamindra

HM King Chulalongkorn laying the foundation stone for Baan Puen Palace in Petchaburi, designed by architect Karl Siegfried Döring.

29th August 1910

My son Lek

I received your letter, saying you had talked to Mr Peel. Yesterday it rained a lot, which was the first and only time. Before that it had rained a fair amount, although only north and south of the river, not in the middle. However, the river went down, even though it rained yesterday and it only came up an inch. It is a great shame.

I plan to make merit for the one year anniversary of Urubongse's death[1], instead of celebrating my own birthday on the 8th and 9th of September. On the 11th, I will come back to Bangkok. The construction work here is going well. If you came to see it, you would be surprised. If it rains over the next few days, the water level should rise.

Siamindra

1. HRH Prince Urubongse Rajasombhoj (1893-1909) had died the previous year, aged only 16, on the same day as the king's birthday.

8th September1910

Your Majesty

I have something I want to tell Your Majesty, which I did not want to discuss when there were a lot of people around and so I beg to send this letter.

When I met with Mr Peel, he told me that he had asked permission to go to London for the coronation of King George[1] and so will not go to Java as originally planned. He talked about it at great length. At the end, he asked who would be representing Your Majesty. I answered that as it was still a long way off, nothing had been decided definitively, but, based on past tradition, one of the senior sons of Your Majesty from the group studying in Europe would attend. He inquired as to who was currently in Europe. I replied that there was my younger brother Daeng[2], whereupon he asked where he was and what he was studying. When I told him, he asked how old he was and when told, exclaimed that he was very young. He asked why someone was not being sent from Bangkok, as going there was not so far or difficult and there was still plenty of time. Could not Toonkramom Toh or myself go instead? I said that, as I had made clear, the matter was not yet decided. And mentioning Daeng was just a guess, based on past practice, as it was easier to send someone from Europe.

Later, I heard from Pi Chira that Mr Peel had asked him what Daeng's rank was. Pi Chira replied that he was a second lieutenant. He then asked about his studies and the matter was closed.

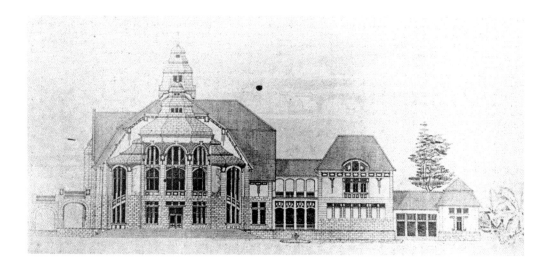

One of the drawings for Baan Puen Palace, only completed in 1916, six years after the King's death.

Having considered this later, I feel that the British government might be surprised if younger brother Daeng was sent as Your Majesty's representative, when there is time to send one of the more senior princes from Bangkok. If we send someone who is still studying, it might look as if we were being stingy. With a sudden event, not known about so far in advance, such as a funeral, it would be quite understandable that someone would go from Europe, but this is not the case. Pi Chira agreed with me. He thought that it should be Toonmom Toh, as this would be a mark of great honour to the British. But on reflection, I think that if Toonmom Toh went, it would require a lot of money, as his entourage would be large and formal receptions would be required all along the way. The money in the royal treasury at this time is not abundant and also we have to receive foreign royals. I am concerned that it will be very expensive. Accordingly, I would like to serve at this event and feel confident that I will not cause Your Majesty's honour to be lessened in any way. Furthermore, no greater expenditure from the royal treasury would be needed, than if younger brother Daeng went, as I would use the royal money only when I was in England on government duty. For my travel, I would go in a private capacity and use my own money.

Since I finished my studies and returned to Bangkok, I have dedicated myself to serving the country in order to repay Your Majesty's goodness to the best of my ability. Now I have an important position, which requires me to plan the workload for the

HM King George V, painted in 1910.

1. George V of England (1865-1937) became King on 6th May 1910 and was crowned on 22nd June 1911. He had been Prince of Wales since the death of Queen Victoria in 1901.

2. HRH Prince Mahidol (nickname Daeng) was the King's son with Queen Savang Vadhana. Later given the title Mahitala Dhibesra Adulyadej Vikrom, he was father to two Kings: King Rama VIII and King Rama IX. At that time, he was 18.

entire department. This has made me feel that the knowledge I gained in Europe is still insufficient in certain areas, because when I was a student I just studied whatever they taught. I did not know what reforms Thailand had implemented previously, how it should progress in the future, and how to plan successfully. There are some areas in which I am deficient, such as map making. I had not dreamt that I would be in the position of being responsible for the Royal Survey Department[3], a subject which I have not studied in detail. I feel there are large gaps in my knowledge and in this I am in line with Your Majesty's view, that one trip to Europe is not enough and two trips are needed. I agree with this assessment wholeheartedly and feel that it applies very much to myself.

I feel very inadequate vis-à-vis Pi Chira in that he has been to Europe twice after finishing his studies. I intend to serve Your Majesty at least as well as Pi Chira and, for that reason, I beg Your Majesty's goodness to allow me to undertake a study tour for my work to the extent that he has.

Should Your Majesty be so gracious as to allow me to go to Europe, if there were matters apart from military ones that Your Majesty desired me to study, such as education, for example, I would be only too happy to serve Your Majesty in this regard.

Furthermore, when I left Russia and said goodbye to the Emperor, I promised to visit him again. I think this is an appropriate moment for me to go and thank him for all his past goodness to me.

When I am in Europe, I swear to Your Majesty that I will do nothing to dishonour Your Majesty's good name or distress you in any way. I beg Your Majesty to grant me this. On this trip, of course, there will be some relaxation, but I feel that I will also gain a lot of new knowledge with which to better serve Your Majesty in the future. I have written this letter in the hope that Your Majesty will be so gracious as to grant permission. If I have overstepped myself in any way. I beg your Majesty's forgiveness.

I beg to remain Your Majesty's obedient servant,

Chakrabongse

P.S. I have not yet spoken to Pi Chira regarding my offer to represent Your Majesty at the coronation, as I wanted to first hear Your Majesty's opinion. Nor have I spoken to anyone else.

Baan Puen, Petchaburi
8th September 1910

Lek

I arrived back and read your letter. This idea is not entirely new and so no one really needs to be consulted. The crown prince does not need to do too much and it would be more expensive for sure. Later on he'll be able to go as king. Now it would not be of much benefit to him. As young Daeng is not old enough, it would probably be unsatisfactory both in their eyes and ours. If you go, I can be confident that everything will be in order and it will be of benefit to your work as well.

The only thing is that people will say because your wife is a *farang*, she can't abide staying in Thailand very long, before begging her husband to go home, every three years at the least as the old saying goes. And some will no doubt worry about criticism. But I have seen a lot of things and I don't think it's that remarkable. The only thing you need to think about is how you will travel. If you don't try and get the better of people, are not too extravagant, nor attempt to raise her up in contravention of local customs, it really won't matter much. You can't take Thai customs as the measure. Besides, whatever the case, the feelings of Thais and *farang* are bound to be different. I am not worried that you will show her off as a princess of this court, as even if you could take her to such functions, royal people would probably not talk to her. I'm sure you are not planning to take her into such situations. But we need to talk about your plan to go like this and how you will deal with this woman. Nearer the time, let's discuss it, so I know what's what and can answer any questions that arise.

Your suggestion to divide the spending, into that which is connected with government work and that which is for your holiday, is totally appropriate. Most of the concern is in that area, while other matters are not so important.

Siamindra

---

3. The Royal Survey school was set up in 1882 with students coming from the Royal Guards. In 1885 it became the Royal Survey Department. Ronald Worthy Giblin was director from 1901-1910. Prince Chakrabongse had oversight of it at this time.

8th September 1910

Your Majesty

I have thought a great deal about the question Your Majesty raised, regarding what I will do with my wife when we are in Europe, but had intended to discuss this when Your Majesty enquired.

In my view, she is a morganatic wife, which the *farang* recognise and understand. Thus, on occasions when the royal husband has to attend royal functions such as an audience with the king, or a visit to other royals, such a wife would not accompany him, nor have anything to do with that event. However, when her royal husband is going about on holiday as an ordinary person, his wife does accompany him. The places where I will be obliged to act as a royal are in Petersburg and in London for the coronation. In Russia, she can behave as a normal person, as it is her homeland. Then when I go to London, there is no need for her to go at all and she will probably stay with her relatives. Apart from in these two places, I will travel as an ordinary person, except when I am going on a fact-finding expedition for my work and need to be royal. My wife has no need to go to such events, or meetings, in any case.

Another thing I have thought about, in order to avoid rumour and speculation that a Thai prince has a foreign wife, is that when I am travelling I will not use my title. This is how many European royals behave, thus King Edward calls himself the Duke of Lancaster, or other royals call themselves Count of this or that. Of course European royals are better known, so the false name is a bit of game, but when I need to use my title, I can just say I'm behaving as the Europeans do for expedience. I think this will be flexible and easy, so as soon as I go on the boat I plan not to use my royal title.

I believe that what I have outlined above will be enough to avoid any complications, but if Your Majesty has any views on this, I can amend my plans accordingly.

I beg to remain Your Majesty's obedient servant,
Chakrabongse

In order to try and be accepted by her husband's family, Katya generally wore Siamese court dress, consisting of a lace blouse and silk jungraben, *as worn by her mother-in-law, Queen Saovabha and other royal ladies.*

Baan Puen, Petchaburi
8th September 1910

Lek

I have received your reply. Your travel plans sound entirely correct, and using a different name is an excellent solution. If anyone knows you, you can own up straight away. I have also done this in the past. It seems we don't need to talk about this, as you understand everything already. However, as your father allow me to speak frankly. You can see that the fact of having a *farang* wife, even if it isn't anything as bad as some may think, is nevertheless something about which both *farang* and Thai feel deep inside is an unsolvable problem. So you must be careful not to fall into awkward situations, or those where you are the object of scorn and derision. You should be able to prevent this, if you think about it beforehand.

Siamindra

28th September 1910

Your Majesty

Monsieur Ramlay, Eeyd Lek's teacher, has asked me to present the results of his exams, so that Your Majesty may be aware of the progress he has made.

The four sheets enclosed with this letter comprise Roman history, Italian history, international law and physics. It can be seen that Eeyd Lek has a good understanding of history and can explain it well, while international law is weak and physics is not good at all, because, according to the teacher, he doesn't like physics. Disliking this subject is strange, because it is very worth knowing, as it describes how things work in the world, which is very interesting and is the cradle of important ideas. Eeyd Lek doesn't like it, because it is a taxing subject. I am disappointed about this, but it's difficult to solve.

I beg to remain Your Majesty's obedient servant
Chakrabongse

Katya, Chula and Prince Chakrabongse, shortly after the death of King Chulalongkorn.

30th September 1910

My son Lek

I have looked at the exam results for Eeyd Lek. Whatever new knowledge he acquires makes me happy. Some things I don't know how to solve, but getting some things better is encouraging.

Siamindra

Three weeks later, King Chulalongkorn died, and so ended a correspondence spanning 14 years and a vast range of topics and emotions. For Katya, she was left to regret she had never met the king and made things all right between them. Prince Chula was too young to know what was going on, but had his picture taken with the sword the king had sent him.
For Prince Chakrabongse, it can only be imagined what conflicting emotions he felt. As shown by the 1910 letters, the anger that the king had expressed after his son's marriage had by then transformed to acceptance. His father had been his most devoted supporter. The next reign was to prove very different.

The last picture taken of King Chulalongkorn.

*Part of the funeral procession for King Chulalongkorn. Prince
Chakrabongse is at the front of the line on the right of the photograph.*

*Part of the Meru for the funeral of King Chulalongkorn.
The actual cremation was held on xxx.*

Prince Chula wearing the uniform and the sword given to him
by King Chulalongkorn, photographed after the king's death.

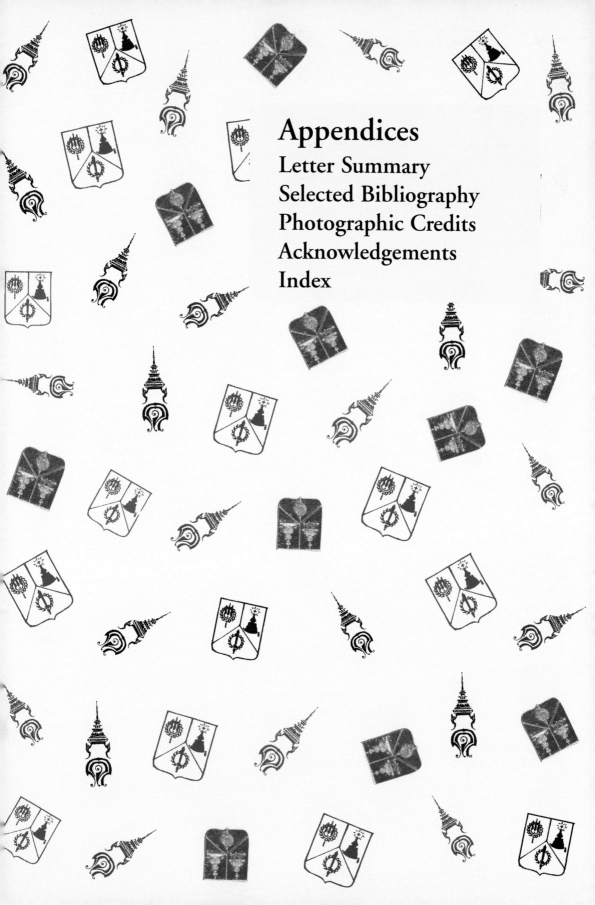

Appendices

Of the almost 300 letters, 280 are summarized below. Those from King Chulalongkorn are in red.

1896 – 6 letters (4 from the King)

23rd May 1896. Lek to King. Colombo. Account of life on board *Saghalien* and impressions of Colombo. p. 14

31st May 1896. Lek to King. Trip to Kandy. The Tooth Relic and scenery on return to Colombo. Trip as far as Aden. p. 16

24th June 1896. King to Lek. Hotel van Horek, Garoet. Account of his trip in Java. Misses Lek a lot. p. 22-24

30th July 1896. King to Lek. Very long description of the trip to Java. Volcanoes. Ruling system and palaces. p. 27-44

3rd August 1896. King to Lek. Hurricane House Singapore. p. 46

25th September 1896. King to Lek. Received cushions Lek sent. Sadly Sadet Yai had already died. Other gifts not arrived. p. 47

1897 – 9 letters (3 from King)

16th February 1897. King To Lek. Only Lek and Paribatra have written that they are looking forward to seeing him. Worried they won't have enough time together. Queen not well, but King thinks trip will be beneficial for the country. p. 50

14th June 1897. King to Lek. In Florence. Having various portraits done. p. 52

18 November 1897. Lek to King. Show at Sandhurst. Studying English as no Russian teacher yet. Checking out possible companion. Likes Nai Poum. p. 54

2nd December 1897. Lek to King. Received letter from Egypt. Studying Russian very hard. p. 55

7th December 1897. King to Lek. Missing him very much. Nervous about welcome home reception. Seasick. p. 66

10th December 1897. Lek to King. Play at Sandhurst. Have decided which student to take to Russia. Have begun riding lessons. p. 67

16th December 1897. Lek to King. Riding lessons in Military Academy. Thinks of King arriving back in Bangkok. p. 67

23rd December 1897. Lek to King. Up to London. Mr Phipps took Lek and Toonmom Toh to visit Lord Bath. p. 68

30th December 1897. Lek to King. Acted in two plays for charity with brothers. Barnums Circus. Saw Jubilee Queen in cinema. Went to Pantomime at Drury Lane but was not a patch on last year. p. 69

1898 – 45 letters (4 from the King)

6th January 1898. Lek to King. Pleased to get letter from Penang. Toro has been over and been fine. Toonmom Toh's birthday. Various brothers to Camberley. Studies begun and doing lots of Russian. p. 72

January 1898. King To Lek. Hasn't been feeling well. Wheezing. Having to meet lots of dignitaries. Still time to choose which student to take. Missing him. p. 73

13th January 1898. Lek to King. Pleased with gifts from Egypt and that Nai Poum has been chosen. Sorry could not take Nai Tiem. Russian exam tomorrow. p. 74

20th January 1898. Lek to King. Lecture in London by Mr Warington Smyth of RGS. Had Russian and English exams. p. 75

27th January 1898. Lek to King. Toonmom Toh starting at Sandhurst. Graitney Debating Society set up. Mr. Hume gives a lecture every week. p. 76

3rd February 1898. Lek to King. Another meeting of debating society. Weather terrible. Fell off riding. p. 76

10th February 1898. Lek to King. Visited Toonmom Toh at Sandhurst. Nai Poum has arrived and started Russian. Should he be part of court? p. 77

17th February 1898. Lek to King. Really pleased to have had a letter. Glad King had great reception on return home. Likes Nai Poum a lot. Worried about whether he'll progress fast enough in Russian. p. 78

18th February 1898. King To Lek. Has had letter from Queen of Spain with photos for Lek. Is pleased that Lek is studying well. French are being quiet. His reception in Bangkok was good in every way. Toro has come back and said he made a scene to get sent home. p. 79

24th February 1898. Lek to King. Hale has joined Russian class. More about King's reception in Bangkok. Doing some photography. p. 80

3rd March 1898. King To Lek. All good wishes for his birthday. Position of Nai Nok Yoong in Russia. Should there be an ambassador or not in St. Petersburg? Will write to Emperor asking him what he has arranged for Lek education. Nothing special in Bangkok. Heat makes everyone lazy. Chira to marry Ying Prawas. Wishes he could go away to Lisbon. p. 80-81

3rd March 1898. Lek to King. Went to concert in Aldershot. Terrible weather. His birthday and not heard from father so a bit upset. p. 82

11th March 1898. Lek to King. Birthday telegram arrived late. Brothers came down for dinner. Various lectures. Russian debating society. Very hard. p. 82

11th March 1898. King To Lek. Has written to Emperor that Lek preparing to leave. Doesn't know how soon he will receive it. Nai Poum will be a cadet. Nai Nok Yoong more difficult as is not a soldier. Russia and England being provocative to each other. p. 83

24th March 1898. Lek to King. Public schools sports day. Boys marched quite badly. Three Thai boys. p. 84

31st March 1898. Lek to King. Pleased to get letter from the King and from King Alfonso. Sorry not to take Nai Tiem. Nai Poum is doing well in Russian. Sends some Russia writing to father. p. 85

15th April 1898. Lek to King. Another schools sport day with gymnastics. Met Duke of Connaught. In evening party for Siamese New Year. Brothers on holiday so down to country. Also to London to theatre. Happy all decided about Nai Poum and Nai Nok Yoong. p. 86

21st April 1898. Lek to King. Letter has been sent to Emperor. Waiting for Phraya Mahibal. Will stop in Berlin on way. p. 87

28th April 1898. Lek to King. Received photos of parents. Vudh came down. Outing on River Thames. p. 87-88

5th May 1898. Lek to King. Seems everything arranged, but is worried date for departure not fixed. Went to evening show at Military academy. p. 88

17th May 1898. Lek to King. Lunch at military academy with Toonmom Toh. Date for arrival in Russia will be 13th June. p. 89

3rd June 1898. Lek to King. Everyone rallying to say goodbye. Has met Mahibal and happy with him. Is a bit anxious. p. 90

10th June 1898. Lek to King. Left London. Stayed in Paris. Then Berlin and saw Toonmom Chai. Says he will do his best in St. Petersburg. p. 90-91

21st June 1898. Lek to King. Train to St. Petersburg. Lessons being planned. Count Keller and Captain Khrulov meet him and take him to Winter Palace. First meeting with Emperor and Empress. Called on Dowager Empress. p. 95-97

4th July 1898. Lek to King. Couldn't write as fell from horse. Emperor and Empress have been to see him. p. 98

12th July 1898. Lek to King. Much better. Emperor and Empress to see him again. Accident covered in all the newspapers and British press. p. 98

20th July 1898. Lek to King. First day out after fall. Went to see Emperor and Empress. Grand Duchess Olga there. Rehearsal for annual cadet review. Presents for doctors who attended him. p. 100

26th July 1898. Lek to King. Lunch for name day of Grand Duchess Olga. Horse racing. Will watch troop review at Krasnoe Selo. King of Romania coming. p. 100

2nd August 1898. Lek to King. Troop review at Krasnoe Selo. Visit of King of Romania. Military review. p. 102

7th August 1898. Lek to King. Name day of Dowager Empress. Observed life boat drill. Lunch in palace. Horse racing at Krasnoe Selo. p. 104

16th August 1898. Lek to King. 14th lunch in palace. Have started studying again. p. 105

23rd August 1898. Lek to King. Sent photos of parents to various nobles. Manoeuvres in St. Petersburg on river Neva with bridge building. Queen of Denmark ill. p. 106-07

30th August 1898. Lek to King. Emperor and Empress to Moscow. Went to see off at station. p. 107

7th September 1898. Lek to King. His impressions of Russia. Met Count Muraviev. Visit of Phraya Cholayut in ship *Siam*. Thavidabhisek ceremony. p. 108-09

13th September 1898. Lek to King. Fall from horse discussed again. Lessons begin. His education. His quarters. Description of first day at school. Austrian Empress shot in Geneva. p. 110

20th September 1898. Lek to King. Party for King's birthday. Admiral Arseniev coming. Life in the Corps, his lessons and other boys. Visit to paper factory. p. 112

27th September 1898. Lek to King. Birthday celebrations for King. Meets Admiral Arseniev and likes him. Count Keller says he can stay at Phraya Mahibal's house at weekends. p. 113

4th October 1898 Lek to King. 30th anniversary of King's accession to throne. Queen of Denmark died. Had party for some school friends. Artillery practice. p. 114

12th October 1898. Lek to King. Shooting near Krasnoe Selo. First snow. Very cold. Shot two rabbits. p. 114-15

18th October 1898. Lek to King. Visit to munitions factory. Went to see Carmen. Very cold and snowy. p. 115

25th October 1898. Lek to King. Visit to porcelain and glass factory. Went to Tsarskoe Selo to see Admiral Arseniev, while he was coming to Petersburg. p. 116

8th November 1898. Lek to King. Anniversary of Emperor's accession. Weather bad and pupils behaving badly. p. 117

15th November 1898. Lek to King. Anniversary of King's coronation. Went marching round city with other pupils. Pupils dislike Count Keller. p. 118

5th December 1898. Lek to King. Dinner for Chao Phraya Abhaya Raja. Arseniev there. Went shooting again. p. 118

27th December 1898. Lek to King. Discussion as to whether Captain Khrulov should go to BKK if Chakrabongse goes home. Not had many letters. Will go on holiday to Moscow. p. 119

1899 – 26 letters (4 from the King)

2nd January 1899. Lek to King. Description of trip to Moscow. Visit to Grand Duke Serge. Ivan Grozny Bell tower. Various churches. p. 122

31st January 1899. Lek to King. Hasn't seen Emperor as he is at Tsarskoe Selo. Dowager Empress in mourning. Weather quite warm. Too warm for trams on frozen river. Description of snow and ice. p. 125

14th February 1899. Lek to King. Concert at Corps des Pages. Balalaika playing very good. Marching around Petersburg with rifles. Arseniev came round then tea at his house. Timing of his trip home. p. 126

26th February 1899. Lek to King. Nothing exciting. Empress pregnant and weak. Dowager Empress in mourning. Emperor came to Corps but Lek not there. No Sunday lunches at palace. p. 127

7th March 1899. Lek to King. Just had birthday, so was party with lucky dip. Pages enjoyed it. One of them has died, so went to funeral. p. 127

14th March 1899. Lek to King. Carnival. Shows on in all theatres and schools shut. Play at Corps des Pages. 10th March school fete day. p. 128

28th March 1899. Lek to King. Finally two letters from father. Shows some conflict with Phraya Suriya. p. 128

English letter. 4th April 1899. Lek to King. Phraya Mahibal said should sometimes write in English to keep it up. King has written letter to Emperor. Khrulov wants to go to BKK with them. p. 129

English letter. 17th April 1899. Lek to King. Pleased with money for birthday and that Emperor is OK with trip home. Will go via Berlin to see Paribatra. Wants Chira to meet him in Singapore. Exams soon. p. 129

English letter. 3rd May 1899. Lek to King. Staying in legation. Emperor and Empress in town for Easter. Lunch in Winter Palace. Discusses telegram from King and his forthcoming trip home. p. 130-31

English letter. 9th May 1899. Lek to King. Talks about Easter. Lunch at Tsarskoe Selo for Empress's saint day. p. 132

21st June 1899. King to Lek. Hasn't been well. Death of Prince Sommatiwongse has upset him greatly. Looking forward to seeing Lek. p. 133

IN BANGKOK UNTIL END OF AUGUST

21st June 1899. King to Lek. Mother is better and has been out riding and seems well. Thinking of him a lot. p. 135

English letter. 30th August 1899. Lek to King. Koh Sichang. Saw Queen Savang, Prince Mahidol and Uncle Svasti. Rangsit on boat with him. Saw Governor Charles Mitchell in Singapore. p. 135-36

1st September 1899. Lek to King. Went to Johor. Nothing much to see. Got rained on. Dinner with the Governor of Singapore. p. 136

English letter. 18th September 1899. Lek to King. On L'Oceanien. Sea very calm and hot. Stopped in Djibouti for coal. Nothing to see. Misses father. p. 137

4th October 1899. King to Lek. Delighted Sultan received him so well. Lonely without Rangsit. DeFrance being difficult. Nothing is as was agreed. Ministerial reshuffle. Mother better and rushing about. p. 138

9th October 1899. Lek to King. Back in Russia. Tells where all the key players are and his arrangements for Rangsit and Thongrod. Pleased Mother is riding. p. 140

11th October 1899. Lek to King. Report on Constantinople. Decorations at King's discretion. Started studying again. p. 140

24th October 1899. Lek to King. Rangsit, Thongrod and Phraya Visudh arrived from Berlin. Visudh should work on education reform. Visit to Alexander Nevsky Monastery. p. 141

29th October 1899. Lek to King. Luang Abhirak (Nai Nok Yoong) going back to Bangkok. Asks who will be his new ADC. p. 146

7th November 1899. Lek to King. Sad about problems with French. Analyses problem. Pleased that Sadet Mother is better. 146-47

14th November 1899. Lek to King. Buddha relic for Russian Buddhists. Prince Ukhtomsky will sort it out. Emperor going shooting in Poland. p. 147

English letter. November 27th 1899. Emperor back at Tsarskoe Selo. 16th birthday lunch for Empress Marie. Private meeting with Emperor and gave cup for Grand Duchess Maria and messages. Lek also brought gifts. Long chat with Emperor giving all the news. Emperor said of course Empress would accept decoration. Asked about Lek's new rooms in Winter Palace. p. 148

9th December 1899. King to Lek. Liked his Constantinople report very much. Decorations for people on trip. Decoration for Empress. Discussion of adjutant. French still problem. Negotiations with British better. 2 *farang* royals about to come. Mother better and planting trees. Feels things are better generally. p. 149

10th December 1899. Lek to King. Ball at Mikhailovsky Artillery Academy. Very hot and crowded. Next day fete for all those who got St. George decoration. p. 150

19th December 1899. Lek to King. Emperor's fete day. Saw Empress Marie for the first time since return. p. 151

1900 – 38 letters (5 from the King)

3rd January 1900. Lek to King. Toonmom Toh visiting St. Petersburg. Dinner for their mother, with Muraviev and various ambassadors. p. 154

12th January 1900. King to Lek. Has been very busy. Decoration for Empress. Enjoyed visit of Prince Henry, disliked visit of Prince Valdemar of Denmark. Burmese and Sri Lankans arrived to receive their relic. Trying to reach agreement with French. Talks with British finished. O (Olarovsky) being difficult. Sankharaj died. Saw end of Northeastern Railway line near Si Kiew. p. 155

17th January 1900. Lek to King. Pleased about agreement with England. Toh left, all went well. Russian New Year sat at Imperial Table together with Grand Duchess Olga and Duke of Leuchtenburg. Emperor very friendly and said he was pleased to see Toonmom Toh. p. 156

22nd January 1900. Lek to KIng. Russian Buddhists came to get relic, led by Prince Ukhtomsky. Small ceremony. Duke of Saxe Coburg on visit without his wife. Started studying again. p. 157

6th February 1900. Lek to King. Went shooting again. Toonmom Chai about to visit. p. 158

20th February 1900. Lek to King. Decoration for Empress not arrived. Emperor's plans for leaving Petersburg. Emperor and Empress came to the Corps. Discussion of Olarovsky. Grand Duke Olga (N's younger sister) ill. Dowager Empress's improved relationship with Empress. p. 159

25th February 1900. Lek to King. Has received long letter from King Alfonso XIII. Emperor went to Corps for a second time. Weather is better. p. 160

26th February 1900. King to Lek. Olarovsky leaving Bangkok and will bring him some things. Complained about Prince Henry and Valdemar again. Pleased Lek received Toh so well. More about Buddhist relic. Will stay at Suan Dusit soon. Wat Benjamabhopit begun. Malaria prevalent. Thinks about Lek a lot. p. 162

5th March 1900. Lek to King. On 26th lunch with Emperor plus Mahibal and Cpt Khrulov. Long chat. Discussion of Kammer Page system. Lek wants to be in the cavalry. Mentions the visit of Valdemar. p. 163

19th March 1900. Lek to King. Toonmom Chai left for Berlin. Visit to Chakrabongse from Adjutant General Espinosa of Spain. p. 164

English letter. 26th March 1900. Lek to King. Empress Marie to Copenhagen. Lunch with Emperor and Empress. Latter said he did well in gun practice at Corps. Emperor will go to Moscow for Easter. p. 165

3rd April 1900. Lek to King. Toonmom Toh and Lek to lunch in palace. Talk about 2nd Boer War. Russians on side of Transvaal. Congratulations for Grand Duke Constantine appointed as Chief of All Military Colleges. Concert at Opera. Grand Duke Constantine to Corps. Pleased the King is happy that he's presented the relic to Russian Buddhists. p. 166-67

16th April 1900. Lek to King. Has been taking Toonmom Toh to various sites: Prison, Deaf Mute School, Pulkovo Observatory, Riding Academy for soldiers. Saw off Emperor and Empress to Moscow. p. 168-69

24th April 1900. Lek to King. Saw off Toonmom Toh back to London. Russian Easter, so on holiday. Says maybe Emperor will write to Queen Victoria suggesting she stops Boer War. p. 170

30th April 1900. Lek to King. Will have exams soon. Description of a Russian wedding. Weather changeable – one minute hot, the next cold. p. 171

15th May 1900. Lek to King. Olarovsky came to see him and Lek was impressed. 7th May, Emperor back from Moscow. Lek went with him to see review of the troops. Afterwards dinner at the Oldenburg palace. 172-73

28th May 1900. Lek to King. Has presented order to Empress. She was very happy. Afterwards had a private lunch and a nice chat. Long description of visit to Naval Dockyard. He has exams all the time. p. 175

7th June 1900. Lek to King. Heard Toonmom Toh was ill, so when exams finished went to England to attend to Toonmom Toh. He has Peritoflitis. Not allowed to see him. Encloses letter to Emperor explaining his absence. Gone to Oxford to be near him. p. 176-77

21st June 1900. Lek to King. A lot about Toonmom Toh and his illness. Has also seen his other brothers. Says he'll stay on in England and keep Toonmom Toh happy. p. 178

28th June 1900. King to Lek. Says hasn't written for long time. Says Thais are interested in Transvaal but more so in China. Talks about Chinese. His trip to seaside. News of Toh being ill. Coming back gets stuck on the Bar. Says has only been able to buy one plot of land for the house [Wang Parus?]. Has stayed at Suan Dusit. Will send photos. Discussions with French have stalled. Will write to Emperor about it. Nai Bus Mahindra and his play which went to Russia. Nakhon Ratchasima train line will open soon. Fancies going to Paris for Great Exhibition but was too tiring last time. p. 179-81

29th June 1900. Lek to King. Toonmom Toh much better. Has been to stay with the Fullers. Mr Verney will give him dinner. p. 181

5th July 1900. Lek to King. From Broadstairs. Dinner given by Mr and Mrs Warr. Mr. Verney has fallen off his bike. Went to see School for Scandal. Discusses Suan Dusit. Hotel in Broadstairs is right on cliff. Toonmom much better but needs sea air. p. 182-83

10th, 17th July 1900, Lek to King. Up to London and met with Prince Paribatra. Dinner in Lek's honour to celebrate his commission into Royal Guards regiment. Back to Broadstairs. Went to Deal and Walmer Castle. Rolin Jacquemyns came down to see Toonmom Toh. p. 183-84

27th July 1900. Lek to King. Dinner to celebrate 7 Royal Guards members being in Europe at same time. p. 184-85

25th July 1900. King to Lek. Refers to Lek's letters. Talks about letter to Emperor. Letter drafted by Phraya Abhai Raja was too pompous, the one by Prince Damrong similar, so had to write it himself. Anxious about asking Emperor for help. Chinese situation and fears of *farang* in Bangkok that protests could spread there. p. 186

7th August 1900. King to Lek. Letter introducing Luang Sorayudh Yothaharn, new ADC. Tells Lek to attend funeral of King Umberto I of Italy. p. 187

10th August 1900. Lek to King. Long letter reporting on the funeral and who he met etc. p. 188-91

16th August 1900. Lek to King. Trip back via Milan and Paris. Staying with Mr Phipps, former guardian. Brief visit to Paris World Fair. p. 191-92

5th September 1900. Lek to King. Much longer visit to Paris World Fair, description of many pavilions. Trip to Berlin and sees Toonmom Chai and Rangsit. p. 192-98

12th September 1900. Lek to King. Has received letter for Emperor, who is in Poland and will then go to Crimea. Will be in special class in the school and undertake guard duties and enter regiment. p. 199

17th September 1900. Lek to King. Luang Surayudh has arrived as ADC and likes him. New classrooms at Corps. Everything will be stricter than before. p. 199

18th September 1900. Lek to King. Forgot to mention Buddhist Tartar monk whom Olarovsky brought to meet him. Very civilised and thrilled with relic. p. 200

7th October 1900. Lek to King. Met Colonel Epanchin, new director of Corps des Pages. Has started law. Emperor still in Crimea. Account of Khmer prince in France criticising French loudly and publicly. p. 200-01

English letter. 14th October 1900. Lek to King. Nothing much going on. The senior class have been appointed pages. Private visits with Epanchin. English not very good [ed. note]. p. 202

20th November 1900. Lek to King. Emperor has been quite ill with typhoid. Speculation could be poison. Sent telegrams to the Emperor to congratulate him on anniversary of his accession. p. 202-03

27th November 1900. Lek to King. More about Emperor's illness and reasons for it. Rumour that Empress is pregnant again. Hopes for a Grand Duke. p. 203

1st December 1900. Lek to King. Has been on guard duty in Corps des Pages. Quite tiring. On 10th November went on marching exercise through the town. People shouted out "The Thai prince!". Thai play by Nai Bus to be shown in two Imperial theatres. Has not heard from King for a long time. p. 204

8th December 1900. Lek to King. Wrote to Empress on behalf of Toonmom Toh and the King asking about Emperor's health. He's better. Very cold and river frozen over. Toonmom Toh planning a visit which Lek hopes will be as successful as first. p. 206

11th December 1900. Lek to King. Emperor's health. Dowager Empress, in Denmark, angry with Empress Alexandra for not tell her he was ill. p. 206-07

English letter. 19th December 1900. Lek to King. Cross because Phraya Suriya trying to organise his holiday programme. Emperor quite better. p. 207

1901 – 32 letters (5 from king)

15th January 1901. Lek to King. Hasn't written for long time. Visit of Toonmom Toh. Saw Grand Duchess Elizabeth, wife of Grand Duke Constantine. 8th January acted in play at embassy. All ambassadors came. 9th Toonmom Toh back to London. 14th was Russian New Year but quiet as Emperor away. Has received Chula Chom Klao First class. Says will honour the decoration always. p. 210-11

English letter. 29th January 1901. Lek to King. Big reception to greet Tsar on his first visit to St. Petersburg after illness. Pages greeted him outside Kazan Cathedral. Met Minister of War Kuropatkin. p. 213

English letter. 5th February 1901. Lek to King. Family lunch with Emperor and Empress. Emperor spoke Russian then changed to English when Empress came in. Emperor very pleased, Lek now in his company. Grand Duchess of Hesse there. Grand Duchess Maria was very curious about Lek. p. 213-14

23rd February 1901. Lek to King. On duty at the Corps. Inspected by Grand Duke Vladimir. Emperor and Empress came to inspect as well. Very tired as hardly any sleep. Concert at Alexandrovsky cadet school. Play at the royal civilian school. Empress there and had tea with her in interval. Gossip about Pi Abha breaking of engagement with one of daughters of Phraya Suriya. p. 215-17

8th March 1901. Lek to King. Letter from Princess of Asturias. Minister of Enlightenment shot. Problem of students in Russian universities. p. 217

English letter. 12th March 1901. Lek to King. Fete day of the Corps. Grand Duke Constantine arrived. Grand Duchess Olga, Tsar's sister, to marry Prince Peter of Oldenburg. p. 218-19

18th March 1901. Lek to King. Engagement between Grand Duchess Olga and Prince of Oldenburg announced. Minister of Education has died. Student unrest People don't know what they want. p. 219-20

English letter. 2nd April 1901. Lek to King. Concert for veteran soldiers by all the military bands. Emperor there. Students quieter and various measures taken against them. Lessons finished, now exams. p. 220

English letter. 10th April 1901. Lek to King. First exams: literature got 12, rules for soldiers and small arms, again 12. All cadets went to see play, Peter the Great, at the Emperor Nicholas II Theatre. p. 221

English letter. 23 April 1901. Lek to King. Geography exam got 12. Russian Easter and invited to ceremony with Emperor and Empress. Then family lunch. Empress gave Lek a stone for the top of a walking stick. Working hard for good marks to be Empress's page. Saw Dowager Empress and received another egg. Olga and Peter of Oldenburg there. Saw other Grand Dukes and Generals. Exam in military tactics – 12. p. 222

English letter. 7th May 1901. Lek to King. Three more exams – Russian language, mechanics and artillery: all 12. Weather too bad for annual parade of troops in St. Petersburg. Went to Fete day of Empress and private family lunch. Visit of Buddhist Cossack and learns one million cossacks are Buddhists. p. 223

8th May 1901. King to Lek. Written from Royal Yacht. *Meru* being done for several people including Prince Maha Vajirunhis and an aunt. Bad asthma. Discusses Lek's infatuation with showgirl at length. Pleased Tsar is better and Empress is pregnant. Should be a boy. Siberians have come to Bangkok. Bus Mahindra affair. Peter of Oldenburg not good enough for Olga. Not keen on Lek being in cavalry. Warns him not to marry a *farang* and to remember the promise he gave his mother. p. 224-26

English letter. 21st May 1901. Lek to King. Exam results: chemistry 12, German 10, natural history 12, French 12, topography 11. Emperor reviewed the troops in St. Petersburg at Champs des Mars. Lek's Corps took part. Lunch at palace of Prince of Oldenburg to which Lek invited. 19th May Emperor's birthday. Lek invited but Empress not there as about to give birth. p. 228-29

3rd June 1901. Lek to King. Eeyd Lek's illness. Volcanic eruption on Java. 12 for last exam – law. Mapping exercise in Peterhof. Sleeping on straw pallets with all the students, but gets special food. p. 230

English letter. 17th June 1901. Lek to King. The King rebuked him so nicely [see letter of 8 May]. Discusses his relationship with Kschessinska. Phraya Suriya has bad intentions towards him. Angry about secrecy and involving Thoonkramom Chai. Apologises for upsetting his

father and mother and says will behave well. p. 231-32

25th June 1901. Lek to King. Explains why wants to be a Hussar. Empress has had another daughter. The Corps on annual camp at Krasnoe Selo. He has separate food. At weekend stays in rented house in Duderhof. p. 232

26th June 1901. King to Lek. Bandung Java. Eeyd Lek's illness. No one knows what's wrong but has a kidney problem. Thai doctors said he would die. King kept calm. Says he may not be able to go to Europe as is sickly. p.233-35

3rd July 1901. Lek to King. Still at camp and exercises with Finnish army. Marching exercises. p. 235-36

22nd July 1901. King to Lek. Royal Yacht Maha Chakri. Complains about lazy officials in Bangkok. Eeyd Lek better. More about the showgirl and Phraya Suriya. Says could well be because of conflict between Suriya and Mahibal. Asks Lek to think about this and weigh up all the angles. p. 236-37

24th July 1901. Lek to King. More exercises with Finnish regiment and Pavlovsky regiment. Sleeping in tents. Various mock battles. Saw Director Epanchin and sightseeing around Tsarskoe Selo. p. 238-39

31st July 1901. Lek to King. Last day of camp. Emperor and both Empresses came to inspect. Dinner in palace for officers and Lek. 28th, name day of Grand Duke Vladimir. 30th, review of all regiments by Emperor and Empresses. Will stay on in Duderhof, then 3rd August will go to London to see Toonkramom Toh. p. 240

6th August 1901. King to Lek. Upset did not send telegram to Emperor about birth of Anastasia. Says Ministry of Foreign affairs does not tell him anything. Not so well since home. Eeyd Lek better but not as strong as normal. p. 241

15th August 1901. Lek to King. 31st July took train to London. Happy to see Toonmom Toh and other brothers. Wedding of Mr. Phipps daughter. Performed in play in embassy. Danai and Tridos are doing well. Stayed with the Verneys. p. 242

29th August 1901. Lek to King. Glasgow exhibition with Toonmom Toh. Stayed in Windsor Hotel. Impressed by engineering exhibition. Visited docks. Russian pavilion large. Back to stay with the Phipps. p. 243

7th September 1901. King to Lek. Sorry Emperor's 4th child is a girl. Doesn't want Lek in cavalry as scared he will fall off again. Discussion of Phraya Mahibal and Captain Khrulov. Eeyd Lek still not fully recovered. p. 244

17th September 1901. Lek to King. On way back stopped in Frankfurt to visit Oon, wife of Phraya Mahibal. In Berlin met Rangsit again. Chinese prince there as ambassador to apologise about German ambassador being killed by Boxers. Back to Petersburg with Prince Vudh. Has a new tutor. Studies recommenced. p. 244-45

25th September 1901. Lek to King. Letter for Emperor arrived but not gift for Anastasia. Emperor's trip to France very good. Emperor shooting in Spala. Studies going well. p. 246

7th October 1901. Lek to King. His German teacher has died. Mock exams. p. 247

30th October 1901. Lek to King. More about Phraya Mahibal lending money to Captain Khrulov. Says Luang Visudh should not come back again, as unsuitable to receive Toonmom Toh. 26th October 1901 appointed as a Chamber Page to the Empress. p. 248-49

20th November 1901. Lek to King. Emperor and Empress back from Spala. Shot huge number of game. Emperor will stay at Tsarskoe Selo until January. Has asked for an audience. Weather very cold and river frozen over earlier than usual. p. 249

10th December 1901. Lek to King. 9th, feast day of St. George and celebrating gallantry order named after this saint. Large ceremony in palace. On page duty. One of pages received award for action against China. Explains about carrying the Empresses's train. The ceremony was at lunch and in evening. His first real duties. p. 250-52

25th December 1901. Lek to King. Emperor's nameday on 19th and Lek there as page. Audience with King of Montenegro who received him well. 22nd, all the new Chamber Pages presented themselves. Emperor and Empress talked about Toonmom Toh's upcoming visit. He will stay in the palace. p. 252-53

1902 – 23 letters (1 from King)

1st January 1902. Lek to King. Questions why Phraya Mahibal is being sent back. Count Lamsdorf may recall Olarovsky. Phraya Suriya prefers Muraviev (former Foreign Minister) but Lek and Emperor thinks this one better. Would be pleased if Olarovsky replaced. p. 256-57

21st January 1902. Lek to King. Toonmom Toh's trip to Russia. Grand Duke Michael met him and many officials. Staying in Winter Palace. Emperor lent him Imperial box in theatre. 12th, lunch with Emperor. Grand Duke George and Grand Duchess Marie there. Discussed regiment for Lek. Emperor said he would decide. Also discussed military academy. Emperor shared his thoughts and said he liked Hussars and Preobrazhensky regiments best. Went back for New Year's celebrations – Toh as guest, Lek as page. 15th Emperor gave a lunch for Toonmom Toh. Finally, trip to Finland. 19th another Russian Fete day. Lek on duty. Tsar confirms he should be in the Hussars. p. 257-61

5th February 1902. Lek to King. Toonmom Toh gone. At American embassy met Lefevre-Pontalis, secretary general at the embassy. French ambassador rather haughty. 28th, State Ball in the palace. Lek on duty. 3,500 people.

Has sent list of tutors to receive royal decorations as studies finished. Can't come home in summer as centenary of Corps des Pages. Asks to go to America with Toonmom Toh. Got most marks of any page in his year – determined to get name on the marble panel. p. 262-63

17th February 1902. Lek to King. Fishing exhibition. Thai exhibit quite good. p. 264

Also 17th February 1902. Lek to King. Visit of Kalmyk group with books and Buddha images for the King. Lots of dances and plays in the palace but lots of people ill with flu. Olarovsky will return to Bangkok as ambassador. Will take photos of Chakrabongse to King. p. 264-65

3rd March 1902. King to Lek. Hasn't written for ages due to asthma. Lots of people unwell. Discusses Phraya Mahibal issue again and next ambassador. Russian ambassador in BKK trying to put Siam under Russian protection. Fears Phraya Mahibal's influence on Lek. So happy at Eeyd Lek's tonsurate, as he almost died. p. 265-66

5th March 1902. Lek to King. Visited Emir of Bukhara, who received him very well, but feels the Russians have received him too well. 20th February, went to barracks of the Royal Guards 1st company and saw drills, weapons stores, kitchens etc. 26th February, Emperor and Empress visited the Corps des Pages. Hasn't had a letter from King for a long time and feels neglected. p. 268-70

12th March 1902. Lek to King. Emir has given Lek decoration and one for King. Lek asks King to give Emir and Crown Prince decorations in return. p. 270

25th March 1902. Lek to King. Very pleased to have letter of 3rd March from King. Wants King to give more money to M. Cuissart (in Petersburg Siamese embassy) so he can marry and entertain and mingle more with Russians. Last day of study in the Corps des Pages. p. 271

8th April 1902. Lek to King. About to take final exams. Lists them. Then will go to Hussar regiment at Tsarskoe Selo. Emperor has given him a room in the palace. Then camp at Karposkoe. Will need a new house and two good horses. Who to accompany him on trip to US? p. 272-73

23rd April 1902. Lek to King. Assassination of Sipyagin and appointment of Phleve. Nevertheless, overall situation in Russia not as bad as made out to be. p. 274

30th April 1902. Lek to King. Explanation of Easter [again]. Big event in palace church. Lek there as page. 27th, visited Dowager Empress. Met Minister of Defence. Mentions Minister has been assassinated and there are troubles in the South. p. 275

12th May 1902. Lek to King. Discussion of what level Thai decorations to give his teachers. Weather bad. Forthcoming visit of French President Loubet. Empress very friendly to him now. Banquet at Grand Duke Vladimir's palace. p. 276-77

17th June 1902. Lek to King. Has had letters from King of 2nd and 8th May [missing]. Decoration for Emir of Bukhara. Explains why needs so much money. His good horse fell, but Emperor lent him one from royal stables. Talks about annoyance in Bangkok. Prince of Bulgaria has been but not received very well. Lek met him. Came top of the class with 11.82 points and name will be engraved. Poum second. Very happy two Thais came top. p. 278-79

22nd July 1902. Lek to King. Continues about visit of King of Italy [previous letter missing]. 14th July, on arrival, went to inspect the camps. Lek was with regiment to receive him. Then major troop review. 16th, inspection of Italian ships in Kronstadt. 17th, reception at palace. Lots of manoeuvres at Krasnoe Selo. Enigmatic comment about Prince Chira. p. 279-80

28th July 1902. Lek to King. In Duderhof. Name day of Grand Duke Vladimir, who was happy with reception of his son Grand Duke Boris in Siam. Grand party at Emperor's palace. Queen of Greece there. Talked to Emperor about Pi Chira, who is in Germany. Asked if Lek was happy in the Hussars. 4th August, German Emperor will go to Ravel on Baltic and meet Emperor for Naval review. End of August, King of Greece to come. p. 281-82

11th August 1902. Lek to King. Karposkoe Village, Hussar regiment. 8th, Chira arrived from Denmark. Met him at Gatchina and brought him to Duderhof. 10th, visited the Emperor at Krasnoe Selo racecourse for regimental races. 13th on, Hussars will be performing military manoeuvres. p. 283

4th September 1902. Lek to King. In Berlin. Has been busy with manoeuvres hence no letters. Extols benefits of cavalry. Emperor also came to watch. At Feodorovsky Pasad Emperor gave out officer ranks to the cadets. Empress was pregnant, so Lek got his orders from Emperor. Also saw King of Greece and Queen. Went to see the Emperor again who said his uniform was well cut. Saw Empress too. 29th, wedding of Prince Nicholas of Greece and Grand Duchess Helen. Met many royals. Description of wedding. More festivities. On 30th left Petersburg for Berlin to see Toonmom Chai. p. 284-87

18th September 1902. Lek to King. Has been to Vienna and Budapest. Liked Vienna and really liked Budapest. Stayed in Hungaria Hotel where King stayed. Pi Pen also there. Back in Berlin on 15th. Empress's miscarriage rather confusing. p. 288-89

13th October 1902. Lek to King. Hotel Arlington Washington. Sea crossing very rough. Been to see the President. Also went to see Russian ambassador. Visited the Capitol and the Library of Congress, train to Annapolis to see the US Naval Academy. Letter from Emperor's personal physician says Empress can still have a child, but rumour of miscarriage was true. p. 290-92

18th November 1902. Lek to King. During US trip no time to write, only now when back in Petersburg. Description of Washington. Accompanied by detectives all the time. Description of Capitol and National Library again, as well as Arlington Cemetery. Home for retired officers. George Washington's former home. Mentions Annapolis naval academy again. From Washington to Wilmington and then Philadelphia with a Mr Potter. Visited Independence Hall, Cramp's Shipyard and Baldwin Locomotive works. New York. Ferry over river. The Mayor. Stock Exchange. Tomb of General Grant. Columbia University library. Underground under construction. Fire stations and Fire brigades. Army College at West Point by river. Toonmom Toh gave dinner for all who'd welcomed them. Trip to Boston. Not impressed by Harvard. 2nd November, had to leave. Formed a very good impression of Americans. Very rough crossing. 16th back in Tsarskoe Selo and gave decoration to Grand Duke Constantine. Emperor and Empress in the Crimea. p. 293-99

25th November 1902. Lek to King. At the Hussars regiment. 19th, annual regimental day. Grand Duke Vladimir there. Later big party with Grand Duke Nicholas. p. 300

30th December 1902. Lek to King. On 24th Emperor back from Crimea for Corps des Pages centenary. Description of festivities. Lek donated a portrait bust of emperor to the school. Banquet in Winter Palace. Celebrations until 28th, when lunched with Emperor and Empress. Talked more with Grand Duke Serge. Somdet Chai and Prince Suriyong came for the holidays. p. 301-02

1903 – 8 letters (those from the King missing)

7th January 1903. Lek to King. Seen Emperor and Empress a lot. Both well. Crown Prince of Germany will come soon. Celebrated Toonmom Toh and Queen's birthday. Grand Duke Boris still delighted with his trip and very friendly as in same regiment. p. 306

4th March 1903. Lek to King. Carnival week. 2-day event with play in palace and costume ball. Audience in period dress of Tsar Alexis period. Went on intelligence corps long-distance march. p. 307-09

18th March 1903. Lek to King. Received letter from king [missing]. Enigmatic mention of a Crown Princess and whether she likes him. Dowager Empress off to Denmark. Emperer to go to Tsarskoe Selo. p. 309

24th March 1903. Lek to King. Asks permission to come home after the annual manoeuvres in time for the King's 50th birthday. Busy with regiment as Commanding Officer coming to inspect training. Will stay with Toonmom Toh in Bangkok.

2nd June 1903. Lek to King. Has received letter of 23rd April [missing]. Pleased about Buddha relic. Very pleased can go home. 22nd May, Emperor and Empress dined at regiment. Stayed till dawn. 28th, 250 anniversary of Uhlan Life Guards. 29th, bi-centenary celebrations of St. Petersburg. Seen the Emperor and Empress very often. p. 310-11

SECOND TRIP HOME. FIVE MONTHS.

17th October 1903. Lek to King. In Siam and has private matter to discuss with the King in person. p. 314

22 October 1903. Lek to King. Begs father to decide if he should go back to study at Military Academy. Pi Chira very against it.

8th December 1903. Lek to King. Reasons why his mother, Queen, has asked him to delay his return. p. 315

1904 – 17 letters (none from the King)

2 January 1904. Lek to King. Thanks for ivory box and begs King to send letter to Emperor. p. 320

6th January 1904. Royal Yacht Maha Chakra, Samut Prakharn. Thanks King for photograph and his good wishes. Feels very sad but says is gaining knowledge in Russia. Concerned about mother's illness. p. 320

10th January 1904. Lek to King. Arrived in Singapore and seen Mr. Anderson. Talk about possibility of Russo-Japanese war. Depressed at going away again. p. 321

11th January 1904. Lek to King. On the ship *Kiautschou*. After talk with Anderson long piece about unfavourable situation in Saibur. Worries that British could use this as an excuse to intervene. p. 322-23

12th January 1904. Lek to King. Arrived in Penang. Talked to Raja Muda about Saiburi, who say things are fine. p. 324-325

16th January 1904. Lek to King. Arrived in Colombo. Everything closed for weekend. Would like another flat, ivory box. p. 325

27th January 1904. Lek to King. Voyage through Red Sea surprisingly cool. Even had some rain. Worried about not hearing any news re Russo-Japanese war possibility. Has seen British naval vessel and Russian ships. All his dreams are of Bangkok at the moment. p. 326-27

3rd February 1904. Arrived in Genoa. Weather is terrible. Has heard Empress is pregnant again. p. 329

10th February 1904. Left Genoa by train. In Berlin heard news about Russo-Japanese war. Emperor to make proclamation in Moscow. Worried about his education. Says everyone very surprised and Russia did not want war. Met Dilok and Rangsit in Berlin. Reiterates war is entirely of Japan's making. p. 330-31

16th February 1904. Lek to King. Met Grand Duke Alexander Michaelovich and his wife in train. Both furious about Japan starting the war. Went to present himself to the regiment. 14th went to see Emperor and Empress for lunch. Presented King's letter. Petersburg full of war talk. Thais seen as siding with Japan. p. 332-33

23rd February 1904. Lek to King. Has been to the regiment and also sorted out his studies thanks to kindness of Emperor and efficiency of Colonel Deguy. Fears other Asian nations will start being looked at askance because of Japanese behaviour. p. 334-35

9th March 1904. Lek to King. Moved back into Winter Palace as easier for teachers. Less excitement about war. Most think Russia will win. p. 335

13th April 1904. Lek to King. Went to say happy Easter to Emperor, who was very friendly. Not much war news. Admiral Makarov has envigorated Russians. Train across Lake Baikal organised. Red Cross scandal with money missing. Press having to be more measured. p. 336-37

3 May 1904. Lek to King. Big welcome for returning sailors from *Varyaz* and *Koreets* ships back from war. Banquet in the palace. Emperor and Empress now back in Tsarskoe. Can see she is pregnant. Pavlovsk has been sunk and Admiral Makarov drowned. p. 337-38

FOUR-MONTH GAP FOR UNKNOWN REASON

21st September 1904. Lek to King. Holiday in San Sebastian. Went to show jumping event and met the royal family by chance, so invited to lunch with Queen Maria Christina and King Alfonso XIII. Had a really relaxed time. p. 339-40

23rd November 1904. Lek to King. Back in St. Petersburg via Berlin. Saw Dilok and Rangsit again. On 20th, lunched with Emperor. Took present King had sent for Tsarevich. Lots of officers have gone to war, so Lek requested to train new recruits. Discussed with Emperor and decided to accept and study less. p. 340-41

26th December 1904. King to Lek. Says hasn't written for a year because of asthma. So upset by the French and the Trat affair. So has been travelling around Thailand more - *tiew ton*. Happy Lek will actually serve in Hussars. Mother not so well but more resigned. p. 341

1905 – 16 letters (3 from the King)

25th January 1905. King to Lek. News from Russia very worrying. Won't force him to come home. Lek is doing a noble and loyal thing by serving, but mustn't overdo and must consider things carefully. Is speaking out of the love of a father and mother. Remember it is someone else's country. Tiw has had tonsurate. Cremation of Pi Nu next month. French have left Chantaburi. p. 346-47

8th February 1905. Lek to King. Pleased King is happy about him training recruits. Tired with all the travelling to Tsarskoe. Feels now French crisis has subsided, should be ready to fight them if necessary. Should follow Japanese example. Thais shouldn't be collecting for Japanese Red Cross. Situation in Russia not good. War has given him much food for thought. p. 347-48

1st March 1905. Lek to King. Sad about death of Somdet YaiYing. Assassination of Grand Duke Sergei. Wonderful behaviour of his wife, Grand Duchess Elizabeth. No one allowed to go to funeral. Discussion of how to solve political situation and problem of inertia. p. 349-351

8th March 1905. Lek to King. Pleased King trusts him to judge situation. Says press exaggerates. Revolution unlikely. Emperor promising some basic constitution. Long analysis of causes of unrest and possible solutions. Asks King to show letter to others to stop them worrying. He cannot behave like a coward. p. 352-53

9th April 1905. King to Lek. He did not want Russia to beat Japan, but sad for Emperor. Relations with French better. Discussion of Lek's mother's illness. Says he is also fed up and wants Lek to come home. Please think about this. p. 354-55

26th April 1905. Lek to King. Pleased to represent him at wedding of Crown Prince of Germany. Discussion of his entourage. Test of new recruits at Hussars. His did very well and he was singled out for special praise by commanding officer. Worries about Russian navy. Domestically situation calmer. p. 356

31st May 1905. Lek to King. Lunched with Emperor before leaving for Crown Prince's wedding. Emperor asked after his studies. Showed him new marble bath. Russian navy defeated again. After wedding will come straight back and holiday in Russia, as is a Russian officer and should not be away long. p. 357-58

11th June 1905. Lek to King. Report on Wedding. Enraged that Kaiser Wilhelm virtually ignored him and did not ask after King Chulalongkorn at all, even though his sons had been to stay in Bangkok. Other royals were very friendly. Not impressed by Japanese prince. p. 359-64

12th June 1905. King to Lek. Discussion of whether he should come back and Toh's role in trying to force him to come and look after mother. Government matters driving him crazy. Eeyd Lek seems to have little knowledge. p. 365

26th June 1905. Lek to King. More about whether he should come home or not. Very angry about Toonmom Toh's role. Says it would be terrible to leave Emperor and Russia now, with studies not finished and at such a time after Emperor has been so kind. Should not abandon a friend in need. p. 366-67

21st July 1905. Lek to King. Emperor would be very upset if he left now. Feels he should leave after studies are finished in December. Hasn't been well and doesn't want to go through Red Sea in summer, but of course will defer to King's command. p. 367-68

25th July 1905. Lek to King. More about when he should leave and wonders why Toonmom Toh has said he is doing nothing. Says work in Russia much harder than for those at university in England. Discussion of arrangments for Eeyd Lek's education in England. p. 368-69

4th August 1905. Lek to King. Arrangements for Eeyd Lek's education. Conflict with Phraya Raja over who is arranging what. Three younger brothers to come to Petersburg in September. Says it's not dangerous. p. 370

17th September 1905. Back to Petersburg after holiday. Another telegram from Toonmom Toh about getting him back has made him very upset More discussion about Phraya Raja and Eeyd Lek's education. Looking forward to seeing brothers. p. 371

3rd October 1905. Lek to King. Went to meet brothers at the station. They are staying at embassy. Will take Eeyd Lek to see Emperor, who is just back from holiday. Thinks Eeyd Lek should study French so will send him to a Belgian family. Studies going well at the Academy. p. 372

8th November 1905. Lek to King. Long letter about fact that there is almost a revolution going on. His view of the major players and reasons for the unrest. p. 374-375

1906 - 6 letters (4 from King)

19th January 1906. Lek to King. On 7th took last exam. In all got highest score achievable and only 3rd time in 100 years that such high marks. Went to see Emperor who was full of praise. Gave him Order of Saint Vladimir 4th class, never given to non-Russians. Emperor said he hoped the King would be pleased with him. Lunched together. Nai Bua, Eeyd Lek's guardian, is unsatisfactory and causing trouble. p. 382

BACK IN SIAM

9th April 1906. King to Lek. Order of White Eagle from King of Serbia. (p. 386)

4th May 1906. King to Lek. Nai Poum has resigned as civil servant. What is meaning of someone calling herself "Madame de Phitsanulok"? p. 386

21st May 1906. Lek to King. Details of the Poum affair. Nothing about Katya in response to king. p. 386

16th June 1906. King to Lek. Very angry and sad letter about Lek marrying Katya and the negative consequences. Says he is very unhappy. p. 388

17th June 1906. King to Lek. More about Lek's failure to understand and analyse consequences of marriage correctly. p. 389

GAP OF ALMOST ONE YEAR DUE EITHER TO ANGER, OR LOSS OF LETTERS, OR BOTH

1907 – The King made second trip to Europe for his health. No letters from father to son

13th February 1907. Lek to King. Will take military cadets to Ratchaburi. p. 390

23rd December 1907. Lek to King. Will take cadets to watch military exercises. p. 390

1908 – 4 letters (1 from King)

2nd April 1908. King to Lek. Will not allow Lek's new-born son to be a member of the royal family. No good deciding now that Lek would like him to be. p. 391

6th April 1908. Lek to King. Sending him a book of writings by Inthara Prasat. p. 393

19th July 1908. Lek to King. Has found some land by the river formerly owned by his mother. Can he knock down part of old city wall and use the bricks? p. 393

24th July 1908. Lek to King. Requests leave to travel to Nakhon Sawan and Phitsanulok. p. 393

1909 – 18 letters (13 from King)

26th February 1909. King to Lek. Touching letter asking him to come and dine with him on Saturdays as he misses him. p. 394

10th March 1909. King to Lek. About ordering furniture for new palace where he wants casual effect. p. 394

15th March 1909. King to Lek. Busy so will have to postpone Saturday dinner. p. 394

18th April 1909. King to Lek. Medi Khan wants to join government service and become Thai. p. 394

17th May 1909. Lek to King. Explains had wanted to become a monk during this rains retreat, but Chira has asked him to be Chief of the General Staff and has agreed. p. 395

17th May 1909. King to Lek. Is delighted he will be Chief of the General Staff. After all can be a monk any time. p. 396

6th July 1909. King to Lek. Pleased Eeyd Lek will go and train at the Military Cadet School. p. 396

7th July 1909. Lek to King. Pleased he can repay King's goodness to him by taking charge of Eeyd Lek's studies. p. 397

8th July 1909. King to Lek. Very satisfied with plans for Eeyd Lek. Says Eeyd Lek still too easily influenced. p. 397

10th August 1909. King to Lek. Pleased Eeyd Lek is studying hard. p. 398

28th August 1909. Lek to King. Eeyd Noi has met with nephew of British ambassador to Siam, Arthur Peel, as both are at Eton. Hopes to go and see King in Petchaburi by boat. p. 398

2nd November 1909. King to Lek. Eeyd Lek not studying so well again. p. 398

10th December 1909. King to Lek. Sadet Mae has pain in ear. Wants Lek to talk to Doctor. p. 398

20th December 1909. King to Lek. Should he write to Emperor about death of Grand Duke Michael? p. 398

24th December 1909. King to Lek. Discussion of banquet being planned for Duke Johann Albrecht of Mecklenburg. p. 399

30th December 1909. Lek to King. List of who is attending which function. p. 400

30th December 1909. King to Lek. Wants to add a guest here and there to banquet list. p. 400

31st December 1909. Lek to King. More about banquet and receptions. p. 400

1910 – 33 letters (24 from the King)

2nd January 1910. Lek to King. Going away to arrange manoeuvres for Johann Albrecht. p. 401

4th January 1910. Lek to King. About Prince Rabi and his refusal to attend receptions. p. 401

12th May 1910. King to Lek. Agrees he can build a pavilion in Paruskavan and has authorised money for it. p. 402

30th May 1910. Lek to King. M. Ramlay's test results for Eeyd Lek. p. 402

3rd June 1910. King to Lek. Note about Chamber of Commerce and transportation. p. 402

4th June 1910. King to Lek. Phraya Yommarat says French want a Chinese man behind various troubles. p. 402

6th June 1910. King to Lek. Investigating troubles in Nan. Prince Prachak not really handling situation. p. 402

9th June 1910. King to Lek. Long and not very clear discussion of Chinese problem. p. 403

15th June 1910. King to Lek. French interested in catching a Vietnamese coup plotter. King feels he could be allowed to slip away. p. 404

15th June 1910. King to Lek. Angry Department of Education don't want a commission established to investigate state of education. Feels very disheartened. p. 404

15th June 1910. King to Lek. Says no one is his equal or works as hard. The Governor of Singapore and beri-beri problem. Everyone passing the buck. How can he find good people? Says all his work of past 43 years in vain and country may not survive. p. 405-06

18th June 1910. King to Lek. Sends a list of people who might be good. Charoon not doing well at Ministry of Justice. Problem of Nai Thiem and the foreign court. p. 407

18th June 1910. King to Lek. Upset Charoon not doing better. More about Nai Thiem, problems with Rabi and intrigues in Ministry of Justice. p. 408

20th June 1910. King to Lek. Arrest of Chinese involved in revolt either against Manchu or French-controlled Vietnam. p. 408-09.

20th June 1910. King to Lek. Liked Lek's letter to French ambassador. More about Charoon and Nai Thiem. p. 409

21st June 1910. King to Lek. More about army material seized from Chinese up North. p. 409

21st June 1910. King to Lek. Short note about Ministry of Justice. p. 410

24th June 1910. King to Lek. Prince Devawongse has asked French ambassador to write report. Luang Sophon introduced new members of Capital Dept. p. 410

1st July 1910. Lek to King. Eeyd Lek to be made company commander to try and make him more responsible. Will go on study tours to various regiments.

1st July 1910. King to Lek. Agrees about Eeyd Lek and hopes he will be more mature. p. 411

5th July 1910. Lek to King. Discusses big guns King wants to buy. French consul and rumours about Nan. Rabi issues continue. p. 411-412

15th July 1910. King to Lek. Pleased with letter about officers to Japan. Shame only one person can speak Japanese. Chinese affair ongoing. p. 412

21st July 1910. Lek to King. More about officers going to Japan. Discussion about the education commission. Everyone likes education. The Chinese are angry because have not achieved their aims. p.413

21 July 1910. King to Lek. Education Department is like a house built without an architect. p. 413-14

13th August 1910. King to Lek. Received book by Mom Narendra. Analyses Narendra's ideas regarding the train line and the Mekong, but asks Lek to remind him that Siam at a disadvantage vis-à-vis France and they have both banks of the Mekong. p. 414-15

19th August 1910. King to Lek. About Eeyd Noi seeing Lady Gage's son, who is also at Eton, and going to stay in Firle place.

29th August 1910. King to Lek. Although has rained, water level still low. Will make merit for one-year anniversary of Prince Urubongse's death instead of celebrating his own birthday.

8th September. Lek to King. Gives all the reasons why neither Prince Mahidol or Toonmom Toh should represent Siam at the Coronation of George V. Says he should go and will pay for travel himself. Wants to gain more knowledge abroad so can serve king better. (p. 416-18)

8th September 1910. King to Lek. Not surprised by Lek's plan. Knows he would do a good job. Only problem is how to deal with Katya.

8th September. Lek to King. Says he will treat Katya as his morganatic wife, a concept *farang* understand. p. 419

8th September 1910. King to Lek. Thinks plans seem fine but he's sure Lek can see problems attached to having such a wife. p. 419

28th September 1910. Lek to King. Sends him the results of Eeyd Lek's exams. Upset he doesn't like Physics. p. 420

30th September 1910. King to Lek. Whatever Eeyd Lek has learnt in addition makes him happy.

SO ENDS THE LAST LETTER

SELECTED BIBLIOGRAPHY

Aldrich, Robert "France and the King of Siam: An Asian King's Visits to the Republican Capital", in *French History and Civilisation, Papers* from the George Rudé Seminar, 2005, H-France

Anake Nawigamune, *Chulalongkorn: The Great Pictures of Thailand's Beloved King,* 2012, Muangboran Printing, Bangkok

http://atieliereline.com/blog/2016/9/15/t5pb796vpa 81k4ys5z1viwerveholh -on Kschinsska

Baker, Christopher and Pasuk Phongpaichit, *A History of Thailand,* 2005, Silkworm

Barchatova, Saburova et al, *A Portrait of Tsarist Russia,* Nishen, 1989

Bautze, Joachim, *Unseen Siam. Early Photography 1860-1910,* River Books, 2016

Brailey, Nigel, *Two Views of Siam on the Eve of the Chakri Reformation: Comments by Robert Laurie Morant and Prince Pritsdang,* Kiscadale Publications, 1989

Burton Holmes Travelogue, Volume 8, *St. Petersburg, Moscow. The Trans-Siberian Railway,* 1917

Chakrabongse, Narisa & Hunter, Eileen, *Katya and the Prince of Siam,* 2016, River Books

Chula Chakrabongse, Prince, *Lords of Life: A History of the Kings of Thailand,* Alvin Redman, 1967

Chula Chakrabongse, Prince, *Kert Wang Parus* (in Thai), 14th edition, 2017

Davidson, Apollon and Filatova, Irina, *The Russians and the Anglo-Boer War,* Human and Rousseau/Combined Book Services

Figes, Orlando, *Natasha's Dance,* A Cultural History of Russia, 2003, Penguin.

Figes, Orlando, *A People's Tragedy: The Russian Revolution: 1891-1924,* Penguin

Finestone, Jeffrey, *The Descendants of King Chulalongkorn,* 1989, Phitsanulok Publishing

Imtip Pattajoti Suharto, *Journeys to Java by a Siamese King* (Jakarta, 2001)

Iroshnikove, M. P, et al, *Before the Revolution - St. Petersburg in Photographs 1890-1914,* 1991, Harry N. Abrams

Jottrand, Emile and Tips, Walter E. J. *In Siam: Diary of a Legal Adviser of King Chulalong-korns's Government,* 1997, White Lotus

Kschessinska, Mathilde, *Dancing in St. Petersburg: The Memoirs of Mathilde Kschessinska,* 2005

Leonowens, Anna Harriette, *The English Governess at the Siamese Court - Being Recollections of Six Years in the Royal Palace at Bangkok,* May 2012

Loos, Tamara, *Bones Around My Neck - The Life and Exile of a Prince Provocatuer,* 2016, Cornell University Press

Massie, Robert K., *Nicholas and Alexandra,* 1967, Atheneum

Melville, Joy, *Diaghilev and Friends,* Haus publishing, 2009

Nish, Ian, *The Origins of the Russo-Japanese War* (Origins Of Modern Wars), 1985, Longman

Ometev, Boris and Stuart, John, *St. Petersburg Portrait of an Imperial City,* 1990, Cassell

Pasuk Phongpaichit and Baker, Chris, *Thailand: Economy and Politics.* 1997, Oxford University Press

Pavie, Auguste, *Pavie Mission Indochina Papers, 1879-1895.* Vol. I. Translated by Walter E. J. Tips.

Peleggi, Maurizio, *Lords of Things: The Fashioning of the Siamese Monarchy's Modern Image,* 2002, University of Hawaii Press

Sebag Montefiore, Simon, *The Romanovs: 1613-1918,* Penguin, 2016.

Ed. Smele, Jonathan D., and Heywood, Anthony, *The Russian Revolution of 1905 - Centenary perspectives,* 2005, Routledge

Terwiel, B. J. *Thailand's Political History. From the 13th Century to Recent Times,* 2014, River Books

Tips, Walter E. J., *HM King Chulalongkorn's 1897 Journey to Europe, Notes on Origins, Background and Significance, based on Private Belgian Archives,* Thai-blogs.com

Tips, Walter E. J., *Siam's Struggle for Survival: Gunboat Incident at Paknam and the Franco-Siamese Treaty of 1893,* 1999, White Lotus

Warington Smyth, H. and Loos, Tamara, *Five Years in Siam,* 1891-1896, Vol. 2: The Malay and Cambodian Peninsulas, With Descriptions of Ruby Mines, 1999, White Lotus

Westwood, J. N., *Russia Against Japan, 1904-1905,* 1986, State University of New York Press

Western-Style Painting and Sculpture in the Thai Royal Court, Volume I, 1993, Amarin Printing Group Co., Ltd., Bangkok,

Yarmolinsky, Avrahm and Witte, Sergei Yulyevich, *The Memoirs of Count Witte,* 2010

Van Der, Kiste, John, *Once a Grand Duchess: Xenia, Sister of Nicolas II,* 2004

As mentioned in the Introduction, all the letters may be viewed on line at the British Library: https://www.bl.uk/collection-guides/chakrabongse-collection-of-thai-royal-letters

ACKNOWLEDGEMENTS

This project has taken such a long time and has been started and then put aside so many times, that it is difficult to remember everyone to thank.

I must start with thanking my grandfather and father, for being brave enough to go against what was expected of them. Firstly, my grandfather dared to elope with and marry my grandmother, and then my father, already looked at askance for being half-Thai and half-Russian, followed his heart and married my English mother. Luckily, along the way, the treasure trove of letters and photographs, which have made this book possible, was preserved, despite my grandfather dying very young, my father being packed off to England aged 12, a revolution in Thailand taking away his family home and much more. The fact that they were almost lost while in my care, makes their survival even more precious.

On the Thai side, without my co-editor, Paisarn Piemmettawat, who has an encyclopedic knowledge of all the main actors in this story, this book would have been impossible. In addition, his wide circle of like-minded friends, has ensured access to many photographs outside my collection and I would like to acknowledge the help of his many friends at this point. Since Paisarn and I first met 30 years ago to work on *The Descendants of King Chulalongkorn*, we have published over 200 books together and for that I owe him a huge debt of gratitude. In this regard, I would also like to thank Suparat Sudcharoen and Ruetairat Nanta of River Books, not only for their work on this book, but their patience, loyalty and skill in carrying out so many projects over the years.

On the Russian side, I must first thank my cousin Masha, Maria Petrova-Desnitsky, who has provided invaluable help in researching and translating significant archive material, not all of which could be included. In particular, her discovery of the Ardachev letters has provided a fascinating perspective of what my grandfather was like as a teenage boy learning Russian in London, before embarking on his exciting life in St. Petersburg. In addition, she has always been ready to carry out additional research and provide biographical details of some of the people mentioned in the text. Following her excellent work in translating my first book, *Katya and the Prince of Siam*, I very much hope that she will translate this volume into Russian. Thanks also to Sergei Trifonov, who has been interested in the Chakrabongse story for many years. More recently, Kirill Barsky, Russian ambassador in Bangkok, has been of great help in obtaining access for my husband, Gee, Paisarn and I to visit the Suvorov Academy where my grandfather once studied when it was the Corps des Pages.

I would also like to thank Yui Chungsiriwat, who carried out extra research late in the day and, my only regret, is I did not have time to incorporate all the fascinating material in this edition. Thanks too, to Billie Phipps Tyndall, who read through and edited the translation one more time. However, errors of transliteration from Thai to English, or any other mistakes are mine alone.

Finally, I would like to thank my family for putting up with me while I was completing the book and, in particular, my husband, Gee Svasti Thomson, who has always been so supportive of all my endeavours.

Opposite: When Prince Chakrabongse returned to Russia in 1911, the Tsar conferred upon him the Order of St. Andrew as a symbol of his friendship.

Votre Altesse Royale. Désirant
offrir à Votre Altesse Royale un
témoignage particulier des sentiments
d'amitié que je Lui porte, je Lui ai
conféré mon Ordre de Saint André.
Je Vous prie d'en revêtir les insignes
comme une preuve de ma sincère
sympathie.
De Votre Altesse Royale
le très affectionné,

Nicolas

Tsarskoé Sélo.
le 25 Mai 1911.

A Son Altesse Royale
le Prince Chakrabong de Siam.

Transliteration of Thai and, to a lesser extent, Russian names is difficult. In Thailand, family members with the same Thai surname, may spell the English version differently from each other. Nicknames are also frequent. I have tried to give the nicknames as used by Prince Chakrabongse. Tsar Nicholas II was mainly called the Emperor by Prince Chakrabongse, so he mainly appears under that title. Figures in bold indicate illustrations.

*Visiting the former Corps des Pages in 2017. 99 years after
my grandfather first walked up these steps.*